T0190339

Lecture Notes in Computer Science   12476

More information about this series at http://www.springer.com/series/7407

Tiziana Margaria · Bernhard Steffen (Eds.)

Leveraging Applications of Formal Methods, Verification and Validation

Verification Principles

9th International Symposium
on Leveraging Applications of Formal Methods, ISoLA 2020
Rhodes, Greece, October 20–30, 2020
Proceedings, Part I

 Springer

Editors
Tiziana Margaria 📵
University of Limerick and Lero
Limerick, Ireland

Bernhard Steffen 📵
TU Dortmund
Dortmund, Germany

ISSN 0302-9743   ISSN 1611-3349   (electronic)
Lecture Notes in Computer Science
ISBN 978-3-030-61361-7   ISBN 978-3-030-61362-4   (eBook)
https://doi.org/10.1007/978-3-030-61362-4

LNCS Sublibrary: SL1 – Theoretical Computer Science and General Issues

This Springer imprint is published by the registered company Springer Nature Switzerland AG
The registered company address is: Gewerbestrasse 11, 6330 Cham, Switzerland

Introduction

It is our responsibility, as general and program chairs, to welcome the participants to the 9th International Symposium on Leveraging Applications of Formal Methods, Verification and Validation (ISoLA), planned to take place in Rhodes, Greece, during October 20–30, 2020, endorsed by the European Association of Software Science and Technology (EASST).

This year's event follows the tradition of its symposia forerunners held in Paphos, Cyprus (2004 and 2006), Chalkidiki, Greece (2008), Crete, Greece (2010 and 2012), Corfu, Greece (2014 and 2016), and most recently in Limassol, Cyprus (2018), and the series of ISoLA workshops in Greenbelt, USA (2005), Poitiers, France (2007), Potsdam, Germany (2009), Vienna, Austria (2011), and Palo Alto, USA (2013).

Considering that this year's situation is unique and unlike any previous one due to the ongoing COVID-19 pandemic, and that ISoLA's symposium touch and feel is much unlike most conventional, paper-based conferences, after much soul searching we are faced with a true dilemma. "Virtualizing" the event, as many conferences have done, violates the true spirit of the symposium, which is rooted in the gathering of communities and the discussions within and across the various communities materialized in the special tracks and satellite events. Keeping with the physical meeting and holding it in a reduced form (as many may not be able to or feel comfortable with travel) under strict social distancing rules may also end up not being feasible. At the time of writing there is a resurgence of cases in several countries, many nations are compiling "green lists" of countries with which they entertain free travel relations, and these lists are updated – most frequently shortened – at short notice, with severe consequence for the travelers. Many governments and universities are again strengthening the travel restrictions for their employees, and many of us would anyway apply caution due to our own specific individual situation.

To be able to react as flexibly as possible to this situation, we decided to split ISoLA 2020 into two parts, one this year and one in October 2021, with the track organizers deciding when their track will take place. So far both dates have promoters, but it may still happen that, in the end, the entire event needs to move. All accepted papers are published in time, but some tracks will present their papers at the 2021 event.

As in the previous editions, ISoLA 2020 provides a forum for developers, users, and researchers to discuss issues related to the adoption and use of rigorous tools and methods for the specification, analysis, verification, certification, construction, test, and maintenance of systems from the point of view of their different application domains. Thus, since 2004, the ISoLA series of events serves the purpose of bridging the gap between designers and developers of rigorous tools on one side, and users in engineering and in other disciplines on the other side. It fosters and exploits synergetic relationships among scientists, engineers, software developers, decision makers, and other critical thinkers in companies and organizations. By providing a specific, dialogue-oriented venue for the discussion of common problems, requirements, algorithms, methodologies, and practices, ISoLA aims in particular at supporting researchers in their quest to improve the usefulness, reliability, flexibility, and efficiency of tools for building systems, and users in their search for adequate solutions to their problems.

The program of the symposium consists of a collection of special tracks devoted to the following hot and emerging topics:

- Reliable Smart Contracts: State-of-the-art, Applications, Challenges and Future Directions
  (Organizers: Gordon Pace, César Sànchez, Gerardo Schneider)
- Engineering of Digital Twins for Cyber-Physical Systems
  (Organizers: John Fitzgerald, Pieter Gorm Larsen, Tiziana Margaria, Jim Woodcock)
- Verification and Validation of Concurrent and Distributed Systems
  (Organizers: Cristina Seceleanu, Marieke Huisman)
- Modularity and (De-)composition in Verification
  (Organizers: Reiner Hähnle, Eduard Kamburjan, Dilian Gurov)
- Software Verification Tools
  (Organizers: Markus Schordan, Dirk Beyer, Irena Boyanova)
- X-by-Construction: Correctness meets Probability
  (Organizers: Maurice H. ter Beek, Loek Cleophas, Axel Legay, Ina Schaefer, Bruce W. Watson)
- Rigorous Engineering of Collective Adaptive Systems
  (Organizers: Rocco De Nicola, Stefan Jähnichen, Martin Wirsing)
- Automated Verification of Embedded Control Software
  (Organizers: Dilian Gurov, Paula Herber, Ina Schaefer)
- Automating Software Re-Engineering
  (Organizers: Serge Demeyer, Reiner Hähnle, Heiko Mantel)
- 30 years of Statistical Model Checking!
  (Organizers: Kim G. Larsen, Axel Legay)
- From Verification to Explanation
  (Organizers: Holger Herrmanns, Christel Baier)
- Formal methods for DIStributed COmputing in future RAILway systems (DisCo-Rail 2020)
  (Organizers: Alessandro Fantechi, Stefania Gnesi, Anne Haxthausen)
- Programming: What is Next?
  (Organizers: Klaus Havelund, Bernhard Steffen)

With the embedded events:

- RERS: Challenge on Rigorous Examination of Reactive Systems (Falk Howar, Markus Schordan, Bernhard Steffen)
- Doctoral Symposium and Poster Session (A. L. Lamprecht)
- Industrial Day (Falk Howar, Johannes Neubauer, Andreas Rausch)

Colocated with the ISoLA symposium is:

- STRESS 2020 – 5th International School on Tool-based Rigorous Engineering of Software Systems (J. Hatcliff, T. Margaria, Robby, B. Steffen)

Altogether the ISoLA 2020 proceedings comprises four volumes, Part 1: Verification Principles, Part 2: Engineering Principles, Part 3: Applications, and Part 4: Tools, Trends, and Tutorials, which also covers the associated events.

We thank the track organizers, the members of the Program Committee and their referees for their effort in selecting the papers to be presented, the local organization chair, Petros Stratis, and the EasyConferences team for their continuous and precious support during the entire two-year period preceding the events, and Springer for being, as usual, a very reliable partner for the proceedings production. Finally, we are grateful to Kyriakos Georgiades for his continuous support for the website and the program, and to Markus Frohme and Julia Rehder for their help with the editorial system Equinocs.

Special thanks are due to the following organization for their endorsement: EASST (European Association of Software Science and Technology) and Lero – The Irish Software Research Centre, and our own institutions – TU Dortmund University and the University of Limerick.

We wish you, as an ISoLA participant, a wonderful experience at this edition, and for you, reading the proceedings at a later occasion, valuable new insights that hopefully contribute to your research and its uptake.

August 2020   Tiziana Margaria
                                                               Bernhard Steffen

Organization

Symposium Chair

Tiziana Margaria   University of Limerick and Lero, Ireland

PC Chair

Bernhard Steffen   TU Dortmund University, Germany

PC Members

Christel Baier	Technische Universität Dresden, Germany
Maurice ter Beek	ISTI-CNR, Italy
Dirk Beyer	LMU Munich, Germany
Irena Bojanova	NIST, USA
Loek Cleophas	Eindhoven University of Technology, The Netherlands
Rocco De Nicola	IMT Lucca, Italy
Serge Demeyer	Universiteit Antwerpen, Belgium
Alessandro Fantechi	University of Florence, Italy
John Fitzgerald	Newcastle University, UK
Stefania Gnesi	CNR, Italy
Kim Guldstrand Larsen	Aalborg University, Denmark
Dilian Gurov	KTH Royal Institute of Technology, Sweden
John Hatcliff	Kansas State University, USA
Klaus Havelund	Jet Propulsion Laboratory, USA
Anne E. Haxthausen	Technical University of Denmark, Denmark
Paula Herber	University of Münster, Germany
Holger Hermanns	Saarland University, Germany
Falk Howar	Dortmund University of Technology and Fraunhofer ISST, Germany
Marieke Huisman	University of Twente, The Netherlands
Reiner Hähnle	Technische Universität Darmstadt, Germany
Stefan Jähnichen	TU Berlin, Germany
Eduard Kamburjan	Technische Universität Darmstadt, Germany
Anna-Lena Lamprecht	Utrecht University, The Netherlands
Peter Gorm Larsen	Aarhus University, Denmark
Axel Legay	Université Catholique de Louvain, Belgium
Heiko Mantel	Technische Universität Darmstadt, Germany
Tiziana Margaria	University of Limerick and Lero, Ireland
Johannes Neubauer	Materna, Germany
Gordon Pace	University of Malta, Malta
Cesar Sanchez	IMDEA Software Institute, Madrid, Spain

Ina Schaefer   TU Braunschweig, Germany
Gerardo Schneider   University of Gothenburg, Sweden
Markus Schordan   Lawrence Livermore National Laboratory, USA
Cristina Seceleanu   Mälardalen University, Sweden
Bernhard Steffen   TU Dortmund University, Germany
Bruce Watson   Stellenbosch University, South Africa
Martin Wirsing   Ludwig-Maximilians-Universität München, Germany
James Woodcock   University of York, UK

Reviewers

Aho, Pekka   Hungar, Hardi
Aichernig, Bernhard   Inverso, Omar
Backeman, Peter   Iosti, Simon
Baranov, Eduard   Jacobs, Bart
Basile, Davide   Jaeger, Manfred
Beckert, Bernhard   Jensen, Peter
Bensalem, Saddek   Johnsen, Einar Broch
Bettini, Lorenzo   Jongmans, Sung-Shik
Beyer, Dirk   Jähnichen, Stefan
Bourr, Khalid   Kanav, Sudeep
Bubel, Richard   Konnov, Igor
Bures, Tomas   Kosak, Oliver
Casadei, Roberto   Kosmatov, Nikolai
Castiglioni, Valentina   Kretinsky, Jan
Ciatto, Giovanni   Könighofer, Bettina
Cimatti, Alessandro   Lanese, Ivan
Damiani, Ferruccio   Lecomte, Thierry
Di Marzo Serugendo, Giovanna   Lluch Lafuente, Alberto
Duong, Tan   Loreti, Michele
Filliâtre, Jean-Christophe   Maggi, Alessandro
Fränzle, Martin   Mariani, Stefano
Gabor, Thomas   Mazzanti, Franco
Gadducci, Fabio   Morichetta, Andrea
Galletta, Letterio   Nyberg, Mattias
Geisler, Signe   Omicini, Andrea
Gerostathopoulos, Ilias   Orlov, Dmitry
Guanciale, Roberto   Pacovsky, Jan
Heinrich, Robert   Parsai, Ali
Hillston, Jane   Peled, Doron
Hnetynka, Petr   Piho, Paul
Hoffmann, Alwin   Pugliese, Rosario

Pun, Violet Ka I
Reisig, Wolfgang
Schlingloff, Holger
Seifermann, Stephan
Soulat, Romain
Steinhöfel, Dominic
Stolz, Volker
Sürmeli, Jan
Tiezzi, Francesco
Tini, Simone
Tognazzi, Stefano
Tribastone, Mirco

Trubiani, Catia
Tuosto, Emilio
Ulbrich, Mattias
Vandin, Andrea
Vercammen, Sten
Viroli, Mirko
Wadler, Philip
Wanninger, Constantin
Weidenbach, Christoph
Wirsing, Martin
Zambonelli, Franco

Contents – Part I

30 Years of Statistical Model Checking!

Verification and Validation of Concurrent and Distributed Systems

Contents – Part II

Contents – Part III

Automated Verification of Embedded Control Software

Formal methods for DIStributed COmputing in future RAILway systems

Modularity and (De-)Composition
in Verification

Who Carries the Burden of Modularity?

Introduction to ISoLA 2020 Track on *Modularity and (De-)composition in Verification*

Dilian Gurov[1]([⊠]), Reiner Hähnle[2]([⊠]), and Eduard Kamburjan[2]([⊠])

[1] KTH Royal Institute of Technology, Stockholm, Sweden
dilian@kth.se
[2] Technische Universität Darmstadt, Darmstadt, Germany
{reiner.haehnle,eduard.kamburjan}@tu-darmstadt.de

Abstract. Modularity and compositionality in verification frameworks occur within different contexts: the model that is the verification target, the specification of the stipulated properties, and the employed verification principle. We give a representative overview of mechanisms to achieve modularity and compositionality along the three mentioned contexts and analyze how mechanisms in different contexts are related. In many verification frameworks one of the contexts carries the main burden. It is important to clarify these relations to understand the potential and limits of the different modularity mechanisms.

1 Introduction

Modularity and compositionality are core principles in all engineering fields and play a major role in verification approaches in Computer Science as well. While the two notions are sometimes used interchangeably, they relate to two slightly differing principles:

Compositionality is a way to break up a problem or system into subproblems or subsystems.

Modularity describes that a subsystem is a module: it has a clear interface and can be exchanged within the overall system with another module that has the same interface.

Hence, modularity is a desirable property of compositional *systems*, which is concerned with the design of interfaces between subsystems.

Modularity and compositionality in verification frameworks occur within different *contexts*. One can clearly distinguish three different contexts: the *model* that is the verification target, the *specification* of the stipulated properties, and the employed *verification principle*. We give a representative overview of mechanisms to achieve modularity and compositionality along the three mentioned contexts and analyze how mechanisms in different contexts are related. In many verification frameworks one of the contexts carries the main burden. It is important to clarify these relations to understand the potential and limits of the various modularity mechanisms.

© Springer Nature Switzerland AG 2020
T. Margaria and B. Steffen (Eds.): ISoLA 2020, LNCS 12476, pp. 3–21, 2020.
https://doi.org/10.1007/978-3-030-61362-4_1

System model: The language in which the verification target is formalized. This could be a mainstream programming language such as JAVA or C, a modeling language such as ABS [78] or PROMELA [71], or a more abstract formalism such as the Actor model [68] or automata [6,56,75]. In any case, we assume that we have as a minimal requirement an executable language with a formal syntax and a precisely stated (though not necessarily formalized) runtime semantics.

System specification: The language in which system properties are expressed. In the simplest case, this means just assertions of Boolean expressions or even a finite set of fixed properties. But in most cases a specification is based on a more expressive logic, such as temporal or first-order logic. Even more expressive safety properties are possible with contract-based languages such as JML [91] or ACSL [15]. Finally, logical frameworks such as Coq [21] or Isabelle [102] permit not only to specify almost any property, but also the syntax and semantics of the system model.

Verification principle: Less obvious than the first two, this concerns the verification methodology used to (dis-)prove properties of the system *model* expressed in the *specification* language. For example, state exploration together with abstraction refinement [43,62] is a popular approach in model checking. Axiomatic approaches based on a calculus for a program logic are common in deductive verification [65]. Symbolic execution [29,38,86] is often the underlying principle in either [3,24]. On the other hand, interactive theorem proving based on structural induction is the main verification principle employed in logical frameworks [21,102] and inductive theorem proving of functional programs [36,121].

In each context, mechanisms for modularity are expressed at differing levels of granularity. Before we discuss and analyze some representative modularity mechanisms, we can already state a few observations at a high level of abstraction:

1. The choice of modularity mechanism in different contexts is *not independent*. For example, a specification language with contracts does not make sense in combination with a system model that knows no procedures, symbolic execution cannot be used to prove properties of abstract programs.
2. Often one of the contexts is *dominant* over the others or can be considered as the starting point of the overall approach. In this case, choosing the modularity mechanism in the "lead" context determines the one in the others.
3. The *burden of modularity* may be unfairly allocated among different contexts: one can restrict an execution model to the extent that modular specification and verification become straightforward, such as the strong encapsulation of Din and Owe [54]. Or one can shift the burden to the power of the underlying verification approach, as the CPAchecker system [23] does. This may or may not be aligned with the dominant context.

2   Modularity and Composition Mechanisms: A Representative Collection

We follow the classification into the three contexts discussed above. Observe that artifacts belonging to different contexts are not necessarily separately formalized entities. For example, in interactive proof assistants the (abstract) syntax of the model, the specification language, and the verification approach are uniformly represented in higher-order formalisms, such type theory [21] and higher-order logic [102]; in dynamic logic [67], programs and their specifications both appear inside formulas, etc. Nevertheless, the context distinction is *conceptually* present and it is useful to make.

2.1   Model

Perhaps the central and most important modularity mechanism in programming is the *method*[1] abstraction. It is a pillar of modularity, because—in principle—one does not need to know the implementation details of a method in order to use it. Rather, it is sufficient to know under which *assumptions* it is supposed to work and what the intended *effects* (side effects and returned result) are.

Methods can be too fine-grained or too coarse-grained to modularize a program's behavior. This is especially true in concurrent systems. For example, a system model may provide full *data encapsulation* via objects [112] or *behavioral encapsulation* via atomic (non-interruptable) code segments [48]. Then all methods of an object *cooperate* to (re-)establish the *object invariant* at return from each call. The actor model is a point in case [4, 34, 54]. Vice versa, in languages such as C, where preemption and direct manipulation of the heap is permitted, one can neither abstract away from the implementation of a method, nor from its execution context.

Packages and modules in the sense of JAVA, C, etc., are important for compositionality at the level of the model, but they are limited to provide syntactic mechanisms for managing the namespace and help with disambiguation. For verification purposes this is not enough, because it is essential to (de-)compose *behavior*.

Some abstract modeling languages have been designed with parallel composition operators that enjoy *algebraic* properties that make reasoning about correctness easy. Such *process calculi* include CCS [96], CSP [70], or the π-calculus [97,98]. The downside is that their concurrency models are not realistic enough to permit efficient implementation. A different class of abstract models with "innate" modularity are *pure functional programs*. By construction, pure functions can be specified and verified independently of each other. Where modularity comes into play is when induction arguments in the proof of complex functions need to be decomposed to become automatically provable. This has

---

[1] There are plethora of synonyms for the same concept in different contexts: function, procedure, routine, etc. In this paper we use the term *method* without committing to a specific execution model.

led to the development of such techniques as *rippling* [37] or *generalization* [119] that help with lemma discovery [77].

Some of the abstract concurrency models use the encapsulation inherent to distributed systems to provide modularity. Choreographies [7,31,105] implement a global view for message passing between services, e.g., in business protocols [39]. A choreography is used as the *endpoint projection* to generate code for single services. This code is guaranteed by construction to realize the order of messages in the choreography. Similarly, orchestration [105] describes a central entity that controls messages between services. It is crucial that the entities are encapsulated and have no other way of communicating. Both notions are deeply connected and choreographies can be used to derive an orchestrator [94]. Choreographies may either commit to one interaction style or mix different interaction styles (e.g., synchronous and asynchronous communication) [10]. The aforementioned actor model is another concurrency model that uses encapsulated distribution to provide modularity.

In software product line engineering (SPLE) modularity is expressed along the composition of features as requested by a product specification [107]. Specifically, in *delta-oriented programming* [109] the implementation of features is associated with *code deltas* specifying the implementation of a feature relative to a given core. A general overview of feature-oriented implementation techniques is [8].

In system engineering and hybrid systems *continuous* state changes, in addition to calls and discrete state changes, are modeled. One compositional technique to do so are components [61]. Components strictly distinguish between the internal *behavior model* and the *interface model* that connects different components via their ports. The interface model can be synchronous or asynchronous and different instances of behavior models are supported. In the area of hybrid systems, (hybrid) I/O automata [93] also offer a basic composition mechanism as a low-level device, albeit only via modeling synchronization on transitions.

2.2 Specification

In the simplest case, a specification consists merely of a generic property, for example, "absence of deadlocks", "(normal) termination", etc. Model-specific properties are mostly expressed in suitable logics. In a basic setup, logical *assertions* are placed at certain locations in the model, where they must hold in any run. When an assertion appears at the syntactic end of a method it functions as a postcondition. Dual to assertions, one can instrument a model with *assumptions*. These are properties that can be assumed to hold in the execution state where they occur. An assumption placed at the syntactic beginning of a program works as a precondition. Hoare logic [69] is based on assumption-program-assertion triples.

Program logics specify not merely a single computation state, but express properties of whole runs and thus can relate multiple execution states. They include temporal logic [12] and dynamic logic [67]. Generic properties, assertions, assumptions, and program logics do not provide any support for modularity in themselves, but assumptions and assertions can be used as elements of modular specification formalisms.

A simple form of modularity are *invariants*. They can take the form of object or loop invariants, but in either case the idea is the same: *assume* that a certain property (the "invariant" I) holds initially. If—under this assumption—the execution of a given model M *asserts* the invariant upon termination in each run, then I is an invariant for M. A simple induction yields that I is also an invariant for an arbitrary number of subsequent executions of M. Now imagine that M is a loop body and I is asserted at the start of the loop. Or M is any method of an object and all constructors assert I. Then I holds whenever the loop or a call to one of the object's methods terminates, respectively. This allows to replace the behavior of a loop or of an object by its invariant during verification and it constitutes a base line of modularity.

Most contemporary deductive verification frameworks (for example, [3, 26, 76, 87, 118]) use a specification language based on the notion of a *method contract*. First introduced by Meyer [95] as *design-by-contract* in the context of runtime verification, a method contract comprises the assumptions under which a method is supposed to work correctly, together with an assertion of its intended effects (side effects and returned result). Thus, contracts can be composed from the building blocks "assertion" and "assumption" over a logical language (usually, typed first-order logic). The requirements that need to hold for a method contract to enter into force are its *precondition*. The stipulated final computation state (including the returned result) after a method terminates is its *postcondition*. The memory locations a method can read are called its *footprint*, the memory locations it can write to are called its *frame*.

Method contracts are a central device to achieve a degree of modularity in specification, because they can characterize the effect of a method call without actually having to analyze the called method. This is essential to make verification of large programs feasible: clearly a program with hundreds of method declarations cannot be analyzed by inlining method calls. Enforcing modularity here also enables local re-verification: changes in one method require one to re-verify the changed method, not the whole system. In the case of recursively defined methods, contracts even enable verification in the first place. In some cases, in particular, in dynamic analyses, the notion of contract is only *implicit*, for example [64] speak of *structural properties* and [60] of *summaries*.

While it is obvious that method contracts must describe the behavior of the called method (the *caller*'s perspective), it is less obvious that one must pay as well attention to the call context (the *callee*'s perspective). The problem arises, whenever the frame or footprint of a method include the heap. Since the callee cannot know in which heap state it is called, the pre- and postcondition have to be expressed so that they are valid in arbitrary states. This means, for example, that the effects of a method on an *unknown* heap that may intersect with its frame and footprint have to be described correctly. A number of techniques to achieve this have been developed, including dynamic frames [85, 111], ownership types [42, 51], boxing [92, 106], and separation logic [103].

The situation worsens in the case of concurrent programs, because of task interleaving. This led to mechanisms such as fractional permissions [30], concurrent separation logic [32], and combinations thereof [28], for low-level concurrency, and to context-aware contracts [83] for concurrency with atomic segments. Assumption-guarantee reasoning is not necessarily bound to method contracts, pairs of pre- and postconditions can also be used to specify processes [99].

It has to be stressed that while various framing theories make it possible to achieve a certain degree of modularity when specifying complex, heap-manipulating software [5,49] this does not mean that the approach is practical yet: often specifications become considerably longer than the specified model and are harder to understand [16].

From a feature-oriented SPLE perspective it makes sense to *compose* contracts. Specification deltas [66] reuse contract elements in analogy to code deltas, but this works smoothly only when behavioral subtyping is assumed. That this is generally not the case is shown in [116], which also contains an overview of feature-oriented contract composition techniques.

Contracts specify the behavior of a method at its endpoints. In particular to specify concurrent models, it may be necessary to expose some of the intermediate behavior. Therefore, it is a natural idea to generalize contracts to symbolic traces [53,81,115]. It remains to be seen, however, whether this leads to improved modularity.

Component contracts were studied to specify the interface level of components [20]. These contracts are also based on assumption-guarantee reasoning, and specify what a component must guarantee *to* the environment and what it can rely on *from* the environment. Component contracts differ from method contracts, as they specify the continuously changing ports of a component at interface level. Component contracts abstract not only from the concrete behavior of a component, but also from the language of its implementation. This allows contracts to inherit the compositional properties of components through contract operators [19], but limits the specifications to boolean assertions over ports. Interface automata [47] are a formalism similar to the aforementioned I/O automata that specify the temporal behavior of automata and have a composition mechanism compatible with open systems: They specify the expected behavior of the environment of an I/O automaton.

One version of program development by step-wise *refinement* works by specifying a series of ever more precise abstract machines [1,2,27,110] that are finally translated into executable code. Such a development can be seen as a series of *modular* specifications.

2.3   Verification

Modularity can occur in several places in the verification context, either by decomposition following another context, e.g., following the structure of contracts or methods, or decompose a problem that is neither specified modularly nor executed modularly.

With *axiomatic decomposition* we denote a verification approach that allows to decompose a verification task into subtasks by way of a decomposition axiom. The *frame rule* of separation logic [103] that allows to localize heap reasoning is a well-known example. Another example can be found in early work on modular verification of simple concurrent programs (without heaps and method calls) in the form of *assumption-guarantee* reasoning [80] and its predecessor, the *Owicki-Gries* composition axiom [104][2]. Similarly, composition of proofs based on the communication between processes has been axiomatized for synchronization based formalisms, such as ADA [9,59]. These principles are implicitly present in many contemporary approaches as well and have been frequently generalized (for example, [57,90]). Being based on axiomatic decomposition, they lend themselves well to deductive verification. In fact, contract-based specification can be seen as a specification language well aligned with assumption-guarantee reasoning.

Not in each case is the underlying logical framework expressive enough to justify a decomposition step. For example, [54,84] prove a meta theorem justifying the problem decomposition. This is more a matter of taste or perhaps the desired degree of mechanization, because it is often possible to justify decomposition in a suitably expressive logic [81,101]. The limitation of axiomatic decomposition is often that the decomposition theorem holds only under certain constraints, which becomes an issue with respect to scalability to complex target languages.

A different decomposition technique is *projection*. Session Types [72,73] are a behavioral type discipline [7,74] using global types to describe protocols. Global types are projected onto a role—this generates a local type for each protocol endpoint. It is similar to projection of choreographies on the modeling level [40] (cf. Sect. 2.1): indeed, global types are used as specifications of choreographies [39]. The target language, where type checking happens, are the local types. Projection is designed in a way that enforces further encapsulation in the concurrency model to ensure modularity: the main verification step is a fully automatic argument that composes adherence to the local types to adherence of the whole system to the global types. Not every global type can be projected and projection depends very much on the concurrency model of the target language. In particular, the notion of an endpoint may correspond to a fixed entity in the concurrency model (for example, for actors [82]), but does not need not to do so (for example, for the π-calculus [73]).

Correctness-by-construction [11,52,63,89,113] is the step-wise development of (simple, usually imperative) programs in a series of refinement steps. Each step is justified in a suitable program logic, so that this can be seen as a modular verification strategy.

Abstraction is a general principle to approximate the behavior of a model and its datastructures during execution. This approach was pioneered by Cousot & Cousot [45] as *abstract interpretation* of programs. It allows to abstract away

---

[2] It is worth noting that the original Owicki-Gries composition axiom verifies all involved processes without encapsulation, i.e., changing one process requires to reprove the composition as well.

Table 1. Mechanisms to achieve modularity and compositionality in different contexts

Context	Model	Specification	Verification
Baseline	unstructured code	assume, assert	**intermediate assertion, cut, interpolant, abstraction**
Mechanism	method, loop	**contract, framing, loop invariant**	axiomatic decomposition, abstract execution
	object, actor, atomic segment	**invariant, symbolic trace**	meta composition
	feature	contract composition	**proof composition**
	(generic)	session type	**projection**
	choreography	(generic)	projection
	component	component contract	(generic)
	process calculus	(generic)	axiomatic decomposition
	functional program	**abstract machine**	refinement
	imperative program	**assume, assert**	
	pure functions	assume, assert	rippling, generalization
	(verification-specific)	(verification-specific)	proof reuse

from intricate data structures or complex behavior, so that a specified property is easier to prove. Of course, it can happen that the property does not hold anymore for the abstract version. In this case, it is desirable to find the exact degree of abstraction where it still holds. *Abstraction refinement* [43,62] allows to determine it in an automated manner. Abstraction is not a modularization technique *per se*, but a base line verification principle.

This is in contrast to *abstract execution* [114], where a program with abstract statements is symbolically executed, so that whatever can be proven about the abstract program holds as well for any of its (legal) instances. It allows to decouple programs from their execution contexts, because the latter can be specified by abstract symbols.

It is also possible to modularize verification problems at the level of proofs. A well-known example is TLA+ [41], where proofs are arranged hierarchically.[3] Similarly, proofs for hybrid systems can be composed if the underlying structure

---

[3] It is also possible to view refinement-based approaches from this angle.

has a component-like structure [100]. *Proof reuse* can also be seen as modularization, for example, lazy symbolic execution [35,55], proof repositories [33], or proof adaptation [18,108,120]. In the context of *family-based* verification approaches in SPLE, a number of proof composition techniques have been explored [14,50,117]. Several of these techniques do not work directly on proofs, which tends to be brittle, but on more abstract representations such as contracts or proof scripts. Even so, these techniques are necessarily tied to a specific verification approach.

3 Alignment of Context and the Burden of Modularity

In Table 1 we summarize some of the modularity mechanisms discussed above. In addition, we attempt to relate them across different contexts. Obviously, this correspondence is neither precise nor exhaustive, but should be seen as a basis for more in-depth investigations or for discussion. In each row we highlight the context that carries the burden of modularity in boldface. Under carrying the burden we mean the burden to provide the modularity that is used by the other contexts.

One can instantiate the table to a wide range of established verification approaches. Just as an example, deductive verification [65] is typically built around the notions of contract and framing of structured pieces of code (blocks, methods, loop bodies).

4 Track Contributions

We briefly discuss the contributions of the ISoLA 2020 track on "Modularity and (De-)composition in Verification" in the light of the classification above and mention where in an approach the burden of modularity lies.

4.1 Modularity in the Context of the Model

Coto et al. [44] (*On Testing Message-Passing Components*) address the problem of generating tests for the components of systems in which the components (or participants) communicate via asynchronous message passing (but where the message buffers do not preserve the order of the messages). The correct coordination of the components is specified by means of global choreographies. Following the (top-down) correctness-by-construction principle, the component test suites are obtained by projecting the choreography suitably along the (interfaces of the) components. The generated tests are guaranteed to be suitable, in the sense that every valid implementation of the given component necessarily passes them. The authors discuss a number of aspects of the considered problem, such as test oracles, efficiency of test generation, and coverage criteria.

4.2 Modularity in the Context of the Specification

Barbanera et al. [13] (*Composing Communicating Systems, Synchronously*) investigate the preservation of generic behavioural properties, and in particular deadlock freedom, under the synchronous composition of systems of communicating finite state machines. A composability condition, two structural constraints, and two types of composition are defined, for which it is proved that composing composable systems satisfying the structural constraints preserves deadlock freedom. The authors argue that the same reasoning can be applied to other generic behavioural properties such as lock freedom and liveness.

Beckert et al. [17] (*Modular Verification of JML Contracts Using Bounded Model Checking*) aim to connect the worlds of contract-based deductive verification (DV) with the one of bounded software model checking (BMC). The burden is in translating JML-annotated JAVA into plain JAVA with asserts and assumes. The latter then can serve as input to the bounded model checker JBMC. Obviously, the translation must be parameterized with a (loop and recursion) bound. Technically, the problem of replacing quantifiers by non-deterministic assignments is a central issue. The translation creates the opportunity to run JBMC on JML-annotated programs. In addition to better efficiency and higher automation, this opens up interesting new scenarios for collaboration of DV and MC the authors point out. It is worth to point out that the suggested tool combination perfectly aligns with the case for integration of verification approaches brought forward in [65].

Further, in the domain of Software Product Line Engineering (SPLE), Damiani et al. [46] (*On Slicing Software Product Line Signatures*) present an abstraction and *decomposition* technique based on slicing. A slice of SPL Signature (SPLS) for some feature set $\mathcal{F}$ is a product line that contains neither implementation details of its classes nor products that depend on features outside $\mathcal{F}$. The paper defines such slices and discusses the challenges for an algorithm that computes the slice manually and efficiently. As the main driver of this approach is the specified feature set $\mathcal{F}$, the burden of modularity lies with the specification and the check that the slice is given correctly.

Johnsen et al. [79] (*Assumption-Commitment Types for Resource Management in Virtually Timed Ambients*) introduce a type system for resource management in the context of nested virtualization. The type system is based on effect/coeffect pairs that specify how much resources a process may consume from its context and how much it must offer to its child process. This allows to type check a process in isolation by specifying a resource interface. Nonetheless, the burden of modularity is only partially with the specification: as the effect/coeffect pairs are derived for the inner processes automatically, it lies also with the verification. However, this is enabled by the structure of the specification.

4.3 Modularity in the Context of Verification

Filliâtre and Paskevich [58] (*Abstraction and Genericity in Why3*) argue that any approach invented for modularity in programming can also be adapted to program verification. The purpose of their contribution is to show how they achieve this in WhyML, the language of the program verification tool Why3. WhyML uses a single concept of module, a collection of abstract and concrete declarations, and a basic operation of cloning which instantiates a module with respect to a given partial substitution, while verifying its soundness. This mechanism brings into WhyML both abstraction and genericity, which the authors illustrate on a small verified Bloom filter implementation.

Then, Beyer and Wehrheim [25] (*Verification Artifacts in Cooperative Verification: Survey and Unifying Component Framework*) give a classification of combinations of verification approaches. The focus is on black-box integration through the exchange of artifacts between multiple tools. The paper discusses the exchange format and different roles that tools can play in a cooperative verification framework. The approach described here places the burden of modularity firmly on the verification.

Beyer and Kanav [22] (*An Interface Theory for Program Verification*) take a verification-centric view: the set of all behaviors of a program P is viewed as a behavioral interface I_P. Verification is then recast as a theory of approximation of behavioral interfaces. As pointed out above, different viewpoints on verification are relevant, because they suggest different decomposition strategies of the verification process. Ideally, this leads to the identification and optimization of core reasoning tasks or to new cooperation strategies. The present paper suggests to use over- and underapproximations of the target program as a uniform mechanism to exchange information between different tools in the form of behavioral interfaces. This leads naturally to a decomposition strategy inspired by gradual specification refinement. A number of known verification approaches are characterized from this angle. The paper provides a uniform view of existing work that invites to think about new ways by which verification tools may cooperate.

Finally, Knüppel et al. [88] (*Scaling Correctness-by-Construction*, CbC) suggest an architectural framework for contract-based, CbC-style program development. While both the target language as well as the current implementation are at the proof-of-concept level, it is a promising start. The CbC approach was until recently characterized by an almost complete lack of tools. The paper describes steps towards scaling mechanized CbC development to more complex programs and to establish a repository of reusable off-the-shelf components. To this end, the authors present a formal framework and open-source tool named ARCHICORC. There, a developer models software components in UML-style with required and provided interfaces. Interface methods are associated to specification contracts and mapped to verified CbC implementations. A code generator backend then emits executable JAVA source code.

5   Conclusion

In this paper we gave an overview of modularity in verification and attempted a classification. Hopefully, this can serve as a starting point for the structural use of modularity principles in verification: First, we hope that the classification helps the research community to transfer ideas between subfields by guiding discussions and reengineering approaches. Abstraction from the technical details of modularity allows the underlying *ideas* to be carried over to fields where the original system is not directly applicable. Second, we believe that the classification has the potential to motivate systematic search for *new* modularity mechanisms. Lastly, a classification may shed light on the structure of existing systems and so may guide their eventual reengineering for an increase of modularity.

Acknowledgements. We thank Marieke Huisman and Wolfgang Ahrendt for their very constructive and valuable feedback on a draft.

References

1. Abrial, J.-R.: The B-Book: Assigning Programs to Meanings. Cambridge University Press, Cambridge (1996)
2. Abrial, J.-R.: Modeling in Event-B - System and Software Engineering. Cambridge University Press, Cambridge (2010)
3. Ahrendt, W., Beckert, B., Bubel, R., Hähnle, R., Schmitt, P.H., Ulbrich, M. (eds.): Deductive Software Verification - The KeY Book - From Theory to Practice. LNCS. Springer, Cham (2016). https://doi.org/10.1007/978-3-319-49812-6
4. Ahrendt, W., Dylla, M.: A verification system for distributed objects with asynchronous method calls. In: Breitman, K., Cavalcanti, A. (eds.) ICFEM 2009. LNCS, vol. 5885, pp. 387–406. Springer, Heidelberg (2009). https://doi.org/10.1007/978-3-642-10373-5_20
5. Alkassar, E., Hillebrand, M.A., Paul, W., Petrova, E.: Automated verification of a small hypervisor. In: Leavens, G.T., O'Hearn, P., Rajamani, S.K. (eds.) VSTTE 2010. LNCS, vol. 6217, pp. 40–54. Springer, Heidelberg (2010). https://doi.org/10.1007/978-3-642-15057-9_3
6. Alur, R., Dill, D.L.: A theory of timed automata. Theor. Comp. Sci. **126**(2), 183–235 (1994)
7. Ancona, D.: Behavioral types in programming languages. Found. Trends Program. Lang. **3**(2–3), 95–230 (2016)
8. Apel, S., Batory, D.S., Kästner, C., Saake, G.: Feature-Oriented Software Product Lines: Concepts and Implementation. Springer, Heidelberg (2013). https://doi.org/10.1007/978-3-642-37521-7
9. Apt, K.R., Francez, N., de Roever, W.P.: A proof system for communicating sequential processes. ACM Trans. Program. Lang. Syst. **2**(3), 359–385 (1980)
10. Arbab, F., Cruz-Filipe, L., Jongmans, S., Montesi, F.: Connectors meet choreographies. CoRR, abs/1804.08976 (2018)
11. Back, R.: A calculus of refinements for program derivations. Acta Informatica **25**(6), 593–624 (1988)
12. Banieqbal, B., Barringer, H., Pnueli, A. (eds.): Temporal Logic in Specification. Springer, Heidelberg (1987). https://doi.org/10.1007/3-540-51803-7
13. Barbanera, F., Lanese, I., Tuosto, E.: Composing communicating systems, synchronously. In: Margaria, T., Steffen, B. (eds.) 9th International Symposium on Leveraging Applications of Formal Methods, Verification and Validation, ISoLA 2020. LNCS, Rhodes, Greece, vol. 12476, pp. 39–59. Springer, Heidelberg (October 2020)

14. Batory, D.S., Börger, E.: Modularizing theorems for software product lines: the Jbook case study. J. Univers. Comput. Sci. **14**(12), 2059–2082 (2008)
15. Baudin, P., et al.: ACSL: ANSI/ISO C Specification Language. CEA LIST and INRIA, Version 1.4 (2010)
16. Baumann, C., Beckert, B., Blasum, H., Bormer, T.: Lessons learned from micro-kernel verification - specification is the new bottleneck. In: Cassez, F., Huuck, R., Klein, G., Schlich, B. (eds.) Proceedings of the 7th Conference on Systems Software Verification. EPTCS, vol. 102, pp. 18–32 (2012)
17. Beckert, B., Kirsten, M., Klamroth, J., Ulbrich, M.: Modular verification of JML contracts using bounded model checking. In: Margaria, T., Steffen, B. (eds.) 9th International Symposium on Leveraging Applications of Formal Methods, Verification and Validation, ISoLA 2020. LNCS, Rhodes, Greece, vol. 12476, pp. 60–80. Springer, Heidelberg (October 2020)
18. Beckert, B., Klebanov, V.: Proof reuse for deductive program verification. In: 2nd International Conference on Software Engineering and Formal Methods (SEFM), Beijing, China, pp. 77–86. IEEE Computer Society (2004)
19. Benveniste, A., Caillaud, B., Elmqvist, H., Ghorbal, K., Otter, M., Pouzet, M.: Multi-mode dae models - challenges, theory and implementation. In: Steffen, B., Woeginger, G. (eds.) Computing and Software Science. LNCS, vol. 10000, pp. 283–310. Springer, Cham (2019). https://doi.org/10.1007/978-3-319-91908-9_16
20. Benveniste, A., Caillaud, B., Ferrari, A., Mangeruca, L., Passerone, R., Sofronis, C.: Multiple viewpoint contract-based specification and design. In: de Boer, F.S., Bonsangue, M.M., Graf, S., de Roever, W.-P. (eds.) FMCO 2007. LNCS, vol. 5382, pp. 200–225. Springer, Heidelberg (2008). https://doi.org/10.1007/978-3-540-92188-2_9
21. Bertot, Y., Castéran, P.: Interactive Theorem Proving and Program Development-Coq'Art: The Calculus of Inductive Constructions. Texts in Theoretical Computer Science. An EATCS Series. Springer, Heidelberg (2004). https://doi.org/10.1007/978-3-662-07964-5
22. Beyer, D., Kanav, S.: An interface theory for program verification (position paper). In: Margaria, T., Steffen, B. (eds.) 9th International Symposium on Leveraging Applications of Formal Methods, Verification and Validation, ISoLA 2020. LNCS, Rhodes, Greece, vol. 12476, pp. 168–186. Springer (October 2020)
23. Beyer, D., Keremoglu, M.E.: CPAchecker: a tool for configurable software verification. In: Gopalakrishnan, G., Qadeer, S. (eds.) CAV 2011. LNCS, vol. 6806, pp. 184–190. Springer, Heidelberg (2011). https://doi.org/10.1007/978-3-642-22110-1_16
24. Beyer, D., Lemberger, T.: Symbolic execution with CEGAR. In: Margaria, T., Steffen, B. (eds.) ISoLA 2016. LNCS, vol. 9952, pp. 195–211. Springer, Cham (2016). https://doi.org/10.1007/978-3-319-47166-2_14
25. Beyer, D., Wehrheim, H.: Verification artifacts in cooperative verification: survey and unifying component framework. In Margaria, T., Steffen, B. (eds.) 9th International Symposium on Leveraging Applications of Formal Methods, Verification and Validation, ISoLA 2020. LNCS, Rhodes, Greece, vol. 12476, pp. 143–167. Springer (October 2020)
26. Blom, S., Darabi, S., Huisman, M., Oortwijn, W.: The VerCors tool set: verification of parallel and concurrent software. In: Polikarpova, N., Schneider, S. (eds.) IFM 2017. LNCS, vol. 10510, pp. 102–110. Springer, Cham (2017). https://doi.org/10.1007/978-3-319-66845-1_7

27. Börger, E., Stärk, R.: Abstract State Machines: A Method for High-Level System Design and Analysis. Springer, Heidelberg (2003). https://doi.org/10.1007/978-3-642-18216-7

28. Bornat, R., Calcagno, C., O'Hearn, P.W., Parkinson, M.J.: Permission accounting in separation logic. In: Palsberg, J., Abadi, M. (eds.) Proceedings of the 32nd ACM SIGPLAN-SIGACT Symposium on Principles of Programming Languages, POPL 2005, Long Beach, California, USA, 12–14 January 2005, pp. 259–270. ACM (2005)

29. Boyer, R.S., Elspas, B., Levitt, K.N.: SELECT–a formal system for testing and debugging programs by symbolic execution. ACM SIGPLAN Not. **10**(6), 234–245 (1975)

30. Boyland, J.: Fractional permissions. In: Clarke, D., Noble, J., Wrigstad, T. (eds.) Aliasing in Object-Oriented Programming. Types, Analysis and Verification. LNCS, vol. 7850, pp. 270–288. Springer, Heidelberg (2013). https://doi.org/10.1007/978-3-642-36946-9_10

31. Bravetti, M., Zavattaro, G.: Towards a unifying theory for choreography conformance and contract compliance. In: Lumpe, M., Vanderperren, W. (eds.) SC 2007. LNCS, vol. 4829, pp. 34–50. Springer, Heidelberg (2007). https://doi.org/10.1007/978-3-540-77351-1_4

32. Brookes, S., O'Hearn, P.W.: Concurrent separation logic. SIGLOG News **3**(3), 47–65 (2016)

33. Bubel, R., et al.: Proof repositories for compositional verification of evolving software systems. In: Steffen, B. (ed.) Transactions on Foundations for Mastering Change I. LNCS, vol. 9960, pp. 130–156. Springer, Cham (2016). https://doi.org/10.1007/978-3-319-46508-1_8

34. Bubel, R., Din, C.C., Hähnle, R., Nakata, K.: A dynamic logic with traces and coinduction. In: De Nivelle, H. (ed.) TABLEAUX 2015. LNCS (LNAI), vol. 9323, pp. 307–322. Springer, Cham (2015). https://doi.org/10.1007/978-3-319-24312-2_21

35. Bubel, R., Hähnle, R., Pelevina, M.: Fully abstract operation contracts. In: Margaria, T., Steffen, B. (eds.) ISoLA 2014. LNCS, vol. 8803, pp. 120–134. Springer, Heidelberg (2014). https://doi.org/10.1007/978-3-662-45231-8_9

36. Bundy, A.: The automation of proof by mathematical induction. In: Robinson, J.A., Voronkov, A. (eds.) Handbook of Automated Reasoning, vol. I, pp. 845–911. Elsevier and MIT Press (2001)

37. Bundy, A., Basin, D., Hutter, D., Ireland, A.: Rippling: Meta-level Guidance for Mathematical Reasoning. Cambridge Tracts in Theoretical Computer Science, vol. 56. Cambridge University Press, Cambridge (2005)

38. Burstall, R.M.: Program proving as hand simulation with a little induction. In: Information Processing, vol. 1974, pp. 308–312. Elsevier/North-Holland (1974)

39. Carbone, M., Honda, K., Yoshida, N.: Structured communication-centered programming for web services. ACM Trans. Program. Lang. Syst. **34**(2), 8:1–8:78 (2012)

40. Castagna, G., Dezani-Ciancaglini, M., Padovani, L.: On global types and multiparty sessions. In: Bruni, R., Dingel, J. (eds.) FMOODS/FORTE-2011. LNCS, vol. 6722, pp. 1–28. Springer, Heidelberg (2011). https://doi.org/10.1007/978-3-642-21461-5_1

41. Chaudhuri, K., Doligez, D., Lamport, L., Merz, S.: A TLA+ proof system. In: Rudnicki, P., Sutcliffe, G., Konev, B., Schmidt, R.A., Schulz, S. (eds.) Proceedings of the LPAR Workshops on Knowledge Exchange: Automated Provers and Proof

Assistants, and the 7th International Workshop on the Implementation of Logics, CEUR Workshop Proceedings, Doha, Qatar, vol. 418. CEUR-WS.org (2008)

42. Clarke, D., Östlund, J., Sergey, I., Wrigstad, T.: Ownership types: a survey. In: Clarke, D., Noble, J., Wrigstad, T. (eds.) Aliasing in Object-Oriented Programming. Types, Analysis and Verification. LNCS, vol. 7850, pp. 15–58. Springer, Heidelberg (2013). https://doi.org/10.1007/978-3-642-36946-9_3

43. Clarke, E., Grumberg, O., Jha, S., Lu, Y., Veith, H.: Counterexample-guided abstraction refinement. In: Emerson, E.A., Sistla, A.P. (eds.) CAV 2000. LNCS, vol. 1855, pp. 154–169. Springer, Heidelberg (2000). https://doi.org/10.1007/10722167_15

44. Coto, A., Guanciale, R., Tuosto, E.: On testing message-passing components. In: Margaria, T., Steffen, B. (eds.) 9th International Symposium on Leveraging Applications of Formal Methods, Verification and Validation, ISoLA 2020. LNCS, Rhodes, Greece, vol. 12476, pp. 22–38. Springer, Heidelberg (October 2020)

45. Cousot, P., Cousot, R.: Abstract interpretation: a unified lattice model for static analysis of programs by construction or approximation of fixpoints. In: 4th ACM Symposium on Principles of Programming Language, Los Angeles, pp. 238–252. ACM Press, New York (January 1977)

46. Damiani, F., Lienhardt, M., Paolini, L.: On slicing software product line signatures. In: Margaria, T., Steffen, B. (eds.) 9th International Symposium on Leveraging Applications of Formal Methods, Verification and Validation, ISoLA 2020. LNCS, Rhodes, Greece, vol. 12476, pp. 81–102. Springer, Heidelberg (October 2020)

47. de Alfaro, L., Henzinger, T.A.: Interface automata. In: Tjoa, A.M., Gruhn, V. (eds.) Proceedings of the 8th European Software Engineering Conference Held Jointly with 9th ACM SIGSOFT International Symposium on Foundations of Software Engineering 2001, Vienna, Austria, 10–14 September 2001, pp. 109–120. ACM (2001)

48. de Boer, F., et al.: A survey of active object languages. ACM Comput. Surv. 50(5), 761–7639 (2017). Article 76

49. De Gouw, S., De Boer, F.S., Bubel, R., Hähnle, R., Rot, J., Steinhöfel, D.: Verifying OpenJDK's sort method for generic collections. J. Autom. Reasoning 62(6), 93–126 (2019). https://doi.org/10.1007/s10817-017-9426-4

50. Delaware, B., Cook, W.R., Batory, D.S.: Product lines of theorems. In: Lopes, C.V., Fisher, K. (eds.) Proceedings of the 26th Annual ACM SIGPLAN Conference on Object-Oriented Programming, Systems, Languages, and Applications, OOPSLA, Portland, OR, USA, pp. 595–608. ACM (2011)

51. Dietl, W., Müller, P.: Universes: lightweight ownership for JML. J. Object Technol. 4(8), 5–32 (2005)

52. Dijkstra, E.W.: A Discipline of Programming. Prentice-Hall, Upper Saddle River (1976)

53. Din, C.C., Hähnle, R., Johnsen, E.B., Pun, K.I., Tapia Tarifa, S.L.: Locally abstract, globally concrete semantics of concurrent programming languages. In: Schmidt, R.A., Nalon, C. (eds.) TABLEAUX 2017. LNCS (LNAI), vol. 10501, pp. 22–43. Springer, Cham (2017). https://doi.org/10.1007/978-3-319-66902-1_2

54. Din, C.C., Owe, O.: Compositional reasoning about active objects with shared futures. Formal Aspects Comput. 27(3), 551–572 (2015)

55. Dovland, J., Johnsen, E.B., Owe, O., Steffen, M.: Incremental reasoning with lazy behavioral subtyping for multiple inheritance. Sci. Comput. Program. 76(10), 915–941 (2011)

56. Emerson, E.A.: Automata, tableaux, and temporal logics. In: Parikh, R. (ed.) Logic of Programs 1985. LNCS, vol. 193, pp. 79–88. Springer, Heidelberg (1985). https://doi.org/10.1007/3-540-15648-8_7

57. Feng, X.: Local rely-guarantee reasoning. In: Shao, Z., Pierce, B.C. (eds.) Proceedings of the 36th ACM SIGPLAN-SIGACT Symposium on Principles of Programming Languages, POPL, Savannah, GA, USA, pp. 315–327. ACM (2009)

58. Filliâtre, J.-C., Paskevich, A.: Abstraction and genericity in Why3. In: Margaria, T., Steffen, B., (eds.) 9th International Symposium on Leveraging Applications of Formal Methods, Verification and Validation, ISoLA 2020. LNCS, Rhodes, Greece, vol. 12476, pp. 122–142. Springer, Heidelberg (October 2020)

59. Gerth, R., de Roever, W.P.: A proof system for concurrent ADA programs. Sci. Comput. Program. 4(2), 159–204 (1984)

60. Godefroid, P., Luchaup, D.: Automatic partial loop summarization in dynamic test generation. In: Dwyer, M.B., Tip, F. (eds.) Proceedings of the 20th International Symposium on Software Testing and Analysis, ISSTA, Toronto, Canada, pp. 23–33. ACM (2011)

61. Gößler, G., Sifakis, J.: Composition for component-based modeling. Sci. Comput. Program. 55(1–3), 161–183 (2005)

62. Graf, S., Saidi, H.: Construction of abstract state graphs with PVS. In: Grumberg, O. (ed.) CAV 1997. LNCS, vol. 1254, pp. 72–83. Springer, Heidelberg (1997). https://doi.org/10.1007/3-540-63166-6_10

63. Gries, D.: The Science of Programming. Texts and Monographs in Computer Science. Springer, New York (1981). https://doi.org/10.1007/978-1-4612-5983-1

64. Gurov, D., Huisman, M.: Reducing behavioural to structural properties of programs with procedures. Theoret. Comput. Sci. 480, 69–103 (2013)

65. Hähnle, R., Huisman, M.: Deductive software verification: from pen-and-paper proofs to industrial tools. In: Steffen, B., Woeginger, G. (eds.) Computing and Software Science. LNCS, vol. 10000, pp. 345–373. Springer, Cham (2019). https://doi.org/10.1007/978-3-319-91908-9_18

66. Hähnle, R., Schaefer, I.: A Liskov principle for delta-oriented programming. In: Margaria, T., Steffen, B. (eds.) ISoLA 2012. LNCS, vol. 7609, pp. 32–46. Springer, Heidelberg (2012). https://doi.org/10.1007/978-3-642-34026-0_4

67. Harel, D., Kozen, D., Tiuryn, J.: Dynamic Logic (Foundations of Computing). MIT Press, Cambridge (2000)

68. Hewitt, C., Bishop, P., Steiger, R.: A universal modular ACTOR formalism for artificial intelligence. In: Proceedings of the 3rd International Joint Conference on Artificial Intelligence, IJCAI 1973, pp. 235–245. Morgan Kaufmann Publishers Inc. (1973)

69. Hoare, C.A.R.: An axiomatic basis for computer programming. Commun. ACM 12(10), 576–580, 583 (1969)

70. Hoare, C.A.R.: Communicating sequential processes. Commun. ACM 21(8), 666–677 (1978)

71. Holzmann, G.J.: The SPIN Model Checker. Pearson Education, London (2003)

72. Honda, K.: Types for dyadic interaction. In: Best, E. (ed.) CONCUR 1993. LNCS, vol. 715, pp. 509–523. Springer, Heidelberg (1993). https://doi.org/10.1007/3-540-57208-2_35

73. Honda, K., Yoshida, N., Carbone, M.: Multiparty asynchronous session types. J. ACM 63(1), 9:1–9:67 (2016)

74. Hüttel, H., et al.: Foundations of session types and behavioural contracts. ACM Comput. Surv. 49(1), 3:1–3:36 (2016)

75. Isberner, M., Howar, F., Steffen, B.: Learning register automata: from languages to program structures. Mach. Learn. **96**(1–2), 65–98 (2014)
76. Jacobs, B., Piessens, F.: The VeriFast program verifier. Technical report CW-520, Department of Computer Science, Katholieke Universiteit Leuven (August 2008)
77. Johansson, M., Dixon, L., Bundy, A.: Dynamic rippling, middle-out reasoning and lemma discovery. In: Siegler, S., Wasser, N. (eds.) Verification, Induction, Termination Analysis. LNCS (LNAI), vol. 6463, pp. 102–116. Springer, Heidelberg (2010). https://doi.org/10.1007/978-3-642-17172-7_6
78. Johnsen, E.B., Hähnle, R., Schäfer, J., Schlatte, R., Steffen, M.: ABS: a core language for abstract behavioral specification. In: Aichernig, B.K., de Boer, F.S., Bonsangue, M.M. (eds.) FMCO 2010. LNCS, vol. 6957, pp. 142–164. Springer, Heidelberg (2011). https://doi.org/10.1007/978-3-642-25271-6_8
79. Johnsen, E.B., Steffen, M., Stumpf, J.B.: Assumption-commitment types for resource management in virtually timed ambients. In: Margaria, T., Steffen, B. (eds.) 9th International Symposium on Leveraging Applications of Formal Methods, Verification and Validation, ISoLA 2020. LNCS, Rhodes, Greece, vol. 12476, pp. 103–121. Springer, Heidelberg (October 2020)
80. Jones, C.B.: Specification and design of (parallel) programs. In; Mason, R.E.A. (ed.) Information Processing 83, Proceedings of the IFIP 9th World Computer Congress, Paris, France, 19–23 September 1983, pp. 321–332. North-Holland (1983)
81. Kamburjan, E.: Behavioral program logic. In: Cerrito, S., Popescu, A. (eds.) TABLEAUX 2019. LNCS (LNAI), vol. 11714, pp. 391–408. Springer, Cham (2019). https://doi.org/10.1007/978-3-030-29026-9_22
82. Kamburjan, E., Chen, T.-C.: Stateful behavioral types for active objects. In: Furia, C.A., Winter, K. (eds.) IFM 2018. LNCS, vol. 11023, pp. 214–235. Springer, Cham (2018). https://doi.org/10.1007/978-3-319-98938-9_13
83. Kamburjan, E.. Din, C.C., Hähnle, R., Johnsen, E.B.: Behavioral contracts for cooperative scheduling. In: Ahrendt, W., Beckert, B., Bubel, R., Hähnle, R., Ulbrich, M. (eds.) Deductive Software Verification: Future Perspectives. LNCS, vol. 12345. Springer, Heidelberg (2020)
84. Kamburjan, E., Hähnle, R., Schön, S.: Formal modeling and analysis of railway operations with Active Objects. Sci. Comput. Program. **166**, 167–193 (2018)
85. Kassios, I.T.: The dynamic frames theory. Formal Aspects Comput. **23**(3), 267–288 (2011)
86. King, J.C.: Symbolic execution and program testing. Commun. ACM **19**(7), 385–394 (1976)
87. Kirchner, F., Kosmatov, N., Prevosto, V., Signoles, J., Yakobowski, B.: Frama-C: a software analysis perspective. Formal Aspects Comput. **27**(3), 573–609 (2015)
88. Knüppel, A., Runge, T., Schaefer, I.: Scaling correctness-by-construction. In: Margaria, T., Steffen, B. (eds.) 9th International Symposium on Leveraging Applications of Formal Methods, Verification and Validation, ISoLA 2020. LNCS, Rhodes, Greece, vol. 12476, pp. 187–207. Springer, Heidelberg (October 2020)
89. Kourie, D.G., Watson, B.W.: The Correctness-by-Construction Approach to Programming. Springer, Heidelberg (2012). https://doi.org/10.1007/978-3-642-27919-5
90. Lahav, O., Vafeiadis, V.: Owicki-Gries reasoning for weak memory models. In: Halldórsson, M.M., Iwama, K., Kobayashi, N., Speckmann, B. (eds.) ICALP 2015. LNCS, vol. 9135, pp. 311–323. Springer, Heidelberg (2015). https://doi.org/10.1007/978-3-662-47666-6_25

91. Leavens, G.T., et al.: JML Reference Manual. Draft revision 2344 (May 2013)
92. Leino, K.R.M., Müller, P., Wallenburg, A.: Flexible immutability with frozen objects. In: Shankar, N., Woodcock, J. (eds.) VSTTE 2008. LNCS, vol. 5295, pp. 192–208. Springer, Heidelberg (2008). https://doi.org/10.1007/978-3-540-87873-5_17
93. Lynch, N., Segala, R., Vaandrager, F., Weinberg, H.B.: Hybrid I/O automata. In: Alur, R., Henzinger, T.A., Sontag, E.D. (eds.) HS 1995. LNCS, vol. 1066, pp. 496–510. Springer, Heidelberg (1996). https://doi.org/10.1007/BFb0020971
94. McIlvenna, S., Dumas, M., Wynn, M.T.: Synthesis of orchestrators from service choreographies. In: Kirchberg, M., Link, S. (eds.) 6th Asia-Pacific Conference on Conceptual Modelling (APCCM), Conceptual Modelling 2009. CRPIT, Wellington, New Zealand, vol. 96, pp. 129–138. Australian Computer Society (2009)
95. Meyer, B.: Applying "design by contract". IEEE Comput. 25(10), 40–51 (1992)
96. Milner, R. (ed.): A Calculus of Communicating Systems. LNCS, vol. 92. Springer, Heidelberg (1980). https://doi.org/10.1007/3-540-10235-3
97. Milner, R., Parrow, J., Walker, D.: A calculus of mobile processes. I. Inf. Comput. 100(1), 1–40 (1992)
98. Milner, R., Parrow, J., Walker, D.: A calculus of mobile processes, II. Inf. Comput. 100(1), 41–77 (1992)
99. Misra, J., Chandy, K.M.: Proofs of networks of processes. IEEE Trans. Softw. Eng. 7(4), 417–426 (1981)
100. Müller, A., Mitsch, S., Retschitzegger, W., Schwinger, W., Platzer, A.: Tactical contract composition for hybrid system component verification. Int. J. Softw. Tools Technol. Transf. 20(6), 615–643 (2018)
101. Nieto, L.P.: The rely-guarantee method in Isabelle/HOL. In: Degano, P. (ed.) ESOP 2003. LNCS, vol. 2618, pp. 348–362. Springer, Heidelberg (2003). https://doi.org/10.1007/3-540-36575-3_24
102. Nipkow, T., Wenzel, M., Paulson, L.C. (eds.): Isabelle/HOL – A Proof Assistant for Higher-Order Logic. LNCS, vol. 2283. Springer, Heidelberg (2002). https://doi.org/10.1007/3-540-45949-9
103. O'Hearn, P.W.: Separation logic. Commun. ACM 62(2), 86–95 (2019)
104. Owicki, S.S., Gries, D.: Verifying properties of parallel programs: an axiomatic approach. Commun. ACM 19(5), 279–285 (1976)
105. Peltz, C.: Web services orchestration and choreography. IEEE Comput. 36(10), 46–52 (2003)
106. Poetzsch-Heffter, A., Schäfer, J.: Modular specification of encapsulated object-oriented components. In: de Boer, F.S., Bonsangue, M.M., Graf, S., de Roever, W.-P. (eds.) FMCO 2005. LNCS, vol. 4111, pp. 313–341. Springer, Heidelberg (2006). https://doi.org/10.1007/11804192_15
107. Pohl, K., Böckle, G., van der Linden, F.J.: Software Product Line Engineering: Foundations Principles and Techniques. Springer, Heidelberg (2005). https://doi.org/10.1007/3-540-28901-1
108. Reif, W., Stenzel, K.: Reuse of proofs in software verification. In: Shyamasundar, R.K. (ed.) FSTTCS 1993. LNCS, vol. 761, pp. 284–293. Springer, Heidelberg (1993). https://doi.org/10.1007/3-540-57529-4_61
109. Schaefer, I., Bettini, L., Bono, V., Damiani, F., Tanzarella, N.: Delta-oriented programming of software product lines. In: Bosch, J., Lee, J. (eds.) SPLC 2010. LNCS, vol. 6287, pp. 77–91. Springer, Heidelberg (2010). https://doi.org/10.1007/978-3-642-15579-6_6
110. Schellhorn, G., Ahrendt, W.: Reasoning about abstract state machines: the WAM case study. J. Univ. Comput. Sci. 3(4), 377–412 (1997)

111. Schmitt, P.H., Ulbrich, M., Weiß, B.: Dynamic frames in Java dynamic logic. In: Beckert, B., Marché, C. (eds.) FoVeOOS 2010. LNCS, vol. 6528, pp. 138–152. Springer, Heidelberg (2011). https://doi.org/10.1007/978-3-642-18070-5_10

112. Sirjani, M., Movaghar, A., Shali, A., de Boer, F.S.: Modeling and verification of reactive systems using Rebeca. Fundamenta Informatica 63(4), 385–410 (2004)

113. Spivey, J.M.: The Z Notation: A Reference Manual, 2nd edn. Prentice Hall International Series in Computer Science, London (1992)

114. Steinhöfel, D., Hähnle, R.: Abstract execution. In: ter Beek, M.H., McIver, A., Oliveira, J.N. (eds.) FM 2019. LNCS, vol. 11800, pp. 319–336. Springer, Cham (2019). https://doi.org/10.1007/978-3-030-30942-8_20

115. Steinhöfel, D., Hähnle, R.: The trace modality. In: Soares Barbosa, L., Baltag, A. (eds.) DALI 2019. LNCS, vol. 12005, pp. 124–140. Springer, Cham (2020). https://doi.org/10.1007/978-3-030-38808-9_8

116. Thüm, T., Knüppel, A., Krüger, S., Bolle, S., Schaefer, I.: Feature-oriented contract composition. J. Syst. Softw. 152, 83–107 (2019)

117. Thüm, T., Schaefer, I., Kuhlemann, M., Apel, S.: Proof composition for deductive verification of software product lines. In: 4th IEEE International Conference on Software Testing, Verification and Validation (Workshop Proceedings), ICST, Berlin, Germany, pp. 270–277. IEEE Computer Society (2011)

118. Tschannen, J., Furia, C.A., Nordio, M., Polikarpova, N.: AutoProof: auto-active functional verification of object-oriented programs. In: Baier, C., Tinelli, C. (eds.) TACAS 2015. LNCS, vol. 9035, pp. 566–580. Springer, Heidelberg (2015). https://doi.org/10.1007/978-3-662-46681-0_53

119. Urso, P., Kounalis, E.: Sound generalizations in mathematical induction. Theoret. Comput. Sci. 323(1–3), 443–471 (2004)

120. Walther, C., Kolbe, T.: Proving theorems by reuse. Artif. Intell. 116(1–2), 17–66 (2000)

121. Walther, C., Schweitzer, S.: About VeriFun. In: Baader, F. (ed.) CADE 2003. LNCS (LNAI), vol. 2741, pp. 322–327. Springer, Heidelberg (2003). https://doi.org/10.1007/978-3-540-45085-6_28

On Testing Message-Passing Components

Alex Coto[1]([✉]) [iD], Roberto Guanciale[2]([✉]) [iD], and Emilio Tuosto[1]([✉]) [iD]

[1] Gran Sasso Science Institute, L'Aquila, Italy
{alex.coto,emilio.tuosto}@gssi.it
[2] KTH, Stockholm, Sweden
robertog@kth.se

Abstract. We instantiate and apply a recently proposed abstract framework featuring an algorithm for the automatic generation of tests for component testing of message-passing systems. We demonstrate the application of a top-down mechanism for test generation. More precisely, we reduce the problem of generating tests for components of message-passing applications to the projection of global views of choreographies. The application of the framework to some examples gives us the pretext to make some considerations about our approach.

1 Introduction

Distributed message-passing applications, as most classes of distributed systems, are hard to develop, reason about, and validate. A principal source of complexity is due to the fact that the state of the computation is scattered across the system. This makes it hard to attain correct coordination of components. Mistakes in the information or control flow may negatively affect the behaviour of the system leading to inconsistent states where a group of components engage in interactions that are not aligned with those of other groups of components. Asynchronous communications and causal dependencies across-components are among the most important hindering factors.

We advocate the combination of model-driven testing with choreographies in order to validate message-passing applications. The notion of choreographies that we adopt is inspired by the one introduced about fifteen years ago by the W3C consortium for WS-CDL [18], a language for specifying service-oriented systems *choreographically*. Key elements introduced in WS-CDL were *global* and *local views* and the notion of a *projection* operation relating these views. Basically, global views are *holistic* descriptions of the behaviour in terms of the interactions among components. The application of the projection operation to global views produces local views, that is, the behaviour of single components in "isolation" that enact the roles of the choreography.

Based on those mechanisms, the community of formal methods developed a so-called *correctness-by-construction* principle. A distinguished example in this

Research partially supported by the EU H2020 RISE programme under the Marie Sklodowska-Curie grant agreement No 778233 , MIUR project PRIN 2017FTXR7S *IT MATTERS* (Methods and Tools for Trustworthy Smart Systems) and the TrustFull project, funded by the Swedish Foundation for Strategic Research.

© Springer Nature Switzerland AG 2020
T. Margaria and B. Steffen (Eds.): ISoLA 2020, LNCS 12476, pp. 22–38, 2020.
https://doi.org/10.1007/978-3-030-61362-4_2

sense is the development of behavioural types [15,17]. The cornerstone of those formal methods is the identification of properties of global views that ensure the correct enactment of the communications they specify. A paramount example is the analysis of distributed choices where participants have to reach consensus about which branch of the choice they have to execute.

These constraints capture suitable notions of *well-formedness* of global views that guarantee the correct exchange of messages for participants projected from the global view. For instance, approaches such as [5,7,9,13,14,16] (to mention but a few) study notions of well-formedness to guarantee the safety of communications, e.g., through awareness of choices. The interesting properties usually are (dead)lock-freedom or no message losses.

We have recently started to investigate the use of choreographic models to test applications [8]. The initial results in [8] feature an abstract framework for component testing of message-passing application, dubbed here CGT, after *choreographies for generation of tests*. More precisely, CGT is based on abstract properties of well-formedness and projection operations to automatically extract tests for a participant from a syntactic presentation of the global views. The generation of tests exploits the local views resulting from a projection operation to identify tests of interest for a fixed component of the choreography. The approach in [8] is abstract in the following sense: instead of concrete project operations, CGT identifies (mild) conditions on them so that a component can be tested. A peculiar aspect of CGT is that it relies on the methods underlying correctness-by-construction approaches of choreographies. In particular, CGT uses well-formedness conditions to generate test suites that any "valid implementation" should pass. Also, CGT is equipped in [8] with an algorithm that generates "meaningful" tests for the component under testing. To some extent, this solves the *oracle problem* for such automatically generated tests.

In this paper, we instantiate CGT on a specific choreographic model and apply it to a non-trivial scenario. This experiment yields another contribution of this paper which is an analysis of testing approaches to message-passing applications as well as a discussion on possible optimisations of the algorithm in [8] as well as some open problems. Despite being a well-established area of software engineering, testing is not widely applied to distributed applications. This domain is indeed quite challenging due to several factors that we discuss (cf. Sect. 5) through some considerations on our experiment.

We apply a model-driven component testing framework for choreography where participants coordinate by asynchronously message-passing. More precisely, we assume that each pair of participants communicate through a unidirectional point-to-point lossless and error-free channel that buffers messages without preserving the order of outputs. As discussed in the paper, we advocate testing to harness the correctness-by-construction principle of choreographies. The main reason for this is that many practices in software development may spoil correctness. We list some situations that may break correctness.

- Often choreographic frameworks abstract away local computations, which therefore require manual intervention.

- Third-party software may not be correct-by-construction.
- Testing may harness those formal settings that do not provide feedback when well-formedness is violated.
- Architects may need to validate choreographies that do not enjoy well-formedness since it is a sufficient but not necessary condition for correctness. Likewise, problems may depend on misbehaviour of underlying communication middlewares rather than applications at hand.
- Software evolution may introduce defects when e.g., a correctly realised component is replaced with a new version because the top-down approach of choreographies is not correctly followed.

Outline. Section 2 surveys background material. Section 3 describes the instantiated framework that we consider here. Section 4 introduces a non-trivial scenario and shows how to apply CGT. Section 5 discusses improvements and some open problems. Section 6 considers related work and draws some conclusions.

2   Background

We briefly sketch the choreographic framework adopted in CGT. Global and local views are respectively formalised in terms of *global choreographies* (g-choreographies) [13] and of a variant of *communicating finite-state machines* (CMFSs) [4]. Both models abstract asynchronous message-passing.

2.1   Global Choreographies

A g-choreography G models the communication protocol of a set of participants. The units of communication are *interactions* representing the exchange of a message between a sender and a receiver. We write A→B: m for the interaction where the sender A sends message (of sort) m to the receiver B which is supposed to receive it. We let $\mathcal{P}$ denote the set of participants and let A, B, ... range over $\mathcal{P}$. Messages (ranged over by m, n, y, ...) represent sorts for data rather than actual values.

We illustrate the problem of well-formedness of g-choreographies informally through the diagram on the right representing an example borrowed from [1]. This g-choreography models the protocol followed by two components, C1 and C2 to control the level of uranium (UR) and nitric acid (NA) for the production of energy in a nuclear power plant. Each component can request variations of the energy production by incrementing or doubling the level of the elements.

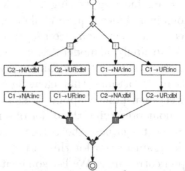

In the diagram, ◇ and its darker variant respectively represent selection and merge of a distributed choice while □ and its darker variant respectively represent the fork and join of concurrent activities in the global view. Note that edges represent causal relations between communication events; for instance, the edge from the interaction C2→NA: dbl and C1→NA: inc means that the former causes/precedes the latter. Intuitively, the intended meaning of the g-choreography above is that either (*i*) both uranium and nitric acid are first doubled and then incremented (left branch of the choice), or (*ii*) they are both first incremented and then doubled (right branch of the choice). In either case, each controller and its respective element execute those operations in parallel. A natural expectation of this protocol is that, upon termination, the levels of the two elements is the same. We anticipate that this is not case when the protocol runs distributively and with asynchronous communications. In fact, UR may first receive and process the message from C1 and then the one from C2 while the one controlling nitric acid may process the messages of the two controllers in the opposite order. This results in one unit of uranium ($2x + 2$) more than nitric acid ($2x + 1$). If the invariant is crucial for maintaining the security of the plant, this behaviour may lead to a catastrophic incident.

The semantics of a g-choreography, written $[\![G]\!]$, is defined in terms of a set of pomsets (i.e. partially ordered multisets). Each pomset represents the causal dependencies among events of a single branch. Events are labelled by communicating actions $l \in \mathcal{L}_{\text{act}}$, where A B!m represents participant A sending message m to B and A B?m represents participant B receiving message m from A. The subject (i.e. $\text{sbj}(l) = A$) of A B!m and A B?m are A and B respectively.

Each pomset represents all possible traces caused by different interleavings of concurrent events. Therefore, the language of a g-choreography, written $\mathcal{L}[G]$, is the closure under prefix of the set of all *linearisations* of $[\![G]\!]$, where a linearisation of a pomset is a permutation of its events that preserves the order of the pomset.

Pomset-based conditions that check well-formedness of g-choreographies have been identified in [26]. The g-choreography above does not satisfy these conditions. The problem arises because both NA and UR make a local choice without communicating with the other partner. For example, it can happen that NA decides to first double and then increment while UR decides for the opposite.

2.2 Communicating Systems

Communicating systems were introduced in [4] as an expressive model of message-passing protocols. Participants of a protocol are modelled as a *communicating finite-state machine* (CFSM), namely a finite state automaton $M = (Q, q_0, \rightarrow)$ where labels are communication actions in $\mathcal{L}_{\text{act}}$. A CFSM is A-*local* if any label l on its transitions is such that $\text{sbj}(l) = A$. Below are two CFSMs corresponding to participants NA and C1 of the example in Sect. 2.1

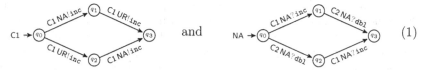

Notice that the parallel composition in the g-choreography is expressed through commuting transitions in the CFSMs. Due to the obvious symmetry, the two

CFSMs corresponding to participants UR and C2 are analogous to the machine corresponding to NA and C1 respectively.

A *(communicating) system* is a map $S = (M_i)_{i \in I}$ where $M_i = (Q_i, q_{0i}, \rightarrow_i)$ is a CFSM for each index $i \in I$. For each pair of participants $A \neq B$ there is a channel AB from A to B formally, $C = \{AB \mid A \neq B \in \mathcal{P}\}$ is the set of *channels*. Each channel $AB \in C$ has an unbounded buffer b_{AB} containing the messages that A has sent to B and from which B consumes the messages sent by A. Here we assume buffers to be finite multisets (in the original definition of CFSMs in [4], buffers are unbounded FIFO queues).

The semantics of a communicating system is a transition system which keeps track of the state of machines and the content of buffers. A *configuration* of S is a pair $s = \langle q \, ; \, b \rangle$ where $q = (q_i)_{i \in I}$ with $q_i \in Q_i$ and $b = (b_{AB})_{AB \in C}$. The *initial* configuration s_0 is the one where, for all $i \in I$, $q_i = q_{0i}$ is the corresponding initial state and all its buffers are empty. A configuration $s = \langle q \, ; \, b \rangle$ *moves* to $s' = \langle q' \, ; \, b' \rangle$, written $s \xrightarrow{l} s'$, if there is a machine that is ready to send a message or if there is a pending message and a machine that is ready to consume it. In both cases, the transition of the machine is fired and the message is either added or removed from the corresponding buffer.

For instance, the following sequence of transitions

$$s \xrightarrow{\text{C1 NA! inc}} s' \xrightarrow{\text{C1 NA? inc}} s'' \qquad (2)$$

is possible in the system containing the CFSMs in (1) where the local states of both C1 and NA is their initial state s while s' and s'' are such that

- the only state changed in s' is the local state of C1, which is set to q_1, and the buffer of C1 NA in s' is obtained by adding an **inc** message to the buffer of C1 NA in s
- s'' equals s but for the local states of the CFSMs C1 and NA which are both q_1 in s''.

Notice that $s' \xrightarrow{\text{C2 NA! dbl}} s'''$ is possible, namely in s' the controller C2 can send the message **dbl** to NA before the latter consumes the message **inc** from the buffer of C1 NA. Obviously $s \xcancel{\xrightarrow{\text{C1 NA? inc}}}$ if the buffer of C1 NA in s does not contain **inc**.

A configuration s is *stable for* $C' \subseteq C$ if all buffers in C' are empty in s (we simply say s *stable* if $C' = C$) and it is a *deadlock* if $s \xcancel{\rightarrow}$ and either there is a machine ready to perform an input or s is not stable.

Let $\Pi(S, s)$ be the set of *runs* of a communicating system S starting from a configuration s of S, that is the set of sequences $\pi = \{(s_i, l_i, s_{i+1})\}_{0 \leq i \leq n}$ with $n \in \mathbb{N} \cup \{\infty\}$ such that $s_0 = s$, and $s_i \xrightarrow{l_i} s_{i+1}$ for every $0 \leq i \leq n$. For instance, the sequence in (2) is a run from s. Also, the run π is *maximal* if $n = \infty$ or $s_n \xcancel{\rightarrow}$. We denote with $\Pi(S)$ the runs of S starting from its initial configuration. The *trace* of a run π is the sequence of actions l_i occurring in it, and the *language of a communicating system S*, written $\mathcal{L}[S]$ is the set of traces of the runs $\Pi(S)$.

3   Instantiating CGT

Well-Formedness and the projection operation are parameters of CGT and are abstracted away by means of some requirements. A *projection* function $\_\lfloor\_$ generates local models from global models. In our case, this intuitively means that $G\lfloor_A$ is a CFSM "reflecting" the communication pattern specified in G for the participant A. The requirements of CGT on well-formedness and projection are that they capture deadlock-free realisable systems, namely that well-formedness of G guarantees

- the existence of a system S realising G, namely that $\mathcal{L}[S] \subseteq \mathcal{L}[G]$ whose runs are deadlock-free;
- and that the projection of G yields a system realising G.

A well-known problem of software testing is to decide when a test is successful. In fact, this decision is application-dependent and usually has to be specified manually [2]. To tackle this problem we appeal to the syntax corresponding to the diagrammatic representation of g-choreographies seen before. It is immaterial to give the actual syntax here; the interested reader is referred to e.g., [13,26]. The procedure assigning the expected outcome to tests is called *oracle*. In our setting, this corresponds to single out configurations of communicating systems according to a sub-tree of a choreography as defined below.

Test success. an *oracle scheme* is a map $\Omega_{G,\lfloor}$ that for each participant A and syntactic subtree of G yields a set of states of the CFSM $G\lfloor_A$ such that for every syntactic subtree τ of G, every maximal run in $\Pi(G\lfloor)$ has a stable configuration where the local state of participant A belongs to $\Omega_{G,\lfloor}(A, \tau)$.

The oracle scheme $\Omega_{G,\lfloor}$ is supposed to "mark" as successful the states that the CSFMs forming a test can possibly reach after having executed the portion of the protocol corresponding to τ. When satisfied, the success requirement establishes that any execution of the test reaches a stable configuration where all the participants are in a successful state. Notice that tests do not check global views; rather they probe (possibly wrong implementations of) local views in order to establish their "compliance" with respect correct global views.

With these ingredients we can define a test for a participant A of G as a map $T = \left(\langle M_i, \underline{Q}_i\rangle\right)_{1\leq i\leq n}$ where $\underline{Q}_i$ is a subset of the states of M_i, which in turn

- is a deterministic CFSM with at most one output transition from each state,
- and the subject of each transition is neither A nor the subject of a transition in a machine M_j with $j \neq i$.

The tests for a participant A of G can be generated from projections by taking all the combinations of CFSMs involving different subjects obtained by "separating" all internal choices until a deterministic machine is attained: i.e., the output transitions from a same state or transitions with the same labels. If, for example, we were to test NA in the choreography in Sect. 2 we could generate the following test machines from C1 in (1):

$$C1 \rightarrow \text{\scriptsize$q_0$} \xrightarrow{\text{C1 NA!inc}} \text{\scriptsize$q_1$} \xrightarrow{\text{C1 UR!inc}} \text{\scriptsize$q_3$} \qquad \text{and} \qquad C1 \rightarrow \text{\scriptsize$q_0$} \xrightarrow{\text{C1 UR!inc}} \text{\scriptsize$q_2$} \xrightarrow{\text{C1 NA!inc}} \text{\scriptsize$q_3$}$$

where the colour-filled states are the successful ones assigned by an oracle scheme. In this case the success of the state disregards anything that happens after that the message C1 UR!inc has been sent.

We instantiate the abstract notions with the well-formedness notion and the projection operation respectively with the predicate $WF(\_)$ and the function $\_\downharpoonright\_$ on g-choreographies defined in [13,26]. For example, if G is the g-choreography in Sect. 1, then as explained $WF(G)$ does not hold, and $G\downharpoonright_{C1}$ and $G\downharpoonright_{NA}$ are the CFSMs in (1). In general, the projection operation $\_\downharpoonright\_$ yields deterministic but not necessarily minimal CFSMs. In the following, we let $G\downharpoonright = (G\downharpoonright_A)_{A\in\mathcal{P}}$ represent the system induced by the projections of G.

It is immaterial to spell out the definitions of well-formedness and projection here; it suffices to note

- that $G\downharpoonright_A$ is a deterministic A-local CFSM for each participant A in G;
- that $WF(G)$ implies $\mathcal{L}[G\downharpoonright] \subseteq \mathcal{L}[G]$, namely $G\downharpoonright$ realises G;
- no run in $\Pi(G\downharpoonright)$ contains a deadlock configuration;

In other words, WF and $\_\downharpoonright\_$ satisfy the soundness requirements of CGT.

Let us now apply the instantiated framework. As said, we need to start from well-formed g-choreographies and the one in Sect. 2 is not. So let us focus on the leftmost parallel composition of the choreography in Sect. 2 that is well-formed and can be syntactically written as

$$G_l = C2{\rightarrow}NA: \text{dbl}; C1{\rightarrow}NA: \text{inc} \mid C2{\rightarrow}UR: \text{dbl}; C1{\rightarrow}UR: \text{inc}$$

Notice that the projections of G_l on C1 and C2 are as those in Sect. 2. We want to test a (wrong) implementation of NA given by the following CFSM:

$$M_{NA} \rightarrow \text{\scriptsize$q_0$} \xrightarrow{\text{C1 NA?inc}} \text{\scriptsize$q_1$} \xrightarrow{\text{C2 NA?inc}} \text{\scriptsize$q_3$}$$

that tries to consume inc from C2. Our tests are of the form

$$T = \left(\langle M_X, \underline{Q}_X \rangle\right)_{X\in\{C1,C2,UR\}} \qquad \text{for some} \quad \underline{Q}_X$$

where each M_X is obtained by applying the algorithm sketched above to $G\downharpoonright_X$. Note that UR is deterministic and has only input transitions, hence the only possible test is $T_{UR} = G\downharpoonright_{UR}$ itself. Instead, the initial states of C1 and C2 both have more than one output transition, so the resulting machines are

$$T_{C1,1} \rightarrow \text{\scriptsize$q_0$} \xrightarrow{\text{C1 NA!inc}} \text{\scriptsize$q_1$} \xrightarrow{\text{C1 UR!inc}} \text{\scriptsize$q_3$} \qquad \text{and} \qquad T_{C1,2} \rightarrow \text{\scriptsize$q_0$} \xrightarrow{\text{C1 UR!inc}} \text{\scriptsize$q_2$} \xrightarrow{\text{C1 NA!inc}} \text{\scriptsize$q_3$}$$

$$T_{C2,1} \rightarrow \text{\scriptsize$q_0$} \xrightarrow{\text{C2 NA!dbl}} \text{\scriptsize$q_1$} \xrightarrow{\text{C2 UR!dbl}} \text{\scriptsize$q_3$} \qquad \text{and} \qquad T_{C2,2} \rightarrow \text{\scriptsize$q_0$} \xrightarrow{\text{C2 UR!dbl}} \text{\scriptsize$q_2$} \xrightarrow{\text{C2 NA!dbl}} \text{\scriptsize$q_3$}$$

We fix the oracle scheme so that (i) the only success state for both C1 and C2 is q_3 and (ii) any state of UR is a success state (in a sense we care only that UR consumes all the messages when C1 and C2 terminate). Now, consider the communicating systems consisting of M_{NA} $T_{\mathsf{C1},i}$, $T_{\mathsf{C2},j}$, and T_{UR} with $i, j \in \{1, 2\}$. It is easy to see that every run of each such system cannot reach a stable configuration where both C1 and C2 are in state q_3 because M_{NA} will never consume the message dbl sent by C2.

4   An Example

We apply CGT to a business-to-business (B2B) example among a customer C, a provider P, a land shipping company T, and maritime shipping company S. The scenario is described by the g-choreography G_{B2B} below. When C buys a product

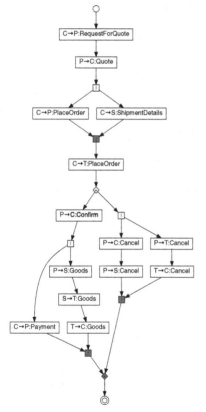

from P, the delivery is outsourced to T and S. The choreography starts with the customer requesting a quote and the provider replying with details of the quote. Notice that the second interaction causally depends on the first one. Then, before[1] booking a truck delivery, in parallel the customer sends the order to the provider and the shipping details to the shipping company.

Once the order has been placed, the transaction can be either successful or cancelled. The latter case may happen because e.g., goods are not available on the date of shipping. In case of a cancelled transaction, the customer is notified by the truck company and the provider. In case of successful transaction, the goods are delivered to the customer while the customer pays the provider.

In order to apply CGT we have to check the well-formedness of G_{B2B}. This is done with the help of Chor-Gram [20], a toolchain for the choreographic development of message-passing applications. Basically, ChorGram confirms that the closure properties hold for G_{B2B}; in fact, all participants are aware of the branch selected by P. Also, ChorGram computes the projections of G_{B2B},

---

[1] This scenario is instrumental to the discussion of Sect. 5; for simplicity we consider only the interesting case when C accepts the quote from P. More realistically, C should decide whether to accept or not the quote (and perhaps bargain with P).

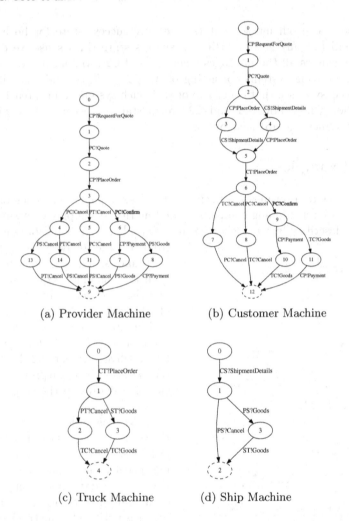

(a) Provider Machine   (b) Customer Machine

(c) Truck Machine   (d) Ship Machine

Fig. 1. Correct machines obtained from projecting G_{B2B}

which are reported in Fig. 1, where dashed states correspond to the completion of the execution of the choreography (as given by an oracle scheme Ω in CGT).

Suppose that the correctness of all components but C has been spoiled due to some modifications. We apply CGT to projections to test the various components.

Testing the Provider. Assume we have the following (faulty) implementation of P (where, for readability, the final state is split in states 5, 8, and 9):

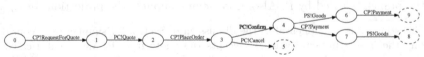

This implementation can bring the whole system to deadlock: suppose the provider decides to cancel the transaction by sending a message to the customer (P C!cancel) and ends it execution on state 5. A correct implementation of S will be expecting either for the goods to arrive from the provider (P S?goods) or for a cancellation message (P S?cancel), and a similar scenario occurs for the truck. A set of machines that can be generated through CGT and can detect this problem is the following:

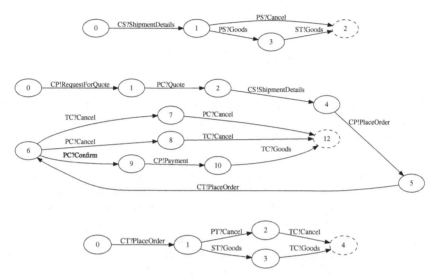

The system composed of the previous wrong implementation of P and the test machines generated by CGT will never reach a success configuration. Notice the execution where P executes P C!cancel and does not also notify the truck and ship of this cancellation (P T!Cancel and P S!Cancel), as required by the original projections. Participant S would then await forever in state 1 either on input P S?goods or on input P S?cancel, whereas T would also be stuck on its state 1, waiting to fire either P T?cancel or S T?goods.

The fact that more than one machine is not in a state marked as final by an oracle scheme means this implementation fails a test. The offending trace can then be used by the developer to better understand and solve the problem.

Testing the Ship. Tests fail also when not all messages of interest are consumed. We see this with the following wrong implementation of S.

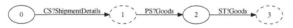

In this case, it might occur that the faulty component decides to finish its execution at state 1, just after receiving the details of the shipment, without ever receiving the goods from the provider, neither sending them to T. This problem would be caught by the following system:

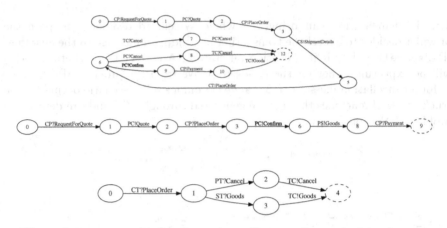

This is because a stable configuration will never be reached in the system, due to the dangling Goods message. A similar example can be derived in the case of T, which we omit for the sake of brevity.

Undetected Errors. There are, however, errors that cannot be detected by the generated tests (as known, tests can reveal the presence of bugs, but not their absence [12]). Indeed, since CGT treats the component under test as a black box, it cannot detect certain interleaving of events of the component under test due to asynchrony. As an example, assume we want to test the C: there is no way to ascertain through testing whether the events C P!PlaceOrder and C S!ShipmentDetails will be done in parallel (instead of e.g. sequentially).

A second example of a scenario where testing might not suffice is when causal dependencies are not preserved. For instance, in Fig. 1c, if we swap the order of events T C!Goods and S T!Goods as follows:

then participant T can send a Goods message before receiving it from S first (as stated in the original g-choreography).

5   Discussion and Open Problems

We now develop some considerations based on the examples presented in the previous sections.

On test generation The mechanisms we used in our examples to test components of message-passing systems hinge on the so called top-down approach featured by an existing choreographic model. A distinctive element of our line of work is the combination of techniques emerged in formal choreographic approaches with model-driven testing. Given mild assumptions on the model, CGT generates tests for component testing of message-passing applications. We remark that the choreographic model adopted, albeit abstract, mimics real programming paradigms, mainly those based on actor models such as Erlang or Akka.

We adopted existing notions of well-formedness and projection. These are the parameters of an abstract test-generation adopted in CGT which fixes the basic notions of test, test feasibility, and test success within the framework of g-choreographies and communicating systems.

The algorithm for test generation discharges inputs in *mixed-choice* states, namely those states with both output and input outgoing transitions. For instance, both Customer and Provider in the shipping example of Sect. 4 have mixed-choice states after the confirmation message is sent by Provider to Customer. Note that mixed-choice states emerge if there is a parallel g-choreography with a participant sending on one thread and receiving on another. The alternative strategy, i.e. discharging outputs of mixed choices, may be problematic and lead to generation of "unsafe" tests. We illustrate this with the following CFSMs:

$$(3)$$

and suppose to use them to test an implementation of A that simply executes A B!m (as expected). The test consisting of the dashed transitions will lead to a deadlock configuration despite the fact that M_A behaves as expected.

There might be alternative approaches to CGT. Firstly, test generation may be done differently when adopting different types of tests. A natural alternative can be obtained by "dualising" projections. Namely, we could take the projection of one component, say M, and consider as test cases the CFSMs obtained by applying our algorithm to the CFSM where all transitions are of M are *dualised* (i.e., each input label is replaced with the corresponding output label and vice versa). Note that this yields a non-local CFSM, which CGT encompasses.

Oracles. Relying on the principled design of the so-called top-down development of choreographic frameworks, we can guarantee that generated tests are suitable, that is they must be passed by valid implementations. This yields a main advantage: CGT solves the oracle problem for the class of generated tests because the oracle scheme can be automatically inferred for a given projection. The problem of determining the expected outcome of a test is indeed well-known in software testing. Usually, this decision problem is application-dependent and requires human intervention [2]. However, there is a trade-off. The exhaustive generation of suitable tests is a source of inefficiency of the algorithm as we argue later.

Efficiency & Feasibility. The theoretical complexity of our test generation algorithm is exponential in the size of the g-choreography. This is essentially due to two main facts.

Firstly, parallel composition of g-choreographies yields an exponential blow-up as it could introduce a number of fictitious internal-choice states in the projections. For instance, consider the variant of the shipping example where, in the parallel composition executed when the order is cancelled, the interactions Provider→Customer: `cancel` and Provider→Ship: `cancel` are in parallel. Then, the algorithm will generate tests that change only for the interleaving of independent outputs. Such tests will be all equivalent and therefore redundant in an asynchronous setting.

Secondly, the exhaustive use of all the syntactic sub-trees yields an high number of tests. This could be unfeasible for large g-choreographies. Note however that the oracle specification is a parameter of our algorithm and, in practice, one can tune it up so to target only "interesting" parts of the g-choreography.

Some optimisations are however possible. A first optimisation can be the reduction of internal choices generated by the parallel composition in our examples. In fact, those tests are redundant and one would be enough in the semantics of communicating systems adopted here (where channels are multisets of messages similar to Erlang's mailboxes). A second optimisation could exploit an analysis of the syntactic structure in order to exclude immaterial sub-trees. For instance, the tree of the whole g-choreography in Sect. 4 is subsumed by the subtree rooted in the second interaction Provider→Customer: `quote`. Indeed any run "going through" the latter tree also goes through the former one. A pre-processing of the oracle specification may therefore improve the efficiency. Note that adopting this approach probably requires a careful transformation of the oracle specification. This may not be easy to attain.

Another optimisation comes from the study of some notion of "dominance" of tests. The discussion above about mixed-choices is an example: in a mixed-choice state, the tests with a bias on first-outputs dominate those starting with inputs. For instance, the test with solid transitions in (3) above dominate the one with dashed transitions.

Quality of Test Suites. In software testing it is widely accepted that it is unfeasible to perform a high number of tests. Hence, test suites are formed by carefully selected tests that satisfy some *coverage* criteria. This yields a number of questions that we did not address yet: What is a good notion of coverage for communicating systems? Can choreographic models help in identifying good coverage measures? What heuristics lead to good coverage? Remarkably, this problem pairs off with the problem of *concretisation* in model-driven testing [23]. Given an abstract test (as the ones we generate), how should it be concretised to test actual implementations? In fact, the abstract notion of coverage only considers distributed choices, but actual implementations may have local branching computations that should also be covered to some extent. This probably requires our approach to be combined with existing approaches to testing.

Semantics, Theory & Practice Obviously, the assumptions on the underlying communication model affect the nature of tests. For instance, the identification of redundant tests discussed above changes if buffers of communicating systems follow a FIFO policy, as per the original definition in [4]. In fact, if one takes such communication model inputs from a same sender become sensitive to the order of the messages. Therefore, a permutation in the sequence of outputs may lead to a deadlock configuration where a receiver cannot consume a message because it is not the top message of the FIFO queue in the buffer.

Studying the semantic aspects of message-passing systems probably requires to develop a suitable theory. An intriguing research direction is indeed the connection between CGT and the theory of testing of communicating systems [10]. This theory has been extended to asynchronous communications [3] and has a natural connection with CGT: the notion of success that we adopt is similar to must-preorder in the theoretical setting. We believe that deeper relations may be unveiled by a systematic study.

Finally, we have started to integrate CGT framework in [20], a toolchain supporting g-choreographies. We believe that tool support is crucial both for experimental analysis and to enable designers to actually adopt CGT.

6   Conclusions and Related Work

We considered component-testing. An intriguing open problem is to apply the ideas of this paper to support integration testing. In fact, one could think of defining *group* projections, namely projection operations that generate communicating systems representing the composition of several participants. We believe that this approach could pay off when the group onto which the g-choreography is projected can be partitioned in a set of "shy" participants that interact only with participants within the group and others that also interact outside the group. The former set of participants basically corresponds to units that are stable parts of the system that and do not need to be (re-)tested as long as the components in the other group pass some tests.

Instead of concretising abstract tests, one could extract CFSMs from actual implementations and run the tests on them. Note that such technique should (i) be more efficient than concretisation (because it does not let abstract tests proliferate into many concrete ones) and (ii) allow to test implemented components for which the source code is not available (e.g., by using some machine learning algorithm to infer the CFSMs). Moreover, another advantage of this approach could be that it enables us to exploit the bottom-up approach of choreographies, where global views are synthesised from local ones (e.g., as in [19,21]). The synthesised choreography can be compared with a reference one to derive tests that are more specific to the implementation at hand. These are definitely interesting alternatives that we plan to explore in the future.

Notoriously, in software engineering, testing is considered *the* tool[2] for verifying software and assuring its quality. The *Software Engineering Book of Knowledge* available from http://www.swebok.org describes *software testing* as (bold text is ours):

> "the dynamic **verification** of the behaviour of a program on a **finite** set of **test cases, suitably selected** from the usually **infinite** executions domain, **against the expected behavior.**"

Our framework reflects the description above[3] for model-driven testing of message-passing systems. An immediate goal of ours is to experimentally check the suitability of the test cases obtained with our algorithm. For this we plan to identify suitable concretisation mechanisms of the abstract tests generated by our algorithm and verify Erlang or Golang programs.

Since message-passing systems fall under the class of *reactive systems* we got inspiration from the work done on model-driven testing of reactive systems [6]. In particular, we showed that choreographic models can, at least to some extend, be used to automatically generate executable tests and as test case specifications [24]. Technically, we exploited the so-called *projection* operation of choreographic models. Here, we gave an abstract notion of projection. A concrete projection was formalised for the first time in [15] (for multi-party session types) and for g-choreographies in [13,14,26], elaborating on the projection of global graphs [11]. As discussed in Sect. 5, in the future we will also explore the use of choreographic model-driven testing to address other problems related to testing message-passing systems.

Traditional testing has been classified [25] according to parameters such as the scale of the system under test, the source from which tests are derived (e.g., requirements, models, or code). There are also classifications according to the specific characteristics being checked [22]; our work can be assigned to the category of behavioural testing.

According to [27], the generation of test cases is one of the ways model-based testing can support software verification. Our model explicitly features a mechanism for test generation paired with the notion of an *oracle scheme* (cf. Sect. 3) as a precise mechanism to identify the expected outcome of test cases. In fact, unlike in most cases, choreographic models contain enough information about the expected behaviour of the system under test in order to make accurate predictions. We believe that this is a peculiarity of our approach.

The use of choreographies in model-driven testing is not new. Model-driven testing exploiting choreography models had been for instance studied in [28]. This work focuses on integration testing rather than component testing. In a

---

[2] Regrettably, barred for few exceptions, rigorous formal methods that aim to show absence of defects rather than their presence are less spread in current practices. We cannot embark in a discussion on this state of the matter here.

[3] Although for simplicity we did not consider iterative g-choreographies in our examples, the algorithm can deal with arbitrary unfolding of the loops, which make infinite the state of possible behaviours of g-choreographies.

sense, our approach complements the one in [28]. In fact, as its authors note, their proposal assumes that component testing has been already performed. A technical difference is that test generation is not attained from the syntax of a global view as we do. Rather, tests are generated in [28] by exploring the resulting transition system. In addition, our approach allows us to generate only valid tests through the oracle scheme we propose.

References

1. Alur, R., Etessami, K., Yannakakis, M.: Inference of message sequence charts. IEEE Trans. Softw. Eng. **29**(7), 623–633 (2003)
2. Barr, E., Harman, M., McMinn, P., Shahbaz, M., Yoo, S.: The oracle problem in software testing: a survey. TOSEM **41**(5), 507–525 (2015)
3. Boreale, M., Nicola, R.D., Pugliese, R.: Trace and testing equivalence on asynchronous processes. Inf. Comput. **172**(2), 139–164 (2002)
4. Brand, D., Zafiropulo, P.: On communicating finite-state machines. J. ACM **30**(2), 323–342 (1983)
5. Bravetti, M., Zavattaro, G.: Contract compliance and choreography conformance in the presence of message queues. In: Bruni, R., Wolf, K. (eds.) WS-FM 2008. LNCS, vol. 5387, pp. 37–54. Springer, Heidelberg (2009). https://doi.org/10.1007/978-3-642-01364-5_3
6. Broy, M., Jonsson, B., Katoen, J., Leucker, M., Pretschner, A. (eds.): Model-Based Testing of Reactive Systems, Advanced Lectures, Lecture Notes in Computer Science, vol. 3472. Springer (2005). https://doi.org/10.1007/b137241
7. Coppo, M., Dezani-Ciancaglini, M., Yoshida, N., Padovani, L.: Global progress for dynamically interleaved multiparty sessions. MSCS **26**(2), 238–302 (2016)
8. Coto, A., Guanciale, R., Tuosto, E.: An abstract framework for choreographic testing. In: Lange, J., Mavridou, A., Safina, L., Scalas, A. (eds.) Proceedings 13th Interaction and Concurrency Experience. Electronic Proceedings in Theoretical Computer Science, vol. 324, pp. 43–60. Open Publishing Association, 19 June 2020. https://doi.org/10.4204/EPTCS.324.5
9. Dalla Preda, M., Gabbrielli, M., Giallorenzo, S., Lanese, I., Jacopo, M.: Dynamic choreographies - safe runtime updates of distributed applications. COORDINATION **2015**, 67–82 (2015). https://doi.org/10.1007/978-3-319-19282-6_5
10. De Nicola, R., Hennessy, M.: Testing equivalences for processes. TCS **34**, 83–133 (1984)
11. Deniélou, P.-M., Yoshida, N.: Multiparty session types meet communicating automata. In: Seidl, H. (ed.) ESOP 2012. LNCS, vol. 7211, pp. 194–213. Springer, Heidelberg (2012). https://doi.org/10.1007/978-3-642-28869-2_10
12. Dijkstra, E.: Notes on structured programming. In: Structure Programming, pp. 1–82. ACM, January 1972
13. Guanciale, R., Tuosto, E.: An abstract semantics of the global view of choreographies. In: Interaction and Concurrency Experience, Electronic Proceedings in Theoretical Computer Science, vol. 223, pp. 67–82, September 2016. https://doi.org/10.4204/EPTCS.223.5, http://arxiv.org/abs/1608.03323
14. Guanciale, R., Tuosto, E.: Semantics of global views of choreographies. J. Logic Algebraic Methods Programm. **95** (2017). Revised and extended version of [13]. Version with proof http://www.cs.le.ac.uk/people/et52/jlamp-with-proofs.pdf

15. Honda, K., Yoshida, N., Carbone, M.: Multiparty asynchronous session types. J. ACM **63**(1), 9:1–9:67 (2016). Extended version of a paper presented at POPL08

16. Honda, K., Yoshida, N., Carbone, M.: Multiparty asynchronous session types. J. ACM **63**(1), 1–67 (2016). https://doi.org/10.1145/2827695. Extended version of a paper presented at POPL08

17. Hüttel, H., et al.: Foundations of session types and behavioural contracts. ACM Comput. Surv. **49**(1), 1–36 (2016). https://doi.org/10.1145/2873052, http://dl.acm.org/citation.cfm?doid=2911992.2873052

18. Kavantzas, N., Burdett, D., Ritzinger, G., Fletcher, T., Lafon, Y.: http://www.w3.org/TR/2004/WD-ws-cdl-10-20041217. Working Draft 17 December 2004

19. Lange, J., Tuosto, E.: Synthesising choreographies from local session types. In: Koutny, M., Ulidowski, I. (eds.) CONCUR 2012. LNCS, vol. 7454, pp. 225–239. Springer, Heidelberg (2012). https://doi.org/10.1007/978-3-642-32940-1_17

20. Lange, J., Tuosto, E.: ChorGram (2015). https://bitbucket.org/emlio_tuosto/chorgram/wiki/Home

21. Lange, J., Tuosto, E., Yoshida, N.: From communicating machines to graphical choreographies. In: SIGPLAN-SIGACT Symposium on Principles of Programming Languages, pp. 221–232 (2015)

22. Oberkampf, W.L., Roy, C.J.: Verification and Validation in Scientific Computing. Cambridge University Press, Cambridge (2010)

23. Pretschner, A., Philipps, J.: Methodological issues in model-based testing. In: Broy, M., Jonsson, B., Katoen, J.P., Leucker, M., Pretschner, A. (eds.) Model-Based Testing of Reactive Systems, vol. 3472, pp. 281–291. Springer, Berlin Heidelberg, Berlin, Heidelberg, October 2005. http://link.springer.com/10.1007/11498490_13

24. Pretschner, A., Philipps, J.: Methodological issues in model-based testing. In: Broy et al. [6], pp. 281–292 (2005)

25. Tretmans, J.: Model-based testing: Property checking for real. In: International Workshop for Construction and Analysis of Safe Secure, and Interoperable Smart Devices (2004)

26. Tuosto, E., Guanciale, R.: Semantics of global view of choreographies. J. Logic Algebraic Methods Program. **95**, 17–40 (2018)

27. Utting, M., Legeard, B.: Practical Model-Based Testing - A Tools Approach. Morgan Kaufmann (2007). http://www.elsevierdirect.com/product.jsp?isbn=9780123725011

28. Wieczorek, S., et al.: Applying model checking to generate model-based integration tests from choreography models. In: Núñez, M., Baker, P., Merayo, M.G. (eds.) FATES/TestCom -2009. LNCS, vol. 5826, pp. 179–194. Springer, Heidelberg (2009). https://doi.org/10.1007/978-3-642-05031-2_12

Composing Communicating Systems, Synchronously

Franco Barbanera[1], Ivan Lanese[2(✉)], and Emilio Tuosto[3,4]

[1] Department of Mathematics and Computer Science, University of Catania, Catania, Italy
[2] Focus Team, University of Bologna/INRIA, Bologna, Italy
ivan.lanese@gmail.com
[3] Gran Sasso Science Institute, L'Aquila, Italy
[4] University of Leicester, Leicester, UK

Abstract. Communicating systems are nowadays part of everyday life, yet programming and analysing them is difficult. One of the many reasons for this difficulty is their size, hence compositional approaches are a need. We discuss how to ensure relevant communication properties such as deadlock freedom in a compositional way. The idea is that communicating systems can be composed by taking two of their participants and transforming them into coupled forwarders connecting the two systems. It has been shown that, for asynchronous communications, if the participants are "compatible" then composition satisfies relevant communication properties provided that the single systems satisfy them. We show that such a result changes considerably for synchronous communications. We also discuss a different form of composition, where a unique forwarder is used.

1 Introduction

The behaviour of systems which communicate via point-to-point message passing can be described in terms of systems of Communicating Finite State Machines (CFSMs) [10], that is systems of finite state automata whose transitions are labelled by sending and receiving actions. Such systems can be then analysed to check whether they enjoy relevant communication properties such as deadlock freedom, lock freedom, etc. (see, e.g., [6,7,16,20,24]).

Traditionally these systems are viewed as *closed*, thus one needs full knowledge of the whole system in order to analyse it. In scenarios such as the Internet, the Cloud or serverless computing, such assumption is less and less realistic.

Research partly supported by the EU H2020 RISE programme under the Marie Skłodowska-Curie grant agreement No 778233, by the MIUR project PRIN 2017FTXR7S "IT-MaTTerS" (Methods and Tools for Trustworthy Smart Systems) and by the Project PTR - UNICT 2016-19. The first and second authors have also been partially supported by INdAM as members of GNCS (Gruppo Nazionale per il Calcolo Scientifico). The authors thanks the reviewers for their helpful comments and also M. Dezani for her support.

© Springer Nature Switzerland AG 2020
T. Margaria and B. Steffen (Eds.): ISoLA 2020, LNCS 12476, pp. 39–59, 2020.
https://doi.org/10.1007/978-3-030-61362-4_3

Recently, an approach to the composition of systems of CFSMs has been proposed [3,4]. The main idea of the approach is to take two systems, select two of their participants (one per system) and transform them into coupled gateways connecting the two systems. More precisely, if a message is sent to one of the gateways, it is forwarded to the other gateway, which sends it to the other system.

Of course, for such a composition to be well-behaved, the two gateways should exhibit behaviours which are essentially dual of each other: when one wants to send a message the other one needs to be willing to receive the same message. Such an intuition has been formalised as a *compatibility* relation. It has also been shown that compatibility, together with conditions of no mixed states and ?!-determinism on the selected participants, ensures that the composition is well-behaved. For instance, if the components are deadlock-free then the system resulting from the composition is deadlock-free too.

In this paper we first revise such results in a setting of synchronous CFSMs, while [3,4] focus on the asynchronous FIFO case. Somehow surprisingly, stricter conditions are required to ensure compositionality of deadlock freedom. We then propose a new composition methodology which replaces the two selected participants with a unique gateway. Beyond saving some communications and simplifying the analysis, this second methodology is also more general since the conditions needed for compositionality of deadlock freedom are slightly weaker. We call this second composition *semi-direct*, to distinguish it also from direct composition as proposed in [5] in a context of multiparty session types [17], which avoids the need for gateways altogether. Notably, two-gateways composition is completely transparent for the participants different from the interface ones, semi-direct composition requires renaming some of their communications, while direct composition may require a non-trivial restructuring of their behaviours.

Structure of the Paper. Section 2 introduces systems of CFSMs and related notions. Composition by gateways and semi-direct composition are discussed in Sect. 3 and Sect. 4, respectively. Conclusions, related and future work are discussed in Sect. 5.

2   Background

Communicating Finite State Machines (CFSMs) [10] are Finite State Automata (FSAs) where transitions are labelled by communications.

Definition 2.1 (FSA). *A* Finite State Automaton *(FSA) is a tuple* $A = \langle S, s_0, \mathcal{L}, \rightarrow \rangle$ *where*

- S *is a finite set of states (ranged over by* $s, q, \ldots$ *);*
- $s_0 \in S$ *is the* initial state*;*
- $\mathcal{L}$ *is a finite set of labels (ranged over by* $l, \lambda, \ldots$ *);*
- $\rightarrow \subseteq S \times \mathcal{L} \times S$ *is a set of transitions.*

We use the usual notation $s_1 \xrightarrow{\lambda} s_2$ for the transition $(s_1, \lambda, s_2) \in \rightarrow$, and $s_1 \rightarrow s_2$ when there exists λ such that $s_1 \xrightarrow{\lambda} s_2$, as well as $\rightarrow^*$ for the reflexive and transitive closure of $\rightarrow$. The set of reachable states of A is $\mathcal{R}(A) = \{\, s \mid s_0 \rightarrow^* s \,\}$.

Let $s \xrightarrow{\lambda} s' \in A$ emphasise that the transition belongs to (the set of transitions of) an FSA A; likewise, $q \in A$ stands for "q belongs to the states of A". A transition $s \xrightarrow{\lambda} s'$ (resp. $s' \xrightarrow{\lambda} s$) is an *outgoing* (resp. *incoming*) transition of s. We write $f[x \mapsto y]$ for the update of the function f in a point x of its domain with the value y. Also, $\mathrm{dom}(f)$ denotes the domain of the function f.

We now define systems of CFSMs, by adapting the definitions in [10] to our context. Let $\mathfrak{P}$ be a set of *participants* (or *roles*, ranged over by A, B, etc.) and $\mathcal{M}$ a set of *messages* (ranged over by m, n, etc.). We take $\mathfrak{P}$ and $\mathcal{M}$ disjoint.

Definition 2.2 (Communicating system). *A communicating finite-state machine (CFSM) is an FSA with labels in the set*

$$\mathcal{L}_{act} = \{\mathsf{A\,B!m}, \mathsf{A\,B?m} \mid \mathsf{A} \neq \mathsf{B} \in \mathfrak{P}, \mathsf{m} \in \mathcal{M}\}$$

of actions. *The* subject *of an output (resp. input) action* $\mathsf{A\,B!m}$ *(resp.* $\mathsf{A\,B?m}$*) is* A *(resp.* B*). A CFSM is* A-local *if all its transitions have subject* A.

A (communicating) system *is a map* $\mathsf{S} = (M_\mathsf{A})_{\mathsf{A} \in \mathcal{P}}$ *assigning an* A-*local CFSM* M_A *to each participant* $\mathsf{A} \in \mathcal{P}$ *where* $\mathcal{P} \subseteq \mathfrak{P}$ *is finite and any participant occurring in a transition of* M_A *is in* $\mathcal{P}$.

Note that systems satisfying the above definition are *closed*: in fact any input or output action does refer to participants belonging to the system itself.

We now define, following [6,7], the synchronous semantics of systems of CFSMs, which is itself an FSA (differently from the asynchronous case, where the set of states can be infinite).

Definition 2.3 (Synchronous semantics). *Let* S *be a communicating system. A* synchronous configuration *of* S *is a map* $s = (q_\mathsf{A})_{\mathsf{A} \in \mathrm{dom}(\mathsf{S})}$ *assigning a* local *state* $q_\mathsf{A} \in \mathsf{S}(\mathsf{A})$ *to each* $\mathsf{A} \in \mathrm{dom}(\mathsf{S})$.

The synchronous semantics *of* S *is the FSA* $[\![\mathsf{S}]\!] = \langle \mathcal{S}, s_0, \mathcal{L}_{int}, \rightarrow \rangle$ *where*

- *$\mathcal{S}$ is the set of synchronous configurations of* S, *as defined above;*
- *$s_0 = (q_{0\mathsf{A}})_{\mathsf{A} \in \mathrm{dom}(\mathsf{S})} \in \mathcal{S}$ is the* initial configuration *where, for each* $\mathsf{A} \in \mathrm{dom}(\mathsf{S})$, $q_{0\mathsf{A}}$ *is the initial state of* $\mathsf{S}(\mathsf{A})$;
- *$\mathcal{L}_{int} = \{\mathsf{A} \rightarrow \mathsf{B}\colon \mathsf{m} \mid \mathsf{A} \neq \mathsf{B} \in \mathfrak{P} \text{ and } \mathsf{m} \in \mathcal{M}\}$ is a set of* interaction labels;
- *$s \xrightarrow{\mathsf{A} \rightarrow \mathsf{B}\colon\, \mathsf{m}} s[\mathsf{A} \mapsto q, \mathsf{B} \mapsto q'] \in [\![\mathsf{S}]\!]$ if $s(\mathsf{A}) \xrightarrow{\mathsf{A\,B!m}} q \in \mathsf{S}(\mathsf{A})$ and $s(\mathsf{B}) \xrightarrow{\mathsf{A\,B?m}} q' \in \mathsf{S}(\mathsf{B})$.*

We say that s enables $q \xrightarrow{\mathsf{A\,B!m}} q' \in \mathsf{S}(\mathsf{A})$ (resp. $q \xrightarrow{\mathsf{B\,A?m}} q' \in \mathsf{S}(\mathsf{A})$) when $s(\mathsf{A}) = q$.

As expected, an interaction $\mathsf{A} {\rightarrow} \mathsf{B}\colon \mathsf{m}$ occurs when A performs an output $\mathsf{A\,B!m}$ and B the corresponding input $\mathsf{A\,B?m}$.

As discussed in the Introduction, in this paper we will study preservation of communication properties under composition. As sample property we choose the well-known notion of deadlock freedom. The definition below adapts the one in [13] to a synchronous setting (as done also in [20,27]).

Definition 2.4 (Deadlock freedom). *Let* S *be a communicating system. A configuration* $s \in \mathcal{R}([\![S]\!])$ *is a* deadlock *if*

- *s has no outgoing transitions in* $[\![S]\!]$ *and*
- *there exists* $A \in \mathcal{P}$ *such that* $s(A)$ *has an outgoing transition in* $S(A)$.

System S *is* deadlock-free *if for each* $s \in \mathcal{R}([\![S]\!])$, *s is not a deadlock.*

3 Composition via Gateways

This section discusses composition of systems of CFSMs via gateways, as introduced in [3,4], and studies its properties under the synchronous semantics. The main idea is that two systems of CFSMs, say S_1 and S_2, can be composed by transforming one participant in each of them into gateways connected to each other. Let us call H the selected participant in S_1 and K the one in S_2. The gateways for H and K are connected to each other and act as forwarders: each message sent to the gateway for H by a participant from the original system S_1 is now forwarded to the gateway for K, that in turn forwards it to the same participant to which K sent it in the original system S_2. The dual will happen to messages that the gateway for K receives from S_2. A main advantage of this approach is that no extension of the CFSM model is needed to transform systems of CFSMs, which are normally closed systems, into open systems that can be composed. Another advantage is that the composition is fully transparent to all participants different from H and K.

We will now define composition via gateways on systems of CFSMs, following the intuition above.

Definition 3.1 (Gateway). *Given a* H-*local CFSM* M *and a participant* K, *the* gateway of M towards K *is the CFSM* $\mathsf{gw}(M, \mathsf{K})$ *obtained by replacing:*

- *each transition* $q \xrightarrow{\mathsf{H\,A!m}} q' \in M$ *with* $q \xrightarrow{\mathsf{K\,H?m}} q'' \xrightarrow{\mathsf{H\,A!m}} q'$ *for some fresh state* q'';
- *each transition* $q \xrightarrow{\mathsf{A\,H?m}} q' \in M$ *with* $q \xrightarrow{\mathsf{A\,H?m}} q'' \xrightarrow{\mathsf{H\,K!m}} q'$ *for some fresh state* q''.

We compose systems with disjoint participants through two of them, say H and K, by taking all the participants of the original systems but H and K, whereas H and K are replaced by their respective gateways.

Definition 3.2 (System composition). *Let* S_1 *and* S_2 *be two systems with disjoint domains. The* composition *of* S_1 *and* S_2 *via* $\mathsf{H} \in \mathrm{dom}(S_1)$ *and* $\mathsf{K} \in \mathrm{dom}(S_2)$ *is defined as*

$$S_1 \mapsto_K S_2 = A \mapsto \begin{cases} S_i(A), & \text{if } A \in \text{dom}(S_i) \setminus \{H, K\} \text{ with } i \in \{1, 2\} \\ \text{gw}(S_1(H), K), & \text{if } A = H \\ \text{gw}(S_2(K), H), & \text{if } A = K \end{cases}$$

(Note that $\text{dom}(S_1 \mapsto_K S_2) = \text{dom}(S_1) \cup \text{dom}(S_2)$.)

We remark again that, by the above approach for composition, we do not actually need to formalise the notion of *open* system. In fact any closed system can be looked at as open by choosing (according to the current necessities) two suitable participants in the "to-be-connected" systems and transforming them into two forwarders.

We also note that the notion of composition above is structural: a corresponding notion of behavioural composition has been studied in [5] in a context of multiparty session types [17].

Example 3.3. Take the systems S_1 and S_2 below

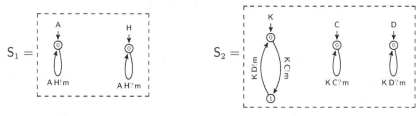

The system consisting of the following CFSMs

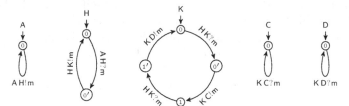

is the composition $S_1 \mapsto_K S_2$.   ◇

Given a configuration of the composition of systems S_1 and S_2 we can retrieve the configurations of the two subsystems by taking only the states of participants in S_i (for $i \in \{1, 2\}$) while avoiding, for the gateways, to take the fresh states introduced by the gateway construction.

Definition 3.4 (Configuration projection). *Let s be a configuration of a composed system $S_1 \mapsto_K S_2$. The projection of s on S_1 is the map $s|_1$ defined by*

$$s|_1 : A \mapsto \begin{cases} s(A), & \text{if } s(A) \text{ is not fresh} \\ q, & \text{if } A = H, \ s(H) \text{ is fresh and } q \xrightarrow{K H ? m} s(H) \in M \\ q, & \text{if } A = H, \ s(H) \text{ is fresh and } s(H) \xrightarrow{H K ! m} q \in M \end{cases}$$

where $M = \text{gw}(S_1(H), K)$. The definition for $s|_2$ is analogous.

Intuitively, in the projection $s|_1$, if H is in a fresh state after receiving from K, then the other participants in S_1 are still not aware of the message arrival, hence to have a coherent configuration we take the state of H before the receive. If instead H is in a fresh state before sending to K, then the other participants in S_1 know that the message has been sent, hence to have a coherent configuration we take the state of H after the send. (A similar intuition applies to $s|_2$.)

Example 3.5. Let us consider the system $S = S_1 \mathbin{\mathsf{H}\!\!-\!\!\mathsf{K}} S_2$ of Example 3.3. Take its configuration $s = (0_A, 0_H, 1'_K, 0_C, 0_D)$. It is easy to check that $s \in \mathcal{R}([\![S]\!])$. In fact

$$s_0 = (0_A, 0_H, 0_K, 0_C, 0_D) \xrightarrow{\text{A}\to\text{H}:\, m} (0_A, 0'_H, 0_K, 0_C, 0_D) \xrightarrow{\text{H}\to\text{K}:\, m} (0_A, 0_H, 0'_K, 0_C, 0_D)$$

$$\xrightarrow{\text{K}\to\text{C}:\, m} (0_A, 0_H, 1_K, 0_C, 0_D) \xrightarrow{\text{A}\to\text{H}:\, m} (0_A, 0'_H, 1_K, 0_C, 0_D) \xrightarrow{\text{H}\to\text{K}:\, m} (0_A, 0_H, 1'_K, 0_C, 0_D)$$

The projections of s on, respectively, S_1 and S_2 are

$$s|_1 = (0_A, 0_H) \quad and \quad s|_2 = (1_K, 0_C, 0_D)$$

Notice that (as we shall prove in Proposition 3.11), from $s \in \mathcal{R}([\![S]\!])$ it is possible to infer that $s|_1 \in \mathcal{R}([\![S_1]\!])$ and $s|_2 \in \mathcal{R}([\![S_2]\!])$.   ◇

Being able to build the composition via gateways does not ensure that the result is well-behaved or that its behaviour is related in any way to the behaviour of the original systems. We provide below sufficient conditions for this to happen. We focus in particular on whether deadlock freedom is preserved under composition. Somehow surprisingly, in the synchronous case preservation of deadlock freedom requires stricter conditions than in the asynchronous one.

Informally, two CFSMs M_1 and M_2 are *compatible* if M_1 is bisimilar to the dual of M_2 provided that the communicating partners are abstracted away. In order to define compatibility, a few simple definitions are handy.
Let $\mathcal{L}_{i/o} = \{\, ?m, !m \mid m \in \mathcal{M} \,\}$ and define the functions

$$\text{io} : \mathcal{L}_{\text{act}} \to \mathcal{L}_{i/o} \quad and \quad \overline{(\cdot)} : \mathcal{L}_{i/o} \to \mathcal{L}_{i/o}$$

by the following clauses

$$\text{io}(\text{A B}?m) = ?m \quad \text{io}(\text{A B}!m) = !m \quad and \quad \overline{?m} = !m \quad \overline{!m} = ?m$$

which extend to CFSMs in the obvious way: given a CFSM $M = \langle S, q_0, \mathcal{L}_{\text{act}}, \to \rangle$, we define $\text{io}(M) = \langle S, q_0, \mathcal{L}_{i/o}, \to' \rangle$ where $\to' = \{\, q \xrightarrow{\text{io}(l)} q' \mid q \xrightarrow{l} q' \in M \,\}$; and likewise for $\overline{M}$.

Definition 3.6 (Compatibility). *Two CFSMs M_1 and M_2 are compatible if $\text{io}(M_1)$ is bisimilar to $\overline{\text{io}(M_2)}$. Given two communicating systems S_1 and S_2, participants $\text{H} \in \text{dom}(S_1)$ and $\text{K} \in \text{dom}(S_2)$ are compatible roles if $S_1(\text{H})$ and $S_2(\text{K})$ are compatible CFSMs.*

We refer to the bisimilarity in Definition 3.6 as *compatibility bisimilarity*. Note that the compatibility bisimilarity between M_1 and M_2 is a relation between their states. It is easy to check that H and K of Example 3.3 are compatible roles.

Definition 3.7. *An* A-*local CFSM M is:*

i) *?-deterministic (resp. !-deterministic) if* $q \xrightarrow{X A ? m} q'$ *and* $q \xrightarrow{Y A ? m} q'' \in M$
   (resp. $q \xrightarrow{A X ! m} q'$ *and* $q \xrightarrow{A Y ! m} q'' \in M$ *) implies* $q' = q''$;
ii) *?!-deterministic if it is both ?-deterministic and !-deterministic;*
iii) *mixed-deterministic if* $m \neq n$ *for all* $q \xrightarrow{X A ? m} q'$ *and* $q \xrightarrow{A Y ! n} q'' \in M$.

A state $q \in M$ is a *sending* (resp. *receiving*) state if it has outgoing transitions, all of which are labelled with sending (resp. receiving) actions; q is a *mixed* state if it has outgoing transitions and q is neither sending nor receiving.

Definition 3.8 ((H, K)-**composability**). *Two systems* S_1 *and* S_2 *with disjoint domains are* (H, K)-*composable if* $H \in \text{dom}(S_1)$ *and* $K \in \text{dom}(S_2)$ *are two compatible roles whose machines have no mixed states and are ?!-deterministic.*

Definition 3.9. *Let* $\text{gw}(M_H, K)$ *be a gateway extracted from an* H-*local CFSM. Function* $\text{nof}_{M_H}(\cdot)$ *maps the states of* $\text{gw}(M_H, K)$ *to the states of* M_H *as follows:*

$$
\text{nof}_{M_H}(q) = \begin{cases} q & \textit{if } q \textit{ is not fresh} \\ q' & \textit{if } q \textit{ is fresh and } q' \xrightarrow{A H ? m} q \in \text{gw}(M_H, K) \textit{ for some } A, m \\ q' & \textit{if } q \textit{ is fresh and } q \xrightarrow{H A ! m} q' \in \text{gw}(M_H, K) \textit{ for some } A, m \end{cases}
$$

Lemma 3.10. *Function* nof_{M_H} *is well-defined.*

Proof. The restriction of nof_{M_H} to the states of M_H is the identity. If q is not a state of M_H, then it is fresh by definition of $\text{gw}(M_H, K)$. By definition of $\text{gw}(M_H, K)$ again, there is a unique q' such that either $q' \xrightarrow{A H ? m} q \in \text{gw}(M_H, K)$ or $q \xrightarrow{H A ! m} q' \in \text{gw}(M_H, K)$. $\square$

In the system $S = S_1 \mathbin{\vdash\!\!\!-\!\!\!\dashv} S_2$ of Example 3.3 it is easy to check, for example, that $\text{nof}_{S(H)}(0) = 0$ and $\text{nof}_{S(K)}(1') = 0$.

Function nof_{M_H} is close to the definition of configuration projection (but for considering a single state instead of a whole configuration) with a main change. Indeed, when $\text{gw}(M_H, K)$ receives a message from its own system S_1 going to some fresh state q'', configuration projection maps it to the next state, since the rest of S_1 is aware of the transition but $\text{gw}(M_H, K)$ will complete the transition only in the next state. Instead, function nof_{M_H} maps q'' to the previous state since S_2, and K in particular, are not yet aware of the transition. Thus, function nof_{M_H} is designed to establish a correspondence with the other system as shown by the next proposition.

Proposition 3.11. *Let* $S = S_1 \mathbin{\vdash\!\!\!-\!\!\!\dashv} S_2$ *be the composition of two* (H, K)-*composable systems* S_1 *and* S_2. *If* $s \in \mathcal{R}([\![S]\!])$ *then exactly one of the following cases hold for* $q_H = s(H)$ *and* $q_K = s(K)$, *the states in* s *of the gateway CFSMs:*

1. *both* q_H *and* q_K *are not fresh;*
2. *either* q_H *is fresh,* q_K *is not fresh,* $q_H \xrightarrow{H K ! m} q \in S_1(H)$, *or, symmetrically,* q_K *is fresh,* q_H *is not fresh,* $q_K \xrightarrow{K H ! m} q \in S_2(K)$;

3. *either q_H is fresh, q_K is not fresh, and there is $A \in \mathrm{dom}(S_1)$ such that $q_H \xrightarrow{H\,A!\,m} q \in S_1(H)$, or, symmetrically, q_K is fresh, q_H is not fresh, and there is $B \in \mathrm{dom}(S_2)$ such that $q_K \xrightarrow{K\,B!\,m} q \in S_2(K)$;*

4. *both q_H and q_K are fresh and either $q_H \xrightarrow{H\,K!\,m} q \in S_1(H)$, and there is $A \in \mathrm{dom}(S_2)$ such that $q_K \xrightarrow{K\,B!\,n} q \in S_2(K)$, or, symmetrically, $q_K \xrightarrow{K\,H!\,m} q \in S_2(K)$, and there is $A \in \mathrm{dom}(S_1)$ such that $q_H \xrightarrow{H\,A!\,n} q \in S_1(H)$.*

Also, $s|_1$ is reachable in S_1, $s|_2$ is reachable in S_2 and $\mathrm{nof}_{M_H}(q_H) \sim \mathrm{nof}_{M_K}(q_K)$.

Proof. The proof is by induction on the number n of transitions performed to reach s. If $n = 0$ then by construction we are in case 1. The conditions on configurations and on bisimulation hold by construction.

Let us assume that we are in one of the cases above and a further transition is performed. Since composition is symmetric for each possibility we do not detail the symmetric case. Also note that in each of the cases, if the transition does not involve the gateways, then we are still in the same case. The condition on configurations hold since the same step can be taken by the same participants in one of the two systems, and the ones of the other system do not move. The condition on bisimulation holds since the state of the gateways does not change.

If we were in case 1, a transition involving a gateway has necessarily the form $s \xrightarrow{A \to H\,:\,m} s'$ (or a similar one for the gateway for K) since an output from a gateway would require a gateway to be in a fresh state. This leads us to case 2. Indeed, the gateway for H goes to the fresh state $s'(H)$ and is willing to execute the gateway communication $s'(H) \xrightarrow{H\,K!\,m} q$, while the state of the gateway for K does not change. The condition on configurations hold by induction on $s|_2$ and holds on $s|_1$ since $s'(H)|_1 = q$ and by construction $s|_1 \xrightarrow{A \to H\,:\,m} s'|_1$. The condition on bisimulation holds by inductive hypothesis since $\mathrm{nof}_{M_H}(q) = s|_1(H)$ and the state of the gateway for K does not change.

In case 2 a transition involving the gateway necessarily is the gateway communication $s \xrightarrow{H \to K\,:\,m} s'$, leading us to case 3. Indeed, the gateway for H cannot perform other transitions and thanks to the condition on compatibility and the fact that gateway roles do not have mixed states K cannot perform any input from its system. Thus, the gateway for H goes to a non-fresh state while the gateway for K goes to a fresh state, willing to execute an output $s'(K) \xrightarrow{K\,B!\,m} q$ towards its system. The condition on configurations holds by inductive hypothesis since projection generates the same configurations as before. The condition on bisimulation holds since the two participants take corresponding steps. The resulting states are in a correspondence thanks to ?!-determinism.

In case 3 for a transition involving a gateway there are two possibilities, according to whether the gateway taking a transition is in a fresh state or not.

- The gateway in a fresh state, say K, takes a transition. By construction it delivers a message m to a participant in its system via a transition $s \xrightarrow{K \to B\,:\,m} s'$. This leads us to case 1. Indeed, K goes to a non-fresh state, while H was in a non-fresh state by hypothesis and does not move. The condition on configurations holds by inductive hypothesis for $s|_1$ and holds for $s|_2$ since B can do the same move as in s and the two moves of the gateway for K (the gateway transition which was not taken into account yet and the delivery of message m) correspond to the complementary move of K in $s|_2$. The condition on bisimulation holds by inductive hypothesis since $\mathrm{nof}_{M_H}(\cdot)$ projects on the same states as before the transition.

– The gateway in a non-fresh state, say H, takes a transition. By construction it takes a message from its own system via a transition $s \xrightarrow{A \to H:\, n} s'$. This leads us to case 4. Indeed, H goes to a fresh state while K was already in a fresh state. Then $s'(K) \xrightarrow{K\,B!m} q$ by inductive hypothesis and $s'(H) \xrightarrow{H\,K!n} q'$ by construction. The reasoning on conditions of configurations and bisimulation is similar to the one of a message taken by the gateway in case 1.

In case 4, when a transition involving a gateway, say K, is performed, it is necessarily of the form $s \xrightarrow{K \to B:\, m} s'$ since the gateway for K by construction cannot take any other action. This leads to case 2. Indeed, H remains in a fresh state and willing to execute a transition $s'(H) \xrightarrow{H\,K!m} q$ while K goes to a non-fresh state. The reasoning for the conditions on configurations and bisimulation is similar to the one for case 3 when K delivers a message to its system. □

Now, one may think that analogously to what happens in [3,4], if two systems are (H, K)-composable and deadlock-free then their composition is deadlock-free too. Unfortunately, this is not the case, as shown by the examples below. The first example is based on an example in [4], that shows that mixed states have to be forbidden and that holds for the synchronous case as well. In the synchronous case, however, we can also exchange some inputs with outputs and obtain the same behaviour *without* mixed states.

Example 3.12. Take the following CFSMs

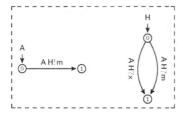 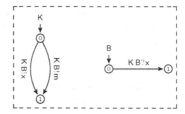

and consider the composition of the system with participants A and H with the one with participants K and B. Clearly, the two systems are (H, K)-composable and deadlock-free, yet their composition has a deadlock; in fact, when the gateway for K receives m, participant B is waiting only for x. By considering the second system alone, this is not a deadlock, since B forces K to select the right branch.

Note that the situation would be different in an asynchronous setting. Indeed, the second system could deadlock. This is due to the fact that K could send m without synchronising with B. ◇

Example 3.13. Take the CFSMs below

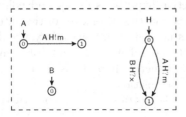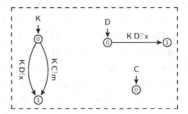

The same reasoning of Example 3.12 can be applied here, to systems with participants A, B, H and C, D, K. Hence, choices made by different participants are problematic as well.   ◇

Example 3.14. Take the CFSMs below

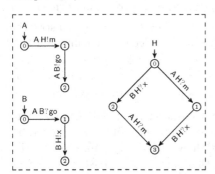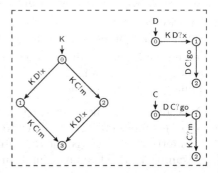

The reasoning is again similar, and shows that the composition of systems A, B, H and K, C, D deadlocks while the two systems in isolation do not. Hence also concurrency diamonds are problematic.   ◇

Given the examples above, it is clear that, differently from the asynchronous case, deadlock freedom can be preserved only under very strict conditions on interface participants. Indeed we show below that it can be preserved if interface participants do not contain choices.

Definition 3.15 (Sequential CFSM). *A CFSM is sequential if each of its states has at most one outgoing transition.*

It is immediate to check that $gw(M, H)$ is sequential if M is so. Moreover, trivially, a sequential M is also ?!-deterministic and with no mixed state (and hence mixed-deterministic).

Theorem 3.16 (Deadlock freedom for sequential interfaces). *Let S_1 and S_2 be two (H, K)-composable and deadlock-free systems, such that $S_1(H)$ and $S_2(K)$ are sequential. Then the composed system $S_1 \Join_K S_2$ is deadlock-free.*

Proof. We show that if the composed system $S_1 \Join_K S_2$ reaches a deadlock configuration s then at least one of $s|_1$ and $s|_2$ is a deadlock. First, we show that if a participant A (say from S_1) is willing to take an action in a configuration s of the composed system then some participant is willing to take an action in $s|_1$ or in $s|_2$ (and the same for participants in S_2). Note that $s|_1$ and $s|_2$ are reachable in, respectively, S_1 and S_2 thanks to the condition on configurations in Proposition 3.11.

If $A \neq H$ then A wants to take the same action by definition of $s|_1$.

If $A = H$ and it is willing to receive from K then, by the definition of $s|_1$ and of gateway, H in $s|_1$ is willing to send a message to some participant in S_1.

If $A = H$ and it is willing to send to K then $\mathsf{nof}_{M_H}(s(H)) \sim \mathsf{nof}_{M_K}(s(K))$ by the condition on bisimulation of Proposition 3.11. By definition of $\mathsf{nof}_{M_H}(\cdot)$ and of gateway, $\mathsf{nof}_{M_H}(s(H))$ is willing to take a message from its own system, hence $\mathsf{nof}_{M_K}(s(K))$ is willing to send such a message to its own system thanks to the definition of bisimulation. By definition of configuration projection $\mathsf{nof}_{M_K}(s(K))$ is also a state in $s|_2$, hence there is a participant willing to take a transition.

Now we show that if no transition is enabled in a configuration s of the composed system then no transition is enabled in $s|_1$ and $s|_2$. We prove the contrapositive, showing that if there is an enabled transition in $s|_1$ or in $s|_2$ then there is a transition enabled in s as well. There are a few cases to consider.

Transition not involving the interface roles: this case follows immediately from the definition of system transition and of configuration projection.

Communication towards an interface role: let A be the sender and H the interface role. The transition is of the form $s|_1 \xrightarrow{A \rightarrow H:\, m} s_1$. There are two possibilities. If the gateway for H is not in a fresh state in s then the same transition can trigger in the composed system thanks to the definition of system transition and of configuration projection.

If it is in a fresh state then thanks to the definition of gateway and of configuration projection it still needs to complete a previous gateway communication. The other gateway, K, may be in a fresh state or not. If it is not, thanks to the definition of $\mathsf{nof}_{M_H}(\cdot)$ and to the condition on bisimulation of Proposition 3.11 it is willing to accept the gateway communication which can thus trigger as desired. If K is in a fresh state then thanks to the definition of configuration projection and of gateway it is willing to deliver a message to S_2. Since S_2 is not a deadlock and a participant is willing to take a transition then a transition can trigger in S_2 too. Thus, we can apply the other cases to find a witness transition in the composed system. Note that the transition in S_2 cannot be towards an interface role thanks to the condition on bisimulation of Proposition 3.11 and since there are no mixed states, hence this reasoning does not cycle.

Communication from an interface role: let K be the interface role and B the target participant. Hence, the transition is of the form $s|_2 \xrightarrow{K \rightarrow B:\, m} s_2$. Thanks to the definition of gateway and of system projection the gateway for K in s is either willing to deliver a message to some participant in S_2 or to receive from the gateway for H. In the first case, since the gateway is sequential then the participant is B and the message m, hence the transition can trigger.

If K is willing to receive from H then thanks to the definition of $\text{nof}_{M_H}(\cdot)$ and the condition on bisimulation of Proposition 3.11 then the gateway for H is willing to receive a message from its system or has just received it and is willing to send it through the gateway. In the last case the gateway communication can occur.

If H is willing to receive a message from some participant in S_1 since S_1 is not a deadlock then there is an enabled transition in S_1 as well. Thus, we can apply the other cases to find a witness transition in the composed system. Note that the transition in S_1 cannot be from an interface role thanks to the condition on bisimulation of Proposition 3.11 and since there are no mixed states, hence this reasoning does not cycle.

Thus, if there is a deadlock configuration s in the composed system then either $s|_1$ or $s|_2$ are deadlocks against the hypothesis. The thesis follows.   □

We can infer deadlock-freedom of the system $S = S_1 \mathbin{\text{H}\!\!-\!\!\text{K}} S_2$ of Example 3.3 by the result above, since S_1 and S_1 are (H, K)-composable and deadlock-free, and $S_1(\text{H})$ and $S_2(\text{K})$ are sequential.

The result above, however, is not fully satisfying since the sequentiality condition is very strict, but, as shown by Examples 3.12, 3.13, and 3.14, any form of choice is problematic.

However, we can complement the result above with an additional one pinpointing where deadlocks can happen when gateways with choices are allowed: deadlocks can only occur in communications from the gateway to its own system.

Equivalently, we can drop the sequentiality condition if the systems are such that, whenever their interface role is willing to send a message, the system is ready to receive it. We formalise this condition by the notion of !live participant.

Definition 3.17 (!live participant). *Let* S *be a system and let* A $\in$ dom(S). *We say that* A *is !live in* S *if, for any* $s \in \mathcal{R}([\![S]\!])$,

$$s(A) \xrightarrow{\text{A B!m}} \text{implies } s \to^* s' \xrightarrow{\text{A}\to\text{B}:\ m} \text{ for some } s'$$

We remark that !liveness is not a property of the gateway but a property of the system to which it belongs.

It is immediate to check that K is not !live in system S_2 of Example 3.12, whereas K is !live in the following system.

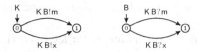

Theorem 3.18 (Deadlock freedom for !live interfaces). *Let* S_1 *and* S_2 *be* (H, K)-*composable and deadlock-free systems. If* $S_1(\text{H})$ *and* $S_2(\text{K})$ *are !live in, respectively,* S_1 *and* S_2 *then the composed system* $S_1 \mathbin{\text{H}\!\!-\!\!\text{K}} S_2$ *is deadlock-free.*

Proof. The proof has the same structure of the one for Theorem 3.16. The only difference is when showing that if there is an enabled transition in $s|_1$ or in $s|_2$ then there is a transition enabled in s as well. Just the case of communication from an interface node changes, in particular when the gateway is willing to deliver some message to some participant in its system. There, !liveness can be used instead of sequentiality to show that indeed some transition can happen. Hence, the thesis follows.   □

4   Semi-direct Composition

One may notice that in the form of composition discussed in the previous section the two gateways simply forward messages, and wonder whether they are strictly needed. Indeed, a form of *direct* composition, where gateways are completely avoided, has been studied in [5] in a multiparty session type [17] setting. It has also been shown that applying this technique has a non trivial impact on the participants in the connected systems. We discuss here a different form of composition where a unique gateway is used, and we call it *semi-direct* composition. This has the advantage of saving one gateway and some communications, and also of simplifying some proofs. Moreover, the conditions for deadlock preservation are weaker when non-sequential interfaces are considered (see Theorem 4.10). On the other hand, participants in the composed systems are affected, but just by a renaming.

Definition 4.1 (Semi-direct gateway).
Let M_1 and M_2 be, respectively, an H- and a K-local CFSM such that

- *M_1 and M_2 are compatible*
- *for all $q_1 \xrightarrow{l_1} q_1' \in M_1$ and $q_2 \xrightarrow{l_2} q_2' \in M_2$ the participants occurring in l_1 are disjoint from those occurring in l_2*

If W is a fresh role then the semi-direct gateway $\mathsf{sgw}(M_1, \mathsf{W}, M_2)$ *is the CFSM* $\langle \mathcal{S}, q_0, \mathcal{L}, \rightarrow \rangle$ *such that*

- *$q_0 = (q_1^0, q_2^0)$ with q_1^0 initial state of M_1 and q_2^0 initial state of M_2;*
- *$\mathcal{S}$ includes all pairs (q_1, q_2) and all triples (q_1, m, q_2) such that q_1 is a state of M_1, q_2 of M_2 and m a message which are reachable from the initial state (q_1^0, q_2^0) via the transitions in $\rightarrow$;*
- *$\rightarrow$ includes, for each $q_1 \in M_1$ and $q_2 \in M_2$ related by the compatibility bisimilarity:*

  - $(q_1, q_2) \xrightarrow{\mathsf{A\,W?m}} (q_1', \mathsf{m}, q_2) \xrightarrow{\mathsf{W\,B!m}} (q_1', q_2')$ *where* $q_1 \xrightarrow{\mathsf{A\,H?m}} q_1' \in M_1$, $q_2 \xrightarrow{\mathsf{K\,B!m}} q_2' \in M_2$,
  - $(q_1, q_2) \xrightarrow{\mathsf{B\,W?m}} (q_1, \mathsf{m}, q_2') \xrightarrow{\mathsf{W\,A!m}} (q_1', q_2')$ *where* $q_2 \xrightarrow{\mathsf{B\,K?m}} q_2' \in M_2$, $q_1 \xrightarrow{\mathsf{H\,A!m}} q_1' \in M_1$.

The semi-direct composition of two systems takes all the machines of the participants in each system (with some channel renaming so to turn communications with H or K into communications with W) but the interface participants, which are replaced by the semi-direct gateway construction of their CFSMs.

Definition 4.2 (Semi-direct system composition). *Given two systems* S_1 *and* S_2 *with disjoint domain, two compatible roles* $H \in \text{dom}(S_1)$ *and* $K \in \text{dom}(S_2)$, *and a fresh role* $W \notin \text{dom}(S_1) \cup \text{dom}(S_2)$, *the system*

$$S_1 \overset{H \underset{W}{\rightleftharpoons} K}{} S_2 : A \mapsto \begin{cases} S_i(A)[W/H][W/K], & \text{if } A \in \text{dom}(S_i) \setminus \{H, K\} \text{ for } i \in \{1, 2\} \\ \text{sgw}(S_1(H), W, S_2(K)), & \text{if } A = W \end{cases}$$

is the W-*composition of* S_1 *and* S_2 *with respect to* H *and* K. *In the definition, the notation* $M[B/A]$ *denotes the machine obtained by replacing role* A *with* B *in all the labels of transitions in* M.

Note that since the gateway construction exploits the compatibility bisimilarity relation then the interface participants need to be compatible for the composition to make sense. This was not the case in the gateway construction in Sect. 3.

In the following simple example we show how the compatibility bisimilarity is exploited in the construction of a semi-direct composition.

Example 4.3. Let us take system S_1 with participants A and H and system S_2 with participants K, C and D as defined in Example 3.3. Participants H and K are trivially compatible. Then the following system

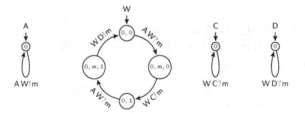

is the semi-direct composition $S_1 \overset{H \underset{W}{\rightleftharpoons} K}{} S_2$.   ◇

We now study systems obtained by semi-direct composition. As in the previous section, we will focus on preservation of deadlock-freedom.

Configurations of a composed system are projected on the two subsystems by taking only the states of their participants and the respective component of the states of the interfaces.

Definition 4.4 (Projection of configurations). *Given a configuration* $s \in \mathcal{R}(\llbracket S_1 \overset{H \underset{W}{\rightleftharpoons} K}{} S_2 \rrbracket)$, *the map* $s|_i$, *for* $i \in \{1, 2\}$, *defined as*

$$s|_i : A \mapsto \begin{cases} s(A), & \text{if } A \in \text{dom}(S_i) \setminus \{H, K\} \\ q_1, & \text{if } A = H \text{ and either } s(W) = (q_1, m, q_2) \text{ or } s(W) = (q_1, q_2) \\ q_2, & \text{if } A = K \text{ and either } s(W) = (q_1, m, q_2) \text{ or } s(W) = (q_1, q_2) \end{cases}$$

is the projection of s on S_i.

As for the composition via gateways we define a notion of state projection to relate the states of the two systems.

Definition 4.5. *Let* $M = \mathsf{sgw}(M_\mathsf{H}, \mathsf{W}, M_\mathsf{K})$ *be a semi-direct gateway. The functions* $\mathsf{nofd}_i(\cdot)$, *where* $i \in \{1, 2\}$, *on the states of* M *are defined as follows*

$$\mathsf{nofd}_i(q) = q_i \text{ if either } q = (q_1, q_2) \text{ or } (q_1, q_2) \xrightarrow{\mathsf{A\,W?m}} (q_1', \mathsf{m}, q_2') = q \text{ for some } \mathsf{m}, \mathsf{A}$$

We can now discuss the properties of composed systems.

Proposition 4.6. *Let* S_1 *and* S_2 *be two systems with disjoint domains and let* $\mathsf{H} \in \mathrm{dom}(\mathsf{S}_1)$ *and* $\mathsf{K} \in \mathrm{dom}(\mathsf{S}_2)$ *be two compatible roles. Then for each* $s \in \mathcal{R}([\![\mathsf{S}_1 \overset{\mathsf{H} \leftrightarrow \mathsf{K}}{\underset{\mathsf{w}}{}} \mathsf{S}_2]\!])$ *we have that*

i) $s\|_1 \in \mathcal{R}([\![\mathsf{S}_1]\!])$, $s\|_2 \in \mathcal{R}([\![\mathsf{S}_2]\!])$ *and* $\mathsf{nofd}_1(s(\mathsf{W})) \sim \mathsf{nofd}_2(s(\mathsf{W}))$;

ii) $s(\mathsf{A}) \xrightarrow{l} q$ *iff one of the following holds*

   (a) $\mathsf{A} \in \mathrm{dom}(\mathsf{S}_i) \setminus \{\mathsf{H}, \mathsf{K}\}$ *and* $s\|_i(\mathsf{A}) \xrightarrow{l} q$ *and* $\mathsf{W} \notin l$, *for* $i \in \{1, 2\}$;

   (b) $\mathsf{A} \in \mathrm{dom}(\mathsf{S}_1) \setminus \{\mathsf{H}\}$ *and* $l = \mathsf{A\,W!m}$ *and* $s\|_1(\mathsf{A}) \xrightarrow{\mathsf{A\,H!m}} q$;

   (c) $\mathsf{A} \in \mathrm{dom}(\mathsf{S}_1) \setminus \{\mathsf{H}\}$ *and* $l = \mathsf{W\,A?m}$ *and* $s\|_1(\mathsf{A}) \xrightarrow{\mathsf{H\,A?m}} q$;

   (d) $\mathsf{A} \in \mathrm{dom}(\mathsf{S}_2) \setminus \{\mathsf{K}\}$ *and* $l = \mathsf{A\,W!m}$ *and* $s\|_2(\mathsf{A}) \xrightarrow{\mathsf{A\,K!m}} q$;

   (e) $\mathsf{A} \in \mathrm{dom}(\mathsf{S}_2) \setminus \{\mathsf{K}\}$ *and* $l = \mathsf{W\,A?m}$ *and* $s\|_2(\mathsf{A}) \xrightarrow{\mathsf{K\,A?m}} q$;

   (f) $\mathsf{A} = \mathsf{W}$ *and* $s\|_1(\mathsf{H}) \xrightarrow{\mathsf{H\,B!m}} q_1$ *and* $s\|_2(\mathsf{K}) = q_2$ *and* $q = (q_1, q_2)$ *and* $l = \mathsf{W\,B!m}$;

   (g) $\mathsf{A} = \mathsf{W}$ *and* $s\|_1(\mathsf{H}) \xrightarrow{\mathsf{B\,H?m}} q_1$ *and* $s\|_2(\mathsf{K}) = q_2$ *and* $q = (q_1, \mathsf{m}, q_2)$ *and* $l = \mathsf{B\,W?m}$;

   (h) $\mathsf{A} = \mathsf{W}$ *and* $s\|_2(\mathsf{K}) \xrightarrow{\mathsf{K\,B!m}} q_2$ *and* $s\|_1(\mathsf{H}) = q_1$ *and* $q = (q_1, q_2)$ *and* $l = \mathsf{W\,B!m}$;

   (i) $\mathsf{A} = \mathsf{W}$ *and* $s\|_2(\mathsf{K}) \xrightarrow{\mathsf{B\,K?m}} q_2$ *and* $s\|_1(\mathsf{K}) = q_1$ *and* $q = (q_1, \mathsf{m}, q_2)$ *and* $l = \mathsf{B\,W?m}$;

Proof. The proof of (i) and (ii) is by simultaneous induction on the number of steps from the initial state. In the initial state (i) and (ii) hold by construction.

Let us consider the inductive case. We consider the following possible cases for the last transition.

$s' \xrightarrow{\mathsf{A \to B:\,m}} s$ with $\mathsf{A}, \mathsf{B} \in \mathrm{dom}(\mathsf{S}_1)$ (the case $\mathsf{A}, \mathsf{B} \in \mathrm{dom}(\mathsf{S}_2)$ can be treated similarly).

By definition of configuration transition, we have that $s'(\mathsf{A}) \xrightarrow{\mathsf{A\,B!m}} s(\mathsf{A})$ and $s'(\mathsf{B}) \xrightarrow{\mathsf{A\,B?m}} s(\mathsf{B})$ and $s'(\mathsf{C}) = s(\mathsf{C})$ for each $\mathsf{C} \in \mathrm{dom}(\mathsf{S}_1) \setminus \{\mathsf{A}, \mathsf{B}\}$. Now, by the induction hypothesis (ii), we have that $s'\|_1(\mathsf{A}) \xrightarrow{\mathsf{A\,B!m}} s(\mathsf{A}) = s\|_1(\mathsf{A})$ and $s'\|_1(\mathsf{B}) \xrightarrow{\mathsf{A\,B?m}} s(\mathsf{B}) = s\|_1(\mathsf{B})$ (where the two equalities can be inferred by definition of configuration projection, since $\mathsf{A}, \mathsf{B} \neq \mathsf{W}$). Hence we have that $s'\|_1 \xrightarrow{\mathsf{A \to B:\,m}} s\|_1$. Now, since by the induction hypothesis we have that $s'\|_1 \in \mathcal{R}([\![\mathsf{S}_1]\!])$, we can infer that $s\|_1 \in \mathcal{R}([\![\mathsf{S}_1]\!])$. We obtain, instead, $s\|_2 \in \mathcal{R}([\![\mathsf{S}_2]\!])$ immediately by the induction hypothesis since, from $\mathsf{A}, \mathsf{B} \in \mathrm{dom}(\mathsf{S}_1)$

and definition of configuration projection we have that $s|_2 = s'|_2$. Also $\mathsf{nofd}_1(s(\mathsf{W})) \sim \mathsf{nofd}_2(s(\mathsf{W}))$ immediately follows from the induction hypothesis since $\mathsf{A}, \mathsf{B} \neq \mathsf{W}$ implies $s(\mathsf{W}) = s'(\mathsf{W})$. Regarding (ii), if $\mathsf{A} \neq \mathsf{W}$ then the same participant wants to take the same action thanks to (i), as desired. If $\mathsf{A} = \mathsf{W}$ is willing to communicate with some participant in S_1 then thanks to (i) and definition of semi-direct gateway, H is willing to do the same in $s|_1$. Symmetrically, if $\mathsf{A} = \mathsf{W}$ is willing to communicate with some participant in S_2 then K is willing to do the same in $s|_2$.

$s' \xrightarrow{\mathsf{A} \rightarrow \mathsf{W}:\, m} s$ with $\mathsf{A} \in \mathsf{dom}(\mathsf{S}_1)$ (the case $\mathsf{A} \in \mathsf{dom}(\mathsf{S}_2)$ can be treated similarly). By definition of system transition, we have that $s'(\mathsf{A}) \xrightarrow{\mathsf{A}\,\mathsf{W}!m} s(\mathsf{A})$ and $s'(\mathsf{W}) \xrightarrow{\mathsf{A}\,\mathsf{W}?m} s(\mathsf{W})$ and $s'(\mathsf{C}) = s(\mathsf{C})$ for each $\mathsf{C} \in \mathsf{dom}(\mathsf{S}_1) \setminus \{\mathsf{A}\}$. Moreover, by the induction hypothesis, $s'|_1 \in \mathcal{R}(\llbracket \mathsf{S}_1 \rrbracket)$, $s'|_2 \in \mathcal{R}(\llbracket \mathsf{S}_2 \rrbracket)$ and $s'|_1(\mathsf{H}) \sim s'|_2(\mathsf{K})$. By definition of configuration projection and of semi-direct gateway construction we have that $s|_2 = s'|_2$, and hence we can immediately infer that $s|_2 \in \mathcal{R}(\llbracket \mathsf{S}_2 \rrbracket)$.

Now, by the induction hypothesis (ii), we have that $s'|_1(\mathsf{A}) \xrightarrow{\mathsf{A}\,\mathsf{H}!m} s(\mathsf{A})$ and $s'|_1(\mathsf{H}) \xrightarrow{\mathsf{A}\,\mathsf{H}?m} q_1$ and $s'|_2(\mathsf{K}) = q_2$ where $s(\mathsf{W}) = (q_1, m, q_2)$. Now, by definition of configuration projection, from $s(\mathsf{W}) = (q_1, m, q_2)$ we obtain that $q_1 = s|_1(\mathsf{W})$. So, by definition of configuration transition, we have that $s'|_1 \xrightarrow{\mathsf{A} \rightarrow \mathsf{W}:\, m} s|_1$, and then $s|_1 \in \mathcal{R}(\llbracket \mathsf{S}_1 \rrbracket)$. For what concerns $\mathsf{nofd}_1(s(\mathsf{W})) \sim \mathsf{nofd}_2(s(\mathsf{W}))$, this is obtained by the induction hypothesis and by definition of $\mathsf{nofd}_{\_}(\cdot)$ and of semi-direct gateway. Also, (ii) holds, as in the previous case, by (i) and definition of semi-direct gateway and of configuration projection.

$s' \xrightarrow{\mathsf{W} \rightarrow \mathsf{A}:\, m} s$ with $\mathsf{A} \in \mathsf{dom}(\mathsf{S}_1)$ or $\mathsf{A} \in \mathsf{dom}(\mathsf{S}_2)$.
Similar to the previous case.   □

We now give a definition of composability for semi-direct composition.

Definition 4.7 (Semi-direct (H, K)-composability). *Two systems S_1 and S_2 with disjoint domains are* semi-directly (H, K)-composable *if $\mathsf{H} \in \mathsf{dom}(\mathsf{S}_1)$ and $\mathsf{K} \in \mathsf{dom}(\mathsf{S}_2)$ are two compatible roles whose machines are ?!-deterministic and mixed-deterministic.*

Notice that semi-direct (H, K)-composability is strictly weaker than (H, K)-composability. In fact, whereas both require ?!-determinism, the former enables some mixed states whereas the latter completely forbids them.

It is easy to check that the counterexamples for deadlock-freedom preservation of Sect. 3 do hold also in case semi-directed gateways are used on (H, K)-composable systems. As before, this forces us to select interface roles which are sequential or which are in systems always willing to receive the messages they send. Before presenting the results we give an auxiliary lemma.

Lemma 4.8. *Let S_1 and S_2 be two semi-directly (H, K)-composable systems. Then for each configuration s of the composed system $\mathsf{S}_1 \overset{\mathsf{H} \leftrightarrow \mathsf{K}}{\underset{\mathsf{W}}{\leftrightarrow}} \mathsf{S}_2$ we have that:*

- *if $s(\mathsf{W}) = (q_1, q_2)$ then q_1, q_2 are in the compatibility bisimilarity;*
- *if $s(\mathsf{W}) = (q_1, \mathsf{m}, q_2)$ then $s(\mathsf{W})$ has a unique transition to and from a state of the form in the item above.*

Proof. By construction. Uniqueness relies on ?!- and mixed-determinism. $\square$

Theorem 4.9 (Deadlock freedom for sequential interfaces). *Let S_1 and S_2 be two semi-directly (H, K)-composable and deadlock-free systems. If $\mathsf{S}_1(\mathsf{H})$ and $\mathsf{S}_2(\mathsf{K})$ are sequential, then the composed system $\mathsf{S}_1 \overset{\mathsf{H} \leftrightharpoons \mathsf{K}}{_{\mathsf{W}}} \mathsf{S}_2$ is deadlock-free.*

Proof. We will show that if $\mathsf{S}_1 \overset{\mathsf{H} \leftrightharpoons \mathsf{K}}{_{\mathsf{W}}} \mathsf{S}_2$ has a deadlock then at least one of S_1 and S_2 has a deadlock as well.

First, Proposition 4.6(ii) immediately yields that for each configuration s of $\mathsf{S}_1 \overset{\mathsf{H} \leftrightharpoons \mathsf{K}}{_{\mathsf{W}}} \mathsf{S}_2$ if there is some participant A such that $s(\mathsf{A})$ has an outgoing transition, then for some participant B either $s\|_1(\mathsf{B})$ or $s\|_2(\mathsf{B})$ has an outgoing transition.

Now we show that if no transition is enabled in a configuration s of $\mathsf{S}_1 \overset{\mathsf{H} \leftrightharpoons \mathsf{K}}{_{\mathsf{W}}} \mathsf{S}_2$ then no transition is enabled in $s\|_1$ and $s\|_2$. We prove the contrapositive, showing that if there is an enabled transition in $s\|_1$ or in $s\|_2$ then there is a transition enabled in s as well. If the transition does not involve H, K this follows from Proposition 4.6. Let us now consider a transition involving H (the case of K is symmetric). If the transition is of the form $s\|_1 \xrightarrow{\mathsf{A} \to \mathsf{H}: \ \mathsf{m}} \hat{s}$ and the state of W in s is a pair, by construction s can perform a transition $s \xrightarrow{\mathsf{A} \to \mathsf{W}: \ \mathsf{m}} s'$ as desired. If the state of W in s is a triple then thanks to Lemma 4.8 and definition of semi-direct gateway, the previous state was in the compatibility bisimilarity with a state of K, which has not changed. Hence K is willing to take a transition and thanks to deadlock-freedom of S_2 we can infer that there is a transition enabled in $s\|_2$. From this we can deduce that there is a transition enabled in s too as shown above, but for the case in which the enabled transition is from K. In this last case thanks to sequentiality the transition towards H and the one from K are complementary, thus S_2 is ready to take the message from the gateway, hence the communication can trigger.

A similar reasoning applies in case the transition is of the form $s\|_1 \xrightarrow{\mathsf{H} \to \mathsf{A}: \ \mathsf{m}} \hat{s}$.

Thus, if there is a deadlock configuration s in the composed system then either $s\|_1$ or $s\|_2$ are deadlocks against the hypothesis. $\square$

Notice that S_1 and S_2 of Example 4.3 are deadlock-free and (H, K)-composable. Besides, both H and K are sequential. Deadlock-freedom of $\mathsf{S}_1 \overset{\mathsf{H} \leftrightharpoons \mathsf{K}}{_{\mathsf{W}}} \mathsf{S}_2$ can hence be inferred by the above result.

As done for the composition via gateways, we can extend the above result by dropping the sequentiality condition in presence of !live interfaces.

Theorem 4.10 (Deadlock freedom for !live interfaces). *Let S_1 and S_2 be two semi-directly (H, K)-composable and deadlock-free systems. Moreover, let $\mathsf{S}_1(\mathsf{H})$ and $\mathsf{S}_2(\mathsf{K})$ be !live, respectively, in S_1 and S_2. Then the composed system $\mathsf{S}_1 \overset{\mathsf{H} \leftrightharpoons \mathsf{K}}{_{\mathsf{W}}} \mathsf{S}_2$ is deadlock-free.*

Proof. The proof is similar to the one of Theorem 4.9. The only difference is that !liveness is used instead of sequentiality when showing that if there is an enabled transition in $s\|_1$ or in $s\|_2$ then there is a transition enabled in s as well.

□

5   Related and Future Work

We have considered the synchronous composition of systems of CFSMs following the approach proposed in [3,4] for asynchronous composition. Quite surprisingly, enforcing that composition preserves deadlock freedom requires very strong conditions on the interface roles, as shown by means of some examples. Indeed, we proved compositionality of deadlock freedom for sequential interface roles only. We hence complemented this result by showing that, if a deadlock occurs, it needs to be when the gateway tries to deliver a message to the other system.

We also discussed semi-direct composition, based on a unique gateway. Beyond sparing some communications, the conditions required to ensure compositionality of deadlock freedom using this second approach are slightly weaker.

While we only discussed deadlock freedom, the same reasonings can be applied to other behavioural properties such as lock freedom [6,18,19] and liveness [6,23].

The above approach to composition has also been discussed in [5], in the setting of systems of processes obtained by projecting well-formed global types [17]. This setting is far less wild than ours, since global types ensure that each send is matched by a receive. Thus, all the counterexamples we showed cannot happen and deadlock freedom is ensured in all typable systems. Thanks to these restrictions they were able to develop a more comprehensive theory, including direct composition, a notion of structural decomposition and notions of behavioural composition and decomposition. Also, they could use as compatibility a relation weaker than bisimilarity. Understanding whether such a theory can be amended to fit in our more general setting is an interesting item for future work.

Compositionality in the setting of global types has been also studied in [22]. There the compositionality mechanism is different since it relies on partial systems, while the approach we use allows one to compose systems which are designed as closed, by transforming some participants into gateways. On the other hand they are able to model ways of interaction more structured than having a single communication channel as in our case. Extending our approach to cope with the composition via multiple interfaces at the same time can be an interesting aim for future work and can contribute to match their expressive power.

A compositional approach for reactive components has been proposed in [12, 25]. Composition is attained by means of a specified protocol regulating the communications between components that are supposed to produce results as soon as they get their inputs. Roughly speaking, this protocol represents the composition interface that rules out, among the communications of components, those not allowed in the composition. In this way, a component may be used in compositions under different protocols if its communications are compliant with (part of) the protocols. A difference with our approach is that the framework in [12,25], as common in session type approaches, requires the specification of a global type from which to derive local types to type check components in order to compose them.

Among the automata-based models in the literature, I/O automata [21], team automata [26], interface automata [15], and BIP [9] are perhaps the closest to communicating systems. In these models composition strategies based on some notion of compatibility have been proposed. However, these approaches differ from ours on a number of aspects.

First, the result of such a composition is a new automaton, not a system as in our case. Correspondingly, our notion of "interface" is more elaborated than in the other models. Indeed, for us an interface is a pair of automata rather than sets of actions of a single automaton.

Second, such automata have a fixed interface, since they distinguish internal from external actions. Instead, we do not fix an explicit interface: the interface is decided in a *relative* fashion. This gives a high degree of flexibility; e.g., we could use as interface a CFSM H′ when composing a system S with a system, say S′, and a different CFSM H″ in S when composing it with another system S″.

As previously pointed out, and related to the previous observations, we could think of our approach as not been based on a notion of "open" systems. We compose *closed* systems by "opening them up" depending on their relative structures, namely on the fact that they possess compatible components.

Extensive studies about compositionality of interacting systems have been conducted in the context of the BIP model [9]. Composition in BIP happens through operators meant to mediate the behaviour of the connected components. The composition can alter the non-deterministic behaviour by suitable priority models. In [1,2] it is shown that, under mild hypothesis, priority models do not spoil deadlock freedom. This requires to compromise on expressiveness. Whether our conditions are expressible in some priority model is open and left for future work. BIP features multi-point synchronisations while CFSMs interactions are point-to-point. Very likely CFSMs can be encoded in BIP without priorities and one could use D-Finder [8] to detect deadlock of composed systems. However, our conditions on interfaces allows us to avoid such analysis.

In the present approach, the transformations generating the gateway(s) from the interface roles do not depend on the rest of the systems to be composed. Besides investigating relaxed notions of compatibility (in the style of [5]), it would also be worth considering the possibility of dropping the compatibility requirement altogether and developing methods to generate ad-hoc gateways (i.e., taking into account the other CFSMs of the two systems to be composed) that preserve deadlock freedom and communication properties in general by construction. It would also be worth investigating whether our approach can be extended to cope with types of message passing communications other than point-to-point, such as multicast [14], broadcast or many-to-many [11].

References

1. Baranov, E., Bliudze, S.: Offer semantics: achieving compositionality, flattening and full expressiveness for the glue operators in BIP. Sci. Comput. Program. **109**, 2–35 (2015)
2. Baranov, E., Bliudze, S.: Expressiveness of component-based frameworks: a study of the expressiveness of BIP. Acta Informatica (2019). https://doi.org/10.1007/s00236-019-00337-7
3. Barbanera, F., de'Liguoro, U., Hennicker, R.: Global types for open systems. In: Bartoletti, M., Knight, S. (eds.) ICE, Volume 279 of EPTCS, pp. 4–20 (2018)
4. Barbanera, F., de'Liguoro, U., Hennicker, R.: Connecting open systems of communicating finite state machines. JLAMP **109** (2019)
5. Barbanera, F., Dezani-Ciancaglini, M., Lanese, I., Tuosto, E.: Composition and decomposition of multiparty sessions. JLAMP (2020). Submitted
6. Barbanera, F., Lanese, I., Tuosto, E.: Choreography automata. In: Bliudze, S., Bocchi, L. (eds.) COORDINATION 2020. LNCS, vol. 12134, pp. 86–106. Springer, Cham (2020). https://doi.org/10.1007/978-3-030-50029-0_6
7. Basu, S., Bultan, T., Ouederni, M.: Deciding choreography realizability. In: POPL, pp. 191–202 (2012)
8. Bensalem, S., Griesmayer, A., Legay, A., Nguyen, T.-H., Sifakis, J., Yan, R.: D-Finder 2: towards efficient correctness of incremental design. In: Bobaru, M., Havelund, K., Holzmann, G.J., Joshi, R. (eds.) NFM 2011. LNCS, vol. 6617, pp. 453–458. Springer, Heidelberg (2011). https://doi.org/10.1007/978-3-642-20398-5_32
9. Bliudze, S., Sifakis, J.: The algebra of connectors: structuring interaction in BIP. In: International Conference on Embedded Software. ACM, September 2020
10. Brand, D., Zafiropulo, P.: On communicating finite-state machines. J. ACM **30**(2), 323–342 (1983)
11. Bruni, R., Corradini, A., Gadducci, F., Melgratti, H., Montanari, U., Tuosto, E.: Data-driven choreographies à la Klaim. In: Boreale, M., Corradini, F., Loreti, M., Pugliese, R. (eds.) Models, Languages, and Tools for Concurrent and Distributed Programming. LNCS, vol. 11665, pp. 170–190. Springer, Cham (2019). https://doi.org/10.1007/978-3-030-21485-2_11
12. Carbone, M., Montesi, F., Vieira, H.T.: Choreographies for reactive programming. CoRR, abs/1801.08107 (2018). http://arxiv.org/abs/1801.08107
13. Cécé, G., Finkel, A.: Verification of programs with half-duplex communication. I&C **202**(2), 166–190 (2005)
14. Coppo, M., Dezani-Ciancaglini, M., Yoshida, N., Padovani, L.: Global progress for dynamically interleaved multiparty sessions. Mathematical structures in computer science **26**(2), 238–302 (2016)
15. De Alfaro, L., Henzinger, T.: Interface automata. ACM SIGSOFT Softw. Eng. Notes **26**(5), 109–120 (2001)
16. Gouda, M.G., Chang, C.: Proving liveness for networks of communicating finite state machines. ACM Trans. Program. Lang. Syst. **8**(1), 154–182 (1986)
17. Hüttel, H., et al.: Foundations of session types and behavioural contracts. ACM Comput. Surv. **49**(1), 3:1–3:36 (2016)
18. Kobayashi, N.: A partially deadlock-free typed process calculus. ACM TOPLAS **20**(2), 436–482 (1998)
19. Kobayashi, N.: Type-based information flow analysis for the pi-calculus. Acta Informatica **42**(4–5), 291–347 (2005)

20. Lange, J., Tuosto, E., Yoshida, N.: From communicating machines to graphical choreographies. In: POPL, pp. 221–232. ACM (2015)
21. Lynch, N., Tuttle, M.: Hierarchical correctness proofs for distributed algorithms. In: ACM Symposium Principles of Distributed Computing, pp. 137–151. ACM (1987)
22. Montesi, F., Yoshida, N.: Compositional choreographies. In: D'Argenio, P.R., Melgratti, H. (eds.) CONCUR 2013. LNCS, vol. 8052, pp. 425–439. Springer, Heidelberg (2013). https://doi.org/10.1007/978-3-642-40184-8_30
23. Padovani, L., Vasconcelos, V.T., Vieira, H.T.: Typing liveness in multiparty communicating systems. In: Kühn, E., Pugliese, R. (eds.) COORDINATION 2014. LNCS, vol. 8459, pp. 147–162. Springer, Heidelberg (2014). https://doi.org/10.1007/978-3-662-43376-8_10
24. Peng, W., Purushothaman, S.: Analysis of a class of communicating finite state machines. Acta Inf. **29**(6/7), 499–522 (1992)
25. Savanović, Z., Vieira, H., Galletta, L.: A type language for message passing component-based systems. In: ICE, EPTCS (2020). To appear
26. ter Beek, M.H., Kleijn, J.: Team automata satisfying compositionality. In: Araki, K., Gnesi, S., Mandrioli, D. (eds.) FME 2003. LNCS, vol. 2805, pp. 381–400. Springer, Heidelberg (2003). https://doi.org/10.1007/978-3-540-45236-2_22
27. Tuosto, E., Guanciale, R.: Semantics of global view of choreographies. JLAMP **95**, 17–40 (2018)

Modular Verification of JML Contracts Using Bounded Model Checking

Bernhard Beckert[1,2(✉)], Michael Kirsten[1(✉)] [ID], Jonas Klamroth[2(✉)], and Mattias Ulbrich[1(✉)]

[1] Karlsruhe Institute of Technology (KIT), Karlsruhe, Germany
{beckert,kirsten,ulbrich}@kit.edu
[2] FZI Research Center for Information Technology, Karlsruhe, Germany
klamroth@fzi.de

Abstract. There are two paradigms for dealing with complex verification targets: Modularization using contract-based specifications and whole-program analysis. In this paper, we present an approach bridging the gap between the two paradigms, introducing concepts from the world of contract-based deductive verification into the domain of software bounded model checking. We present a transformation that takes Java programs annotated with contracts written in the Java Modeling Language and turns them into Java programs that can be read by the bounded model checker JBMC. A central idea of the translation is to make use of nondeterministic value assignments to eliminate JML quantifiers. We have implemented our approach and discuss an evaluation, which shows the advantages of the presented approach.

Keywords: Software verification · Modular design · Design by contract · Software bounded model checking

1 Introduction

Over the last decades, the reach and power of formal methods for program verification has increased considerably. However, at some point, one has to face the complexities of real-world systems. There are two paradigms for dealing with complex verification targets. (1) Modularization and (de-)composition using contract-based specifications: Components – typically methods or functions – are verified separately, and can then be replaced by their abstract contracts for verifying the overall system. (2) Whole-program analysis, where the search space is restricted by over- or under-approximating the set of reachable states. While modular verification is most often performed using a deductive verification engine relying on some form of theorem prover, whole-program verification applies techniques like predicate abstraction, abstract interpretation or bounded model checking to reduce the size of the state space.

Here, we focus on bounded model checking where the search space is restricted using bounds on the number of loop iterations and the size of data

© Springer Nature Switzerland AG 2020
T. Margaria and B. Steffen (Eds.): ISoLA 2020, LNCS 12476, pp. 60–80, 2020.
https://doi.org/10.1007/978-3-030-61362-4_4

structures. While modularization requires user interaction to specify the components, software bounded model checking is fully automatic, but comes at the cost of potential false negatives that miss program failures beyond the chosen bounds. In this paper, we present an approach that bridges the gap between the two paradigms by introducing concepts from the world of contract-based deductive verification [12,23] into the domain of software bounded model checking [5]. Our method enables a software bounded model checker to verify properties of components (methods) written in a contract-based specification language. This allows for modular proofs in a software bounded model checking context. The proofs can also be hybrid where only some parts are modular in an otherwise monolithic proof. We envision three main application areas: (1) The reach of software bounded model checking is extended. While many program parts can be dealt with using exhaustive search, other parts need to be decomposed in order to verify them for non-trivial bounds. This may even allow for an increase of the bounds for the non-modular parts to the point where the software bounded model checker can explore the full search space. (2) Software bounded model checking can be combined with deductive program verification, where those components that – even after decomposition – cannot be handled by a model checker can be verified using a deductive verification tool. (3) Our bridging approach has the potential of being a valuable tool during the engineering phase of a deductive proof. Typically, formulating contracts and constructing a proof in a deductive verification tool requires several iterations of adjusting either code or specification until a proof is found. A software bounded model checker that can handle contracts may be used to spot bugs in the specification and the code before a full deductive verification is started.

While the concepts behind our approach apply to a range of languages and tools, in the following we target the Java programming language, bringing together two important players in formal methods for Java: The Java Bounded Model Checker (JBMC) [10] meets the Java Modeling Language (JML) [19]. We present a transformation that takes Java programs annotated with contracts written in JML and turns them into Java programs that can be read by JBMC, i.e., the JML specifications are turned into Java code and annotations in the form of `assume` and `assert` statements understood by JBMC. A central idea of the translation is to make use of nondeterministic value assignments 'x = *'[1] to eliminate (part of the) JML 'forall' and 'exists' quantifiers. Therefore, the resulting programs are not executable, but can be handled by JBMC more efficiently.

The rest of this paper starts with a brief introduction to software (bounded) model checking, deductive verification, as well as the syntax and semantics of JML in Sect. 2. Then, Sect. 3 shows the main ideas of our approach, and Sect. 4 illustrates our translation from Java with JML into Java with assertions, assumptions and nondeterministic assignments. In Sect. 5, we present a prototypical

---

[1] The notation x = *; (and semantics) are borrowed from nondeterministic assignment in dynamic logic [15]. Boogie, e.g., often refers to this as the **havoc** statement.

implementation[2] and evaluate our approach on multiple case studies in Sect. 6. We discuss related work in Sect. 7 and conclude in Sect. 8.

2 Background

Software Bounded Model Checking (SBMC) is a formal program verification technique that, given a program and a software property to be checked, verifies fully automatically whether the program satisfies the property [5]. In a nutshell, that question is translated into a reachability problem w.r.t. the given program. SBMC symbolically, i.e., without the need for concrete values, executes the program and exhaustively checks it for errors that could violate the given property within some given bounds that restrict the number of loop iterations and recursive method calls. Using these bounds, SBMC limits all runs through the program to a bounded length and can thereby unroll the control flow graph of the program and transform it into static single assignment form [8]. This bounded program is then translated into a formula in a decidable logic, e.g., an instance of the SAT problem. The formula is satisfiable if and only if a program run exists that violates the given software property within the given bounds. Modern SAT or SMT solvers [2,13] can be used to check whether such a program run exists, in which case the SBMC tool constructs the corresponding problematic input and presents the counterexample to the user. If no such program run is found, that may be either because the property is actually satisfied, or because it is invalid only for runs exceeding the given bounds. In some cases, SBMC is also able to infer statically which bounds are sufficient, in order to come to a definitive conclusion. SBMC tools also permit to extend the program with nondeterministic value assignments and **assume** statements in order to restrict the values and states that are to be considered. The properties to be checked are given in the form of **assert** statements. Hence, SBMC checks whether there are any runs through the program that satisfy all encountered **assume** statements but violate an **assert** statement.

Deductive Program Verification is based on a logical (program) calculus to construct a proof for a formula expressing that a program satisfies its specification [12,23]. Typically, deductive verification uses invariants and induction to handle loops. In order to mitigate complexity, most deductive approaches employ design by contract [21], where functions resp. methods are specified with formal pre- and postconditions. These additional annotations enable a modular verification[3], where each method is individually proved to satisfy its contract. To this end, each method – together with its contract – is translated into a formula, e.g., using some form of weakest precondition computation [11]. Method calls are replaced by the contract of the called method (instead of the method body), and loops are replaced by their invariants (instead of loop unwinding). The resulting formulas are either discharged using automatic theorem provers, e.g., SMT solvers [2], or shown to the user for interactive proof construction.

---

[2] The source code is available at https://github.com/JonasKlamroth/JJBMC.

```
/*@ requires 0 <= x1;
  @ ensures \result == x1 * x2;
  @ assignable \nothing;
  @*/
public int mult(int x1, int x2) {
  int res = 0;
  /*@ loop_invariant 0 <= i && i <= x1 && res == i * x2;
    @ decreases x1 - i;
    @ assignable \nothing;
    @*/
  for (int i = 0; i < x1; ++i) res += x2;
  return res;
}
```

Listing 1. An example of a method specified with JML.

The Java Modeling Language (JML) is a specification language for Java programs that follows the design-by-contract paradigm and enables the user to annotate Java programs with modular specifications, e.g., method contracts and loop invariants [19]. JML annotations are written in Java comments that are initiated with the character sequence "/*@". The syntax and semantics for JML expressions are equivalent to those of Java expressions, which additionally permits universal and existential quantifiers as well as special keywords, e.g., \old that enables the postcondition to refer to expressions before executing the method.

Consider, for example, Listing 1, where the method mult multiplies two integers using repeated addition. The precondition (indicated by **requires**) requires that both integers are non-negative; the postcondition (indicated by **ensures**) demands that the returned value (indicated by \result) is the product of the two parameters x1 and x2. Note that, even though this program may produce an integer overflow, the specification is still correct, as JML and Java have the same integer semantics. Moreover, the **assignable** clause restricts the heap locations which the method may change. The keyword \nothing requires that no heap location may be changed. In case we allow the method to change existing heap locations, we would specify a sequence of *storage references* (either field accesses o.f, object accesses o.* meaning that all fields of o may be written, or array access ranges a[$i..j$] meaning that any index between i and j in array a may be written). JML also permits to give auxiliary specifications, e.g., loop invariants to specify the behavior of a loop, that are specified inside the method body. The loop invariant in Listing 1 specifies that, for each loop execution, the currently computed result **res** is equal to the value of the loop variable multiplied by the second parameter x2. Loop invariants may also be extended by a **decreases** clause that specifies an integer expression which must strictly decrease in every loop iteration and never become negative. Since infinite strictly decreasing sequences are not possible within the domain of the natural numbers, this clause permits to prove termination of the loop. While JML encompasses many more concepts, we assume in the rest of this paper that method contracts are desugared, i.e., they adhere to the description from above [1,19].

There are two deductive verification tools available for JML-annotated Java code: the KeY tool and OpenJML. The KeY tool supports both automatic and interactive verification [1]. KeY's support for user interaction permits deductive verification w.r.t. expressive specifications. OpenJML is an automatic verification tool for verifying JML annotations [9]. The JML proof obligations are first reduced to SMT formulas which are then discharged by SMT solvers.

The Java Bounded Model Checker (JBMC) is an extension of the C Bounded Model Checker (CBMC) and performs (software) bounded model checking on Java bytecode for a bit-accurate verification of Java programs by combining SAT/SMT solving with a full symbolic state-space exploration [10]. It includes an exact and verification-friendly model of standard Java library classes. Behavioral subtyping is handled by conducting a case distinction over all possible implementations expanding their respective method bodies. JBMC supports all control flow mechanisms of Java including exceptions. The tool is fully automatic and its scalability depends mainly on the complexity of string operations, loops, recursion and floating-point arithmetic in the analyzed code.

3   The Main Ideas Behind the Approach

At the base of our approach is the assumption that the reach of software bounded model checking is extended when modularization is added, which comes with three individual arguments as following. (1) While many program parts can be dealt with using exhaustive search, other parts need to be decomposed in order to verify them for non-trivial bounds. (2) For devising a formal program specification, it is often worthwhile to early on either gain trust in its validity or uncover its incorrectness already for a bounded domain or scope. Exploiting this *small scope hypothesis* [16] lets us do effective program verification within a bounded scope and mitigate the otherwise common state space explosion. However, prominent examples such as the TimSort algorithm show that the more labor-intensive deductive program verification within a universal scope is generally desirable [14]. (3) With the approach taken in this paper, we enable a powerful combination of both methodologies on a modular level, such that a verification engineer can avoid wasting time in labor-intensive interactive verification when guarantees within a bounded scope suffice. The bounded scope in our case does not only refer to unwindings and recursion inlinings, but also to data structures. With data always being finite, program verification becomes a theoretically decidable and in many cases practically manageable problem. Our approach gives the user a fine-grained control as to which degree or which parts and how much of the program to verify either within a bounded scope or deductively. The communication between both verification techniques happens on specification level via method contracts, loop invariants, or block contracts, making use of the design-by-contract paradigm (see Sect. 2).

Consider, e.g., the common case where the user develops a method together with some inner helper method. For the deductive verification scenario, the outer method would have a method contract corresponding to its API. However, also the inner method would need a contract, which is not known yet when it is still being developed. In this early development stage, the user can rapidly gain confidence in possible contracts for this inner method by employing a modular proof within a bounded scope, as no user interaction is needed. Once the development of the method is finished, the user can opt for employing an unbounded modular proof, after gaining confidence that the proof will succeed. Often, the size of modules for SBMC can be considerably larger than that for deductive verification scenarios where every small method is individually specified. We automatically translate proof obligations induced by modular specification contracts into special code constructs that let the SBMC tool restrict the state space to the one defined by the precondition and insert assertions into the code that are equivalent to the postcondition. This relieves us from manually creating an execution harness for the whole-program approach that SBMC otherwise takes, which inlines method invocations. Similar to the technique of runtime assertion checking or runtime verification, the necessary abstractions from, e.g., method contracts are automatically encoded in assertions that are inserted into the program (see Sect. 7). However, unlike in runtime verification, we insert statements into the code that are only useful for static verification, namely **assume** statements and nondeterministic value assignments. These additional statements enhance the expressiveness and efficiency for static verification, but alter the execution semantics of the program. Quantifiers that cannot be represented by nondeterminism are translated into loops that iterate over the quantified domain. We evaluate such expressions in additional statements that implement side computations.

Within our formal translation rules described in Sect. 4, we reflect the distinction of side computations and computing the value of an expression E by splitting the translation E into two parts: (a) a command translation $[\![E]\!]^{cmd}$ and (b) a value translation $[\![E]\!]^{val}$. We make use of nondeterministic assignment when translating quantifiers by using a form of skolemization – instead of translating into a loop with many assertions. In order to express, e.g., that all elements of an array a are positive, instead of

```
for (int i = 0; i < a.length; i++){ assert 0 < a[i]; },
```

we generate the following more efficient, yet equivalently valid translation:

```
int i := *; assert !(0 <= i && i < a.length) || 0 < a[i];
```

The latter encoding makes use of the builtin nondeterministic choice operation of SBMC to make sure that all possible valuations are covered, whereas the former translation makes this explicit by iterating over all possible values. For the latter encoding, the assertion is violated once there exists a value within the bounds which makes the assertion invalid. The advantage of nondeterministic choice is that the instantiation task is given to a SAT or SMT solver that is optimized to cover all cases in a more clever way than by naive explicit enumeration.

4   Translating JML Annotations

Basics. This section describes how a Java program with JML annotations (in particular method contracts and loop invariants) can be translated into Java code ready for the analysis with the bounded model checker JBMC. The target language is Java code without JML annotations as the annotations are replaced by additional Java statements. The additional Java code includes statements that are interpreted by the model checker in a particular way: `assume` statements and nondeterministic value assignments. While we present them as keyword statements in this paper, they are expressed as special method invocations in the actual implementation. The meaning of an assertion `assert c;` is the usual one of Java: A program run is considered failing if the assertion is reached and the evaluation of the `assert`ed proposition c evaluates to false. In contrast, if in the statement `assume c;` the condition c evaluates to false, then the program run is not considered failing, but irrelevant. One may think of this as a graceful, but abrupt termination of the program at this point. The nondeterministic assignment `x = *;` assigns an arbitrary, nondeterministically chosen, not further constrained value of `x`'s static type to `x`. When such an assignment is reached multiply during a program run, each time a different value may be chosen.

Formally, our translation is defined as a syntactical replacement function

$$[\![\cdot]\!] : JML \cup Java \rightarrow Java$$

that takes Java annotated with JML and returns Java constructs without JML (but with assumptions and nondeterministic assignments). The translation is recursively applied as a rewriting rule to the program in a top-down fashion. In the following subsections, we present the most noteworthy rewriting rules that define $[\![\cdot]\!]$, but refrain from providing a complete list due to space limitations. We focus on a subset of Java and JML, where

- method calls only appear standalone in the form $lhs = o.\mathtt{m}(a_1, a_2, \ldots)$,
- `break` and `continue` statements do not occur, and
- `try-catch` statements do not occur.

This is not a fundamental restriction; additional rules for handling these features can easily be added. Our implementation, in fact, supports already a considerably larger subset of Java and JML than shown in this paper (see Sect. 5).

4.1   Translating Method Contracts

As design by contract targets individual methods (and not the whole program) for a method-modular program analysis, we start with a translation pattern in (1) that covers blocks of pre- and postconditions for method contracts. This easily extends to classes by applying the translation to all methods in a class.

$$
\left[\!\!\left[\begin{array}{l} \text{/*@ requires } R; \\ \text{@ ensures } E; \\ \text{@*/} \\ \{ \ B \ \} \end{array}\right]\!\!\right] \quad = \ \{ \ [\![\text{assume } R]\!]; \ [\![B]\!]; \ [\![\text{assert } E]\!]; \ \} \quad (1)
$$

The translation of the precondition R is assumed before the block and the translation of the postcondition E is asserted after its execution. The translation's goal is that any program that satisfies the block contract on the left does not fail any assert in the program on the right and vice versa. This encoding schema is also the basis for the translation schema for methods with contracts. However, it is important that the control flow in B does not bypass the assertion at the end of the block (e.g., by throwing an exception).

$$
\left[\!\!\left[\begin{array}{l} \text{/*@ requires } R; \\ \text{@ ensures } E; \\ \text{@ assignable } M; \\ \text{@*/} \\ T \ m(P) \text{ throws } S \ \{ \\ \quad B \\ \} \end{array}\right]\!\!\right] = \left(\begin{array}{l} T \ m(P) \text{ throws } S \ \{ \\ \quad [\![\text{ assume } R \ ]\!]; \\ \quad T \text{ result}; \\ \quad saveOld(E, B); \\ \quad \text{try } \{ \ [\![B]\!] \ \} \\ \quad \text{catch (ReturnExc e) } \{\} \\ \quad [\![\text{ assert } E \ ]\!]; \\ \quad \text{return result}; \\ \} \end{array}\right) \quad (2)
$$

The specified method m is translated into a method with the same signature, embedding the pre- and postcondition as assumption and assertion, respectively. Moreover, we need additional statements and declarations. New variables are initialized in $saveOld(E, B)$ to enable the translation of \old that refers to values at method entry. We add the variable result for the return value of the method. Together with the exception ReturnExc, this encodes return statements. The correctness of the translation is captured by the following claim:

Correctness of Translation. A JML-annotated Java method m satisfies its JML contract if and only if the translation of m does not fail[3] any of its assertions for any initial state, argument values, nondeterministically chosen values and bound on the number of loop iterations.

This claim has been shown for a simple while language, but remains to be proven for the full semantics of Java and JML [17]. Most Java statements s in a method body B are translated by the identity ($[\![s]\!] = s$), i.e., are left unchanged. The translation differs only for modularity-related aspects, e.g., modular handling of loops, assignable clauses, and abstractions of method calls using contracts, which are covered in Sect. 4.4 and 4.5.

---

[3] Failure means that an exception is thrown when evaluating the assertion.

For methods, we furthermore need to translate assert, assume and return statements. The former two occur directly in the method's translation, and the latter one is required for a control flow that contains the explicit cast of an exception. In order to evaluate conditions in assertions and assumptions, we need to know their "polarity", which depends on whether they occur within an assumption or an assertion, and changes within negated expressions. As an example, the translation of quantifiers requires to distinguish their polarity. For expressions, there are several different translation functions for the contexts in which the expression occurs. Depending on the polarity of the expression (i.e., whether it occurs negated or not and whether it is assumed or asserted), we translate expressions differently (indicated by the *assert* or *assume* subscript). Moreover, some expressions require that code is executed before their evaluation. There is, hence, for both modes another translation function that gives the code to evaluate the expression (it is denoted by the superscript *cmd* while the superscript *val* indicates the code for the expression itself). This distinction enables a more efficient treatment of quantifiers as shown in Sect. 4.3.

$$[\text{assert } A] = \{[A]_{assert}^{cmd} \; ; \; \text{assert } [A]_{assert}^{val} \; ; \}$$

$$[\text{assume } A] = \{[A]_{assume}^{cmd} \; ; \; \text{assume } [A]_{assume}^{val} \; ; \}$$

$$[\text{return } E] = \{\text{result} = E; \text{ throw new ReturnException}(); \}$$

4.2   Translating JML Expressions

The expression language in JML extends the side-effect-free expressions in Java. In most cases, the translation operator is simply propagated to all subexpressions. For literals and local variables, the translation is the identity. We hence give rules for the majority of all binary operations $\circ$, such as + or ==:

$$[A \circ B]^{val} = [A]^{val} \circ [B]^{val} \qquad [A \circ B]^{cmd} = [A]^{cmd} \; ; [B]^{cmd}$$

$$[x]^{val} = x \qquad\qquad\qquad [x]^{cmd} = \{\}$$

The translation of unary operators, field and array accesses, etc., follows the same principle. Special attention must be given to the case of binary Boolean connectives that have a short-circuit semantics in Java, i.e., the second operand is only evaluated if the result is not determined by the value of the first one. This applies to Java operators such as "&&" and "||", but also to the implication "==>" in JML (see Sect. 4.6). The rules are the same both for *assert* and *assume*:

$$[A \;\&\&\; B]^{val} = [A]^{val} \;\&\&\; [B]^{val} \qquad [A \;||\; B]^{val} = [A]^{val} \;||\; [B]^{val}$$

$$[A \texttt{ ==> } B]^{val} = [!A]^{val} \;||\; [B]^{val}$$

$$[A \;\&\&\; B]^{cmd} = [A]^{cmd} \; ; \; \text{if}(\; [A]^{val})\{ \; [B]^{cmd} \; \}$$

$$[A \;||\; B]^{cmd} = [A]^{cmd} \; ; \; \text{if}(\; [!A]^{val})\{ \; [B]^{cmd} \; \}$$

$$[A \texttt{ ==> } B]^{cmd} = [A]^{cmd} \; ; \; \text{if}(\; [A]^{val})\{ \; [B]^{cmd} \; \}$$

An additional twist occurs with operators that modify polarity, most notably negation. In that case, *assert* gets switched to *assume* and vice versa:

$$[\![!A]\!]_{assert}^{val} = \; ! [\![A]\!]_{assume}^{val} \qquad\qquad [\![!A]\!]_{assert}^{cmd} = [\![A]\!]_{assume}^{cmd}$$

$$[\![!A]\!]_{assume}^{val} = \; ! [\![A]\!]_{assert}^{val} \qquad\qquad [\![!A]\!]_{assume}^{cmd} = [\![A]\!]_{assert}^{cmd}$$

The ternary conditional operator $(C \; ? \; T \; : \; E)$ is special, since the condition C occurs both positive (as a guard for T in case C is true) and negative (as a guard for E in case C is false). Furthermore, we introduce another mode *demonic* which makes sure that the optimizations proposed in Sect. 4.3 are not applied (there are also the dual rules to the following ones for *assert*):

$$[\![C \; ? \; T \; : \; E]\!]_{assume}^{val} = [\![C]\!]_{demonic}^{val} \; ? \; [\![T]\!]_{assume}^{val} \; : \; [\![E]\!]_{assert}^{val}$$

$$[\![C \; ? \; T \; : \; E]\!]_{assume}^{cmd} =$$
$$[\![C]\!]_{assume}^{cmd} \; ; \; \mathtt{if(} \, [\![C]\!]_{assume}^{val} \, \mathtt{)\{} \, [\![T]\!]_{assume}^{cmd} \, \mathtt{\}} \; \mathtt{else} \; \mathtt{\{} \, [\![E]\!]_{assume}^{cmd} \, \mathtt{\}}$$

Apart from pure Java, also JML-specific constructs, e.g., implications as shown in the beginning of this subsection, may occur within specifications. We support the \old(E) construct which can be used to refer to the value of an expression E in the state at the beginning of the current method invocation. This semantics is achieved by storing the prestate value of all expressions used as arguments for this operator in fresh variables before executing the method (as done for *saveOld* in (2)). The keyword \result can be used in postconditions to refer to the result of the method invocation. We translate it into the new variable result during the translation of the method body in (2).

$$[\![\backslash\mathtt{result}]\!]^{val} = \mathtt{result} \qquad\qquad [\![\backslash\mathtt{result}]\!]^{cmd} = \mathtt{\{\}}$$

$$[\![\backslash\mathtt{old}(E)]\!]^{val} = oldVar(E) \qquad\qquad [\![\backslash\mathtt{old}(E)]\!]_{x}^{cmd} = [\![E]\!]_{x}^{cmd}$$

The symbol x is used as a placeholder for either *assume* or *assert* mode. Moreover, we require special treatment when \old(E) occurs within a quantified expression if it contains the quantified variable.

4.3 Translating Quantifiers

JML also supports universally and existentially quantified expressions, and although JML permits to quantify over objects and unbounded ranges, the following rules only cover bounded integer ranges, where for an integer variable i bounded by L and H, and the quantified expression E, expressions are as follows:

$$(\backslash\mathtt{forall} \; \mathtt{int} \; i; \; L <= i \; \&\& \; i < H; \; E)$$
$$(\backslash\mathtt{exists} \; \mathtt{int} \; i; \; L <= i \; \&\& \; i < H; \; E)$$

In JBMC's semantics, assert statements can be seen as implicitly universally quantified and assume statements as implicitly existentially quantified (see Sect. 2). Hence, we translate the JML clause

```
ensures (\forall int i; 0 <= i && i < 10; 0 <= a[i]);
```

by assigning a nondeterministic value to i and eliminating the quantifier:

```
int i = *; assert !(0 <= i && i < 10) || 0 <= a[i];
```

Note that this also works for unbounded quantifiers. By the duality of the quantifiers, an equivalent translation exists for the assumption of existentially quantified expressions. We denote such quantifiers that may be translated in this way as "angelic" quantifiers, since they are the "easy" case regarding translation.

$$[\![(\texttt{\textbackslash forall int } i;\ L <= i\ \&\&\ i < H;\ E)]\!]^{cmd}_{assert} = \texttt{int } i\texttt{=*; } [\![E]\!]^{cmd}_{assert}$$

$$[\![(\texttt{\textbackslash forall int } i;\ L <= i\ \&\&\ i < H;\ E)]\!]^{val}_{assert} =$$
$$[\![(L <= i\ \&\&\ i < H)\ \texttt{==>}\ E]\!]^{val}_{assert}$$

$$[\![(\texttt{\textbackslash exists int } i;\ L <= i\ \&\&\ i < H;\ E)]\!]^{cmd}_{assume} = \texttt{int } i\texttt{=*; } [\![E]\!]^{cmd}_{assume}$$

$$[\![(\texttt{\textbackslash exists int } i;\ L <= i\ \&\&\ i < H;\ E)]\!]^{val}_{assume} =$$
$$[\![(L <= i\ \&\&\ i < H)\ \&\&\ E]\!]^{val}_{assume}$$

The integer expressions for the bounds L and H of the index variable i are not subject to the translation $[\![\cdot]\!]^{cmd}$ and must not contain quantifiers. Special care must be given to quantifiers that cannot be translated by implicit semantics, i.e., universal quantifiers within assume and existential quantifier within assert. We call these quantifiers "demonic quantifiers", as these are more problematic and we need an explicit loop within our translation:[4]

$$\left[\!\!\left[\begin{array}{l} (\texttt{\textbackslash exists int } i;\\ \quad L <= i\ \&\&\ i < H;\\ \quad E) \end{array} \right]\!\!\right]^{cmd}_{assert} = \left(\begin{array}{l} \texttt{b = false;}\\ \texttt{for (int } i = L;\ i < H;\ \texttt{++}i) \ \{\\ \quad [\![E]\!]^{cmd}_{assert}\\ \quad \texttt{b = (b || } [\![E]\!]^{val}_{assert})\\ \texttt{\}} \end{array} \right)$$

$$\left[\!\!\left[\begin{array}{l} (\texttt{\textbackslash forall int } i;\\ \quad L <= i\ \&\&\ i < H;\\ \quad E) \end{array} \right]\!\!\right]^{cmd}_{assume} = \left(\begin{array}{l} \texttt{b = true;}\\ \texttt{for (int } i = L;\ i < H;\ \texttt{++}i) \ \{\\ \quad [\![E]\!]^{cmd}_{assume}\\ \quad \texttt{b = (b \&\& } [\![E]\!]^{val}_{assume})\\ \texttt{\}} \end{array} \right)$$

---

[4] Using the demonic translation also for angelic quantifiers would be sound, yet less efficient. Hence, we use it in the *demonic* mode of the ternary operator.

$$[\![(\verb|\exists int i;| \; L \; \verb|<=| \; \verb|i| \; \verb|&&| \; \verb|i| \; \verb|<| \; H; \; E)]\!]_{assert}^{val} \; = \; \verb|b|$$

$$[\![(\verb|\forall int i;| \; L \; \verb|<=| \; \verb|i| \; \verb|&&| \; \verb|i| \; \verb|<| \; H; \; E)]\!]_{assume}^{val} \; = \; \verb|b|$$

In this translation, `b` is a fresh Boolean variable that does not occur in the program, and is assumed to be declared at the beginning of the program. The translations of `\forall` and `\exists` differ in the initialization value of `b` and the Boolean operation in the loop body. The requirement of bounded integer ranges is crucial (the loop must terminate). Although this translation may be more intuitive, it is significantly less efficient for verification and hence only used when necessary. Note that the quantified range must not only be bounded, but must also be of the expected form. Consider, e.g., the set of even integers smaller than 10. This set is clearly bounded, but it does not fit the expected form, as there is an additional constraint in the guard. This can, however, always be fixed by moving the additional constraint to the inner expression within the quantifier.

4.4   Translating Frame Conditions

So far, we only considered the translation of pre- and postconditions. In JML, however, method contracts also contain frame conditions, which are specified within `assignable` clauses (see Sect. 2). The basic idea is to add an assertion for each assignment that fails if and only if the assignment violates the frame condition (for the sake of simplicity, we only consider assignments, but our approach also applies to other state-changing operations). Note that these rules only cover assignments to arrays and object fields, as assignments to local variables are always permitted. If '`assignable` a_1, a_2, ..., a_n' is the assignable clause for the enclosing method, the translation rules for an assignment to a left-hand side of the form $O.f$, where O is of type OT, as well as a left-hand side of the form $A[I]$, where A is of array type $AT[]$, are as follows:

$$[\![O.f\texttt{=}E;]\!] = \begin{pmatrix} OT \; \texttt{n0} \; \texttt{=} \; O; \\ \texttt{assert} \; mc(\texttt{n0}.f, \verb|\old|(a_1)) \; \texttt{||} \; ... \; \texttt{||} \\ \qquad mc(\texttt{n0}.f, \verb|\old|(a_n)); \\ \texttt{n0.f} \; \texttt{=} \; E; \end{pmatrix}$$

$$[\![A[I]\texttt{=}E;]\!] = \begin{pmatrix} AT[] \; \texttt{nA} \; \texttt{=} \; A; \\ \texttt{assert} \; mc(\texttt{nA}[I], \verb|\old|(a_1)) \; \texttt{||} \; ... \; \texttt{||} \\ \qquad mc(\texttt{nA}[I], \verb|\old|(a_n))); \\ \texttt{nA}[I] \; \texttt{=} \; E; \end{pmatrix}$$

The predicate $mc(l, a)$ determines whether an assignment to location l (a field access $o.f$ or an array access $a[i]$) is justified by a storage reference a in the assignable clauses. This predicate is defined as follows, where for all other combinations not explicitly mentioned, mc is `false`:

$$mc(o.\mathtt{f},\ p.\mathtt{g}) \Leftrightarrow \mathtt{false} \qquad mc(o.\mathtt{f},\ p.\mathtt{f}) \Leftrightarrow o\mathord{=}\mathord{=}p \qquad mc(o.\mathtt{f},\ p.\mathtt{*}) \Leftrightarrow o\mathord{=}\mathord{=}p$$
$$mc(a[i],\ b[l..h]) \Leftrightarrow (a \mathrel{\mathtt{==}} b\ \mathtt{\&\&}\ l \mathrel{\mathtt{<=}} i\ \mathtt{\&\&}\ i \mathrel{\mathtt{<}} h)$$

The above translation is sound, but produces false positives for newly created objects. Consider, e.g., a method annotated by 'assignable \nothing;' that starts by creating a new object, then stores this object in a local variable, and finally assigns a new value to one of the object's fields. Our translation would lead to a frame-condition violation being reported as there is no storage reference in the assignable clause that justifies this assignment. In order to fix this problem, we introduce a predicate that we call $newObj$, which we `assume` for each new object. We are then able to adapt our assertions by requiring that an assignment is permitted by the assignable clause (as before) *or* the $newObj$ predicate is true for the left-hand side of the assignment.

4.5   Translating Method Invocations

So far, we have seen how to translate JML expressions and use that to translate method contracts. However, in order to achieve a truly modular approach, we need to replace parts of Java code by their contracts, namely method calls. In this section, we moreover show how loops can be replaced by loop invariants, as the general idea for both method calls and loops is very similar: First, the precondition (or the invariant) is `assert`ed, then the parts of the state that are modifiable by the method call (or the loop) according to the JML assignable clause are anonymized, and finally the post condition is `assumed`. The same translation technique can be applied for block contracts and statement contracts (not shown here). The standard treatment for method calls in JBMC is to inline the method body. We can exploit this behavior, as we replace the original definition of the method by a "symbolic" definition, which contains the method contract instead of the method body. Once the symbolic method body gets inlined, it takes care of all necessary assertions and assumptions. The transformation of the method definition is contained in the following rule:

$$
\left\llbracket
\begin{array}{l}
\mathtt{/*@\ requires}\ R; \\
\quad \mathtt{@\ ensures}\ E; \\
\quad \mathtt{@\ assignable}\ A; \\
\quad \mathtt{@*/} \\
T\ m(P)\ \mathtt{throws}\ S\ \{ \\
\quad B \\
\}
\end{array}
\right\rrbracket
=
\left(
\begin{array}{l}
T\ m\mathtt{Contract}(P)\ \mathtt{throws}\ S\ \{ \\
\quad \llbracket\ \mathtt{assert}\ R\ \rrbracket; \\
\quad T\ \mathtt{result}; \\
\quad saveOld(E, B); \\
\quad havoc(A); \\
\quad \llbracket\ \mathtt{assume}\ E\ \rrbracket; \\
\quad \mathtt{return\ result}; \\
\}
\end{array}
\right)
$$

The "normal" translation of a method contract, as shown in the beginning of this section, is used to prove that a method satisfies its contract, while the above translation uses the contract and assumes its correctness. Both translations use the method *saveOld* to store values of variables which may be referred from thereon via the keyword \old. We introduce a variable for the return value before the postcondition is assumed, since the postcondition may contain restrictions to the returned value. Moreover, we introduce the translation method $havoc(A)$, which anonymizes the values of all location sets of the assignable clause A. "Havocing" for primitive types is equivalent to assigning a nondeterministic value of that type. We must also assume and enable that, if A contains locations of object type, then $havoc(A)$ may nondeterministically generate new objects, which may be used in the assignments and cannot be easily reduced to a nondeterministic assignment for JBMC (see Sect. 5). Remember that, as to provide a compact representation for our rules, we do not permit method calls to occur as sub-expressions but only in assignments to local variables. Thus, the translation rule for method calls extends the rule for Java statements (see Sect. 4.1) and is as follows:

$$[\![var=m(P);]\!] \; = \; var=m\texttt{Contract}(\, [\![P]\!] \,);$$

Therein, the assignment to the local variable *var* is optional. The same as for method calls can be applied to loops. Verifying loops is inherently challenging, in particular if no bound on the number of loop iterations is known beforehand. For this matter, we can use loop invariants, which can be understood as the contract for a loop, as a loop invariant must be guaranteed and can be assumed for the whole loop execution. A loop invariant acts both as a pre- and a postcondition for the loop, as it must hold before and after each loop iteration.

$$
\left[\!\!\left[
\begin{array}{l}
\texttt{/*@ loop\_invariant } I; \\
\texttt{@ assignable } A; \\
\texttt{@ decreases } D; \\
\texttt{@*/} \\
\texttt{while } (C) \; \{ \; B \; \}
\end{array}
\right]\!\!\right]
\;=\;
\left(
\begin{array}{l}
\texttt{int oldD = } D; \\
[\![\texttt{ assert } I \,]\!]; \\
\quad havoc(A); \\
[\![\texttt{ assume } I \,]\!]; \\
\texttt{if } (C) \; \{ \\
\quad [\![B]\!]; \\
\quad [\![\texttt{ assert } I \,]\!]; \\
\quad \texttt{assert } D \texttt{ < oldD \&\& 0 <= } D \texttt{ ;} \\
\quad \texttt{assume false;} \\
\texttt{\}}
\end{array}
\right)
$$

On the right side of the above rule (a similar rule is defined for `for`-loops), we (1) `assert` the invariant, then (2) we "havoc" the assignable set of the loop that replaces all loop iterations that may already have occurred, then (3) `assume` the invariant, (4) execute the loop body once, and finally, (5) `assert` the invariant again. Steps (1) to (3) make use of the invariant to replace multiple loop iterations, while Steps (3) to (5) prove the inductive invariant. Proving the invariant for a single loop execution suffices to establish its validity. Additionally, we prove that the loop terminates by asserting that the decreases clause does indeed decrease and is still greater than zero.

Finally, we append the statement "`assume false;`" to the loop body, as we chose an arbitrary loop iteration, but all assertions after the loop must only hold in case the loop is fully executed. Essentially, as long as the loop body is executed, we prevent the model checker from reporting any assertion violations, since this is not a valid program run.

4.6   Ensuring Correct Behavior for Boolean Operators

As seen in Sect. 4.2, binary Boolean connectives that have a short-circuit semantics in Java need special consideration during the translation. According to JML's semantics, if an exception is raised during the evaluation of an expression, then the whole clause is considered to have failed, i.e., the program does not satisfy that clause [7]. Thus, no method can satisfy the ill-defined specification '`ensures 1/0 == 0;`'. However, the definition uses the short-circuit semantics of Java operators, so that every method satisfies '`ensures true || (1/0 == 0);`' In most cases, our translation easily leads to the right behavior of the resulting code. For example, '`ensures 1/0 == 0;`' becomes '`assert 1/0 == 0;`', which brings the invalid postcondition directly to the Java code in form of an assertion whose evaluation throws an exception.

However, we need to be careful when translating short-circuit behavior in combination with "demonic" quantifiers. Consider, for example, the following postcondition:

```
ensures (true || (\exists int i; 0 <= i && i < 1; 1/i == 0));
```

Due to the short-circuit semantics of `||`, and since the first operand is `true`, we never evaluate the second operand, and the whole expression evaluates to `true`, which is trivially satisfied by any method. If the special behavior of `||` were not considered, our translation would produce the following (wrong) result:

```
b = false;
for (int i = 0; i < 1; ++i) { b = (b || 1/i == 0); } // WRONG
assert true || b;
```

However, this translation is wrong, since the `for`-loop throws an exception when i equals 0 in the first iteration, which would falsely indicate a failure. Hence, in order to deal with such behavior, our translation adheres to the rules presented in Sect. 4.2, and the code $[\![B]\!]^{cmd}$ for the second operand B of a disjunction is only evaluated if the first operand A evaluates to `false`. Consequently, our translation produces the following code with the desired behavior, where the loop is not executed and no exception is thrown:

```
if (!true) {
  b = false;
  for (int i = 0; i < 1; ++i) { b = (b || 1/i == 0); }
}
assert true || b;
```

5   Implementation

We provide a prototypical implementation of our approach in form of the command-line application JJBMC.[5] It translates a Java source file annotated with JML specifications into a Java file to be read by JBMC. The implementation makes use of the OpenJML back end (see Sect. 2) to parse and manipulate the given Java/JML. The user can choose to either verify only a single method or all methods in the given Java file. Furthermore, they can pass any JBMC options for a customized behavior, e.g., concerning various bounds for objects, arrays, or object structures, as well as the handling of exceptions, the employed SAT or SMT solver, or the output format. If JBMC is able to find a counterexample for the given specification and program, the counterexample is parsed and provided as a program trace, i.e., the sequence of program states up to the violated assertion (with concrete instantiations for the nondeterministic values). The output is optimized from the original JBMC output such that the user may (relatively) easily understand and analyze the semantics. We provide additional options for the user to choose whether auxiliary specifications (contracts of called methods and loop invariants) or inlining shall be used. Even though ignoring contracts seems to contradict our modular approach, it is sometimes useful to try verification that way first, so that unnecessary modularization may be avoided. Inlining also allows the user to flexibly distinguish between errors in the top-level specification and individual auxiliary specifications. Note that our implementation is still prototypical and does currently not support full JML and Java. However, we provide a clear user feedback whenever unsupported features are used, in order to maintain the soundness of our approach. For full (sequential) Java, everything except for catching exceptions, **break** and **continues** statements, and inheritance is supported. For JML, we currently support preconditions, postconditions, loop invariants, frame conditions (limited to fields and array ranges) for contracts and loops, assertions, assumptions, \old (with similar restrictions as for frame conditions), and universal and existential quantifiers.

Given that both SBMC and runtime assertion checking do not involve the full abstraction from JML contracts, tasks that require to distinguish different heap states or specify object anonymization are new and challenging for JBMC's semantics. Consider, e.g., the keyword \old that "remembers" a variable's value before method execution. Java lacks support for deep copies of objects, which hinders the implementation of such a concept. Furthermore, JBMC's semantics

---

[5] The source code is available at https://github.com/JonasKlamroth/JJBMC.

```
/*@ requires a != null && a.length <= 5;
  @ ensures \result <= a.length * 32;
  @ assignable \nothing;
  @*/
int naiveHammingWeight(int[] a) {
  int result = 0;
  /*@ loop_invariant result <= i * 32;
    @ loop_invariant 0 <= i && i <= a.length;
    @ assignable result;
    @*/
  for (int i = 0; i < a.length; i++) {
    int x = a[i];
    while (x != 0) { result += x&1; x = x >>> 1; }
  }
  return result;
}
```

Listing 2. Calculation of the hamming weight for an array.

of nondeterministic value assignments for objects is not sufficient to implement anonymization of heap locations: JBMC interprets a nondeterministic object as a new object with nondeterministic values assigned to its fields. JML, however, demands that this "anonymous" object may or may not be new, and its fields may or may not point to existing or new objects. For implementing such semantics, we would need an explicit model of all objects within the Java program, such that we can do a nondeterministic selection among all those objects.

6   Evaluation

We evaluated our translation and its implementation on a selection of JML-annotated Java examples[6] that are shipped with the KeY tool [1], which illustrate a variety of JML's and KeY's features. The goal of our evaluation was to demonstrate correctness and feasibility of our approach, i.e., that JML annotations are translated into programs which are correctly read and verified by JBMC. Using a bound of 5 on the number of loop iterations and array sizes, all verification tasks were successfully performed by JBMC within a few seconds. Besides simple examples, our evaluation included algorithms that perform array manipulations, e.g., sorting algorithms, and algorithms with bit-operations.

Let us first consider the program given in Listing 2, which calculates the hamming weight of an integer array by iterating over all array elements and adding together their respective hamming weights. Each hamming weight is – very inefficiently – calculated by iterating over every bit and checking whether it is zero or not. The program contains two loops, but a loop invariant is only provided for the outer one. This is what an engineer may do in practice, as the

---

[6] All case studies are available at https://github.com/JonasKlamroth/JJBMC.

inner loop is guaranteed to run at most 32 times (for each bit of the integer value) and is thus a prime suspect for loop unrolling, since it does not necessarily require a loop invariant. In contrast, the outer loop iterates over array elements, where the number of iterations is unknown. Using our translation, JBMC verifies this program for our default upper bound with an array size of 5. Note that, for very large arrays, the postcondition is actually not satisfied, as a.length * 32 may overflow. The fact that this is not discovered by JBMC is due to the inherently bounded nature of *bounded* model checking and does not mean that our translation is incorrect. In addition to this inefficient hamming weight calculation, we also implemented and verified a more efficient version that uses a sequence of bit operations without the need for an inner loop.

Let us further consider bubble sort[7], which performs array manipulations. The JML contract demands that the result array is sorted, i.e., each entry is less than or equal to the consecutive entry. The program contains two nested loops that iterate over the array and move the greatest remaining element to the end of the unsorted part of the array. Element swaps are carried out by a method swap(int[] a, int i, int j) which swaps a[i] and a[j] and is implemented as an in-place xor-operation. For this example, we evaluated different levels of modularity. In the first step, we verified the (translation of the) top-level specification of bubble sort with JBMC by unrolling the loops and inlining the swap method, i.e., a (non-modular) whole-program verification. In the next step, we used the contract of the swap method instead of its implementation and then, in the final step, we also used two loop invariants. This demonstrates that our approach may support finding both the right specification and implementation without the need of having everything ready from the beginning.

7   Related Work

Pnueli and Shahar present a verification system that combines both deductive verification and bounded model checking, where they verify finite-state systems w.r.t. constraints in linear temporal logic (LTL) [22]. Moreover, Shankar examines the interrelations between the two paradigms by exploring various examples for their combination, and illustrates the advantages [24]. The synergy of such a combination is also discussed by Beckert et al. on the verification of C programs, who focus, however, on combining two tools rather than doing program transformation [3]. Lourenço et al. present a minimal model as a combined theoretical basis for the two paradigms [4]. Similar to our work, they capture both concrete loop unrollings and abstract loop invariants. Whereas their model works on a simple while language, we target the Java programming language that comes with a richer semantics. Furthermore, the field of runtime verification also translates program specifications into assertions that are checked at runtime. Burdy et al. present a tool that translates JML annotations into runtime assertion checks for Java programs [6]. They encounter similar challenges as we do, e.g., interpreting well-definedness of specifications and translating quantifiers.

---

[7] We do not print the code, as we used the well-known standard implementation.

Their translation covers the quantification over iterable collections and other forms of quantifiers such as \sum. While Burdy et al. focus on runtime checks, we use the translation as input for static verification, and instead of translating into pure Java, our output is extended by assertions and assumptions. The underlying idea, however, namely that "JML accommodates both runtime assertion checking and formal verification" is the same [20]. Chalin et al. discuss this approach for the strong-validity semantics of JML [7]. Similar work has been conducted by Kosmatov et al. for C programs and ACSL specifications [18].

8   Conclusion and Future Work

We presented a translation of JML-annotated Java code into Java programs that can be read by the software bounded model checker JBMC, which enables JBMC to check JML annotations at an early stage when developing the specification. This extends JBMC's reach such that it may use method contracts and loop invariants additionally to (mere) method body inlining or unwinding loops. Finally, we presented a prototypical implementation which we evaluated on first case studies that can be read and verified by JBMC.

As future work, we plan to extend our approach to support further features of Java and JML, e.g., full exception handling and abrupt termination within loops. We also plan to extend our translation to fully capture JML's semantics of heap anonymization or "havocing", as we are currently restricted by JMBC's default semantics of nondeterminism that excludes previously created objects. Moreover, we plan to evaluate and improve both the performance and the usability of our implementation, e.g., the readability of reported counterexamples. Finally, we performed first experiments for the verification of stability properties for floating-point operations such as addition, which we plan to extend.

References

1. Ahrendt, W., Beckert, B., Bubel, R., Hähnle, R., Schmitt, P.H., Ulbrich, M. (eds.): Deductive Software Verification - The KeY Book: From Theory to Practice. LNCS, vol. 10001. Springer, Cham (2016). https://doi.org/10.1007/978-3-319-49812-6
2. Barrett, C., Tinelli, C.: Satisfiability modulo theories. In: Clarke, E., Henzinger, T., Veith, H., Bloem, R. (eds.) Handbook of Model Checking, pp. 305–343. Springer, Cham (2018). https://doi.org/10.1007/978-3-319-10575-8_11
3. Beckert, B., Bormer, T., Merz, F., Sinz, C.: Integration of bounded model checking and deductive verification. In: Beckert, B., Damiani, F., Gurov, D. (eds.) FoVeOOS 2011. LNCS, vol. 7421, pp. 86–104. Springer, Heidelberg (2012). https://doi.org/10.1007/978-3-642-31762-0_7
4. Belo Lourenço, C., Frade, M.J., Sousa Pinto, J.: A generalized program verification workflow based on loop elimination and SA form. In: 7th International Workshop on Formal Methods in Software Engineering, FormaliSE 2019, pp. 75–84. IEEE/ACM (2019). https://doi.org/10.1109/FormaliSE.2019.00017
5. Biere, A., Kröning, D.: SAT-based model checking. In: Clarke, E., Henzinger, T., Veith, H., Bloem, R. (eds.) Handbook of Model Checking, pp. 277–303. Springer, Cham (2018). https://doi.org/10.1007/978-3-319-10575-8_10

6. Burdy, L.: An overview of JML tools and applications. Int. J. Softw. Tools Technol. Transf. **7**(3), 212–232 (2004). https://doi.org/10.1007/s10009-004-0167-4
7. Chalin, P., Rioux, F.: JML runtime assertion checking: improved error reporting and efficiency using strong validity. In: Cuellar, J., Maibaum, T., Sere, K. (eds.) FM 2008. LNCS, vol. 5014, pp. 246–261. Springer, Heidelberg (2008). https://doi.org/10.1007/978-3-540-68237-0_18
8. Clarke, E.M., Kroening, D., Yorav, K.: Behavioral consistency of C and Verilog programs using bounded model checking. In: 40th Design Automation Conference, DAC 2003, pp. 368–371. ACM (2003). https://doi.org/10.1145/775832.775928
9. Cok, D.R.: OpenJML: JML for Java 7 by extending OpenJDK. In: Bobaru, M., Havelund, K., Holzmann, G.J., Joshi, R. (eds.) NFM 2011. LNCS, vol. 6617, pp. 472–479. Springer, Heidelberg (2011). https://doi.org/10.1007/978-3-642-20398-5_35
10. Cordeiro, L., Kesseli, P., Kroening, D., Schrammel, P., Trtik, M.: JBMC: a bounded model checking tool for verifying Java bytecode. In: Chockler, H., Weissenbacher, G. (eds.) CAV 2018. LNCS, vol. 10981, pp. 183–190. Springer, Cham (2018). https://doi.org/10.1007/978-3-319-96145-3_10
11. Dijkstra, E.W.: Guarded commands, nondeterminacy and formal derivation of programs. Commun. ACM **18**(8), 453–457 (1975). https://doi.org/10.1145/360933.360975
12. Filliâtre, J.: Deductive software verification. Int. J. Softw. Tools Technol. Transf. **13**(5), 397–403 (2011). https://doi.org/10.1007/s10009-011-0211-0
13. Gomes, C.P., Kautz, H.A., Sabharwal, A., Selman, B.: Satisfiability solvers. In: Handbook of Knowledge Representation, FAI, vol. 3, pp. 89–134. Elsevier (2008). https://doi.org/10.1016/S1574-6526(07)03002-7
14. de Gouw, S., Rot, J., de Boer, F.S., Bubel, R., Hähnle, R.: OpenJDK's Java.utils.Collection.sort() is broken: the good, the bad and the worst case. In: Kroening, D., Păsăreanu, C.S. (eds.) CAV 2015. LNCS, vol. 9206, pp. 273–289. Springer, Cham (2015). https://doi.org/10.1007/978-3-319-21690-4_16
15. Harel, D.: Dynamic logic. In: Gabbay, D., Guenthner, F. (eds.) Handbook of Philosophical Logic, vol. 165, pp. 497–604. Springer, Dordrecht (1984). https://doi.org/10.1007/978-94-009-6259-0_10
16. Jackson, D., Vaziri, M.: Finding bugs with a constraint solver. In: International Symposium on Software Testing and Analysis, ISSTA 2000, pp. 14–25. ACM (2000). https://doi.org/10.1145/347324.383378
17. Klamroth, J.: Modular Verification of JML Contracts Using Bounded Model Checking. Master's thesis, Karlsruhe Institute of Technology (KIT) (2019). https://doi.org/10.5445/IR/1000122228
18. Kosmatov, N., Signoles, J.: Runtime assertion checking and its combinations with static and dynamic analyses. In: Seidl, M., Tillmann, N. (eds.) TAP 2014. LNCS, vol. 8570, pp. 165–168. Springer, Cham (2014). https://doi.org/10.1007/978-3-319-09099-3_13
19. Leavens, G.T., Baker, A.L., Ruby, C.: Preliminary design of JML: a behavioral interface specification language for Java. SIGSOFT Softw. Eng. Notes **31**(3), 1–38 (2006). https://doi.org/10.1145/1127878.1127884
20. Leavens, G.T., Cheon, Y., Clifton, C., Ruby, C., Cok, D.R.: How the design of JML accommodates both runtime assertion checking and formal verification. Sci. Comput. Program. **55**(1–3), 185–208 (2005). https://doi.org/10.1016/j.scico.2004.05.015
21. Meyer, B.: Applying "design by contract". IEEE Comput. **25**(10), 40–51 (1992). https://doi.org/10.1109/2.161279

22. Pnueli, A., Shahar, E.: A platform for combining deductive with algorithmic verification. In: Alur, R., Henzinger, T.A. (eds.) CAV 1996. LNCS, vol. 1102, pp. 184–195. Springer, Heidelberg (1996). https://doi.org/10.1007/3-540-61474-5_68
23. Shankar, N.: Automated deduction for verification. ACM Comput. Surv. **41**(4), 20:1–20:56 (2009). https://doi.org/10.1145/1592434.1592437
24. Shankar, N.: Combining model checking and deduction. In: Clarke, E., Henzinger, T., Veith, H., Bloem, R. (eds.) Handbook of Model Checking, pp. 651–684. Springer, Cham (2018). https://doi.org/10.1007/978-3-319-10575-8_20

On Slicing Software Product Line Signatures

Ferruccio Damiani[1]($\boxtimes$) (ID), Michael Lienhardt[2], and Luca Paolini[1] (ID)

[1] University of Turin, Turin, Italy
{ferruccio.damiani,luca.paolini}@unito.it
[2] ONERA, Palaiseau, France
michael.lienhardt@onera.fr

Abstract. A Software Product Line (SPL) is a family of similar programs (called variants) generated from a common artifact base. Variability in an SPL can be documented in terms of abstract description of functionalities (called features): a feature model (FM) identifies each variant by a set of features (called a product). Delta-orientation is a flexible approach to implement SPLs. An SPL Signature (SPLS) is a variability-aware Application Programming Interface (API), i.e., an SPL where each variant is the API of a program. In this paper we introduce and formalize, by abstracting from SPL implementation approaches, the notion of slice of an SPLS K for a set of features F (i.e., an SPLS obtained from by K by hiding the features that are not in F). Moreover, we formulate the challenge of defining an efficient algorithm that, given a delta-oriented SPLS K and a set of features F, sreturns a delta-oriented SPLS that is an slice of K for F. Thus paving the way for further research on devising such an algorithm. The proposed notions are formalized for SPLs of programs written in an imperative version of Featherweight Java.

1 Introduction

A *Software Product Line* (SPLs) is a family of similar programs, called *variants*, that have a well-documented variability and are generated from a common artifact base [3,10,39]. An SPL can be structured into: (i) a *feature model* describing the variants in terms of *features* (each feature is a name representing an abstract description of functionality and each variant is identified by a set of features, called a *product*); (ii) an *artifact base* comprising language dependent reusable code artifacts that are used to build the variants; and (iii) *configuration knowledge* connecting feature model and artifact base by specifying how, given a product, the corresponding a variant can be derived from the code artifacts—thus inducing a mapping from products to variants, called the *generator* of the SPL.

An interface can be understood as a partial specification of the functionalities of a system. Such a notion of interface provides a valuable support for modularity. If a system can be decomposed in subsystems in such a way that all the uses of each subsystem by the other subsystems are mediated by interfaces

© Springer Nature Switzerland AG 2020
T. Margaria and B. Steffen (Eds.): ISoLA 2020, LNCS 12476, pp. 81–102, 2020.
https://doi.org/10.1007/978-3-030-61362-4_5

of the subsystem, then subsystem changes that do not break the interfaces are transparent (with respect to the specifications expressed by the interfaces) to the other subsystems.

In this paper we formalize, by abstracting from SPL implementation approaches, the problem of designing an efficient algorithm that, given an SPL and subset F of it features, extracts an interface for the SPL that exposes only the functionalities associated to the features in F. We build on the notions of signature and interface of an SPL introduced in [17] (see also [19]). An *SPL Signature* (SPLS) is a variability-aware *Application Programming Interface* (API), i.e., an SPL where each variant is a program API. The *signature of an SPL* L is an SPLS Z where: (i) the features are the same of L; (ii) the products are the same of L; and (iii) each variant is the *program signature* (i.e., a program API that exposes all the functionalities) of the corresponding variant of L. An SPLS Z_1 is:

- an *interface of an SPLS* Z_2 iff[1] (i) the features of Z_1 are a subset of the features of Z_2; (ii) the products of Z_1 are obtained for the products of Z_2 by dropping the features that are not in Z_1; and (iii) for each product p_1 of Z_1, its associated variant is an interface of all the variants associated to the products of Z_2 from which p_1 can be obtained by dropping the features that are not in Z_1; and
- an *interface of an SPL* L iff it is an interface of the signature of L.

The contribution of this paper is twofold.

1. We introduce and formalize, by abstracting from SPL implementation approaches, the notion of *slice of an SPLS for a set of features* $\mathcal{F}$. *It* lifts to SPLs the notion of *slice of a FM* introduced in [1] (see also [43]). Namely, we define an operator that given an SPLS Z and a set of features $\mathcal{F}$ returns an SPLS that has exactly the features in $\mathcal{F}$ and is an interface of Z.
2. We introduce and formalize the problem of devising a feasible algorithm that takes as input a delta-oriented SPLS Z [19] and a set of features $\mathcal{F}$, and yields as output a delta-oriented SPLS that is a slice of Z for $\mathcal{F}$. Thus paving the way for further research on devising such an algorithm.

Since extracting the signature of a delta-oriented SPL is quite straightforward [17], an algorithm like the one described in point 2 above would provide a way to extract from an SPL an interface that exposes only the functionalities associated to a given set of features. This would enable refactoring a delta-oriented SPL by decomposing it into a *Multi SPL* (MPL), that is a set of interdependent SPLs that need to be managed in a decentralized fashion by multiple teams and stakeholders [29], and performing compositional analysis of delta-oriented MPLs [19]. Moreover, the implementation-independent formalization described in point 1 above might foster further research on MPLs comprising SPLs implemented according to different approaches (see, e.g., [3,42,47] for a presentation of different SPL implementation approaches).

---

[1] In [19] the phrase "subsignature of an SPLS" is used instead of "interface of an SPLS".

Organisation of the Paper. Section 2 provides the necessary background on SPLs, SPLSs and interfaces. Section 3 provides a definition of the SPLS slice operator that abstracts from SPL implementation approaches. Section 4 recalls delta-oriented SPLs and illustrates the problem of devising a feasible algorithm for slicing delta-oriented SPLSs. Related work is discussed in Sect. 5, and Sect. 6 concludes the paper by outlining possible future work.

2   A Recollection of SPLs, SPL Signatures and Interfaces

2.1   Feature Models, Feature Module Slices and Interfaces

The following definition provides an extensional account on the notion of feature model, namely a feature model is represented as a pair "(set of features, set of products)", thus allowing to abstract from implementation approaches—see e.g. [4] for a discussion on possible representations of feature models.

Definition 1 (Feature model, extensional representation). *A* feature model $\mathcal{M}$ *is a pair* $(\mathcal{F}, \mathcal{P})$ *where* $\mathcal{F}$ *is a set of features and* $\mathcal{P} \subseteq 2^{\mathcal{F}}$ *is a set of products.*

The slice operator for feature models introduced by Acher et al. [1], given a feature model $\mathcal{M}$ and a set of features Y, returns the feature model obtained from $\mathcal{M}$ by removing the features not in Y.

Definition 2 (Feature model slice operator). *Let* $\mathcal{M} = (\mathcal{F}, \mathcal{P})$ *be a feature model. The* slice *operator* Π_Y *on feature models, where* Y *is a set of features, is defined by:* $\Pi_Y(\mathcal{M}) = (\mathcal{F} \cap Y, \{p \cap Y \mid p \in \mathcal{P}\})$.

More recently, Schröter et al. [43] introduced the slice function $\mathbf{S}$ such that $\mathbf{S}(\mathcal{M}, Y) = \Pi_{\mathcal{F} \setminus Y}(\mathcal{M})$ Schröter et al. [43] also introduced the following notion of feature model interface.

Definition 3 (Interface relation for feature models). *A feature model* $\mathcal{M}_0 = (\mathcal{F}_0, \mathcal{P}_0)$ *is an* interface *of feature model* $\mathcal{M} = (\mathcal{F}, \mathcal{P})$, *denoted as* $\mathcal{M}_0 \preceq \mathcal{M}$, *whenever both* $\mathcal{F}_0 \subseteq \mathcal{F}$ *and* $\mathcal{P}_0 = \{p \cap \mathcal{F}_0 \mid p \in \mathcal{P}\}$ *hold.*

It is worth observing that $\mathcal{M}_0 \preceq \mathcal{M}$ holds if and only if $\mathcal{M}_0 = \Pi_Y(\mathcal{M})$, where Y are features of $\mathcal{M}_0$. Moreover, the interface relation for feature models is reflexive, transitive and anti-symmetric.

Given a product p, we define $\mathcal{I}_p(x) = \begin{cases} \textbf{true} & \text{if } x \in p, \\ \textbf{false} & \text{otherwise} \end{cases}$ and, given a *propositional formula over features* (i.e., where propositional variable are feature names) ϕ, we wrote $\mathcal{I}_p \models \phi$ to mean that ϕ evaluates to **true** by replacing its variables according to $\mathcal{I}_p$.

Example 1 (Slicing the Expression Feature Model). Consider the propositional formula $\phi_{\text{EPL}} = \text{Lit} \wedge (\text{Print} \vee \text{Eval})$. The feature model $\mathcal{M}_{\text{EPL}} = (\mathcal{F}_{\text{EPL}}, \mathcal{P}_{\text{EPL}})$ has 4 features $\mathcal{F}_{\text{EPL}} = \{\text{Lit}, \text{Add}, \text{Print}, \text{Eval}\}$ and 8 products $\mathcal{P}_{\text{EPL}} = \{ p \mid p \subseteq$

$$
\begin{array}{llr}
P & ::= \overline{CD} & \text{Program} \\
CD & ::= \textbf{class } \texttt{C} \textbf{ extends } \texttt{C} \ \{ \ \overline{AD} \ \} & \text{Class Declaration} \\
AD & ::= FD \ | \ MD & \text{Attribute (Field or Method) Declaration} \\
FD & ::= \texttt{C f} & \text{Field Declaration} \\
MH & ::= \texttt{C m}(\overline{\texttt{C x}}) & \text{Method Header} \\
MD & ::= MH \ \{\textbf{return } e; \} & \text{Method Declaration} \\
e & ::= \texttt{x} \ | \ e.\texttt{f} \ | \ e.\texttt{m}(\overline{e}) \ | \ \textbf{new } \texttt{C()} \ | \ (\texttt{C})e \ | \ e.\texttt{f} = e \ | \ \textbf{null} & \text{Expression}
\end{array}
$$

Fig. 1. IFJ programs

$\mathcal{F}_{\text{EPL}}$ and $\mathcal{I}_p \models \phi_{\text{EPL}}\}$. It describes a family of programs implementing an expression datatype where Literals are mandatory and Additions are optional, and where either a Print operation or an Evaluation operation must be supported. Let $\mathcal{F}_{\text{EPL}_0} = \{\text{Lit}, \text{Add}, \text{Print}\}$, then we have that $\Pi_{\mathcal{F}_{\text{EPL}_0}}(\mathcal{M}_{\text{EPL}}) = \mathcal{M}_{\text{EPL}_0} = (\mathcal{F}_{\text{EPL}_0}, \mathcal{P}_{\text{EPL}_0})$, where $\mathcal{P}_{\text{EPL}_0} = \{\, p_{\text{I}}, p_{\text{II}}, p_{\text{III}}, p_{\text{IV}} \,\}$ with $p_{\text{I}} = \{\text{Lit}\}$, $p_{\text{II}} = \{\text{Lit}, \text{Add}\}$, $p_{\text{III}} = \{\text{Lit}, \text{Print}\}$, $p_{\text{IV}} = \mathcal{F}_{\text{EPL}_0}$.

2.2   SPLs of IFJ Programs

Imperative Featherweight Java (IFJ) [7] is an imperative version of *Featherweight Java* (FJ) [30]. The abstract syntax of IFJ *programs* is given in Fig. 1. Following Igarashi et al. [30], we use the overline notation for (possibly empty) sequences of elements—e.g., $\overline{e}$ stands for a sequence of expressions $e_1, \dots, e_n$ $(n \geq 0)$—and we denote the empty sequence by $\emptyset$.

A program P is a sequence of class declarations $\overline{CD}$. A class declaration comprises the name $\texttt{C}$ of the class, the name of the superclass (which must always be specified, even if it is the built-in class $\textbf{Object}$) and a list of attribute (field or method) declarations $\overline{AD}$. Variables $\texttt{x}$ include the special variable $\textbf{this}$ (implicitly bound in any method declaration MD), which may not be used as the name of a method's formal parameter. All fields and methods are public, there is no field shadowing, there is no method overloading, and each class is assumed to have an implicit constructor that initialized all fields to **null**.

An *attribute name* $\texttt{a}$ is either a field name $\texttt{f}$ or a method name $\texttt{m}$. Given a program P, a class name $\texttt{C}$ and an attribute name $\texttt{a}$, we write $\text{dom}(P)$, $P(\texttt{C})$, $\text{dom}_P(\texttt{C})$, $\leq_{:P}$, $CD(\texttt{a})$, and $lookup_P(\texttt{a}, \texttt{C})$ to denote, respectively: the set of class names declared in P; the declaration of $\texttt{C}$ in P when it exists; the set of attribute names declared in $P(\texttt{C})$; the subtyping relation in P (i.e., the reflexive and transitive closure of the immediate **extends** relation); the declaration of attribute $\texttt{a}$ in CD; and the declaration of the attribute $\texttt{a}$ in the closest superclass of $\texttt{C}$ (including $\texttt{C}$ itself) that contains a declaration for $\texttt{a}$ in P, when it exists. We write $<_{:P}$ to denote the strict subtyping relation in P, defined by: $\texttt{C}_1 <_{:P} \texttt{C}_2$ if and only if $\texttt{C}_1 \leq_{:P} \texttt{C}_2$ and $\texttt{C}_1 \neq \texttt{C}_2$.

As usual, we identify two IFJ programs P_1 and P_2 (written $P_1 = P_2$) up to: (i) the order of class declarations and attribute declarations, and (ii) renaming of the formal parameters of methods. The following notational convention entails the assumption that the classes declared in a program have distinct names, the attributes declared in a class have distinct names, and the formal parameter declared in a method have distinct names.

Convention 1 (On sequences of named declarations). *Whenever we write a sequence of named declarations $\overline{N}$ (e.g., classes, attributes, parameters, etc.) we assume that they have pairwise distinct names. We write names$(\overline{N})$ to denote the sequence of the names of the declarations in $\overline{N}$. Moreover, when no confusion may arise, we sometimes identify sequences of pairwise distinct elements with sets, e.g., we write $\overline{e}$ as short for $\{e_1, \ldots, e_n\}$.*

We require that every IFJ program P satisfies the following *sanity conditions*:

SC1: For every class name C (except Object) appearing anywhere in P, we have $C \in \text{dom}(P)$.
SC2: The strict subtyping relation $<:_P$ is acyclic.
SC3: If $C_2 <:_P C_1$, then $\text{dom}(P(C_1)) \cap \text{dom}(P(C_2))$ does not contain field names.
SC4: If $C_2 <:_P C_1$ then for all method names $m \in \text{dom}(P(C_1)) \cap \text{dom}(P(C_2))$ the methods $P(C_1)(m)$ and $P(C_2)(m)$ have the same header (up to renaming of the formal parameters).

Note that **SC3** and **SC4** formalize the requirements "there is no field shadowing" and "there is no method overloading", respectively. Type system, operational semantics, and type soundness for IFJ are given in [7].

Remark 1 (Sugared IFJ syntax). To improve readability, in the examples we use Java syntax for field initialization, primitive data types, strings and sequential composition. Encoding in IFJ syntax a program written in such a *sugared IFJ syntax* is straightforward (see [7]).

Example 2 (The Expression Program). Figure 2 illustrates a sugared IFJ program called the Expression Program (EP for short), that encodes the following grammar of numerical expressions:

Exp ::= Lit | Add   Lit ::= non-negative-integers   Add ::= Exp "+" Exp

The EP consists of: (i) a class Exp representing all expressions; (ii) a class Lit representing literals; and, (iii) a class Add representing an addition between two expressions. All these classes implement a method toInt that computes the value of the expression, and a method toString that gives a textual representation of the expression. Note that the concept of expression is too general to provide a meaningful implementation of these methods, and thus the class Exp is supposed to be used as a type and should never be instantiated.

The following definition (taken form [35]) provides an extensional account on the notion of SPL, thus allowing to abstract from implementation approaches— see e.g. [42,47] for a survey on SPL implementation approaches.

```
class Exp extends Object {                      class Lit extends Exp {
  String name = "Exp";                            Int val;
  Int toInt() { return null; }                    Lit setLit(Int x) { this.val=x; return this; }
  String toString() { return name; }              Int toInt() { return this.val; }
}                                                 String toString() { return this.val.toString(); }
                                                }

class Add extends Exp {
  Exp a; Exp b;
  Int toInt() { return this.a.toInt().add(this.b.toInt()); }
  String toString() { return this.a.toString() + "+" + this.b.toString(); }
}
```

Fig. 2. The expression program

Definition 4 (SPL, extensional representation). *An SPL* L *is a pair* $(\mathcal{M}_L, \mathcal{G}_L)$ *where* $\mathcal{M}_L = (\mathcal{F}_L, \mathcal{P}_L)$ *is the feature model of the SPL and* $\mathcal{G}_L$ *is the generator of the SPL, i.e., a function from the products in* $\mathcal{P}_L$ *to the variants.*[2]

Type system, operational semantics, and type soundness for IFJ are given in [7]. We say that the extensional representation of an SPL of IFJ programs is well typed to mean that the variants are well-typed IFJ programs.

Example 3 (The Expression Product Line). The Expression Product Line (EPL) is the SPL EPL = $(\mathcal{M}_{EPL}, \mathcal{G}_{EPL})$ where $\mathcal{M}_{EPL} = (\mathcal{F}_{EPL}, \mathcal{P}_{EPL})$ is as in Example 1, $\mathcal{G}_{EPL}(\mathcal{F}_{EPL})$ is the program EP in Example 2, and the other 7 variants are obtained from EP by dropping class Add whenever feature Add is not selected and by dropping methods toString and toInt whenever features Print and Eval are not selected, respectively.

2.3   Signatures and Interfaces for SPLs of IFJ Programs

The abstract syntax of IFJ *program signatures* is given Fig. 3. From a syntactic perspective, a program signature is essentially a program deprived of method bodies, and a class signature is a class deprived of method bodies. The *signature of a program P*, denoted as ***signature***(P), is the program signature obtained from P by dropping the body of its methods.

Remark 2 (On the signature of a sugared IFJ program). The signature of a program written in sugared IFJ syntax (introduced Remark 1) is obtained by dropping the body of the methods and the initialization of the field declarations. Notably, the signature of a sugared IFJ program is an IFJ program signature.

Given a program signature *PS*, a class name C, a class signature *CS* and an attribute name a, we write dom(*PS*), *PS*(C), dom$_{PS}$(C), $\leq:_{PS}$, *CS*(a), and *lookup$_{PS}$*(a, C) to denote, respectively: the set of class names declared in *PS*; the

---

[2] In [35] the generator is modeled as a partial function in order to encompass ill-formed SPLs where, for some product, the generation of the associated variant fails. In this paper we focus on well-formed SPLs, so we consider a total generator.

$PS ::= \overline{CS}$ Program Signature
$CS ::= \textbf{class C extends C} \{ \overline{AS} \}$ Class Signature
$AS ::= FD \mid MH$ Attribute (Field or Method) Signature

Fig. 3. IFJ program signatures

declaration of the class signature of C in PS when it exists; the set of attribute names declared in $PS(\text{C})$; the subtyping relation in PS; the set of attribute names declared in CS; and the signature of the attribute a in the closest supertype of C (including itself) that contains a declaration for a in PS, when it exists. We write $<:_{PS}$ to denote the strict subtyping relation in PS, defined by: $\text{C}_1 <:_{PS} \text{C}_2$ if and only if $\text{C}_1 \leq:_{PS} \text{C}_2$ and $\text{C}_1 \neq \text{C}_2$.

We require that every IFJ program signature PS satisfies the *sanity conditions* listed below.

SCi: For every class name C (except `Object`) appearing in an **extends** clause in PS, we have $\text{C} \in \text{dom}(PS)$.
SCii: The strict subtyping relation $<:_{PS}$ is acyclic.
SCiii: If $\text{C}_2 <:_{PS} \text{C}_1$, then for all attributes $\text{a} \in \text{dom}(PS(\text{C}_1)) \cup \text{dom}(PS(\text{C}_2))$ we have $PS(\text{C}_1)(\text{a}) = PS(\text{C}_2)(\text{a})$.

It is worth noticing that sanity condition **SCi** is weaker than **SC1**: a program signature is not required to provide a declaration for the class names occurring in attribute declarations. Recall that in IFJ field shadowing if forbidden (cf. sanity condition **SC3**). For the sake of simplicity, in program signatures there is no such a restriction: field and method signatures are treated uniformly.

A program signature PS can be understood as an API that expresses requirements on programs. I.e., *program signature PS is an interface of program P if P provides at least all the classes, attributes and subtyping relations in PS.* Similarly, *program signature PS is an interface*[3] *of program signature PS_0 if PS_0 provides at least all the classes, attributes and subtyping relations in PS.* These notions are formalized by the following definitions.

Definition 5 (Interface relation for program signatures). *A program signature PS_1 is an* interface *of a program signature PS_2, denoted as $PS_1 \preceq PS_2$, iff: (i) $\text{dom}(PS_1) \subseteq \text{dom}(PS_2)$; (ii) $\leq:_{PS_1} \subseteq \leq:_{PS_2}$; and (iii) for all class name $\text{C} \in \text{dom}(PS_1)$, for all attribute a, we have that if $lookup_{PS_1}(\text{a}, \text{C})$ is defined then $lookup_{PS_2}(\text{a}, \text{C})$ is defined and $lookup_{PS_1}(\text{a}, \text{C}) = lookup_{PS_2}(\text{a}, \text{C})$.*

Definition 6 (Interface relation between signatures and programs). *A program signature PS is an* interface *of program P, denoted as $PS \preceq P$, iff $PS \preceq \textbf{signature}(P)$ holds.*

The interface relation for program signatures is a preorder. Namely, it is reflexive (which implies $\textbf{signature}(P) \preceq P$), transitive, and (due to the possibility of overriding of attribute signatures) not antisymmetric (i.e., $PS_1 \preceq PS_2$

---
[3] In [19] the word "subsignature" is used instead of "interface".

and $PS_2 \preceq PS_1$ do not imply $PS_1 = PS_2$). Since $\preceq$ is a preorder, the relation $\approx = (\preceq \cap \succeq)$ is an equivalence relation, and the relation $\preceq$ can be understood as a partial order (reflexive, transitive and antisymmetric) on the set of $\approx$-equivalence classes. The (equivalence class of the) empty program signature $\emptyset$ is the bottom element with respect to $\preceq$.

Example 4 (Signature and interfaces of the Expression Program). Let EP be the program illustrated in Fig. 2. Given the following three signatures

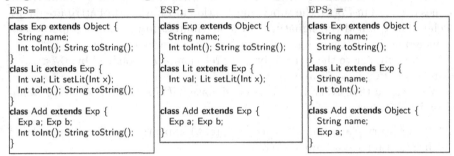

EPS=
```
class Exp extends Object {
    String name;
    Int toInt(); String toString();
}
class Lit extends Exp {
    Int val; Lit setLit(Int x);
    Int toInt(); String toString();
}
class Add extends Exp {
    Exp a; Exp b;
    Int toInt(); String toString();
}
```

ESP$_1$ =
```
class Exp extends Object {
    String name;
    Int toInt(); String toString();
}
class Lit extends Exp {
    Int val; Lit setLit(Int x);
}
class Add extends Exp {
    Exp a; Exp b;
}
```

EPS$_2$ =
```
class Exp extends Object {
    String name;
    String toString();
}
class Lit extends Exp {
    String name;
    Int toInt();
}
class Add extends Object {
    String name;
    Exp a;
}
```

we have: EPS = $\textbf{\textit{signature}}(\text{EP})$, EPS$_1 \approx$ EPS, EPS$_2 \preceq$ EPS, and EPS $\not\preceq$ EPS$_2$.

The notion of *SPL signature* (SPLS) [19] describes the API of an SPL, i.e., the APIs of the variants generated by the SPL. Namely, an SPLS is an SPL where the variants are program signatures instead of programs. The following definition provides an extensional account of this notion.

Definition 7 (SPLS, extensional representation). *An SPLS* Z *is a pair* $(\mathcal{M}_Z, \mathcal{G}_Z)$ *where* $\mathcal{M}_Z = (\mathcal{F}_Z, \mathcal{P}_Z)$ *is the feature model of the SPLS and* $\mathcal{G}_Z$ *is the generator of the SPLS, i.e., a mapping from the products in* $\mathcal{P}_Z$ *to variant signatures.*

The notion of *signature of an SPL* [19] naturally lifts that of signature of a program. Namely, the *signature of an SPL* L $= (\mathcal{M}_L, \mathcal{G}_L)$ is the SPLS defined by $\textbf{\textit{signature}}(L) = (\mathcal{M}_L, \textbf{\textit{signature}}(\mathcal{G}_L))$, where $\textbf{\textit{signature}}(\mathcal{G}_L)$ is defined by

$$\textbf{\textit{signature}}(\mathcal{G}_L)(p) = \textbf{\textit{signature}}(\mathcal{G}_L(p)), \text{ for all } p \in \mathcal{P}_L.$$

The notion of *interface of an SPLS* [19] naturally lifts the one of interface of a program signature (in Definition 5) by combining it with the notion of feature model interface (in Definition 3).

Definition 8 (Interface relation for SPLSs). *An SPLS* Z_1 *is a interface of an SPLS* Z_2, *denoted as* $Z_1 \preceq Z_2$, *iff: (i)* $\mathcal{M}_{Z_1} \preceq \mathcal{M}_{Z_2}$; *and (ii) for each* $p \in \mathcal{P}_{Z_2}$, $\mathcal{G}_{Z_1}(p \cap \mathcal{F}_{Z_1}) \preceq \mathcal{G}_{Z_2}(p)$.

Similarly, the notion of *interface of an SPL* lifts the notion interface of a program (in Definition 6).

Definition 9 (Interface relation between SPLs and SPLSs). *An SPLS* Z *is an* interface *of an SPL* L, *denoted as* $Z \preceq L$, *iff* $Z \preceq signature(L)$ *holds.*

It is worth observing that the interface relation for SPLSs has two degrees of freedom: it allows to hide features from the feature model (as described in Definition 3), and it allows to hide declarations from the SPLS variants (as described in Definition 5). Additionally, note that the interface relation for SPLSs, like the one for program signatures (see the explanation after Definition 6), is reflexive, transitive and not anti-symmetric. We say that two SPLSs Z_1 and Z_2 are *equivalent*, denoted as $Z_1 \cong Z_2$, to mean that both $Z_1 \preceq Z_2$ and $Z_2 \preceq Z_1$ hold.

Example 5 (Signature and interfaces of the EPL). Consider the signature of the EPL of Example 3: $signature(\text{EPL}) = \text{EPLS} = (\mathcal{M}_{\text{EPLS}}, \mathcal{G}_{\text{EPLS}})$. Let $\text{EPLS}' = (\mathcal{M}_{\text{EPL}}, \mathcal{G}_{\text{EPLS}'})$, where $\mathcal{G}_{\text{EPLS}'}(p) = \begin{cases} \text{EPS}_1 \text{ (see Example 4)} & \text{if } p = \mathcal{F}_{\text{EPL}}, \\ \mathcal{G}_{\text{EPLS}}(p) & \text{otherwise.} \end{cases}$
We have $\text{EPLS}' \cong \text{EPLS}$. Moreover, let $\text{EPLS}'' = (\mathcal{M}_{\text{EPL}}, \mathcal{G}_{\text{EPLS}''})$, where $\mathcal{G}_{\text{EPLS}''}(p) = \begin{cases} \text{EPS}_2 \text{ (see Example 4)} & \text{if } p = \mathcal{F}_{\text{EPL}}, \\ \mathcal{G}_{\text{EPLS}}(p) & \text{otherwise.} \end{cases}$ We have $\text{EPLS}'' \preceq \text{EPLS}$ and $\text{EPLS} \npreceq \text{EPLS}''$. Consider also the following four program signatures

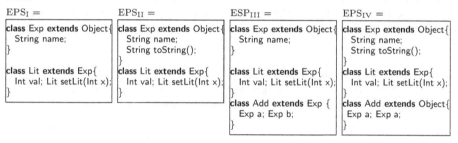

and the SPLS $\text{EPLS}_0 = (\mathcal{M}_{\text{EPL}_0}, \mathcal{G}_{\text{EPLS}_0})$ where $\mathcal{M}_{\text{EPL}_0} = (\mathcal{F}_{\text{EPL}_0}, \mathcal{P}_{\text{EPL}_0})$ is as in Example 1 and $\mathcal{G}_{\text{EPLS}_0}(p_i) = \text{EPLS}_i$ for $i \in \{\text{I}, \text{II}, \text{III}, \text{IV}\}$. We have $\text{EPLS}_0 \preceq$ EPLS and $\text{EPLS} \npreceq \text{EPLS}_0$.

Let EPS'_{I}, EPS'_{II}, EPS'_{III}, EPS'_{IV} be the program signatures obtained from EPS_{I}, EPS_{II}, EPS_{III}, EPS_{IV} by dropping all the fields (respectively), and let $\text{EPLS}'_0 = (\mathcal{M}_{\text{EPL}_0}, \mathcal{G}_{\text{EPLS}'_0})$ be the SPLS such that $\mathcal{M}_{\text{EPL}_0}$ is as above and $\mathcal{G}_{\text{EPLS}'_0}(p_i) = \text{EPLS}'_i$ for $i \in \{\text{I}, \text{II}, \text{III}, \text{IV}\}$. We have $\text{EPLS}'_0 \preceq \text{EPLS}_0$ and $\text{EPLS}_0 \npreceq \text{EPLS}'_0$.

3 The Slice Operator for SPLSs of IFJ Programs

In this section we lift the feature model slice operator to SPLs in extensional form. In order to do this, we first introduce some auxiliary notions.

Given a feature model $\mathcal{M} = (\mathcal{F}, \mathcal{P})$ and a set $\mathcal{F}_0$ of features, the slice $\Pi_{\mathcal{F}_0}(\mathcal{M}) = \mathcal{M}_0 = (\mathcal{F}_0, \mathcal{P}_0)$ determines a partition of $\mathcal{P}$. Namely, let $\mathbf{cpl}_{\mathcal{F}_0, \mathcal{M}} : \mathcal{P}_0 \to 2^{\mathcal{P}}$ be the function that maps each sliced product $p_0 \in \mathcal{P}_0$ to the set of products $\{p \mid p \in \mathcal{P} \text{ and } p_0 = p \cap \mathcal{F}_0\}$ that complete it, then:

1. $\mathbf{cpl}_{\mathcal{F}_0,\mathcal{M}}(p_0)$ is non-empty, for all $p_0 \in \mathcal{P}_0$;
2. $p' \neq p''$ implies $\mathbf{cpl}_{\mathcal{F}_0,\mathcal{M}}(p') \cap \mathbf{cpl}_{\mathcal{F}_0,\mathcal{M}}(p'') = \emptyset$, for all $p', p'' \in \mathcal{P}_0$; and
3. $\bigcup_{p \in \mathcal{P}_0} \mathbf{cpl}_{\mathcal{F}_0,\mathcal{M}}(p) = \mathcal{P}$.

The following definition introduces a canonical form for the elements of the equivalence classes of the relation $\approx$ between program signatures (introduced immediately after Definition 6).

Definition 10 (Thin program signatures). *We say that a program signature PS is in* thin *form (thin for short) to mean that, for all classes* $\mathsf{C}_1, \mathsf{C}_2 \in \mathrm{dom}(PS)$ *and for all attributes* $\mathtt{a} \in \mathrm{dom}(PS(\mathsf{C}_1))$, *if* $\mathsf{C}_2 <:_{PS} \mathsf{C}_1$ *then* $\mathtt{a} \notin \mathrm{dom}(PS(\mathsf{C}_2))$. *We denote* **thin**$(PS)$ *the thin form of a program signature PS.*

Example 6 (Thin signature of the Expression Program). Recall the program EP and the signatures EPS and EPS_1 considered in Example 4, where EPS = **signature**(EP). It is straightforward to check $\mathrm{EPS}_1 = $ **thin**(EPS) holds.

Given a non-empty set of program signatures $\overline{PS} = PS_1, ..., PS_n$ ($n \geq 1$) we write $\bigwedge \overline{PS}$ to denote the thin program signature that is the infimum (a.k.a. greatest lower bound) of $\overline{PS}$ with respect to the interface relation—it is a program signature (which is unique modulo program signature equivalence $\approx$) that exposes exactly the (classes, fields, methods and subtyping) declarations that are present in all the program signatures $\overline{PS}$. The following theorem states that $\bigwedge \overline{PS}$ is always defined.

Theorem 1 (Infimum for program signatures w.r.t. $\preceq$). *The thin program signature* $\bigwedge \overline{PS}$ *that is the infimum with respect to* $\preceq$ *of a non empty set of program signature* $\overline{PS} = PS_1, ..., PS_n$ ($n \geq 1$) *is always defined.*

Proof. See Appendix A.   □

The following definition lifts the feature model slice operator $\Pi_{\mathcal{F}_0}$ (Definition 2) to SPLSs.

Definition 11 (SPLS slice). *Let* $\mathcal{F}_0$ *be a set of features and, let* $\mathsf{Z} = (\mathcal{M}_\mathsf{Z}, \mathcal{G}_\mathsf{Z})$ *be an SPLS with feature model* $\mathcal{M}_\mathsf{Z} = (\mathcal{F}_\mathsf{Z}, \mathcal{P}_\mathsf{Z})$ *and generator* $\mathcal{G}_\mathsf{Z}$. *The slice operator* $\Pi_{\mathcal{F}_0}$ *on SPLSs returns the SPLS* $\Pi_{\mathcal{F}_0}(\mathsf{Z}) = (\mathcal{M}_0, \mathcal{G}_0)$ *where*

(i) $\mathcal{M}_0 = (\mathcal{F}_0, \mathcal{P}_0) = \Pi_{\mathcal{F}_0}(\mathcal{M}_\mathsf{Z})$; *and*
(ii) for each $p_0 \in \mathcal{P}_0$ *we have that* $\mathcal{G}_0(p_0) = \bigwedge_{p \in \mathbf{cpl}_{\mathcal{F}_0,\mathcal{M}_\mathsf{Z}}(p_0)} \mathcal{G}_\mathsf{Z}(p)$.

Note that not all the interfaces of an SPLS Z are slices of Z (cf. the observation immediately after Definition 3). Namely, $\Pi_{\mathcal{F}_0}(\mathsf{Z})$ is an interface (which is unique modulo SPLS equivalence $\approx$) that is the greatest (with respect to the $\preceq$ relation between SPLSs) interface of Z with exactly the features of Z that are in $\mathcal{F}_0$ I.e., if $\mathsf{Z}_1 \preceq \mathsf{Z}$ and Z_1 has exactly the features of Z that are in $\mathcal{F}_0$, then $\mathsf{Z}_1 \preceq \Pi_{\mathcal{F}_0}(\mathsf{Z})$. The SPLS slice operator induces therefore a restriction of the SPLS interface operator by limiting the possibility to hide declarations from SPLS variants (cf.

the second degree of freedom discussed immediately after Definition 9). Namely, if $\Pi_{\mathcal{F}_0}((\mathcal{F}_z, \mathcal{P}_z), \mathcal{G}_z)) = ((\mathcal{M}_0, \mathcal{P}_0), \mathcal{G}_0)$ then, for all $p_0 \in \mathcal{P}_0$, we have that $\mathcal{G}_0(p_0)$ exposes exactly the declarations that are present in all the program signatures $\mathcal{G}_z(p)$ such that $p \in \mathbf{cpl}_{\mathcal{F}_0, (\mathcal{F}_z, \mathcal{P}_z)}(p_0)$.

The SPL slice is an operator that given an SPL and a set of features returns its greatest interface with exactly the given features. It is defined as follows.

Definition 12 (SPL slice). *Given an SPL* L *and a set of features* $\mathcal{F}_0$ *we define* $\Pi_{\mathcal{F}_0}(\mathrm{L})$ *as* $\Pi_{\mathcal{F}_0}(\mathbf{signature}(\mathrm{L}))$.

Example 7 (Slicing the EPL). Consider the SPL EPL of Example 3 and the SPLSs EPLS, EPLS$_0$ and EPLS$'_0$ of Example 5. We have that EPLS$_0$ is a slice of both EPLS and EPL. Namely, EPLS$_0 = \Pi_{Y_0}(\text{EPLS}) = \Pi_{Y_0}(\text{EPL})$, where $Y_0 = \{\mathsf{Lit}, \mathsf{Add}, \mathsf{Print}\}$ are the features of EPLS$_0$. Instead, EPLS$'_0$ is not a slice of EPLS.

4 On Slicing Delta-Oriented SPLSs of IFJ Programs

The extensional representation of SPLs allowed us to formulate notion of slice of an SPLS by abstracting from SPL implementation details. However, in order to investigate a practical slicing algorithm, we need to consider a representation of SPLs that reflects some implementation approach. To this aim, we first recall the propositional presentation of feature models (in Sect. 4.1) and the delta-oriented approach to implement SPLs, the definition delta-oriented SPL of IFJ programs, and the corresponding definition of SPLS (in Sect. 4.2). Then we illustrate the problem of devising a feasible algorithm for slicing delta-oriented SPLSs where the feature model is represented in propositional form (in Sect. 4.3).

4.1 Propositional Representation of Feature Models

The propositional representation of feature models works well in practice [6, 36, 38, 47]. In this representation, a feature model is given by a pair $(\mathcal{F}, \phi)$ where:

- $\mathcal{F}$ is a set of features, and
- ϕ is a propositional formula where the variables x are feature names:

$$\phi ::= x \mid \phi \wedge \phi \mid \phi \vee \phi \mid \phi \rightarrow \phi \mid \neg\phi.$$

A propositional formula ϕ over a set of features $\mathcal{F}$ represents the feature models whose products are configurations $\{x_1, ..., x_n\} \subseteq \mathcal{F}$ $(n \geq 0)$ such that ϕ is satisfied by assigning value true to the variables x_i $(1 \leq i \leq n)$ and false to all other variables. More formally, given the propositional representation $\mathcal{M} = (\mathcal{F}, \phi)$ of a feature model, we denote $\mathcal{E}(\mathcal{M})$ its extensional representation, i.e, the feature model $(\mathcal{F}, \mathcal{E}(\phi))$ with $\mathcal{E}(\phi) = \{p \mid p \subseteq \mathcal{F} \text{ and } \mathcal{I}_p \models \phi\}$.

Example 8 (A proposition representation of the Expression Feature Model). Consider the feature model $\mathcal{M}_{\mathrm{EPL}} = (\mathcal{F}_{\mathrm{EPL}}, \mathcal{P}_{\mathrm{EPL}})$ and the propositional formula ϕ_{EPL} introduced in Example 1. Then $(\mathcal{F}_{\mathrm{EPL}}, \phi_{\mathrm{EPL}})$ is a propositional representation of the feature model $\mathcal{M}_{\mathrm{EPL}}$, i.e., $\mathcal{E}((\mathcal{F}_{\mathrm{EPL}}, \phi_{\mathrm{EPL}})) = \mathcal{M}_{\mathrm{EPL}}$.

$$AB ::= P \, \overline{DD} \qquad\qquad\qquad\qquad\qquad\qquad\qquad \text{Artifact Base}$$
$$DD ::= \textbf{delta } \text{d}\{\overline{CO}\} \qquad\qquad\qquad\qquad\qquad\qquad \text{Delta Declaration}$$
$$CO ::= \textbf{adds } CD \mid \textbf{removes } \text{C} \mid \textbf{modifies } \text{C}[\textbf{extends } \text{C}']\{\overline{AO}\} \qquad \text{Class Operation}$$
$$AO ::= \textbf{adds } AD \mid \textbf{removes } \text{a} \mid \textbf{modifies } MD \qquad\qquad \text{Attribute Operation}$$

Fig. 4. Syntax of IFΔJ SPL artifact base

4.2 Delta-Oriented SPLs and SPLSs

Delta-Oriented Programming (DOP) [40,41], [3, Sect. 6.6.1] is a transformational approach to implement SPLs. The artifact base of a delta-oriented SPL consists of a *base program* (that might be empty) and of a set of *delta modules* (*deltas* for short). A delta is a container of program modifications (e.g., for IFJ programs, a delta can add, remove or modify classes). The configuration knowledge of a delta-oriented SPL associates to each delta an *activation condition* (determining the set of products for which that delta is activated) and specifies an *application ordering* between deltas: once a product is selected, the corresponding variant can be automatically generated by applying the activated deltas to the base program according to the application ordering. It is worth mentioning that the *Feature-Oriented Programming* (FOP) [5], [3, Sect. 6.1] approach to implement SPLs can be understood as the restriction of DOP where deltas correspond one-to-one to features and do not contain remove operations.

4.2.1 Delta-Oriented SPLs of IFJ Programs

Imperative Featherweight Delta Java (IFDJ) [7] is a core calculus for delta-oriented SPLs of IFJ programs. The abstract syntax of the artifact base of an IFDJ SPL is given in Fig. 4. The artifact base comprises a (possibly empty) IFJ program P, and a set of deltas $\overline{DD}$. A delta declaration DD comprises the name d of the delta and class operations $\overline{CO}$ representing the transformations performed when the delta is applied to an IFJ program. A class operation can add, remove, or modify a class. A class can be modified by (possibly) changing its super class and performing attribute operations $\overline{AO}$ on its body. An attribute operation can add or remove fields and methods, and modify the implementation of a method by replacing its body. The new body may call the special method name `original`, which is implicitly bound to the previous implementation of the method.

Recall that, according to Convention 1, we assume that the deltas declared in an artifact base have distinct names, the class operations in each delta act on distinct classes, the attribute operations in each class operation act on distinct attributes, etc.

If the feature model of a delta-oriented SPL L is in propositional representation $(\mathcal{F}, \phi)$, then the configuration knowledge of L can be conveniently represented by a pair $\mathcal{K} = (\alpha, <)$ where:

- α (the *delta activation map*) is a function that associates to each delta d a propositional formula ϕ_d such that $\phi \wedge \phi_d$ represents the set of products that activate it; and
- $<$ (the *delta application order*) is a partial ordering between delta names.[4]

Therefore an IFΔJ SPL can be represented by a triple $L = ((\mathcal{F}, \phi), AB, \mathcal{K})$.

The generator of L, denoted by $\mathcal{G}_L$, is a total function that associates each product p in $\mathcal{M}_L$ with the IFJ program $d_n(\cdots d_1(P) \cdots)$, where P is the base program of L and $d_1 \ldots, d_n$ ($n \geq 0$) are the deltas of L activated by p (they are applied to P according to a total ordering that is compatible with the application order).[5]

In most presentation of delta-oriented SPLs (see, e.g, [40,41]), the generator is considered to be a partial function in order to encompass ill-formed SPLs where, for some product, the generation of the associated variant fails. Recall that we focus on well-formed SPLs,[6] where generators are total functions and the generated products are well-typed IFJ programs—see [13,24] for effective means to ensure the well-formedness of IFΔJ SPLs.

The extensional representation a delta-oriented SPL L, denoted by $\mathcal{E}(L)$, is the SPL $(\mathcal{M}_L, \mathcal{G}_L)$ where $\mathcal{M}_L$ and $\mathcal{G}_L$ are the feature model and the generator of L, respectively.

4.2.2 Delta-Oriented SPLSs of IFJ Programs

A delta-oriented SPLS [19] can be understood as a delta-oriented SPL where the variants are program signatures. The abstract syntax of the artifact base of an IFΔJ SPLSs [19], *called artifact base signature,* is given in Fig. 5. An artifact base signature ABS comprises a program signature PS and a set of *delta signatures* $\overline{DS}$ that are deltas deprived of method-modifies operations and method bodies.

If the feature model of a delta-oriented SPLS Z is in propositional representation $(\mathcal{F}, \phi)$, then the configuration knowledge of Z can be represented by a pair $\mathcal{K} = (\alpha, <)$ defined similarly to the configuration knowledge of a delta-oriented SPL. Therefore the IFΔJ SPLS can be represented by a triple $Z = ((\mathcal{F}, \phi), ABS, \mathcal{K})$.

Also generator of a delta-oriented SPLS Z, denoted by $\mathcal{G}_Z$, and the extensional representation a delta-oriented SPLS Z, denoted by $\mathcal{E}(Z)$, are defined as for delta-oriented SPLs.

Given two delta-oriented SPLSs Z_1 and Z_2 we say that:

- Z_1 and Z_2 are *extensional equivalent* to mean that their extensional representations are equivalent, i.e., $\mathcal{E}(Z_1) \cong \mathcal{E}(Z_2)$; and
- Z_1 is an interface of Z_2 (written $Z_1 \preceq Z_2$) to mean that $\mathcal{E}(Z_1) \preceq \mathcal{E}(Z_2)$.

---

[4] As pointed out in [40,41], the delta application order $<_L$ is defined as a partial ordering to avoid over specification.

[5] We assume that all the total orders that are compatible with $<_L$ yield the same generator—see [7,34] for effective means to enforce this constraint.

[6] See footnote 2.

$$ABS ::= PS \; \overline{DS} \hspace{4cm} \text{AB Signature}$$
$$DS \;\; ::= \textbf{delta d} \; \{ \; \overline{COS} \; \} \hspace{3.2cm} \text{Delta Signature}$$
$$COS ::= \textbf{adds } CS \; \mid \; \textbf{removes } \mathtt{C} \; \mid \; \textbf{modifies } \mathtt{C} \; [\textbf{extends } \mathtt{C'}]\{\overline{AOS}\} \hspace{0.5cm} \text{CO Signature}$$
$$AOS ::= \textbf{adds } AS \; \mid \; \textbf{removes a} \hspace{2.8cm} \text{AO Signature}$$

Fig. 5. Syntax of IFΔJ SPLS artifact base signature

The *signature of an IFΔJ SPL* L, denoted as $\textbf{\textit{signature}}(\mathtt{L})$, is the SPLS obtained from L by dropping the method-modifies operations and the body of the methods in the artifact base. Note that the notion of signature of a delta-oriented SPL is consistent with the notion of signature defined for extensionally represented SPLs (introduced immediately after Definition 7). Namely, for all IFΔJ SPLs L we have that:

$$\mathcal{E}(\textbf{\textit{signature}}(\mathtt{L})) = \textbf{\textit{signature}}(\mathcal{E}(\mathtt{L})).$$

Given a delta-oriented SPLS Z and a delta-oriented SPL L, we say that Z is an interface of L (written $\mathtt{Z} \preceq \mathtt{L}$) to mean that $\mathcal{E}(\mathtt{Z}) \preceq \mathcal{E}(\textbf{\textit{signature}}(\mathtt{L}))$.

Recently [19], we have presented an algorithm for checking the interface relation between IFΔJ SPLSs where the feature model is represented in propositional form. The algorithm encodes interface checking into a boolean formula such that the formula is valid if and only of the interface relation holds. Then a SAT solver can be used to check whether a propositional formula is valid by checking whether its negation is unsatisfiable. Although this is a co-NP problem, similar translations into SAT constraints have been applied in practice for several SPL analysis with good results [26,37,46,47].

4.3   On Devising an Algorithm for Slicing Delta-Oriented SPLSs

Given a set of features $\mathcal{F}_0$ and delta-oriented SPL L where the feature model is represented in propositional form, manually writing a delta-oriented SPLS Z that is a slice of $\textbf{\textit{signature}}(\mathtt{L})$ for $\mathcal{F}_0$ is a tedious and error-prone task. In this section we illustrate the problem of devising a feasible algorithm for slicing delta-oriented SPLSs where the feature model is represented in propositional form.

We first focus on slicing a feature model represented in propositional form (in Sect. 4.3.1), then we consider slicing an IFΔJ SPLS (in Sect. 4.3.2).

4.3.1   Slicing Feature Models in Propositional Form

Given a set of features $X = \{x_1, ..., x_n\}$ ($n \geq 0$) and a feature model in propositional representation $(\mathcal{F}, \phi)$, the slicing algorithm *slice* is defined by:

$$\textbf{\textit{slice}}_X((\mathcal{F}, \phi)) = (\mathcal{F} \cap X, \textbf{\textit{sliceBF}}_{\mathcal{F}/X}(\phi))$$

where the algorithm $\textbf{\textit{sliceBF}}$ is defined by:

$$\textbf{\textit{sliceBF}}_\emptyset(\phi) = \phi$$
$$\textbf{\textit{sliceBF}}_{\{x_1,...,x_n\}}(\phi) = \textbf{\textit{sliceBF}}_{\{x_2,...,x_n\}}(\phi[x_1 := \textbf{true}]) \vee (\phi[x_1 := \textbf{false}])).$$

The following theorem states that the slicing algorithm *slice* is correct.

Theorem 2 (Correctness of the *slice* algorithm for feature models). *For all set of features X and for all feature models in propositional representation $(\mathcal{F}, \phi)$, we have that $\mathcal{E}(\textbf{slice}_X(\mathcal{F}, \phi))) = \Pi_X(\mathcal{E}((\mathcal{F}, \phi)))$.*

Proof. Straightforward by induction on the number of features in $\mathcal{F} \setminus X$. □

By construction, the size of feature model $\textbf{slice}_X((\mathcal{F}, \phi))$ can grow as 2^n, where n is the number of variables in X. In order to avoid this exponential growth, we modify the notion of propositional representation of feature model (introduced in Sect. 4.1) by replacing the Boolean formula ϕ by an (existentially) Quantified-Boolean formula σ defined by:

$$\sigma ::= \exists \bar{x}.\phi, \quad \text{where } \bar{x} \text{ may be empty, i.e., } \sigma = \phi.$$

Given a set of features $X = \{x_1, ..., x_n\}$ ($n \geq 0$) and a feature model in propositional representation $(\mathcal{F}, \sigma)$, the slicing algorithm *sliceE* is defined by:

$$\textit{sliceE}_X((\mathcal{F}, \exists \bar{y}.\phi)) = (\mathcal{F} \cap X, \exists \bar{w}.\phi)), \quad \text{where } \bar{w} \text{ are the elements of} \{\bar{y}\} \cup (\mathcal{F} \setminus X).$$

The following theorem states that the slicing algorithm *sliceE* is correct.

Theorem 3 (Correctness of the *sliceE* algorithm for feature models). *For all set of features X and for all feature models in propositional representation $(\mathcal{F}, \sigma)$, we have that $\mathcal{E}(\textbf{sliceE}_X(\mathcal{F}, \sigma))) = \Pi_X(\mathcal{E}((\mathcal{F}, \sigma)))$.*

Proof. Straightforward by induction on the number of features in $\mathcal{F} \setminus X$. □

Example 9 (Computing a slice of the Expression Feature Model). Consider the feature model $(\mathcal{F}_{\text{EPL}}, \phi_{\text{EPL}})$ introduced in Example 8 and the set of features $Y_0 = \{\text{Lit}, \text{Add}, \text{Print}\}$ introduced in Example 7. We have: $\textbf{slice}_{Y_0}(\mathcal{F}_{\text{EPL}}, \phi_{\text{EPL}}) = (Y_0, \phi_{\text{EPL}_0})$ and $\textbf{sliceE}_{Y_0}(\mathcal{F}_{\text{EPL}}, \phi_{\text{EPL}}) = (Y_0, \sigma_{\text{EPL}_0})$, where both $\phi_{\text{EPL}_0} = (\text{Lit} \wedge (\text{Print} \vee \textbf{true})) \vee (\text{Lit} \wedge (\text{Print} \vee \textbf{false}))$ and $\sigma_{\text{EPL}_0} = \exists x.\text{Lit} \wedge (\text{Print} \vee x)$ are logically equivalent to Lit.

Although the fact that slicing a feature model in propositional representation corresponds to performing an existential quantification on the dropped feature variables was already know in the literature (e.g., we have exploited it Sect. 5 of [19]), we are not aware of other authors that have published slicing algorithms like $\textbf{slice}_X$ and $\textbf{sliceE}_X$ above.

4.3.2 On the Problem of Slicing IFΔJ SPLSs

We aim at devising an algorithm such that:

- given an IFΔJ SPLS $\mathsf{Z} = ((\mathcal{F}, \sigma), ABS, \mathcal{K})$ and a set of features X,
- returns an IFΔJ SPLS $\mathsf{Z}' = ((\mathcal{F}', \sigma'), ABS', \mathcal{K}')$ that is a slice of Z for X and is such that:
  1. $(\mathcal{F}', \sigma') = \textbf{sliceE}_X(\mathcal{F}, \sigma)$,

2. the size of the artifact base ABS' is linear in the size of ABS, and
3. the size of the configuration knowledge $\mathcal{K}'$ is linear in the size of $\mathcal{K}$.

Note that requirements 2 and 3 above rule out any algorithm that returns an IFΔJ SPLS where the artifact base and configuration knowledge are the straightforward encoding of the generation mapping $\mathcal{G}_Z$ of Definition 11 (i.e., a delta for each product, activated if and only if the product is selected).

Although we don't know whether an algorithm that satisfies requirements 2 and 3 exists, we conjecture that it exists at least for some significant classes of delta-oriented SPLs. We leave the investigating of such an algorithm for future work, and conclude this section by an example.

Example 10 (On slicing a delta-oriented implementation of the EPLS). Consider the IFΔJ SPLS $Z = (\mathcal{M}_{\mathrm{EPL}}, ABS, \mathcal{K})$ where: $\mathcal{M}_{\mathrm{EPL}}$ is the feature model $(\mathcal{F}_{\mathrm{EPL}}, \phi_{\mathrm{EPL}})$ introduced in Example 8; the artifact base signature ABS is

EPS$_1$ // the program signature introduced in Example 4
delta d_1 { **removes** Add }
delta d_2 { **modifies** Exp {**removes** toString} }   **delta** d_3 { **modifies** Exp {**removes** toInt} }

and the configuration knowledge $\mathcal{K}$ comprises the activation mapping $\{d_1 \mapsto \neg\mathsf{Add}, d_2 \mapsto \neg\mathsf{Print}, d_3 \mapsto \neg\mathsf{Eval}\}$ and the flat application order (i.e., d_1, d_2 and d_3 can be applied in any order). Note that $\mathcal{E}(Z) \cong \mathrm{EPLS}_1$, where EPLS_1 is as in Example 5.

The slicing of Z w.r.t. the set of features $Y_0 = \{\mathsf{Lit}, \mathsf{Add}, \mathsf{Print}\}$ introduced in Example 5 is represented by the IFΔJ SPLS $Z_0 = (\mathcal{M}_{\mathrm{EPL}_0}, ABS_0, \mathcal{K}_0)$ where: $\mathcal{M}_{\mathrm{EPL}_0}$ is the feature model (Y_0, Lit) introduced in Example 9; the artifact base signature ABS_0 is

EPS$_{\mathrm{IV}}$ // the program signature introduced in Example 5
delta d_1 { **removes** Add }
delta d_2 { **modifies** Exp {**removes** toString} }

and the configuration knowledge $\mathcal{K}$ comprises the activation mapping $\{d_1 \mapsto \neg\mathsf{Add}, d_2 \mapsto \neg\mathsf{Print}\}$ and the flat application order. Note that $\mathcal{E}(Z_0) \cong \mathrm{EPLS}_0$, where EPLS_0 is as in Example 7.

5   Related Work

The notion of SPLS considered in this paper can be used to introduce a support for MPLs on top of a given approach for implementing SPL. For instance, in [19] we have exploited it to to define a formal model for delta-oriented MPLs. Previous work [25] informally outlined an extension of delta-oriented programming to implement MPLs, which does not enforce any boundaries between different SPLs and therefore is not suitable for supporting compositional analyses. In contrast, as illustrated in [19], SPLSs can be used to support compostional type-checking of MPLs of IFJ programs.

Schröter et al. [44] advocated investigating interface constructs for supporting compositional analyses of MPLs at different stages of the development process. In particular, they informally introduced the notion of syntactical interfaces (which generalizes feature model interfaces to provide a view of reusable programming artifacts) and the notion of behavioral interface (which generalizes syntactical interfaces to support formal verification). The notion of SPLS considered in this paper is (according to terminology of [44]) a syntactical interface.

Schröter et al. [45] also proposed the notion of feature-context interfaces in order to support preventing type errors while developing SPLs with the FOP approach. A feature-context interface provides an invariable API specifying classes and members of the feature modules that are intended to be accessible in the context of a given set of features. In contrast, an SPLS represents a variability-aware API.

The notion of slice of an SPLS for a set of features introduced and formalized in this paper lifts to SPLs the notion of slice of a feature model introduced in [1] (see also [43]). We are not aware of any other proposal for lifting to SPLs the notion of slice of a feature model.

6 Conclusions and Future Work

We have defined the notion of slice of an SPLS by abstracting from SPL(S) implementation approaches, and we have formulated the problem of defining an efficient algorithm that given a delta-oriented SPLS K and a set of features F returns a delta-oriented SPLS that is an slice of K for F.

In future work we would like to investigate a efficient algorithm for slicing delta-oriented SPLSs. In particular, we are planning to devise an algorithm for refactoring IFΔJ SPLSs to some normal form that is suitable for performing a slice. A starting point for this investigation could be represented by the algorithms for refactoring IFΔJ SPLs presented in [14,15,18]. The Abstract Behavioural Specification (ABS) language [9,16,31] is a delta-oriented modeling language has been successfully used in the context of industrial use cases [2,11,28,32]. DeltaJava [33,48] is a delta-oriented programming language designed to comfortably create SPLs within the Java environment. In future work we would like to exploit the notions of SPLS and slice for adding support for MPLs and support for deductive verification proof reuse [8,20,27] to the ABS toolchain (https://abs-models.org/) and to the DeltaJava toochain (http://deltajava.org/). We also plan the exploit the notion of SPLS to increase modularity in mechanisms that extend delta-oriented programming to support dynamic SPLs [23] (see also [21,22]) and interoperability between variants of the same SPL [12].

Acknowledgments. We thank the anonymous reviewers for comments and suggestions for improving the presentation.

A   Proof of Theorem 1

Recall that, although $\mathtt{Object} \notin \mathrm{dom}(PS)$, class $\mathtt{Object}$ is used in every non-empty program PS. Therefore, $\leq_{:PS}$ is a relation on $\widehat{\mathrm{dom}}(PS)$, where $\widehat{\mathrm{dom}}(PS)$ is a shortening for $\mathrm{dom}(PS) \cup \{\mathtt{Object}\}$.

Definition 13 (Subtyping path). *Given a program signature PS and a class $\mathtt{C} \in \mathrm{dom}(PS)$, we denote* PATH$(\mathtt{C}, PS)$ *the restriction of $\leq_{:PS}$ to the supertypes of $\mathtt{C}$ viz. the set $\{(\mathtt{C}', \mathtt{C}'') \mid \mathtt{C}' \leq_{:PS} \mathtt{C}''\ and\ \mathtt{C} \leq_{:PS} \mathtt{C}'\}$.*

We remark that PATH$(\mathtt{C}, PS)$ is an order relation that identifies (uniquely) a linearly ordered sequence of classes, with $\mathtt{C}$ as bottom and $\mathtt{Object}$ as top. No path can be empty, since it has to include at least the pair $(\mathtt{Object}, \mathtt{Object})$.

The following definition and lemma exploit a canonical form for the elements of the equivalence classes of the relation $\approx$ between program signatures that is more convenient than the thin form (given in Definition 10) for writing the proofs.

Definition 14 (Fat program signatures and *fatInf* operator). *We say that a program signature PS is in fat form (fat for short) to mean that, for all classes $\mathtt{C} \in \mathrm{dom}(PS)$ and for all attributes $\mathtt{a} \in \mathrm{dom}(PS(\mathtt{C}))$, if $lookup_{PS}(\mathtt{a}, \mathtt{C}) = AS$ then $PS(\mathtt{C})(\mathtt{a}) = AS$. We write **fat**$(PS)$ to denote the fat form of a program signature PS. Let $\overline{PS}$ be a (non empty) set of program signatures.*

1. *We write $\bigcap_{\overline{PS}} \mathrm{dom}(PS)$ to shorten $\bigcap_{PS \in \overline{PS}} \mathrm{dom}(PS)$. Note that $\mathtt{Object}$ is never included in this intersection.*
2. *Let $\mathtt{C} \in \bigcap_{\overline{PS}} \mathrm{dom}(PS)$.*
   (a) PATH$_{\overline{PS}}(\mathtt{C})$ *is the linear order relation $\bigcap\{$PATH$(\mathtt{C}, PS_i) \mid PS_i \in \overline{PS}\}$.*
   (b) PATH$^{\not{\mathtt{C}}}_{\overline{PS}}(\mathtt{C})$ *is the order relation obtained by PATH$_{\overline{PS}}(\mathtt{C})$ removing $\mathtt{C}$.*
   (c) $mcs(\mathtt{C})$ *(minimum common superclass of $\mathtt{C}$) is the bottom of* PATH$^{\not{\mathtt{C}}}_{\overline{PS}}(\mathtt{C})$.
   (d) MCFD$(\overline{PS}, \mathtt{C})$ *is the (maximum) set of common field declarations, viz. the set of all field declarations of the shape $\mathtt{C}_* \mathtt{f}_*$ such that: for all $PS_i \in \overline{PS}$, $lookup_{PS_i}(\mathtt{f}_*, \mathtt{C}) = \mathtt{C}_* \mathtt{f}_*$.*
   (e) MCMD$(\overline{PS}, \mathtt{C})$ *is the (maximum) set of common method declarations, viz. the set of all field declarations of the shape $\mathtt{C}_* \mathtt{m}_*(\overline{\mathtt{C}_\mathtt{x}\ \mathtt{x}})$ such that: for all $PS_i \in \overline{PS}$, $lookup_{PS_i}(\mathtt{m}_*, \mathtt{C}) = \mathtt{C}_* \mathtt{m}_*(\overline{\mathtt{C}_\mathtt{x}\ \mathtt{x}'})$ for some variable names $\mathtt{x}'$ (the type sequences have to match but, as usual, the names of arguments do not matter).*
3. *We denote **fatInf**$(\overline{PS})$ the in $\overline{PS}$, viz. the program signature such that, for all and only $\mathtt{C} \in \bigcap_{\overline{PS}} \mathrm{dom}(PS)$ includes all and only the declarations:*

$$\mathbf{class}\ \mathtt{C}\ \mathbf{extends}\ mcs(\mathtt{C})\ \{\ \text{MCMD}(\overline{PS}, \mathtt{C})\ \ \text{MCFD}(\overline{PS}, \mathtt{C})\ \}\ .$$

Lemma 1 (*fatInf* characterizes $\bigwedge$). *For every (non empty) set of program signatures $\overline{PS}$, it holds that **fatInf**$(\overline{PS}) = \mathbf{fat}(\bigwedge \overline{PS})$.*

Proof. It is straightforward to see that $fatInf(\overline{PS})$ is always defined and that $fatInf(\overline{PS}) \preceq PS_i$ for all $PS_i \in \overline{PS}$ (since it is build as a restriction of them). Therefore $fatInf(\overline{PS})$ is a lower bound for $\overline{PS}$ and we can conclude the proof by showing that it is the greater between the lower bounds for $\overline{PS}$, namely if $PS^\star \preceq PS_i$ for all $PS_i \in \overline{PS}$ then $PS^\star \preceq fatInf(\overline{PS})$ has to hold. In accordance with Definition 5, we have to prove that the following three conditions hold.

(i) If $\mathsf{C} \in \mathrm{dom}(PS^\star)$ then it has to be $\mathsf{C} \in \mathrm{dom}(PS_i)$ for all $PS_i \in \overline{PS}$. Therefore, $\mathsf{C} \in fatInf(\overline{PS})$ by construction.

(ii) Let $\mathsf{C_1, C_2} \in \mathrm{dom}(PS^\star)$. If $\mathsf{C_0} <:_{P\star} \mathsf{C_1}$ then it has to be $\mathsf{C_0} <:_{P_i} \mathsf{C_1}$ for all $PS_i \in \overline{PS}$, viz. $(\mathsf{C_0, C_1}) \in \mathrm{PATH}_{\overline{PS}_i}(\mathsf{C_0})$. Therefore, $(\mathsf{C_0, C_1}) \in \mathrm{PATH}_{(\overline{PS})}(\mathsf{C})$ by construction.

(iii) Let $\mathsf{C} \in \mathrm{dom}(PS^\star)$ and a be an attribute such that $lookup_{PS^\star}(\mathsf{a, C})$ is defined. But $PS^\star \preceq \overline{PS}$ implies that, for all $PS_i \in \overline{PS}$, $lookup_{PS_i}(\mathsf{a, C})$ is defined and $lookup_{PS_i}(\mathsf{a, C}) = lookup_{PS^\star}(\mathsf{a, C})$. Since $\mathrm{MCFD}(\overline{PS}, \mathsf{C})$ and $\mathrm{MCMD}(\overline{PS}, \mathsf{C})$ have been defined to grasp the maximum set of common attribute declarations, the proof follows by construction. □

Proof (of Theorem 1). Straightforward by Lemma 1. □

References

1. Acher, M., Collet, P., Lahire, P., France, R.B.: Slicing feature models. In: 26th IEEE/ACM International Conference on Automated Software Engineering (ASE), pp. 424–427 (2011). https://doi.org/10.1109/ASE.2011.6100089

2. Albert, E., et al.: Formal modeling and analysis of resource management for cloud architectures: an industrial case study using real-time ABS. Serv. Oriented Comput. Appl. **8**(4), 323–339 (2014). https://doi.org/10.1007/s11761-013-0148-0

3. Apel, S., Batory, D.S., Kästner, C., Saake, G.: Feature-Oriented Software Product Lines: Concepts and Implementation. Springer, Heidelberg (2013)

4. Batory, D.: Feature models, grammars, and propositional formulas. In: Obbink, H., Pohl, K. (eds.) SPLC 2005. LNCS, vol. 3714, pp. 7–20. Springer, Heidelberg (2005). https://doi.org/10.1007/11554844_3

5. Batory, D., Sarvela, J.N., Rauschmayer, A.: Scaling step-wise refinement. IEEE Trans. Softw. Eng. **30**, 355–371 (2004). https://doi.org/10.1109/TSE.2004.23

6. Benavides, D., Segura, S., Ruiz-Cortés, A.: Automated analysis of feature models 20 years later: a literature review. Inf. Syst. **35**(6), 615–636 (2010). https://doi.org/10.1016/j.is.2010.01.001

7. Bettini, L., Damiani, F., Schaefer, I.: Compositional type checking of delta-oriented software product lines. Acta Informatica **50**(2), 77–122 (2013). https://doi.org/10.1007/s00236-012-0173-z

8. Bubel, R., et al.: Proof repositories for compositional verification of evolving software systems - managing change when proving software correct. Trans. Found. Mastering Change **I**(1), 130–156 (2016). https://doi.org/10.1007/978-3-319-46508-1_8

9. Clarke, D., et al.: Modeling spatial and temporal variability with the HATS abstract behavioral modeling language. In: Bernardo, M., Issarny, V. (eds.) SFM 2011. LNCS, vol. 6659, pp. 417–457. Springer, Heidelberg (2011). https://doi.org/10.1007/978-3-642-21455-4_13

10. Clements, P., Northrop, L.: Software Product Lines: Practices & Patterns. Addison Wesley Longman, Boston (2001)
11. Damiani, F., Hähnle, R., Kamburjan, E., Lienhardt, M.: A unified and formal programming model for deltas and traits. In: Huisman, M., Rubin, J. (eds.) FASE 2017. LNCS, vol. 10202, pp. 424–441. Springer, Heidelberg (2017). https://doi.org/10.1007/978-3-662-54494-5_25
12. Damiani, F., Hähnle, R., Kamburjan, E., Lienhardt, M.: Interoperability of software product line variants. In: Proceedings of the 22nd International Systems and Software Product Line Conference SPLC 2018, vol. 1, pp. 264–268. Association for Computing Machinery, New York (2018). https://doi.org/10.1145/3233027.3236401
13. Damiani, F., Lienhardt, M.: On type checking delta-oriented product lines. In: Ábrahám, E., Huisman, M. (eds.) IFM 2016. LNCS, vol. 9681, pp. 47–62. Springer, Cham (2016). https://doi.org/10.1007/978-3-319-33693-0_4
14. Damiani, F., Lienhardt, M.: Refactoring delta-oriented product lines to achieve monotonicity. In: Proceedings 7th International Workshop on Formal Methods and Analysis in Software Product Line Engineering, FMSPLE@ETAPS 2016 EPTCS, Eindhoven, The Netherlands, 3 April 201, vol. 206, pp. 2–16 (2016). https://doi.org/10.4204/EPTCS.206.2
15. Damiani, F., Lienhardt, M.: Refactoring delta-oriented product lines to enforce guidelines for efficient type-checking. In: Margaria, T., Steffen, B. (eds.) ISoLA 2016, Part II. LNCS, vol. 9953, pp. 579–596. Springer, Cham (2016). https://doi.org/10.1007/978-3-319-47169-3_45
16. Damiani, F., Lienhardt, M., Muschevici, R., Schaefer, I.: An extension of the ABS toolchain with a mechanism for type checking SPLs. In: Polikarpova, N., Schneider, S. (eds.) IFM 2017. LNCS, vol. 10510, pp. 111–126. Springer, Cham (2017). https://doi.org/10.1007/978-3-319-66845-1_8
17. Damiani, F., Lienhardt, M., Paolini, L.: A formal model for multi SPLs. In: Dastani, M., Sirjani, M. (eds.) FSEN 2017. LNCS, vol. 10522, pp. 67–83. Springer, Cham (2017). https://doi.org/10.1007/978-3-319-68972-2_5
18. Damiani, F., Lienhardt, M., Paolini, L.: Automatic refactoring of delta-oriented SPLs to remove-free form and replace-free form. Int. J. Softw. Tools Technol. Transf. **21**(6), 691–707 (2019). https://doi.org/10.1007/s10009-019-00534-2
19. Damiani, F., Lienhardt, M., Paolini, L.: A formal model for multi software product lines. Sci. Comput. Program. **172**, 203–231 (2019). https://doi.org/10.1016/j.scico.2018.11.005
20. Damiani, F., Owe, O., Dovland, J., Schaefer, I., Johnsen, E.B., Yu, I.C.: A transformational proof system for delta-oriented programming. In: Proceedings of SPLC 2012, vol. 2, pp. 53–60. ACM (2012). https://doi.org/10.1145/2364412.2364422
21. Damiani, F., Padovani, L., Schaefer, I.: A formal foundation for dynamic delta-oriented software product lines. In: Proceedings of the 11th International Conference on Generative Programming and Component Engineering GPCE 2012, pp. 1–10. ACM, New York (2012). https://doi.org/10.1145/2371401.2371403
22. Damiani, F., Padovani, L., Schaefer, I., Seidl, C.: A core calculus for dynamic delta-oriented programming. Acta Informatica **55**(4), 269–307 (2018). https://doi.org/10.1007/s00236-017-0293-6
23. Damiani, F., Schaefer, I.: Dynamic delta-oriented programming. In: Proceedings of the 15th International Software Product Line Conference SPLC 2011, vol. 2, pp. 34:1–34:8. ACM, New York (2011). https://doi.org/10.1145/2019136.2019175

24. Damiani, F., Schaefer, I.: Family-based analysis of type safety for delta-oriented software product lines. In: Margaria, T., Steffen, B. (eds.) ISoLA 2012, Part I. LNCS, vol. 7609, pp. 193–207. Springer, Heidelberg (2012). https://doi.org/10.1007/978-3-642-34026-0_15

25. Damiani, F., Schaefer, I., Winkelmann, T.: Delta-oriented multi software product lines. In: Proceedings of the 18th International Software Product Line Conference SPLC 2014, vol. 1, pp. 232–236. ACM (2014). https://doi.org/10.1145/2648511.2648536

26. Delaware, B., Cook, W.R., Batory, D.: Fitting the pieces together: a machine-checked model of safe composition. In: ESEC/FSE, pp. 243–252. ACM (2009). https://doi.org/10.1145/1595696.1595733

27. Din, C.C., Johnsen, E.B., Owe, O., Yu, I.C.: A modular reasoning system using uninterpreted predicates for code reuse. J. Log. Algebraic Methods Program. **95**, 82–102 (2018). https://doi.org/10.1016/j.jlamp.2017.11.004

28. Helvensteijn, M., Muschevici, R., Wong, P.Y.H.: Delta modeling in practice: a Fredhopper case study. In: Proceedings of VAMOS 2012, pp. 139–148. ACM (2012). https://doi.org/10.1145/2110147.2110163

29. Holl, G., Grünbacher, P., Rabiser, R.: A systematic review and an expert survey on capabilities supporting multi product lines. Inf. Softw. Technol. **54**(8), 828–852 (2012). https://doi.org/10.1016/j.infsof.2012.02.002

30. Igarashi, A., Pierce, B., Wadler, P.: Featherweight Java: a minimal core calculus for Java and GJ. ACM TOPLAS **23**(3), 396–450 (2001). https://doi.org/10.1145/503502.503505

31. Johnsen, E.B., Hähnle, R., Schäfer, J., Schlatte, R., Steffen, M.: ABS: a core language for abstract behavioral specification. In: Aichernig, B.K., de Boer, F.S., Bonsangue, M.M. (eds.) FMCO 2010. LNCS, vol. 6957, pp. 142–164. Springer, Heidelberg (2011). https://doi.org/10.1007/978-3-642-25271-6_8

32. Kamburjan, E., Hähnle, R.: Uniform modeling of railway operations. In: Artho, C., Ölveczky, P.C. (eds.) FTSCS 2016. CCIS, vol. 694, pp. 55–71. Springer, Cham (2017). https://doi.org/10.1007/978-3-319-53946-1_4

33. Koscielny, J., Holthusen, S., Schaefer, I., Schulze, S., Bettini, L., Damiani, F.: DeltaJ 1.5: delta-oriented programming for Java. In: International Conference on Principles and Practices of Programming on the Java Platform Virtual Machines, Languages and Tools, PPPJ 2014, pp. 63–74 (2014). https://doi.org/10.1145/2647508.2647512

34. Lienhardt, M., Clarke, D.: Conflict detection in delta-oriented programming. In: Margaria, T., Steffen, B. (eds.) ISoLA 2012, Part I. LNCS, vol. 7609, pp. 178–192. Springer, Heidelberg (2012). https://doi.org/10.1007/978-3-642-34026-0_14

35. Lienhardt, M., Damiani, F., Donetti, S., Paolini, L.: Multi software product lines in the wild. In: Proceedings of the 12th International Workshop on Variability Modelling of Software-Intensive Systems VAMOS 2018, pp. 89–96. ACM, New York (2018). https://doi.org/10.1145/3168365.3170425

36. Lienhardt, M., Damiani, F., Johnsen, E.B., Mauro, J.: Lazy product discovery in huge configuration spaces. In: Proceedings of the 42th International Conference on Software Engineering ICSE 2020. ACM (2020). https://doi.org/10.1145/3377811.3380372

37. Lienhardt, M., Damiani, F., Testa, L., Turin, G.: On checking delta-oriented product lines of statecharts. Sci. Comput. Program. **166**, 3–34 (2018). https://doi.org/10.1016/j.scico.2018.05.007

38. Mendonca, M., Wasowski, A., Czarnecki, K.: SAT-based analysis of feature models is easy. In: Muthig, D., McGregor, J.D. (eds.) Proceedings of the 13th International Software Product Line Conference. ACM International Conference Proceeding Series, vol. 446, pp. 231–240. ACM (2009)

39. Pohl, K., Böckle, G., van der Linden, F.: Software Product Line Engineering - Foundations, Principles, and Techniques. Springer, Heidelberg (2005). https://doi.org/10.1007/3-540-28901-1

40. Schaefer, I., Bettini, L., Bono, V., Damiani, F., Tanzarella, N.: Delta-oriented programming of software product lines. In: Bosch, J., Lee, J. (eds.) SPLC 2010. LNCS, vol. 6287, pp. 77–91. Springer, Heidelberg (2010). https://doi.org/10.1007/978-3-642-15579-6_6

41. Schaefer, I., Damiani, F.: Pure delta-oriented programming. In: Proceedings of the 2nd International Workshop on Feature-Oriented Software Development, pp. 49–56. ACM (2010). https://doi.org/10.1145/1868688.1868696

42. Schaefer, I., et al.: Software diversity: state of the art and perspectives. Int. J. Softw. Tools Technol. Transfer 14(5), 477–495 (2012). https://doi.org/10.1007/s10009-012-0253-y

43. Schröter, R., Krieter, S., Thüm, T., Benduhn, F., Saake, G.: Feature-model interfaces: the highway to compositional analyses of highly-configurable systems. In: Proceedings of the 38th International Conference on Software Engineering ICSE 2016, pp. 667–678. ACM (2016). https://doi.org/10.1145/2884781.2884823

44. Schröter, R., Siegmund, N., Thüm, T.: Towards modular analysis of multi product lines. In: Proceedings of the 17th International Software Product Line Conference Co-located Workshops SPLC 2013, pp. 96–99. ACM (2013). https://doi.org/10.1145/2499777.2500719

45. Schröter, R., Siegmund, N., Thüm, T., Saake, G.: Feature-context interfaces: tailored programming interfaces for SPLs. In: Proceedings of the 18th International Software Product Line Conference SPLC 2014, vol. 1, pp. 102–111. ACM (2014). https://doi.org/10.1145/2648511.2648522

46. Thaker, S., Batory, D., Kitchin, D., Cook, W.: Safe composition of product lines. In: GPCE 2007, pp. 95–104. ACM (2007). https://doi.org/10.1145/1289971.1289989

47. Thüm, T., Apel, S., Kästner, C., Schaefer, I., Saake, G.: A classification and survey of analysis strategies for software product lines. ACM Comput. Surv. 47(1), 6:1–6:45 (2014). https://doi.org/10.1145/2580950

48. Winkelmann, T., Koscielny, J., Seidl, C., Schuster, S., Damiani, F., Schaefer, I.: Parametric DeltaJ 1.5: propagating feature attributes into implementation artifacts. In: Gemeinsamer Tagungsband der Workshops der Tagung Software Engineering 2016 (SE 2016), Wien, 23–26 February 2016. CEUR Workshop Proceedings, vol. 1559, pp. 40–54. CEUR-WS.org (2016)

Assumption-Commitment Types for Resource Management in Virtually Timed Ambients

Einar Broch Johnsen$^{(\boxtimes)}$, Martin Steffen$^{(\boxtimes)}$, and Johanna Beate Stumpf

University of Oslo, Oslo, Norway
{einarj,msteffen,johanbst}@ifi.uio.no

Abstract. This paper introduces a type system for resource management in the context of nested virtualization. With nested virtualization, virtual machines compete with other processes for the resources of their host environment in order to provision their own processes, which could again be virtual machines. The calculus of virtually timed ambients formalizes such resource provisioning, extending the capabilities of mobile ambients to model the dynamic creation, migration, and destruction of virtual machines. The proposed type system is compositional as it uses assumptions about the outside of a virtually timed ambient to guarantee resource provisioning on the inside. We prove subject reduction and progress for well-typed virtually timed ambients, expressing that upper bounds on resource needs are preserved by reduction and that processes do not run out of resources.

1 Introduction

Virtualization enables the resources of an execution environment to be represented as a software layer, a so-called *virtual machine.* Software processes are agnostic to whether they run on a virtual machine or directly on physical hardware. A virtual machine is itself such a process, which can be executed on another virtual machine. Technologies such as VirtualBox, VMWare ESXi, Ravello HVX, Microsoft Hyper-V, and the open-source Xen hypervisor increasingly support running virtual machines inside each other in this way. This *nested virtualization,* originally introduced by Goldberg [1], is necessary to host virtual machines with operating systems which themselves support virtualization [2], such as Microsoft Windows 7 and Linux KVM. Use cases for nested virtualization include end-user virtualization for guests, software development, and deployment testing. Nested virtualization is also a crucial technology to support the hybrid cloud, as it enables virtual machines to migrate between different cloud providers [3].

To study the logical behavior of virtual machines in the context of nested virtualization, this paper introduces a type-based analysis for a calculus of virtual machines. An essential feature of virtual machines, captured by this calculus, is that a virtual machine competes with other processes for the resources available in their execution environment, in order to provision resources to the processes *inside* the virtual machine. Another essential feature of virtual machines is

© Springer Nature Switzerland AG 2020
T. Margaria and B. Steffen (Eds.): ISoLA 2020, LNCS 12476, pp. 103–121, 2020.
https://doi.org/10.1007/978-3-030-61362-4_6

migration. From an abstract perspective, virtual machines can be seen as mobile processes which can move between positions in a hierarchy of nested locations.

We develop the type system for *virtually timed ambients* [4], a calculus of mobile virtual locations with explicit resource provisioning, based on mobile ambients [5]. The goal is to statically approximate an upper bound on resource consumption for systems of virtual machines expressed in this calculus. The calculus features a resource called *virtual time*, reflecting local execution capacity, which is provisioned to an ambient by its parent ambient, similar to time slices that an operating system provisions to its processes. With several levels of nested virtualization, virtual time becomes a *local* notion which depends on an ambient's position in the location hierarchy. Virtually timed ambients are mobile, reflecting that virtual machines may migrate between host virtual machines. Migration affects the execution speed of processes inside the virtually timed ambient which is moving as well as in its host before and after the move. Consequently, the resources required by a process change dynamically when the topology changes.

The distinction between the inside and outside of a virtually timed ambient (or a virtual machine) is a challenge for compositional analysis; we have knowledge of the current contents of the virtual machine, but not of what can happen outside its borders. This challenge is addressed in our type system by distinguishing *assumptions* about ambients on the outside of the virtually timed ambient from *commitments* to ambients on the inside. To statically approximate the effects of migration, an ambient's type imposes a bound on the ambients it can host. If type checking fails, the ability to provision resources for an incoming ambient in a timely way cannot be statically guaranteed in our type system.

The ambient calculus has previously been enriched with types (e.g., [6]). Exploiting the explicit notion of resource provisioning in virtually timed ambients (including a fair resource distribution and competition for resources between processes), our type system captures the resource capacity of a virtually timed ambient and an upper bound on the number of its subambients. The type system thereby provides concrete results on resource consumption in an operational framework. Resource dependency in the type system is expressed using *coeffects*. The term coeffect was coined by Petricek, Orchard, and Mycroft [7,8] to capture how a computation depends on an environment rather than how it affects the environment. In our setting, coeffects capture how a process depends on its environment by an upper bound on the resources needed by the process.

Contributions. The main technical contributions of this paper are

- an *assumption commitment type system* with *effects* and *coeffects*, which provides a static approximation of constraints regarding the capacity of virtually timed ambients and an upper bound on their resource usage; and
- a proof of the *soundness of resource management* for well-typed virtually timed ambients in terms of a *subject reduction* theorem which expresses that the upper bounds on resources and on the number of subambients are preserved under reduction, and a *progress* theorem which expresses that well-typed virtually timed ambients will not run out of resources.

To the best of our knowledge, this is the first assumption commitment style type system for resource types and nested locations.

Paper Overview. Section 2 introduces virtually timed ambients. Section 3 presents the type system for resource management. In Sect. 4, we prove the soundness of the type system in terms of subject reduction and progress. We discuss related work and conclude in Sects. 5 and 6.

2   Virtually Timed Ambients

Mobile ambients [5] are processes with a concept of location, arranged in a hierarchy which may change dynamically. Interpreting these locations as places of deployment, *virtually timed ambients* [4,9] extend mobile ambients with notions of virtual time and resource consumption. The timed behavior of a process depends on the one hand on the *local* timed behavior, and on the other hand on the placement or deployment of the process in the hierarchical ambient structure. Virtually timed ambients combine timed processes and timed capabilities with the mobility and location properties of the mobile ambient calculus.

Compared to Johnsen *et al.* [4,9], we here present a slightly simplified version of virtually timed ambients which assumes a uniform speed for all ambients in the hierarchy. This simplification does not mean the ambients proceed uniformly with respect to time: the progress of an ambient still depends on its position in the hierarchy and the number of sibling ambients that compete for time slices at the given level. When discussing the reduction rules from Table 1 later, we provide further details on how the more general non-uniform setting relates to the presentation here. Since an ambient system can change its structure, i.e., its hierarchy, an ambient's local access to time slices may also dynamically change. Thus, the simplification by uniform speed is not conceptual, but it allows a simpler formulation of the type system by removing fractional representations of speed in scheduling and the resulting (easy but cumbersome) calculations.

Definition 1 (Virtually timed ambients). *The syntax of virtually timed ambients is as follows:*

$$P ::= \mathbf{0} \mid (\nu n)\, P \mid P \mid P \mid\ !C.P \ \mid C.P \mid n[P]$$
$$C ::= \mathbf{in}\, n \mid \mathbf{out}\, n \mid \mathbf{open}\, n \mid \mathbf{c}$$

The syntax is almost unchanged from that of standard mobile ambients (e.g., [5]); the only syntactic addition is an additional capability **c** explained below. In the sequel, we mostly omit the qualification "timed" or "virtually timed" when speaking about processes, capabilities, etc. Processes include the inactive process **0**, parallel composition $P \mid P$ and replication $!C.P$, the latter conceptually represents an unbounded parallel composition of a process, with capability C as "guard". The ν-binder or restriction operator, makes the name n local, as in the π-calculus, ambient calculus, and related formalisms. *Ambients* $n[P]$ are named processes. The standard mobile ambient *capabilities* **in**, **out**, and **open** allow a process to change the nested ambient structure by moving an ambient into or out of another ambient, or by dissolving an ambient altogether.

The additional capability **c** is specific for the virtually timed extension and abstractly represents the need of the process for a *resource* in order to continue its execution (i.e., **c** can be read as "consume"). Thus, the consume capability relates to resource cost in frameworks for cost analysis (e.g., [10, 11]). In our setting, the **c**-capabilities consume resources which can be thought of as time slices and which are governed by a scheduler. A scheduler is *local* to an ambient and its responsibility is to schedule resources to the processes directly contained in this ambient. Since ambients are nested, the scheduler also has to allocate time slices or resources to subambients, thereby delegating the allocation of time slices at the level of the subambients to their respective schedulers. To achieve a fair distribution of resources, the semantics adopts a simple round-based scheduling strategy. Intuitively, no process is served twice, unless all other processes that need resources at that level have been served at least once. This *round-based scheme* is slightly more refined in that the number of processes per ambient is not fixed as ambients may move inside the hierarchy and even dissolve.

To capture the outlined scheduling strategy in operational rules working on the syntax of ambients, we *augment* the grammar of Definition 1 with additional *run-time* syntax (highlighted below). When needed, we refer to the original syntax from Definition 1 as *static* syntax. The run-time syntax uses the notation $\widecheck{}$ to indicate that processes, including ambients, are *frozen* and $\overline{n}$ to denote either n or $\widecheck{n}$.

$$P ::= \mathbf{0} \mid (\nu n)\,P \mid P \mid P \mid {!}C.P \mid \textbf{tick?} \mid \textbf{tick!} \mid \overline{n}[P] \mid C.P$$
$$\overline{n} ::= n \mid \widecheck{n}$$
$$\gamma ::= \mathbf{c} \mid \widecheck{\mathbf{c}}$$
$$C ::= \textbf{in}\,n \mid \textbf{out}\,n \mid \textbf{open}\,n \mid \textbf{tick?} \mid \gamma$$

Frozen processes are not eligible for scheduling. For regular (non-ambient) processes, only processes prefixed by the consume capability **c** will be controlled in this way; other processes are unconditionally enabled. Consequently, we only need as additional run-time syntax $\widecheck{\mathbf{c}}$, capturing a deactivated resource capability. Similarly $\widecheck{n}[P]$ denotes a timed ambient which is not eligible for scheduling. Apart from scheduling, a frozen ambient $\widecheck{n}[P]$ is treated as any other ambient $n[P]$: the ordinary, untimed capabilities address ambients by their name without the additional scheduling annotation. Likewise, ν-binders and corresponding renaming and algebraic equivalences treat names $\widecheck{n}$ as identical to n. Unless explicitly mentioned, we assume in the following run-time syntax, i.e., P may contain occurrences of $\widecheck{n}$ and $\widecheck{\mathbf{c}}$. Time slices are denoted by ticks, and come in two forms **tick?** and **tick!**. We may think of the first form **tick?** as representing incoming ticks into an ambient, typically from the parent ambient, the second form **tick!** represents time slices handed out to the local processes by the local scheduler. The **tick?**-capability similarly accepts an incoming tick. Let *names*(P) denote the set of names for ambients contained in P.

Semantics. The semantics of virtually timed ambients is given as a *reduction* relation $P \twoheadrightarrow Q$ (see Tables 1 and 2). Processes are considered up-to structural congruence $P \equiv Q$ and reduction is defined modulo $\equiv$. The corresponding rule is omitted here, as is the standard axiomatization of $P \equiv Q$. We further omit the standard congruence rules (e.g., $P \twoheadrightarrow P' \Rightarrow \overline{n}[P] \twoheadrightarrow \overline{n}[P']$), which also correspond to those for mobile ambients. The rules in Table 1 (with rule names to the left) cover ambient reconfiguration. Apart from the annotations used for scheduling, the rules are exactly the ones for the (untimed) mobile ambients [5].

Table 1. Reduction rules (1). The symbol $\bar{m}$ occuring both on the left and the right side of a reduction rule represents either $\check{m}$ on both sides, or else m on both sides.

(R-In)	$\overline{n}[\mathbf{in}\ m.P_1 \mid P_2] \mid \overline{m}[Q] \twoheadrightarrow \overline{m}[Q \mid \check{n}[P_1 \mid P_2]]$
(R-Out)	$\overline{m}[\overline{n}[\mathbf{out}\ m.P_1 \mid P_2] \mid Q] \twoheadrightarrow \check{n}[P_1 \mid P_2] \mid \overline{m}[Q]$
(R-Open)	$\mathbf{open}\ n.P_1 \mid \overline{n}[P_2] \twoheadrightarrow P_1 \mid \check{P}_2$

Ambients can undergo restructuring in three different ways. First, an ambient can move horizontally or laterally by entering a sibling ambient (rule R-In). Second, it can move vertically up the tree, leaving its parent ambient (rule R-Out). Finally, a process can cause the dissolution of its surrounding ambient (rule R-Open). These forms of restructuring are *untimed* in that they incur no resource cost. If an ambient changes its place, the scheduler of the target ambient will, from that point on, become responsible for the new ambient, and the treatment is simple: Being frozen, the newcomer will not be served in the current round of the scheduler, but waits for the next round. Considering the source ambient (i.e., the ambient which contained the process executing the **out** or **in** capability), no process inside the source ambient looses or changes its status. A similar discipline is followed (for P_1) when opening an ambient in rule R-Open (the interpretation of $\widehat{P}_2$ as opposed to P_2 follows shortly). Note that a process in an ambient can execute a capability **in**, **out**, or **open** independent of the status of the affected ambient, which is indicated in the rules by $\overline{n}$ and $\overline{m}$.

Scheduling, in particular the handling of ticks and the resource capabilities, is covered by the reduction rules in Table 2. Scheduling ultimately means to discriminate and select between processes which are allowed to proceed at a given point, and those which are not. To capture that distinction in the rules, $\widehat{P}$ represents the former, i.e. P is eligible for a new time-slice ("unfrozen"). Dually, $\check{P}$ represents P after having been served ("frozen"). The exact formulation of the freeze and unfreeze operation will be given in Definition 3 below, after discussing the rules themselves. The first rule translates "incoming" ticks to ticks available for local processes. The translation ratio is uniform; i.e., one incoming tick produces one outgoing tick (this is the simplification compared to previous work mentioned earlier, where the ratio between incoming and local ticks could more generally be a rational number). A **tick!** process can be consumed in two ways. First by scheduling a **c**-prefixed process which undergoes the steps $c.P \twoheadrightarrow \textbf{tick?}.P \twoheadrightarrow \check{P}$ (consuming $\textbf{tick!}$ in the second step).[1] Second, by scheduling a subambient, such that an incoming tick $\textbf{tick?}$ occurs one level down in the hierarchy. To ensure the round-based scheduling, the scheduled entity must not have been served yet in the current round. For this purpose, the process before the transition must be of the form $\textbf{tick?}.P$ or $n[P]$, and after the transition the continuation of the process is frozen, using Definition 3. The last rule completes one scheduling round and initiates the next round by changing the ambient's processes P to $\hat{P}$. This unfreezing step can be done only if all the ambient's processes have been served, which is captured be the rule's negative premise, stipulating that no process at the level of n can proceed.

Table 2. Reduction rules (2)

$\textbf{tick?} \twoheadrightarrow \textbf{tick!}$	$\textbf{tick!} \mid \textbf{tick?}.P \twoheadrightarrow \check{P}$	$\dfrac{\text{not } P \text{ }_{\textbf{tick?}}}{\overline{n}[P] \twoheadrightarrow \overline{n}[\hat{P}]}$
$c.P \twoheadrightarrow \textbf{tick?}.P$	$\textbf{tick!} \mid n[P] \twoheadrightarrow \check{n}[\textbf{tick?} \mid P]$	

This inability to proceed by a tick-step at the end of a round is formulated using the notion of *observables,* also known as *barbs*. Barbs, originally introduced for the π-calculus [12], capture a notion of immediate observability. In the ambient calculus, these observations concern the presence of a top-level ambient whose name is not restricted [13]. In our context, the barbs are adapted to express *top-level* schedulability, i.e., an ambient's ability to receive a tick. Later, to formulate progress properties, we will additionally need to capture the same condition for t a sub-process deeper inside the system and not necessarily at top-level. For that, we denote by $\mathcal{C}[\cdot]$ (or simply by $\mathcal{C}$) a *context*, i.e., a process with a (unique) hole $[\cdot]$ in place of a process, and write $\mathcal{C}[P]$ for the context with its hole replaced by P (for the formal definition, see [13]). The observability predicates (or "tick-barbs") $\downarrow_{\textbf{tick?}}$ resp. $\downarrow^{\mathcal{C}}_{\textbf{tick?}}$ are then defined as follows, where $\tilde{m}$ is a tuple of names:

Definition 2 (Barbs). *A process P has a strong barb on $\textbf{tick?}$, written $P\downarrow_{\textbf{tick?}}$, if $P \equiv (\nu\tilde{m})(n[P_1] \mid P_2)$ or $P \equiv (\nu\tilde{m})(\textbf{tick?}.P_1 \mid P_2)$. A process P has a strong barb on $\textbf{tick?}$ in context $\mathcal{C}$, written $P\downarrow^{\mathcal{C}}_{\textbf{tick?}}$, if $P = \mathcal{C}[P']$ for some process P' with $P'\downarrow_{\textbf{tick?}}$.*

Note that the ambient name n may well be hidden, i.e., mentioned in $\tilde{m}$. Barbing on the ambient name n, written $P\downarrow_n$, would require that $P \equiv (\nu\tilde{m})(n[P_1] \mid P_2)$ where $n \notin \tilde{m}$, in contrast to the definition of $P\downarrow_{\textbf{tick?}}$. This more conventional notion of strong barbs [13] expresses that an ambient is available for interaction

---

[1] The rules and the calculus may be simplified, e.g., by avoiding the two-step behavior just described. The formulation here was chosen as it more aligned with versions of virtually timed ambients allowing non-uniform speeds across ambients, mentioned earlier in this section. Thus, the type system here would allow a more straightforward generalization to ambients with non-uniform speed.

with the standard ambient capabilities; ambients whose name is unknown are not available to be contacted by other ambients and therefore, their name is excluded in the observability predicate $\downarrow_n$. In contrast, strong barbs as defined in Definition 2 capture an ambient's ability to receive ticks and thus, the definition will allow hidden ambients to be served by the local scheduler. However, the name of the ambient must *not* be frozen $\check{n}$: ambients that have been served a tick in the current round are not eligible for another allocation before a new round has started, in which case the ambient's name has "changed" to n.

To complete the presentation of the semantics, we provide the operations used in the rules that allow processes to conceptually switch back and forth between waiting to be served in the current round, and having been served and thus waiting for the next round to begin.

Definition 3 (Freezing and unfreezing). *Let $\check{P}$ denote the process where all top-level occurrences of $n[Q]$ are replaced by $\check{n}[Q]$ and all top-level occurrences of c replaced by $\check{c}$. Conversely, let $\hat{P}$ denote the process where all top-level occurrences of $\check{c}$ are replaced by c and all top-level occurrences of $\check{n}[Q]$ replaced by $n[Q]$. Define $\check{P}$ by induction on the syntactic structure as follows:*

$$\widetilde{(\nu n)\,P} = (\nu n)\,\check{P} \qquad\qquad \check{\check{c}} = \check{c}$$
$$\widetilde{P_1 \mid P_2} = \widetilde{P_1} \mid \widetilde{P_2} \qquad\qquad \check{\check{c}} = \check{c}$$
$$\widetilde{n[P]} = \check{n}[P] \qquad\qquad \check{\check{n}} = \check{n}$$
$$\widetilde{\gamma.P} = \check{\gamma}.P \qquad\qquad \check{\check{n}} = \check{n}$$
$$\widetilde{C.P} = C.\check{P} \qquad C \neq \gamma$$
$$\check{P} = P \qquad\qquad otherwise$$

The definition of $\hat{P}$ is analogous (e.g., $\hat{\hat{c}} = c$) and omitted here.

Remark that the congruence relation, which is part of the reduction semantics, works with scheduling in the sense that both operations defined in Definition 3 are preserved under congruence: $P_1 \equiv P_2$ implies $\widetilde{P_1} \equiv \widetilde{P_2}$ and $\widehat{P_1} \equiv \widehat{P_2}$.

Example 1. Consider the process $cloud\,[\mathbf{0}] \mid vm[\mathbf{in}\ cloud.\mathbf{c}.\mathbf{0}]$. If we place this process in a context $root$ with one **tick**! process, three reduction steps become possible, as **tick**! can propagate to either ambients and ambient vm can move into $cloud$. One way this process can reduce, is as follows:

$root[\mathbf{tick}! \mid cloud\,[\mathbf{0}] \mid vm[\mathbf{in}\ cloud.\mathbf{c}.\mathbf{0}]] \twoheadrightarrow root[\mathbf{tick}! \mid cloud\,[\mathbf{0} \mid v\check{m}[\mathbf{c}.\mathbf{0}]]]$
$\twoheadrightarrow root[cl\check{o}ud\,[\mathbf{tick}? \mid \mathbf{0} \mid v\check{m}[\mathbf{c}.\mathbf{0}]]] \twoheadrightarrow root[cl\check{o}ud\,[\mathbf{tick}! \mid \mathbf{0} \mid vm[\mathbf{c}.\mathbf{0}]]]$
$\twoheadrightarrow root[cl\check{o}ud\,[\mathbf{0} \mid v\check{m}[\mathbf{tick}? \mid \mathbf{c}.\mathbf{0}]]] \twoheadrightarrow root[cl\check{o}ud\,[\mathbf{0} \mid v\check{m}[\mathbf{tick}! \mid \mathbf{c}.\mathbf{0}]]]$
$\twoheadrightarrow root[cl\check{o}ud\,[\mathbf{0} \mid v\check{m}[\mathbf{tick}! \mid \mathbf{tick}?.\mathbf{0}]]] \twoheadrightarrow root[cl\check{o}ud\,[\mathbf{0} \mid v\check{m}[\mathbf{0}]]].$

However, the time slice could also enter the ambient vm, and move with this ambient, resulting in a reduction sequence starting as follows:

$root[\mathbf{tick}! \mid cloud\,[\mathbf{0}] \mid vm[\mathbf{in}\ cloud.\mathbf{c}.\mathbf{0}]]$
$\twoheadrightarrow root[cloud\,[\mathbf{0}] \mid v\check{m}[\mathbf{tick}? \mid \mathbf{in}\ cloud.\mathbf{c}.\mathbf{0}]]$
$\twoheadrightarrow root[cloud\,[\mathbf{0} \mid v\check{m}[\mathbf{tick}? \mid \mathbf{c}.\mathbf{0}]]] \twoheadrightarrow \dots$

Generally, a process P will be placed in a runtime environment which provisions it with a given amount of resources (e.g., *root* in Example 1 with one **tick**!). When executed in a surrounding ambient without enough resources, some sub-process of P may not receive a sufficient number of resources and may get "stuck". This inability to progress for lack of resources can be captured by (contextually) having a barb on an irreducible process: $P \not\rightarrow$ and $P \downarrow^C_{\mathbf{tick?}}$ for some C, i.e., P cannot proceed despite the fact that there is a sub-process that could proceed by consuming a resource, if one were still available. This intuition is used to formulate progress (Theorem 2), stipulating that well-typed processes will not get stuck.

3   An Assumption-Commitment Type System

We consider a type system which analyzes the timed behavior of virtually timed ambients in terms of the movement and resource consumption of a given process. Statically estimating the timed behavior is complicated because the placement of an ambient in the process hierarchy influences its resource consumption, and movements inside the hierarchy change the relative speed of the ambients. The proposed type system is loosely based on Cardelli, Ghelli, and Gordon's movement control types for mobile ambients [14]; however, its purpose is quite different, and therefore the technical formulation will be rather different as well.

Types and Typing Contexts. Processes will be typed with respect to nominal resource contracts for virtually timed ambients, which are tuples of the form

$$T = \langle cap, bnd, tkn \rangle.$$

Here, $cap \in \mathbb{N}$ specifies the ambient's *resource capacity*, i.e., the upper bound on the number of resources that the subprocesses of the ambient are allowed to require; $bnd \in \mathbb{N}$ specifies the ambient's *hosting capacity*, i.e., the upper bound on the number of timed subambients and timed processes allowed inside this ambient; and $tkn \in \mathbb{N}$ specifies the ambient's *currently hosted processes*, i.e., the number of taken slots within the ambient's hosting capacity. The number of currently hosted processes inside an ambient can change dynamically, due to the movements of ambients. These changes must be captured in the type system. In this sense, a type for ambient names T contains an accumulated effect mapping.

Typing *environments* or contexts associate ambient names with resource contracts. They are finite lists of associations of the form $n : T$. In the type system, when analyzing an ambient or process, a typing environment will play a role as an *assumption*, expressing requirements about the ambients *outside* the current process. Dually, facts about ambients which are part of the current process are captured in another typing environment which plays the role of a *commitment*. Notationally, we use Γ for assumption and Δ for commitment environments. We write $\varnothing$ for the empty environment, and $\Gamma, n : T$ for the extension of Γ by a new binding $n : T$. We assume that ambient names n are unique in environments, so n is not already bound in Γ. Conversely, $\Gamma \backslash n : T$ represents an environment coinciding with Γ except that the binding for n is removed. If n is not declared in Γ, the removal has no effect. The typing judgment for names is given as $\Gamma \vdash n : T$. Since each name occurs at most once, an environment Γ can be seen as a finite mapping; we use $\Gamma(n)$ to denote the ambient type associated with n in Γ and write $dom(\Gamma)$ for all names bound in Γ. In the typing rules, the typing environment Γ may need to capture the ambient in which the current process resides; this ambient will conventionally be denoted by the *reserved name* **this**.

We now define domain equivalence, context addition, error-free environments, and an ordering relation on types and environments to capture subtyping.

Definition 4 (Domain equivalence). *Two contexts Γ_1 and Γ_2 are* domain equivalent, *denoted $\Gamma_1 \sim \Gamma_2$, iff $dom(\Gamma_1) = dom(\Gamma_2)$.*

Definition 5 (Additivity of contexts). *Let Γ_1 and Γ_2 be contexts such that $\Gamma_1 \sim \Gamma_2$, and $\Gamma_i(n) = \langle cap, bnd, tkn_i \rangle$ for $n \in dom(\Gamma_1)$ and $i = 1, 2$. The context $\Gamma_1 \oplus \Gamma_2$ with domain $dom(\Gamma_1)$ is defined as follows: for $n \in dom(\Gamma_1)$*

$$(\Gamma_1 \oplus \Gamma_2)(n) = \langle cap, bnd, tkn_1 + tkn_2 \rangle.$$

If the number of currently hosted ambients is smaller than the hosting capacity of all ambients in an environment, we say that the environment is error-free:

Definition 6. (Error-free environments) *An environment Γ is* error-free, *denoted $\vdash \Gamma : \mathbf{ok}$ if $tkn \leq bnd$ for all $n \in dom(\Gamma)$ and $\Gamma(n) = \langle cap, bnd, tkn \rangle$.*

Resource contracts can be ordered by their contents and environments by their resource contracts. The bottom type $\bot$ is a subtype of all resource contracts.

Definition 7 (Ordering of resource contracts and environments). *Let $T_1 = \langle cap_1, bnd_1, tkn_1 \rangle$ and $T_2 = \langle cap_2, bnd_2, tkn_2 \rangle$ be resource contracts. Then T_1 is a subtype of T_2, written $T_1 \leq T_2$, if and only if $cap_1 \leq cap_2$, $bnd_1 \leq bnd_2$ and $tkn_1 \geq tkn_2$. Typing environments Γ_1 and Γ_2 are ordered by the subtype relation as follows: $\Gamma_1 \sqsubseteq \Gamma_2$ if and only if $dom(\Gamma_1) \subseteq dom(\Gamma_2)$ and $\Gamma_1(n) \leq \Gamma_2(n)$, for all $n \in dom(\Gamma_1)$.*

Typing Judgments. A typing judgment for a process P has the form

$$\Gamma; req \vdash P : \mathbf{ok}\langle prov, subs \rangle; \Delta$$

where *req* and *prov* are the required and provided resources for P, *subs* is the number of subambients of P, and Γ and Δ are the assumptions and commitments of P, respectively. Scheduling is reflected in the type rules by the calculation of the required resources *req*, which capture the number of resources a process will need to make progress. We call *req* the *coeffect* of the process. Coeffects [7,8] capture how a computation depends on an environment rather than how it affects this environment. We use the perspective of coeffects since a computation may require resources from its environment to terminate. Similarly, *prov* is the number of provided resources in P; these resources are available in P independent of its environment, and *subs* approximates the number of subambients in P. We may think of $\langle prov, subs \rangle$ as the *effect* of the typing judgment, where effects express what the process P potentially provides to its environment.

For each process, the domain of the assumptions is assumed to contain all names which are not in the domain of the commitments; i.e., for two parallel processes P_1 and P_2 such that $\Gamma_1; req_1 \vdash P_1 : \mathbf{ok}\langle prov_1, subs_1 \rangle; \Delta_1$ and $\Gamma_2; req_2 \vdash P_2 : \mathbf{ok}\langle prov_2, subs_2 \rangle; \Delta_2$, we will have that $\Delta_2 \subseteq \Gamma_1$, $\Delta_1 \subseteq \Gamma_2$ and $dom(\Delta_1) \cap dom(\Delta_2) = \varnothing$. Since ambient names are assumed to be unique, it follows for type judgments that $dom(\Delta) \cap dom(\Gamma) = \varnothing$, as an ambient is either inside the process and has its contract in the commitments, or outside and has its contract in the assumptions. Further, $dom(\Delta) \subseteq names(P)$.

In Table 3, Rule T-ZERO types the inactive process, which does not require nor provide any time slices. Rule T-TICK1 expresses the availability of **tick!** and Rule T-TICK2 that a time slice **tick?** is ready to be consumed. Both judgments express that a time slice is provided without requiring any time slice. The assumption rule T-ASS types an ambient with the resource contract it has in the environment. The restriction rule T-RES removes the resource contract assumption in the environment for the restricted name. Subsumption relates different resource contracts; e.g., in subtypes (T-TSUB), the subsumption rule T-SUB allows a higher number of required resources, a lower number of provided resources and a higher number of subambients to be assumed in a process.

For the typing of ambients in Rule T-AMB, the reserved name **this** is used to denote the *current environment* of P in the premise of the rule; the assumed typing of **this** becomes the typing of n in the commitment of the conclusion. Note that the required resources in the co-effect of the premise may be smaller than the *bnd* of the contract; for example, n may already have received the time slices *prov*. Furthermore, the number of resources a process P requires changes if it becomes enclosed in an ambient n; i.e., we move to the resource contract T of n, provided the process P satisfies its part of the contract.

The parallel composition rule T-PAR makes use of the fairness of the scheduling of time slices in virtually timed ambients. While the branches agree on the required resources *req*, the provided resources and subambients accumulate. It follows from T-PAR that several ambients in parallel will at most need as many resources *req* from the parent ambient as the slowest of them. Furthermore, T-PAR changes assumptions and commitments depending on the assumptions and the commitments of the composed processes, using the context composition operator from Definition 5 to compose environments. We have $dom(\Delta_P) \cap dom(\Delta_Q) = \varnothing$, which is a consequence of the uniqueness of ambient names. The assumptions of the branches split the resource contracts of the environment Γ between the type judgments for P_1 and P_2 and the commitments split such that Δ_1' is the assumption for P_1 and vice versa. The replication rule T-REP imposes the restriction that the process being replicated does not incur any cost; allowing that would amount to an unbounded resource need, which cannot be provisioned in a setting with a finite amount of resources.

Table 3. Type rules for the virtually timed ambients.

$$\frac{}{\varnothing;\, 0 \vdash \mathbf{0} : \mathbf{ok}\langle 0,0\rangle;\, \varnothing} \; \text{(T-Zero)} \qquad \frac{}{\varnothing;\, 0 \vdash \mathbf{tick?} : \mathbf{ok}\langle 1,0\rangle;\, \varnothing} \; \text{(T-Tick1)} \qquad \frac{}{\varnothing;\, 0 \vdash \mathbf{tick!} : \mathbf{ok}\langle 1,0\rangle;\, \varnothing} \; \text{(T-Tick2)}$$

(T-Ass)
$$\frac{\Gamma(n) = T}{\Gamma \vdash n : T}$$

(T-Res)
$$\frac{\Gamma, k : T;\, req \vdash P : \mathbf{ok}\langle prov, subs\rangle;\, \Delta}{\Gamma;\, req \vdash (\nu k : T)P : \mathbf{ok}\langle prov, subs\rangle;\, \Delta}$$

(T-Tsub)
$$\frac{\Gamma \vdash n : T_1 \qquad T_1 \leqslant T_2}{\Gamma \vdash n : T_2}$$

(T-Amb)
$$\frac{\begin{array}{c} T'=\langle cap, bnd, tkn+subs\rangle \quad req \times bnd \leqslant cap+prov \\ tkn+subs \leqslant bnd \quad \Gamma';\, req \vdash P : \mathbf{ok}\langle prov, subs\rangle;\, \Delta \\ \Gamma' = \Gamma, n{:}\langle cap, bnd, tkn\rangle, \mathbf{this}{:}\langle cap, bnd, tkn\rangle \end{array}}{\Gamma;\, cap \vdash \bar{n}[P] : \mathbf{ok}\langle 0, bnd + 1\rangle;\, n{:}T', \Delta}$$

(T-Sub)
$$\frac{\begin{array}{c} req' \leqslant req \quad prov \leqslant prov' \\ \Gamma' \subseteq \Gamma \quad \Delta \subseteq \Delta' \quad subs' \leqslant subs \\ \Gamma';\, req' \vdash P : \mathbf{ok}\langle prov', subs'\rangle;\, \Delta' \end{array}}{\Gamma;\, req \vdash P : \mathbf{ok}\langle prov, subs\rangle;\, \Delta}$$

(T-Par)
$$\frac{\begin{array}{c} \Delta_1 \sim \Delta_1' \qquad \Delta_2 \sim \Delta_2' \qquad \vdash \Gamma : \mathbf{ok} \qquad \vdash \Delta : \mathbf{ok} \\ \Gamma = \Gamma_1 \oplus \Gamma_2 \qquad \Gamma_1 \sim \Gamma_2 \qquad \Gamma_1, \Delta_2';\, req \vdash P_1 : \mathbf{ok}\langle prov_1, subs_1\rangle;\, \Delta_1 \\ \Delta = (\Delta_1 \oplus \Delta_1'), (\Delta_2 \oplus \Delta_2') \qquad \Gamma_2, \Delta_1';\, req \vdash P_2 : \mathbf{ok}\langle prov_2, subs_2\rangle;\, \Delta_2 \end{array}}{\Gamma;\, req \vdash P_1 \mid P_2 : \mathbf{ok}\langle prov_1 + prov_2, subs_1 + subs_2\rangle;\, \Delta}$$

(T-Consume1)
$$\frac{subs' = \max\{subs, 1\} \qquad \Gamma;\, req \vdash P : \mathbf{ok}\langle prov, subs\rangle, \Delta}{\Gamma;\, req + 1 \vdash \mathbf{c}.P : \mathbf{ok}\langle prov, subs'\rangle, \Delta}$$

(T-Consume2)
$$\frac{subs' = \max\{subs, 1\} \qquad \Gamma;\, req \vdash P : \mathbf{ok}\langle prov, subs\rangle, \Delta}{\Gamma;\, req + 1 \vdash \mathbf{tick?}.P : \mathbf{ok}\langle prov, subs'\rangle, \Delta}$$

(T-In)
$$\frac{\begin{array}{c} T = \langle cap, bnd, tkn\rangle \qquad T' = \langle cap, bnd, tkn + bnd' + 1\rangle \\ \Gamma, m{:}T;\, req \vdash P : \mathbf{ok}\langle prov, subs\rangle, \Delta \qquad bnd \times req \leqslant cap \\ \Gamma \vdash \mathbf{this} : \langle cap', bnd', tkn'\rangle \qquad tkn + bnd' + 1 \leqslant bnd \end{array}}{\Gamma, m{:}T';\, req \vdash \mathbf{in}\, m.P : \mathbf{ok}\langle prov, subs\rangle;\, \Delta}$$

(T-Rep)
$$\frac{\Gamma;\, 0 \vdash P : \mathbf{ok}\langle 0, 0\rangle, \Delta_P \qquad C \in \{\mathbf{in}\, n, \mathbf{out}\, n, \mathbf{open}\, n\}}{\Gamma;\, 0 \vdash !C.P : \mathbf{ok}\langle 0, 0\rangle, \Delta_P}$$

(T-Out)
$$\frac{\Gamma;\, req \vdash P : \mathbf{ok}\langle prov, subs\rangle, \Delta}{\Gamma;\, req \vdash \mathbf{out}\, m.P : \mathbf{ok}\langle prov, subs\rangle, \Delta}$$

(T-Open)
$$\frac{\Gamma;\, req \vdash P : \mathbf{ok}\langle prov, subs\rangle, \Delta}{\Gamma;\, req \vdash \mathbf{open}\, m.P : \mathbf{ok}\langle prov, subs\rangle, \Delta}$$

Now consider the capability rules. In T-Consume, the resource consumption is a requirement to the environment, expressed by increasing the coeffect to $req + 1$. Since the process requires a time slice, it is counted among the currently hosted processes. If it was already counted as a timed process, $subs$ remains unchanged, but since it could have been untimed, we let $subs' = \max\{subs, 1\}$.

Rule T-In derives an assumption about ambient m under which the movement $\mathbf{in}\,m.P$ can be typed. Since the movement involves all processes co-located with $\mathbf{in}\,m.P$, the rule depends on the resource contract of $\mathbf{this}$, the ambient in which the current process is located. The rule has a premise expressing that if P can be typed with a resource contract T for m, then $\mathbf{in}\,m.P$ can be typed with the resource contract T' for m. In addition, the hosting capacity bnd' of $\mathbf{this}$ and $\mathbf{this}$ itself are added to the assumed currently hosted processes tkn of the premise. The premise $bnd \times req \leqslant cap$ expresses that the required resources req must be within the resource capacity cap if scheduled to all processes within the hosting capacity bnd of m. The effect and co-effect carry over directly from the premise, as the movement does not modify the required or provided resources or subambients of P. In contrast, rules T-Open and T-Out simply preserve the co-effect and effect of its premise, since the actual movement is captured by the worst-case assumption in T-Amb.

Example 2 (Typing of in-capabilities). We revisit Example 1 to illustrate the typing of $cloud\,[\mathbf{0}] \mid vm[\mathbf{in}\,cloud.\mathbf{c}.\mathbf{0}]$. From T-Zero and T-Consume1, we get $\varnothing; 1 \vdash \mathbf{c}.\mathbf{0} : \mathbf{ok}\langle 0,1\rangle; \varnothing$. The $\mathbf{in}$-capability will move the ambient containing this process, which is captured by $\mathbf{this}$ in the typing environment. Let us type $\mathbf{this}$ by $T = \langle 1,1,1\rangle$. In this case $cloud$ will need a hosting capacity of at least 2, so let us type $cloud$ by $T' = \langle 2,2,2\rangle$. Then, from T-In, we get

$$cloud : T', \mathbf{this} : T; 1 \vdash \mathbf{in}\,cloud.\mathbf{c}.\mathbf{0} : \mathbf{ok}\langle 0,1\rangle; \varnothing.$$

By T-Amb, we get $cloud : T'; 1 \vdash vm[\mathbf{in}\ cloud.\mathbf{c}.\mathbf{0}] : \mathbf{ok}\langle 0,2\rangle; vm : T$. Similarly, $\varnothing; 2 \vdash cloud\,[\mathbf{0}] : \mathbf{ok}\langle 0,1\rangle; cloud : \langle 2,2,0\rangle$ and T-Par gives us

$$\varnothing; 2 \vdash cloud\,[\mathbf{0}] \mid vm[\mathbf{in}\,cloud.\mathbf{c}.\mathbf{0}] : \mathbf{ok}\langle 0,3\rangle; vm : T, cloud : T';$$

Example 3 (Typing of open-capabilities). We consider the typing of a process $cloud\,[\mathbf{open}\ vm.\mathbf{0} \mid vm[\mathbf{c}.\mathbf{0}]]$. From T-Zero and T-Consume, we get $\varnothing; 1 \vdash \mathbf{c}.\mathbf{0} : \mathbf{ok}\langle 0,1\rangle; \varnothing$. Let vm have type $T = \langle 1,1,1\rangle$. Then, by T-Amb,

$$\varnothing; 1 \vdash vm[\mathbf{c}.\mathbf{0}] : \mathbf{ok}\langle 0,2\rangle; vm : T.$$

By T-Zero, T-Open and T-Sub, we have $\varnothing; 1 \vdash \mathbf{open}\ vm.\mathbf{0} : \mathbf{ok}\langle 0,0\rangle; \varnothing$. By T-Par, we obtain $\varnothing; 1 \vdash \mathbf{open}\ vm.\mathbf{0} \mid vm[\mathbf{c}.\mathbf{0}] : \mathbf{ok}\langle 0,2\rangle; vm : T$. Let $cloud$ have type $T' = \langle 2,2,2\rangle$. By T-Amb, we get

$$\varnothing; 2 \vdash cloud\,[\mathbf{open}\ vm.\mathbf{0} \mid vm[\mathbf{c}.\mathbf{0}]] : \mathbf{ok}\langle 0,3\rangle; vm : T, cloud : T'.$$

Example 4 (Typing of out-capabilities). We consider the typing of a process

$$cloud[vm[\mathbf{out}\ cloud.\mathbf{c}.\mathbf{0}] \mid \mathbf{0}]$$

By T-Zero and T-Consume, we have $\varnothing; 1 \vdash \mathbf{c}.\mathbf{0} : \mathbf{ok}\langle 0,1\rangle; \varnothing$, and by T-Out we get

$$\varnothing; 1 \vdash \mathbf{out}\ cloud.\mathbf{c}.\mathbf{0} : \mathbf{ok}\langle 0,1\rangle; \varnothing$$

Let $T = \langle 1, 1, 1 \rangle$. We can type vm by

$$\varnothing; 1 \vdash vm[\textbf{out } cloud.\textbf{c}.\textbf{0}] : \textbf{ok}\langle 0, 2 \rangle; vm : T$$

and, with $T' = \langle 2, 2, 2 \rangle$, we get

$$\varnothing; 2 \vdash cloud[vm[\textbf{out } cloud.\textbf{c}.\textbf{0}] \mid \textbf{0}] : \textbf{ok}\langle 0, 3 \rangle; vm : T, cloud : T'$$

Example 5 (Failure of type checking). Type checking fails if the provisioning of resources for an incoming ambient in a timely way cannot be statically guaranteed. This can occur for different reasons. One reason is that an ambient may lack *sufficient hosting capacity* to take in the processes that want to enter. Let $T' = \langle 2, 2, 2 \rangle$ as before and consider again the process $cloud[\textbf{0}] \mid vm[\textbf{in } cloud.\textbf{c}.\textbf{0}]$ from Example 2. Now assume a second virtual machine $vm_2[\textbf{in } cloud.\textbf{c}.\textbf{0}]$ which aims to enter the *cloud* ambient, resulting in the parallel process

$$cloud[\textbf{0}] \mid vm[\textbf{in } cloud.\textbf{c}.\textbf{0}] \mid vm_2[\textbf{in } cloud.\textbf{c}.\textbf{0}]$$

We can type vm_2 similarly to vm in Example 2.:

$$cloud : T'; 1 \vdash vm_2[\textbf{in } cloud.\textbf{c}.\textbf{0}] : \textbf{ok}\langle 0, 2 \rangle; vm_2 : T.$$

In contrast to Example 2, the hosting capacity for *cloud* in T' cannot accommodate both vm and vm_2; type checking fails when giving *cloud* the resource contract T'. (Remark that type checking would succeed if *cloud* get more resources, e.g., the resource contract $\langle 4, 4, 4 \rangle$.)

Another reason is that the resource contract of *cloud* may have a *too low resource capacity*. Consider a third virtual machine $vm_3[\textbf{in } cloud.\textbf{c}.\textbf{c}.\textbf{c}.\textbf{0}]$ which can be typed with the resource contract $\langle 3, 1, 1 \rangle$ for vm_3. Again, type checking $cloud[\textbf{0}] \mid vm_3[\textbf{in } cloud.\textbf{c}.\textbf{c}.\textbf{c}.\textbf{0}]$ fails if *cloud* were given the resource contract T', since the resource capacity of *cloud* must here be at least 6 with hosting capacity 2. (Here, *cloud* would need a resource contract such as $\langle 6, 2, 2 \rangle$ for the expression to be well-typed.)

Example 6 (Capacity of an ambient). Assume that the process

$$n_1[\textbf{in } m.P_1] \mid n_2[\textbf{in } m.P_2] \mid m[Q]$$

is well-typed. Let resource contracts $T_1 = \langle cap, bnd, tkn_1 \rangle$, $T_2 = \langle cap, bnd, tkn_2 \rangle$ and $T_3 = \langle cap, bnd, tkn_3 \rangle$ be such that

$$m : T_i; req_i \vdash n_i[\textbf{in } m.P_i] : \textbf{ok}\langle prov_i, subs_i \rangle; \Delta_i$$

for $i \in \{1, 2\}$, and $\varnothing; req_3 \vdash m[Q] : \textbf{ok}\langle prov_3, subs_3 \rangle; m : T_3$. Now let $r_{12} = \max(r_1, r_2)$ and $T_{12} = \langle cap, bnd, tkn_1 \oplus tkn_2 \rangle$. Since $n_1[\textbf{in } m.P_1] \mid n_2[\textbf{in } m.P_2]$ is well-typed, we have $tkn_1 \oplus tkn_2 \leqslant bnd$ and, by T-PAR,

$$m : T_{12}; req_{12} \vdash n_1[\textbf{in } m.P_1] \mid n_2[\textbf{in } m.P_2] : \textbf{ok}\langle prov_{12}, subs_{12} \rangle; \Delta_{12}$$

where $prov_{12} = prov_1 + prov_2$, $subs_{12} = subs_1 + subs_2$ and $\Delta = \Delta_1, \Delta_2$. By applying T-PAR again, we get

$$\varnothing; req \vdash n_1[\textbf{in } m.P_1] \mid n_2[\textbf{in } m.P_2] \mid m[Q] : \textbf{ok}\langle prov, subs \rangle; m : T, \Delta$$

where $req = \max\{req_{12}, req_3\}$, $prov = prov_{12} + prov_3$, $subs = subs_{12} + subs_3$ and $T = \langle cap, bnd, tkn_{12} + tkn_3 \rangle$. Thus, the weakest resource contract which types m and allows both n_1 and n_2 to enter, will have $bnd = tkn_{12} + tkn_3$ and $cap = bnd \times req$.

4   Soundness of Resource Management

The soundness of resource management can be perceived similarly to that of message exchange [14]. We prove a subject reduction theorem, stating that the number of resources required for a boxed process to make progress is preserved under reduction.

Theorem 1 (Subject Reduction).   *Assume $\Gamma, req \vdash n[P] : \textbf{ok}\langle prov, subs \rangle; \Delta$ and $n[P] \twoheadrightarrow n[Q]$, then there are environments $\Gamma' \leqslant \Gamma$ and $\Delta' \leqslant \Delta$ such that $\Gamma', req' \vdash n[Q] : \textbf{ok}\langle prov', subs' \rangle; \Delta'$ and $req' \leqslant req$ or $req' = req \wedge prov' \geqslant prov$.*

Proof. By induction on the derivation of $n[P] \twoheadrightarrow n[Q]$.   □

Further, we prove a progress theorem, which shows that a well-typed boxed process which receives the approximated number of resources from its environment will not get stuck due to missing resources. Obviously, a well-typed process may be non-progressing due to other reasons. For instance, the terminated process **0** cannot "proceed" no matter how many ticks it may be served. To characterize a situation where inside the process, there is a sub-process in need of a tick to proceed, be it an unserved ambient or a process guarded by a **tick**?-capability, we use the contextual variant of barbs from Definition 2.

Theorem 2 (Tick progress).   *Assume $\Gamma; req \vdash P : \textbf{ok}\langle prov, subs \rangle; \Delta$ where $P = m[R]$, and let $Q = \bar{n}[P \mid \textbf{tick}! \mid \ldots \mid \textbf{tick}!]$, where P is running in parallel with req occurrences of $\textbf{tick}!$ inside some enclosing ambient. If $Q \downarrow_{\textbf{tick}?}^{\mathcal{C}}$ for some context $\mathcal{C}$, then $Q \twoheadrightarrow Q'$ for some process Q'.*

Proof sketch. This follows from the definition of the typing rules. If P contains the subprocess $\textbf{c}.P'$ it follows from the typing rule for the consume capability that $req \geqslant 1$. From the other typing rules it the number of resources is sufficient to trigger the reduction $\textbf{c}.P' \twoheadrightarrow P'$. Thus, Q can reduce to Q'.   □

With the properties of subject reduction and progress the type system guarantees the soundness of resource management.

Corollary 1 (Soundness).   *The type system guarantees the soundness of resource management, i.e., the transitive closure of the progress result holds.*

5   Related Work

We first discuss related work on modeling virtualization, time and resources, mainly focusing on process algebra, and then related work on type systems.

The calculus presented here differs from Stumpf *et al*'s original work on virtually timed ambients [4,9] by assuming uniform time and by the use of freezing and unfreezing operations, which allow a significantly simpler formulation of the calculus. The behavior of the original calculus, with non-uniform time, can be recaptured by modifying the rule **tick**? $\rightarrow$ **tick**! to cater for different numbers of input and output ticks, and to contextualize the rule for specific ambients. Stumpf *et al.* provide more elaborate examples of how aspects of virtualization (such as scaling and load balancing) can be modeled in virtually timed ambients (e.g., [4,9]). For the original calculus of virtually timed ambients, a modal logic with somewhere and sometime modalities [15] captures aspects of reachability for these ambients. Whereas this work can express more complex properties of a given process than the contract-based types in our paper, the logic cannot capture properties for all processes, in contrast to our work.

Gordon proposed a simple formalism for virtualization loosely based on mobile ambients [16]. Virtually timed ambients [4] stay closer to the syntax of the original ambient calculus, while including notions of time and resources. This model of resources as processing capacity over time builds on deployment components [17,18], a modeling abstraction for cloud computing in ABS [19]. Compared to virtually timed ambients, ABS does not support nested deployment components nor the timed capabilities of ambients.

Timers have been studied both for the distributed π-calculus [20,21] and mobile ambients (e.g., [22]) to express the possibility of a timeout, controlled by a global clock. In membrane computing, rule execution similarly takes exactly one time unit, as given by a global clock [23]. Timed P systems [24] overcome this restriction by associating with each rule an integer representing the time needed to complete its execution. This resembles the timer approach on mobile ambients [22]. In contrast, schedulers in virtually timed ambients recursively control the execution power of the nested location structure. Modeling timeouts is a straightforward extension of virtually timed ambients.

The process algebra ACSR [25] features resources as primitives. In contrast to the **c**-capability in virtually timed ambients, ACSR uses a set of consume actions with a priority relation, which can be used to encode, e.g., scheduling policies. PADS [26] extends ACSR with hierarchical approaches to scheduling, making the provisioning of resources explicit and introducing refinement relations on supply and demand. PARS [27] similarly uses explicit resource provisioning to specify that process needs, e.g., one processor and 100 units of memory for a given duration. Neither of these calculi combine resources with locations and mobility. The Kell calculus [28] supports mobility, inspired by mobile ambients, through higher order communication, but does not model resource provisioning. Whereas Kell has a type system to enforce the uniqueness of names [28], none of these calculi provide contract-based abstractions for resource analyses such as our type system for resource contracts.

A type system for the ambient calculus was defined in [14] to control communication and mobility. For communication, a basic ambient type captures the kind of messages that can be exchanged within. For mobility, the type system controls which ambients can enter. Types are often enriched with effects to capture the aspects of computation which are not purely functional. In process algebra, session types have been used to capture communication in the π-calculus [29]. Orchard and Yoshida have shown that effects and session types are similar concepts as they can be expressed in terms of each other [30]. Session types have been defined for boxed ambients in [31] and behavioral effects for the ambient calculus in [32], where the original communication types by Cardelli and Gordon are enhanced by movement behavior. This is captured with traces, the flow-sensitivity hereby results from the copying of the capabilities in the type. Type-based resource control for resources in the form of locks has been proposed for process algebras in general [33] and for the π-calculus in particular [34,35].

The idea of assumptions and commitments (or relies and guarantees) is quite old, but has mainly been explored for specification and compositional reasoning about concurrent or parallel processes (e.g., [36–38]). Assumption commitment style type systems have previously been used for multi-threaded concurrency [39, 40]; the resources controlled by the effect-type system there are locks and a general form of futures, in contrast to our work.

To capture how a computation depends on an environment instead of how the computation affects it, Petricek, Orchard and Mycroft suggest the term *coeffect* as a notion of *context-dependent* computation [7,8]. Dual to effects, which can be modeled monadically, the semantics of coeffects is provided by indexed comonads [41,42]. We use coeffects to control time and resources. An approach to control timing via types can be found in [43], which develops types and typed timers for the timed π-calculus. Another approach to resource control without coeffects can be found in [44], which proposes a type system to restrict resource access for the distributed π-calculus. In [45] a type system for resource control for a fragment of the mobile ambients is defined by adding capacity and weight to communication types for controlled ambients. Simplified non-modifiable mobile ambients with resources, and types to control migration and resource distribution are proposed in [46]. Another fragment of the ambient calculus, finite control ambients with only finite parallel composition, are covered in [47]. Here the types are a bound to the number of allowed active outputs in an ambient.

6   Concluding Remarks

Virtualization opens for new and interesting models of computation by explicitly emphasizing deployment and resource management. This paper introduces a type system based on resource contracts for virtually timed ambients, a calculus of hierarchical locations of execution with explicit resource provisioning. Resource provisioning in this calculus is based on virtual time, a local notion of time reminiscent of time slices provisioned by operating systems in the context of nested virtualization. The proposed assumption-commitment type system with effects and coeffects enables static checking of timing and resource constraints for ambients and gives an upper bound on the resources used by a process. The type system supports subsumption, which allows relating subtypes to supertypes. We show that the proposed type system is sound in terms of subject reduction and a progress property. Although these are core properties for type systems, the results are here given for a non-standard assumption-commitment setting in an operational framework. The type system further provides reusable properties as it supports abstraction and the results would also hold for other operational accounts of fair resource distribution. The challenge of how to further generalize the distribution strategy and type system for, e.g., earliest deadline first or priority-based scheduling policies, remains.

The virtually timed ambients used for the models in this paper extend the basic ambient calculus without channel communication. Introducing channels would lead to additional synchronization, which could potentially be exploited to derive more precise estimations about resource consumption. Such an extension would be non-trivial as the analysis of the communication structure would interfere with scheduling.

References

1. Goldberg, R.P.: Survey of virtual machine research. IEEE Comput. **7**(6), 34–45 (1974)
2. Ben-Yehuda, M., et al.: The turtles project: design and implementation of nested virtualization. In: Proceedings 9th USENIX Symposium on Operating Systems Design and Implementation (OSDI 2010), pp. 423–436. USENIX Association (2010)
3. Williams, D., Jamjoom, H., Weatherspoon, H.: The Xen-Blanket: virtualize once, run everywhere. In: Proceedings 7th European Conference on Computer Systems (EuroSys 2012), pp. 113–126. ACM (2012)
4. Johnsen, E.B., Steffen, M., Stumpf, J.B.: A calculus of virtually timed ambients. In: James, P., Roggenbach, M. (eds.) WADT 2016. LNCS, vol. 10644, pp. 88–103. Springer, Cham (2017). https://doi.org/10.1007/978-3-319-72044-9_7
5. Cardelli, L., Gordon, A.D.: Mobile ambients. Theoret. Comput. Sci. **240**(1), 177–213 (2000)
6. Giovannetti, E.: Ambient calculi with types: a tutorial. In: Priami, C. (ed.) GC 2003. LNCS, vol. 2874, pp. 151–191. Springer, Heidelberg (2003). https://doi.org/10.1007/978-3-540-40042-4_5
7. Petricek, T., Orchard, D., Mycroft, A.: Coeffects: a calculus of context-dependent computation. In: Jeuring, J., Chakravarty, M.M.T. (eds.) Proceedings of the International Conference on Functional Programming (ICFP 2014). ACM (2014)
8. Petricek, T., Orchard, D., Mycroft, A.: Coeffects: unified static analysis of context-dependence. In: Fomin, F.V., Freivalds, R., Kwiatkowska, M., Peleg, D. (eds.) ICALP 2013. LNCS, vol. 7966, pp. 385–397. Springer, Heidelberg (2013). https://doi.org/10.1007/978-3-642-39212-2_35
9. Johnsen, E.B., Steffen, M., Stumpf, J.B.: Virtually timed ambients: a calculus of nested virtualization. J. Log. Algebraic Methods Program. **94**, 109–127 (2018)
10. Albert, E., Arenas, P., Genaim, S., Puebla, G., Zanardini, D.: Cost analysis of java bytecode. In: De Nicola, R. (ed.) ESOP 2007. LNCS, vol. 4421, pp. 157–172. Springer, Heidelberg (2007). https://doi.org/10.1007/978-3-540-71316-6_12

11. Albert, E., Correas, J., Johnsen, E.B., Pun, V.K.I., Román-Díez, G.: Parallel cost analysis. ACM Trans. Comput. Log. **19**(4), 31:1–31:37 (2018)
12. Milner, R., Sangiorgi, D.: Barbed bisimulation. In: Kuich, W. (ed.) ICALP 1992. LNCS, vol. 623, pp. 685–695. Springer, Heidelberg (1992). https://doi.org/10.1007/3-540-55719-9_114
13. Merro, M., Zappa Nardelli, F.: Behavioral theory for mobile ambients. J. ACM **52**(6), 961–1023 (2005)
14. Cardelli, L., Ghelli, G., Gordon, A.D.: Types for the ambient calculus. Inf. Comput. **177**(2), 160–194 (2002)
15. Johnsen, E.B., Steffen, M., Stumpf, J.B., Tveito, L.: Checking modal contracts for virtually timed ambients. In: Fischer, B., Uustalu, T. (eds.) ICTAC 2018. LNCS, vol. 11187, pp. 252–272. Springer, Cham (2018). https://doi.org/10.1007/978-3-030-02508-3_14
16. Gordon, A.D.: V for virtual. Electr. Notes Theoret. Comput. Sci. **162**, 177–181 (2006)
17. Johnsen, E.B., Schlatte, R., Tapia Tarifa, S.L.: Integrating deployment architectures and resource consumption in timed object-oriented models. J. Logic Algebraic Methods Program. **84**(1), 67–91 (2015)
18. Albert, E., et al.: Formal modeling and analysis of resource management for cloud architectures: an industrial case study using Real-Time ABS. J. Serv.-Oriented Comput. Appl. **8**(4), 323–339 (2014). https://doi.org/10.1007/s11761-013-0148-0
19. Johnsen, E.B., Hähnle, R., Schäfer, J., Schlatte, R., Steffen, M.: ABS: a core language for abstract behavioral specification. In: Aichernig, B.K., de Boer, F.S., Bonsangue, M.M. (eds.) FMCO 2010. LNCS, vol. 6957, pp. 142–164. Springer, Heidelberg (2011). https://doi.org/10.1007/978-3-642-25271-6_8
20. Berger, M.: Towards Abstractions for Distributed Systems. Ph.D. thesis, University of London, Imperial College (2004)
21. Prisacariu, C.: Timed distributed pi-calculus. In: Modelling and Verifying of Parallel Processes (MOVEP06), pp. 348–354 (2006)
22. Aman, B., Ciobanu, G.: Mobile ambients with timers and types. In: Jones, C.B., Liu, Z., Woodcock, J. (eds.) ICTAC 2007. LNCS, vol. 4711, pp. 50–63. Springer, Heidelberg (2007). https://doi.org/10.1007/978-3-540-75292-9_4
23. Paun, G., Rozenberg, G., Salomaa, A.: The Oxford Handbook of Membrane Computing. Oxford University Press, Oxford (2010)
24. Cavaliere, M., Sburlan, D.: Time–independent P systems. In: Mauri, G., Păun, G., Pérez-Jiménez, M.J., Rozenberg, G., Salomaa, A. (eds.) WMC 2004. LNCS, vol. 3365, pp. 239–258. Springer, Heidelberg (2005). https://doi.org/10.1007/978-3-540-31837-8_14
25. Lee, I., Philippou, A., Sokolsky, O.: Resources in process algebra. J. Logic Algebraic Program. **72**(1), 98–122 (2007)
26. Philippou, A., Lee, I., Sokolsky, O.: PADS: an approach to modeling resource demand and supply for the formal analysis of hierarchical scheduling. Theor. Comput. Sci. **413**(1), 2–20 (2012)
27. Mousavi, M.R., Reniers, M.A., Basten, T., Chaudron, M.R.V.: PARS: a process algebraic approach to resources and schedulers. In: Alexander, M., Gardner, W. (eds.) Process Algebra for Parallel and Distributed Processing. Chapman and Hall/CRC (2008)
28. Bidinger, P., Stefani, J.-B.: The Kell calculus: operational semantics and type system. In: Najm, E., Nestmann, U., Stevens, P. (eds.) FMOODS 2003. LNCS, vol. 2884, pp. 109–123. Springer, Heidelberg (2003). https://doi.org/10.1007/978-3-540-39958-2_8

29. Honda, K.: Types for dyadic interaction. In: Best, E. (ed.) CONCUR 1993. LNCS, vol. 715, pp. 509–523. Springer, Heidelberg (1993). https://doi.org/10.1007/3-540-57208-2_35
30. Orchard, D., Yoshida, N.: Effects as sessions, sessions as effects. In: POPL 2016. ACM Press (2016)
31. Garralda, P., Compagnoni, A., Dezani-Ciancaglini, M.: BASS: boxed ambients with safe sessions. In Maher, M. (ed.) PPDP 2006, pp. 61–72. ACM Press (2006)
32. Amtoft, T.: Flow-sensitive type systems and the ambient calculus. Higher-Order Symb. Comput. **21**(4), 411–442 (2008)
33. Igarashi, A., Kobayashi, N.: Resource usage analysis. ACM Trans. Program. Lang. Syst. **27**(2), 264–313 (2005)
34. Kobayashi, N., Suenaga, K., Wischik, L.: Resource usage analysis for the π-calculus. Log. Methods Comput. Sci. **2**(3) (2006)
35. Kobayashi, N., Sangiorgi, D.: A hybrid type system for lock-freedom of mobile processes. ACM Trans. Program. Lang. Syst. **32**(5), 16:1–16:49 (2010)
36. Abadi, M., Lamport, L.: Conjoining specifications. ACM Trans. Program. Lang. Syst. **17**(3), 507–534 (1995)
37. Jones, C.B.: Tentative steps towards a development method for interfering programs. ACM Trans. Program. Lang. Syst. **5**(4), 596–619 (1983)
38. Misra, J., Chandy, K.M.: Proofs of networks of processes. IEEE Trans. Softw. Eng. **7**, 417–426 (1981)
39. Ábrahám, E., Grabe, I., Grüner, A., Steffen, M.: Behavioral interface description of an object-oriented language with futures and promises. J. Logic Algebraic Program. **78**(7), 491–518 (2009)
40. Ábrahám, E., Grüner, A., Steffen, M.: Heap-abstraction for an object-oriented calculus with thread classes. In: Beckmann, A., Berger, U., Löwe, B., Tucker, J.V. (eds.) CiE 2006. LNCS, vol. 3988, pp. 1–10. Springer, Heidelberg (2006). https://doi.org/10.1007/11780342_1
41. Katsumata, S.: Parametric effect monads and semantics of effect systems. In: Proceedings of POPL 2014, pp. 633–645. ACM (2014)
42. Uustalu, T., Vene, V.: Comonadic notions of computation. Electr. Notes Theoret. Comput. Sci. **203**, 263–284 (2008). Proceedings 9th Intl. Workshop on Coalgebraic Methods in Computer Science (CMCS 2008)
43. Berger, M., Yoshida, N.: Timed, distributed, probabilistic, typed processes. In: Shao, Z. (ed.) APLAS 2007. LNCS, vol. 4807, pp. 158–174. Springer, Heidelberg (2007). https://doi.org/10.1007/978-3-540-76637-7_11
44. Hennessy, M., Riely, J.: Resource access control in systems of mobile agents. Inf. Comput. **173**(1), 82–120 (2002)
45. Teller, D., Zimmer, P., Hirschkoff, D.: Using ambients to control resources*. In: Brim, L., Křetínský, M., Kučera, A., Jančar, P. (eds.) CONCUR 2002. LNCS, vol. 2421, pp. 288–303. Springer, Heidelberg (2002). https://doi.org/10.1007/3-540-45694-5_20
46. Godskesen, J.C., Hildebrandt, T., Sassone, V.: A calculus of mobile resources*. In: Brim, L., Křetínský, M., Kučera, A., Jančar, P. (eds.) CONCUR 2002. LNCS, vol. 2421, pp. 272–287. Springer, Heidelberg (2002). https://doi.org/10.1007/3-540-45694-5_19
47. Charatonik, W., Gordon, A.D., Talbot, J.-M.: Finite-control mobile ambients. In: Le Métayer, D. (ed.) ESOP 2002. LNCS, vol. 2305, pp. 295–313. Springer, Heidelberg (2002). https://doi.org/10.1007/3-540-45927-8_21

Abstraction and Genericity in Why3

Jean-Christophe Filliâtre$^{(\boxtimes)}$ and Andrei Paskevich$^{(\boxtimes)}$

Université Paris-Saclay, CNRS, Inria, LRI, 91405 Orsay, France
{jean-christophe.filliatre,andrei}@lri.fr

Abstract. The benefits of modularity in programming—abstraction barriers, which allow hiding implementation details behind an opaque interface, and genericity, which allows specializing a single implementation to a variety of underlying data types—apply just as well to deductive program verification, with the additional advantage of helping the automated proof search procedures by reducing the size and complexity of the premises and by instantiating and reusing once-proved properties in a variety of contexts

In this paper, we demonstrate the modularity features of WhyML, the language of the program verification tool Why3. Instead of separating abstract interfaces and fully elaborated implementations, WhyML uses a single concept of *module*, a collection of abstract and concrete declarations, and a basic operation of *cloning* which instantiates a module with respect to a given partial substitution, while verifying its soundness. This mechanism brings into WhyML both abstraction and genericity, which we illustrate on a small verified Bloom filter implementation, translated into executable idiomatic C code.

1 Introduction

When Alice writes code that uses hash tables, she does not need direct access to the actual implementation of that data structure—only to the handful of operations provided by it. Truth be told, she would rather not have that access: less risk to break her data structure by mistake, and she can also swap one implementation for another, provided that the offered operations behave in the same way. What she needs, however, is hash tables for cabbages and hash tables for kings, and hash tables for whatever other data type she has in her code, for which she has written a hash function and an equality test[1].

If Alice also wants to formally verify her program, then *not having* access to the implementation may easily become a necessary requirement for her success. The automated provers are more stubborn than smart, and they will happily drown in all the minute properties of the implementation, whereas they could easily succeed in their proof, were they given just the simple specifications of

---

[1] "Cabbage hash can be delicious," said Alice, "but I would never dare to hash a king.".

A. Paskevich—This research was partly supported by the French National Research Organization (project VOCAL ANR-15-CE25-008) and by the Inria-Mitsubishi Electric bilateral contract "ProofInUse-MERCE".

© Springer Nature Switzerland AG 2020
T. Margaria and B. Steffen (Eds.): ISoLA 2020, LNCS 12476, pp. 122–142, 2020.
https://doi.org/10.1007/978-3-030-61362-4_7

hash table operations. The best way to get an automated proof of anything is to give the prover very little data written in very simple terms (incidentally, this also helps if at some later point you need to slightly change your problem and be able to prove it again). And then, if you do get the proof, just make sure that it somehow still holds if your terms are not as simple and your problem is actually much larger than what you let your prover believe.

What this means for Alice, is that she would prefer to verify her code without knowing anything about how hash tables are implemented, and if she also verified her implementation of hash tables, she would prefer to do it just once, without giving her prover any details about the type of the objects to store, only that there is an equality test and a hash function for them. If her verification framework is done right, this should be enough to guarantee that her final executable—where sophisticated and highly performant hash tables are reused for ships and shoes and sealing-wax sticks—is flawless.

Probably, any approach invented for modularity in programming can be adapted to program verification. The purpose of this work is to show how we do it in WhyML, the language of the program verification tool Why3 [6].

Our framework is inspired by theorem proving just as much as by programming. In classical, non-constructive, logic, the difference between full implementation and partial specification is just how much you say about your type, function, or program. Also, apart from some symbols that are given a fixed meaning in your formalism (equality predicate or integer type), everything else is just an identifier bound by some quantifier, explicitly or implicitly, up in the scope. And finally, we need to break our formalizations into many small pieces, to keep the proof tasks within reach of automated provers.

This has led us to quite a minimalistic system of modules, which are simple collections of specifications and code, with only two basic operations: (a) link module A from module B so that B can have access to the contents of A, and (b) put a fresh copy of module A inside module B, while replacing some symbols introduced in A with the symbols from B. The second operation we call *module cloning*, and it turned out to be surprisingly (not that surprisingly, if one comes from classical logic) versatile. One of the first cloning instructions we wrote was in the standard library of integers, where we imported the ring axioms by cloning the generic library of rings, replacing the abstract domain t with int, abstract function plus with +, etc. We did not need to say that the module of generic rings was a functor parametrized by that type and those operations. Instead we simply declared an abstract type and three abstract functions on it. And Why3 allows us to instantiate any abstract symbol (or none at all) when cloning a module, on condition that we respect its properties.

Module cloning can help us create abstraction barriers. Write a module A with abstract types and abstract functions, described only by their specifications—this is your interface. Client code may link to A or clone it (to have a fresh instantiated copy), and be verified without knowing anything about the implementation. Write an implementation—a module B with fully defined types and fully implemented operations, and then clone A into B while instantiating every abstract symbol from the interface with its implementation. Why3 will check the types and the side effects, and will generate verification conditions for you to prove in order to ensure that the implementation respects the interface.

Module cloning can help us implement generic code. Rings and integers cited above are just one example. Write a module A with all the parameters as abstract symbols—this is your functor. State (and prove) all the generic properties you may need. Clone A into the client code while instantiating the abstract symbols with concrete types and concrete operations. Why3 will transfer all the properties you have proved in the generic module to the client code without requiring you to reprove them.

Below, we present the modules in WhyML (Sect. 2) and show their use on an example of a Bloom filter library (Sect. 3), where proofs performed in minimal contexts lead us to a fully implemented correct-by-construction C program (Sect. 4). The complete formalization of this case study is available at the companion web page http://why3.lri.fr/isola-2020/. Our account, though detailed, stays informal: we bring up the soundness properties of the framework but do not try to prove them.

2   WhyML Modules

A building block of a WhyML development is a *declaration*. A declaration can introduce a data type, a mathematical symbol, a logical proposition or a program function. Some declarations provide full information about the symbols they introduce: the structure of a data type is fully exposed, a mathematical symbol is given a sound definition, a proposition is proved, a program function is implemented. Other declarations give us a partial view: we only get to know some fields of a data type, a mathematical symbol is only given a name and a type signature, a proposition is posited without a proof, and a program function shows its specification but the actual implementation is unknown. Mixing concrete and abstract declarations is best suited for program verification, as we get to freely choose the level of abstraction for each element involved. Of course, if we intend to obtain executable code at the end, we must be able to refine the abstract portions into concrete implementations, while preserving the properties obtained through proof.

Declarations are structured using *scopes* and *modules*. Scopes help us to manage namespaces. Let us say, we declare a function symbol f in a scope S:

```
scope S
  function f ...
end
```

After closing the scope S, we can refer to f by using a qualifier:

```
lemma L: ... S.f ...
```

or by temporarily opening S inside a WhyML expression:

```
predicate p = ... S.( ... f ... ) ...
```

or by importing S into the current namespace until the end of the current scope:

```
import S
constant c = ... f ...
```

Sometimes we want to import a scope right away:

```
scope import T     (* the same as writing 'import T'... *)
  predicate q ...   (* ...right after closing the scope *)
end
```

This is useful if there is some other symbol named q declared in the current scope. WhyML forbids giving the same name to two symbols declared in the same scope, but permits shadowing with imported names.

Scopes can be nested and reopened. They are only used for name resolution and do not affect the logical or operational semantics of WhyML declarations.

Modules, on the other hand, provide the semantic structure of a WhyML program. Each module contains a sequence of declarations and scopes and references to other modules. These references are of two kinds.

First, a module N can bring another module M in its logical context, and thus get access to the contents of M, through the operation use:

```
module M                      module N
  type t                        use M
  function h (x: int): t        constant d: t = h 5
end                           end
```

Module M shares its contents with all modules that use it, either directly or indirectly. For example, if some third module uses both M and N, it will get access to the same type t and function h through both of them.

The other way to reference a module is by *cloning* it. This operation makes a full copy of the contents of the cloned module while simultaneously replacing some of its abstract symbols with suitable refinements:

```
module P
  clone M
  constant e: t     (* this is not the same type as t in M *)
end

module Q
  clone M with type t = int
  lemma idem: forall z: int. h (h z) = h z    (* h returns int *)
end
```

When cloning M in the module P above, the programmer does not specify any substitution to be performed. Thus the contents of M is copied into P verbatim. However, the copied declarations are now part of P and they are distinct from the original declarations in M. If some other module uses both M and P, it will get two different types named t: one from M and another from P.

As for the module Q in the same example, it copies the contents of M while replacing every occurrence of the type t with int. Since type t is abstract, this substitution is allowed. Still, if M contains any axioms about t, they may come in contradiction with the properties of type int (e.g., t could be axiomatized as a finite type in M), thus creating an inconsistency. This is why all axioms from a cloned module appear by default as *lemmas* in the cloning module, obliging the programmer either to prove them or to deliberately override the default.

Cloning a module does not affect the symbols that were added to it through the use command. For example, if we clone module N, we get access to the same type t and function h as if we have used module M directly. Informally, one can see use as creating a window into another module. On the other hand, the symbols introduced with clone belong to the cloning module (and Why3 does actually put the instantiated declarations inside the cloning module), and thus can be further instantiated during subsequent clone commands. For example, one can write clone P with type M.t = real.

When we use or clone a module, we introduce new symbols to the logical context and thus, new names. In their shortest form, with no modifiers, both use and clone will put these names in a new scope, named after the module in question, and import that scope. Operations use export and clone export do not open a new scope, and put all the new names in the current namespace instead. For example, module P above can be equivalently written as follows:

```
module P
  scope import M      (* gets the name of the cloned module *)
    clone export M
  end
  constant e: t       (* we can also write 'M.t' here *)
end
```

We can choose a different name for the new scope by writing use M as A or clone M as B. In this form, the new scope is not imported automatically:

```
module P_alt_1
  clone M as B        (* scope B is not imported *)
  constant e: B.t     (* qualifier is required *)
end
```

unless we add the import modifier:

```
module P_alt_2
  clone import M as B   (* scope B is imported *)
  constant e: t         (* both 't' and 'B.t' work *)
end
```

It is important to note that module names can only appear in use or clone operations. In particular, it is impossible to refer to a symbol from a module that has not been added to the current context either through use or through clone. Once it is done, the scope structure will determine the fully qualified name for each symbol that came with that module.

In what follows, we discuss in more detail various aspects of cloning, paying most attention to the checks and verifications required to ensure the soundness of symbol instantiations. The cloning mechanism guarantees that all properties that have been established in the module being cloned—proved lemmas, verified program contracts, etc.—stay valid after instantiation and can be incorporated into the cloning module without creating a contradiction. This does not mean that cloning a module is always a conservative extension: as we have seen earlier, Why3 does not guarantee that the instantiated *axioms* of the cloned module are consistent with the current logical context (which is why it incites the programmer to prove them after instantiation). However, whatever has been *proved* in the cloned module must stay provable after cloning.

We call "original" the module being cloned and the symbols declared in it: type symbols, mathematical symbols, program symbols, etc. The substitution in a `clone` operation we call a "refinement", the original symbols on the left-hand side being "refined", and the ones on the right-hand side, which replace the originals in the cloned declarations, being "refining". Symbols that are given a full definition in the original module cannot be refined, and are simply transferred into the new context. Their definitions, however, are still instantiated with respect to the cloning substitution, similarly to how in module Q above, type t is replaced with `int` in the signature of the cloned function h.

Type Declarations. Fully defined types in Why3 are sum types, non-private records, type aliases, and special numeric types:

```
type list 'a = Nil | Cons 'a (list 'a)
type ref 'a = { mutable contents: 'a }
type point = (real, real)
type int8 = <range -128 127>
```

Being fully defined, these types cannot be replaced by cloning instructions. The only refinable types are private records:

```
type queue 'a = private { ghost mutable elts: list 'a }
```

WhyML programs can read the values of private records' fields, but cannot directly construct such records or modify their mutable fields through a direct assignment. Instead, a module that declares a private type like `queue` should also declare functions to create and manipulate the objects of this type: allocate a new empty queue, add an element to a queue, etc. These functions ought to be implemented in the refining modules that provide a full definition for the type.

A type without definition is considered to be a private record with no fields:

```
type t   (* the same as 'type t = private {}' *)
```

A private type whose fields are all ghost (meaning that they can only be used in specifications and in ghost computations, but cannot influence the observable program behaviour) is called "abstract". For example, the definition of type `queue` above can be equivalently written as follows:

```
type queue 'a = abstract { mutable elts: list 'a }
```

Both private and non-private records can be equipped with a type invariant:

```
type clock = abstract { mutable h: int; mutable m: int }
              invariant { 0 <= h < 24 /\ 0 <= m < 60 }
```

A type invariant is essentially an axiom that restricts possible values of the fields of a record type. Only the variables representing these fields are allowed to be free in the invariant; the quantifiers over the new type are also forbidden. Why3 requires type invariants to be satisfiable and generates appropriate proof obligations. Private records, records with mutable fields, and records with type invariants cannot be recursive in WhyML.

A cloning operation can instantiate a private record with a different type. The following restrictions apply:

1. The refining type must have the same number of type parameters as the original type.
2. All fields of the original type must be present in the refining type and have the same type. Here, as before, "the same type" is meant modulo instantiation: that is, if the field's type in the original record is `ref t` and the cloning substitution replaces `t` with `int`, the corresponding field in the refining type must have type `ref int`.
3. A mutable (respectively, immutable) field in the original type must be mutable (respectively, immutable) in the refining type.
4. A ghost field in the original type may become non-ghost in the refining type but not vice-versa.
5. New fields can be added, which can be mutable and/or ghost. Mutable fields, however, can only be added when the original type is explicitly declared as mutable or has mutable fields of its own.
6. The (instantiated) original invariant must hold for each value of the refining type; Why3 generates an appropriate proof obligation. One possible way to satisfy this requirement is to include the original invariant in the invariant of the refining type.
7. An original field with a mutable type that is not mentioned in the original type invariant cannot occur in the invariant of the refining type either.

The last item deserves some discussion. Let us consider the following declaration:

```
type ptr 'a = private { segment: array 'a;
                mutable offset:  int }
```

and a variable p of type `ptr`. Since `ptr` is private, modification of the mutable field `p.offset` is only possible through abstract functions operating on values of type `ptr`. What about `p.segment`, an immutable field containing a mutable value? One possibility is to treat it in the same way as `p.offset`, that is, to forbid direct modification of the array. Another is to allow writes into `p.segment`. In the latter case, however, we must ensure that any such write does not break the invariant of the `ptr` type. The problem, of course, is that `ptr` is a private type and its invariant can be strengthened during refinement. Since we do not know the full invariant of `ptr` right now, we cannot formulate an invariant preservation condition for the writes into `p.segment`. We can work around this problem by forbidding to constrain the values of the `segment` field in the current and *all future* type invariants of `ptr`, so that no state of `p.segment` can break the integrity of `p`. An easy way to ensure this is to forbid mentioning the field in the invariant altogether.

Thus, the presence or the absence of a field with a mutable type (such as `segment`) in the type invariant of a private type serves as an indication of the user intention: If the field is mentioned in the type invariant (even in a trivially tautological way, like `segment = segment`), then it becomes non-modifiable[2]; otherwise, it can be written into, but must not appear in the invariants of the refining types, ensuring that modifications are always safe.

Mathematical Functions and Predicates. Here, the rules are simple, because functions and predicates in WhyML are either provided with a (consistent, total, and unambiguous) definition:

```
predicate mem (x: 'a) (l: list 'a) = match l with
  | Nil      -> false
  | Cons y r -> x = y \/ mem x r
  end
```

or declared as abstract symbols, with only their name and type signature:

```
function length (s: string): int
```

The defined functions and predicates cannot be refined and their definitions are simply transferred to the current module. An abstract function or predicate is refinable, and the refining symbol must have the exact same type signature modulo instantiation.

For example, the following module clones module M above, and refines both type `t` and function `h`:

```
module R
  use list.List
  function singleton (n: int): list int = Cons n Nil
  clone M with type t = list int, function h = singleton
end
```

Refinement of functions and predicates does not produce proof obligations.

Logical Propositions. Axioms, lemmas, and goals are not refinable: they cannot be replaced with some other propositions. However, Why3 allows the programmer to specify how they should be treated in the cloning module.

The goals in the original module are not transferred to the current module at all. Indeed, they have already been proved in the original module and thus

---

[2] In this case, due to the specifics of state handling in WhyML, not even abstract functions are allowed to announce a potential write in the `segment` field, which limits the usefulness of this kind of construction. This may be relaxed in the future.

do not need to be reproved after instantiation. And since they are not added to the logical context as premises (contrary to lemmas), the cloning module has no need for the original goals.

The original lemmas are cloned as lemmas; however, since they have already been proved in the original module, Why3 will not generate a proof obligation for them. If we do not want to keep a cloned lemma as a premise in the logical context (e.g., because it duplicates an existing premise), we can "recast" it as a goal by writing with goal L in the cloning substitution (where L is the name of the original lemma). Then lemma L will not be copied to the current module.

Axioms require caution, because, as we have noted above, simply copying an original axiom into the new context may create an inconsistency. To prevent this from happening, WhyML clones axioms as lemmas by default (and generates proof obligations for them), and the programmer must explicitly specify which axioms of the original module are to be kept as axioms:

```
clone relations.PreOrder with axiom Refl, axiom Trans
```

This instruction clones the `PreOrder` module from the file `relations.mlw` from the standard library of Why3. It adds to the current module declarations of a new abstract type `t` and a new binary relation `rel` on `t` together with the axioms of reflexivity and transitivity of `rel`.

When cloning modules with numerous axioms, listing all of them would be tedious. Therefore, WhyML provides a shortcut `with axiom .` which preserves every axiom in the original module unless it is converted into a lemma or a goal elsewhere in the cloning substitution.

Program Functions. Only the abstract program functions, characterized by their type signature and their contract, can be refined in a cloning substitution. However, due to the large variety of possible side effects in the original and refining functions, the required checks are rather complex. For example, consider the code in Fig. 1 (we omit the references to the standard library of lists). The `Queue` module declares an abstract type of mutable queues and an abstract enqueuing function. The `TwoListQueue` module implements the queue type and the enqueue operation, and then clones `Queue`, refining the two symbols.

After checking the correctness of the type refinement (remember that in an abstract record all fields are ghost and thus field `elts` is allowed to stay ghost in the implementation), Why3 proceeds to the refinement of `enqueue`.

The procedure starts with instantiating the prototype of the original abstract function. This step does not take the refining function into consideration; in fact, the same rules are applied when we simply transfer an abstract function into the cloning module without refining it. Prototype instantiation is non-trivial because the types in the original type signature, notably those involved in the side effects, may have been refined, revealing new mutable fields and new fields with mutable components. This is the case in our example: the modified parameter `q` has gained two new mutable fields, `front` and `back`.

Why3 applies the following rules when instantiating the "writes" annotations for the modified mutable values whose type is refined (remember that all side

```
module Queue
  type queue 'a = abstract { mutable elts: list 'a }

  val enqueue (q: queue 'a) (x: 'a) : unit
    writes   { q.elts }
    ensures  { q.elts = (old q.elts) ++ Cons x Nil }
end

module TwoListQueue
  type queue 'a = { mutable front: list 'a;
                    mutable back:  list 'a;
              ghost mutable elts:  list 'a }
    invariant { elts = front ++ reverse back }

  let enqueue (q: queue 'a) (x: 'a) : unit
    writes   { q.back, q.elts }
    ensures  { q.elts = (old q.elts) ++ Cons x Nil }
  =
    q.back <- Cons x q.back;
    q.elts <- q.elts ++ Cons x Nil

  clone Queue with type queue = queue, val enqueue = enqueue
end
```

Fig. 1. Queues: interface and implementation.

effects in these annotations are latent and do not have to actually happen in any implementation):

1. All original mutable fields marked as written in the original prototype are considered written in the instantiated prototype.
2. All original fields not marked as written in the original prototype are not considered written in the instantiated prototype.
3. All new mutable fields are considered written in the instantiated prototype.
4. All mutable components of the new fields are considered written in the instantiated prototype.

Mutable values that are not modified in the original prototype, are not modified in the instantiated prototype either, regardless of how their type is refined.

According to these rules, the instantiated prototype of the original function enqueue is as follows:

```
val enqueue (q: queue 'a) (x: 'a): unit
  writes   { q.front, q.back, q.elts }
  ensures  { q.elts = (old q.elts) ++ Cons x Nil }
```

Indeed, q.elts is considered written, as it was already marked as such in the original prototype (rule 1). The fields front and back are added to the write effect, since they are new mutable fields in a modified parameter q (rule 3). If the added fields `front` and `back` were not mutable but had a mutable type (say, `array'a`), they would also appear in the instantiated effect by rule 4.

To sum up, the instantiated effect annotation stays the same with respect to what is known by the original module (rules 1, 2, and 5). However, each announced write effect extends to all added fields of the affected values. This allows the implementations of the original `enqueue` function to modify the new fields `front` and `back`.

Now that we have the instantiated prototype of the original abstract function, we need to compare it with the proposed refinement and verify that the instantiation is legal. This requires multiple checks:

1. The type signatures must coincide.
2. Ghost parameters of the original should be ghost in the refinement (an implementation cannot depend on ghost data passed from the client code).
3. Ghost results of the refinement should be ghost in the original (an implementation cannot pass ghost data to client code unbeknown to it).
4. The refining function must not have effects unlisted in the instantiated prototype of the original.
5. The refining function must not create memory aliases that are not required by the original.
6. The refinement must satisfy the instantiated contract of the original, that is, have a weaker (or equivalent) precondition and a stronger (or equivalent) postcondition.

In order to check these conditions, Why3 creates and verifies (and then throws out) a WhyML function whose specification comes from the instantiated original prototype and whose implementation consists in calling the refining function with the same parameters. The type-checking system of Why3 and its verification condition generator perform the necessary checks and produce an appropriate proof obligation for the last item. In the case of `enqueue`, this proof obligation is an easily provable tautology.

While the rules for prototype instantiation introduce new latent write effects, these effects only concern the values that are already marked as modified in the original prototype, and they are limited to the new fields. Since a caller of the abstract function only knows the fields in the original type declaration, it can only observe a modification in the new fields as a non-specific change of the whole value—which is covered by the effect annotation in the original prototype.

It is crucial for the soundness of cloning that no aliases exist between the values accessible to the caller and the "hidden state" represented by the added fields. Such an alias can only be created through a refinement of an abstract program function in the original module, and this is prevented by rule 5 above.

In the next section, we show how to use modules in a fully developed example, going from abstract specifications to executable C code. In particular, we demonstrate how module cloning expresses: (a) the relation between an interface and an implementation; (b) the relation between a generic module and its parameters; and (c) specialization of a generic module.

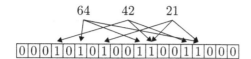

Fig. 2. A Bloom filter for integers, using $m = 19$ and $k = 3$.

3   Example: Bloom Filters

A Bloom filter [4] is a data structure that implements a set and provides two operations: one to insert an element into the set and one to query the presence of an element in the set. The latter must always give a correct positive answer for elements that have been indeed inserted into the set, but it may return a false answer for the elements not in the set. In other words, false positives are allowed but false negatives are not.

A Bloom filter makes use of a bitmap (a Boolean array) of a given size m and of k hash functions $h_1, \ldots, h_k$ mapping the elements to integers between 0 and $m - 1$. When inserting an element x, we set the bits at indices $h_1(x), \ldots, h_k(x)$. When querying the presence of x, we return true if and only if *all* bits at indices $h_1(x), \ldots, h_k(x)$ are set.

Figure 2 illustrates a Bloom filter for integer elements where we use an array of 19 bits and 3 hash functions $h_1(x) = 34x$, $h_2(x) = 55x$, and $h_3(x) = 89x$ (all considered modulo 19). We insert three elements into the set, namely 21, 42, and 64. It results in seven bits being set (bits at indices 3, 5, 7, 10, 11, 14, and 15 in the array). If we now query the filter for the element 82, it reports that it is not in the set. Indeed, element 82 is mapped to bits 2, 7, and 14 and, though bits 7 and 14 are set, bit 2 is not and thus 82 does not belong to the set. But if we now query the filter for the element 80, it checks for bits 3, 11, and 14, which are all set, and thus reports that 80 belongs to the set. This is a false positive. If we query the filter for all elements between 0 and 99, it reports 17 positives: the three elements we added and 14 false positives. For the remaining 83 elements, we know for sure they do not belong to the set.

Despite being imprecise, a Bloom filter is a genuinely useful data structure. One good application is the following. Say we are implementing a storage whose operations are expensive, because they involve disk or network access. A Bloom filter can be conveniently placed between the storage and its client. When an element is added to the storage, it is added to the filter as well. Whenever the storage needs to be queried, we first query the filter. If the filter reports that the element is not in the storage, the answer is guaranteed to be correct and we avoid a costly operation. By themselves, Bloom filters are efficient data structures, in both space and time. With suitable choices of m and k, a Bloom filter can achieve an error ratio less than 1% with less than 10 bits per element [13].

It is worth pointing out that unlike a traditional hash table, a Bloom filter cannot be resized to accommodate an increasing number of elements. Indeed, the elements themselves are not kept in the Bloom filter and thus there is no

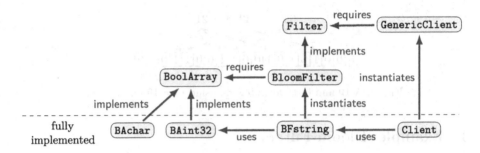

Fig. 3. Bloom filters in Why3: the module map.

way to rehash them into a larger array. This means that we must make an estimation of the expected size of the element set in advance, and pick the value of m accordingly. Similarly, there is no way to remove an element from a Bloom filter. Indeed, by clearing the bits corresponding to an element, we could remove other elements from the set, which would make the filter unsound. This is not a problem, since removing an element from the actual storage without updating the Bloom filter would merely lead to another false positive, which is allowed. If need be, the filter can be reconstructed from the storage on regular intervals, without compromising the asymptotic complexity.

Let us implement a Bloom filter with Why3. Our final objective is to get a verified C library of Bloom filters. We decompose the code into eight modules, shown in Fig. 3. Notice that the verbs "requires", "implements", and "instantiates" are all realized using the `clone` operation, as will be demonstrated throughout this section. Here is a short overview of the diagram:

- On the left side of the figure, we have three modules related to Boolean arrays. Module `BoolArray` is an interface and modules `BAchar` and `BAint32` are two implementations of this interface. The former implements a Boolean array rather naïvely, using one byte per element. The latter uses an array of 32-bit integers, using one bit per element.
- On the central part of the figure, we have three modules related to filters. Module `Filter` is an interface. It provides an abstract data type and three operations `create`, `add`, and `mem`. Module `BloomFilter` implements Bloom filters on the basis of various parameters: an implementation of Boolean arrays, values for m and k, a data type for the elements, and a set of hash functions. Then module `BFstring` instantiates all these parameters to get a fully implemented Bloom filter for strings.
- Finally, on the right side of the figure, we have two modules to make a quick test of the library. Module `GenericClient` uses the interface `Filter` to build a filter and perform a few additions and membership queries. Then module `Client` instantiates this generic client using module `BFstring`.

The four modules at the bottom of the figure are fully implemented and can be translated to compilable C code (this is described in the next section).

Boolean Arrays. We start with an interface `BoolArray`, which declares a type t together with three operations `create`, `get`, and `set`.

```
module BoolArray
  type t = abstract { mutable contents: seq bool; }
  val create (size: uint32): t
  val get (a: t) (i: uint32): bool
  val set (a: t) (i: uint32): unit
end
```

We omit various details here, such as the modules imported from the standard library and the contracts for the three operations. The type t is an abstract record data type, with a single field named `contents`. Since all fields of an abstract type are ghost, the field `contents` can be used within any specification element, such as a function contract, but cannot be used in actual computation in the code. In other words, it serves as a *model* for the type t, but not as a part of its implementation. This model is a sequence of Boolean values (type `seq`, from Why3 standard library, can be seen as a purely applicative array) and this is all we need to provide suitable contracts to our three operations. For instance, operation `get` is given the following contract:

```
val get (a: t) (i: uint32): bool
  requires { i < length a.contents }
  ensures  { result = a.contents[i] }
```

For convenience, WhyML allows us to declare `contents` a coercion symbol, so that we can write simply a instead of `a.contents`. Module `BoolArray` does not incur any verification condition.

We now provide two different implementations of this interface. We start with a rather simple implementation with one byte per bit. We do this in a separate module `BAchar`. It also contains declarations for a type t and three operations `create`, `get`, and `set`.

```
module BAchar
  type t = { mutable ghost contents: seq bool;
                                  arr: ptr uchar; }
    invariant { ... }
  let create (size: uint32): t = ...
  let get (a: t) (i: uint32): bool = ...
  let set (a: t) (i: uint32): unit = ...
  ...
```

This time, however, our types and functions are fully implemented. Type t is still a record data type with a ghost field `contents`. But it also contains a non-ghost field `arr` that holds a pointer to an array of bytes (type `uchar` from Why3 standard library). A gluing invariant (omitted here) makes the connection between field `contents` (the model) and field `arr` (the implementation). The type t is not abstract anymore, which means we are now allowed to construct instances of that type. This is precisely what function `create` does.

Operations `create`, `get`, and `set` are now given definitions (omitted here). Their contracts are identical to those of module `BoolArray`. In particular, they only refer to field `contents`. Their definitions, of course, do make use of field `arr`. Why3 generates suitable verification conditions for these three definitions to be correct with respect to their contracts.

Finally, we show that module `BAchar` is indeed an implementation of the interface `BoolArray`. This is done with the help of a `clone` instruction:

```
    ...
  clone BoolArray with type t, val create, val get, val set
end
```

Here, we use a syntactical shortcut that allows us to write only the left-hand side of the substitution when the refining symbol has the same name as the original. That is, we substitute the type `t` of module `BoolArray` with the type `t` we just defined, and similarly for the three operations.

This `clone` command generates several verification conditions. They are all rather trivial, as there is no invariant on type `BoolArray.t` and the contracts for the three operations are the same in the interface and the implementation.

Apart from this last `clone`, module `BAchar` is completely independent of `BoolArray`. The `clone` instruction matches the definitions in `BAchar` to the declarations in `BoolArray` and verifies that the former can indeed serve as an implementation of the latter. It is perfectly possible for a module to implement several different interfaces.

We also provide a second implementation of `BoolArray` in a module called `BAint32`. It is a more efficient implementation that uses an array of 32-bit integers, where each element packs 32 Boolean values.

Filters. We proceed in a similar way for filters, though using two layers of refinement instead of one. We start with an interface, `Filter`, which declares types for elements and filters and three operations:

```
module Filter
  type elt
  type filter = abstract { mutable contents: fset elt; }
  val create (m: uint32): filter
  val add (x: elt) (s: filter): unit
  val mem (x: elt) (s: filter): bool
end
```

This is similar to what we did earlier with module `BoolArray`. Here, the contents of type `filter` is modeled using a finite set. Then we implement Bloom filters in a second module `BloomFilter`. We start by introducing parameters for the type of elements and the family of k hash functions.

```
module BloomFilter
  type elt
  val constant k: uint32
  val function hash (i: uint32) (e: elt): uint32
```

The individual hash functions are identified with an index i in $0 \ldots k - 1$. Then we move to the implementation of type `filter`. For that, we need a Boolean array, and so we bring a copy of `BoolArray` into the context.

```
clone BoolArray
```

It is worth pointing out that this module is merely an *interface* for Boolean arrays. This means that our implementation of Bloom filters does not depend on a particular implementation of that data structure, and can be instantiated to use any of them. We can now define type `filter` on top of `BoolArray.t`.

```
type filter = {
  mutable ghost contents: fset elt;
                     m: uint32;
                  barr: BoolArray.t; }
invariant { length barr = m > 0 }
invariant { forall x. mem x contents ->
               forall i. i < k -> barr[(hash i x) % m] }
```

The gluing invariant makes the connection between the model field `contents` and the implementation fields `m` and `barr`. Now we can implement the three operations over Bloom filters:

```
let bloom_filter (m: uint32): filter = ...
let add (x: elt) (s: filter): unit  = ...
let mem (x: elt) (s: filter): bool  = ...
```

Note that, despite being defined, these functions still depend on parameters `elt`, `k`, and `hash`. Thus, they are not executable.

Last, as we did with module `BAint32`, we check that this module refines module `Filter`, using a `clone` command.

```
clone Filter with type elt, type filter,
   val create = bloom_filter, val add, val mem
end
```

Again, this generates VCs that are all easily discharged.

In order to obtain executable code, we further refine module `BloomFilter` to produce a filter for strings. Here, we choose to use three hash functions.

```
module BFstring
  type elt = string
  let constant k: uint32 = 3
  let function hash (h: uint32) (x: elt): uint32 = ...
```

The actual implementation of `hash`, omitted here, is based on Fowler-Noll-Vo hash functions, following Louridas [12]. The remaining part is a `clone` command to instantiate `BloomFilter` with these parameters and with module `BAint32`:

```
use BAint32
clone export BloomFilter with val k, type elt, val hash,
```

```
      type BoolArray.t = BAint32.t,
      val BoolArray.create = BAint32.create,
      val BoolArray.get = BAint32.get,
      val BoolArray.set = BAint32.set
   end
```

Though for Why3 this `clone` command is no different from the previous two, from the programmer's point of view it is of a rather different flavor. Instead of claiming that module `BFstring` implements `BloomFilter`, it rather *instantiates* module `BloomFilter` with actual parameters. Notice that we write `export` in order to have the Bloom filter operations in the top namespace of `BFstring`.

Client. We conclude this example with a tiny client code. The main purpose is to check the usability of our contracts before going any further. We start with a client for module `Filter`, which we instantiate on string elements.

```
   module GenericClient
      clone Filter with type elt = string
```

Then a test function builds a filter of a given size, inserts some strings, and checks for membership:

```
      let main () =
        let f = Filter.create 0x10000 in
        Filter.add "foo" f;
        Filter.add "bar" f;
        let b = Filter.mem "foo" f in
        assert { b };
        ...
   end
```

Once this is done, and verified, we can `clone` this generic client with a specific implementation of `Filter`, namely module `BFstring` we built earlier.

```
   module Client
      use BFstring
      clone export GenericClient with type Filter.filter = filter,
        val Filter.create = bloom_filter, val Filter.add = add,
        val Filter.mem = mem
   end
```

This verification passes, too, as we have already checked that `BFstring` implements `Filter`. (As for now, Why3 unnecessarily generates the same VCs a second time; this will be improved in the future.) Module `Client` is fully implemented and we will be able to translate it into executable C code, as shown in the next section. If we look again at the right-hand size of Fig. 3, we can see that the correctness of the `Client` module is ensured by the correctness of `GenericClient` and the fact that `BFstring` correctly refines `Filter`. A similar relation exists between modules `BFstring`, `BloomFilter`, `BAint32`, and `BoolArray`.

```
uint32_t * create(uint32_t size) {
  uint32_t n, i, o;
  uint32_t * p;
  n = 1U + (size - 1U) / 32U;
  p = malloc(n * sizeof(uint32_t));
  assert (p);
  o = n - 1U;
  for (i = 0U; ; ++i) {
    p[(int32_t)i] = 0u;
    if (i == o) {
      break;
    }
  }
  return p;
}
```

Fig. 4. Generated C code for function `create` from module `BAint32`.

4 C Library

Once verification is complete, Why3 can automatically translate WhyML code to C [14]. The resulting C code is composed of three files:

- `baint32.c`, a translation of module `BAint32`;
- `bfstring.c`, a translation of module `BFstring`;
- `client.c`, a translation of module `Client`.

File `bfstring.c` makes use of functions from `baint32.c` and file `client.c` makes use of functions from `bfstring.c`. Each C file comes with a corresponding header file (`.h`). These files are available at http://why3.lri.fr/isola-2020/. Figure 4 contains the C code for function `create` from file `baint32.c`, resulting from the translation of function `create` from module `BAint32`. We can make two comments regarding this code. First, `assert` is used so that we can assume that the value returned by `malloc` is not `NULL` in the following, without having to test it. This is reflected on the Why3 side with an `assert` function that ensures (in its postcondition) that p is not `NULL`. Second, the rather unusual form of the `for` loop, using a `break` statement, ensures that even a loop up to the maximum representable value is sound with respect to the WhyML semantics. In this case, the loop is bounded by `n-1` so a traditional loop would be fine but Why3 does not make any effort to figure that out.

It is worth pointing out that each generated header file exposes *all* declarations from the corresponding WhyML module. For instance, file `baint32.h` declares the functions `create`, `get`, and `set`, as expected, but also "internal" functions `one_bit`, `bit_set`, and `set_bit`. Similarly, file `bfstring.h` declares the structure `filter` and the functions `bloom_filter`, `add`, and `mem`, but also the global variable `k` and the functions `hash` and `bit`. We translate all declarations because the translation is made on per-module basis. In WhyML, modules do not have dedicated interfaces and any module using module `Baint32` has access to all of its declarations. Thus, this ability must not be lost in translation.

An argument can be made that it is not crucial to ensure any abstraction barrier in the translated code since we have already made use of it on the WhyML side. This argument is less applicable when we develop a verified library for the target language, which is the case of `bfstring`. Indeed, the development will be pursued in the target language and thus it would be nice to hide the translated code behind a suitable interface. The simplest way to achieve it is just to remove unnecessary declarations from the generated header files. Finally, when translating to C, the whole discussion is moot since there is no proper encapsulation in C (it is always possible to bypass header files).

5   Related Work

The idea of conducting verification through stepwise refinements is not new. It is at the basis of Abrial's B method [1] for instance. In this context, abstract machines, which can be seen as interfaces, are gradually refined into fully executable machines, which are implementations. This is quite close to what we do: for instance, when we start with an interface `Filter` and refine it into an implementation `BFstring` in two steps. Proper modularity is also offered by the B method, as a machine is referring to the abstract version of another machine (its interface) and not to its refinements. Again, this is similar to what we do, for instance with our `GenericClient` referring to the interface `Filter`. Yet, there are fundamental differences between B machines and Why3 modules, the main being that B machines are state machines. Though Why3 modules can definitely be used to specify and implement state machines, they are not limited to this usage. Why3 modules may provide data types (as Boolean arrays and filters in our example) and this has no counterpart in the B method.

Abstraction and genericity are handled in programming languages in various ways. Most of these solutions can be readily used or adapted for use in program verifiers. When a program verifier is built for an existing programming language, such as Java for instance, it is natural to apply the abstraction and genericity mechanisms (e.g., object-oriented programming, visibility modifiers, generic types) to the specification/verification level. This is done in tools such as VeriFast [7] or KeY [2] for instance. When a program verifier is providing its own programming language, it is nonetheless possible to reuse mechanisms from the programming community. The Coq proof assistant, for instance, implements both a module system inspired by that of OCaml [5, 11] and type classes inspired by those of Haskell [16, 17].

Why3 modules are not a direct implementation of a concept from any programming language. Yet, they have obvious connections with traits [15] and mixins [3], even if they are not cast in some object-oriented context. Indeed, Why3 modules mix declarations and definitions, may require parameters to come with some operations (by cloning suitable "interfaces"), and may provide new definitions on top of these parameters (in modules to be later cloned in suitable contexts). The comparison stops at some point, however, as Why3 modules are not centered around types. A parameter of a Why3 module can be a constant, a function, etc., which means more flexibility. On the other hand, Why3 modules cannot be used to require that a type parameter of a polymorphic type or function provides some operations, contrary to traits or type classes.

Closest to our work is likely to be Dafny [9], where modules are used to organize the namespace and to restrict visibility of symbols or symbol definitions [10]. Thus it provides adequate abstraction during the verification of client code, though this is done by hiding implementation details rather than having the client exposed to an interface only. There is a notion of module refinement in Dafny [8]. As in Why3, it allows declarations to be refined with definitions and it permits data refinement, though it is class-based in Dafny and record-based in Why3. Dafny goes a step forward in program refinement, allowing reduction of nondeterminism in program statements during refinement.

6 Conclusion

We have shown how abstraction and genericity are provided in the Why3 program verifier through a notion of modules and a module cloning operation. The latter performs a partial substitution on a module, replacing some of its abstract declarations with concrete ones, and generates suitable verification conditions to guarantee correctness. In this paper, we demonstrated this mechanism on a library of Bloom filters, using several modules and refinement steps.

The module system of Why3, despite being usable (and extensively used), can still be improved in several regards.

First, we should avoid redundant verification conditions (such as ones generated for the `clone` instruction in the `Client` module) by taking into account the previously made refinements. In practice, these redundant VCs are usually easy to discharge, but it is preferable not to produce them at all.

Second, we should add support for scope-level cloning substitutions, which would allow us to write simply `clone GenericClient with scope Filter = BFstring`, and avoid long and tedious enumeration of individual refinements.

Third, it would be convenient to annotate an "implementation" module with its designated interface, e.g., by writing `module BAint32 : BoolArray`. This notation should automatically add an appropriate cloning instruction at the end of `BAint32`, ensuring that it indeed refines `BoolArray`. Furthermore, any subsequent `use` of `BAint32` in the client code should only add to the logical context the contents of `BoolArray`, acting as an abstraction barrier (of course, translation into executable code would still use the concrete definitions from `BAint32`). This can be achieved by implicitly replacing such `use` instructions with cloning of `BoolArray`, like we did in the `BloomFilter` module above; also, renaming substitutions should be applied to ensure symbol sharing where necessary.

Acknowledgments. We are grateful to Claude Marché, Jacques-Henri Jourdan, and Rustan Leino for their insightful remarks and suggestions.

References

1. Abrial, J.-R.: The B-Book, Assigning Programs to Meaning. Cambridge University Press, Cambridge (1996)
2. Ahrendt, W., Beckert, B., Bubel, R., Hähnle, R., Schmitt, P.H., Ulbrich, M. (eds.): Deductive Software Verification - The KeY Book - From Theory to Practice. LNCS, vol. 10001. Springer, Cham (2016). https://doi.org/10.1007/978-3-319-49812-6
3. Ancona, D., Zucca, E.: An algebraic approach to mixins and modularity. In: Hanus, M., Rodríguez-Artalejo, M. (eds.) ALP 1996. LNCS, vol. 1139, pp. 179–193. Springer, Heidelberg (1996). https://doi.org/10.1007/3-540-61735-3_12
4. Bloom, B.H.: Space/time trade-offs in hash coding with allowable errors. Commun. ACM **13**(7), 422–426 (1970)
5. Chrzaszcz, J.: Modules in Type Theoryx with Generative Definitions. Ph.D. thesis, Warsaw University, Poland and Université de Paris-Sud (January 2004)
6. Filliâtre, J.-C., Paskevich, A.: Why3—where programs meet provers. In: Felleisen, M., Gardner, P. (eds.) ESOP 2013. LNCS, vol. 7792, pp. 125–128. Springer, Heidelberg (2013). https://doi.org/10.1007/978-3-642-37036-6_8
7. Jacobs, B., Smans, J., Philippaerts, P., Vogels, F., Penninckx, W., Piessens, F.: VeriFast: a powerful, sound, predictable, fast verifier for C and Java. In: Bobaru, M., Havelund, K., Holzmann, G.J., Joshi, R. (eds.) NFM 2011. LNCS, vol. 6617, pp. 41–55. Springer, Heidelberg (2011). https://doi.org/10.1007/978-3-642-20398-5_4
8. Koenig, J., Rustan, K., Leino, M.: Programming language features for refinement. In: Derrick, J., Boiten, E.A., Reeves, S. (eds.) Proceedings of 17th International Workshop on Refinement, Refine@FM 2015. EPTCS, Oslo, Norway, 22 June 2015, vol. 209, pp. 87–106 (2015)
9. Leino, K.R.M.: Dafny: an automatic program verifier for functional correctness. In: Clarke, E.M., Voronkov, A. (eds.) LPAR 2010. LNCS (LNAI), vol. 6355, pp. 348–370. Springer, Heidelberg (2010). https://doi.org/10.1007/978-3-642-17511-4_20
10. Leino, K.R.M., Matichuk, D.: Modular verification scopes via export sets and translucent exports. In: Müller, P., Schaefer, I. (eds.) Principled Software Development, pp. 185–202. Springer, Cham (2018). https://doi.org/10.1007/978-3-319-98047-8_12
11. Leroy, X.: A modular module system. J. Funct. Program. **10**(3), 269–303 (2000)
12. Louridas, P.: Real-World Algorithms: A Beginner's Guide. The MIT Press, Cambridge (2017)
13. Mitzenmacher, M., Upfal, E.: Probability and Computing: Randomized Algorithms and Probabilistic Analysis. Cambridge University Press, New York (2005)
14. Rieu-Helft, R., Marché, C., Melquiond, G.: How to get an efficient yet verified arbitrary-precision integer library. In: Paskevich, A., Wies, T. (eds.) VSTTE 2017. LNCS, vol. 10712, pp. 84–101. Springer, Cham (2017). https://doi.org/10.1007/978-3-319-72308-2_6
15. Schärli, N., Ducasse, S., Nierstrasz, O., Black, A.P.: Traits: composable units of behaviour. In: Cardelli, L. (ed.) ECOOP 2003. LNCS, vol. 2743, pp. 248–274. Springer, Heidelberg (2003). https://doi.org/10.1007/978-3-540-45070-2_12
16. Mohamed, O.A., Muñoz, C., Tahar, S. (eds.): TPHOLs 2008. LNCS, vol. 5170. Springer, Heidelberg (2008). https://doi.org/10.1007/978-3-540-71067-7
17. Wadler, P., Blott. S.: How to make ad-hoc polymorphism less ad hoc. In: Proceedings of the 16th ACM SIGPLAN-SIGACT Symposium on Principles of Programming Languages, POPL 1889, pp. 60–76. ACM, New York (1989)

Verification Artifacts in Cooperative Verification: Survey and Unifying Component Framework

Dirk Beyer[1] and Heike Wehrheim[2]

[1] LMU Munich, Munich, Germany
[2] Paderborn University, Paderborn, Germany

Abstract. The goal of *cooperative* verification is to combine verification approaches in such a way that they work together to verify a system model. In particular, cooperative verifiers *provide* exchangeable information (verification artifacts) *to* other verifiers or *consume* such information *from* other verifiers with the goal of increasing the overall effectiveness and efficiency of the verification process.

This paper first gives an overview over approaches for leveraging strengths of different techniques, algorithms, and tools in order to increase the power and abilities of the state of the art in software verification. To limit the scope, we restrict our overview to tools and approaches for automatic program analysis. Second, we specifically outline cooperative verification approaches and discuss their employed verification artifacts. Third, we formalize all artifacts in a uniform way, thereby fixing their semantics and providing verifiers with a precise meaning of the exchanged information.

Keywords: Cooperative verification · Software verification · Conditional model checking · Verification witness · Exchange format · Partial verification · Reducer · Execution report · Tool combination

1 Introduction

The area of software verification studies methods and constructs tools for automatically proving program properties. The recent past has seen an enormous improvement in this area, in particular with respect to scalability, precision, and the handling of different programming-language features. Today's software-verification tools employ a variety of different techniques, ranging from data-flow analysis [69] over symbolic execution [70] to SAT-based approaches [16,33]. As all these techniques have their particular strengths and weaknesses, a number of tools *tightly* integrate different —usually two— approaches into one tool (see [17] for an overview). For instance, the integration of techniques that under- and over-approximate the state space of the program is a frequent combination. Such combinations typically improve over pure approaches. However, such conceptual integrations also require new tool implementations for every additional integration

---

A preliminary version of this article appeared as technical report [30].
Funded in part by the Deutsche Forschungsgemeinschaft (DFG) – 418257054 (Coop)

T. Margaria and B. Steffen (Eds.): ISoLA 2020, LNCS 12476, pp. 143–167, 2020.
https://doi.org/10.1007/978-3-030-61362-4_8

of techniques. Portfolio combinations *loosely* integrate different tools: There is no communication between the approaches and the resulting combination can be composed from off-the-shelf components. Algorithm selection combines different approaches into one by first analyzing the input problem and then choosing the approach that will most likely (according to some heuristics) succeed.

In contrast to these extremely tight or extremely loose combinations, *cooperative verification* is a combination of approaches that *cooperate*, that is, work together to achieve the verification goal, but leave the existing tools (mostly) untouched. Cooperative verifiers *communicate* with each other in order to maximize the common strength, in particular, by exchanging information about intermediate results. In a framework for cooperative verification, the integration of a new technique might require some implementation to make it understand the communication, viz. be able to use intermediate results, but it can avoid a new re-implementation of the combination — from the conceptual as well as from the practical viewpoint. If the intermediate results come in a format already accepted by the tool (e.g. as a program), the tool can even be employed as is.

In this paper, we provide a classification of verification approaches according to the interface and type of combination employed; we briefly survey combination approaches, for portfolio, selection, cooperative, and conceptual combination of verification approaches. We then discuss a number of aspects relevant to cooperative verification, in particular its objectives and prerequisites.

2   Classification of Verification Approaches

In the following, we provide a classification of verification approaches according to their way of interfacing and combining verification components. By the term "verification approach" we understand an automatic or automatable formal method for solving *verification tasks*, i.e., for evaluating the proposition "Program p satisfies behavioral specification φ_b" and returning a result r, which can be TRUE ($p \models \varphi_b$), FALSE ($p \not\models \varphi_b$), or UNKNOWN, and an (optional) witness ω, which contains proof hints, as depicted in Fig. 1.

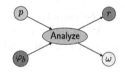

Fig. 1. Formal verification

2.1   Overview over Interfaces

Output. The goal of a verification tool is to solve a verification task and to deliver the computed results to either a verification engineer for manual inspection or to a machine for further automated processing (Fig. 2). Depending on how the results are consumed (by human or by machine), the tool needs to use different formats.

Fig. 2. Output Interfaces

While researchers mainly concentrated on improving the (internal) verification algorithms during the past two decades, it is understood since recently that it is (at least) equally important to provide not only TRUE/FALSE answers, but more details about the reasoning and the process of the verification.

Human. Almost all verification tools provide some kind of statistics to the user, for example, about the number of iterations, of number of proof facts, or consumed resources. *Execution reports* [34] present an underapproximation of the successfully verified state space to the user. There are also approaches to support interactive inspection of verification results, e.g., by visualization of error paths [81] and verification-aided debugging [11].

Machine. In order to make it possible to validate verification results in an automated way, *verification witnesses* were introduced [8,31], a machine-readable exchange format (XML based). Verification witnesses make it possible to independently re-verify the program based on knowledge that another verifier has produced. This can increase trust in the results, can spread the risk of verification errors, and can help making internal knowledge from the verification engine accessible for the user (error paths, program invariants). *Violation witnesses* [14] enhance the answer FALSE by a description of the state space that contains an error path (a program path that violates the specification), while *correctness witnesses* [13] enhance the answer TRUE by a description of program invariants that are helpful to prove that the program satisfies the specification. It is known since 15 years that test cases can be derived from error paths [9,96], but this approach was rarely used in practice and only since recently it is possible to output and exchange this kind of information via a standard format.

   While the previous approaches, as the name indicates, witness the verification result, it is also important to make intermediate results and partial results accessible to further processing. *Conditional model checking* [19] reads as input and writes as output a description of the already verified state space. That is, a conditional verifier outputs a condition that describes the work already done, i.e, the parts of the state space that are already verified. Another kind of intermediate output for machines to later reuse is the *abstraction precision* [23,29,86]. In CEGAR-based approaches [38] an abstract model is automatically constructed by finding abstraction facts in refinement steps which are added to the precision of the analysis (the more abstraction facts are added to the precision, the finer the abstract model). Full abstract models can be used as certificate of correctness [66] or in order to speed up later verification runs for different versions of the same program during regression verification [60].

Input. Similar to the output, there are different interfaces for the kind of input that is given to the verification tools, some from users, some from machines, see Fig. 3.

Fig. 3. Input Interfaces

Human. From the very beginning of programming, assertions were added to programs [94] in order to make it easier to prove correctness. Nowadays, assertions, invariants, pre- and post-conditions, are annotated in programs in a way that machines (inter-active verifiers) can read [5,59]. There are several languages and tools that support this, and a nice overview over such tools and their application opportunities are given in the annual competition on interactive software verification VerifyThis [49].

There were also attempts to support the splitting of specifications and pro-grams into modular parts, in order to make the verification task for the model checkers easier, such as in the BLAST query language [10,87]. There are also testing and analysis tools which ask the user for help [98]. Last not least, and this is one of the most difficult parts, each verifier expects a set of parameters that the user has to set, in order to choose how the verifier should solve its task. However, finding the right parameters is a challenging task, which could use tool support itself (such as SMAC [64] or Tuner [92]).

Machine. A classic approach to make additional information available to a tool is by transforming the original input, e.g., by simplification or enhancement. The advantage is that there is no additional input (no extra parser, no need to imple-ment additional features). For example, the first software model checkers did not have a specification language, but the specification was weaved into the program in a preprocessing step (as was done for the SLAM [3] specification language SLIC [2] and the BLAST [18] query language [10]). Even programs were made simpler [78].

Verification witnesses and conditions were discussed already above as example implementations for output interfaces. Verification witnesses can be taken as input by validation tools that re-establish the verification result using independent tech-nology. Also, the error path described by the violation witness can be replayed and a test case can be derived from the path constraints along the found error path [15].

Conditional model checking is not widespread yet because it was considered difficult to extend a verifier such that it understands conditions as input and reduces the state space accordingly before running the verification engine. This problem was solved by the reducer-based construction of conditional verifiers: *Reducers* [25,45] can be used to construct (without implementation effort) condi-tional model checkers from off-the-shelf verifiers that do not understand conditions themselves, by reducing the original input program to a residual program that contains all the behavior that is not yet covered by the condition and removes as much as possible from the already-verified state space.

2.2   Overview over Combinations

In the early days of automatic program verification, tools implemented a single technique for verification (e.g., explicit enumeration of state space or data-flow analysis using a fixed abstract domain). In our classification (see Fig. 4) these are represented as **Basic**. Later, the tools implementing these techniques were considerably generalized, for instance by allowing abstract domains to be flexibly set via tool parameters. Still, during one verification run a sin-gle basic technique was employed.

It soon turned out that a single verification technique may work well for some verification tasks, but fail for others. This immediately triggered the ap-plication of **Combination** techniques, in order to benefit from the different

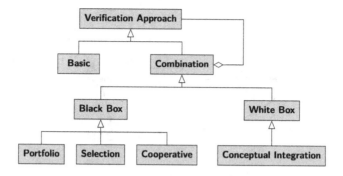

Fig. 4. Hierarchy of verification approaches (using UML notation)

strengths. Combinations can come in two sorts: A combination either treats techniques or tools as **Black Box** objects and runs them (mainly) as they are without implementation-specific integrations for which it matters what's inside the box, or a combination views a component as **White Box**, conceptually integrating two or more techniques within a new tool. We distinguish three forms of black-box combinations, without and with communication, and classify all white-box approaches into one category.

Portfolio combinations are motivated by the portfolio idea from economics [63], which is a means for distributing the risk: if one investment (here: of computational resources in a certain technique) fails, there are other investments (techniques) that will be successful. A portfolio combination has a number of approaches available, and on a given verification task executes the approaches in a fixed order sequentially (Fig. 5, top), or runs all approaches in parallel (Fig. 5, bottom). The overall approach terminates if one component analysis was successful in obtaining the result.

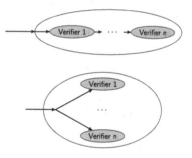

Fig. 5. Portfolio approaches (top: sequential, bottom: parallel)

The big advantage of this approach is that it requires no knowledge about the components and there is almost no effort for implementing the combination. Therefore, we placed this most loosely coupled approach on the very left in the bottom row of Fig. 4. The big disadvantage of portfolio approaches is that the resources invested on unsuccessful tools or approaches are lost.

Algorithm **Selection** [85] is a solution to the problem of wasted resources of portfolio approaches: Algorithm-selection approaches have a number of approaches available, and on a given verification task choose one and execute it (Fig. 6). That is, before starting an approach, a selection model is extracted from the input, based on which a selector function predicts which approach would be best, and only the potentially best approach is selected and executed. This requires some knowledge about the (black box) characterization of the components, but does not require any change of the implementation of the components.

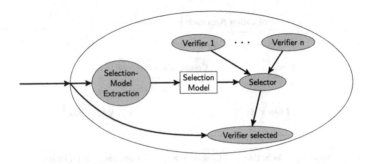

Fig. 6. Algorithm selection

Portfolio and selection approaches run the component tools independently from each other, without any form of information exchange between the approaches. The goal of combining strengths of different approaches and at the same time avoiding to waste resources inspired the development of *cooperative* combinations of verification approaches.

Cooperation approaches enable the possibility of solving the problem *together*. Typically, tools exchange intermediate results (e.g., the state space which has already been searched) in order to achieve a division of labor. Such cooperative combinations range from two or more basic techniques running in parallel and combining the information obtained for certain program locations (e.g., combining partial verification results to proof witnesses [67]) to approaches executing different tools in turns with each specializing to specific tasks (e.g., a testing tool trying to achieve coverage together with a model checker constructing counter examples to non-reachability [46]).

Conceptual Integration is the most intensively coupled approach and therefore put on the very right end of the bottom row in Fig. 4. The components are not communicating via clear interfaces, but are tightly integrated and exchange data structures via procedure calls and not via interfaces that could be externalized [17].

In the following subsections, we describe some forms of non-cooperative verification approaches in more detail. In the next section we explain some examples for cooperative verification approaches.

2.3 Examples for Portfolio Combinations

While it seems obvious that portfolio combinations of verification techniques have a large potential, the topic has not yet been systematically investigated for software verification, although it is used in other areas since many years [63].

Sequential Combinations. Examples of sequential combinations are SDV and CPACHECKER. The static driver verification (SDV) [4] tool chain at Microsoft used a sequential combination (described in [93]) which first runs Corral [71] for up to 1 400 s and then Yogi [80]. CPACHECKER [26] won the competition on software verification 2013 (SV-COMP'13, [7]) using a sequential combination [97] that started with explicit-state model checking for up to 100 s and then switched to a predicate analysis [27].

Parallel Combinations. Examples of parallel combinations are the verifiers UFO [57] and PREDATORHP [77], which start several different strategies simultaneously and take the result from the approach that terminates first.

2.4   Examples for Algorithm Selection

Algorithm selection [85] first extracts a *selection model* from the input. In the case of software verification, the input is the verification task (program and its specification). The selection model describes some characteristics of the verification task, for example, feature vectors (measurement values for certain measures that map verification tasks to values). Based on the selection model, the *strategy selector* chooses one strategy from a set of given verification strategies.

Approaches without Machine Learning. Strategy selection can be very simple and yet effective. For example, a recent work has shown that it is possible with a few boolean features to effectively improve the overall verification progress [12]. The disadvantage is that the strategy selector needs to be explicitly defined by the developer or user. This leads to approaches that use machine learning, in order to automatically learn the strategy selector from training instances.

Machine-Learning-Based Approaches. The technique MUX [93] can be used to synthesize a strategy selector for a set of features of the input program and a given number of strategies. The strategies are verification tools in this case, and the feature values for the selection model are statically extracted from the source code of the input program. Later, a technique that uses more sophisticated features was proposed [47,48]. While the above techniques use explicit features (defined by measures on the source code), a more recently developed technique [44] leaves it up to the machine learning to obtain insights from the input program. The advantage is that there is no need to define the features: the learner is given the control-flow graph, the data-dependency graph, and the abstract syntax tree, and automatically derives internally the characteristics that it needs. Also, the technique predicts a ranking, that is, the strategy selector is not a function that maps verification tasks to a strategy, but to a sequence of strategies.

2.5   Examples for Conceptual Integrations

Conceptual integrations tightly combine two or more approaches into a new tool, typically re-implementing the basic techniques. A frequent combination of this type is integrating an overapproximating (static) may-analysis with an underapproximating (dynamic) must-analysis. The tool SMASH [54] at the same time maintains an over- and an under-approximation of the state space of programs. Building on the same idea, Yogi [6] (first proposal of the algorithm was under the name SYNERGY [55]) in addition specifically employs testing to derive alias information which is costly to precisely compute by a static analysis.

A second form of conceptual integration is offered by tools running different analysis in parallel in a form of "product" construction. For example, the verification framework CPACHECKER [26] provides the possibility of specifying and running *composite* analyses. A composite analysis could for instance combine two sorts of data-flow analyses (e.g., an interval analysis and an available-expression analysis). The analyses are then jointly run and jointly derive analysis information for program locations. The same idea was classically hard-coded as reduced product [40] and further improved [22,39,43,50,56,72].

All those combinations have in common that they exchange information, but they are configured, intertwined, or even hardcoded combinations, rather than interface-based black-box combinations. More approaches are described in the Handbook on Model Checking, in the chapters on combining model checking with data-flow analysis [17], with deductive verification [88], and with testing [53].

2.6   Verification as a Web Service

Orthogonally to the above combinations, approaches can be combined by providing them as web services. The *Electronic Tools Integration* platform (ETI) [91] was developed for experimenting with, presenting, evaluating, conserving, and coordinating tools. Later, the approach was extended to make it possible to use the tools via a web site [74–76], such that the user does not need to install any software. ETI uses LTL as specification language, and the systems to be verified can be software systems or models of systems (e.g., times automata). The central point of information of ETI is important, as otherwise, it is time-consuming to collect the URLs of web services to different tool providers, such as, for example, CPACHECKER[1], DAFNY[2], and ULTIMATE[3]. It is even more difficult to get them to cooperate if the tools are distributed, using different interfaces. Unfortunately, the ETI initiative was discontinued, according to Steffen [90] because of the manual integration effort at the ETI site in Dortmund and because tool providers hesitated to provide their tools.

3   Cooperative Verification Approaches

In the following, we discuss approaches for cooperative verification, structured according to the kind of information objects that are exchanged, and then explain a few applications and their effects.

3.1   Exchangeable Objects for Communication and Information Transfer

We now classify the approaches for cooperative verification according to the kinds of communication interfaces that they use. While our text always refers to software verification for concrete examples, cooperative verification is in no way limited to software.

---

[1] https://vcloud.sosy-lab.org/cpachecker/webclient/run/

[2] https://rise4fun.com/Dafny/

[3] https://monteverdi.informatik.uni-freiburg.de/tomcat/Website/

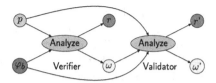

Fig. 7. Witness-based results validation

Conditions and Residual Programs. Conditional model checking (CMC) [19] means to produce a condition as output that describes the state-space that was successfully verified. The (temporal) condition can be represented as an automaton. This information can be passed on to another verifier as input, instructing this verifier to not verify again those parts of the state space that are covered by the condition. Using a *reducer* [25], a program can be reduced to those parts of its state space that still has to be verified; the result is called *residual program*. Symbiotic [36] can be seen as reducer-based cooperation (slicer + KLEE). Inspired by CMC, comprehensive failure characterization (CFC) [51] computes a condition that represents failure paths, using several tools that cooperate on the task. Alternating conditional analysis (implemented in the tool ALPACA [52][4]) is a generalization of CFC and involves a portfolio of 14 tools for program analysis.

Witnesses. Exchangeable witnesses serve as envelopes for error paths and invariants in a way that makes it possible to exchange the information between different tools. A *violation witness* [8,14,31] explains the specification violation, by describing a path through the program that violates the specification. A *correctness witness* [13] explains why the program satisfied the specification, by describing invariants that are useful to have in a correctness proof. Figure 7 illustrates the process: The first analyzer verifies the program p according to specification φ_b, and produces a result r and a witness ω. The second analyzer (re-)verifies the same program and specification using information from the witness. If the result r matches the result r', then the result is confirmed.

Precisions. Verification approaches that are based on counterexample-guided abstraction refinement (CEGAR) [38] iteratively construct an abstract model of the system. The "abstraction facts" that define the level of abstraction are often formalized and expressed as *precision* [23,29,31,86]. The precision can be exported as output, such that later verification runs can start from such a given definition of the abstraction level.

Abstract States / Certificates. Extreme model checking [60] dumps the abstract reachability graph (ARG) to a file when the verification process terminates. Configurable certificates [66] are sets of abstract states that cover all reachable states of the system. ARGs and configurable certificates can be used by a different verifier to check their validity (completeness and soundness).

Path Programs and Path Invariants. Path programs [21] are programs (for example, written in the same programming language as the input program) that

---

[4] https://bitbucket.org/mgerrard/alpaca/

were invented to incorporate external invariant generators into CEGAR-based approaches and are produced after a verifier has found an infeasible error path (often called infeasible counterexample). The path program contains that path in question, but usually also longer paths that use the same program operations, that is, unrollings of a certain loop. The path program can now be given to a tool for invariant synthesis (e.g., [20]) in order to obtain *path invariants* [21], which are invariants for the whole path program, but in particular also for the original path. The path invariants can then be fed back into the CEGAR-based approach that was encountering the original path.

Taint-Analysis Queries and Answers. Taint analyses perform a specific sort of software verification. They do not look at the satisfaction of behavioral specifications, but at the *flow of information* (typically within smartphone applications) from private sources to public sinks. In this area of software analysis, numerous tools with complementary strengths exist which has already lead to the proposal of a cooperative taint-analysis tool [83]. Information exchange among tools is therein performed via the AQL (Android-App Analysis Query Language [82]) which allows to state task queries as well as answers to these queries.

Evidential Tool Bus. The evidential tool bus [41,42] is a tool-integration framework, which is based on a variant of Datalog [1,35] as a meta language. Artifacts like claims, rules, and evidence are described in this language, as well as verification workflows. The idea is to compose assurance claims (certificates) based on evidence artifacts contributed by different tools, which interact in the evidential tool bus using scripts, queries, and evidence artifacts. Artifacts for models and programs are stored together with evidence artifacts. The intended application area is not only software verification, but the verification of systems in general (that is, models of systems).

Program Annotations. Assertions [94] and other information about the behavior of the program can be added to the program as annotations [5]. An overview over behavioral interface specification languages can be found in the literature [59].

3.2   Objectives and Applications

Having exchangeable objects about (partial) verification results [32] available is important to overcome a variety of practical problems. In the following, we highlight a few of the objectives and applications that we can aim for.

Improvement of Effectiveness and Efficiency. Storing intermediate results can be used to improve the effectiveness and efficiency of the verification process.

Stateful Verification and Reuse. Storing (exchangeable) objects that contain information about intermediate verification results can be considered as a *state* of the verification process, i.e., making the verification process *stateful.*

Precisions that are stored and in later verification runs read and reused can significantly improve the performance of regression verification [29,86]. The setup of this strategy is the following: the first version of a module is verified and at the end, the precision is written to a file. When the i-th version is verified, then the verifier reads the precision that the verification run for version $i-1$ has written, in order to save time discovering the right abstraction level for the abstract model.

Configurable certificates [66] can reduce the validation time, because the verifier that performs the validation of the certificate "only" needs to check for the set of abstract states that all initial states are contained and that the set is closed under successor transitions.

Also *caching-based approaches* to improve the efficiency can be seen as a stateful way of performing computation. For example, Green [95] makes symbolic execution more efficient by caching previous intermediate results.

Stateless Verification and Parallelization. The previous argument was based on having a state that contains the intermediate results. It is also possible to speed up verification processes in a *stateless* way. The technique of conditional model checking is used to split programs into parts that can be independently verified [89].

Improvement of Precision and Confidence. *Witness-based results validation* [13,14] can be used to increase the confidence in the results of verification tools, because it is possible to take a witness-based results validator to "replay" the verification. That is, for a violation witness, the validator tries to find and confirm the error path that the witness describes, and for a correctness witness, the validator tries to use the invariants in the witness to re-establish the proof of correctness.

Execution-based results validation [15] extracts a test case from a violation witness and executes it, in order to confirm that the specification violation is observable in the executed program as well.

Explainability. The existence and availability of exchangeable objects with information about the verification process makes it possible to develop approaches for *explaining* what the verification process did and why the user should be more confident about the verification result. There are preliminary results on explaining and visualizing counterexamples, e.g., for SPIN models [73] and for C programs [11,81], but due to the exchangeable witness format, many more approaches are possible.

4   Verification Artifacts

This section outlines a construction framework for cooperation. We study verification *artifacts*, classify several verification tools as verification *actors* according to their usage of artifacts, and define the *semantics* of some important artifacts.

4.1   Artifacts of Verification Tools

Verification artifacts are central to cooperation as they provide the means of information exchange. A number of artifacts exist already, most notably of course the programs themselves. We identified the following artifacts:

Program p. Defines the implemented behavior of the system. **Syntax**: C programming language (for example). We represent programs as control-flow automata in Sect. 4.3.

Behavior Specification φ_b. Defines requirements that all executions of a given program have to satisfy, often as conjunction of several properties. **Syntax:** The competition SV-COMP established a minimal set of properties that participants of the competition have to support[5], which is based on LTL [84], but some tools also support monitor automata as specification. We represent properties by property automata in Sect. 4.3.

Test Specification φ_t. Defines requirements that a given test suite has to satisfy. **Syntax:** The competition Test-Comp established a minimal set of coverage criteria that participants of the competition have to support[6], which is based on FQL [61,62]; some tools offer parameters for hard-coded coverage criteria. We represent coverage criteria by test-goal automata in Sect. 4.3.

Verification Result r. Verification tools return an evaluation of the statement "Program p satisfies specification φ_b." as answer. **Syntax:** The answer is from the set {TRUE, FALSE, UNKNOWN}.

Witness ω. Verification witnesses are used to witness an outcome of a verification run, and thus can come in the form of violation and correctness witnesses. **Syntax:** XML-based witness format[7] that is supported by all available validators of verification results.

Test case t. Defines a sequence of values for all calls of external functions, i.e., inputs for the program. **Syntax:** XML-based test-case format[8] that is supported by all test-case generators that participate in Test-Comp.

Condition ψ. Defines the part of the program behavior that does not need to be further explored. For verification, ψ describes the already verified parts. For testing, ψ describes the parts of the program that are already covered by an existing test suite. **Syntax:** Condition automata using a notation similar to the BLAST query lang. [10] for verification and test-goal sets for testing [28].

We use the corresponding capital letters to denote the types (i.e., sets of artifacts of a kind), for example, the type P is the set of all C programs. Many tools generate different forms of verification artifacts, but currently only very few understand more than the artifact "program" as input.

4.2 Classification of Verification Tools as Actors

Based on the identified artifacts, we classify existing tools according to their usage of artifacts into three sorts of verification actors:

Analyzers. Produce new knowledge about programs, for example verification results or test suites.

Transformers. Translate one artifact into another, in order to implement a certain feature or support cooperation.

Presenters. Prepare information from artifacts such that it can be presented in a human-readable form.

---

[5] https://sv-comp.sosy-lab.org/2019/rules.php

[6] https://test-comp.sosy-lab.org/2019/rules.php

[7] https://github.com/sosy-lab/sv-witnesses

[8] https://gitlab.com/sosy-lab/software/test-format

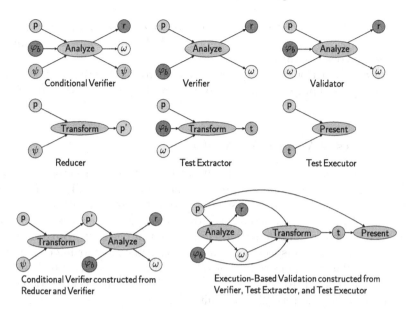

Fig. 8. Graphical visualization of the component framework

To convey a better understanding of these concepts, consider the following examples: A *verifier* is an analyzer of type $P \times \Phi_b \to R \times \Omega$, which takes as input a program p and a behavior specification φ_b, and produces as output a result r and a witness ω[9]. A *conditional verifier* is of type $P \times \Phi_b \times \Psi \to R \times \Omega \times \Psi$, i.e., a verifier that supports also input and output conditions. A *validator* is of type $P \times \Phi_b \times \Omega \to R \times \Omega$, i.e., a verifier that takes as input in addition a witness. A *test-case generator* is also an analyzer, but of type $P \times \Phi_t \to 2^T$, which takes as input a program p and a test specification φ_t, and produces as output a set $ts \in 2^T$ of test cases.

Transformers are largely lacking today, only a few exist already [15,25,58,79]. Transformers are, however, key to cooperation: only if a transformer can bring the artifact into a form understandable by the next tool without implementing an extension of this tool, cooperation can be put into practice. A *test-case extractor* is a transformer of type $P \times \Phi_b \times \Omega \to T$, which translates a program, specification, and violation witness to a test case. The identity function is also a transformer (for any given type). A *reducer* is a transformer of type $P \times \Psi \to P$, which takes a program and a condition as input, and transforms it to a residual program.

Presenters form the interface to the user. A *test-case executor* is a presenter of type $P \times T \to \{\}$, which takes a program p and a test case t as input, and shows a particular program execution (perhaps with a crash) to the software engineer.

Now we can construct, for example, a conditional verifier from a reducer *red* and an off-the-shelf verifier *ver* by composition. For inputs p, φ_b, and ψ, the expression $ver(red(p, \psi), \varphi_b)$ runs the construction. For a verification with an execution-based result validation based on a given verifier *ver*, test extractor *wit2test*,

---

[9] All verifiers that participate in the competition SV-COMP are analyzers of this form.

and test executor $exec$, we can write $exec(p, wit2test(p, \varphi_b, ver(p, \varphi_b).\omega))$. Figure 8 shows a graphical visualization of the individual components and the two mentioned constructions.

With our construction framework, it is possible to identify the gaps of meaningful transformers, and propose solutions to close these gaps, as far as needed for cooperation.

4.3   Semantics of Verification Artifacts

We now develop the theoretical foundations of artifacts and actors. Artifacts describe some information about a program (or a program itself), and for sound cooperation we need to define the *semantics* of artifacts. For instance, a violation witness of a program describes a path of the program on which a specific specification is violated, a condition describes a set of paths of a program which have (or have not been) inspected by an analyzer. When employing cooperation as a means for sharing the work load of validation, the cooperating tools need to agree on the meaning of the exchanged artifacts. Without this, cooperation might easily get unsound, e.g., returning a result TRUE for a program and specification although the combined usage of tools has failed to inspect the whole state space of the program. By defining the semantics of artifacts, we also implicitly define the desired semantics of the various actors operating on artifacts.

All of the artifacts given below are a variation of finite-state automata. The reasons for choosing automata as our formalization are twofold: First, artifacts arising in software verification naturally incorporate the sequencing of actions or events as specifiable via automata (e.g., programs have control flow, paths or counterexamples are sequences of operations), and second, a number of verification tools already accept or produce artifacts which are some sort of automata (e.g., violation or correctness witnesses).

We start the formalization of artifacts with the definition of programs, our prime artifact. We denote the set of all program locations by Loc. Formally, a program p is described by a *control-flow automaton* (CFA) $A_p = (L, \ell_0, G)$ that consists of a set of locations $L \subseteq Loc$, an initial location $\ell_0 \in L$, and a set of control-flow edges $G \subseteq L \times Ops \times L$, where Ops is the set of operations. Operations can be (a) assignments, (b) assume statements (arising out of branches), and (c) calls to functions retrieving inputs. Here, we assume to have a single such function, called input. We let $\mathcal{G} = L \times Ops \times L$ be the set of all control-flow edges.

We let X be the set of variables occurring in the operations Ops. For simplicity, we restrict the type of variables to integers. A *concrete data state* $c : X \rightharpoonup \mathbb{Z}$ is thus a partial mapping from X to $\mathbb{Z}$. In the left of Fig. 9 we see our running example of the simple program p and its control-flow automaton on the right. The program starts by retrieving an input for variable x, sets variables a and b to 0, and then increments both while the value of a is less than that of x.

A *concrete program path* of a program $A_p = (L, \ell_0, G)$ is a sequence $(c_0, \ell_0) \xrightarrow{g_1} \ldots \xrightarrow{g_n} (c_n, \ell_n)$, where the initial concrete data state $c_0 = \emptyset$ assigns no value, $g_i = (\ell_{i-1}, op_i, \ell_i) \in G$, and $c_{i-1} \xrightarrow{op_i} c_i$, i.e., (a) in case of assume

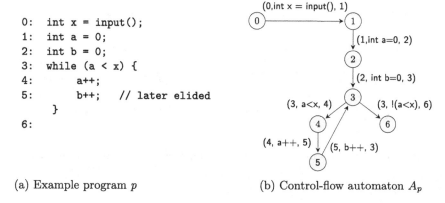

```
0:    int x = input();
1:    int a = 0;
2:    int b = 0;
3:    while (a < x) {
4:        a++;
5:        b++;  // later elided
      }
6:
```

(a) Example program p (b) Control-flow automaton A_p

Fig. 9. Example program and its control-flow automaton

operations, $c_{i-1} \models op_i$ (op_i is a boolean condition) and $c_{i-1} = c_i$, (b) in case of assignments, $c_i = \mathsf{SP}_{op_i}(c_{i-1})$, where SP is the strongest-post operator of the operational semantics, and (c) in case of inputs of the form $x = \texttt{input}()$, $c_i(x) \in \mathbb{Z}$ (nondeterministic choice of input) and $c_i(y) = c_{i-1}(y)$ for all $y \neq x$. An edge g is *contained* in a concrete program path $\pi = (c_0, \ell_0) \xrightarrow{g_1} \ldots \xrightarrow{g_n} (c_n, \ell_n)$ if $g = g_i$ for some $i \in [1, n]$. We let $paths(A_p)$ be the set of all concrete program paths.

We allow artifacts to state *assumptions* and *invariants* on program variables. These are given as state conditions (from a set Φ of predicates over a certain theory). We write $c \models \psi$ and $c \models \varphi$ to say that a concrete state c satisfies an assumption $\psi \in \Phi$ and an invariant $\varphi \in \Phi$, respectively.

Artifacts on a program p are represented by protocol automata [14]:

Definition 1. *A **protocol automaton** $A = (Q, \Sigma, \delta, q_0, F)$ for a program CFA $A_p = (L, \ell_0, G)$ consists of*

- *a finite set $Q \subseteq \Omega \times \Phi$ of states, each being a pair of a name and an invariant, and an initial state $q_0 \in Q$,*
- *an alphabet $\Sigma \subseteq 2^G \times \Phi$,*
- *a transition relation $\delta \subseteq Q \times \Sigma \times Q$, and*
- *a set $F \subseteq Q$ of final states.*

We write $q \xrightarrow{(D, \psi)} q'$ for $(q, (D, \psi), q') \in \delta$. In figures, we often elide invariants at states and assumptions at edges when they are *true*. We furthermore elide the set notation when the element of 2^G is a singleton.

Protocol automata describe paths of a program.[10] Depending on the sort of protocol automaton, these could for instance be paths allowed or disallowed by a specification, or paths already checked by a verifier. A path of the program can be *accepted* (if the automaton reaches a final state) or *covered* by the automaton.

---

[10] Note: Each CFA (L, ℓ_0, G) induces a protocol automaton (where $\top$ denotes *true*) $\big(L \times \{\top\}, \{(\{g\}, \top) \mid g \in G\}, \{(l, (\{g\}, \top), l') \mid g = (l, op, l') \in G\}, (\ell_0, \top), L \times \{\top\}\big)$.

(a) Property automaton $A_{\neg \varphi_b}$ (b) Test-goal automaton A_{φ_t}

Fig. 10. Automata for a property and a test-goal specification

Definition 2. *A protocol automaton $A = (Q, \Sigma, \delta, q_0, F)$ **matches** a path $\pi = (c_0, \ell_0) \xrightarrow{g_1} \dots \xrightarrow{g_n} (c_n, \ell_n)$ if there is a run $\rho = q_0 \xrightarrow{(G_1, \psi_1)} \dots \xrightarrow{(G_k, \psi_k)} q_k$ in A, with $k \in [0, n]$, s.t.*

1. *$\forall i \in [1, k] : g_i \in G_i$,*
2. *$\forall i \in [0, k] : c_i \models \varphi$, for $q_i = (\cdot, \varphi)$ and*
3. *$\forall i \in [1, k] : c_i \models \psi_i$.*

*The protocol automaton A **accepts** the path π if A matches π and $q_k \in F$, and A **covers** π if A matches π and $k = n$.*

We let $L(A)$ be the set of paths accepted by the automaton A (its *language*) and *paths*(A) be the set of paths covered by A. As we will see below, some protocol automata might have an empty set of final states and just describe a set of paths that they cover.

Protocol Automata as Representation of Artifacts. We consider different specializations of protocol automata and use the notation A_s to denote the automaton that represents the syntactical object s.

(1) A **property automaton** (or, observer automaton) $A_{\neg \varphi_b} = (Q, \Sigma, \delta, q_0, F)$ is a protocol automaton that satisfies the following conditions:

1. $\forall (\cdot, \varphi) \in Q : \varphi = true$,
2. $\forall q \in Q \setminus F, \forall g \in G : \bigvee \left\{ \psi \mid \exists q \xrightarrow{(D, \psi)} q' \in \delta : g \in D \right\} = true$
    (assuming $\bigvee \emptyset = false$).

Condition 2 ensures that property automata only observe the state of the program (when running in parallel with the program). They do not block, except for the case when the final state is reached where blocking is allowed. Final states denote the reaching of property violations (or, targets).

(2) A **test-goal automaton** $A_{\varphi_t} = (Q, \Sigma, \delta, q_0, F)$ is a protocol automaton that has only trivial state invariants, i.e., $\forall (\cdot, \varphi) \in Q : \varphi = true$. If a final state is reached, the test goal is fulfilled.

Figure 10 shows two specification automata: In Fig. 10a we see a property automaton specifying that variables a and b have to be equal when the loop terminates, i.e., the error state is reached if there is a transition from location 3 to 6 at which $a \neq b$. The label o/w (otherwise) denotes all transitions other

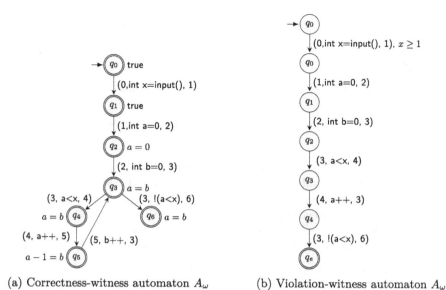

(a) Correctness-witness automaton A_ω (b) Violation-witness automaton A_ω

Fig. 11. Automata for a correctness witness for program p and a violation witness for p without line 5, both wrt. behavior specification φ_b of Fig. 10a.

than the ones explicitly depicted. Figure 10b depicts a test-goal automaton for the branch condition entering the loop.

(3) A **violation-witness automaton** $A_\omega = (Q, \Sigma, \delta, q_0, F)$ is a protocol automaton with trivial state invariants only, i.e., $\forall (\cdot, \varphi) \in Q : \varphi = true.$

Violation witnesses are used to describe the part of a program's state space which contains the error. The final state is reached if an error is detected. Counterexamples are a specific form of violation witnesses which describe a single path.

(4) A **correctness-witness automaton** $A_\omega = (Q, \Sigma, \delta, q_0, F)$ is a protocol automaton that has only trivial transition assumptions, that is, $\forall (q, (D, \psi), q') \in \delta : \psi = true$, and all states are final states ($F = Q$). A correctness witness typically gives information about the state space of the program (like a loop invariant) in order to facilitate its verification.

In Fig. 11 we see both a correctness and a violation witness. The correctness witness belongs to program p and, e.g., certifies that at location 3 variables a and b are equal (via the invariant for q_3). The violation witness on the right belongs to program p with line 5 removed, i.e., a program which does not satisfy the property stated in Fig. 10a. The violation witness states that an input value of x being greater or equal to 1 is needed for directing the verifier towards the error.

(5) A **condition automaton** $A_\psi = (Q, \Sigma, \delta, q_0, F)$ is a protocol automaton that satisfies

1. $\forall (\cdot, \varphi) \in Q : \varphi = true$ (no invariants at states) and
2. $\neg \exists (q_f, \cdot, q) \in \delta$ with $q_f \in F$ (no transitions leaving final states).

(a) Condition automaton A_ψ

(b) Test-case automaton A_t

Fig. 12. Automata for a condition and a test case

A condition is typically used to describe parts of the state space of a program, e.g., the part already explored during verification. Final states are thus used to fix which paths have already been explored.

A test case is a sequence of input values consecutively supplied to the calls of function **input**. Such a test case is encoded as protocol automaton using a special template variable χ that can be instantiated with every program variable.

(6) A **test-case automaton** $A_t = (Q, \Sigma, \delta, q_0, F)$ for a test case $\langle z_1, \ldots, z_n \rangle$ is a protocol automaton with the following components: $Q = \{q_0, \ldots, q_n\}$, $q_{i-1} \xrightarrow{((*, \chi = \text{input}(), *), \chi = z_i)} q_i$, $q_0 \xrightarrow{o/w} q_0$, $q_i \xrightarrow{o/w} q_i$ $(i \in [1, n])$ and $F = Q$. For matching these special transitions $(G_i, \psi_i) = ((\cdot, \chi = \text{input}(), \cdot), \chi = z)$ with program paths, the program transitions g_i have to be of the form $(\ell, x = \text{input}(), \ell')$ and the next state needs to satisfy $c_i(x) = z$, $c_i(y) = c_{i-1}(y)$ for $y \neq x$.

Figure 12a gives a condition stating the exploration of the state space for inputs less or equal to 0. This could for instance be the output of a verifier having checked that the property holds for inputs $x \leq 0$. Figure 12b is the test-case automaton for the test case $\langle 4 \rangle$.

Semantics of Protocol Automata. The above definitions fix the syntactical structure of protocol automata. In addition, we need to state their semantics, i.e., the meaning of particular artifacts for a given program. In the following, we let $A_p = (L, \ell_0, G)$ be the CFA for a program p and $A_{\neg\varphi_b}$, A_ω, and A_{φ_t} be protocol automata.

(i) The program p *fulfills* a property specification φ_b if $paths(A_p) \cap L(A_{\neg\varphi_b}) = \emptyset$. Our running example p fulfills the property of Fig. 10a.

(ii) A correctness witness ω is *valid* for a program p and property specification φ_b if $paths(A_p) \subseteq paths(A_\omega) \wedge paths(A_p) \cap L(A_{\neg\varphi_b}) = \emptyset$. We see here that a correctness witnesses can thus be used to facilitate verification: when we run program, property, and correctness witness in parallel in order to check the emptiness of $paths(A_p) \cap L(A_{\neg\varphi_b})$, the correctness witness helps in proving the program correct. The correctness witness in Fig. 11a is valid for p and the property in Fig. 10a.

(iii) A violation witness ω is *valid* for a program p and a property specification φ_b if $paths(A_p) \cap L(A_\omega) \cap L(A_{\neg\varphi_b}) \neq \emptyset$. During verification, violation witnesses can thus steer the state-space exploration towards the property violation. Looking again at the running example: If we elide the statement in location 5 of our program, the automaton in Fig. 11b is a valid violation witness. It restricts the state-space exploration to inputs for variable x which are greater or equal to 1.

(iv) A condition ψ is *correct* for a program p and property φ_b if $\boxed{paths(A_p) \cap L(A_\psi) \cap L(A_{\neg\varphi_b}) = \emptyset}$. All program paths accepted by the condition fulfill the specification given by the property automaton. The condition in Fig. 12a describes all paths of the program p which initially started with input x less or equal to 0. This condition is correct for p and the property automaton in Fig. 10a.

(v) A test-case t for a program p *covers* a goal of a test-goal specification φ_t if $\boxed{paths(A_p) \cap paths(A_t) \cap L(A_{\varphi_t}) \neq \emptyset}$. Basically, we require that the inputs provided by the test case guarantee the program execution to reach (at least one) test goal. If there are more than one final state in the test-goal automaton (or the final state can be reached via different paths), the test-goal automaton specifies several test goals. In this case, the test case covers only some of these goals. The test-case automaton in Fig. 12b for p covers the (single) goal of the test-goal automaton in Fig. 10b.

5   Conclusion

Different verification approaches have different strengths, and the only way to benefit from a variety of approaches is to combine them. The two classic approaches of combining approaches either in white-box manner via a tight conceptual integration or in black-bock manner via loosely coupled combinations, such as portfolio or selection, are both insufficient.

We propose that *cooperation* is the right direction to go: a loosely-coupled combination of tools that interact via clear interfaces and exchange formats, in order to achieve the verification goal together. To this end, we provide a classification and an overview of existing techniques, which we briefly describe, while giving most importance to cooperative approaches. We add definitions of several useful artifacts, actors, and their semantics.

As future work we see the development of tool combinations putting the outlined cooperation approach into practice. Since a number of tools already generate some of the discussed artifacts, they are "ready for cooperation". Ultimately, we aim at assembling a pool of actors which can be combined in various ways and where some combination can be easily defined by users, e.g., with the help of a domain-specific combination language.

References

1. Abiteboul, S., Hull, R., Vianu, V.: Foundations of Databases. Addison-Wesley (1995)
2. Ball, T., Rajamani, S.K.: SLIC: A specification language for interface checking (of C). Technical report MSR-TR-2001-21, Microsoft Research (2002)

3. Ball, T., Rajamani, S.K.: The SLAM project: Debugging system software via static analysis. In: Proc. POPL, pp. 1–3. ACM (2002). https://doi.org/10.1145/503272.503274

4. Ball, T., Bounimova, E., Kumar, R., Levin, V.: SLAM2: Static driver verification with under 4% false alarms. In: Proc. FMCAD, pp. 35–42. IEEE (2010)

5. Baudin, P., Cuoq, P., Filliâtre, J.C., Marché, C., Monate, B., Moy, Y., Prevosto, V.: ACSL: ANSI/ISO C specification language version 1.15 (2020)

6. Beckman, N.E., Nori, A.V., Rajamani, S.K., Simmons, R.J., Tetali, S., Thakur, A.V.: Proofs from tests. IEEE Trans. Softw. Eng. 36(4), 495–508 (2010). https://doi.org/10.1109/TSE.2010.49

7. Beyer, D.: Second competition on software verification (Summary of SV-COMP 2013). In: Proc. TACAS. LNCS, vol. 7795, pp. 594–609. Springer (2013). https://doi.org/10.1007/978-3-642-36742-7_43

8. Beyer, D.: Software verification and verifiable witnesses (Report on SV-COMP 2015). In: Proc. TACAS. LNCS, vol. 9035, pp. 401–416. Springer (2015). https://doi.org/10.1007/978-3-662-46681-0_31

9. Beyer, D., Chlipala, A.J., Henzinger, T.A., Jhala, R., Majumdar, R.: Generating tests from counterexamples. In: Proc. ICSE, pp. 326–335. IEEE (2004). https://doi.org/10.1109/ICSE.2004.1317455

10. Beyer, D., Chlipala, A.J., Henzinger, T.A., Jhala, R., Majumdar, R.: The BLAST query language for software verification. In: Proc. SAS. LNCS, vol. 3148, pp. 2–18. Springer (2004). https://doi.org/10.1007/978-3-540-27864-1_2

11. Beyer, D., Dangl, M.: Verification-aided debugging: An interactive web-service for exploring error witnesses. In: Proc. CAV (2). LNCS, vol. 9780, pp. 502–509. Springer (2016). https://doi.org/10.1007/978-3-319-41540-6_28

12. Beyer, D., Dangl, M.: Strategy selection for software verification based on Boolean features: A simple but effective approach. In: Proc. ISoLA. LNCS, vol. 11245, pp. 144–159. Springer (2018). https://doi.org/10.1007/978-3-030-03421-4_11

13. Beyer, D., Dangl, M., Dietsch, D., Heizmann, M.: Correctness witnesses: Exchanging verification results between verifiers. In: Proc. FSE, pp. 326–337. ACM (2016). https://doi.org/10.1145/2950290.2950351

14. Beyer, D., Dangl, M., Dietsch, D., Heizmann, M., Stahlbauer, A.: Witness validation and stepwise testification across software verifiers. In: Proc. FSE, pp. 721–733. ACM (2015). https://doi.org/10.1145/2786805.2786867

15. Beyer, D., Dangl, M., Lemberger, T., Tautschnig, M.: Tests from witnesses: Execution-based validation of verification results. In: Proc. TAP. LNCS, vol. 10889, pp. 3–23. Springer (2018). https://doi.org/10.1007/978-3-319-92994-1_1

16. Beyer, D., Dangl, M., Wendler, P.: A unifying view on SMT-based software verification. J. Autom. Reasoning 60(3), 299–335 (2018). https://doi.org/10.1007/s10817-017-9432-6

17. Beyer, D., Gulwani, S., Schmidt, D.: Combining model checking and data-flow analysis. In: Handbook of Model Checking, pp. 493–540. Springer (2018). https://doi.org/10.1007/978-3-319-10575-8_16

18. Beyer, D., Henzinger, T.A., Jhala, R., Majumdar, R.: The software model checker BLAST. Int. J. Softw. Tools Technol. Transf. 9(5-6), 505–525 (2007). https://doi.org/10.1007/s10009-007-0044-z

19. Beyer, D., Henzinger, T.A., Keremoglu, M.E., Wendler, P.: Conditional model checking: A technique to pass information between verifiers. In: Proc. FSE. ACM (2012). https://doi.org/10.1145/2393596.2393664

20. Beyer, D., Henzinger, T.A., Majumdar, R., Rybalchenko, A.: Invariant synthesis for combined theories. In: Proc. VMCAI. LNCS, vol. 4349, pp. 378–394. Springer (2007). https://doi.org/10.1007/978-3-540-69738-1_27

21. Beyer, D., Henzinger, T.A., Majumdar, R., Rybalchenko, A.: Path invariants. In: Proc. PLDI, pp. 300–309. ACM (2007). https://doi.org/10.1145/1250734.1250769

22. Beyer, D., Henzinger, T.A., Théoduloz, G.: Lazy shape analysis. In: Proc. CAV. LNCS, vol. 4144, pp. 532–546. Springer (2006). https://doi.org/10.1007/11817963_48

23. Beyer, D., Henzinger, T.A., Théoduloz, G.: Program analysis with dynamic precision adjustment. In: Proc. ASE, pp. 29–38. IEEE (2008). https://doi.org/10.1109/ASE.2008.13

24. Beyer, D., Jakobs, M.C.: CoVeriTest: Cooperative verifier-based testing. In: Proc. FASE. LNCS, vol. 11424, pp. 389–408. Springer (2019). https://doi.org/10.1007/978-3-030-16722-6_23

25. Beyer, D., Jakobs, M.C., Lemberger, T., Wehrheim, H.: Reducer-based construction of conditional verifiers. In: Proc. ICSE, pp. 1182–1193. ACM (2018). https://doi.org/10.1145/3180155.3180259

26. Beyer, D., Keremoglu, M.E.: CPAchecker: A tool for configurable software verification. In: Proc. CAV. LNCS, vol. 6806, pp. 184–190. Springer (2011). https://doi.org/10.1007/978-3-642-22110-1_16

27. Beyer, D., Keremoglu, M.E., Wendler, P.: Predicate abstraction with adjustable-block encoding. In: Proc. FMCAD, pp. 189–197. FMCAD (2010)

28. Beyer, D., Lemberger, T.: Conditional testing: Off-the-shelf combination of testcase generators. In: Proc. ATVA. LNCS, vol. 11781, pp. 189–208. Springer (2019). https://doi.org/10.1007/978-3-030-31784-3_11

29. Beyer, D., Löwe, S., Novikov, E., Stahlbauer, A., Wendler, P.: Precision reuse for efficient regression verification. In: Proc. FSE, pp. 389–399. ACM (2013). https://doi.org/10.1145/2491411.2491429

30. Beyer, D., Wehrheim, H.: Verification artifacts in cooperative verification: Survey and unifying component framework. arXiv/CoRR 1905(08505), May 2019. https://arxiv.org/abs/1905.08505

31. Beyer, D., Wendler, P.: Reuse of verification results: Conditional model checking, precision reuse, and verification witnesses. In: Proc. SPIN. LNCS, vol. 7976, pp. 1–17. Springer (2013). https://doi.org/10.1007/978-3-642-39176-7_1

32. Beyer, D.: Partial verification and intermediate results as a solution to combine automatic and interactive verification techniques. In: Proc. ISoLA. LNCS, vol. 9952, pp. 874–880. Springer (2016). https://doi.org/10.1007/978-3-319-47166-2

33. Biere, A., Cimatti, A., Clarke, E.M., Zhu, Y.: Symbolic model checking without BDDs. In: Proc. TACAS. LNCS, vol. 1579, pp. 193–207. Springer (1999). https://doi.org/10.1007/3-540-49059-0_14

34. Castaño, R., Braberman, V.A., Garbervetsky, D., Uchitel, S.: Model checker execution reports. In: Proc. ASE, pp. 200–205. IEEE (2017). https://doi.org/10.1109/ASE.2017.8115633

35. Ceri, S., Gottlob, G., Tanca, L.: What you always wanted to know about Datalog (and never dared to ask). IEEE Trans. Knowl. Data Eng. 1(1), 146–166 (1989)

36. Chalupa, M., Vitovská, M., Strejcek, J.: Symbiotic 5: Boosted instrumentation (competition contribution). In: Proc. TACAS. LNCS, vol. 10806. Springer (2018). https://doi.org/10.1007/978-3-319-89963-3_29

37. Christakis, M., Müller, P., Wüstholz, V.: Guiding dynamic symbolic execution toward unverified program executions. In: Proc. ICSE, pp. 144–155. ACM (2016). https://doi.org/10.1145/2884781.2884843

38. Clarke, E.M., Grumberg, O., Jha, S., Lu, Y., Veith, H.: Counterexample-guided abstraction refinement for symbolic model checking. J. ACM **50**(5), 752–794 (2003). https://doi.org/10.1145/876638.876643
39. Codish, M., Mulkers, A., Bruynooghe, M., de la Banda, M.G., Hermenegildo, M.: Improving abstract interpretations by combining domains. In: Proc. PEPM, pp. 194–205. ACM (1993). https://doi.org/10.1145/154630.154650
40. Cousot, P., Cousot, R.: Systematic design of program-analysis frameworks. In: Proc. POPL, pp. 269–282. ACM (1979). https://doi.org/10.1145/567752.567778
41. Cruanes, S., Hamon, G., Owre, S., Shankar, N.: Tool integration with the Evidential Tool Bus. In: Proc. VMCAI. LNCS, vol. 7737, pp. 275–294. Springer (2013). https://doi.org/10.1007/978-3-642-35873-9_18
42. Cruanes, S., Heymans, S., Mason, I., Owre, S., Shankar, N.: The semantics of Datalog for the Evidential Tool Bus. In: Specification, Algebra, and Software, pp. 256–275. Springer (2014)
43. Cuoq, P., Kirchner, F., Kosmatov, N., Prevosto, V., Signoles, J., Yakobowski, B.: Frama-C. In: Proc. SEFM, pp. 233–247. Springer (2012). https://doi.org/10.1007/978-3-642-33826-7_16
44. Czech, M., Hüllermeier, E., Jakobs, M., Wehrheim, H.: Predicting rankings of software verification tools. In: Proc. SWAN, pp. 23–26. ACM (2017). https://doi.org/10.1145/3121257.3121262
45. Czech, M., Jakobs, M., Wehrheim, H.: Just test what you cannot verify! In: Proc. FASE. LNCS, vol. 9033, pp. 100–114. Springer (2015). https://doi.org/10.1007/978-3-662-46675-9_7
46. Daca, P., Gupta, A., Henzinger, T.A.: Abstraction-driven concolic testing. In: Proc. VMCAI. LNCS, vol. 9583, pp. 328–347. Springer (2016). https://doi.org/10.1007/978-3-662-49122-5_16
47. Demyanova, Y., Pani, T., Veith, H., Zuleger, F.: Empirical software metrics for benchmarking of verification tools. In: Proc. CAV. LNCS, vol. 9206, pp. 561–579. Springer (2015). https://doi.org/10.1007/978-3-319-21690-4_39
48. Demyanova, Y., Pani, T., Veith, H., Zuleger, F.: Empirical software metrics for benchmarking of verification tools. Formal Methods Syst. Des. **50**(2–3), 289–316 (2017). https://doi.org/10.1007/s10703-016-0264-5
49. Ernst, G., Huisman, M., Mostowski, W., Ulbrich, M.: VerifyThis: Verification competition with a human factor. In: Proc. TACAS. LNCS, vol. 11429, pp. 176–195. Springer (2019). https://doi.org/10.1007/978-3-030-17502-3_12
50. Fischer, J., Jhala, R., Majumdar, R.: Joining data flow with predicates. In: Proc. FSE, pp. 227–236. ACM (2005). https://doi.org/10.1145/1081706.1081742
51. Gerrard, M.J., Dwyer, M.B.: Comprehensive failure characterization. In: Proc. ASE, pp. 365–376. IEEE (2017). https://doi.org/10.1109/ASE.2017.8115649
52. Gerrard, M.J., Dwyer, M.B.: ALPACA: A large portfolio-based alternating conditional analysis. In: Proc. ICSE, pp. 35–38. IEEE (2019). https://doi.org/10.1109/ICSE-Companion.2019.00032
53. Godefroid, P., Sen, K.: Combining model checking and testing. In: Handbook of Model Checking, pp. 613–649. Springer (2018). https://doi.org/10.1007/978-3-319-10575-8_19
54. Godefroid, P., Nori, A.V., Rajamani, S.K., Tetali, S.: Compositional may-must program analysis: unleashing the power of alternation. In: Proc. POPL, pp. 43–56. ACM (2010). https://doi.org/10.1145/1706299.1706307
55. Gulavani, B.S., Henzinger, T.A., Kannan, Y., Nori, A.V., Rajamani, S.K.: SYNERGY: A new algorithm for property checking. In: Proc. FSE, pp. 117–127. ACM (2006). https://doi.org/10.1145/1181775.1181790

56. Gulwani, S., Tiwari, A.: Combining abstract interpreters. In: Proc. PLDI, pp. 376–386. ACM (2006). https://doi.org/10.1145/1133981.1134026
57. Gurfinkel, A., Albarghouthi, A., Chaki, S., Li, Y., Chechik, M.: UFO: Verification with interpolants and abstract interpretation (competition contribution). In: Proc. TACAS. LNCS, vol. 7795, pp. 637–640. Springer (2013). https://doi.org/10.1007/978-3-642-36742-7_52
58. Harman, M., Hu, L., Hierons, R.M., Wegener, J., Sthamer, H., Baresel, A., Roper, M.: Testability transformation. IEEE Trans. Softw. Eng. **30**(1), 3–16 (2004). https://doi.org/10.1109/TSE.2004.1265732
59. Hatcliff, J., Leavens, G.T., Leino, K.R.M., Müller, P., Parkinson, M.: Behavioral interface specification languages. ACM Comput. Surv. **44**(3) (2012). https://doi.org/10.1145/2187671.2187678
60. Henzinger, T.A., Jhala, R., Majumdar, R., Sanvido, M.A.A.: Extreme model checking. In: Verification: Theory and Practice, pp. 332–358 (2003). https://doi.org/10.1007/978-3-540-39910-0_16
61. Holzer, A., Schallhart, C., Tautschnig, M., Veith, H.: Query-driven program testing. In: Proc. VMCAI. LNCS, vol. 5403, pp. 151–166. Springer (2009). https://doi.org/10.1007/978-3-540-93900-9_15
62. Holzer, A., Schallhart, C., Tautschnig, M., Veith, H.: How did you specify your test suite. In: Proc. ASE, pp. 407–416. ACM (2010). https://doi.org/10.1145/1858996.1859084
63. Huberman, B.A., Lukose, R.M., Hogg, T.: An economics approach to hard computational problems. Science **275**(7), 51–54 (1997)
64. Hutter, F., Hoos, H.H., Leyton-Brown, K.: Sequential model-based optimization for general algorithm configuration. In: Proc. LION. LNCS, vol. 6683, pp. 507–523. Springer (2011). https://doi.org/10.1007/978-3-642-25566-3_40
65. Jakobs, M.C.: Speed up configurable certificate validation by certificate reduction and partitioning. In: Proc. SEFM. LNCS, vol. 9276, pp. 159–174. Springer (2015). https://doi.org/10.1007/978-3-319-22969-0_12
66. Jakobs, M.C., Wehrheim, H.: Certification for configurable program analysis. In: Proc. SPIN, pp. 30–39. ACM (2014). https://doi.org/10.1145/2632362.2632372
67. Jakobs, M.: PART_{PW} : From partial analysis results to a proof witness. In: Proc. SEFM. LNCS, vol. 10469, pp. 120–135. Springer (2017). https://doi.org/10.1007/978-3-319-66197-1_8
68. Jakobs, M., Wehrheim, H.: Compact proof witnesses. In: Proc. NFM. LNCS, vol. 10227, pp. 389–403. Springer (2017). https://doi.org/10.1007/978-3-319-57288-8_28
69. Kildall, G.A.: A unified approach to global program optimization. In: Proc. POPL, pp. 194–206. ACM (1973). https://doi.org/10.1145/512927.512945
70. King, J.C.: Symbolic execution and program testing. Commun. ACM **19**(7), 385–394 (1976). https://doi.org/10.1145/360248.360252
71. Lal, A., Qadeer, S., Lahiri, S.K.: A solver for reachability modulo theories. In: Proc. CAV. LNCS, vol. 7358, pp. 427–443. Springer (2012). https://doi.org/10.1007/978-3-642-31424-7_32
72. Lerner, S., Grove, D., Chambers, C.: Composing data-flow analyses and transformations. In: Proc. POPL, pp. 270–282. ACM (2002). https://doi.org/10.1145/503272.503298
73. Leue, S., Befrouei, M.T.: Counterexample explanation by anomaly detection. In: Proc. SPIN. LNCS, vol. 7385, pp. 24–42. Springer (2012). https://doi.org/10.1007/978-3-642-31759-0_5

74. Margaria, T., Nagel, R., Steffen, B.: Remote integration and coordination of verification tools in jETI. In: Proc. ECBS, pp. 431–436 (2005). https://doi.org/10.1109/ECBS.2005.59

75. Margaria, T.: Web services-based tool-integration in the ETI platform. Softw. Syst. Modeling 4(2), 141–156 (2005). https://doi.org/10.1007/s10270-004-0072-z

76. Margaria, T., Nagel, R., Steffen, B.: jETI: A tool for remote tool integration. In: Proc. TACAS. LNCS, vol. 3440, pp. 557–562. Springer (2005). https://doi.org/10.1007/978-3-540-31980-1_38

77. Müller, P., Peringer, P., Vojnar, T.: Predator hunting party (competition contribution). In: Proc. TACAS. LNCS, vol. 9035, pp. 443–446. Springer (2015). https://doi.org/10.1007/978-3-662-46681-0_40

78. Necula, G.C., McPeak, S., Rahul, S.P., Weimer, W.: Cil: Intermediate language and tools for analysis and transformation of C programs. In: Proc. CC. LNCS, vol. 2304, pp. 213–228. Springer (2002)

79. Necula, G.C., McPeak, S., Weimer, W.: CCured: Type-safe retrofitting of legacy code. In: Proc. POPL, pp. 128–139. ACM (2002). https://doi.org/10.1145/503272.503286

80. Nori, A.V., Rajamani, S.K., Tetali, S., Thakur, A.V.: The Yogi Project: Software property checking via static analysis and testing. In: Proc. TACAS. LNCS, vol. 5505, pp. 178–181. Springer (2009). https://doi.org/10.1007/978-3-642-00768-2_17

81. Novikov, E., Zakharov, I.S.: Towards automated static verification of GNU C programs. In: Proc. PSI. LNCS, vol. 10742, pp. 402–416. Springer (2017). https://doi.org/10.1007/978-3-319-74313-4_30

82. Pauck, F., Bodden, E., Wehrheim, H.: Do Android taint-analysis tools keep their promises? In: Proc. ESEC/FSE, pp. 331–341. ACM (2018). https://doi.org/10.1145/3236024.3236029

83. Pauck, F., Wehrheim, H.: Together strong: Cooperative Android App analysis. In: Proc. ESEC/FSE, pp. 374–384. ACM (2019). https://doi.org/10.1145/3338906.3338915

84. Piterman, N., Pnueli, A.: Temporal logic and fair discrete systems. In: Handbook of Model Checking, pp. 27–73. Springer (2018). https://doi.org/10.1007/978-3-319-10575-8_2

85. Rice, J.R.: The algorithm selection problem. Adv. Comput. 15, 65–118 (1976). https://doi.org/10.1016/S0065-2458(08)60520-3

86. Rothenberg, B., Dietsch, D., Heizmann, M.: Incremental verification using trace abstraction. In: Proc. SAS. LNCS, vol. 11002, pp. 364–382. Springer (2018). https://doi.org/10.1007/978-3-319-99725-4_22

87. Serý, O.: Enhanced property specification and verification in Blast. In: Proc. FASE. LNCS, vol. 5503, pp. 456–469. Springer (2009). https://doi.org/10.1007/978-3-642-00593-0_32

88. Shankar, N.: Combining model checking and deduction. In: Handbook of Model Checking, pp. 651–684. Springer (2018). https://doi.org/10.1007/978-3-319-10575-8_20

89. Sherman, E., Dwyer, M.B.: Structurally defined conditional data-flow static analysis. In: Proc. TACAS (2). LNCS, vol. 10806, pp. 249–265. Springer (2018). https://doi.org/10.1007/978-3-319-89963-3_15

90. Steffen, B.: The physics of software tools: SWOT analysis and vision. Int. J. Softw. Tools Technol. Transf. 19(1), 1–7 (2017). https://doi.org/10.1007/s10009-016-0446-x

91. Steffen, B., Margaria, T., Braun, V.: The Electronic Tool Integration platform: Concepts and design. STTT **1**(1–2), 9–30 (1997). https://doi.org/10.1007/s100090050003

92. Torsney-Weir, T., Saad, A., Möller, T., Hege, H., Weber, B., Verbavatz, J.: Tuner: Principled parameter finding for image segmentation algorithms using visual response surface exploration. IEEE Trans. Vis. Comput. Graph. **17**(12), 1892–1901 (2011). https://doi.org/10.1109/TVCG.2011.248

93. Tulsian, V., Kanade, A., Kumar, R., Lal, A., Nori, A.V.: MUX: Algorithm selection for software model checkers. In: Proc. MSR. ACM (2014). https://doi.org/10.1145/2597073.2597080

94. Turing, A.: Checking a large routine. In: Report on a Conference on High Speed Automatic Calculating Machines, pp. 67–69. Cambridge Univ. Math. Lab. (1949)

95. Visser, W., Geldenhuys, J., Dwyer, M.B.: GREEN: Reducing, reusing, and recycling constraints in program analysis. In: Proc. FSE, pp. 58:1–58:11. ACM (2012). https://doi.org/10.1145/2393596.2393665

96. Visser, W., Păsăreanu, C.S., Khurshid, S.: Test-input generation with Java PATHFINDER. In: Proc. ISSTA, pp. 97–107. ACM (2004). https://doi.org/10.1145/1007512.1007526

97. Wendler, P.: CPACHECKER with sequential combination of explicit-state analysis and predicate analysis (competition contribution). In: Proc. TACAS. LNCS, vol. 7795, pp. 613–615. Springer (2013). https://doi.org/10.1007/978-3-642-36742-7_45

98. Xie, T., Zhang, L., Xiao, X., Xiong, Y., Hao, D.: Cooperative software testing and analysis: Advances and challenges. J. Comput. Sci. Technol. **29**(4), 713–723 (2014). https://doi.org/10.1007/s11390-014-1461-6

An Interface Theory for Program Verification

Dirk Beyer[ID] and Sudeep Kanav[ID]

LMU Munich, Munich, Germany

Abstract. Program verification is the problem, for a given program P and a specification ϕ, of constructing a proof of correctness for the statement "program P satisfies specification ϕ" ($P \models \phi$) or a proof of violation ($P \not\models \phi$). Usually, a correctness proof is based on inductive invariants, and a violation proof on a violating program trace. Verification engineers typically expect that a verification tool exports these proof artifacts. We propose to view the task of program verification as constructing a behavioral interface (represented e.g. by an automaton). We start with the interface I_P of the program itself, which represents all traces of program executions. To prove correctness, we try to construct a more abstract interface I_C of the program (overapproximation) that satisfies the specification. This interface, if found, represents more traces than I_P that are all *correct* (satisfying the specification). Ultimately, we want a compact representation of the program behavior as a *correctness interface* I_C in terms of *inductive invariants*. We can then extract a correctness witness, in standard exchange format, out of such a correctness interface. Symmetrically, to prove violation, we try to construct a more concrete interface I_V of the program (underapproximation) that violates the specification. This interface, if found, represents fewer traces than I_P that are all *feasible* (can be executed). Ultimately, we want a compact representation of the program behavior as a *violation interface* I_V in terms of a *violating program trace*. We can then extract a violation witness, in standard exchange format, out of such a violation interface. This viewpoint exposes the duality of these two tasks — proving correctness and violation. It enables the decomposition of the verification process, and its tools, into (at least!) three components: interface synthesizers, refinement checkers, and specification checkers. We hope the reader finds this viewpoint useful, although the underlying ideas are not novel. We see it as a framework towards modular program verification.

Keywords: Program verification · Interface theory · Cooperative verification · Software verification · Verification interface · Verification witness · Conditional model checking · Tool combination · Modular verification

1 Introduction

Software verification solves the problem of finding out, for a given program P and a behavioral specification ϕ, whether the program fulfills the specification, writ-

Funded in part by Deutsche Forschungsgemeinschaft (DFG) – 378803395 (ConVeY).

T. Margaria and B. Steffen (Eds.): ISoLA 2020, LNCS 12476, pp. 168–186, 2020.
https://doi.org/10.1007/978-3-030-61362-4_9

ten $P \models \phi$, or not, written $P \not\models \phi$. The problem is in general undecidable [26,48], but we can create verification tools that solve some practical instances of the problem with reasonable performance. The society and industry depends on correctly working software. As often with difficult problems, there are many different heuristics that lead to different verification tools with different strengths [7,15,37]. Software verification is applied more and more to industry-scale software [5,24,29,39].

Our motivation is to decompose the problem of software verification in such a way that parts of the problem can be given to different verification tools, which can be specialized to solve their part of the problem. Tools for software verification usually work on an internal representation of the program, which is an overapproximation (to prove correctness), or an underapproximation (to prove violation), or neither of the two (intermediate result). We call these internal representations *verification interfaces*, and we would like to make them explicit and ideally export them to the user, such that the verification problem can be composed into sub-problems that can be solved by different tools.

In theory, the answer to the verification problem is TRUE or FALSE, and early tools only reported those answers. It became clear quickly that in practice, the value lays not in the short answer, but in the explanation —a verification witness— that describes the answer TRUE or FALSE in more detail. Thus, model checkers started exporting counterexamples when the answer was FALSE [28]. It took another 20 years to make counterexamples exchangeable using a standard XML format for violation witnesses [11]. The format was quickly adopted by many publicly available tools for software verification[1] and got extended to correctness witnesses later [10]. Exporting witnesses for decisions computed by algorithms seems to be standard also in other areas [42,50].

Contributions. As a first step towards the decomposition of verification tools, we define interfaces, state the interface theorems (known from refinement calculus [44] and interface automata [3]) to enable modular verification, discuss the various proof flows, including the connection to verification witnesses, and discuss a few approaches as we see them through the lens of interfaces.

Related Work. The insights in this paper stem from our work on capturing the essence of the program-verification process in verification witnesses [10,11], which is a large project that started seven years ago [21]. The basic idea is to summarize, materialize, and conserve the information that the verification system uses internally for the proof of correctness or violation.

The foundational ideas that we use in this paper are well-known, such as seeing the correctness proofs as a modular two-step approach that consists of (i) capturing the semantics and deduct specification satisfaction (e.g., using a correctness logic [34] or an incorrectness logic [45]) and (ii) base the proof on refinements [44].

The inspiration to call the objects of interest *interface* comes from the interface theories for concurrent systems [3], for timed systems [4], for resources [25], for web services [8], and for program APIs [17,33].

---

[1] For C programs: https://gitlab.com/sosy-lab/sv-comp/archives-2020/-/tree/svcomp20/2020

2   Verification via Interfaces

For simplicity, we restrict our consideration to specifications of safety properties, and to programs that contain only variables of type integer and no function calls. The theory can be extended naturally.

2.1   Verification Interfaces

A program P is usually represented as a control-flow graph (CFA) [1,40] or control-flow automaton [15,16]. A control-flow automaton $P = (L, l_0, G)$ consists of a set L of program locations, an initial program location l_0, and a set $G \subseteq L \times Ops \times L$ of control-flow edges, which transfer from one program location to another on a program operation from Ops. The program operations operate on a set of program variables X. For defining interfaces, we use protocol automata from the literature on verification witnesses [11,20], in order to emphasis the similarity of verification interfaces with verification witnesses.

A *verification interface* $(Q, \Sigma, \delta, q_{init}, F)$ for a program P is a nondeterministic finite automaton and its components are defined as follows (the set Φ contains all predicates of a given theory over the set X of variables of P):

1. The set $Q \subseteq \Gamma \times \Phi$ is a finite set of control states, where each control state $(\gamma, \varphi) \in Q$ has a name γ from a set Γ of names, which can be used to uniquely identify a control state q within Q, and an invariant $\varphi \in \Phi$, which is a predicate over program variables that evaluates to *true* whenever a program path reaches a program location that is matched by this control state.[2]
2. The set $\Sigma \subseteq 2^G \times \Phi$ is the alphabet, in which each symbol $\sigma \in \Sigma$ is a pair (S, ψ) that comprises a finite set $S \subseteq G$ of CFA edges and a state condition $\psi \in \Phi$.
3. The set $\delta \subseteq Q \times \Sigma \times Q$ contains the transitions between control states, where each transition is a triple (q, σ, q') with a source state $q \in Q$, a target state $q' \in Q$, and a guard $\sigma = (S, \psi) \in \Sigma$ comprising a *source-code guard* S (syntax), which restricts a transition to the specific set $S \subseteq G$ of CFA edges, and a *state-space guard* $\psi \in \Phi$ (semantics), which restricts the state space to be considered by an analysis that consumes the protocol automaton. We also write $q \xrightarrow{\sigma} q'$ for $(q, \sigma, q') \in \delta$.
4. The control state $q_{init} \in Q$ is the initial control state of the automaton.
5. The subset $F \subseteq Q$ contains the accepting control states.

For a given interface $(Q, \Sigma, \delta, q_{init}, F)$, a sequence $\langle q_0, \ldots \rangle$ of states from Q is called *path* if it starts in the initial state, i.e., $q_0 = q_{init}$, and there exists a transition between successive control states, i.e., $q_i \xrightarrow{\cdot} q_{i+1}$ for all $i \in [0, n-1]$. A *test vector* [9] specifies the values for input variables of a program. A path p is called *P-feasible*, if a test vector exists[3] for which p can be executed in P,

---

[2] For example, an invariant that is matched for a loop-head location is called *loop invariant* of the program.

[3] Note that a test vector can have length zero if no input values are necessary to execute a path.

```
1  x = nondet();
2  if (x < −10)
3     exit(1);
4
5  if (x < 0)
6     x = −x;
7
8  if (x >= 0)
9     return x;
10 else
11    error();
12
```

Listing 1. Correct program

```
1  x = nondet();
2  if (x < −10)
3     exit(1);
4
5  if (x > 0)
6     x = −x;
7
8  if (x >= 0)
9     return x;
10 else
11    error();
12
```

Listing 2. Violating program

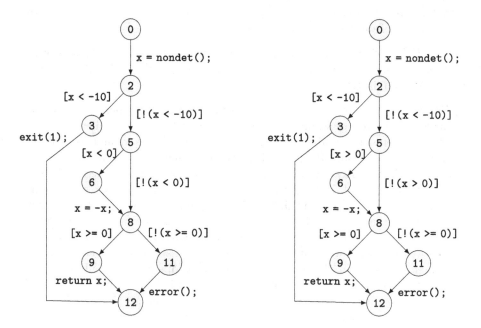

Fig. 1. Program interface for Listing 1   **Fig. 2.** Program interface Listing 2

otherwise the path is called *P-infeasible*. The *semantics* $L(I)$ of a verification interface I is defined as the set of all paths of I.

Refinement. Given two verification interfaces I_1 and I_2, we say that I_1 *refines* I_2, written $I_1 \preceq I_2$, if $L(I_1) \subseteq L(I_2)$.

Program Interface. If our goal is to reason about interfaces, we need to be able to represent the control-flow automaton of a program also as an interface. For a given program P, the corresponding program interface $I_P = (Q_P, \Sigma_P, \rightarrow_P, (l_0, true), Q_P)$ consists of the following components:

1. The set $Q_P = L \times \{true\}$ of control states represents the program locations, where the set L models the program-counter values, and the invariant is $true$ for all program locations.
2. The set $\Sigma_P = G_P \times \{true\}$ of alphabet symbols represents the program operations, where the set $G_P = \{\{g\} \mid g \in G\}$ models the program operations when control flows from one location to the next, and the guard is $true$ for all operations. Each transition is labeled with exactly one control-flow edge (therefore the singleton construction above).
3. The set $\to_P \subseteq Q_P \times \Sigma_P \times Q_P$ of transitions represents the control-flow edges of the program.
4. The initial control state $(l_0, true) \in Q_P$ consists of the program-entry location and the invariant $true$.
5. The set of final control states is the set Q_P of all control states, which models that the program executions can potentially end at any given time (e.g., by termination from the operating system).

The set $L(I_P)$ of paths in I_P contains (by definition) exactly the paths of P, in other words, each program execution corresponds to a P-feasible path of the verification interface I_P.

Example 1. We consider as example a program that is supposed to compute the absolute value of an integer number, if the value is not smaller than -10. The program first reads an integer value into variable x, and exits if the value is smaller than -10. Then, if the value is smaller than zero, the value is inverted. If the operation was successful, the new value is returned, otherwise an error is signaled. Listings 1 and 2 show two C programs, one correct and one with a typo as bug: in line 5, the programmer mistyped the less-than as a larger-than. Figures 1 and 2 show the program interfaces for the two C programs from Listings 1 and 2. We use a compact notation for a transition label (S, ψ), where we omit the set braces for the set S of CFA edges, if S is a singleton, we omit the source and target control states and only print the operation, and we omit the state-space guard if it is $true$. The background color of a control state indicates membership in the set F: gray for final (accepting) and light-red for non-final (non-accepting) control states.

Specification Interface. Specifications are typically given as LTL formulas [46] or as monitor automata [15,47]. Since we focus on safety specifications, we use monitor automata. In order to use a uniform formalism, we use interfaces here also. A specification interface $I_\phi = (Q_\phi, \Sigma_\phi, \to_\phi, q_{init}, F_\phi)$ consists of the following components:

1. The set $Q_\phi \subseteq \Gamma \times \{true\}$ of control states (all state invariants are $true$).
2. The set $\Sigma_\phi = 2^G \times \{true\}$ of labels that match control-flow edges, where each label has a set of control-flow edges for the matching, and the guard is $true$ for all transitions.
3. The set $\to_S \subseteq Q_\phi \times \Sigma_\phi \times Q_\phi$ of transitions represents the state changes according to the monitored control-flow edges of the program.

4. The initial control state is $q_{init} \in Q_\phi$, with the invariant *true*, i.e., $q_{init} = (\cdot, true)$.
5. The set $F_\phi \subseteq Q_\phi$ of final control states are those control states in which the interface accepts the path, that is, the represented specification is satisfied.

Correctness and Violation. Given a verification interface I and a specification ϕ, the verification interface is *correct*, written as $I \models \phi$, if $L(I) \subseteq L(I_\phi)$, or, using the notion of refinement of verification interfaces, $I \preceq I_\phi$, otherwise the verification interface is *violating*.

Verification Problem. Given a program P and a specification ϕ, *verification* is the problem of finding either a correctness proof for $P \models \phi$ or a violation proof for $P \not\models \phi$.

Since we know that the program interface I_P is path-equivalent to the program P, and that the specification interface I_ϕ represents a monitor automaton for the specification ϕ, we can restate the verification problem in terms of verification interfaces:

Given a program P and a specification ϕ, verification is the problem of finding either a correctness proof for $I_P \preceq I_\phi$ or a violation proof for $I_P \not\preceq I_\phi$.[4]

Traditionally, the verification problem is solved in one monolithic procedure, or in an alternating sequence of attempts to prove $P \models \phi$ or $P \not\models \phi$. Our goal is to decompose the proof-finding process into smaller parts.

Figure 3 illustrates the space of verification interfaces. Each node represents an interface and each dotted line represents that the lower interface refines the upper interface. On the very top, we have the interface $I_\top$, which accepts all paths, and $I \preceq I_\top$ holds for all interfaces I. On the very bottom, we have the interface $I_\bot$, which accepts no paths, and $I_\bot \preceq I$ holds for all interfaces I. These two parts of the picture are not interesting and we will not revisit them.

The program interface I_P is the center of the interface space, and the verification problem is to answer the question whether it belongs to the area of *correctness interfaces* (marked by $\models \phi$, light blue) or to the area of the *violation interfaces* (marked by $\not\models \phi$, red).

The specification interface I_ϕ is the top-most element in the refinement hierarchy inside the area of correctness interfaces, that is, I_ϕ is the most abstract correctness interface. If $I_P \preceq I_\phi$ holds, then there exists is a refinement path through the area of correctness interfaces from the program interface to the specification interface. This is well-known from refinement calculus [44] and is applied for proving correctness. There is a symmetry for proving violation, which was not yet emphasized in the literature:

The test-vector interface I_T contains one feasible violating path and is the bottom-most element in the refinement hierarchy inside the area of violation

---

[4] There are various ways for reasoning in order to obtain a proof, for example, strongest post-conditions [34] are traditionally used for correctness proofs and incorrectness logic [45] was recently proposed for violation proofs.

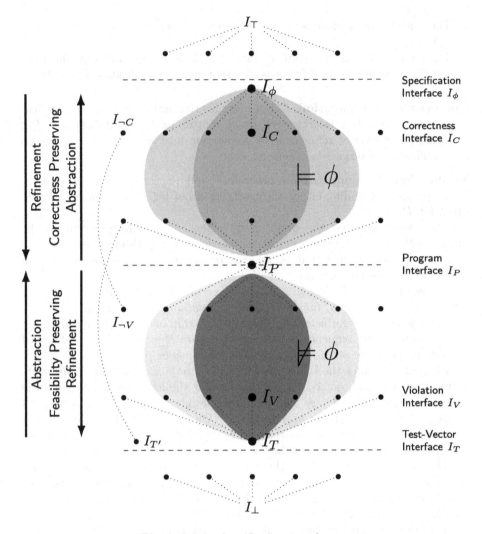

Fig. 3. Space of verification interfaces

interfaces, that is, I_T is the most concrete violation interface.[5] If $I_T \preceq I_P$ holds, then there exists is a refinement path through the area of violation interfaces from the test-vector interface to the program interface.

---

[5] There might be several violating test-vectors for different bugs (as there might be different specifications for the overall correctness of the program), but let us assume for simplicity that there is only one violating test vector.

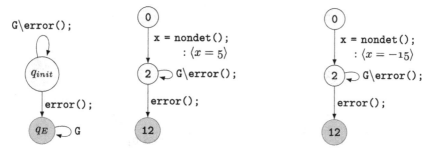

Fig. 4. Specification interface

Fig. 5. Feasible interface (test vector for Listing 2)

Fig. 6. Infeasible interface (test vector for Listing 2)

Example 2. Figure 4 shows an example specification interface (I_ϕ in Fig. 3) for representing a safety specification. The specification interface starts from an initial state q_{init} and transitions to the non-final (non-accepting, violating) control state q_E when it encounters a call to function error. A program is *correct* if the non-accepting state is never reached during any execution, otherwise it is said to *violate* the specification.

Figure 5 shows an example interface (I_T in Fig. 3) representing a test vector for our violating example program in Listing 2. Here, the test vector assumes that variable x was assigned the value 5 (expressed by the state-space guard after the colon) by the call to function nondet. Note that the label of a transition is a pair (S, ψ) and here we have S is the set $\{(0, \text{x} = \text{nondet}();, 2)\}$ and ψ is the predicate $x = 5$. Then, the automaton either keeps on looping in control state 2, or transitions to the non-accepting (violating) control state 12 on a call to function error.

Figure 6 shows an example test-vector interface ($I_{T'}$ in Fig. 3) that is infeasible for our violating example program in Listing 2. Here, the test vector assumes that variable x was assigned the value -15 by the call to function nondet. Then, the automaton either keeps on looping in the control state 2, or transitions to the non-accepting (violating) control state 12 on a call to function error. This interface is infeasible because our program would exit (line 3 of Listing 2) if x was assigned -15.

2.2 Modular Verification using Interfaces

As illustrated in Fig. 3, there are intermediate correctness interfaces between the program and the specification, and there are intermediate violation interfaces between the program interface and the test-vector interface.

Theorem 1 (Refinement Preserves Correctness). *Given a program P, a specification ϕ, and an interface I_C, if $I_C \models \phi$ and $I_P \preceq I_C$, then $P \models \phi$.*

According to Theorem 1 [44], we can now use an intermediate correctness interface to construct a correctness proof via the interface: Given a program P, a specifi-

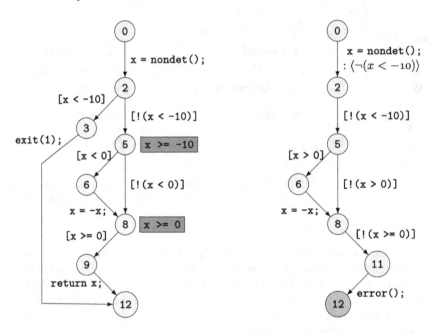

Fig. 7. Correctness interface for correct program (Listing 1)

Fig. 8. Violation interface for violating program (Listing 2)

cation ϕ, and an interface I_C, to prove $P \models \phi$ it is sufficient to prove (i) $I_C \models \phi$ and (ii) $I_P \preceq I_C$. An intermediate correctness interface I_C is also drawn in Fig. 3.

The requirement for constructing correctness interfaces is to represent (a) only correct program paths (satisfying the specification) and (b) try to enlarge the set of paths until a compact form is reached. The quality of a correctness interface I_1 is often felt better than the quality of I_2, if $I_2 \preceq I_1$, or $L(I_2) \subseteq L(I_1)$. Requirement (a) can be proven with a Hoare logic [34].

To construct an induction proof, we would like to add another requirement: (c) *all* the invariants in the control states of the correctness interfaces are *inductive*. Therefore, Fig. 3 has two marked areas between the program and the specification interface: The large (light-blue) area represents all correctness interfaces, the smaller (green) area represents all correctness interfaces whose invariants are *inductive*. We use the notion of *inductive invariants* as used in the literature [30].

Example 3. Figure 7 shows an example correctness interface I_C for the program in Listing 1. The green rectangles at control states show the state invariants. The paths leading to the violating program location (i.e., taking the violating transition) in the program interface of Fig. 1 are not contained in the correctness interface because they are infeasible.

To emphasize the symmetry between correctness and violation proofs, we write the below text using a wording as close as possible to the above.

Theorem 2 (Abstraction Preserves Violation). *Given a program P, a specification ϕ, and an interface I_V, if $I_V \not\models \phi$ and $I_V \preceq I_P$, then $P \not\models \phi$.*

According to Theorem 2, we can now use an intermediate violation interface to construct a violation proof via the interface: Given a program P, a specification ϕ, and an interface I_V, to prove $P \not\models \phi$ it is sufficient to prove (i) $I_V \not\models \phi$ and (ii) $I_V \preceq I_P$. An intermediate violation interface I_V is also drawn in Fig. 3.

The requirement for constructing violation proofs is to represent (a) only feasible program paths (being executable) and (b) try to reduce the set of paths until only one is left. The quality of a violation interface I_1 is often felt better than the quality of I_2, if $I_1 \preceq I_2$, or $L(I_1) \subseteq L(I_2)$. Requirement (a) can be proven with an incorrectness logic [45].

To construct a counterexample proof, we would like to add another requirement: (c) *all* the feasible paths of the violation interfaces are *violating*. Therefore, Fig. 3 has two marked areas between the program and the test-vector interface: The large (light gray) area represents all feasible interfaces, the smaller (red) area represents all violation interfaces that contain *only violating* paths.

Example 4. Figure 8 shows an example violation interface I_V for the program in Listing 2. This interface only shows the paths leading to the non-accepting (violating) control state (i.e., taking the violating transition) in Fig. 2.

Theorem 3 (Substitutivity of Interfaces). *Given two verification interfaces I_1 and I_2 with $I_1 \preceq I_2$ and a specification ϕ, if $I_2 \models \phi$, then $I_1 \models \phi$ (and if $I_1 \not\models \phi$, then $I_2 \not\models \phi$).*

Using Theorem 3, we can use the concept of step-wise refinement in proofs of correctness [44] and in proofs of violation [11]. Theorem 3 lets us *substitute* one interface by another one while preserving the (dis-) satisfaction of the specification.

2.3 Proof Flows using Interfaces and Witnesses

Figure 9 illustrates the possible ways to construct proofs. In the interface domain on the left, the figure shows the program interface I_P, a correctness interface I_C, and a violation interface I_V. In the domain of the software engineer, we have the specification ϕ, the program P, the test vector T, and two verification witnesses W_C and W_V. The correctness witness W_C [10] is a representation of the verification results if the verification tool constructed a correctness proof; the violation witness W_V [11] is a representation of the verification results if the verification tool constructed a violation proof.

Proving Correctness. To prove the correctness $P \models \phi$ for a given program P and a specification ϕ, we can use interfaces in the following way: First we embed the program P into the interface domain by constructing I_P. This is simply done by applying the definition. The creative part of the proof construction is to come up with the correctness interface I_C that contains invariants that are inductive. So the actual proof consists of three steps: (a) construct I_C, (b) show $I_P \preceq I_C$,

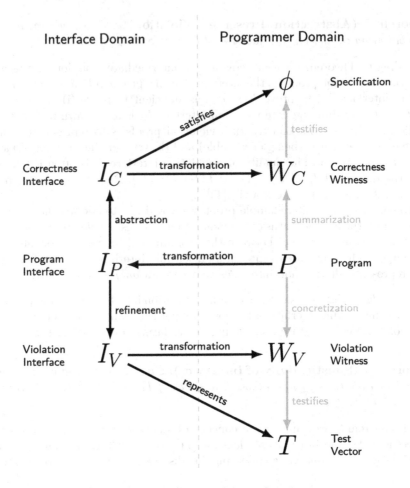

Fig. 9. Proof flows using the interface domain

and (c) show $I_C \models \phi$. At the end, we can extract a correctness witness W_C in an exchange format to share with tools and users.

A correctness witness overapproximates the correctness interface that it is extracted from. The intention of a correctness witness is to represent useful information to help reconstructing a correctness proof [10], but it might be overapproximating too much, that is, having invariants that are not inductive, or even weaker than the specification. In other words, a correctness witness might describe a set of paths that includes also violating paths, while a correctness interface is guaranteed to represent only correct (and inductive) paths.

Proving Violation. To prove the violation $P \not\models \phi$ for a given program P and a specification ϕ, we can use interfaces in the following way: First we embed the program P into the interface domain by constructing I_P. Again, this is simply done by applying the definition. The creative part of the proof construction is to come up with the violation interface I_V that describes paths that all violate the specification. So the actual proof consists of three steps: (a) construct I_V, (b) show $I_V \preceq I_P$, and (c) show $I_V \not\models \phi$. At the end, we can extract a violation witness W_V in an exchange format to share with tools and users.

A violation witness overapproximates the violation interface that it is extracted from. The intention of a violation witness is to represent useful information to help reconstructing a violation proof [11], but it might be overapproximating too much, that is, including paths that are not violating, or not even feasible. In other words, a violation witness might describe a set of paths that includes also correct paths, while a violation interface is guaranteed to represent only feasible (and violating) paths.

3   Decomposing Verification and Cooperative Verification

The original goal of our work is to find ways to decompose verification tasks in such a way that several tools, written by different development teams, cooperate to solve the verification task. In fact, the proof flows that were explained in the previous section are actually used in practice, but their three steps are usually hidden under the hood of the verification engine, and the flow is mostly implemented in a monolithic way.

Our proposal is to make the interfaces eminent, and to explicitly separate the steps of the overall proof. From this it follows that the steps need not necessarily be taken care of by the same verifier. The idea is to decompose the overall verification process into parts that can be performed by specific tools, optimized for their part of the proof. Verification interfaces are a great tool to make program verification compositional, involving different tools that solve the problem together in a cooperative manner [20]. Thus, we need three kinds of tools:

- Interface synthesizers, to construct an interface
- Refinement checkers, to check $I_1 \preceq I_2$
- Specification checkers, to check $I \models \phi$

In the following, we put new and existing approaches to verification into the perspective of interfaces, by motivating their existence (for new or recent ones) and by trying to explain the internal working of some existing approaches.

3.1   Decomposed Approaches

Learning and Approximate Methods. Classically, we need approaches to construct interfaces that are valid, that is, interfaces with inductive invariants for correctness proofs and interfaces that are feasible and validating for violation proofs. But given existing checkers as explained above, we can use approximate methods to construct interfaces that are not guaranteed to be helpful for the proof construction. Since the interfaces can be checked, it is easy to refute them or prove that they are indeed useful. Also, such interfaces might

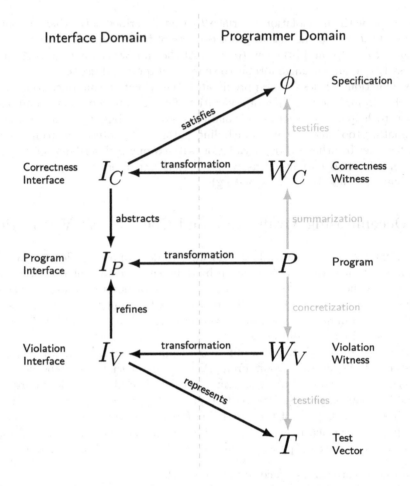

Fig. 10. Validation flows using the interface domain

be helpful to be further refined or abstracted to become more useful for the proof process. Furthermore, it might be interesting to come up with violation interfaces via learning-based testing [43].

Refiners. Besides the above-mentioned checkers, we can imagine tools that take an interface I_1 as input and refine (e.g., reduce) it in order to construct a new interface I_2 such that $I_2 \preceq I_1$. This idea is already used in the context of conditional model checking [18] (Reducers).

Abstracters. For the other direction, we can imagine tools that take an interface I_1 as input and abstract (e.g., extend, slice) it in order to construct a new interface I_2 such that $I_1 \preceq I_2$. This is an old but effective idea and used in program slicing [49].

Interactive Verification. The process of interactively constructing a proof in software verification using tools like Dafny [41], KeY [2], and Why3 [31] can be seen through the interface lens as follows: The human defines the correctness interface, usually by injecting the invariants in the program source code using annotations, and the verifier checks the refinement and specification satisfaction.

Witness-Based Results Validation. A validator for verification results takes the correctness witness W_C and transforms it to the internal interface representation I_C, that is, the validator does not need to come up with I_C (and the contained invariants) but applies only a (syntactic) transformation. Figure 10 tries to illustrate this flow. Then, the validator tries to prove $I_P \preccurlyeq I_C$ and $I_C \models \phi$. Symmetrically, for validating a violation result, the validator takes the violation witness W_V and transforms it to the internal interface representation I_V, which ideally describes an error path that it can easily replay and check for feasibility and violation, i.e., $I_V \preccurlyeq I_P$ and $I_V \not\models \phi$. Regarding multi-threaded programs, there is support for verification witnesses and their validation already [14].

k-Induction. There are verification approaches that consist of two engines, (a) an invariant-generator and (b) an inductiveness checker [12,13,38]. The former constructs the most essential parts of the correctness interface I_C (the invariants, done in parallel in an isolated separate process), while the latter performs the checks $I_P \preccurlyeq I_C$ and $I_C \models \phi$, with ever increasing values for length k of the inductive-step.

3.2   Integrated Approaches

CEGAR — Explained using Interfaces. Counterexample-guided abstraction refinement (CEGAR) [27] is an approach that uses the following steps in a loop until a proof of either correctness or violation is constructed:

1. construct an abstract model I_a using a given precision
2. check $I_a \models \phi$; if it holds, terminate with answer (TRUE, W_C) (the interface I_a corresponds to an interface I_C in Fig. 3, the correctness witness W_C in Fig. 9 is an abstraction of I_C)
3. extract counterexample interface I_b from I_a (interface I_a corresponds to interface $I_{\neg C}$ in Fig. 3)
4. check $I_b \not\models \phi$; if it holds, terminate with answer (FALSE, W_V) (the interface I_b corresponds to an interface I_V in Fig. 3, the violation witness W_V in Fig. 9 is an abstraction of I_V)
5. extract new facts to refine the precision (derived from the infeasibility of I_b) and continue with step (1); (the interface I_b corresponds to an interface $I_{\neg V}$ in Fig. 3)

Theorems 1 and 2 explain the correctness of CEGAR-based software model checking: The interfaces I_C and I_V can be used to prove the correctness and violation, respectively, using an internal specification checker and feasibility checker. Note that the feasibility checker in CEGAR is given by the above-described refinement checker (all refinements of the program interface I_P are

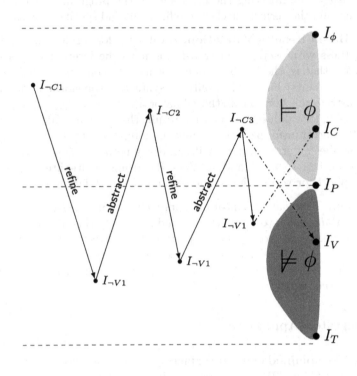

Fig. 11. Explaining CEGAR using interfaces

feasible, see Fig. 3). Figure 11 illustrates the alternation of the CEGAR loop between trying to prove correctness and trying to prove violation.

The resulting correctness interface I_C (in case of outcome TRUE) contains predicates describing inductive invariants (overapproximation of I_P), and the resulting violation interface I_V (in case of outcome FALSE) contains (at least one) feasible and violating path (underapproximation of I_P).

Test Generation. Theorem 2 explains the process of symbolic-execution-based test generation (as done, e.g., by KLEE [23]): The approaches leverage concretization mechanisms to construct a refined interface (constraints describing error paths, underapproximation) and the process must ensure feasibility, until a violating interface is found.

Explicit-State Model Checking. In some approaches to verification, the complete state space is exhaustively enumerated and checked [6,19,32,36]. When proving correctness of a program, those approaches operate on the same level of abstraction as the program itself, there is neither over- nor under-approximation. Thus, the most compact correctness interface used by such a verifier is the program interface I_P — these approaches cannot benefit from abstraction. However, when proving violation of a program, once an error path is encountered, the verifier can terminate the exploration and the partially explored state space can be seen as violation interface (which represents only a subset of all paths). Similar observations hold for SMT-based bounded model checking [22].

4   Conclusion

Software verification is a grand challenge of computer science [35]. Many powerful tools and approaches have been developed for program verification. Different approaches come with different strengths, and in order to join forces, we need to investigate ways to combine approaches. We are looking into possibilities to decompose a verification problem into smaller sub-problems in such a way that we can assign them to different tools (cooperative verification [20]). To achieve this, we extended the schema for proving correctness from refinement calculus by a symmetric schema for proving violation of program specifications. We hope that our interface-based viewpoint stimulates discussion on how we can achieve more modularity and decomposition in software verification. As future work, we plan to integrate compositional proofs into CoVeriTeam[6] — a tool to compose verification actors.

References

1. Aho, A.V., Sethi, R., Ullman, J.D.: Compilers: Principles, Techniques, and Tools. Addison-Wesley (1986)
2. Ahrendt, W., Baar, T., Beckert, B., Bubel, R., Giese, M., Hähnle, R., Menzel, W., Mostowski, W., Roth, A., Schlager, S., Schmitt, P.H.: The KeY tool. Softw. Syst. Model. **4**(1), 32–54 (2005). https://doi.org/10.1007/s10270-004-0058-x
3. de Alfaro, L., Henzinger, T.A.: Interface automata. In: Proc. FSE, pp. 109–120. ACM (2001). https://doi.org/10.1145/503271.503226
4. de Alfaro, L., Henzinger, T.A., Stoelinga, M.: Timed interfaces. In: Proc. EMSOFT, LNCS, vol. 2491, pp. 108–122. Springer (2002). https://doi.org/10.1007/3-540-45828-x_9
5. Ball, T., Levin, V., Rajamani, S.K.: A decade of software model checking with SLAM. Commun. ACM **54**(7), 68–76 (2011). https://doi.org/10.1145/1965724.1965743
6. Baranová, Z., Barnat, J., Kejstová, K., Kučera, T., Lauko, H., Mrázek, J., Ročkai, P., Štill, V.: Model checking of C and C++ with DIVINE 4. In: Proc. ATVA, LNCS, vol. 10482, pp. 201–207. Springer (2017). https://doi.org/10.1007/978-3-319-68167-2_14
7. Beckert, B., Hähnle, R.: Reasoning and verification: State of the art and current trends. IEEE Intell. Syst. **29**(1), 20–29 (2014). https://doi.org/10.1109/MIS.2014.3
8. Beyer, D., Chakrabarti, A., Henzinger, T.A.: Web service interfaces. In: Proc. WWW, pp. 148–159. ACM (2005). https://doi.org/10.1145/1060745.1060770

---

[6] https://gitlab.com/sosy-lab/software/coveriteam/

9. Beyer, D., Chlipala, A.J., Henzinger, T.A., Jhala, R., Majumdar, R.: Generating tests from counterexamples. In: Proc. ICSE, pp. 326–335. IEEE (2004). https://doi.org/10.1109/ICSE.2004.1317455

10. Beyer, D., Dangl, M., Dietsch, D., Heizmann, M.: Correctness witnesses: Exchanging verification results between verifiers. In: Proc. FSE, pp. 326–337. ACM (2016). https://doi.org/10.1145/2950290.2950351

11. Beyer, D., Dangl, M., Dietsch, D., Heizmann, M., Stahlbauer, A.: Witness validation and stepwise testification across software verifiers. In: Proc. FSE, pp. 721–733. ACM (2015). https://doi.org/10.1145/2786805.2786867

12. Beyer, D., Dangl, M., Wendler, P.: Boosting k-induction with continuously-refined invariants. In: Proc. CAV, LNCS, vol. 9206, pp. 622–640. Springer (2015). https://doi.org/10.1007/978-3-319-21690-4_42

13. Beyer, D., Dangl, M., Wendler, P.: A unifying view on SMT-based software verification. J. Autom. Reason. **60**(3), 299–335 (2018). https://doi.org/10.1007/s10817-017-9432-6

14. Beyer, D., Friedberger, K.: Violation witnesses and result validation for multithreaded programs. In: Proc. ISoLA, LNCS. Springer (2020)

15. Beyer, D., Gulwani, S., Schmidt, D.: Combining model checking and data-flow analysis. In: Handbook of Model Checking, pp. 493–540. Springer (2018). https://doi.org/10.1007/978-3-319-10575-8_16

16. Beyer, D., Henzinger, T.A., Jhala, R., Majumdar, R.: The software model checker BLAST. Int. J. Softw. Tools Technol. Transfer **9**(5–6), 505–525 (2007). https://doi.org/10.1007/s10009-007-0044-z

17. Beyer, D., Henzinger, T.A., Singh, V.: Algorithms for interface synthesis. In: Proc. CAV, LNCS, vol. 4590, pp. 4–19. Springer (2007). https://doi.org/10.1007/978-3-540-73368-3_4

18. Beyer, D., Jakobs, M.C., Lemberger, T., Wehrheim, H.: Reducer-based construction of conditional verifiers. In: Proc. ICSE, pp. 1182–1193. ACM (2018). https://doi.org/10.1145/3180155.3180259

19. Beyer, D., Löwe, S.: Explicit-state software model checking based on CEGAR and interpolation. In: Proc. FASE, LNCS, vol. 7793, pp. 146–162. Springer (2013). https://doi.org/10.1007/978-3-642-37057-1_11

20. Beyer, D., Wehrheim, H.: Verification artifacts in cooperative verification: Survey and unifying component framework. In: Proc. ISoLA, LNCS. Springer (2020)

21. Beyer, D., Wendler, P.: Reuse of verification results: Conditional model checking, precision reuse, and verification witnesses. In: Proc. SPIN, LNCS, vol. 7976, pp. 1–17. Springer (2013). https://doi.org/10.1007/978-3-642-39176-7_1

22. Biere, A., Cimatti, A., Clarke, E.M., Zhu, Y.: Symbolic model checking without BDDs. In: Proc. TACAS, LNCS, vol. 1579, pp. 193–207. Springer (1999). https://doi.org/10.1007/3-540-49059-0_14

23. Cadar, C., Dunbar, D., Engler, D.R.: KLEE: Unassisted and automatic generation of high-coverage tests for complex systems programs. In: Proc. OSDI, pp. 209–224. USENIX Association (2008)

24. Calcagno, C., Distefano, D., Dubreil, J., Gabi, D., Hooimeijer, P., Luca, M., O'Hearn, P.W., Papakonstantinou, I., Purbrick, J., Rodriguez, D.: Moving fast with software verification. In: Proc. NFM, LNCS, vol. 9058, pp. 3–11. Springer (2015). https://doi.org/10.1007/978-3-319-17524-9_1

25. Chakrabarti, A., de Alfaro, L., Henzinger, T.A., Stoelinga, M.: Resource interfaces. In: Proc. EMSOFT, LNCS, vol. 2855. Springer (2003). https://doi.org/10.1007/978-3-540-45212-6_9

26. Church, A.: A note on the Entscheidungsproblem. J. Symb. Logic **1**(1), 40–41 (1936). https://doi.org/10.2307/2269326

27. Clarke, E.M., Grumberg, O., Jha, S., Lu, Y., Veith, H.: Counterexample-guided abstraction refinement for symbolic model checking. J. ACM **50**(5), 752–794 (2003). https://doi.org/10.1145/876638.876643

28. Clarke, E.M., Grumberg, O., McMillan, K.L., Zhao, X.: Efficient generation of counterexamples and witnesses in symbolic model checking. In: Proc. DAC, pp. 427–432. ACM (1995). https://doi.org/10.1145/217474.217565

29. Cook, B.: Formal reasoning about the security of Amazon web services. In: Proc. CAV (2), LNCS, vol. 10981, pp. 38–47. Springer (2018). https://doi.org/10.1007/978-3-319-96145-3_3

30. Cousot, P.: On fixpoint/iteration/variant induction principles for proving total correctness of programs with denotational semantics. In: Proc. LOPSTR 2019, LNCS, vol. 12042, pp. 3–18. Springer (2020). https://doi.org/10.1007/978-3-030-45260-5_1

31. Filliâtre, J.C., Paskevich, A.: Why3: Where programs meet provers. In: Programming Languages and Systems, pp. 125–128. Springer (2013). https://doi.org/10.1007/978-3-642-37036-6_8

32. Havelund, K., Pressburger, T.: Model checking Java programs using Java PATHFINDER. Int. J. Softw. Tools Technol. Transfer **2**(4), 366–381 (2000)

33. Henzinger, T.A., Jhala, R., Majumdar, R.: Permissive interfaces. In: Proc. FSE, pp. 31–40. ACM (2005). https://doi.org/10.1145/1095430.1081713

34. Hoare, C.A.R.: An axiomatic basis for computer programming. Commun. ACM **12**(10), 576–580 (1969). https://doi.org/10.1145/363235.363259

35. Hoare, C.A.R.: The verifying compiler: A grand challenge for computing research. J. ACM **50**(1), 63–69 (2003)

36. Holzmann, G.J.: The SPIN model checker. IEEE Trans. Softw. Eng. **23**(5), 279–295 (1997)

37. Jhala, R., Majumdar, R.: Software model checking. ACM Comput. Surv. **41**(4) (2009). https://doi.org/10.1145/1592434.1592438

38. Kahsai, T., Tinelli, C.: PKIND: A parallel k-induction based model checker. In: Proc. Int. Workshop on Parallel and Distributed Methods in Verification, EPTCS, vol. 72, pp. 55–62 (2011). https://doi.org/10.4204/EPTCS.72.6

39. Khoroshilov, A.V., Mutilin, V.S., Petrenko, A.K., Zakharov, V.: Establishing Linux driver verification process. In: Proc. Ershov Memorial Conference, LNCS, vol. 5947, pp. 165–176. Springer (2009). https://doi.org/10.1007/978-3-642-11486-1_14

40. Kildall, G.A.: A unified approach to global program optimization. In: Proc. POPL, pp. 194–206. ACM (1973). https://doi.org/10.1145/512927.512945

41. Leino, K.R.M.: Dafny: An automatic program verifier for functional correctness. In: Proc. LPAR, LNCS, vol. 6355, pp. 348–370. Springer (2010). https://doi.org/10.1007/978-3-642-17511-4_20

42. McConnell, R.M., Mehlhorn, K., Näher, S., Schweitzer, P.: Certifying algorithms. Comput. Sci. Rev. **5**(2), 119–161 (2011). https://doi.org/10.1016/j.cosrev.2010.09.009

43. Meinke, K.: Learning-based testing: Recent progress and future prospects. In: Machine Learning for Dynamic Software Analysis: Potentials and Limits, LNCS, vol. 11026, pp. 53–73. Springer (2018). https://doi.org/10.1007/978-3-319-96562-8_2

44. Morris, J.M.: A theoretical basis for stepwise refinement and the programming calculus. Sci. Comput. Program. **9**(3), 287–306 (1987). https://doi.org/10.1016/0167-6423(87)90011-6

45. O'Hearn, P.W.: Incorrectness logic. Proc. ACM Program. Lang. **4**(POPL) (2020). https://doi.org/10.1145/3371078
46. Piterman, N., Pnueli, A.: Temporal logic and fair discrete systems. In: Handbook of Model Checking, pp. 27–73. Springer (2018). https://doi.org/10.1007/978-3-319-10575-8_2
47. Schneider, F.B.: Enforceable security policies. ACM Trans. Inf. Syst. Secur. **3**(1), 30–50 (2000). https://doi.org/10.1145/353323.353382
48. Turing, A.: On computable numbers, with an application to the Entscheidungsproblem. In: Proc. LMS, vol. s2–42, pp. 230–265. London Mathematical Society (1937). https://doi.org/10.1112/plms/s2-42.1.230
49. Weiser, M.: Program slicing. IEEE Trans. Softw. Eng. **10**(4), 352–357 (1984). https://doi.org/10.1109/tse.1984.5010248
50. Wetzler, N., Heule, M.J.H., Hunt Jr., W.A.: DRAT-TRIM: Efficient checking and trimming using expressive clausal proofs. In: Proc. SAT, LNCS, vol. 8561, pp. 422–429. Springer (2014). https://doi.org/10.1007/978-3-319-09284-3_31

Scaling Correctness-by-Construction

Alexander Knüppel$^{(\boxtimes)}$ (ID), Tobias Runge$^{(\boxtimes)}$, and Ina Schaefer$^{(\boxtimes)}$

TU Braunschweig, Braunschweig, Germany
{a.knueppel,tobias.runge,i.schaefer}@tu-braunschweig.de

Abstract. The correctness-by-construction paradigm allows developers to derive formally correct programs from a pair of first-order precondition and postcondition. Although tool support has been proposed recently, and thus correctness-by-construction has left the period of pen-and-paper proofs, it is still applied in an unstructured manner to independent algorithmic problems only. To scale correctness-by-construction to more complex programs and to establish a *repository* of reusable off-the-shelf *components*, we present a formal framework and open-source tool support called ARCHICORC. In ARCHICORC, a developer models UML-style software *components* comprising *required* and *provided interfaces*, where methods contained in interfaces are associated to *specification contracts* and mapped to correct-by-construction implementations. We describe our proposed mathematical model for the horizontal and vertical composition of correct-by-construction components, and identify properties that allow to reuse them across different projects. Finally, we demonstrate feasibility of our approach on a case study and discuss future research directions related to the integration of correct-by-construction components into software engineering practices.

Keywords: Correctness-by-construction · Deductive verification · Architecture · UML components · Design-by-contract

1 Introduction

As a promising methodology to guarantee the *correct* implementation of algorithms, the correctness-by-construction approach [10,11,17,23] has been proposed to support the incremental development of *correct* programs with respect to some specification. Starting with a Hoare triple $\{\phi\}\mathcal{P}\{\psi\}$ comprising precondition ϕ, postcondition ψ, and abstract program P, a developer refines this triple into code using small, tractable, and provably correct *refinement rules*. Applying correctness-by-construction promises to introduce little to no defects [17]. However, despite its advantages, missing adequate tool support is one of the reasons that this approach is not a prevalent style of software development.

To mitigate these challenges and leave the period of pen-and-paper proofs, CORC [32] has been recently introduced by some of the authors as a hands-on software development environment for constructing programs following the correctness-by-construction paradigm. Moreover, in a recent empirical study [33],

© Springer Nature Switzerland AG 2020
T. Margaria and B. Steffen (Eds.): ISoLA 2020, LNCS 12476, pp. 187–207, 2020.
https://doi.org/10.1007/978-3-030-61362-4_10

CORC showed that good tool support renders the correctness-by-construction paradigm as a real alternative to post-hoc verification. In particular, CORC provides a hybrid textual-graphical editor to develop single programs on the granularity level of *procedures* (i.e., methods). Additionally, a refinement rule for method calls has been introduced, which allows to call subroutines in a modular manner and to build larger programs. However, large-scale software development using CORC and correctness-by-construction is still in its infancy, as, currently, correctness-by-construction is not well integrated into existing software development methodologies.

As a first step towards software engineering practices and correctness-by-construction in concert, we propose ARCHICORC, a framework that extends the principles of CORC and structures correct-by-construction programs into *components* with defined *provided* and *required interfaces*. Such interfaces represent sets of method signatures specified following the *design by contract* principle [22]. That is, each method signature m is associated to a contract $c = \{\phi\}m\{\psi\}$ with precondition $\{\phi\}$ and postcondition $\{\psi\}$. When a basic component is developed, each method contract $c = \{\phi\}m\{\psi\}$ of its provided interfaces is mapped to a CORC implementation that satisfies the contract $\{\phi'\}\mathcal{P}\{\psi'\}$. Compatibility is ensured by following behavioral subtyping [21]. That is, precondition ϕ' is only allowed to be weaker (i.e., $\phi \implies \phi'$), whereas postcondition ψ' is only allowed to be stronger (i.e., $\psi' \implies \psi$). One additional particularity of ARCHICORC is that CORC implementations associated to a component are only allowed to invoke methods that are part of the component's required interface. Moreover, component *connectors* link *compatible* provided and required interfaces of two components together, such that during execution of an implementation the respective method is invoked.

Following the hierarchical nature and reuse potential of component-based software [35], more complex components called *composite components* can be constructed from simpler ones by *component composition*. To this end, so called *delegation connectors* wire interfaces from higher-level components to interfaces of the lower-level components. Only basic components (i.e., components that cannot be decomposed any further) are realised by the implementing CORC implemenations. An advantage of composite components is their hiding of implementation details and their reuse potential in different contexts. We provide an open source implementation of ARCHICORC that offers a hybrid graphical-textual IDE and integrates CORC as part of its tool suite. Methods in component interfaces are annotated by contracts written in a syntax resembling the Java Modeling Language [19]. In summary, the contribution of this work is threefold.

- We propose a framework for specifying and reasoning about UML-style *components* based on Hoare logic [14] and correctness-by-construction [10,11,17].
- We provide a practical open-source implementation, ARCHICORC, that connects component modeling, specification, and code generation facilities with CORC [32].
- We showcase our theoretical framework on a case study that has been created with ARCHICORC.

2   The Correctness-by-Construction Approach

Correctness-by-Construction [17] is a paradigm to derive formally correct programs in an incremental process guided by a specification. Specifications are represented as Hoare triples [14] of the form $\{\phi\}P\{\psi\}$ comprising a precondition ϕ asserting the initial state, an *abstract statement* P that is concretized during program construction, and a postcondition ψ asserting the final state after the program is executed. Hoare triples represent *total correctness assertions* that valuate only to *true* if, beginning from the precondition, the postcondition is met after executing the eventually defined concrete program *and* the program terminates. Therefore, in each step, the Hoare triple $\{\phi\}P\{\psi\}$ is refined to a primed Hoare triple $\{\phi\}P'\{\psi\}$ using a set of allowed and provably correct refinement rules. $\{\phi\}P'\{\psi\}$ is thus true for a subset of programs represented by $\{\phi\}P\{\psi\}$. Finally, all abstract statements are replaced by concrete statements and the derived concrete program is guaranteed to be correct by construction.

Recently, CORC [32] has been proposed, which is a graphical and textual development environment for creating programs following the correctness-by-construction approach. Following the CORC language, preconditions and postconditions are written in a flavor of *first-order logic* following the *design-by-contract* methodology [22], and programs are written in an adapted version of the *guarded command language* [9]. Incremental derivation of concrete programs from abstract statements is accomplished by means of *refinement rules*. These rules are based on a constructive calculus, such that developers are able to establish the correctness of each individual step (e.g., to faster identify nonconformance of program and specification), as opposed to the classical post-hoc verification of complete programs.

In Fig. 1, we show the six core refinement rules currently supported by the CORC language. For the *composition* rule and the *repetition* rule, additional manual specification is typically required. For the composition rule, an *intermediate condition* M has to be provided, which valuates to true after P_1 is executed and needs to be strong enough to serve as the precondition for P_2. For the repetition rule, a *loop invariant* I and a variant V have to be provided. To show termination, the evolution of variant V needs to be strictly monotonically decreasing with each execution of P until a lower bound of zero is reached. The *method call rule* omits side effects (i.e., call by value) and is applicable iff the callee's specification complies with the respective statement's specification.

Contrary to the purely imperative guarded command language, the CORC language introduces a simple object model similar to the one used in ABS [15]. That is, there exists no inheritance and no subtyping. Moreover, each CORC program is part of an object definition by exhibiting a *method* as declared in classical object-oriented languages (e.g., JAVA). In particular, all referenced variables in a program are labeled as either *argument, return value,* or *local variable.* As we will extend CORC programs with *class* membership for grouping purposes, we additionally allow to label variables as shared *class variables.* Besides primitive types, such variables are allowed to have an *interface type,* which comprises further accessible correct-by-construction methods (cf. method call rule

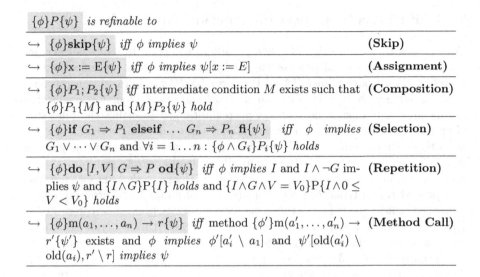

$\{\phi\}P\{\psi\}$ *is refinable to*

$\hookrightarrow$ $\{\phi\}\textbf{skip}\{\psi\}$ *iff* ϕ *implies* ψ **(Skip)**

$\hookrightarrow$ $\{\phi\}\text{x} := \text{E}\{\psi\}$ *iff* ϕ *implies* $\psi[x := E]$ **(Assignment)**

$\hookrightarrow$ $\{\phi\}P_1; P_2\{\psi\}$ *iff* intermediate condition M exists such that   **(Composition)**
$\{\phi\}P_1\{M\}$ and $\{M\}P_2\{\psi\}$ *hold*

$\hookrightarrow$ $\{\phi\}\textbf{if}\ G_1 \Rightarrow P_1\ \textbf{elseif}\ \dots\ G_n \Rightarrow P_n\ \textbf{fi}\{\psi\}$ *iff* ϕ *implies* **(Selection)**
$G_1 \vee \cdots \vee G_n$ and $\forall i = 1 \dots n : \{\phi \wedge G_i\}P_i\{\psi\}$ *holds*

$\hookrightarrow$ $\{\phi\}\textbf{do}\ [I, V]\ G \Rightarrow P\ \textbf{od}\{\psi\}$ *iff* ϕ *implies* I and $I \wedge \neg G$ im-   **(Repetition)**
plies ψ and $\{I \wedge G\}\text{P}\{I\}$ *holds* and $\{I \wedge G \wedge V = V_0\}\text{P}\{I \wedge 0 \leq V < V_0\}$ *holds*

$\hookrightarrow$ $\{\phi\}\text{m}(a_1, \dots, a_n) \rightarrow r\{\psi\}$ *iff* method $\{\phi'\}\text{m}(a'_1, \dots, a'_n) \rightarrow$ **(Method Call)**
$r'\{\psi'\}$ *exists* and ϕ *implies* $\phi'[a'_i \setminus a_1]$ and $\psi'[\text{old}(a'_i) \setminus \text{old}(a_i), r' \setminus r]$ *implies* ψ

Fig. 1. Refinement Rules Following the Correctness-By-Construction Approach [32]

in Fig. 1). The precondition of the top-level specification is allowed to reference arguments and class variables, whereas the postcondition is additionally allowed reference return values. Class variables can be seen as the equivalent of private class fields in object-oriented programming languages. Hence, class variables are shared among all CORC methods associated to the same interface type.

3   Overview and Motivating Example

In this section, we present an overview and the key ideas of ARCHICORC. One main goal is to purposefully *bundle* correct-by-construction implementations into reusable components with defined interfaces to establish a repository of correct-by-construction components. In particular, our proposed framework is based on the following elements:

Key Elements of ArchiCorC

1. A *component and interface description language* to describe the interconnection in terms of provided and required interfaces between components based on design by contract.
2. A *construction technique* that allows to refine method signatures of provided interfaces to provably correct implementations using the correctness-by-construction approach.
3. An *integrated formal reasoning framework* in order to establish hierarchical and vertical compatibility of composed components.
4. A *code generation method* for correct-by-construction JAVA implementations from ARCHICORC components.

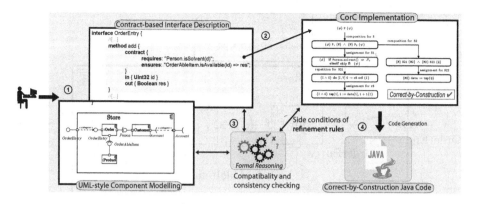

Fig. 2. Schematic Workflow of the ARCHICORC Development Process

As shown in Fig. 2, a developer starts by designing an initial, high-level structure of a component including its required and provided interfaces. Interfaces represent sets of *method signatures* that are either needed or provided and are specified by a pair of precondition and postcondition ①. In the following, we refer to *Hoare triples* consisting of a method signature and a pair of precondition and postcondition as *contracts*. In ARCHICORC, we distinguish two types of components: *basic* and *composite* components. Composite components are hierarchically composed of sub-components and do not have an explicit mapping of method signatures of provided interfaces to CORC implementations. Instead, only basic components have that mapping, but are not decomposed any further. Both basic and composite components can be part of a enclosing composite component and propagate their provided interfaces to the enclosing composite component if a delegation between the interfaces exists.

Subsequently, a developer maps provided method signatures of basic components to either existing CORC implementations from an already established repository or tries to construct a new provably-correct program starting from the method contract ②. External methods that are used in these CORC implementations by applying the *method call rule* (cf. Fig. 1) must be part of the required interface of this component.

Basic components represent correct-by-construction implementations in a strictly defined way. Through the construction of composite components in concert with assume-guarantee reasoning, a developer is able to correctly assemble smaller existing CORC implementations to larger ones, while also hiding functionality ③. Valid compositions are established through contracts, which enable both *horizontal* and *vertical* reasoning. Horizontal reasoning ensures compatibility between connected components by proving that each component satisfies the assumptions of any component it provides input to. Vertical reasoning ensures substitutability by allowing the replacement of a component k by any other component k', whose contract is subsumed by the contract of component k. Finally, ARCHICORC allows to generate correct-by-construction JAVA implementations

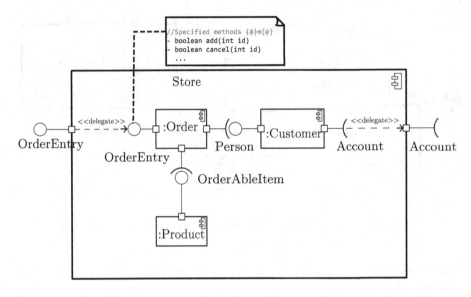

Fig. 3. Illustration of Composite Component Store

from components including JML annotations, which can be used in typical JAVA projects ④.

Motivating Example. To illustrate the described concepts, we have chosen a simple composite component Store, depicted in Fig. 3, consisting of three basic components, namely Order, Customer, and Product. Externally, composite component Store only provides interface OrderEntry to place a new order, for which it depends on interface Account. Internally, method signatures of interfaces associated to basic components are mapped to CORC implementations and are possibly delegated to the external interfaces. In particular, part of interface OrderEntry is method add(int id) that adds a new product to the cart identified by a unique id. An excerpt of a corresponding CORC implementation is presented in Fig. 4. As highlighted, the program uses the *method call rule* to access method isSolvent of interface Person, which is only possible, as Person is a required interface of component Order. A developer can hide many implementations details by developing composite components, while provided methods of such components also retain their correctness. Users of such components need to satisfy the required interfaces, but can rely on the correctness of provided methods in their own software projects.

4   Formalizing ArchiCorC Components

A software component in the sense of ARCHICORC is similar to a UML-style software component [35] such that it provides a static view on an encapsulated

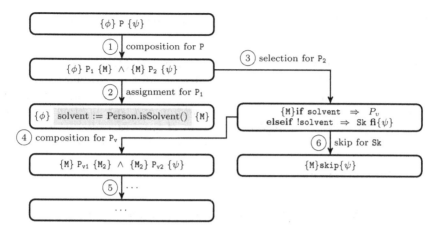

Fig. 4. Excerpt of a CORC Implementation for Method OrderEntry.add(int id)

piece of software with explicit interfaces to its environment. In the following, we give the necessary formal definitions of ARCHICORC's component model.

4.1 Interface Definition

In this regard, a ARCHICORC component provides *methods* (i.e., *functionality*) to other components through its *provided interfaces* and possibly requires methods specified by its *required* interfaces to be even able to provide such functionality. Provided and required interfaces of ARCHICORC components comprise specified method signatures, which are associated to Hoare triples of the form $c = \{\phi\}m\{\psi\}$, where ϕ and ψ are the respective precondition and postcondition. As mentioned before, we refer to such Hoare triples as *method contracts* and denote by $\mathcal{C}$ the universe of all existing contracts.

The specification language used for formalizing method contracts is based on a simple version of the Java Modeling Language [19] (JML). That is, specification expressions used in method contracts must be side-effect free, which means that assignment and increment expressions are not permitted. Additionally, method contracts may refer to some variables in their specification, which have to be resolved when the corresponding method is implemented. Therefore, we allow the declaration of fields in our interface definitions similar to *model fields* as used in JML. Technically, when code generation takes place, **get** and **set** methods are generated for field declarations in a provided interface. Fields in required interfaces are accessible in CORC implementations through their **get** and **set** methods.

Importantly, the introduction of fields is only necessary when the intended application is stateful. Contrary, a stateless application (e.g., RESTful API's) follows a functional programming style, which means that no fields are needed. Finally, it is possible to call *pure* methods in method contracts. A method is *pure* if the state is not altered when executing the method. We define an *interface* as follows.

Definition 1 (Interface). *An* interface I *is a pair* $\langle M, \mathcal{F} \rangle$. *$M$ is a set of method signatures of the form* {req : ϕ}m(**in** : $\overline{T}\,\overline{a}$, **out** : $U\,b$){guar : ψ}, *where m is the name of the method, $\overline{a}$ of types $\overline{T}$ are the passed arguments, $\overline{b}$ of type $\overline{U}$ are the result values, and ϕ, ψ are the precondition and postcondition of method signature m, respectively. Moreover, $\mathcal{F}$ is a set of typed variables, which we will refer to as* fields. *An interface specification has the following form:*

Interface Specification

Interface I:

      Method m_1: {req : ϕ_1} m_1(**in** : $\overline{T_1}\,\overline{a_1}$, **out** : $U_1\,b_1$){guar : ψ_1}

             $\vdots$

      Method m_k: {req : ϕ_k} m_k(**in** : $\overline{T_k}\,\overline{a_k}$, **out** : $U_k\,b_k$){guar : ψ_k}

      Fields: $\overline{T}\,\overline{f}$

As apparent in the interface specification, all arguments, the return value, and fields have a type. However, for the sake of presentation we discard the introduction of a type system and assume only primitive data types and standard typing rules (e.g., as introduced by Pierce [27]). Moreover, to increase flexibility in our formalism, we allow that multiple components may in fact provide a part of a required interface of a another component. We therefore introduce an operator that merges *composable* interfaces together to match the required interface.

Definition 2 (Interface Merging). *Let $I = \{I_1, ..., I_n\}$ with $I_i = \langle M_i, \mathcal{F}_i \rangle$ be a finite set of composable interfaces. That is, interfaces are* composable *if equally named methods have identical signatures and method contracts, and equally named fields are equally typed. Then, their merging is defined as*

$$\texttt{merge}\,I = \langle \bigcup M_i, \bigcup \mathcal{F}_i \rangle. \tag{1}$$

Similarly, we may want to be able to provide only a subset of methods to different clients of a component. Therefore, we allow to hide methods and fields in an interface to render them invisible.

Definition 3 (Method Hiding). *Let $I = \langle M, \mathcal{F} \rangle$ be an interface. Further, let $M' \subset M$ a set of method signatures and $\mathcal{F}' \subset \mathcal{F}$ a set of fields we want to hide. Then, we denote by $I' = \langle M \setminus M', \mathcal{F} \setminus \mathcal{F}' \rangle$ the interface after removal of all methods M' and fields $\mathcal{F}'$ from I.*

4.2 Contract Compatibility

Method signatures of our interface definition and contracts as used in CORC implementations are conceptually identical, which we exploit to define a valid mapping between both concepts. Indeed, each method signature m of an interface I has to be associated to a method contract $c = \{\phi\}m\{\psi\} \in \mathcal{C}$ that we use as the lingua franca in our formalism. Known as behavioral subtyping [21], a contract may *preserve* the behavior of another contract. Informally, a contract c can be replaced by a contract c' if each behavior specified by contract c is also specified by contract c'. In this case, we say that contract c' is *compatible* to contract c. This property is important, as it (1) allows a developer to link a method signature in a provided interface of a basic component to a CORC implementation that preserves the behavior, and (2) provides a provable condition for the valid connection of a provided and required interface. For a method signature m that satisfies a contract c, we say that a CORC implementation c' is *compatible* to m iff c' is compatible to c. That is, (1) c and c' have the same arguments and return values, and (2) c's precondition is only allowed to be stronger than c''s precondition and c's postcondition is only allowed to be weaker than c''s postcondition. Formally, we define contract compatibility as follows.

Definition 4 (Contract Compatibility). *Let $c, c' \in \mathcal{C}$ be two contracts with $c = \{\phi\}m\{\psi\}$ and $c' = \{\phi'\}m'\{\psi'\}$. We say that contract c' is* compatible *to contract c, denoted by $c' \preceq c$, iff* $\mathsf{arg}_m = \mathsf{arg}_{m'}$ *and* $\mathsf{ret}_m = \mathsf{ret}_{m'}$, *where* arg *and* ret *are sets associated to the arguments and return values of a method, respectively, and the following condition holds:*

$$\vdash \phi \Rightarrow \phi' \wedge \psi' \Rightarrow \psi. \tag{2}$$

Compatibility has also to be guaranteed between required and provided interfaces. In essence, each method signature of a required interface has to be connected to a *compatible* method signature of a provided interface, which means that the provided method signature has to fulfill the corresponding required method signature. The following definition lifts *contract compatibility* to the level of interfaces.

Definition 5 (Interface Compatibility). *Let $I = \langle M, \mathcal{F} \rangle$ and $I' = \langle M', \mathcal{F}' \rangle$ be two interfaces. We say that interface I' is* compatible *to interface I, denoted by $I' \preceq I$, iff*

$$\forall m' \in M' \, \exists m \in M \text{ such that } m' \preceq m \wedge \mathcal{F}' \subseteq \mathcal{F} \tag{3}$$

4.3 Component Definition and Composition

We consider a *basic* component to be a black-box comprising an optional required interface and a mandatory provided interface. Furthermore, basic components map method signatures of their provided interface to compatible CORC implementations from a set of existing programs $\mathcal{P} \subset \mathcal{C}$. Formally, we define basic components as follows.

Definition 6 (Basic Component). *A basic component k_b is a triple $\langle I_p, I_r, \mathsf{Impl} \rangle$ consisting of: (i) the provided interface I_p, (ii) the possibly empty* *required interface I_r, and (iii) a mapping* Impl $: I_p \to \mathcal{P}$ *associating each method signature in* $m \in I_p$ *with a valid* CORC *implementation* $c \in \mathcal{P}$. *We say that* k_b *is well-formed iff* $\forall c = \{\phi\}m\{\psi\} \in I_p.M :$ Impl$(m) \preceq c$.

Furthermore, we introduce composite components that hierarchically structure sub-components to reuse already implemented functionality, but also to hide unneeded method signatures. Opposed to basic components, composite components do not establish any mapping from their provided interfaces to CORC implementations. Instead, delegate connectors link the external method signatures (i.e., the required and provided interfaces) of the composite component to the respective interfaces of sub-components (cf. Sect. 2). Formally, we define composite components as follows.

Definition 7 (Composite Component). *A composite component k_c is a tuple* $\langle I_p, I_r, K_{sub}, $ Conn, Dele$_{req/prov}\rangle$ *consisting of: (i) the provided interface I_p, (ii) the required interface I_r, (iii) a finite set of sub-components $K_{sub} = \{k_1, \ldots, k_n\}$, where each k_i is either basic or a composite, (iv) a finite set of connections* Conn $\subseteq \{k.I_p \,|\, k \in K_{sub}\} \times \{k.I_r \,|\, k \in K_{sub}\}$ *between provided and required interfaces of sub-components, and (v) two finite sets* Dele$_{req} \subseteq \{k.I_r \,|\, k \in K_{sub}\}$ *and* Dele$_{prov} \subseteq \{k.I_p \,|\, k \in K_{sub}\}$ *of delegate connectors.*

In ARCHICORC, we assume that connected top-level components are implicitly part of a composite component. To specify a link between components on the same hierarchy, *component connectors* associate provided interfaces of a component with required interfaces of another one. The connection can only be established when the provided interface is compatible to the required interface (cf. Definition 4). Furthermore, a *well-formed* composite component consists of only well-formed sub-component and has to ensure that its required and provided interface is correctly linked to sub-components. In the following, we give a formal definition of a well-formed composite component.

Definition 8 (Well-Formed Composite Component). *Let $k_c = \langle I_p, I_r, K_{sub}, $ Conn, Dele$_{req/prov}\rangle$ be a composite component. Composite component k_c is* well-formed *iff the following conditions hold.*

- *Each method of a required interface of a sub-component is linked to either a provided method signature of a sub-component or to a method of the composite's required interface through a delegate connector. The sub-component's interface has therefore to be compatible to the merge of all interfaces of connected sub-components and the composite's required interface (i.e., $\forall k' \in K_{sub} : k'.I_r \preceq$ merge $\{I'_p \,|\, (k'.I_r, I'_p) \in$ Conn$\} \cup$ Dele$_{req}$).*
- *Each method of the provided interface I_p is linked to a method of a provided interface of a sub-component through a delegate connector. Therefore, I_p has to be compatible to all connected sub-components (i.e., $I_p \preceq$ merge Dele$_{out}$).*
- *All sub-components in K_{sub} are well-formed.*

5   Code Generation and Validation

For using correct-by-construction components in arbitrary software projects, ARCHICORC provides facilities for code generation. The tooling translates composite components to a JAVA implementation, where methods are additonally annotated with JML [19] contracts. Using the generated code then amounts to importing the respective JAVA package. Following the principles of ARCHICORC, only provided methods of the composite component are visible and accessible, while implementation details are hidden. Moreover, our aim is to retain correctness during the code generation, which is trivially accomplished for all methods that are implemented with CORC, as CORC implementations already resemble valid JAVA code. However, if the composite component requires methods through its required interface, these methods have to be provided by a user and contract conformance has to be checked separately.

In Table 1, we show the formal constructs of our component model and the corresponding translation to JAVA code. The complete interfaces and classes of a ARCHICORC component are generated in the same JAVA package. Provided interfaces are translated to classical JAVA interfaces, where methods are additionally annotated with the corresponding method contract. Furthermore, actual components are translated to classes that implement the containing provided interface. Top-level components are publicly visible, whereas lower-level components are only visible inside the *package*. For each PROVIDED field of the provided interface, a private field together with its **set** and **get** method is generated. Moreover, a reference for each component and delegate connector that is connected to the required interface is generated.

Methods of a basic component's provided interface are implemented by the corresponding CORC implementation. Methods of a composite component's provided interface delegate all method calls to the respective sub-components (i.e., specified with a delegate connector) through method chaining. Furthermore, all referenced variables in the specification are (both basic and composite components) and CORC implementations (only basic components) are resolved and replaced with the respective **set** and **get** methods.

As mentioned in Sect. 2, CORC implementations label referenced variables as either arguments, return values, local variables, and class variables. During code generation, it is checked that all mapped CORC implementations indeed satisfy the specification of the corresponding interface method. That is, (1) arguments and the return value have to match, and (2) class variables have to form a subset of the fields that are part of the respective provided interface.

6   Bank Account Case Study

In this section, we demonstrate the applicability of ARCHICORC on a part of a *bank account* application. In Fig. 5, we depict the corresponding component diagram of a banking account together with a module for financial transaction between two accounts. Composite component DailyAccountComposite provides the interface DailyAccount to a client for managing accounts with a fixed daily

Table 1. Excerpt of Code Translation from ARCHICORC Components to Correct-by-Construction JAVA Code

Formal Construct	Transformation

Provided interface $I_p = \langle M, \mathcal{F}\rangle$	```interface I_p {```
	$\forall\{\phi\}m(\overline{Ta}, Ub)\{\psi\} \in M :$
	```//@ requires φ;```
	```//@ ensures ψ;```
	```public U m(Ta);```
	```}```

Component K with provided interface $I_p = \langle M_p, \mathcal{F}_p\rangle$, required interface $I_r = \langle M_r, \mathcal{F}_r\rangle$, which is part of a composite component $K^* = \langle I_p^*, I_r^*, K_{sub}^*, \mathsf{Conn}, \mathsf{Dele}_{req/prov}\rangle$	```modifier class K implements I_p {```
	$\forall f \in \mathcal{F}_p$ with type $T:$
	```private Tf;```
	```//@ ensures \result == f;```
	```public T get_f();```
	```//@ ensures f == f';```
	```public void set_f(Tf');```
	$\forall(k.I_p, I_r) \in \mathsf{Conn} \wedge \forall k'.I_p \in \mathsf{Dele}_{req}:$
	```private k.I_p Object_i = new k.I_p();```
	```private k'.I_p Object_j = new k'.I_p();```
	```//method implementations ...```
	```}```

Top-level component?	```modifier = public else modifier = ε```

Method implementation for basic component $\langle I_p, I_r, \mathsf{Impl}\rangle$ with $I_p = \langle M_p, \mathcal{F}_p\rangle$ and $I_r = \langle M_r, \mathcal{F}_r\rangle$	```...```
	$\forall\{\phi\}m(\overline{Ta}, Ub)\{\psi\} \in M_p :$
	```//@ requires``` $\phi[f \in \mathcal{F}_r \mapsto I_r.\mathsf{get\_}f];$
	```//@ ensures``` $\psi[f \in \mathcal{F}_r \mapsto I_r.\mathsf{get\_}f];$
	```public U m(Ta) {```
	```//Resolve CORC implementation```
	```Impl(m)```
	```}```
	```...```

Method implementation for composite component $\langle I_p, I_r, K_{sub}, \mathsf{Conn}, \mathsf{Dele}_{req/prov}\rangle$ with $I_p = \langle M_p, \mathcal{F}_p\rangle$ and $I_r = \langle M_r, \mathcal{F}_r\rangle$	```...```
	$\forall\{\phi\}m(\overline{Ta}, Ub)\{\psi\} \in M_p :$
	```//@ requires``` $\phi[f \in \mathcal{F}_r \mapsto I_r.\mathsf{get\_}f];$
	```//@ ensures``` $\psi[f \in \mathcal{F}_r \mapsto I_r.\mathsf{get\_}f];$
	```public U m(Ta) {```
	$k'.m \in \mathsf{Dele}_{prov}$ with $m' \preceq m:$
	```return k'.m(Ta);```
	```}```
	```...```

Enclosing composite component $K = \langle I_p, I_r, K_{sub}, \mathsf{Conn}, \mathsf{Dele}_{req/prov}\rangle$ with non-empty required interface $I_r = \langle M_r, \mathcal{F}_r\rangle$	```...```
	```I_r req;```
	```public K(I_r arg) { //constr.```
	```req = arg;```
	```}```
	```...```

withdrawal limit. In particular, DailyAccountComposite consists of three basic sub-components, namely Account, DailyLimit, and DailyAccount. Account provides basic functionality to alter the balance of an account (e.g., to withdraw a specific amount of money). DailyLimit is used to set withdrawal limits for

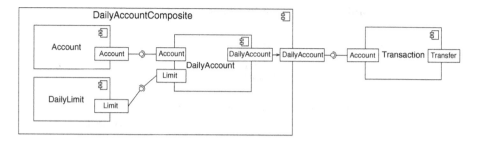

Fig. 5. Component Diagram of a Banking Account Application

an account. Both components are required by DailyAccount to provide updates for an account considering the daily withdrawal limit. Whereas the interfaces of both components Account and DailyLimit are only accessible internally, DailyAccount's equally-named interface is delegated to the DailyAccountComposite composite component and therefore accessible by any client. The basic component Transaction provides functionality to transfer money from one account to another. Therefore, it requires the Account interface to operate on two accounts.

For our evaluation, we constructed this component diagram in ARCHICORC[1]. ARCHICORC is a graphical editor written in Java. The graphical interface is implemented with Graphiti[2]. The components and interfaces can be added by drag and drop from a palette at the side of the editor. Required and provided interfaces are connected with UML lollipop notation. Additionally, the provided interfaces can be specified with contracts for each method. To establish behavior of methods of provided interfaces, the methods are mapped to CORC implementations and ARCHICORC verifies automatically that the CORC implementation is compatible to the corresponding method contracts using the SMTSolver Z3 [8].

In Table 2, we present the mapping of each method of a provided interface of Fig. 5 to the corresponding CORC implementation. Correctness is ensured by proving that (1) the Hoare triple of each CORC implementation is compatible to the method signature's contract, and (2) that connected interfaces are also *compatible* (cf. Definition 5). In particular, provided interface DailyAccount of component DailyAccountComposite is connected to required interface Account of component Transaction, which is only valid as interfaces DailyAccount and Account respect the compatibility property defined in Definition 5.

As an example for a visualization of a correct-by-construction program developed in CORC, an excerpt of the implementation of method update of component Account is shown in Fig. 6. The method computes the new balance of an account, while checking whether input argument x exceeds the overdraft limit of the account. The method returns true if the update was successful and false otherwise. The top-level specification is shown in the top node and the complete implementation is constructed using refinement rules (i.e., each refinement is visualized by one node). In this excerpt, a total of three refinements starting

---

[1] https://github.com/TUBS-ISF/ArchiCorC.
[2] https://eclipse.org/graphiti/.

Table 2. Mapping of Interfaces to CorC-Programs

Component	Interface	Method	CorC-Program
Transaction	Transfer	boolean transfer(Account a, Account b, int x)	transfer
DailyAccount	DailyAccount	boolean update(int x)	updateDaily
		boolean undoUpdate()	undoUpdateDaily
Account	Account	boolean update(int x)	update
		boolean undoUpdate()	undoUpdate
DailyLimit	Limit	int getLimit()	getLimit
		void nextDay()	nextDay
		void nextYear()	nextYear

from the top-level specification are shown. First, a composition statement splits the program into a calculation of old_balance and newBalance with an assignment statement, and a second part. The second, shortened, part uses a selection statement to check whether newBalance exceeds the *overdraft limit*, which is represented by a **provided** field OVERDRAFT_LIMIT of interface Account. In the complete implementation, both cases of the selection statement are refined to satisfying assignment statements to ensure that the complete implementation is constructed correctly.

In the following, we show the basic interface description of interface Account. Alongside the two aforementioned methods update and undoUpdate, Account declared the two integer fields balance and OVERDRAFT_LIMIT, which are accessible in the CORC implementation. Keyword old E refers to the state of expression E before method execution and is translated to old_E to match the specification of the corresponding CORC implementation.

Interface Specification: Account

- update(in : int x, out : boolean res)   (Method)
  req : {true}
  guar : {res ⇒ balance = old balance + x} ∧ {!res ⇒ balance = old balance}
- undoUpdate(in : int x, out : boolean res)   (Method)
  req : {true}
  guar : {res ⇒ balance = old balance − x} ∧ {!res ⇒ balance = old balance}
- int balance   (Field)

- int OVERDRAFT_LIMIT   (Field)

Interface DailyAccount extends the interface description of Account by a daily withdrawal limit, such that withdrawing money is only allowed, when the limit is not yet reached. Therefore, a new attribute withdraw is added and, as highlighted in the following, the specification is also extended. Internally, the corresponding CORC implementation updateDaily and undoUpdateDaily access the DAILY_LIMIT attribute of interface Limit through the generated **get** method of

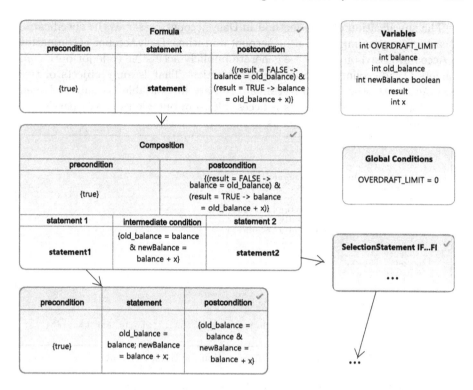

Fig. 6. Excerpt of Basic Update Method in the Graphical CORC Editor

component DailyLimit. DAILY_LIMIT is only accessible, as components DailyLimit and DailyAccount are connected. Visibility of methods and attributes is also ensured by a checking mechanism during the development of the CORC implementation when using ARCHICORC.

Interface Specification: DailyAccount

– update(in : int x, out : boolean res)   (Method)
  req : {true}
  guar : {res ⇒ balance = old balance + x} ∧ {!res ⇒ balance = old balance}
  ∧ {res ⇒ withdraw ≤ old withdraw} ∧ {!res ⇒ withdraw = old withraw}

– undoUpdate(in : int x, out : boolean res)   (Method)
  req : {true}
  guar : {res ⇒ balance = old balance − x} ∧ {!res ⇒ balance = old balance}
  ∧ {res ⇒ withdraw ≥ old withdraw} ∧ {!res ⇒ withdraw = old withraw}

– int balance   (Field)

– int OVERDRAFT_LIMIT   (Field)

– int withdraw   (Field)

The specification of each method in DailyAccount preserves the specification of each corresponding method in Account and, thus, DailyAccount is compatible to Account. Based on Fig. 5, we generate publicly accessible code for both components DailyAccountComposite and Transaction. That is, only objects of type DailyAccountComposite and Transaction are instantiable, as only code generated for top-level components is accessible from outside the JAVA package. A basic application may then look as illustrated in Listing 1.

```
1  package Application;
2
3  //Auto-generated packages
4  import DailyAccount.DailyAccount;
5  import Transaction.Transfer;
6
7  public static void main(String[] args) {
8      DailyAccount a = new DailyAccount();
9      DailyAccount b = new DailyAccount();
10
11     // Correct-by-construction update method
12     a.update(500);
13     b.update(400);
14
15     // Correct-by-construction transfer method
16     (new Transfer()).transfer(a,b,100);
17
18     asssert a.balance == 400 && b.balance == 500 : "Should not happen";
19  }
```

Listing 1. Example Application for Bank Account

By implementing every method in CORC and mapping the components to these implementations, we can guarantee correctness of the complete component diagram, as all required interfaces are satisfied and all provided interfaces are correctly implemented.

7 Discussion

Our considerations exhibit only a starting point for the integrated development of correct software following the correct-by-construction philosophy. In this section, we discuss current limitations, how they might be mitigated, and future directions of ARCHICORC.

7.1 Beyond Preconditions and Postconditions

For brevity, our formulations in Sects. 2 and 4 only focused on simple contracts consisting of pairs of exactly one precondition and one postcondition as introduced by Meyer [22]. However, there are advanced specification concepts in alignment with the notion of contracts that may further support developers with the challenging task of specifying software and are possibly required for practical usage.

Framing Conditions. As introduced in Sect. 2, *class variables* express class fields that can be shared among multiple CORC programs that belong to the same class. With the introduction of method calls and the abstraction with the respective contract, it is necessary to inform the verifier, which locations a method may modify and which locations remain unmodified. These additional conditions are referred to as framing conditions [2,12,16]. Currently, these conditions have to be encoded as $\bigwedge_i \texttt{old}(v_i) = v_i$ for every class variable v_i that is not altered (i.e., specifying which variables remain unmodified). To reduce specification effort, prominent specification languages provide syntactic sugar (e.g., keyword `assignable` in JML [19]) to simply express in a set-theoretic notion, which locations might be modified. In the future, ARCHICORC will integrate the concept of framing conditions and desugar them when required (e.g., to be compatible with CORC, which currently does not provide syntactic sugar for framing itself).

Specification Cases. Specification languages such as JML support the definition of multiple contracts for a single method by connecting them with keyword `also` [7]. Specification cases allow to define different expected behaviors based on different assumptions (i.e., preconditions). That is, integrating such a concept into ARCHICORC would allow to specify multiple contracts for an interface method, such that different (and smaller) CORC programs would be compatible. In fact, such a concept is already integrated in the current version of ARCHICORC, as specification cases are, again, just syntactic sugar. Given n separated specification cases with their respective precondition ϕ_i and postcondition ψ_i, desugaring all specification cases into a single contract results in precondition $\bigvee_i^n \phi_i$ and postcondition $\bigwedge_i^n \texttt{old}(\phi_i) \Rightarrow \psi_i$. Compatibility between this contract and the possible CORC implementations then follows from Definition 4. However, an explicit notion for specification cases (e.g., separation by keyword `also`) would certainly improve the readability of specifications and is part of future work.

Class Invariants. Apart from method contracts, specification languages for object-oriented languages allow to define conditions for complete classes referred to as *class invariants* [20]. Class invariants are defined once per class and consequently apply to all of its methods by implicitly adding them in conjunction to each precondition and postcondition. CORC already provides the definition of such conditions and refers to them as *global conditions* [32]. Instead of redundantly adding such conditions manually to each precondition and postcondition, we plan to add a designated keyword to ARCHICORC's interface description language for describing such invariants as part of future work. Global conditions of connected CORC programs then have to be implied by the invariants as specified in the respective interfaces or are otherwise rejected as incompatible.

7.2 Liskov-Style Compatibility

The intended application of ARCHICORC is management of correct-by-construction library functions, for which we group interfaces into components and implement interface methods by CORC programs adhering to a notion of refinement and *compatibility* (cf. Definition 4). The most crucial step is the last refinement step, which involves a switch from the specification language to the implementation language. Consequently, *abstract* data types of the specification language have to be concretized to data types of the implementation language, which enables the rise of potential (unrecognized) errors. For instance, integer types of specification languages are usually of infinite domain, whereas programming languages, such as JAVA, bound their integers to a finite domain.

There are three possible solutions to this problem [4]. First, we may change the implementation level to support equal operation as provided by the specification language. Second, we may restrict domains of data types to the same domains as provided by the implementation language. Third, it is possible to introduce a notion of *controlled incorrectness*, referred to as *retrenchment* [3,4], in our refinement rules. A retrenchment framework may additionally prove the absence of cases where such mismatches could occur, albeit possible based on the different type definitions of specification and implementation language.

ARCHICORC shifts this problem to CORC, as its focus is primarily on the specification language and code generation. CORC itself overcomes this limitation (i.e., does not violate the refinement from specification to implementation) by closely following the JML specification language and by integrating the verifier KEY as part of its tool suite. That is, the second solution is applied by using implementation level data types in the specification language to avoid any mismatch between the two. However, as identified by Beckert and Schlager [4], this solution comes with certain drawbacks, such that the hiding of implementation details is reduced or that not all implementation details are even known during the specification phase, which consequently limits applicability of such a specification language.

A future direction could be to study the notion of retrenchment in combination with the correctness-by-construction paradigm. First, as our vision is to support *software developers* in their daily practices with writing correct software, retrenchment already follows the idea of implementation hiding and focusing on adequately abstract specifications for refinement calculi. Second, humans typically think of types as mathematical objects with infinite domains. Hence, a natural consequence is to not restrict the domains of data types of the specification language. As lifting the data types of many programming languages to infinite domains seems infeasible due to scalability and compatibility reasons, keeping infinite domains for data types of the specification language is only sufficiently addressed by the third solution mentioned before (i.e., applying retrenchment).

8   Related Work

The primary goal of ARCHICORC is to scale the correctness-by-construction paradigm to large scale software projects following the design-by-contract paradigm. As such, the component model of ARCHICORC is simpler compared to most existing component models applied in practice, as it follows a UML-style modularization to separate concerns and realize reusable components. More recent contract theories are applied at the level of embedded systems and aim at supporting heterogeneous systems [13, 29] (i.e., contracts over systems that comprise multiple domains, such as software, hardware, mechanical, and electrical parts). In particular, component models in such theories [5, 6, 34] are comprised of a set of ports and an implementation, and contracts follow the assume-guarantee paradigm similar to design-by-contract. In contrast to ARCHICORC, these components are typical dynamic in the sense that they follow a trace-based semantics and their state changes over time.

Besides ARCHICORC, there exist other tools for specifying software architectures as component models that apply the design-by-contract principle in their description language. Examples of such tools include CBABEL [28], RADL [30], XCD [26] and its visual extension VXCD [25], and X-MAN [18]. However, our programming model for components greatly differs from the mentioned tools, as their primary focus is the interaction model between components, whereas our focus is to establish a repository of correct-by-construction library functions following the component-based design model.

In this work, we applied correctness-by-construction to implement methods of provided interfaces. Related to the correctness-by-construction approach is Event-B [1], which provides a formal language together with a notion of refinement. Other refinement-inspired tools include ARCANGEL [24], which is based on Morgan's refinement calculus [23]. To apply correctness-by-construction, we integrated CORC into ARCHICORC. Recently, CORC was extended to enable information flow control-by-construction [31].

9   Conclusion

Our vision is to bring correctness-by-construction into the realm of mainstream software developers by providing sophisticated tool support. We believe that ARCHICORC exhibits a promising starting point for integrating correctness-by-construction into software engineering processes. Specifically, we implemented ARCHICORC as an extension to CORC with the goal to scale the correctness-by-construction paradigm to large scale software development. ARCHICORC lets developers model UML-style software components consisting of required and provided interfaces, while methods of provided interfaces are implemented with CORC. Consequently, deployed ARCHICORC components bundle functionality in a modular way, while correctness is provably established per construction. Moreover, by generating valid JAVA code, such components can be imported and used in various software projects as-is. We defined the valid composition of components and demonstrated the capabilities of ARCHICORC on the bank account case study.

For future work, we aim at extending the tool support even further to establish a repository of correct-by-construction components. For instance, as mentioned before, our proposed methodology has potential to be used for implementing stateless web services and therefore to derive a process for developing correct-by-construction services. Moreover, our code generation is prone to changes in the component model, as the complete JAVA code has to be re-generated. This can be solved with more sophisticated design patterns. A second package for future work is to conduct more case and user studies to evaluate ARCHICORC's improvement over just CORC for constructing larger programs using correctness-by-construction.

References

1. Abrial, J.-R.: Modeling in Event-B: System and Software Engineering. Cambridge University Press, Cambridge (2010)
2. Ahrendt, W., Beckert, B., Bubel, R., Hähnle, R., Schmitt, P.H., Ulbrich, M.: Deductive Software Verification-The KeY Book. Lecture Notes in Computer Science. Springer, Heidelberg (2016). https://doi.org/10.1007/978-3-319-49812-6
3. Banach, R., Poppleton, M.: Retrenchment: an engineering variation on refinement. In: Bert, D. (ed.) B 1998. LNCS, vol. 1393, pp. 129–147. Springer, Heidelberg (1998). https://doi.org/10.1007/BFb0053358
4. Beckert, B., Schlager, S.: Refinement and retrenchment for programming language data types. Formal Aspects Comput. **17**(4), 423–442 (2005)
5. Benveniste, A., Caillaud, B., Ferrari, A., Mangeruca, L., Passerone, R., Sofronis, C.: Multiple viewpoint contract-based specification and design. In: de Boer, F.S., Bonsangue, M.M., Graf, S., de Roever, W.-P. (eds.) FMCO 2007. LNCS, vol. 5382, pp. 200–225. Springer, Heidelberg (2008). https://doi.org/10.1007/978-3-540-92188-2_9
6. Benveniste, A., Caillaud, B., Passerone, R.: Multi-Viewpoint State Machines for Rich Component Models. Model-Based Design of Heterogeneous Embedded Systems (2009)
7. Chalin, P., Kiniry, J.R., Leavens, G.T., Poll, E.: Beyond assertions: advanced specification and verification with JML and ESC/Java2. In: de Boer, F.S., Bonsangue, M.M., Graf, S., de Roever, W.-P. (eds.) FMCO 2005. LNCS, vol. 4111, pp. 342–363. Springer, Heidelberg (2006). https://doi.org/10.1007/11804192_16
8. de Moura, L., Bjørner, N.: Z3: an efficient SMT solver. In: Ramakrishnan, C.R., Rehof, J. (eds.) TACAS 2008. LNCS, vol. 4963, pp. 337–340. Springer, Heidelberg (2008). https://doi.org/10.1007/978-3-540-78800-3_24
9. Dijkstra, E.W.: Guarded commands, non-determinacy and formal derivation of programs. Comm. ACM **18**(8), 453–457 (1975)
10. Dijkstra, E.W.: A Discipline of Programming, 1st edn. Prentice Hall PTR, Upper Saddle River (1976)
11. Gries, D.: The Science of Programming, 1st edn. Springer, Secaucus (1981). https://doi.org/10.1007/978-1-4612-5983-1
12. Hatcliff, J., Leavens, G.T., Leino, K.R.M., Müller, P., Parkinson, M.: Behavioral interface specification languages. ACM Comput. Surv. (CSUR) **44**(3), 1–58 (2012)
13. Henzinger, T.A., Sifakis, J.: The discipline of embedded systems design. Computer **40**(10), 32–40 (2007)
14. Hoare, C.A.R.: An axiomatic basis for computer programming. Commun. ACM **12**(10), 576–580 (1969)
15. Johnsen, E.B., Hähnle, R., Schäfer, J., Schlatte, R., Steffen, M.: ABS: a core language for abstract behavioral specification. In: Aichernig, B.K., de Boer, F.S., Bonsangue, M.M. (eds.) FMCO 2010. LNCS, vol. 6957, pp. 142–164. Springer, Heidelberg (2011). https://doi.org/10.1007/978-3-642-25271-6_8

16. Kassios, I.T.: Dynamic frames: support for framing, dependencies and sharing without restrictions. In: Misra, J., Nipkow, T., Sekerinski, E. (eds.) FM 2006. LNCS, vol. 4085, pp. 268–283. Springer, Heidelberg (2006). https://doi.org/10.1007/11813040_19

17. Kourie, D.G., Watson, B.W.: The Correctness-by-Construction Approach to Programming. Springer, Heidelberg (2012). https://doi.org/10.1007/978-3-642-27919-5

18. Lau, K.-K., Tran, C.M.: X-MAN: an MDE tool for component-based system development. In: 2012 38th EUROMICRO Conference on Software Engineering and Advanced Applications, pp. 158–165. IEEE (2012)

19. Leavens, G.T., Baker, A.L., Ruby, C.: JML: a Java modeling language. In: Formal Underpinnings of Java Workshop (at OOPSLA 1998), pp. 404–420. Citeseer (1998)

20. Leavens, G.T., Muller, P.: Information hiding and visibility in interface specifications. In: 29th International Conference on Software Engineering (ICSE 2007), pp. 385–395. IEEE (2007)

21. Liskov, B.H., Wing, J.M.: A behavioral notion of subtyping. ACM Trans. Programm. Lang. Syst. (TOPLAS) 16(6), 1811–1841 (1994)

22. Meyer, B.: Applying design by contract. IEEE Comput. 25(10), 40–51 (1992)

23. Morgan, C.: Programming from Specifications. Prentice Hall, Upper Saddle River (1994)

24. Oliveira, M., Cavalcanti, A., Woodcock, J.: ArcAngel: a Tactic Language For Refinement. Formal Aspects Comput. 15(1), 28–47 (2003)

25. Ozkaya, M.: Visual specification and analysis of contract-based software architectures. J. Comput. Sci. Technol. 32(5), 1025–1043 (2017). https://doi.org/10.1007/s11390-017-1779-y

26. Ozkaya, M., Kloukinas, C.: Design-by-contract for reusable components and realizable architectures. In: Proceedings of the 17th International ACM SIGSOFT Symposium on Component-Based Software Engineering, pp. 129–138 (2014)

27. Pierce, B.C.: Types and Programming Languages. MIT Press, Cambridge (2002)

28. Rademaker, A., Braga, C., Sztajnberg, A.: A rewriting semantics for a software architecture description language. Electron. Notes Theor. Comput. Sci. 130, 345–377 (2005)

29. Rawat, D.B., Rodrigues, J.J., Stojmenovic, I.: Cyber-Physical Systems: From Theory to Practice. CRC Press, Boca Raton (2015)

30. Reussner, R.H., Schmidt, H.W., Poernomo, I.H.: Reliability prediction for component-based software architectures. J. Syst. Softw. 66(3), 241–252 (2003)

31. Runge, T., Knüppel, A., Thüm, T., Schaefer, I.: Lattice-based information flow control-by-construction for security-by-design. In: FormaliSE 2020. IEEE (2020)

32. Runge, T., Schaefer, I., Cleophas, L., Thüm, T., Kourie, D., Watson, B.W.: Tool support for correctness-by-construction. In: Hähnle, R., van der Aalst, W. (eds.) FASE 2019. LNCS, vol. 11424, pp. 25–42. Springer, Cham (2019). https://doi.org/10.1007/978-3-030-16722-6_2

33. Runge, T., Thüm, T., Cleophas, L., Schaefer, I., Watson, B.W.: Comparing correctness-by-construction with post-hoc verification—a qualitative user study. In: Sekerinski, E., et al. (eds.) FM 2019. LNCS, vol. 12233, pp. 388–405. Springer, Cham (2020). https://doi.org/10.1007/978-3-030-54997-8_25

34. Sangiovanni-Vincentelli, A., Damm, W., Passerone, R.: Taming Dr. Frankenstein: contract-based design for cyber-physical systems. Eur. J. Control 18(3), 217–238 (2012)

35. Szyperski, C., Gruntz, D., Murer, S.: Component Software: Beyond Object-Oriented Programming. Pearson Education, London (2002)

X-by-Construction: Correctness Meets Probability

X-by-Construction

Correctness Meets Probability

Maurice H. ter Beek[1(✉)], Loek Cleophas[2,5(✉)], Axel Legay[3], Ina Schaefer[4], and Bruce W. Watson[5,6]

[1] ISTI–CNR, Pisa, Italy
maurice.terbeek@isti.cnr.it
[2] TU Eindhoven, Eindhoven, The Netherlands
l.g.w.a.cleophas@tue.nl
[3] UC Louvain, Louvain-la-Neuve, Belgium
axel.legay@uclouvain.be
[4] TU Braunschweig, Braunschweig, Germany
i.schaefer@tu-braunschweig.de
[5] Stellenbosch University, Stellenbosch, South Africa
bwwatson@sun.ac.za
[6] CAIR, Stellenbosch, South Africa

Abstract. In recent years, researchers have started to investigate X-by-Construction (XbC) as a refinement approach to engineer systems that by-construction satisfy certain non-functional properties, beyond correctness as considered by the more traditional Correctness-by-Construction (CbC). In line with increasing attention for fault-tolerance and the use of machine-learning techniques in modern software systems, in which even correctness is hard to establish, this track brings together researchers and practitioners that are interested in XbC in particular in the setting of probabilistic properties.

1 Motivation and Aim

Correctness-by-Construction (CbC) approaches the development of software (systems) as a true form of Engineering, with a capital 'E'. CbC advertises a step-wise refinement process from specification to code, ideally by CbC design tools that automatically generate error-free software (system) implementations from rigorous and unambiguous specifications of requirements. Afterwards, testing only serves to validate the CbC process rather than to find bugs. (Of course, bugs might still be present outside the boundaries of the verified system: in libraries, compilers, hardware, the CbC design tools themselves, etc.)

A lot of progress has been made in this domain, implying it is time to look further than correctness and investigate a move from CbC to *XbC*, i.e., by considering also *non-functional properties*. XbC is thus concerned with a step-wise refinement process from specification to code that automatically generates software (system) implementations that *by-construction* satisfy specific non-functional

© Springer Nature Switzerland AG 2020
T. Margaria and B. Steffen (Eds.): ISoLA 2020, LNCS 12476, pp. 211–215, 2020.
https://doi.org/10.1007/978-3-030-61362-4_11

properties concerning security, dependability, reliability or resource/energy consumption, etc. A track on XbC was organised at ISoLA 2018 [2], in turn building on an ISoLA 2016 track focusing on the combination of post-hoc verification with CbC [3]. The 2018 XbC track brought together researchers and practitioners interested in CbC and the promise of XbC, with a particular emphasis on security-by-construction.

Building on the highly successful ISoLA 2018 track, the aim of this track is to once again bring together researchers and practitioners that are interested in CbC and XbC. In line with the growing attention to fault-tolerance (thanks to increasingly common failures in hardware and software) and the increasing use of machine-learning techniques in modern software systems—in both of these contexts, *guaranteed properties* are hard to establish—we particularly emphasise XbC in the setting of probabilistic properties.

We therefore invited researchers and practitioners working in the following communities to share their views on (moving from CbC to) XbC:

- People working on system-of-systems, who address modelling and verification (correctness, but also non-functional properties concerning security, reliability, resilience, energy consumption, performance, and sustainability) of networks of interacting legacy and new software systems, and who are interested in applying XbC techniques in this domain in order to prove—potentially probabilistic—non-functional properties of systems-of-systems by construction (from their constituent systems satisfying these properties).
- People working on quantitative modelling and analysis, e.g., through probabilistic or real-time systems and probabilistic or statistical model checking, in particular in the specific setting of dynamic, adaptive or (runtime) reconfigurable systems with variability. These people work on lifting successful formal methods and verification tools from single systems to families of systems, i.e., modelling and analysis techniques that need to cope with the complexity of systems stemming from behaviour, variability, and randomness—and which focus not only on correctness but also on non-functional properties concerning safety, security, performance, or dependability properties. As such, they may be interested in applying XbC techniques in this domain to prove non-functional properties of families of systems by construction (from their individual family members satisfying these properties).
- People working on systems involving components that employ machine-learning (ML) or other artificial-intelligence (AI) approaches. In these settings, models and behaviour are typically dependent on what is learned from large data sets, and may change dynamically based on yet more data being processed. As a result, guaranteeing properties (whether functional or non-functional ones) becomes hard, and probabilistic reasoning needs to be applied instead with respect to such properties for the components employing ML or AI approaches, and as a consequence, for systems involving such components as well.
- People working on generative software development, who are concerned with the automatic generation of software from specifications given in general for-

mal languages or domain-specific languages, leading to families of related software (systems). Also in this setting, the emphasis so far has typically been on functional correctness, but the restricted scope of the specifications—especially for domain-specific languages—may offer a suitable ground for reasoning about non-functional properties, and for using XbC techniques to guarantee such properties.

☑ People working on systems security, privacy, and algorithmic transparency and accountability, who care about more than correctness. The application of XbC techniques could provide certain guarantees from the outset when designing critical systems. It could also enforce transparency when developing algorithms for automated decision-making, in particular those based on data analytics—thus reducing algorithmic bias by avoiding opaque algorithms.

2   Contributions

In their keynote contribution, McIver and Morgan [8] describe a correct-by-construction proof method for probabilistic programming. It is based on their probabilistic extension pGCL of Dijkstra's Guarded-Command Language, which allows to describe program correctness by a generalisation of Hoare logic that includes quantitative analysis, and to develop programs by refinement such that both functional and probabilistic properties are preserved. They demonstrate how to apply their method by deriving a fair-coin implementation of any given discrete probability distribution in a systematic, layered way such that the reasoning in each layer does not depend on earlier layers nor affect later ones. Moreover, in the special case of simulating a fair die, the authors show how one final correctness-preserving step allows them to obtain Knuth and Yao's optimal die-roll algorithm.

In the context of probabilistic component-based systems that interact via synchronised execution of shared actions, Baier et al. [1] present different notions of (component) suitability, results on their decidability for restricted classed, and associated algorithmic analysis procedures. The basic notion of suitability is provided through threshold suitability that determines whether each one of the given quantitative properties exceeds a given threshold, while weighting quantitative properties leads to a quantitative measure of degrees of suitability. The applicability of the resulting notions of quantitative suitability analysis is illustrated with a case study of vehicle components with features for different road conditions, which is particularly appealing due to its feature-oriented nature.

Fahrenberg and Legay [4] consider the notion of behavioural specification theories, giving an overview of the underlying theoretical concepts, as well as various kinds of behavioural specification theories, with examples for most of them. To make the connection to this specific XbC track, they include three different behavioural specification theories for modelling real-time and probabilistic systems. The survey emphasises commonalities and differences between the various specification and modelling formalisms in such theories, leading to a taxonomy in the form of a table showing the different behavioural specification theories and their properties.

Jaeger et al. [6] consider the resolution of control problems under uncertainty and continuous domains. For doing so, they rely on finite-state imprecise Markov decision processes that can be used to approximate the behaviour of these infinite models. The authors address two questions. First, they investigate what kind of approximation guarantees are obtained when the process is approximated by finite-state approximations induced by increasingly fine partitions of the continuous state space. They show that for cost functions over finite time horizons the approximations become arbitrarily precise. Second, they use imprecise Markov decision process approximations as a tool to analyse and validate cost functions and strategies obtained by reinforcement learning. Finally, the authors compare this constructive process with classical learning-based solutions.

Könighofer et al. [7] present an overview of shield synthesis approaches in order to ensure that policies learned using reinforcement learning do not make incorrect or unsafe actions. They discuss the approaches of pre-shielding where the set of possible actions an agent can take are filtered before decision making, to only include correct actions and post-shielding where the selected action after decision making is corrected in case it is incorrect. The paper reviews existing work for shield synthesis for temporal, probabilistic and timed properties and presents examples and evaluation results for each of the reviewed approaches.

Performance is an important non-functional property that, being related to metrics like response time and throughput, directly affects end-user perception of the quality of a software system. Therefore, controlling a software system's performance is an important endeavour in today's engineering practice. Incerto et al. [5] argue that the performance-by-construction development paradigm by which executable code carries some kind of performance guarantees, as opposed to the current practice in software engineering where performance concerns are left to later stages of the development process by means of profiling or testing, needs to support techniques that are probabilistic in nature, leveraging accurate models for the analysis. To this aim, they present a literature review and a classification of methods that can form the basis of such performance-by-construction development approaches, focussing on methods where performance information is extracted directly from the code. This is a line of research that has apparently been less explored by the software performance engineering community. They conclude by discussing limitations of the state of the art.

References

1. Baier, C., et al.: Components in probabilistic systems: suitable by construction. In: Margaria, T., Steffen, B. (eds.) ISoLA 2020, Part I. LNCS, vol. 12476, pp. 240–261. Springer, Cham (2020). https://doi.org/10.1007/978-3-030-61362-4_13
2. ter Beek, M.H., Cleophas, L., Schaefer, I., Watson, B.W.: X-by-construction. In: Margaria, T., Steffen, B. (eds.) ISoLA 2018. LNCS, vol. 11244, pp. 359–364. Springer, Cham (2018). https://doi.org/10.1007/978-3-030-03418-4_21
3. ter Beek, M.H., Hähnle, R., Schaefer, I.: Correctness-by-construction and post-hoc verification: friends or foes? In: Margaria, T., Steffen, B. (eds.) ISoLA 2016. LNCS, vol. 9952, pp. 723–729. Springer, Cham (2016). https://doi.org/10.1007/978-3-319-47166-2_51

4. Fahrenberg, U., Legay, A.: Behavioral specification theories: an algebraic taxonomy. In: Margaria, T., Steffen, B. (eds.) ISoLA 2020, Part I. LNCS, vol. 12476, pp. 262–274. Springer, Cham (2020). https://doi.org/10.1007/978-3-030-61362-4_14

5. Incerto, E., Napolitano, A., Tribastone, M.: Inferring performance from code: a review. In: Margaria, T., Steffen, B. (eds.) ISoLA 2020, Part I. LNCS, vol. 12476, pp. 307–322. Springer, Cham (2020). https://doi.org/10.1007/978-3-030-61362-4_17

6. Jaeger, M., Bacci, G., Bacci, G., Larsen, K.G., Jensen, P.G.: Approximating euclidean by imprecise Markov decision processes. In: Margaria, T., Steffen, B. (eds.) ISoLA 2020, Part I. LNCS, vol. 12476, pp. 275–289. Springer, Cham (2020). https://doi.org/10.1007/978-3-030-61362-4_15

7. Könighofer, B., Lorber, F., Jansen, N., Bloem, R.: Shield synthesis for reinforcement learning. In: Margaria, T., Steffen, B. (eds.) ISoLA 2020, Part I. LNCS, vol. 12476, pp. 209–306. Springer, Cham (2020). https://doi.org/10.1007/978-3-030-61362-4_16

8. McIver, A., Morgan, C.: Correctness by construction for probabilistic programs. In: Margaria, T., Steffen, B. (eds.) ISoLA 2020, Part I. LNCS, vol. 12476, pp. 216–239. Springer, Cham (2020). https://doi.org/10.1007/978-3-030-61362-4_12

Correctness by Construction
for Probabilistic Programs

Annabelle McIver[1(✉)] and Carroll Morgan[2(✉)]

[1] Macquarie University, Sydney, Australia
annabelle.mciver@mq.edu.au
[2] University of New South Wales and Trustworthy Systems, Data61, CSIRO,
Sydney, Australia
carroll.morgan@unsw.edu.au

Abstract. The "correct by construction" paradigm is an important component of modern Formal Methods, and here we use the probabilistic Guarded-Command Language *pGCL* to illustrate its application to *probabilistic* programming.

pGCL extends Dijkstra's guarded-command language *GCL* with probabilistic choice, and is equipped with a correctness-preserving refinement relation ($\sqsubseteq$) that enables compact, abstract specifications of probabilistic properties to be transformed gradually to concrete, executable code by applying mathematical insights in a systematic and layered way.

Characteristically for correctness by construction, as far as possible the reasoning in each refinement-step layer does not depend on earlier layers, and does not affect later ones.

We demonstrate the technique by deriving a fair-coin implementation of any given discrete probability distribution. In the special case of simulating a fair die, our correct-by-construction algorithm turns out to be "within spitting distance" of Knuth and Yao's optimal solution.

1 Testing Probabilistic Programs?

Edsger Dijkstra argued [1, p. 3] that the construction of *correct* programs requires mathematical proof, since "... program testing can be used very effectively to show the presence of bugs but never to show their absence." But for programs that are constructed to exhibit some form of randomisation, regular testing can't even establish that *presence*: surprising, unexpected program traces are bound to turn up even in *correctly* operating probabilistic systems.

Thus evidence of quantitative errors in probabilistic systems could require many, many traces to be subjected to detailed statistical analysis—yet even then debugging probabilistic programs is a challenge once that evidence has been assembled. Unlike standard (non-probabilistic) programs, where a single failed test can often pinpoint the source of the offending error in the code, it's not easy

---

We are grateful for the support of the Australian Research Council.

T. Margaria and B. Steffen (Eds.): ISoLA 2020, LNCS 12476, pp. 216–239, 2020.
https://doi.org/10.1007/978-3-030-61362-4_12

to figure out what to change in the implementation of probabilistic programs in order to move closer towards "correctness" rather than further away.

Without that unambiguous relationship between failed tests and the coding errors that cause them, Dijkstra's caution regarding proofs of programs is even more apposite. In this paper we describe such a proof method for probability: *correctness by construction*. In a sentence, to apply "*CbC*" one constructs the program and its proof at the same time, letting the requirement that there *be* a proof guide the design decisions taken while constructing the program.

Like standard programs, probabilistic programs incorporate mathematical insights into algorithms, and a correctness-by-construction method should allow a program developer to refer rigorously to those insights by applying development steps that preserve "probabilistic correctness". Probabilistic correctness is however notoriously unintuitive. For example, the solution of the infamous Monty Hall problem caused such a ruckus in the mathematical community that even Paul Erdös questioned the correct analysis [14].[1] Yet once coded up as a program [10, p. 22], the Monty Hall problem is only four lines long! More generally though, many widely relied-upon probabilistic programs in security are quite short, and yet still pose significant challenges for correctness.

We describe correctness by construction in the context of *pGCL*, a small programming language which restores demonic choice to Kozen's landmark (purely) probabilistic semantics [7,8] while using the syntax of Dijkstra's *GCL* [2]. Its basic principles are that correctness for programs can be described by a generalisation of Hoare logic that includes *quantitative* analysis; and it has a definition of refinement that allows programs to be developed in such a way that both functional and probabilistic properties are preserved.[2]

2   Enabling Correctness by Construction—*pGCL*

The setting for correctness by construction of probabilistic programs is provided by *pGCL* –the probabilistic Guarded-Command Language– which contains both abstraction and (stepwise) refinement [10]. We begin by reviewing its origins, then its treatment of probabilistic choice and demonic choice, and finally its realisation of *CbC*.

(This section can be skimmed on first reading: just collect *pGCL* syntax from Figs. 2, 3, and 4, and then skip directly to Sect. 3.)

As we will not be treating non-terminating programs, we can base our description here on quite simple models for sequential (non-reactive) programs. The

---

[1] A game-show host, Monty Hall, exhibits three curtains, behind one of which sits a Cadillac; the other two curtains conceal goats. The contestant guesses which curtain hides the prize, and Monty then opens another, making sure however that it reveals a goat. The contestant is allowed to change his mind. Should he?

[2] If the program is a mathematical object, then as Andrew Vazonyi [14] pointed out: "I'm not interested in *ad hoc* solutions invented by clever people. I want a method that works for lots of problems... One that mere mortals can use. Which is what a correctness-by-construction method should be.".

state space is some set S and, in its simplest terms, a program takes an initial state to a final state: it (its semantics) therefore has type $S \to S$.

The three subsections that follow describe logics based on successive enrichments of this, the simplest model, and even the youngest of those logics is by now almost 25 years old: thus we will be "reviewing" rather than inventing.

The first enrichment, Sect. 2.1, is based on the model $S \to \mathbb{P}S$ that allows demonic nondeterminism,[3] so facilitating abstraction; then in Sect. 2.2 the model $S \to \mathbb{D}S$ replaces demonic nondeterminism by probabilistic choice, losing abstraction (temporarily) but in its place gaining the ability to describe probabilistic outcomes; and finally in Sect. 2.3 the model $S \to \mathbb{PD}S$ restores demonic nondeterminism, allowing programs that can abstract from precise probabilities. Using syntax we will make more precise in those sections, we give here some simple examples of the three increments in expressivity:

(1)   x := H   Set variable x to H (as in any sequential language);

(2)   x :∈ {H,T}   Set x's value demonically from the set {H,T};

(3)   x :∈ H $_{2/3}\oplus$ T   Set x's value from the set {H,T} with probability $2/3$ for H and $1/3$ for T, a "biased coin"; and

(4)   x :∈ H $_{1/3}\oplus_{1/3}$ T   Set x from the set {H,T} with probability *at least* $1/3$ each way, a "capricious coin".

The last example of those (4) is the most general: for (3) is x :∈ H $_{2/3}\oplus_{1/3}$ T; and (2) is x :∈ H $_0\oplus_0$ T; and finally (1) is x :∈ H $_1\oplus_0$ T.

2.1   Floyd/Hoare/DijKstra: Pre- and Postconditions: (1, 2) Above

We assume a typical sequential programming language with variables, expressions over those variables, assignment (of expressions to variables), sequential composition (semicolon or line break), conditionals and loops. It is more or less Dijkstra's *guarded command language* [2], and is based on the model $S \to \mathbb{P}S$, where $\mathbb{P}S$ is the set of all subsets of S.

The *weakest precondition* of program *Prog* in such a language, with respect to a postcondition *post* given as a first-order formula over the program variables, is written wp(*Prog*,*post*) and means

the weakest formula (again on the program variables) that must hold *before* *Prog* executes in order to ensure that *post* holds *after* *Prog* executes [2].

In a typical compositional style, the wp of a whole program is determined by the wp of its components.

We group Dijkstra, Hoare and Floyd together because the Dijkstra-style implication *pre* $\Rightarrow$ wp(*Prog*,*post*) has the same meaning as the Hoare-style triple {*pre*} *Prog* {*post*} which in turn has the same meaning as the original Floyd-style flowchart annotation, as shown in Fig. 1 [3,4]. All three mean "If *pre* holds of the state before execution of *Prog*, then *post* will hold afterwards."

---

[3] Constructor $\mathbb{P}$ is "subsets of" and $\mathbb{D}$ is "discrete distributions on".

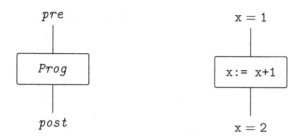

At left is a "generic" Floyd annotation of a flowchart containing only one program element. If the annotation *pre* holds "on the way in" to the program *Prog*, then annotation *post* will hold on the way out. At right is an example with specific annotations and a specific program.

In the Hoare style the right-hand example would be written

$$\{x = 1\} \;\; \texttt{x:= x+1} \;\; \{x = 2\} \;\; .$$

In the Dijsktra style it would be written $\texttt{x=1} \Rightarrow \textsf{wp}(\texttt{x:= x+1, x=2})$.
They all three have the same meaning.

Fig. 1. Floyd-style annotated flowchart

Finally, a notable –but incidental– feature of Dijkstra's approach was that (demonic) nondeterminism arose naturally, as an abstraction from possible concrete implementations.[4] That is why we use $S \to \mathbb{P}S$ rather than $S \to S$ here. In later work (by others) that abstraction was made more explicit by including explicit syntax for a binary "demonic choice" between program fragments, a composition *Left* $\sqcap$ *Right* that could behave either as the program *Left* or as the program *Right*. But that operator ($\sqcap$) was not really an extension of Dijkstra's work, because his (more verbose) conditional

```
IF   True  →  Left    – If True holds, then this branch may be taken.
[]   True  →  Right   – If True holds, then also this branch may be taken.
FI                    – (Dijkstra terminated all IF's with FI's.)
```

was there in his original guarded-command language, introducing demonic choice naturally as an artefact of the program-design process—and it expressed exactly the same thing. The ($\sqcap$) merely made it explicit.

2.2 Kozen: Probabilistic Program Logic: (3) Above

Kozen extended Dijkstra-style semantics to probabilistic programs, again over a sequential programming language but now based on the model $S \to \mathbb{D}S$, where

---

[4] See Sect. 3.5 for a further discussion of this.

$\mathbb{D}S$ is set of all discrete distributions in S.[5] He replaced Dijkstra's demonic non-determinism ($\sqcap$) by a "probabilistic nondeterminism" operator ($_p\oplus$) between programs, understood so that *Left* $_p\oplus$ *Right* means "Execute *Left* with probability p and *Right* with probability $1-p$." The probability p is (very) often $1/2$ so that `coin:= Heads` $_{1/2}\oplus$ `coin:= Tails` means "Flip a fair coin." But probability p can more generally be any real number, and more generally still it can even be an expression in the program variables.

Kozen's corresponding extension of Floyd/Hoare/Dijkstra [7,8] replaced Dijkstra's logical formulae with real-valued expressions (still over the program variables); we give examples below. The "original" Dijkstra-style formulae remain as a special case where real number 1 represents *True* and 0 represents *False*; and Dijkstra's definitions of wp simply carry through essentially as they are... except that an extra definition is necessary, for the new construct ($_p\oplus$), where Kozen defines that

$$\mathsf{wp}(\textit{Left } _p\oplus \textit{Right}, \textit{post})$$

is $\quad p \cdot \mathsf{wp}(\textit{Left}, \textit{post}) \; + \; (1-p) \cdot \mathsf{wp}(\textit{Right}, \textit{post}).$

With this single elegant extension, it turns out that in general $\mathsf{wp}(\textit{Prog}, \textit{post})$ is the *expected value*, given as a (real valued) expression over the *initial* state, of what *post* will be in the *final* state, i.e. after *Prog* has finished executing from that initial state. (The initial/final emphasis simply reminds us that it is the same as for Dijkstra: the weakest precondition is what must be true in the *initial* state for the postcondition to be true in the *final* state.) For example we have that

$$\mathsf{wp}(\mathtt{x:=}\ \mathtt{1-y}\, _{1/3}\oplus\ \mathtt{x:=}\ \mathtt{3*x}, \quad \mathtt{x}+3) \quad \text{is} \quad 1/3(1-\mathtt{y}+3) \; + \; 2/3(3\mathtt{x}+3),$$

that is the real-valued expression $3\frac{1}{3} + 2\mathtt{x} - \mathtt{y}/3$ in which both $\mathtt{x}$ and $\mathtt{y}$ refer to their values in the initial state.

More impressive though is that if we introduce the convention that brackets $[-]$ convert Booleans to numbers, i.e. that $[\textit{True}] = 1$ and $[\textit{False}] = 0$, we have in general for *Boolean*-valued *prop* the convenient idiom [6]

$$\mathsf{wp}(\textit{Prog}, [\textit{prop}])$$

is   "the probability that *Prog* establishes property *prop*",   (1)

And if –further– it happens that the "probabilistic" program *Prog* actually contains no probabilistic choices at all, then (1) just above has value 1 just when

---

[5] Kozen's work did not restrict to discrete distributions; but that is all we need here.

[6] The expected value of the characteristic function $[\textit{prop}]$ of an event *prop* is equal to the probability that *prop* itself holds.

Prog is guaranteed to establish *post*, and is 0 otherwise: it is in that sense that the Dijkstra-style semantics "carries through" into the Kozen extension. That is, if *Prog* contains no probabilistic choice, and *post* is a conventional (Boolean valued) formula, then we have that[7]

$$\begin{array}{lll} & \textit{Dijkstra style} & [\, \mathsf{wp}(\textit{Prog}, \textit{post}\,)\,] \\ \text{is the same as} & \textit{Kozen style} & \mathsf{wp}(\textit{Prog}, [\,\textit{post}\,]). \end{array}$$

The full power of the Kozen approach, however, starts to appear in examples like this one below: we flip two fair coins and ask for the probability that they show the same face afterwards. Using the (Dijkstra) weakest-precondition rule that $\mathsf{wp}(\textit{Prog1}\,;\textit{Prog2},\textit{post})$ is simply $\mathsf{wp}(\textit{Prog1}, \mathsf{wp}(\textit{Prog2},\textit{post}))$,[8] we can calculate

$$\begin{array}{rl} & \mathsf{wp}(\mathtt{c1}:= \mathtt{H}\ _{1/2}\!\oplus\ \mathtt{c1}:= \mathtt{T};\ \mathtt{c2}:= \mathtt{H}\ _{1/2}\!\oplus\ \mathtt{c2}:= \mathtt{T},\ \ [\mathtt{c1}=\mathtt{c2}]) \\ = & \mathsf{wp}(\mathtt{c1}:= \mathtt{H}\ _{1/2}\!\oplus\ \mathtt{c1}:= \mathtt{T},\ \ \mathsf{wp}(\mathtt{c2}:= \mathtt{H}\ _{1/2}\!\oplus\ \mathtt{c2}:= \mathtt{T}, [\mathtt{c1}=\mathtt{c2}])) \\ = & \mathsf{wp}(\mathtt{c1}:= \mathtt{H}\ _{1/2}\!\oplus\ \mathtt{c1}:= \mathtt{T},\ \ 1/2[\mathtt{c1}=\mathtt{H}] + (1-1/2)[\mathtt{c1}=\mathtt{T}]) \\ = & 1/2(1/2[\mathtt{H}=\mathtt{H}] + 1/2[H=\mathtt{T}]) + 1/2(1/2[\mathtt{T}=\mathtt{H}] + 1/2[\mathtt{T}=\mathtt{T}]) \\ = & 1/2(1/2 \cdot 1 + 1/2 \cdot 0) + 1/2(1/2 \cdot 0 + 1/2 \cdot 1) \\ = & 1/4 + 1/4 \\ = & 1/2\ ,\quad \text{that is that the probability that }\mathtt{c1}=\mathtt{c2}\text{ is }1/2. \end{array}$$

A nice further exercise for seeing this probabilistic wp at work is to repeat the above calculation when one of the coins uses $(_p\!\oplus)$ but $(_{1/2}\!\oplus)$ is retained for the other, confirming that the answer is still $1/2$.

2.3 McIver/Morgan: Pre- and Post-expectations

Following Kozen's probabilistic semantics at Sect. 2.2 just above (which itself turned out later to be a special case of Jones and Plotkin's probabilistic powerdomain construction [5]) we restored demonic choice to the programming language and called it *pGCL* [10,12]. It contains both demonic $(\sqcap)$ and probabilistic $(_p\!\oplus)$ choices; its model is $S \to \mathbb{P}\mathbb{D}S$; and it is the language we will use for the correct-by-construction program development we begin in Sect. 3 below [10]. Figures 2, 3, and 4 summarise its syntax and its wp-logic.

To illustrate demonic- vs. probabilistic choice, we'll revisit the two-coin program from above. This time, one coin will have a probability-p bias for some constant $0 \le p \le 1$ (thus acting as a fair coin just when p is $1/2$). The other choice will be purely demonic.

We start with the (two-statement) program

```
c1:= H  _p⊕  c1:= H
c2:= H   ⊓   c2:= T    ,
```

---

[7] Note that if *Prog* contains $(_p\!\oplus)$ somewhere, the above does not apply: Dijkstra semantics has no definition for $(_p\!\oplus)$.

[8] This is particularly compelling when wp is Curried: sequential composition $\mathsf{wp}(\textit{Prog1}\,;\textit{Prog2})$ is then the functional composition $\mathsf{wp}(\textit{Prog1}) \circ \mathsf{wp}(\textit{Prog2})$.

name	syntax	semantics
expectation *post*	real-valued expression over the program variables	(the usual)
expression E	expression over the program variables (of any type)	(the usual)
condition C	Boolean-valued expression over the program variables	(the usual)
substitution	$E1\,[x \backslash E2]$	Replace all free occurrences of x in $E1$ by $E2$ (with the usual caveats.)

---

assignment	$x := E$	Evaluate E; assign it to x. $\text{wp}(x := E, post) = post\,[x \backslash E]$
sequential composition	$Prog1\,;Prog2$	Execute $Prog1$ then $Prog2$.

$$\text{wp}(Prog1\,;Prog2,\ post) = \text{wp}(Prog1,\ \text{wp}(Prog2, post))$$

conditional	IF C THEN $Prog1$ ELSE $Prog2$	Evaluate Boolean C, then execute $Prog1$ or $Prog2$ accordingly.

$$\text{wp}(\text{IF } C \text{ THEN } Prog1 \text{ ELSE } Prog2,\ post)$$
$$= \quad [C]\cdot\text{wp}(Prog1, post) + [\neg C]\cdot\text{wp}(Prog2, post)$$

loop	WHILE C DO $Prog$	Evaluate Boolean C, then execute $Prog$ (and repeat), or exit, accordingly.

The usual least fixed point, based on

$$\text{WHILE } C \text{ DO } Prog \quad = \quad \text{IF } C \text{ THEN } (Prog;\ \text{WHILE } C \text{ DO } Prog)$$

The above cases cover the constructs of *pGCL* without probabilistic- or demonic choice, but nevertheless defined with Kozen-style "numeric" wp's which, applied to "post-expectations" give "pre-expectations".

Fig. 2. Syntax and wp-semantics for "restricted" *pGCL*

where the first statement is probabilistic and the second is demonic, and ask, as earlier, "What is the probability that the two coins end up equal?" We calculate

$$
\begin{aligned}
&\ \ \text{wp}(\text{c1} := \text{H } {}_p\oplus \text{ c1} := \text{T};\ \text{c2} := \text{H} \sqcap \text{c2} := \text{T},\ \ [\text{c1} = \text{c2}]) \\
=&\ \ \text{wp}(\text{c1} := \text{H } {}_p\oplus \text{ c1} := \text{T},\ \ \text{wp}(\text{c2} := \text{H} \sqcap \text{c2} := \text{T},\ [\text{c1} = \text{c2}])) \\
=&\ \ \text{wp}(\text{c1} := \text{H } {}_p\oplus \text{ c1} := \text{T},\ \ [\text{c1} = \text{H}] \text{ min } [\text{c1} = \text{T}]) \\
=&\ \ p\cdot([\text{H} = \text{H}] \text{ min } [\text{H} = \text{T}]) + (1{-}p)\cdot([\text{T} = \text{H}] \text{ min } [\text{T} = \text{T}]) \\
=&\ \ p\cdot(1 \text{ min } 0) + (1{-}p)\cdot(0 \text{ min } 1) \\
=&\ \ p\cdot 0 + (1{-}p)\cdot 0 \\
=&\ \ 0\ \ ,
\end{aligned}
$$

name	syntax	semantics
probabilistic choice	*Prog1* $_p\oplus$ *Prog2*	Evaluate p, which must be in $[0,1]$, then execute *Prog1* with that probability; otherwise execute *Prog2*.

$$\mathsf{wp}(\textit{Prog1}\,_p\oplus\,\textit{Prog2},\,\textit{post}) \;=\; p\cdot\mathsf{wp}(\textit{Prog1},\textit{post})+(1\!-\!p)\cdot\mathsf{wp}(\textit{Prog2},\textit{post})$$

name	syntax	semantics
demonic choice	*Prog1* $\sqcap$ *Prog2*	Choose demonically whether to execute *Prog1* or *Prog2*.

$$\mathsf{wp}(\textit{Prog1}\sqcap\textit{Prog2},\,\textit{post}) \;=\; \mathsf{wp}(\textit{Prog1},\textit{post})\;\min\;\mathsf{wp}(\textit{Prog2},\textit{post})$$

These "extra" cases cover the probabilistic- and demonic choice constructs of $pGCL$.

Fig. 3. Syntax and wp-semantics for $pGCL$'s choice constructs

to reach the conclusion that the probability of the two coins' being equal finally... is zero. And that highlights the way demonic choice is usually treated: it's a worst-case outcome. The "demon" –thought of as an agent– always tries to make the outcome as bad as possible: here because our desired outcome is that the coins be equal, the demon always sets the coin c_2 so they will differ. If we were to repeat the above calculation with postcondition $c_1{\neq}c_2$ instead, the result would *again* be zero: if we change our minds, want the coins to differ, then the demon will change his mind too, and act to make them the same.[9]

Implicit in the above treatment is that the c_2 demon knows the outcome of the c_1 flip—which is reasonable because that flip has already happened by the time it's the demon's turn.

Now we reverse the statements, so that the demon goes first: it must set c_2 without knowing beforehand what c_1 will be. The program becomes

$$c_2:=\;H\;\;\sqcap\;\;c_2:=\;T$$
$$c_1:=\;H\;\,_p\oplus\;c_1:=\;T\quad,$$

and we calculate

$$\mathsf{wp}(c_2:=\;H\;\sqcap\,c_2:=\;T;\;c_1:=\;H\;_p\oplus\;c_1:=\;T,\;\;[c_1=c_2])$$
$$=\quad\mathsf{wp}(c_2:=\;H\;\sqcap\,c_2:=\;T,\;\;\mathsf{wp}(c_1:=\;H\;_p\oplus\;c_1:=\;T,\;[c_1=c_2]))$$
$$=\quad\mathsf{wp}(c_2:=\;H\;\sqcap\,c_2:=\;T,\;\;p\cdot[H=c_2]+(1{-}p)\cdot[T=c_2])$$
$$=\quad p\cdot[H=H]+(1{-}p)\cdot[T=H]\;\;\min\;\;p\cdot[H=T]+(1{-}p)\cdot[T=T]$$
$$=\quad p\cdot1+(1{-}p)\cdot0\;\;\min\;\;p\cdot0+(1{-}p)\cdot1$$
$$=\quad p\;\min\;(1{-}p).$$

---

[9] This is not a novelty: demonic choice is usually treated that way in semantics—that's why it's called "demonic".

name	syntax	semantics
do nothing	SKIP	$\mathrm{wp}(\mathtt{SKIP}, post) = post$.
fail	ABORT	$\mathrm{wp}(\mathtt{ABORT}, post) = 0$.
probabilistic assignment	$x :\in E1\ {}_p\oplus E2$	As for $(x := E1)\ {}_p\oplus\ (x := E2)$.
demonic assignment	$x :\in E1 \sqcap E2$	As for $(x := E1)\ \sqcap\ (x := E2)$.
probabilistic conditional	IF p THEN *Prog1* ELSE *Prog2*	As for *Prog1* ${}_p\oplus$ *Prog2* .
probabilistic loop	WHILE p DO *Prog*	As for ordinary loop, but using probabilistic conditional.

The cases above introduce special abbreviations and "syntactic sugar" for *pGCL*.

Command SKIP allows an "ELSE-less" conditional, as used e.g. in Fig. 2, to be defined in the usual way as IF C THEN *Prog1* ELSE SKIP.

Command ABORT allows $\mathrm{wp}(\mathtt{WHILE}\ C\ \mathtt{DO}\ Prog, post)$, as a least fixed point, to be defined as the supremum of

$\mathrm{wp}(\mathtt{ABORT}, post)$
$\mathrm{wp}(\mathtt{IF}\ C\ \mathtt{THEN}\ (Prog\,;\mathtt{ABORT}), post)$
$\mathrm{wp}(\mathtt{IF}\ C\ \mathtt{THEN}\ (Prog\,;(\mathtt{IF}\ C\ \mathtt{THEN}\ (Prog\,;\mathtt{ABORT}))), post)$
$\vdots$,

which exists (in spite of the reals' being unbounded) because it can be shown by structural induction that

$$\mathrm{wp}(Prog, post) \ \leq\ post \ ,$$

and that $\mathrm{wp}(Prog, -)$ is continuous, for all programs *Prog*. The above is therefore a chain, is dominated by *post* itself, and attains the limit at ω.

Fig. 4. Syntax and wp-semantics for *pGCL*'s choice constructs

Since the demon set flip c2 *without* knowing what the c1-flip would be (because it had not happened yet), the worst it can do is to choose c2 to be the value that it is known c1 is least likely to be—which is just the result above, the lesser of p and $1-p$. If –as before– we changed our minds and decided instead that we would like the coins to be different, then the demon would adapt by choosing c2 to be the value that c1 is *most* likely to be.

Either way, the probability our postcondition will be achieved, the pre-expectation of its characteristic function, is the same p min $(1-p)$—so that only when $p = 1/2$, i.e. when $p = (1-p)$, does the demon gain no advantage.

3   Probabilistic *Correctness by Construction* in Action[10]

Our first example problem conceptually will be to achieve a binary choice of arbitrary bias using only a fair coin. With the apparatus of Sect. 2.3 however, we can immediately move from conception to precision:

> We must write a *pGCL* program that implements *Left* ${}_p\oplus$ *Right* , under the constraint that the only probabilistic choice operator we are allowed to use in the final (*pGCL*) program is $({}_{1/2}\oplus)$.

This is not a hard problem mathematically: the probabilistic calculation that solves it is elementary. Our point here is to use this simple problem to show how such solutions can be calculated within a programming-language context, while maintaining rigour (possibly machine-checkable) at every step.

The final program is given at (8) in Sect. 3.5.

3.1   Step 1—A Simplification

We'll start by simplifying the problem slightly, instantiating the programs *Left* and *Right* to x:= 1 and x:= 0 respectively. Our goal is thus to implement

$$x:\in 1 \,{}_p\oplus\, 0, \tag{2}$$

for arbitrary p, and our first step is to create two other distributions $1 \,{}_q\oplus\, 0$ and $1 \,{}_r\oplus\, 0$ whose average is $1 \,{}_p\oplus\, 0$—that is

$$1/2 \times (\, (1 \,{}_q\oplus\, 0) + (1 \,{}_r\oplus\, 0)\,) \quad = \quad (1 \,{}_p\oplus\, 0). \tag{3}$$

A fair coin will then decide whether to carry on with $1 \,{}_q\oplus\, 0$ or with $1 \,{}_r\oplus\, 0$.

Trivially (3) holds just when $(q+r)/2 = p$, and if we represent p, q, r as variables in our program, we can achieve (3) by the double assignment[11]

$$
\begin{array}{l}
\text{IF } \text{p}\le 1/2 \;\rightarrow\; \text{q,r:= 0,2p} \\
\;[\!]\;\;\; \text{p}\ge 1/2 \;\rightarrow\; \text{q,r:= 2p-1,1} \\
\text{FI} \\
\{\, \text{p} = (\text{q}+\text{r})/2\,\},
\end{array}
\tag{4}
$$

whose postcondition indicates what the assignment has established. If we follow that with a fair-coin flip between continuing with q or with r, viz.

$$
\begin{array}{ll}
\text{IF } \text{p}\le 1/2 \;\rightarrow\; \text{q,r:= 0,2p} & \text{– Here q is 0.} \\
\;[\!]\;\;\; \text{p}\ge 1/2 \;\rightarrow\; \text{q,r:= 2p-1,1} & \text{– Here r is 1.} \\
\text{FI} \\
(\text{x}:\in 1 \,{}_q\oplus\, 0) \;\;{}_{1/2}\oplus\;\; (\text{x}:\in 1 \,{}_r\oplus\, 0) & \text{– The fair coin } ({}_{1/2}\oplus) \text{ here is permitted.}
\end{array}
\tag{5}
$$

---

[10] This intent of this section can be understood based on the syntax given in Figs. 2, 3, and 4.

[11] We will sometimes include Dijkstra's closing FI.

then we should have implemented Program (2). But what have we gained?

The gain is that, whichever branch of the conditional is taken, there is a $1/2$ probability that the problem we have *yet* to solve will be either $(_0\oplus)$ or $(_1\oplus)$, both of which are trivial. If we were unlucky, well. . . then we just try again. But how do we show rigorously that Program (2) and Program (5) are equal?

If we look back at Program (4), we find the assertion $\{\,p = (q+r)/2\,\}$ which is easy to establish by conventional Hoare-logic or Dijkstra-wp reasoning from the conditional just before it. (We removed it from Program (5) just to reduce clutter.) Rigour is achieved by calculating

$$\mathsf{wp}((\mathsf{x}:\in 1\ _q\oplus 0)\ _{1/2}\oplus\ (\mathsf{x}:\in 1\ _r\oplus 0),\quad post\,)$$

$$= \quad 1/2\,\mathsf{wp}((\mathsf{x}:\in 1\ _q\oplus 0), post\,)\ +\ 1/2\,\mathsf{wp}((\mathsf{x}:\in 1\ _r\oplus 0), post\,)$$

$$= \quad q/2\cdot post\,[\mathsf{x}\backslash 1] + (1-q)/2\cdot post\,[\mathsf{x}\backslash 0] + r/2\cdot post\,[\mathsf{x}\backslash 1] + (1-r)/2\cdot post\,[\mathsf{x}\backslash 0]$$

$$= \quad (q{+}r)/2\cdot post\,[\mathsf{x}\backslash 1]\ +\ (1-(q{+}r)/2)\cdot post\,[\mathsf{x}\backslash 0]$$

$$= \quad p\cdot post\,[\mathsf{x}\backslash 1]\ +\ (1{-}p)\cdot post\,[\mathsf{x}\backslash 0]\qquad\qquad\text{``}\{\,p = (q{+}r)/2\,\}\text{''}$$

$$= \quad \mathsf{wp}(\mathsf{x}:\in 1\ _p\oplus 0,\quad post\,),$$

for arbitrary postcondition *post* where at the end we used $\{\,p = (q+r)/2\,\}$. Thus $(2) = (5)$ because for any *post* their pre-expectations agree.

3.2   Step 2—Intuition Suggests a Loop

We now return to the remark "... then we just try again." If we replace the final fair-coin flip $(\mathsf{x}:\in 1\ _q\oplus 0)\ _{1/2}\oplus\ (\mathsf{x}:\in 1\ _r\oplus 0)$ by $\mathsf{p}:\in\mathsf{q}\ _{1/2}\oplus\mathsf{r}$ then –intuitively– we are in a position to "try again" with $\mathsf{x}:\in 1\ _p\oplus 0$. Although it is the same as the statement we started with, we have made progress because variable p has been updated—and with probability $1/2$ it is either 0 or 1 and we are done. If it is not, then we arrange for a second execution of

$$
\begin{aligned}
&\texttt{IF } \mathsf{p}\leq 1/2\ \rightarrow\ \mathsf{q,r:=}\ 0,2\mathsf{p}\\
&[]\ \ \mathsf{p}\geq 1/2\ \rightarrow\ \mathsf{q,r:=}\ 2\mathsf{p}{-}1,1\\
&\texttt{FI}\\
&\mathsf{p}:\in\mathsf{q}\ _{1/2}\oplus\mathsf{r}
\end{aligned}
\tag{6}
$$

and, if *still* p is neither 0 nor 1, then ... we need a loop.

3.3   Step 3—Introduce a Loop

We have already shown that

$$Program\,(2)\quad =\quad Program\,(6);\ Program\,(2).$$

A general equality for sequential programs (including probabilistic) tells us that in that case also we have [12]

$$Program\,(2)\quad =\quad \texttt{WHILE } C \texttt{ DO } Program\,(6)\ \texttt{OD};\ Program\,(2)$$

---

[12] As before, we usually use Dijkstra's loop-closing OD.

for any loop condition C, provided the loop terminates. Intuitively that is clear because, if Program (2) can annihilate Program (6) once from the right, then it can do so any number of times. A rigorous argument appeals to the fixed-point definition of WHILE, which is where termination is used. (If C were False, so that the loop did not terminate, the *rhs* would be Abort, thus providing a clear counter-example.)

For probabilistic loops, the usual "certain" termination is replaced with *almost-sure* termination, abbreviated *AST*, which means that the loop terminates with probability one: put the other way, that would be that the probability of iterating forever is zero. For example the program

$$c := H; \text{ WHILE } c=H \text{ DO } c :\in H_{1/2} \oplus T \text{ OD.}$$

terminates almost surely because the probability of flipping T forever is zero.

A reasonably good *AST* rule for probabilistic loops is that the variant is (as usual) a natural number, but must be bounded above; and instead of having to decrease on every iteration, it is sufficient to have a non-zero probability of doing so [10,13].[13] The variant for our example loop just above is [c=H], which has probability $1/2$ of decreasing from [H=H], that is 1, to [T=H] on each iteration.

The loop condition C for our program will be $0 < p < 1$ and the variant comes directly from there: it is [0<p<1], which has probability of $1/2$ of decreasing from 1 to 0 on each iteration: and when it is 0, that is $0 < p < 1$ is false, the loop must exit. With that, we have established that our original Program (2) equals the looping program

```
WHILE 0 < p < 1 DO
    IF p ≤ ½ → q,r:= 0,2p
    ▯  p ≥ ½ → q,r:= 2p-1,1
    FI
    p:∈ q 1/2⊕ r
OD
{ p = 1 ∨ p = 0 }
x:∈ 1 p⊕ 0,
```

where the assertion at the loop's end is the negation of the loop guard.

3.4 Step 4—Use the Loop's Postcondition

There is still the final $x :\in 1_p \oplus 0$ to be dealt with, at the end; but the assertion $\{ p = 1 \vee p = 0 \}$ just before it means that it executes only when p is zero or one. So it can be replaced by IF p=0 THEN $x :\in 1_1 \oplus 0$ ELSE $x :\in 1_0 \oplus 0$, i.e. with

---

[13] By "reasonably good" we mean that it deals with most loops, but not all: it is sound, but not complete. There are more complex rules for dealing with more complex situations [11]. Strictly speaking, over infinite state spaces "non-zero" must be strengthened to "bounded away from zero" [13].

just $x := p$. Mathematically, that would be checked by showing for all post-expectations $post$ that

$$p = 1 \lor p = 0 \quad \Rightarrow \quad \mathsf{wp}(x :\in 1 {}_p \oplus 0, post) = \mathsf{wp}(x := p, post).$$

But it's a simple-enough step just to believe (unless you were using mechanical assistance, in which case it *would* be checked).

And so now the program is complete: we have implemented $x :\in 1_p \oplus 0$ by a step-by-step correctness-by-construction process that delivers the program

```
WHILE 0<p<1 DO
   IF p≤1/2 → q,r:= 0,2p
   ▯ p≥1/2 → q,r:= 2p-1,1                          (7)
   FI
     p:∈ q 1/2⊕ r
OD
x:= p
```

in which only fair choices appear. And each step is provably correct.

3.5   Step 5—After-the-Fact Optimisation

There is still one more thing that can (provably) be done with this program, and it's typical of this process: only when the pieces are finally brought together do you notice a further opportunity. It makes little difference—but it is irresistible.

Before carrying it out, however, we should be reminded of the way in which these five steps are isolated from each other, how all the layers are independent. This is an essential part of CbC, that the reasoning can be carried out in small, localised areas, and that it does not matter –for correctness– where the reasoning's target came from; nor does it matter where it is going.

Thus even if we had absolutely no idea what Program (7) was supposed to be doing, still we would be able to see that if we are replacing x by p at the end, we could just as easily replace it at the beginning; and then we can remove the variable p altogether. That gives

```
   – Now p is again a parameter, as it was in the original specification.
   x:= p
   WHILE 0<x<1 DO
      IF x≤1/2 → q,r:= 0,2x          – When x=1/2, these two
      ▯ x≥1/2 → q,r:= 2x-1,1     – branches have the same effect.   (8)
      FI
        x:∈ q 1/2⊕ r
   OD,
   – The above implements x:∈ 1_p⊕0 for any 0≤p≤1.
```

and we are done. When p is 0 or 1, it takes no flips at all; when p is $1/2$, it takes exactly one flip; and for all other values the expected number of flips is 2.

We notice that Program (8) appears to contain demonic choice, in that when $x = 1/2$ the conditional could take either branch. The nondeterminism is real— even though the *effect* is the same in either case, that q,r:= 0,1 occurs. But genuinely different computations are carried out to get there: in the first branch $2(1/2) - 1$ is evaluated to 0; and in the second branch $2(1/2)$ is evaluated to 1.

This is not an accident: we recall from Sect. 2.1 that for Dijkstra such nondeterminism arises naturally as part of the program-construction process. Where did it come from in this case?

The specification from which this conditional IF $\cdots$ FI arose was set out much earlier, at (3) which given p has many possible solutions in q, r. One of them for example is $q = r = p$ which however would have later given a loop whose non-termination would prevent Step 3 at Sect. 3.3. With an eye on loop termination, therefore, we took a design decision that at least one of q, r should be "extreme", that is 0 or 1. To end up with $q = 0$, what is the largest that p could be without sending r out of range, that is strictly more than 1? It's $p = 1/2$, and so the first IF-condition is $p \leq 1/2$. The other condition $p \geq 1/2$ arises similarly, and it absolutely does not matter that they overlap: the program will be correct whichever IF-branch taken in that case.

And, in the end –in (8) just above– we see that indeed that is so.

4   Implementing *any* Discrete Choice with a Fair Coin

Suppose instead of trying to implement a biased coin (as we have been doing so far), we want to implement a general (discrete) probabilistic choice of x's value from its type, say a finite set $\mathcal{X}$, but still using only a fair coin in the implementation. An example would be choosing x uniformly from $\{x_0, x_1, x_2\}$, i.e. a three-way fair choice. But what we develop below will work for any discrete distribution on a finite set $\mathcal{X}$ of values: it does not have to be uniform.

The combination of probability *and* abstraction allows a development like the one in Sect. 3 just above to be replayed, but a greater level of generality. We begin with a variable d of type $\mathbb{D}\mathcal{X}$,[14] where we recall that $\mathcal{X}$ is the type of x; and our specification is x:$\in$ d , that is "Set x according to distribution d."

4.1   Replaying Earlier Steps from Sect. 3

Our first step –Step 1– is to declare two more $\mathbb{D}\mathcal{X}$-typed variables d0 and d1, and –as in Sect. 3.1– specify that they must be chosen so that their average is the original distribution d; for that we use the *pGCL* nondeterministic-choice construct "assign such that" (with syntax borrowed from Dafny [9]), from Fig. 5, to write

$$\text{d0,d1:}|\ \text{d} = (\text{d0+d1})/2 \quad \text{– Choose d0,d1 so that their average is d.} \tag{9}$$

---

[14] Recall from Sect. 2.2 that $\mathbb{D}\mathcal{X}$ is the set of discrete distributions over finite set $\mathcal{X}$.

name	syntax	semantics

choose from set $\quad x :\in set$

$$wp(x :\in set, post) = (\min e \mid e \in set . post [x\backslash e])$$

assign "such that" $\quad x :\mid property (x)$

$$wp(x :\mid property (x), post) = (\min e \mid property (e). post [x\backslash e])$$

The above generalise to more than a single variable, and are consistent with the earlier definitions: thus

$$\begin{array}{ll} & x:= a \sqcap x:= b \\ = & x :\in \{a,b\} \\ = & x :\mid x \in \{a,b\} \quad . \end{array}$$

By analogy with "choose from set" (but not itself an abstraction) we have also

name	syntax	semantics

choose from distribution $\qquad x :\in dist$

$$wp(x :\in dist, post) = (\textstyle\sum e \mid e \in \lceil dist \rceil . dist (e) \cdot post [x\backslash e]) \quad ,$$

where $dist (e)$ is the probability that $dist$ assigns to e and $\lceil dist \rceil$ is the *support* of $dist$, the set of elements to which it assigns non-zero probability. 15

It is just the expected value of $post$, considered as a function of x, over the distribution $dist$ on x. (Since $E1 \,_p{\oplus}\, E2$ is a distribution, the definition above agrees with the earlier meaning of $x :\in E1 \,_p{\oplus}\, E2$ that we gave in Fig. 4 as an abbreviation.)

Fig. 5. Abstraction in *pGCL*.

The analogy with our earlier development is that there the distribution d was specifically $1 \,_p{\oplus}\, 0$, and we assigned

$$\begin{array}{lll} \text{if } p \leq 1/2 & d0, d1 = (1 \,_0{\oplus}\, 0), & (1 \,_{2p}{\oplus}\, 0) \\ \text{if } p \geq 1/2 & d0, d1 = (1 \,_{2p-1}{\oplus}\, 0), & (1 \,_1{\oplus}\, 0), \end{array}$$

which is a refinement ($\sqsubseteq$) of (9).

Our second step is to re-establish the $x :\in d$ -annihilating property that

$$\text{Program (9)} ; \quad d :\in d0 \,_{1/2}{\oplus}\, d1; \quad x :\in d \quad = \quad x :\in d, \tag{10}$$

---

15 Summing over all possible values e of x would give the same result, since the extra values have probability zero anyway. Some find this formulation more intuitive.

which is proved using wp-calculations against a general post-expectation *post*, just as before: instead of the assertion $\{\, p = (q + r)/2 \,\}$ used at the end of Step 1, we use the assertion $\{\, d = (d0+d1)/2 \,\}$ established by the assign-such-that.

The third step is again to introduce a loop. But we recall from Step 3 earlier that the loop must be almost-surely terminating and, to show that, we need a variant function. Here we have no q,r that might be set to 0 or 1; we have instead d0,d1. Our variant will be that the "size" of one of these distributions must decrease strictly, where we define the *size* of a discrete distribution to be the number of elements to which it assigns non-zero probability.[16] But our specification d0,d1:| $d = (d0+d1)/2$ above does not require that decrease; and so we must backtrack in our *CbC* and make sure that it does.

And we have made an important point, that developments following *CbC* rarely proceed as they are finally presented: the dead-ends are cut off, and only the successful path is left for the audit trail. It highlights the multiple uses of *CbC*—that on the one hand, used for teaching, the dead-ends are shown in order to learn how to avoid them; used in production, the successful path remains so that it can be modified in the case that requirements change.[17]

Thus to establish *AST* of the loop –that it terminates with probability one– we strengthen the split of d achieved by   d0,d1:| $(d0+d1)/2 = d$ with the decreasing-variant requirement, that either $|d0| < |d|$ or $|d1| < |d|$, where we are writing $|-|$ for "size of". Then the variant $|d|$ is guaranteed strictly to decrease with probabililty $1/2$ on each iteration. That is we now write

$$\text{d0,d1:|}\quad (d0+d1)/2 = d \ \wedge\ (|d0| < |d| \vee |d1| < |d|), \tag{11}$$

replacing (9), for the nondeterministic choice of d0 and d1. We do not have to re-prove its annihilation property, because the new statement (11) is a refinement of the (9) from before (It has a stronger postcondition.) and so preserves all its functional properties. In fact that is the definition of refinement.

Our next step is to reduce the nondeterminism in (11) somewhat, choosing a particular way of achieving it: to "split" d into two parts d0,d1 such that the size of at least one part is smaller, we choose two subsets X_0, X_1 of $\mathcal{X}$ whose intersection contains at most one element. That is illustrated in Fig. 6, where $X_0 = \{A, B, C\}$ and $X_1 = \{C, D\}$. Further, we require that the probabilities $d(X_0)$ and $d(X_1)$ assigned by d to $X_0 - X_1$ and $X_1 - X_0$ are both no more than $1/2$.[18] Those constraints mean that we can always arrange the subsets so that the "$1/2$-line" of Fig. 6 either goes strictly through $X_0 \cap X_1$ (if they overlap) or runs between them (if they do not).[19]

---

[16] In probability theory this would be the cardinality of its support.

[17] And if an error was made in the *CbC* proofs, the "successful" path can be audited to see what the mistake was, why it was made, and how to fix it.

[18] Applying d to a set means the sum of the d-probabilities of the elements of the set.

[19] If for example C were much smaller, so that the dividing line went through D, the new distribution d0 would have support 4, the same as d itself. But $|d1|$ would then have support 1, strictly smaller.

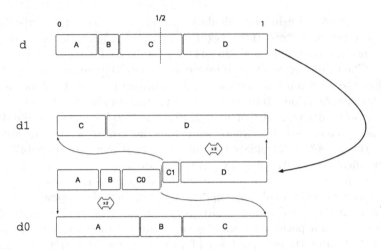

Suppose that $\mathcal{X}$ is $\{A, B, C, D\}$, and that the distribution d in $\mathcal{X}$ that we start with is indicated by the size of the rectangles: the size $|d|$ of d here is therefore 4, because it contains 4 rectangles. We choose X_0 to be $\{A, B, C\}$ and X_1 to be $\{C, D\}$, so that $X_0 - X_1$ is $\{A, B\}$ and $X_1 - X_0$ is $\{D\}$, and both $d(X_0 - X_1)$ and $d(X_1 - X_0)$ are no more than $1/2$. Their overlap is $\{C\}$, whose probability the "$1/2$-line" splits into two pieces: one piece joins $d0$ and the other piece joins $d1$.

Thus by dividing the overall rectangle (representing $\mathcal{X}$ itself) exactly in the middle, at least one side must contain strictly fewer than $|d|$ rectangles — and if we double the size of each small rectangle, we get our two distributions $d1$ and $d2$ such that $d = (d0 + d1)/2$ and either $|d0| < |d|$ or $|d1| < |d|$.

Fig. 6. Dividing a discrete distribution into two pieces.

We then construct $d0$ by restricting d to just X_0, then doubling all the probabilities in that restriction; if they sum to more than 1, we then trim any excess from the one element in $X_0 \cap X_1$ that X_0 shares with X_1. The analogous procedure is applied to generate $d1$. In Fig. 6 for example we chose sizes 0.2, 0.1, 0.3 and 0.4 for the four regions, and the $1/2$ line went through the third one. On the left, the 0.2 and 0.1 and 0.3 are doubled to 0.4 and 0.2 and 0.6, summing to 1.2; thus 0.2 is trimmed from the 0.6, leaving 0.4 assigned to C. And the analogous procedure applies on the right.

4.2 "Decomposition of Data into Data Structures"

The quote is from Wirth [15]. Our program is currently

```
WHILE |d|≠1 DO
    d0,d1:|  (d0+d1)/2 = d  ∧  (|d0| < |d| ∨ |d1| < |d|)
    d:∈ d0 1/2⊕ d1                                          (12)
OD
x:∈ d // This is a trivial choice, because |d|=1 here.
```

And it is correct: it does refine $x :\in d$—but it is rather abstract. Our next development step will be to make it concrete by realising the distribution-typed variables and the subsets of $\mathcal{X}$ as "ordinary" datatypes using scalars and lists. In CbC this is done by deciding, before that translation process begins, what the realisations will be—and only then is the abstract program transformed, piece by piece. The relation between the abstract- and concrete types is called a *coupling invariant*.

Although an obvious approach is to order the type $\mathcal{X}$, say as $x_1, x_2, \ldots, x_N$ and then to realise discrete distributions as lists of length N of probabilities (summing to 1), a more concise representation is suggested by the fact that for example we represent a *two*-point distribution $x_1 \, {}_p\oplus \, x_2$ as just *one* number p, with the $1-p$ implied. Thus we will represent the distribution $p_1, p_2, \ldots p_N$ as the list of length $N-1$ of "accumulated" probabilities: in this case for p we would have a list

$$p_1, \quad p_1+p_2, \quad \ldots, \quad \sum_{n=1}^{N-1} p_n,$$

leaving off the Nth element of the list since it would always be 1 anyway. Subsets of $\mathcal{X}$ will be pairs low,high of indices, meaning $\{x_{\text{low}}, \ldots, x_{\text{high}}\}$, and although that can't represent *all* subsets of $\mathcal{X}$, contiguous subsets are all we will need. Carrying out that transformation gives following concrete version of our abstract Program (12) below, where the abstract d is represented as the concrete dL[low:high] , which is the coupling invariant.[20]

And in Program (13) of Fig. 7 we have, finally, a concrete program that can actually be run. Notice that it has exactly the same *structure* as Program (12): split (the realisations of) d into d0 and d1; overwrite d with one of them; exit the loop when $|d|$ is one.

Nevertheless, as earlier in Sect. 3.5, further development steps might still be possible now that everything is together in one place:[21] and indeed, recognising that only one of dL0,dL1 will be *used*, we can rearrange Program (13)'s body so that only one of them will be *calculated*—and it can be updated as we go. That gives our really-final-this-time program (14) in Fig. 8, which will -without further intervention- use a fair coin to choose a value x_n according to *any* given discrete distribution d on finite $\mathcal{X}$. Its expected number of coin flips is no worse than $2N-2$, where N is the size of $\mathcal{X}$, thus agreeing with expected 2 flips for the program (8) in Sect. 3.5 that dealt with the simpler case $d = (1 \, {}_p\oplus \, 0)$ where $\mathcal{X}$ was $\{1, 0\}$.

It's again worth emphasising –because it is the main point– that the correctness arguments for all of these steps are isolated from each other: in CbC every step's correctness is determined by looking at that step alone. Thus for example nothing in the translation process just above involved reasoning about the earlier steps, whether Program (12) actually implemented the $x :\in d$ that

---

[20] The range low:high is inclusive-exclusive (as in Python). A similar coupling invariant applies to d0 and d1. All three invariants are applied at once.

[21] Note the necessity of keeping this as two steps: first data-refine, then (if you can) optimise algorithmically.

– Discrete distribution d in $\mathcal{X}$ of size N is realised here as dL (for "d-list").
low,high:= 1, N – Initial support is all of $\mathcal{X}$.
WHILE low $\neq$ high DO   – low = high means support is $\{x_{low}\}$
  – Current support is $\{x_{low}, \dots, x_{high}\}$.

  – Find X_0 by examining the probabilities of $x_1, x_2, \dots$
  n:= low   – Determine dL0 as in *lhs* of Fig. 6.
  WHILE n<high $\wedge$ dL[n]<1/2 DO dL0[n]:= 2*dL[n]; n:= n+1 OD
  low0,high0:= low,n   – Subset X_0 is $\{x_{low0}, \dots, x_{high0}\}$.

                                                                              (13)

  – Find X_1 by examining the probabilities of $x_N, x_{N-1}, \dots$
  n:= high-1   – Determine dL1 as in *rhs* of Fig. 6.
  WHILE low$\leq$n $\wedge$ 1/2<dL[n] DO dL1[n]:= 2*dL[n]-1; n:= n-1 OD
  low1,high1:= n+1,high   – Subset X_1 is $\{x_{low1}, \dots, x_{high1}\}$.

  – Use fair coin to choose between dL0 and dL1.
  (dL,low,high):$\in$ (dL0,low0,high0) $_{1/2}\oplus$ (dL1,low1,high1)

OD
x:= x_{low} – Extract sole element of point distribution's support.

Fig. 7. Implement any discrete choice using only a fair coin.

– Assume discrete distribution d over $\mathcal{X} = \{x_1, \dots, x_N\}$ of size N
– has been represented cumulatively in list dL, as described above.

low,high:= 1, N – Initial support is all of $\mathcal{X}$.
WHILE low $\neq$ high DO   – low = high means support is $\{x_{low}\}$
  – Fair coin flipped here. (Recall Fig. 4.)
  IF 1/2 THEN   – Then update dL as in *lhs* of Fig. 6.
    n:= low
    WHILE n<high $\wedge$ dL[n]<1/2 DO dL[n]:= 2*dL[n]; n:= n+1 OD   (14)
    high:= n
  ELSE   – Else update dL as in *rhs* of Fig. 6.
    n:= high-1
    WHILE low$\leq$n $\wedge$ 1/2<dL[n] DO dL[n]:= 2*dL[n]-1; n:= n-1 OD
    low:= n+1
  FI
OD
x:= x_{low} – Extract sole element of point distribution dL's support.

Fig. 8. Optimisation of Program (13)

we started with: we didn't care, and we didn't check. We just translated Program (12) into Program (13) regardless. And the subsequent rearrangement of (13) into Program (14) similarly made no use of Program (13)'s provenence.

All that is to be contrasted with the more common approach in which *only* intuition (and experience, and skill) is used, that is in which our final Program (14) might be written all at once at this concrete level, only then checking (testing, debugging, hoping) afterwards that our intuitions were correct. A transliteration of Program (14) into Python is given in Appendix A.

5   An Everyday Application: Simulating a Fair Die Using only a Fair Coin

Program (14) of the previous section works for any discrete distribution, without having to adapt the program in any way. However if the distribution's probabilities are not too bizarre, then the number of different values for low and d and high might be quite small—and then the program's behaviour for that distribution in particular can be set out as a small probabilistic state machine.

In Fig. 9 we take d to be the uniform distribution over the possible die-roll outcomes $\{1, 2, 3, 4, 5, 6\}$, and show the state machine that results. For that state machine in particular, we propose one last correctness-preserving step: it takes us to the optimal die-roll algorithm of Knuth and Yao [6].

6   Why Was This "Correctness by Construction"?

The programs here are not themselves remarkable in any way. (The optimality of the Knuth/Yao algorithm is not our contribution.) Even the mathematical insights used in their construction are well known, examples of elementary probability theory. *CbC* means however applying those insights in a systematic, layered way so that the reasoning in each layer does not depend on earlier layers, and does not affect later ones. The steps were specifically

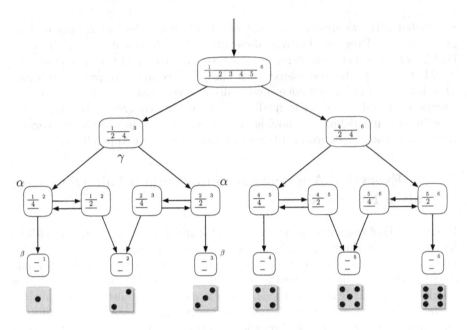

Each interior node has two possible successors chosen with equal probability, and each final-die node is reached with the same probability $1/6$. There are 17 nodes, and the expected number of coin flips is 4.

The nodes' origins are shown by labelling them with `low`, `d` and `high` from the states in the generating program that gave rise to them, representing the current probability distribution `d` yet to be realised over over the remaining subset $\{\texttt{low}, \ldots, \texttt{high}\}$ of possible results. With probabilities normalised out of 6 for neatness, a typical label is

$$\overset{\text{low} \qquad\qquad\qquad \text{high}}{\underset{\longleftarrow \ 6{\times}\mathtt{d} \ \longrightarrow}{\rule{5cm}{0.4pt}}} ,$$

where we recall that `d` gives the *sum* of the probabilities for $x_{\texttt{low}}, x_{\texttt{low}+1}, \ldots, x_{\texttt{high}-1}$ and that `d` for $x_{\texttt{high}}$ is left out, because it is always 1. Thus for example `low` = 2 and `high` = 3 and `d` = [4] represents the distribution over support $\{2,3\}$ of $4/6$ for 2 and $1-4/6$ for 3, that is $2 \ _{2/3}{\oplus} \ 3$.

The well-known (optimal) algorithm of Knuth and Yao for simulating a die with a fair coin has 13 states and $11/3$ expected coin flips [6] — and it can be obtained from here by one last correctness-preserving step. Eliminate the choice γ, so that the two α and the two β nodes are merged; since that also merges the two die-rolls 1 and 3, restore the γ choice as a new fair choice γ' over $\{1,3\}$, just below the merged β's. (The nodes leading to die-roll 2 are merged as well, but it makes no difference.)

Concentrating on the left (justified by symmetry), we see that the original γ choice must be done every time; but its replacement γ' is done only $2/3$ of the time. That realises exactly the $1/3$ efficiency advantage that Knuth/Yao optimal algorithm has over the one synthesised here by our general Program (14).

Fig. 9. Simulating a fair die with a fair coin

1. Start with the *specification* x :∈ d at the beginning of Sect. 4.
2. Prove a one-step annihilation property (10) for that specification.
3. Use a general loop rule to prove loop-annihilation Program (12), after Strengthening Program (9) to Program (11) to establish *AST*.
4. Propose strategy Fig. 6 for the loop body of Program (12).
5. Propose data representation of finite discrete distributions as lists, in Sect. 4.2, realising the strategy of Fig. 6 in the code of Program (13).
6. Rearrange Program (13) to produce a more efficient final program Program (14).
7. Note that **correctness by construction guarantees** that Program (14) refines x :∈ d for any d.
8. Apply Program (14) to the fair die, to produce state chart of Fig. 9.
9. Modify Fig. 9 to produce the Knuth/Yao (optimal) algorithm [6].
10. Note that **correctness by construction guarantees** that the Knuth/Yao (optimal) algorithm implements a fair die.

CbC also means that since all those steps are done explicitly and separately, they can be checked easily as you go along, and audited afterwards. But to apply *CbC* effectively, and *honestly*, one must have a rigorous semantics that justifies every single development step made. In our example here, that was supplied here by the semantics of *pGCL* [10]. But working in any "wide spectrum" language, right from the (abstract) start all the way to the (concrete) finish, means that many of those rigorous steps can be checked by theorem provers.

A   Program (14) implemented in Python

```
#    Run 1,000,000 trials on a fair-die simulation.
#
#    bash-3.2$ python ISoLA.py
#    1000000
#    1 1 1 1 1 1
#    Relative frequencies
#        0.998154 1.00092   0.996474 0.998664 1.004928   1.00086
#    realised, using 4.001938 flips on average.


import sys
from random import randrange

# Number of runs, an integer on the first line by itself.
runs = int(sys.stdin.readline())

# Discrete distribution unnormalised, as many subsequent integers as needed.
# Then EOT.
d= []
for line in sys.stdin.readlines():
    for word in line.split(): d.append(int(word))
sizeX= len(d) # Size of initial distribution's support.
```

```
# Construct distribution's representation as accumulated list dL_Init.
# Note that length of dL_Init is sizeX-1,
#    because final (normalised) entry of 1 is implied.
# Do not normalise, however: makes the arithmetic clearer.
sum,dL_Init= d[0],[]
for n in range(sizeX-1): dL_Init= dL_Init+[sum]; sum= sum+d[n+1]

tallies= []
for n in range(sizeX): tallies= tallies+[0]

allFlips= 0 # For counting average number of flips.
for r in range(runs):
    flips= 0

    ### Program (14) starts here.
    low,high,dL= 0,sizeX-1,dL_Init[:] # Must clone dL_Init.
    # print "Start:", low, dL[low:high], high

    while low<high:
        flip= randrange(2) # One fair-coin flip.
        flips= flips+1

        if flip==0:
            n= low
            while n<high and 2*dL[n]<sum: dL[n]= 2*dL[n]; n= n+1
            high= n # Implied dL0[high]=1 performs trimming automatically.
            # print "Took dL0:", low, dL[low:high], high # dL0 has overwritten dL.

        else: # flip==1
            n= high-1
            while low<=n and 2*dL[n]>sum: dL[n]= 2*dL[n]-sum; n= n-1
            low= n+1 # Implied dL1[low]=0 performs trimming automatically.
            # print "Took dL1", low, dL[low:high], high # dL1 has overwritten dL.

    # print "Rolled", low, "in", flips, "flips."
    ### Program (14) ends here.

    tallies[low]= tallies[low]+1
    allFlips= allFlips+flips

print "Relative frequencies"
for n in range(sizeX): print "     ", float(tallies[n])/runs * sum
print "realised, using", float(allFlips)/runs, "flips on average."
```

References

1. Dijkstra, E.W.: On the reliability of programs (EWD303)
2. Dijkstra, E.W.: A Discipline of Programming. Prentice-Hall, Upper Saddle River (1976)
3. Floyd, R.W.: Assigning meanings to programs. In: Schwartz, J.T. (ed.) Mathematical Aspects of Computer Science. Proceedings of Symposium on Applied Mathematics, vol. 19, pp. 19–32. American Mathematical Society (1967)
4. Hoare, C.A.R.: An axiomatic basis for computer programming. Comm. ACM **12**(10), 576–580 (1969)
5. Jones, C.B., Plotkin, G.: A probabilistic powerdomain of evaluations. In: Proceedings of the IEEE 4th Annual Symposium on Logic in Computer Science, Los Alamitos, CA, pp. 186–195. Computer Society Press (1989)
6. Knuth, D., Yao, A.: The complexity of nonuniform random number generation. In: Algorithms and Complexity: New Directions and Recent Results. Academic Press (1976)
7. Kozen, D.: Semantics of probabilistic programs. J. Comput. Syst. Sci. **22**, 328–350 (1981)
8. Kozen, D.: A probabilistic PDL. In: Proceedings of the 15th ACM Symposium on Theory of Computing, pp. 291–297. ACM, New York (1983)
9. Leino, K.R.M.: Dafny: an automatic program verifier for functional correctness. In: Clarke, E.M., Voronkov, A. (eds.) LPAR 2010. LNCS (LNAI), vol. 6355, pp. 348–370. Springer, Heidelberg (2010). https://doi.org/10.1007/978-3-642-17511-4_20
10. McIver, A.K., Morgan, C.C.: Abstraction, Refinement and Proof for Probabilistic Systems. Monographs in Computer Science. Springer, New York (2005). https://doi.org/10.1007/b138392
11. McIver, A.K., Morgan, C.C., Kaminski, B.-L., Katoen, J.-P.: A new proof rule for almost-sure termination. Proc. ACM Program. Lang. **2**(POPL), 1–28 (2017)
12. Morgan, C.C., McIver, A.K., Seidel, K.: Probabilistic predicate transformers. ACM Trans. Program. Lang. Syst. **18**(3), 325–353 (1996)
13. Morgan, C.C.: Proof rules for probabilistic loops. In: Jifeng, H., Cooke, J., Wallis, P. (eds.) Proceedings of the BCS-FACS 7th Refinement Workshop, Workshops in Computing. Springer, Heidelberg (July 1996). http://www.bcs.org/upload/pdf/ewicrw96paper10.pdf
14. Vazsonyi, A.: Which Door has the Cadillac: Adventures of a Real-Life Mathematician. Writers Club Press (2002)
15. Wirth, N.: Program development by stepwise refinement. Commun. ACM **14**(4), 221–227 (1971)

Components in Probabilistic Systems: Suitable by Construction

Christel Baier[1]([✉])(iD), Clemens Dubslaff[1]([✉])(iD), Holger Hermanns[2,3]([✉])(iD),
Michaela Klauck[2]([✉])(iD), Sascha Klüppelholz[1]([✉])(iD),
and Maximilian A. Köhl[2]([✉])(iD)

[1] Technische Universität Dresden, Dresden, Germany
baier@tcs.inf.tu-dresden.de,
{clemens.dubslaff,sascha.klueppelholz}@tu-dresden.de
[2] Saarland University, Saarland Informatics Campus, Saarbrücken, Germany
{hermanns,klauck,mkoehl}@cs.uni-saarland.de
[3] Institute of Intelligent Software, Guangzhou, China

Abstract. This paper focusses on the question when and to what extent a particular system component can be considered *suitable* to use in the context of the dynamics of a larger technical system. We introduce different notions of *suitability* that arise naturally in the context of probabilistic nondeterministic systems that interact through the exchange of messages in the style of input-output automata. Besides discussing algorithmic aspects for an analysis following our notions of suitability, we demonstrate practical usability of our concepts by means of experiments on a concrete use case.

1 Introduction

The structured composition of systems from smaller entities is a key technique across many engineering disciplines. For instance, in the field of architecture, it is well understood how the structural properties of construction stones translate into structural properties of walls and thus of houses. This concept also is extremely appealing for the engineering of *cyber-physical systems (CPSs)*, typically built up of components that interact and exchange information [3,30]. For CPSs, the compositional approach poses a number of challenges, stemming first and foremost from the notoriously complex dynamics of even simple CPSs placed in only partially controllable or partially known environments. But also the semantic heterogeneity of computational, physical, and human aspects for modelling the CPS, together with algorithmic and technical challenges in a

Authors are listed in alphabetical order. This work was partially supported by the DFG under the projects TRR 248 (see https://perspicuous-computing.science, project ID 389792660), EXC 2050/1 (CeTI, project ID 390696704, as part of Germany's Excellence Strategy), BA-1679/11-1, and BA-1679/12-1, the ERC Advanced Investigators Grant 695614 (POWVER), and the Key-Area Research and Development Program Grant 2018B010107004 of Guangdong Province.

© Springer Nature Switzerland AG 2020
T. Margaria and B. Steffen (Eds.): ISoLA 2020, LNCS 12476, pp. 240–261, 2020.
https://doi.org/10.1007/978-3-030-61362-4_13

model-based engineering process render the modelling and analysis of composite CPSs an exigent task.

The present paper contributes to the quest for methods and tools to construct, abstract, compose, and evaluate CPS models that summarise the crucial aspects of components' quantitative behaviour, together with support for design-time evaluation of alternatives. Our long-term vision is a methodology to devise, verify, and compose *summaries of component characteristics*, and to provide means that enable the comparative analysis of such characteristics. To this end, we aim at deepening the known concepts of interfaces and service contracts in that they come with rigid semantic interpretations, and are supported by effective algorithmic analysis techniques. In doing so, we focus on component models that can exhibit probabilistic behaviour while engaging in interaction via inputs and outputs. The central notion that we study in this paper is *suitability*. We explore the spectrum of meaningful notions of suitability of a component with respect to a set of quantitative properties representing what is considered important in a specific context. In this, we concentrate on probabilistic aspects of suitability.

Concurrency, Composition, and Probability. The questions in how far component characteristics affect a larger context is entrenched with the question how the components interact, i.e., what the composition of components and contexts actually mean semantically. Process calculi like CSP [26] or CCS [34] are at the roots of generic and expressive ways to piece up larger systems from concurrent interacting components. Segala [38] lifted these ideas to the setting of probabilistic automata, nowadays the standard composition for Markov decision processes (MDPs) [37] also used in analysis tools such as PRISM [29]. Earlier seminal work on probabilistic concurrency [24] has put in focus the importance of a generative/reactive view on probabilities. This echoes the separation of component activities into inputs and outputs, a central concept especially in the works on I/O automata [32]. In this modelling approach, component inputs are always enabled, meaning that no component can block the output of another component by not accepting it as input. This simple assumption is natural in many contexts: if in place, it is intuitively easy to add more components to an existing system, since none of them will block the behaviour already present. In a probabilistic setting with inputs and outputs, it is furthermore natural to associate to outputs a generative probabilistic effect: different outputs of a component can be generated according to a probability distribution (local to the output component), while inputs are reactive in the sense that for all inputs the component is able to react with a probabilistic effect. This idea was first worked out in probabilistic I/O automata [40], and later adapted to the setting of probabilistic automata [11,14,23].

Probabilistic Input-Output Systems (PIOSs). In this paper, we strive towards notions for the suitability of components to be composed with a larger context. To benefit from the compositional advantages detailed above, we work with a very expressive formalism for interacting probabilistic components and their composition based on the compositional framework of *interleaved probabilistic I/O system (IPIOA)* [23]. This formalism is a conservative extension of input-output automata [32] to the setting of discrete probabilities. We further enhance IPIOA slightly by a more flexible concept of observability, leading to the framework of *partially observable PIOSs (PO-PIOSs)*. While the use of I/O formalisms as in PO-PIOSs is common for many compositional specification theories, input-enabledness is sometimes not natural for tightly interacting systems. However, our concept of suitability does not explicitly rely on the input-enabledness assumption in PO-PIOSs and can be adapted to other compositional MDP-based formalisms.

Notions of Suitability. Stepwise and with an increasing intricacy, we introduce several notions of suitability formalised for the setting of PO-PIOS. Our basic instance is provided through *threshold suitability* that determines whether each one of the given quantitative properties exceeds a given threshold. This notion has similarities to conjunctive multi-objective properties in MDPs [12,19–21]. Weighting quantitative properties for the CPS leads to a single quantitative measure of *suitability degree*, which then might be used to relate different components with respect to their suitability. That is, we call a component *more suitable* than another if executed in the same context CPS all possible executions achieve a higher suitability degree. For all of our notions, we present *universal* and *existential* versions, differing in the ability of the component investigated with respect to its ability to react on the other components of the CPS.

Suitability Evaluation. Algorithmically, the notions of suitability we introduce for PO-PIOS are closely related to threshold properties for IPIOA [23], and to verification problems on partially-observable MDPs [8,31,33,35], all of which are known to be undecidable already under mild assumptions. As we illustrate in this paper, this leaves little room for decidable suitability problems in the general case. Therefore, restricted classes of PO-PIOSs, properties, and schedulers have to be considered to establish decidable instances of our suitability problems. The problem instances for which we establish positive results comprise PO-PIOSs with full observability and restrictions on the nondeterminism that is present in the components. While these instances appear to be quite restricted at the first glance, our case study shows that they provide useful contributions to estimate suitability of components in CPSs.

Suitability in Action. Despite our definitions of suitability being a priori developed in a theoretical context, and despite the challenges in algorithmically capturing the concepts, we put them to a first practical litmus test. For this, we instantiated them in a concrete example context, known as the *Racetrack* case study across the automated planning community [9,10,36], here augmented with probabilistic noise [25]. Within this case study, a car that comprises multiple components such as an engine, tank, and a track with different types of ground, aims to reach a target position while meeting time, energy, and CO_2-emission constraints. We work on a feature-oriented model of the car where the model family consists of multiple car and environment configurations, e.g. differing in the engine variant, the tank size and the ground the car drives on. Specifically, we show that a more powerful engine is *existentially threshold suitable* on tarmac but not on sand and that a less powerful engine is *more suitable* in terms of its *suitability degree* than a more powerful engine.

Contributions. In a nutshell, this paper (i) develops a spectrum of suitability notions for probabilistic components with inputs and outputs, (ii) provides results regarding decidability for the notions considered, and (iii) illustrates the notions and their effect in the context of a case study with vehicle components.

2 Partially Observable Probabilistic I/O Systems

This section discusses the basic concepts of the compositional framework of *probabilistic I/O automata* originally proposed by Giro et al. [23], enhanced with a notion of partial observability.

Markov Decision Processes. For a finite set S, we denote by $Dist(S)$ the set of all the probability distributions over the set S, i.e. functions $\mu\colon S \to [0,1]$ such that $\sum_{s \in S} \mu(s) = 1$. We write $\delta(s)$ for the *Dirac distribution* where $\delta(s)(s) = 1$.

Definition 1 (Markov Decision Process (MDP)). *A Markov Decision Process (MDP) is a tuple* $(S, \mathcal{A}, \mathcal{T}, s_0)$ *where* S *and* $\mathcal{A}$ *are sets of states and actions, respectively,* $\mathcal{T} \subseteq S \times \mathcal{A} \times Dist(S)$ *is a transition probability relation, and* $s_0 \in S$ *is an initial state.*

Let $\mathcal{M} = (S, \mathcal{A}, \mathcal{T}, s_0)$ be an MDP as above. We say that action $a \in \mathcal{A}$ is *applicable* in state $s \in S$ if $(s, a, \mu) \in \mathcal{T}$ for some $\mu \in Dist(S)$. By $\mathcal{A}(s) \subseteq \mathcal{A}$ we denote the set of actions applicable in s. We assume w.l.o.g. that $\mathcal{A}(s)$ is nonempty for all $s \in S$. Furthermore, we require that for all $(s, a, \mu), (s, a, \mu') \in \mathcal{T}$ we have $\mu = \mu'$. A *finite path* in $\mathcal{M}$ is an alternating sequence of states and transitions $\pi = s_0\, t_0\, s_1\, t_1\, \dots\, t_{k-1}\, s_k$ where $s_1, \dots, s_k \in S$ and where for each index $i \in \{0, 1, \dots, k-1\}$, $t_i = (s_i, a_i, \mu_i) \in \mathcal{T}$ such that $\mu_i(s_{i+1}) > 0$. We denote by $Paths(\mathcal{M})$ the set of all finite paths in $\mathcal{M}$. By $last(\pi)$ we denote the last state of π, i.e. $last(\pi) = s_k$. Infinite paths are defined accordingly, collected in a set $IPaths(\mathcal{M})$. A (randomised) *scheduler* for $\mathcal{M}$ is a function $\mathfrak{S}\colon Paths(\mathcal{M}) \to Dist(\mathcal{A})$ that resolves the nondeterminism in an execution of the MDP $\mathcal{M}$, i.e. for any path $\pi \in Paths(\mathcal{M})$ we have $\mathfrak{S}(\pi) \in Dist(\mathcal{A}(last(\pi)))$. $\mathfrak{S}$ is called *memoryless* in case for all paths $\pi_1, \pi_2 \in Paths(\mathcal{M})$ with $last(\pi_1) = last(\pi_2)$ we have $\mathfrak{S}(\pi_1) = \mathfrak{S}(\pi_2)$, and *deterministic* if all distributions in $\mathfrak{S}$ are Dirac. We define the probability measure $\mathrm{Pr}_{\mathcal{M}}^{\mathfrak{S}}$ on $\mathcal{M}$ with respect to a scheduler $\mathfrak{S}$ in the standard way, assigning a probability to measurable sets of paths in $\mathcal{M}$. Here, the fact that any scheduler resolves the nondeterminism in the given MDP towards a Markov chain [37] is exploited.

Observability in MDPs. A flexible notion of observation will allow us to map states and actions to *observables*.

Definition 2 (Observation Function). *An* observation function *for an MDP* $\mathcal{M} = (\mathcal{S}, \mathcal{A}, \mathcal{T}, s_0)$ *over a set of atomic observables Obs is a function obs:* $(\mathcal{S} \cup \mathcal{A}) \rightarrow (Obs \cup \{\varepsilon\})$, *where* $obs(x) = \varepsilon$ *stands for unobservability of state or action* x.

We refer to observation function *obs* as *totally observable* in case $Obs = \mathcal{S} \cup \mathcal{A}$ and $obs(x) = x$ for all $x \in \mathcal{S} \cup \mathcal{A}$. For a transition $t = (s, a, \mu) \in \mathcal{T}$ we denote by $obs(t)$ the observation $obs(a)$ of the action of t. Observation functions *obs* are extended to functions from paths $\pi = s_0 t_0 s_1 t_1 \ldots t_{k-1} s_k$ to strings over the alphabet *Obs*, given by

$$obs(\pi) \quad = \quad obs(s_0)\, obs(t_0)\, obs(s_1) \ldots obs(t_{k-1})\, obs(s_k).$$

For an observation function *obs* as above, a function ρ defined on paths of $\mathcal{M}$ is said to be *obs-complying* if for all finite paths $\pi_1, \pi_2 \in Paths(\mathcal{M})$ we have that

$$obs(\pi_1) = obs(\pi_2) \text{ implies } \rho(\pi_1) = \rho(\pi_2).$$

Probabilistic I/O Systems. To introduce the PIOS framework [23], we first need to define reactive and generative structures for outputs and inputs, respectively: Given a set *Act* of action labels and a set *States* of states, a *generative output transition relation* G is a subset of $States \times Dist(Act \times States)$, and an *input reactive transition function* R is a function of the form $States \times Act \rightarrow Dist(States)$. Intuitively, executing a generative output transition $(s, \kappa) \in G$ available in some state s means choosing both an action a to output and a state s' with joint probability $\kappa(a, s)$. In a composed setting, action a will serve as an output broadcasted to other participants. Receiving input a while being in state t triggers a unique reaction $R(t, a)$ according to the input reactive transition function R, mapping to a distribution over successor states.

Definition 3 (Probabilistic Input/Output System (PIOS)). *A probabilistic I/O* component *is a tuple* $(States, Act, G, R, init)$, *where*

- *States is a finite set of states,*
- *Act is a finite set of action labels,*
- $G \subseteq States \times Dist(Act \times States)$ *is a generative output transition relation,*
- $R: States \times Act \rightarrow Dist(States)$ *is a reactive transition function, and*
- $init \in States$ *is an initial state.*

A probabilistic I/O system (PIOS) *is a finite vector* $\mathcal{P} = (\alpha_1, \ldots, \alpha_n)$ *of components* α_i, $i \in \{1, \ldots, n\}$.

Note that since $R: States \times Act \rightarrow Dist(States)$ is a total function, every component is input-deterministic and input-enabled. We use the indices of components also for their elements, e.g. refer to the states of α_i by $States_i$.

Definition 4 (MDP induced by PIOS). *Any PIOS $\mathcal{P} = (\alpha_1, \ldots, \alpha_n)$ gives rise to an MDP $[\![\mathcal{P}]\!] = (\mathcal{S}, \mathcal{A}, \mathcal{T}, s_0)$ as follows:*

- $\mathcal{S} = \times_{i=1}^{n} States_i$
- $\mathcal{A} = Dist(\bigcup_{i=1}^{n} Act_i)$
- $\mathcal{T} \subseteq \mathcal{S} \times \mathcal{A} \times Dist(\mathcal{S})$ *is the smallest set of transitions* $((s_1, \ldots, s_n), \kappa, \mu)$ *for which there is an $i \in \{1, \ldots, n\}$ and $\kappa_i \in Dist(Act_i \times States_i)$ such that*
  - $(s_i, \kappa_i) \in G_i$,
  - *for all $a \in Act_i$ we have $\kappa(a) = \sum_{s \in States_i} \kappa_i(a, s)$, and*
  - *for all $(s'_1, \ldots, s'_n) \in \mathcal{S}$ we have*

$$\mu(s'_1, \ldots, s'_n) = \sum_{a \in Act_i} \kappa_i(a, s'_i) \prod_{\substack{j=1 \\ j \neq i}}^{n} \mu_j^a(s'_j)$$

  where $\mu_j^a = \delta(s_j)$ provided $a \notin Act_j$ and otherwise $\mu_j^a = R_j(s_j, a)$.
- $s_0 = (init_1, \ldots, init_n)$

Remark 1. In the MDP defined above, output distributions appear as action labels of MDP transitions. This slightly differs from the semantics of PIOSs defined in [23], where the operational behaviour is specified through *compound transitions*, explicitly comprising generative and reactive transitions as well as the action label. ∎

Observability in PIOSs. In the following, we assume a fixed PIOS $\mathcal{P} = (\alpha_1, \ldots, \alpha_n)$ with the induced MDP semantics $[\![\mathcal{P}]\!] = (\mathcal{S}, \mathcal{A}, \mathcal{T}, s_0)$ as per Definition 4. Let α_i be a component of $\mathcal{P}$ and $\mathsf{s} = (s_1, \ldots, s_n)$ a global state of $\mathcal{P}$, i.e. a state in the MDP $[\![\mathcal{P}]\!]$. By $\mathsf{s}|_i = s_i$ we denote the *state projection* of s to the i-th local state. The set of atomic observables Obs_i collects the observations a component α_i of $\mathcal{P}$ can make on global states and actions. Suppose that for all $i \in \{1, \ldots, n\}$ we are given a *local observation function* obs_i, for which we require that global states of $\mathcal{P}$ with different local states for component α_i have different observables. Formally,

$$\text{if } obs_i(\mathsf{s}) = obs_i(\mathsf{s}') \text{ then } \mathsf{s}|_i = \mathsf{s}'|_i.$$

We call obs_i *purely locally observable* in case $Obs_i = States_i \cup Dist(Act_i)$ where $obs_i(\mathsf{s}) = \mathsf{s}|_i$ for any $\mathsf{s} \in \mathcal{S}$ and for all $\mu \in \mathcal{A}$ we have $obs_i(\mu)(a) = \mu(a)/\sum_{a \in Act_i} \mu(a)$ for $a \in Act_i$ and $obs_i(\mu)(a) = \varepsilon$ for $a \notin Act_i$. Intuitively, a purely local observation function observes only the local state of component α_i and the normalised action distribution on its local actions.

Partially Observable PIOS. We define *observation profiles* $\mathfrak{D}$ for $\mathcal{P}$ as tuples

$$\mathfrak{D} = (obs_1, \ldots, obs_n, obs)$$

where obs_i are local observation functions for each component α_i, $i \in \{1, \ldots, n\}$ as defined above, and obs is a global observation function. The tuple $\mathcal{Q} = (\mathcal{P}, \mathfrak{D})$ is called *partially observable PIOS (PO-PIOS)*.

Strategies for Partially Observable PIOSs. Let $(\mathcal{P}, \mathfrak{O})$ be a PO-PIOS with $\mathfrak{O} = (obs_1, \ldots, obs_n, obs_{intl})$. A *local strategy* for component α_i is a scheduler σ_i for $\llbracket \mathcal{P} \rrbracket$ where for all paths π in $\llbracket \mathcal{P} \rrbracket$ there is $(last(\pi)|_i, \mu) \in G_i$ such that $\sigma_i(\pi)(a) = \sum_{s \in States_i} \mu(a, s)$ for all $a \in Act_i$.

We also consider *interleaving strategies* for $\mathcal{P}$ as functions $\sigma_{intl} \colon Paths(\llbracket \mathcal{P} \rrbracket) \to Dist(\{1, \ldots, n\})$ where for each path π in $\llbracket \mathcal{P} \rrbracket$ with $\sigma_{intl}(\pi)(i) > 0$ there is some $\mu \in Dist(States_i \times Act_i)$ such that $(last(\pi)|_i, \mu) \in G_i$. An interleaving strategy σ_{intl} is *deterministic* if all distributions of σ_{intl} are Dirac. Intuitively, an interleaving strategy selects the component to choose the next move, i.e. for a path $\pi \in Paths(\llbracket \mathcal{P} \rrbracket)$ and $i \in \{1, \ldots, n\}$ the component α_i is scheduled with probability $\sigma_{intl}(\pi)(i)$ to select and perform one of its generative output transitions.

Strategy Profiles. We restrict our attention to those schedulers for $\llbracket \mathcal{P} \rrbracket$ that arise by composing an interleaving strategy σ_{intl} for $\mathcal{P}$ and local strategies σ_i for component α_i for all $i \in \{1, \ldots, n\}$. To formalise the composition for PO-PIOSs, i.e. also take observability into account, we define *strategy profiles* to be tuples

$$\mathfrak{P} = (\sigma_1, \ldots, \sigma_n, \sigma_{intl})$$

where σ_i is an obs_i-complying strategy for component α_i for each $i = \{1, \ldots, n\}$ and σ_{intl} is an obs_{intl}-complying interleaving strategy.

Strategy profiles can be understood as a class of observation-based schedulers for $\llbracket \mathcal{P} \rrbracket$. The scheduler $\mathfrak{S}_{\mathfrak{P}} \colon Paths(\llbracket \mathcal{P} \rrbracket) \to Dist(\mathcal{A})$ for $\llbracket \mathcal{P} \rrbracket$ induced by a strategy profile $\mathfrak{P}$ is a function that assigns to any finite path $\pi = s_0 \, t_0 \, s_1 \ldots t_{k-1} \, s_k$ in $\llbracket \mathcal{P} \rrbracket$ an action $a \in Act$ with probability

$$\mathfrak{S}_{\mathfrak{P}}(\pi)(a) = \sum_{i=1}^{n} \sigma_{intl}(\pi)(i) \cdot \sigma_i(\pi)(a).$$

We denote by $\mathrm{Pr}_{\mathcal{P}}^{\mathfrak{P}}$ the probability measure $\mathrm{Pr}_{\llbracket \mathcal{P} \rrbracket}^{\mathfrak{S}_{\mathfrak{P}}}$.

Remark 2 (On observability in [23]). For defining strategy profiles, we followed the approach of [23] by composing interleaving and local strategies, called "interleaving schedulers" and "output schedulers". The class of observation-based schedulers $\mathfrak{S}_{\mathfrak{P}}$ that arises from strategy profiles $\mathfrak{P}$ for PO-PIOS where the global observation function provides total observability and local observation functions are purely locally observable is similar however not equivalent to the class of *distributed schedulers*. The restricted class of *strongly distributed schedulers* that imposes constraints on the component distribution of interleaving schedulers corresponds to variants of $\mathfrak{S}_{\mathfrak{P}}$ where the global observation function is not totally observable. ∎

Remark 3 (Observability by the interleaving strategy). It appears reasonable to assume that interleaving strategies have access to the local information available to the components. Formally,

- if $s, s' \in S$ such that $obs_{intl}(s) = obs_{intl}(s') \neq \varepsilon$ then $obs_i(s) = obs_i(s')$ for all $i \in \{1, \ldots, n\}$, and
- if $a, a' \in A$ such that $obs_{intl}(a) = obs_{intl}(a') \neq \varepsilon$ then $obs_i(a) = obs_i(a')$ for all $i \in \{1, \ldots, n\}$. ∎

3 Notions of Suitability

We now turn our attention to the question of how far some component κ can be considered suitable to use in combination with a given system. For this, let us consider a fixed PO-PIOS $\mathcal{Q} = (\mathcal{P}, \mathfrak{O})$ where $\mathcal{P} = (\alpha_1, \ldots, \alpha_n)$ is a PIOS with observation profile $\mathfrak{O} = (obs_1, \ldots, obs_n, obs_{intl})$. Furthermore, we follow the convention of the last section, denoting by $\mathfrak{P}$ a not necessarily fixed strategy profile for $\mathcal{Q}$. For any fresh component κ not contained in $\mathcal{P}$ we assume furthermore an observability function obs_κ and denote by $\kappa \| \mathcal{Q}$ the PO-PIOS $((\kappa, \mathcal{P}), (obs_\kappa, \mathfrak{O}))$.

Properties and Their Values. In what follows, suppose that we are given a set Φ of properties or quantitative measures (e.g. defined using some temporal logics). For the definition of suitability notions, the type and syntax of these properties is irrelevant as we shall take an abstract view and deal with *valuation functions* $val^{\mathfrak{P}} : \Phi \to \mathbb{R}$ for strategy profiles $\mathfrak{P}$ for $\mathcal{Q}$.

Example 1. We exemplify several variants for value functions:

(i) If ϕ is a (P)CTL-like state property, then $val^{\mathfrak{P}}(\phi)$ could be defined as Boolean value not directly depending on $\mathfrak{P}$, i.e. 1 ("true") if $s_0 \models \phi$ in $[\![\mathcal{P}]\!]$ and 0 ("false") otherwise. In case ϕ is a PCTL property, the semantics of the probability operator could be restricted to range over all strategy profiles only, rather than over arbitrary schedulers for the MDP $[\![\mathcal{P}]\!]$.

(ii) If ϕ is an LTL formula or more generally an ω-regular path property, then $val^{\mathfrak{P}}(\phi)$ could be $\mathrm{Pr}_{\mathcal{Q}}^{\mathfrak{P}}(\phi)$, the probability of the set of infinite paths that satisfy ϕ under the probability measure induced by $\mathfrak{S}_{\mathfrak{P}}$.

(iii) If ϕ is a random variable of type $IPaths([\![\mathcal{P}]\!]) \to \mathbb{R}$, then $val^{\mathfrak{P}}(\phi)$ could be the expectation of ϕ on $\mathfrak{S}_{\mathfrak{P}}$-paths in $[\![\mathcal{P}]\!]$. This, of course, requires a side constraint to ensure the existence of the expectation or a default value if the expectation does not exist. Examples for such random variables are the accumulated weight until reaching a target state set, or the mean payoff when weights are attached to the transitions of $[\![\mathcal{P}]\!]$. ∎

To ease the notations that follow, we suppose that high satisfaction values are desirable in the sense that the objective is to increase values $val^{\mathfrak{P}}(\phi)$ of properties $\phi \in \Phi$ whenever possible. Furthermore, when analysing multiple objectives, we might annotate the kind of valuation function on the property. For instance, we allow for a property set $\Phi = \{\mathsf{P}(ok \mathsf{U} goal), \mathsf{E}[cost](\Diamond goal)\}$ to describe that the LTL formula $ok \mathsf{U} goal$ and $\Diamond goal$ should be evaluated with respect to their probability $\mathrm{Pr}_{\mathcal{Q}}^{\mathfrak{P}}(ok \mathsf{U} goal)$ and expected costs $\mathrm{Exp}_{\mathcal{Q}}^{\mathfrak{P}}(\Diamond goal)$, respectively.

Remark 4. Note that if instead one aims at minimising objectives regarding a state or path property ϕ one can switch to its complement $\neg\phi$ and consider the maximising objective instead. Likewise, in a weighted setting with accumulated, discounted, or instantaneous weights, weights can be multiplied by -1 turning the meaning of weights to costs to be paid rather than rewards to be earned. ■

Remark 5 (Observation-compatible properties). It appears natural to assume that the properties fit with the observations, in the sense that if ϕ is a path property then ϕ does not distinguish between paths with identical observations. Formally, for $\pi_1, \pi_2 \in IPaths(\llbracket \mathcal{P} \rrbracket)$ with $obs_i(\pi_1) = obs_i(\pi_2)$ for $i \in \{1, \dots, n\} \cup \{intl\}$ and $\pi_1 \models \phi$, then $\pi_2 \models \phi$. Similarly, if ϕ is a random variable formalising a reward to be earned along paths one might require that paths with the same observation have the same value under ϕ. ■

3.1   Threshold Suitability

We are now in the position to propose formal criteria for a component β to be suitable in the context of other components. Suitability of β and $\mathcal{Q}$ is defined by imposing conditions on the PO-PIOS $\beta \| \mathcal{Q}$.

Definition 5 (Universal Threshold Suitability (∀TS)). *Let Φ be a set of properties with a valuation function for the PO-PIOS $\beta \| \mathcal{Q}$ and let $\vartheta = (\vartheta_\phi)_{\phi \in \Phi}$ be a real vector assigning a threshold value for each property $\phi \in \Phi$. β and $\mathcal{Q}$ are said to be* universally threshold-suitable *with respect to (Φ, ϑ) if for all strategy profiles $\mathfrak{P}$ for $\beta \| \mathcal{Q}$ and for each property $\phi \in \Phi$ we have*

$$val^{\mathfrak{P}}(\phi) \; > \; \vartheta_\phi.$$

In a nutshell, the definition says that $\beta \| \mathcal{Q}$ will meet all the criteria being part of $val^{\mathfrak{P}}(\cdot)$ regardless of what happens to the system, in terms of the strategy profiles imaginable. An alternative definition arises when β has the freedom to choose its strategy depending on the decisions of global control and other components.

Definition 6 (Existential Threshold Suitability (∃TS)). *Let Φ be a set of properties with a valuation function for the PO-PIOS $\beta \| \mathcal{Q}$ and let $\vartheta = (\vartheta_\phi)_{\phi \in \Phi}$ be a real vector assigning a threshold value for each property $\phi \in \Phi$. Then, β and $\mathcal{Q}$ are said to be* existentially threshold-suitable *with respect to (Φ, ϑ) if*

for all obs_i-complying strategies σ_i for α_i, $i \in \{1, \dots, n\}$ and
for all obs_{intl}-complying interleaving strategies σ_{intl}
there exists an obs_β-complying strategy σ_β for β

such that with $\mathfrak{P} = (\sigma_\beta, \sigma_1, \dots, \sigma_n, \sigma_{intl})$ for each property $\phi \in \Phi$ we have

$$val^{\mathfrak{P}}(\phi) \; > \; \vartheta_\phi.$$

A practical example for threshold suitability are *Real Driving Emissions* (RDE) tests where it is required that the amount of emitted pollutants is below certain thresholds for all reasonable driver behaviours [28]. In terms of threshold suitability, a driver behaviour corresponds to a strategy and the system could constrain nondeterministic choices to those that are reasonable as required. Universal threshold suitability then asks whether the emitted pollutants are below their respective thresholds for all possible RDE tests as required by the RDE regulation. In contrast, existential threshold suitability asks whether it is possible to pass an individual test by driving accordingly.

3.2   Degree of Suitability

To provide a more fine-grained mechanism to quantify how suitable components behave, we go beyond the simple discrimination discussed thus far, i.e. whether or not they are suitable. For this, we introduce measures of *degrees of suitability*, which rely on an aggregation function $f \colon \mathbb{R}^\Phi \to \mathbb{R} \cup \{\pm\infty\}$ for the potential satisfaction values of properties. Here, $\mathbb{R}^\Phi$ stands for the set of real-valued vectors $(v_\phi)_{\phi \in \Phi}$ over a set of properties Φ.

Example 2 Typical candidates for an aggregation function f are:

(i) Weighted sums $f(v) = \sum_{\phi \in \Phi} w_\phi \cdot v_\phi$ of the individual satisfaction values defined over vectors $v = (v_\phi)_{\phi \in \Phi}$ for a finite set of properties Φ. This corresponds to the switch to a composite valuation function

$$(\mathfrak{P}, \Phi) \mapsto \sum_{\phi \in \Phi} w_\phi \cdot val^{\mathfrak{P}}(\phi)$$

(ii) The valuation function of a (single) distinguished property $\psi \in \Phi$ under threshold conditions for the values for all other properties, and $-\infty$ otherwise. That is:

$$f(v) = \begin{cases} v_\psi & \text{if } v_\phi > \vartheta_\phi \text{ for all } \phi \in \Phi \setminus \{\psi\} \\ -\infty & \text{otherwise} \end{cases}$$

where ϑ_ϕ are thresholds as in Definition 5 or Definition 6.

(iii) Combinations of (i) and (ii).

In practical situations, the latter are all but uncommon. For instance, when consumer organisations like the Dutch *Consumentenbond* and the German *Stifung Warentest* [1] carry out safety tests of consumer products, it is very common to have some criteria where a certain threshold must be met in order to be considered eligible, and that the other criteria are weighted with percentages and mapped into a scalar of normed range. This principle is also behind the European car safety performance assessment programme *EuroNCAP* [2].   ■

Definition 7 (Universal Degree of Suitability ($\forall$DS)**).** *Let Φ be a set of properties with a valuation function for the PO-PIOS $\beta \| \mathcal{Q}$ and let $f \colon \mathbb{R}^\Phi \to \mathbb{R} \cup \{\pm\infty\}$ be an aggregation function. Then, the universal degree of suitability of β with respect to $\mathcal{Q}$ is defined as*

$$\inf_{\mathfrak{P}} \ f\Big(\big(val^{\mathfrak{P}}(\phi) \big)_{\phi \in \Phi} \Big)$$

where the infimum ranges over all strategy profiles $\mathfrak{P}$ for $\beta \| \mathcal{Q}$.

As in the case for threshold suitability, we also present an existential version of suitability degrees where component β has the freedom of choosing a strategy depending on the interleaving strategy and local strategies of other components.

Definition 8 (Existential Degree of Suitability ($\exists$DS)). *Let Φ be a set of properties with a valuation function for the PO-PIOS $\beta\|\mathcal{Q}$ and let $f\colon \mathbb{R}^\Phi \to \mathbb{R} \cup \{\pm\infty\}$ be an aggregation function. Then, the* existential degree of suitability *of β with respect to $\mathcal{Q}$ is defined as*

$$\sup_{\sigma_\beta} \inf_{\mathfrak{P}[\beta]} f\Big(\big(val^{\mathfrak{P}[\beta]}(\phi)\big)_{\phi\in\Phi} \Big)$$

where the supremum ranges over all obs_β-complying strategies σ_β for β and the infimum ranges over all strategy profiles $\mathfrak{P}[\beta] = (\sigma_\beta, \sigma_1, \ldots, \sigma_n, \sigma_{intl})$ for $\beta\|\mathcal{Q}$.

It is conceivable to combine both of the above notions in a weighted setting, but we do not spell out the details here. For instance, one may be interested in the average emissions in the best and the worst case.

3.3 Suitability Relations

We now consider two composite PO-PIOS $\beta\|\mathcal{Q}$ and $\gamma\|\mathcal{Q}$ and introduce formal notions that spell out in what sense β is *more suitable* than γ when running in the context of $\mathcal{Q}$ with respect to a given set Φ of properties with valuation functions $val^{\mathfrak{P}}\colon \Phi \to \mathbb{R}$ and aggregation functions $f\colon \mathbb{R}^\Phi \to \mathbb{R} \cup \{\pm\infty\}$ for both $\beta\|\mathcal{Q}$ and $\gamma\|\mathcal{Q}$. Although β and γ can have different observables, we suppose here that all the corresponding observation functions of $\beta\|\mathcal{Q}$ and $\gamma\|\mathcal{Q}$ coincide. Furthermore, we assume the following requirements for the observation functions of $\kappa\|\mathcal{Q}$, $\kappa \in \{\beta, \gamma\}$:

(Loc) We assume that the components of $\mathcal{Q}$ do not have information on the local states of κ in the sense that the observable of global state $(s_\kappa, s_1, \ldots, s_n)$ in $[\![\kappa\|\mathcal{Q}]\!]$ only depends on $(s_1, \ldots, s_n)$ but not on s_κ. Likewise, we suppose that actions in $Act_\kappa \setminus Act_i$ are invisible for all α_i, $i = 1, \ldots, n$.

(Intl) Global observation functions for $\kappa\|\mathcal{Q}$ do not have access to the local state of κ and cannot see the actions in $(Act_\beta \setminus Act_\gamma) \cup (Act_\gamma \setminus Act_\beta)$. Formally,

- $obs_{intl}(s_\kappa, s_1, \ldots, s_n) = obs_{intl}(s'_\kappa, s_1, \ldots, s_n)$ for all states $s_\kappa, s'_\kappa \in States_\kappa$ and $s_i \in States_i$ for $i = 1, \ldots, n$, and
- $obs_{intl}(a) = \varepsilon$ for each action $a \in (Act_\beta \setminus Act_\gamma) \cup (Act_\gamma \setminus Act_\beta)$.

Assumption **Loc** implies that if $\mathcal{P} = (\alpha_1, \ldots, \alpha_n)$ then any obs_i-complying strategy for α_i in $\beta\|\mathcal{P}$ is also an obs_i-complying strategy for α_i in $\gamma\|\mathcal{P}$, and vice versa. Note that here, we regard strategies as functions that take as input an observation sequence. Assumption **Intl** ensures that $\beta\|\mathcal{Q}$ and $\gamma\|\mathcal{Q}$ have the same interleaving strategies. While assumption **Loc** is a fairly natural and standard assumption in the partial information setting, assumption **Intl** appears technically rather strong. In an exemplary setting, **Loc** means that when testing the performance of two cars, we do not exploit that one of them offers the possibility to turn on and off "boost mode" while the other one does not. **Intl** then corresponds to the idea that the behaviour considered relevant is observed from the outside, and does not refer to particularities of the components to be compared, such as a warning light only available in one of the cars.

Definition 9 (Universally More Suitable ($\forall$MS)). *Let Φ be a set of properties with a valuation function for the PO-PIOS $\beta\|Q$ and let $f\colon \mathbb{R}^\Phi \to \mathbb{R} \cup \{\pm\infty\}$ be an aggregation function. Under the assumptions **Loc** and **Intl**, β is said to be* universally more suitable *than γ if for all strategy profiles $\mathfrak{P}[\gamma] = (\sigma_\gamma, \sigma_1, \ldots, \sigma_n, \sigma_{intl})$ for $\gamma\|Q$ and for all obs_β-complying strategies σ_β for β we have*

$$f\left(\left(val^{\mathfrak{P}[\beta]}(\phi)\right)_{\phi\in\Phi} \right) \;>\; f\left(\left(val^{\mathfrak{P}[\gamma]}(\phi)\right)_{\phi\in\Phi} \right)$$

where $\mathfrak{P}[\beta] = (\sigma_\beta, \sigma_1, \ldots, \sigma_n, \sigma_{intl})$.

Note that due to the assumption **Intl**, for any obs_β-complying strategy for β we have that $\mathfrak{P}[\beta]$ is indeed a strategy profile for $\beta\|Q$. Intuitively, a component β is universally more suitable than γ if for all strategy profiles $\mathfrak{P}[\beta]$ for $\beta\|Q$, we cannot find a local strategy σ_γ for γ that leads to a higher degree of suitability in $\gamma\|Q$ when replacing σ_β in $\mathfrak{P}[\beta]$ by σ_γ.

Similar as for the notions of threshold suitability and the degrees of suitability, we also introduce an existential version of the "more suitable" relation that allows σ_β to react on behaviour imposed by σ_γ.

Definition 10 (Existentially More Suitable $\exists$MS). *Let Φ be a set of properties with a valuation function for the PO-PIOS $\beta\|Q$ and let $f\colon \mathbb{R}^\Phi \to \mathbb{R} \cup \{\pm\infty\}$ be an aggregation function. Under the assumptions **Loc** and **Intl**, β is said to be* existentially more suitable *than γ if for all strategy profiles $\mathfrak{P}[\gamma] = (\sigma_\gamma, \sigma_1, \ldots, \sigma_n, \sigma_{intl})$ for $\gamma\|Q$ there is an obs_β-complying strategy for β such that*

$$f\left(\left(val^{\mathfrak{P}[\beta]}(\phi)\right)_{\phi\in\Phi} \right) \;>\; f\left(\left(val^{\mathfrak{P}[\gamma]}(\phi)\right)_{\phi\in\Phi} \right)$$

where $\mathfrak{P}[\beta] = (\sigma_\beta, \sigma_1, \ldots, \sigma_n, \sigma_{intl})$.

To determine the $\forall$MS- and $\exists$MS-relations provided in Definitions 9 and 10, we have to evaluate aggregated valuations with respect to an observation-based scheduler for both, $[\![\beta\|Q]\!]$ and $[\![\gamma\|Q]\!]$. Since this might require more involved analysis techniques, an independent analysis of $[\![\beta\|Q]\!]$ and $[\![\gamma\|Q]\!]$ towards deriving a more strict notion of suitability is desirable.

Definition 11 (Strictly More Suitable (SMS)). *Let Φ be a set of properties with a valuation function for the PO-PIOS $\beta\|Q$ and let $f\colon \mathbb{R}^\Phi \to \mathbb{R} \cup \{\pm\infty\}$ be an aggregation function. Then, β is said to be* strictly more suitable *than γ if*

$$\inf_{\mathfrak{P}[\beta]} f\left(\left(val^{\mathfrak{P}[\beta]}(\phi)\right)_{\phi\in\Phi} \right) \;>\; \sup_{\mathfrak{P}[\gamma]} f\left(\left(val^{\mathfrak{P}[\gamma]}(\phi)\right)_{\phi\in\Phi} \right)$$

where the infimum ranges over all strategy profiles $\mathfrak{P}[\beta]$ for $\beta\|Q$ and the supremum ranges over all strategy profiles $\mathfrak{P}[\gamma]$ for $\gamma\|Q$.

Note that if β is strictly more suitable than γ, then β is also universally and existentially more suitable than γ.

4   Suitability Analysis

We now turn to the algorithmic side of the definitions proposed. Assume we are given an input PO-PIOS $\mathcal{Q} = (\mathcal{P}, \mathfrak{O})$, two components β and γ, a set of properties Φ with a valuation function $val^{\mathfrak{P}} \colon \Phi \to \mathbb{R}$, and an aggregation function $f \colon \mathbb{R}^{\Phi} \to \mathbb{R} \cup \{\pm\infty\}$. Then we consider the following decision problems:

(a) For a threshold vector $\vartheta = (\vartheta_{\phi})_{\phi \in \Phi}$ decide whether β and $\mathcal{Q}$ are threshold suitable with respect to (Φ, ϑ) as defined in Definitions 5 and 6.
(b) For a threshold $\vartheta \in \mathbb{R}$ decide whether the suitability degree of β with respect to $\mathcal{Q}$ exceeds ϑ for notions defined in Definitions 7 and 8.
(c) Decide whether β is more suitable than γ with respect to $\mathcal{Q}$ as defined in Definitions 9, 10, and 11.

In the sequel, we provide positive and negative answers for the above decision problems. Due to the lack of space, we moved full proofs to the appendix.

Theorem 1. *The problems (a)–(c) are undecidable for all valuation functions of Example 1 and all aggregation functions of Example 2.*

Due to the above theorem, one has to consider restrictions of strategy profiles, PO-PIOSs, and/or valuation functions in order to enable the analysis of suitability notions. A natural candidate for a restriction would be to only consider strategy profiles that are composed of strategies whose decisions can be represented as a finite-state machine. Existing results on IPIOAs [23] suggest that this direction is indeed worth to consider. In this paper, we do not a priori restrict the class of schedulers, but restrict the PO-PIOSs making up the system.

Threshold and Degree of Suitability Analysis. We arrive at a positive decidability result by restricting to total observation.

Proposition 1. *For all valuation functions of Example 1 and all aggregation functions of Example 2, problems (a) and (b) are decidable if all observation functions in the observation profile of $\beta \| \mathcal{Q}$ are totally observable.*

The above proposition relies on the fact that the class of observation-based schedulers $\mathfrak{S}_{\mathfrak{P}}$ for observation profiles consisting of totally observable observation functions in $\beta \| \mathcal{Q}$ coincides with the full class of schedulers for $[\![\beta \| \mathcal{Q}]\!]$. Thus, threshold suitability and deciding degree of suitability questions boil down to multi-objective analysis tasks for MDPs [12, 19, 21] in case of universal notions of suitability and $2\frac{1}{2}$-player games in case of existential notions of suitability [13].

More Suitable Relation Analysis. For problem (c), totally observable observation functions in observation profiles violate conditions (**Loc**) and (**Intl**), such that we present different conditions to provide decidability.

Proposition 2. *For all valuation functions of Example 1 and all aggregation functions of Example 2, problems (a)–(c) are decidable if*

(i) all components in $\mathcal{Q}$ are not containing any generative input transition, and
(ii) the observation function for β, respectively γ, in the observation profile of $\beta\|\mathcal{Q}$, respectively $\gamma\|\mathcal{Q}$, is totally observable.

Due to (i), β and γ contain all generative input transitions and the interleaving strategies for $\beta\|\mathcal{Q}$ and $\gamma\|\mathcal{Q}$ agree in the sense that they are independent from the global state, always picking component β, respectively γ, to perform the next move. To this end, the only nondeterminism in the composite system stems from the components β or γ, respectively. In combination with condition (ii), solving problem (c) reduces to multi-objective analysis tasks for MDPs [12,19,21].

5   Racetrack – A Case Study

In this section, we explain and illustrate the applicability of the theoretical concepts discussed above by means of a simple scenario known as *Racetrack* [22]. For the fragment that can be reduced to standard methods for MDPs, we present initial experimental results obtained with PRISM [29]. The tooling as well as the obtained results are made available for download[1]. The computation of the results shown in this section took less than 40 min on a standard laptop.

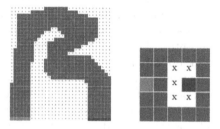

Fig. 1. Two example maps with start line in green, goals in red, and walls marked with **x**. (Color figure online)

5.1   Racetrack Scenario

Originally, Racetrack is a pen and paper game [22], comprising a *vehicle* which has to manoeuvre through a given two-dimensional discrete *track* with a designated start and goal, walls on the boundaries, and barriers on the track. The vehicle starts with no initial velocity from a starting position, with the objective to reach the goal as fast as possible without crashing into a wall or barrier. We extend this setting with costs for time steps, fuel consumption and CO_2-emission yielding a trade-off between costs and reaching the goal fast. To this end, the *driver* modifies the current velocity vector by means of acceleration and steering actions. Apart from those nondeterministic actions, we extend our setting

---

[1] https://doi.org/10.5281/zenodo.3970766 [6].

to a probabilistic environment such that actions may fail with a certain probability. We obtain a PIOS-based model with MDP semantics that allows, e.g. emulating slippery road conditions, where the driver's action may not induce the intended change in the velocity or direction. As a consequence, the vehicle will be unable to almost surely reach the goal, even when considering the best driver (namely a maximising scheduler for the underlying MDP). Stochastic variants of the racetrack scenario have traditionally served as benchmarks for MDP algorithms in the AI community [9,10,36] and lately also considered in the context of statistical model checking [25].

For our case study, we generalised the racetrack scenario by choosing a feature-oriented modelling approach [4,5] in the probabilistic variant introduced in [15,18]. To this end, features encapsulate the behavioural descriptions and characteristics for different road conditions (in the following: tarmac, sand, and ice), tank sizes (here: small, medium, large) with different fuel capacities, and engine variants, which are characterised by a maximal velocity v_{max} and maximal acceleration a_{max} (here as values from the set $\{1, 2, 3\}$). This feature model then gives rise to an entire family of PIOS (rather than just one) with three components: the *engine*, the *tank*, and the *map*. In our case we end up with $3^4 = 81$ family members, standing for separate models for each setting. The engine component controls the acceleration and thereby the speed of the car by generative input transitions corresponding to acceleration changes. A driver is in control of the car by selecting acceleration actions in x- and y-dimension. The tank updates its fuel level in reaction to the engine's acceleration decisions and gets trapped in a failure state once all fuel is entirely used up. Note that PIOS components have to be input-enabled and, hence, the tank has to be able to react to all acceleration decisions independent on whether there is enough fuel left for the required acceleration change. Finally, the map models the terrain as a grid with fixed road conditions and with starting cells, road cells, barrier cells and goal cells. Throughout this section we use a tiny map of size 5×5 as depicted on the right of Fig. 1, which is included in the available artefacts. Depending on the drivers choices, i.e. in reaction to the engine's generative transitions, the map then updates the car's position on the track under the given road conditions. As the engine is the only generative component in this setting, our assumptions with regard to the case study are fulfilled and the system is completely determined by the driver's strategy for the engine. Following the decidability result of Proposition 2, this allows to use existing tooling for the analysis of MDPs.

5.2   A New Car

Imagine that we would like to purchase a new car which we primarily need to drive to the office every day. Hence, the map and in particular the possible routes to the office are fixed, while the road conditions may vary from day to day. Now, the car salesman asks us which tank and engine variant we would like to purchase. Obviously, we want to configure our new car such that it suits our needs and here our suitability notions come into play. To apply them, we first have to fix a context $\mathcal{Q}$ and decide on the component(s) for which we would like to analyse suitability. Assume that we already decided that we would like a medium sized tank, but we are still uncertain about the engine variant. Hence, we are interested in the suitability of engine variants. Notably, this scenario entails that the road conditions are part of the fixed context as well. However, we can still carry out the analysis for different contexts to cover threshold suitability. For instance, in case we are interested in whether a particular engine variant is threshold suitable for all road conditions.

Threshold Suitability. Threshold suitability allows us to define *minimal requirements* for our new car. Imagine that we would like the probability of reaching our office (without running out of fuel or crashing into walls or barriers) to be at least 0.55. At the same time, we want the expected number of time steps to be less than 20, the expected fuel consumption to be less than 39 and the expected CO_2-emission to be less than 35. Formally, these requirements manifest in the set of properties

$$\Phi = \{ \ \mathsf{P}(status\_ok \,\mathsf{U}\, office), \ \mathsf{E}[timesteps](\Diamond\, office),$$
$$\mathsf{E}[fuel](\Diamond\, office), \ \mathsf{E}[CO_2](\Diamond\, office) \ \}$$

and respective thresholds ϑ_ϕ for each property.

Threshold suitability allows us to decide whether a car with a particular engine variant β as characterised by a maximal velocity $v_{\max}$ and acceleration $a_{\max}$ fulfils these thresholds in context Q by considering $\beta \| Q$. As $(\forall TS)$ quantifies over all strategy profiles and β is nondeterministic with regard to the acceleration vector, it tells us whether the thresholds will be satisfied independent of the driver, i.e. it essentially assumes the worst possible driver. In contrast, $(\exists TS)$ merely requires that there exists a strategy profile for which all thresholds are satisfied and thereby assumes the best possible driver. Intuitively $(\forall TS)$ is not particularly helpful in our case as even with the best car, the worst possible driver can waste all fuel driving in circles, never reaching the office. The same phenomenon also applies to the other notions of universal suitability.

For our analysis we considered all engine variants with $a_{\max}, v_{\max} \in \{1, 2, 3\}$ on sand and on tarmac with a medium sized tank. For all variants we computed a multi-objective with a lower bound on reaching the goal without crashing and upper bounds on the expected fuel consumption, time steps and CO_2-emission. We refer to Sect. 5.3 for the technical details of the multi-objective analysis. From the analysis we can conclude that all engine variants with $a_{\max} = 1$ are existentially threshold suitable on sand, while all the others are not. On tarmac, however, all engine variants with $a_{\max} \in \{1, 2\}$ are existentially threshold suitable while all the others, i.e. with $a_{\max} = 3$, are not. If we would like to go off-road with our car we should thus purchase a car with an engine variant satisfying $a_{\max} = 1$. Otherwise, every engine variant with $a_{\max} \in \{1, 2\}$ is just fine. The full result, including the numbers for icy road conditions are included in the available artifacts.

Degree of Suitability. While threshold suitability is a purely qualitative notion, the degree of suitability provides a quantitative measure. Coming back to our example, multiple engine variants meet our minimal requirements as set by our thresholds, however, one of them may for instance be more fuel efficient than the others. Here suitability degrees come into play.

To apply (∃DS) and (∀DS) we first need to specify an aggregation function combining the values for the different properties into a single value depending on our requirements. Assume that it is more important for us to save time than it is to preserve fuel and that it is more important for us to preserve fuel than to emit less CO_2. In this case, we may define an aggregation function f as a weighted sum giving weight -50 to the time it takes, -30 to the fuel consumption, and -20 to the CO_2 emissions with the set of properties being:

$$\Phi = \{ \; \mathsf{E}[timesteps](\lozenge office), \; \mathsf{E}[fuel](\lozenge office), \; \mathsf{E}[CO_2](\lozenge office) \; \}.$$

Note that we weighted all properties with negative values as all these properties are subject to minimisation (cf. Remark 4). Analogously to threshold suitability, (∀DS) and (∃DS) provide a suitability degree assuming the worst, respectively best, driver behaviour.

For tarmac and the medium sized tank we determined the following suitability degrees: if $a_{max} = 1$ then the suitability degree is -1450, if $a_{max} = 2$ then the suitability degree is -1900, and if $a_{max} = 3$ then the suitability degree is -2350. This is explained by the fact that an engine with a higher a_{max} is assumed to consume more fuel than a weaker engine. While all engine variants with $a_{max} \in \{1, 2\}$ are existentially threshold suitable for tarmac, the engines with $a_{max} = 1$ are more economical. Hence, we conclude that we should purchase a car with $a_{max} = 1$. The technical details can again be found in Sect. 5.3.

More Suitable Relations. In addition to the already discussed notions of suitability, we defined *more suitable* relations that directly compare two variants. While one may use suitability degrees to compare two engine variants, this assumes the worst respectively best driver behaviour for both variants. Instead, the *more suitable* relations compare the worst strategy profile for one component with the best for the other (cf. Definition 9) or, as a more relaxed existential notion, the best component behaviour assuming the worst system behaviour with the best strategy profile for the other component (cf. Definition 10). We are not aware of tool support for these notions.

The strict variation (cf. Definition 11) is merely a comparison of the best degree for one component with the worst degree for the other. Specifically, the worst degree will always be $-\infty$ because the worst driver can just drive in a circle. Hence, while easier to analyse, this notion of suitability is too coarse for our example. The result would be that no engine variant is strictly dominating.

5.3   Implementation and Technical Aspects

We now present the technical details regarding the analysis for existential threshold suitability and degree of suitability as discussed in the previous section using standard methods for MDPs as provided by PRISM.

Threshold Suitability. Using PRISM's multi-objective engine [20] and manually translating the family of PIOS to their corresponding MDPs we were able to obtain experimental results for (∃TS) and using the following numerical multi-objective query:

```
multi(
  P>=PBound["ap_status_ok" U "ap_office"],
  R{"fuel"}<=FBound[C], R{"timesteps"}<=TBound[C],
  R{"CO2"}<=CBound[C]
);
```

Note that in the above query, we used non-strict bounds on the valuation functions as opposed to our theoretical framework. This is due to the current tool support provided by PRISM. Furthermore, encoding (∃TS) into a numerical multi-objective query required us to switch from the expected reachability rewards to total accumulated rewards, as expected rewards are not yet supported by the multi-objective engine. This change is reasonable, because the total accumulated rewards are all finite due to the fact that the number of time steps is bounded until the car can no longer move and one ends up in a trap state where no further reward is gained. Furthermore, the goal states, when the office is reached and the car stops, and the crashed states enjoy this property. Also the actual bounds used within the total reward properties can be scaled with a factor PBound. This is due to the fact that the multi-objective engine computes optimal weights for each property and the computed scheduler is in fact a randomised scheduler that balances out the individual objectives. Hence, the upper bounds for the total expected costs (fuel and CO_2) used within the multi-objective query were scaled down by multiplying with PBound and rounding.

While (∀TS) does not seem to be as important as (∃TS) in our case study, let us note that there is tool support by PRISM to decide (∀TS) for our set of properties. For this, one can solve (∀TS) by considering a dual problem on multiple (∃TS) questions of single properties [21].

Degree of Suitability. To the best of our knowledge, there exists no tool support for aggregating and weighting properties over a particular scheduler and then searching for a scheduler which minimises respectively maximises this aggregation. But in case of probability and expectation properties, we can transform the model from a multi-reward into a single-reward model by pulling inwards the aggregation function, so that we arrive at weighted sums as rewards on edges. This is justified by the distributivity law, and results in the following transition reward structure:

```
reward "wsum" := (50 * c_timestep) + (30 * f_fuel_consumption)
                                   + (20 * f_co2_production)
```

Note that we switched here to positive weights, because PRISM hardly supports negative rewards. Now, by computing the minimal expected reward for finally reaching the goal, we compute how *unsuitable* the system is in the best case. In the end, we have to invert the result in order to obtain the actual existential suitability degree as specified with the negative weights above. Please note that the expected reachability reward will be ∞ for all soils different from tarmac, as the probability of reaching the goal is strictly less than one.

Feature-Oriented Analysis and Scalability. Using our feature-based modelling approach, the analysis for different contexts could be in principle carried out separately one-by-one per context or in a single run by means of an all-in-one analysis [4,15,16,39]. The latter relies on our family model that encodes all settings in a single model. It is well known (see, e.g. [16,17,39]) that all-in-one approaches can mitigate the exponential blowup of feature combinations in the number of features by exploiting similarities of behaviours within different settings using symbolic analysis techniques such as implemented in PRISM's MTBDD engine. However, as the current implementation of PRISM to analyse multi-objective properties does not fully support family models and symbolic engines, we had to follow a one-by-one analysis approach to compute results for different notions of suitability. The lack of such a support is also the reason why we used a comparably small case-study setup with the 5x5 map shown on the right of Fig. 1. The map on the left of Fig. 1 is an example of realistically sized map that is also considered in the automated planning community [9]. Here, the PRISM family model contained $6 \cdot 81 = 486$ family members and led to a model with more than $1.1 \cdot 10^9$ states. As this model could not be explicitly represented in memory, we considered a symbolic representation with $1.4 \cdot 10^6$ MTBDD nodes.[2] Using PRISM's MTBDD engine applied on the family model, an all-in-one analysis of single-objective threshold suitability was possible for this larger map, checking ($\forall$TS) for $\Phi = \{\mathsf{P}(status\_ok \mathsf{U} office)\}$ with $\vartheta_\Phi = 0.35$ in less than 14 min, equivalent to about 10 s per configuration. A corresponding one-by-one analysis required around 10 h in total, i.e. in average more than 7 min per configuration. This comparison shows the potential of our feature-based modelling and analysis approach.

6   Concluding Remarks

This paper has introduced notions formalising the suitability of components in the context of probabilistic systems given as PO-PIOSs. We presented undecidability results for the general case of suitability notions and established decidability for restricted classes of PO-PIOSs that we used in our case study. Further positive results on suitability notions could be expected with respect to restricted classes of strategy profiles, e.g. where all strategies in a profile are finite-memory strategies [23].

Many facets of these suitability notions can be seen as future work. The definitions presented rely on strict comparisons in the case of threshold suitability and "more suitable" formalisations. Instead one may also consider relations that implement "at least as suitable", i.e. replace the strict comparison $>$ relation by

---

[2] Also exploiting variable-reordering techniques from [27] on the generated model.

$\geqslant$ in our formal definitions. For this, it is an open question whether threshold suitability is decidable for simple valuation functions. In addition, further kinds of valuation and aggregation functions could be investigated, e.g. by including energy-utility trade-offs into the measure of suitability or rely on conditional probabilities and expectations [7].

On the evaluation and practical side, an implementation of the multi-objective engine of PRISM supporting family models would enable to exploit the benefits of our family-based approach towards an all-in-one suitability analysis.

References

1. Test-ablauf - So testet die Stiftung Warentest. https://www.test.de/unternehmen/testablauf-5017344-0/. Accessed 30 June 2020
2. The Official Site of The European New Car Assessment Programme. https://www.euroncap.com/en/. Accessed 30 June 2020
3. Alur, R.: Principles of Cyber-Physical Systems. The MIT Press, Cambridge (2015)
4. Apel, S., Batory, D., Kästner, C., Saake, G.: Feature-Oriented Software Product Lines: Concepts and Implementation. Springer, Heidelberg (2013). https://doi.org/10.1007/978-3-642-37521-7
5. Apel, S., Kästner, C.: An overview of feature-oriented software development. J. Object Technol. **8**, 49–84 (2009)
6. Baier, C., Dubslaff, C., Hermanns, H., Klauck, M., Klüppelholz, S., Köhl, M.A.: Tooling, Data and Results for "Components in Probabilistic Systems: Suitable by Construction" (2020). https://doi.org/10.5281/zenodo.3970766
7. Baier, C., Dubslaff, C., Klüppelholz, S.: Trade-off analysis meets probabilistic model checking. In: Proceedings of the 23rd Conference on Computer Science Logic and the 29th Symposium on Logic in Computer Science (CSL-LICS), pp. 1:1–1:10. ACM (2014)
8. Baier, C., Größer, M., Bertrand, N.: Probabilistic ω-automata. J. ACM **59**(1), 1:1–1:52 (2012)
9. Barto, A.G., Bradtke, S.J., Singh, S.P.: Learning to act using real-time dynamic programming. Artif. Intell. **72**(1–2), 81–138 (1995)
10. Bonet, B., Geffner, H.: Labeled RTDP: improving the convergence of real-time dynamic programming. In: ICAPS, pp. 12–21 (2003)
11. Canetti, R., et al.: Task-structured probabilistic I/O automata. J. Comput. Syst. Sci. **94**, 63–97 (2018). https://doi.org/10.1016/j.jcss.2017.09.007
12. Chatterjee, K., Majumdar, R., Henzinger, T.: Markov decision processes with multiple objectives. In: STACS, February 2006. http://chess.eecs.berkeley.edu/pubs/81.html
13. Chen, T., Forejt, V., Kwiatkowska, M., Simaitis, A., Wiltsche, C.: On stochastic games with multiple objectives. In: Chatterjee, K., Sgall, J. (eds.) MFCS 2013. LNCS, vol. 8087, pp. 266–277. Springer, Heidelberg (2013). https://doi.org/10.1007/978-3-642-40313-2_25
14. Cheung, L., Lynch, N.A., Segala, R., Vaandrager, F.W.: Switched PIOA: parallel composition via distributed scheduling. Theor. Comput. Sci. **365**(1–2), 83–108 (2006). https://doi.org/10.1016/j.tcs.2006.07.033
15. Chrszon, P., Dubslaff, C., Klüppelholz, S., Baier, C.: ProFeat: feature-oriented engineering for family-based probabilistic model checking. Formal Aspects Comput. **30**(1), 45–75 (2018). https://doi.org/10.1007/s00165-017-0432-4

16. Classen, A., Heymans, P., Schobbens, P.Y., Legay, A., Raskin, J.F.: Model checking lots of systems: efficient verification of temporal properties in software product lines. In: Proceedings of ICSE 2010, pp. 335–344. ACM (2010)

17. Czarnecki, K., Eisenecker, U.W.: Generative Programming: Methods, Tools, and Applications. ACM Press/Addison-Wesley Publishing Co., New York (2000)

18. Dubslaff, C., Baier, C., Klüppelholz, S.: Probabilistic model checking for feature-oriented systems. Trans. Aspect-Oriented Softw. Dev. **12**, 180–220 (2015). https://doi.org/10.1007/978-3-662-46734-3_5

19. Etessami, K., Kwiatkowska, M., Vardi, M., Yannakakis, M.: Multi-objective model checking of Markov decision processes. Log. Methods Comput. Sci. **4**(4), 1–21 (2008)

20. Forejt, V., Kwiatkowska, M., Parker, D.: Pareto curves for probabilistic model checking. In: Chakraborty, S., Mukund, M. (eds.) ATVA 2012. LNCS, pp. 317–332. Springer, Heidelberg (2012). https://doi.org/10.1007/978-3-642-33386-6_25

21. Forejt, V., Kwiatkowska, M.Z., Norman, G., Parker, D., Qu, H.: Quantitative multi-objective verification for probabilistic systems. In: Abdulla, P.A., Leino, K.R.M. (eds.) TACAS 2011. LNCS, vol. 6605, pp. 112–127. Springer, Heidelberg (2011). https://doi.org/10.1007/978-3-642-19835-9_11

22. Gardner, M.: Mathematical games. Sci. Am. **229**, 118–121 (1973)

23. Giro, S., D'Argenio, P.R., Fioriti, L.M.F.: Distributed probabilistic input/output automata: expressiveness, (un)decidability and algorithms. Theor. Comput. Sci. **538**, 84–102 (2014). https://doi.org/10.1016/j.tcs.2013.07.017. Quantitative Aspects of Programming Languages and Systems (2011–12)

24. van Glabbeek, R.J., Smolka, S.A., Steffen, B.: Reactive, generative and stratified models of probabilistic processes. Inf. Comput. **121**(1), 59–80 (1995). https://doi.org/10.1006/inco.1995.1123

25. Gros, T.P., Hermanns, H., Hoffmann, J., Klauck, M., Steinmetz, M.: Deep statistical model checking. In: Gotsman, A., Sokolova, A. (eds.) FORTE 2020. LNCS, vol. 12136, pp. 96–114. Springer, Cham (2020). https://doi.org/10.1007/978-3-030-50086-3_6

26. Hoare, C.A.R.: Communicating sequential processes. Commun. ACM **21**(8), 666–677 (1978). https://doi.org/10.1145/359576.359585

27. Klein, J., et al.: Advances in probabilistic model checking with PRISM: variable reordering, quantiles and weak deterministic Büchi automata. Int. J. Softw. Tools Technol. Transf. **20**(2), 179–194 (2017). https://doi.org/10.1007/s10009-017-0456-3

28. Köhl, M.A., Hermanns, H., Biewer, S.: Efficient monitoring of real driving emissions. In: Colombo, C., Leucker, M. (eds.) RV 2018. LNCS, vol. 11237, pp. 299–315. Springer, Cham (2018). https://doi.org/10.1007/978-3-030-03769-7_17

29. Kwiatkowska, M., Norman, G., Parker, D.: PRISM 4.0: verification of probabilistic real-time systems. In: Gopalakrishnan, G., Qadeer, S. (eds.) CAV 2011. LNCS, vol. 6806, pp. 585–591. Springer, Heidelberg (2011). https://doi.org/10.1007/978-3-642-22110-1_47

30. Lee, E.A.: Cyber physical systems: design challenges. In: 2008 11th IEEE International Symposium on Object and Component-Oriented Real-Time Distributed Computing (ISORC), pp. 363–369 (2008)

31. Lovejoy, W.S.: A survey of algorithmic methods for partially observable Markov decision processes. Ann. Oper. Res. **28**(1), 47–65 (1991)

32. Lynch, N., Tuttle, M.: An introduction to input/output automata. CWI Q. **2**(3), 219–246 (1989)

33. Madani, O., Hanks, S., Condon, A.: On the undecidability of probabilistic planning and related stochastic optimization problems. Artif. Intell. **147**(1–2), 5–34 (2003)
34. Milner, R.: Communication and Concurrency. PHI Series in Computer Science. Prentice Hall, Upper Saddle River (1989)
35. Papadimitriou, C., Tsitsiklis, J.: The complexity of Markov decision processes. Math. Oper. Res. **12**(3), 441–450 (1987)
36. Pineda, L.E., Zilberstein, S.: Planning under uncertainty using reduced models: revisiting determinization. In: ICAPS (2014)
37. Puterman, M.: Markov Decision Processes: Discrete Stochastic Dynamic Programming. Wiley, New York (1994)
38. Segala, R.: Modeling and verification of randomized distributed real-time systems. Ph.D. thesis, Massachusetts Institute of Technology (1995)
39. Thüm, T., Apel, S., Kästner, C., Schaefer, I., Saake, G.: A classification and survey of analysis strategies for software product lines. ACM Comput. Surv. **47**(1s), 6:1–6:45 (2014)
40. Wu, S., Smolka, S.A., Stark, E.W.: Composition and behaviors of probabilistic I/O automata. Theor. Comput. Sci. **176**(1–2), 1–38 (1997). https://doi.org/10.1016/S0304-3975(97)00056-X

Behavioral Specification Theories: An Algebraic Taxonomy

Uli Fahrenberg[1]([✉]) and Axel Legay[2]([✉])

[1] École polytechnique, Palaiseau, France
uli@lix.polytechnique.fr
[2] Université Catholique de Louvain, Louvain-la-Neuve, Belgium
axel.legay@uclouvain.be

Abstract. We develop a taxonomy of different behavioral specification theories and expose their algebraic properties. We start by clarifying what precisely constitutes a behavioral specification theory and then introduce logical and structural operations and develop the resulting algebraic properties. In order to motivate our developments, we give plenty of examples of behavioral specification theories with different operations.

1 Introduction

Behavioral specification theories are specification formalisms for formal models which are enriched with logical and structural operations. This allows for incremental and compositional design and verification and has shown itself to be a viable way to avoid the habitual state-space explosion problems associated with the verification of complex models.

Behavioral specification theories have seen significant attention in recent years [1,6,8,12–14,17–19,40,41,44,46]. Generally speaking, they have the property that the specification formalism is an extension of the modeling formalism, so that specifications have an operational interpretation and models are verified by comparing their operational behavior against the specification's behavior.

Popular examples of behavioral specification theories are modal transition systems [6,18,40], disjunctive modal transition systems [12–14,17–32,44], and acceptance automata [19,46]. Also relations to contracts and interfaces have been exposed [8,47], as have extensions for real-time, probabilistic, and quantitative specifications and for models with data [9–11,15,20,22,23,27–29].

Except for the work by Vogler *et al.* in [17,18] and our own [31], behavioral specification theories have been developed only to characterize bisimilarity (or variants like timed or probabilistic bisimilarity). While bisimilarity is an important equivalence relation on models, there are many others which also are of interest. Examples include nested and k-nested simulation [2,34], ready or $\frac{2}{3}$-simulation [43], trace equivalence [36], impossible futures [51], or the failure semantics of [16–18,45,50] and others. We have addressed some of these equivalences in [31].

© Springer Nature Switzerland AG 2020
T. Margaria and B. Steffen (Eds.): ISoLA 2020, LNCS 12476, pp. 262–274, 2020.
https://doi.org/10.1007/978-3-030-61362-4_14

In this survey we take a step back and develop a *systemization* or *taxonomy* of different behavioral specification theories and expose their *algebraic* properties. As an example, the most basic ingredient of a behavioral specification theory is a preorder of *refinement* on specifications, turning the set of specifications into a partial order up to $\equiv$, the equivalence generated by refinement. Now if the refinement preorder admits least upper bounds, then this binary operation is usually called *conjunction*, and the set of specifications becomes a meet-semilattice up to $\equiv$. Conjunction is a useful ingredient of any specification theory, but some also admit *disjunctions*, thus turning them into *distributive lattices* up to $\equiv$.

We believe that a systemization as we set out for here is useful to clarify which properties one needs or expects of behavioral specification theories, and that it may help in developing new behavioral specification theories, both for equivalence relations different from bisimilarity and for more intricate models such as real-time, probabilistic, or hybrid systems.

To develop our systemization, we first have to clarify what precisely *is* a behavioral specification theory. Here we follow the seminal work of Pnueli [45], Hennessy and Milner [35], and Larsen [41] and argue that a behavioral specification theory is built on an *adequate* and *expressive* specification formalism equipped with a mapping from models to their *characteristic formulae*, which provides the extension of the modeling formalism by the specification formalism. This is the theme of Sects. 2 and 3.

Section 4 then introduces behavioral specification theories, and Sect. 5 makes precise what it means to have logical operations on specifications. Section 6 is concerned with *structural* operations on specifications: composition and quotient. When present in a specification theory, these can be used for compositional design and verification. Algebraically, a specification theory which has all the logical and structural operations forms a *residuated lattice* up to $\equiv$, a well-understood algebraic structure [37] which also appears in linear logic [33] and other areas.

All throughout Sects. 2 to 6, we give plenty of examples, taken from our own work in [14,27,31], of specification theories which have the required operations. In the final Sect. 7 we survey a few other behavioral specification theories, for real-time and probabilistic models, in order to expose their particular algebraic properties. We make no claim to completeness of this survey; indeed there are many other examples which we do not treat here. The paper finishes with a scheme which sums up the relevant algebraic structures and an overview of the properties of the different behavioral specification theories encountered.

2   Models and Specifications

Let Spec be a set of *specifications*, Mod a set of *models*, $\models\ \subseteq$ Mod $\times$ Spec a relation between specifications and models, and $\sim\ \subseteq$ Mod $\times$ Mod an equivalence relation on Mod. The intuition is that Spec is to provide specifications for the models in Mod through the relation $\models$, but *up to* $\sim$, so that two models which are equivalent cannot be distinguished by their specifications. We will make this precise below.

We will generally use $\mathcal{S}$ for specifications and $\mathcal{M}$ for models. For $\mathcal{S} \in$ Spec, let $[\![\mathcal{S}]\!] = \{\mathcal{M} \in$ Mod $\mid \mathcal{M} \models \mathcal{S}\}$ denote its *set of implementations*. For $\mathcal{M} \in$ Mod, let $\mathsf{Th}(\mathcal{M}) = \{\mathcal{S} \in$ Spec $\mid \mathcal{M} \models \mathcal{S}\}$ denote its *set of theories*. We record the following trivial fact:

Lemma 1. *For any $\mathcal{S} \in$ Spec and $\mathcal{M} \in$ Mod, the following are equivalent:*

(1) $\mathcal{M} \models \mathcal{S}$;
(2) $\mathcal{M} \in [\![\mathcal{S}]\!]$;
(3) $\mathcal{S} \in \mathsf{Th}(\mathcal{M})$.

Example 2. A common type of models is given by *labeled transition systems* (LTS). These are structures $\mathcal{M} = (S, s^0, T)$ consisting of a finite set of states S, an initial state $s^0 \in S$, and transitions $T \subseteq S \times \Sigma \times S$ labeled with symbols from a fixed finite set Σ.

LTS are often considered modulo *bisimilarity*: A *bisimulation* between two LTS $\mathcal{M}_1 = (S_1, s_1^0, T_1)$ and $\mathcal{M}_2 = (S_2, s_2^0, T_2)$ is a relation $R \subseteq S_1 \times S_2$ such that $(s_1^0, s_2^0) \in R$ and for any $(s_1, s_2) \in R$,

(1) for all $(s_1, a, s_1') \in T_1$ there exists $(s_2, a, s_2') \in T_2$ such that $(s_1', s_2') \in R$;
(2) for all $(s_2, a, s_2') \in T_2$ there exists $(s_1, a, s_1') \in T_1$ such that $(s_1', s_2') \in R$;

and then $\mathcal{M}_1$ and $\mathcal{M}_2$ are said to be *bisimilar* if there exists a bisimulation between them.

A common specification formalism for LTS is *Hennessy-Milner logic* [35]. It consists of formulae generated by the abstract syntax

$$\mathsf{HML} \ni \phi, \psi ::= \mathbf{tt} \mid \mathbf{ff} \mid \phi \wedge \psi \mid \phi \vee \psi \mid \langle a \rangle \phi \mid [a]\phi \quad (a \in \Sigma),$$

with semantics defined by $[\![\mathbf{tt}]\!] = \mathsf{LTS}$, $[\![\mathbf{ff}]\!] = \emptyset$, $[\![\phi \wedge \psi]\!] = [\![\phi]\!] \cap [\![\psi]\!]$, $[\![\phi \vee \psi]\!] = [\![\phi]\!] \cup [\![\psi]\!]$, and

$$[\![\langle a \rangle \phi]\!] = \{(S, s^0, T) \in \mathsf{LTS} \mid \exists (s^0, a, s) \in T : (S, s, T) \in [\![\phi]\!]\};$$
$$[\![[a]\phi]\!] = \{(S, s^0, T) \in \mathsf{LTS} \mid \forall (s^0, a, s) \in T : (S, s, T) \in [\![\phi]\!]\}.$$

The Hennessy-Milner theorem [35] then states that HML specifies LTS up to bisimilarity, that is, $\mathcal{M}_1 \sim \mathcal{M}_2$ precisely when $\mathsf{Th}(\mathcal{M}_1) = \mathsf{Th}(\mathcal{M}_2)$.   □

Definition 3 [35]. (Spec, $\models$) *is* adequate *for* (Mod, $\sim$) *if it holds for any $\mathcal{M}_1, \mathcal{M}_2 \in$ Mod that $\mathcal{M}_1 \sim \mathcal{M}_2$ iff $\mathsf{Th}(\mathcal{M}_1) = \mathsf{Th}(\mathcal{M}_2)$.*

3   Characteristic Formulae

Let $\mathcal{M} \in$ Mod. A specification $\mathcal{S} \in$ Spec is a *characteristic formula for* $\mathcal{M}$ [45] if it holds for any $\mathcal{M}' \in$ Mod that $\mathcal{M}' \models \mathcal{S}$ iff $\mathsf{Th}(\mathcal{M}') = \mathsf{Th}(\mathcal{M})$.

Lemma 4. *If $\mathcal{S}_1, \mathcal{S}_2 \in$ Spec are characteristic formulae for $\mathcal{M} \in$ Mod, then $[\![\mathcal{S}_1]\!] = [\![\mathcal{S}_2]\!]$.*

Proof. For any $\mathcal{M}' \in \mathsf{Mod}$, $\mathcal{M}' \in [\![\mathcal{S}_1]\!]$ iff $\mathsf{Th}(\mathcal{M}') = \mathsf{Th}(\mathcal{M})$, iff $\mathcal{M}' \in [\![\mathcal{S}_2]\!]$.   □

Definition 5 [45]. (Spec, $\models$) *is* expressive *for* (Mod, $\sim$) *if every* $\mathcal{M} \in \mathsf{Mod}$ *admits a characteristic formula.*

Example 6. It is known [3] that HML is *not* expressive for LTS with bisimilarity. Indeed, the simple transition system $(\{s^0\}, s^0, (s^0, a, s^0))$ consisting only of a loop at the initial state does not admit a characteristic formula in HML.

The standard remedy [42] for this expressivity failure is to add recursion and maximal fixed points to the logic. For a finite set X of variables, let $\mathsf{HML}(X)$ be the set of formulae generated as follows:

$$\mathsf{HML}(X) \ni \phi, \psi ::= \mathbf{tt} \mid \mathbf{ff} \mid \phi \wedge \psi \mid \phi \vee \psi \mid \langle a \rangle \phi \mid [a]\phi \mid x \quad (a \in \Sigma, x \in X)$$

That is, $\mathsf{HML}(X)$ formulae are HML formulae which additionally may contain variables from X.

A *recursive Hennessy-Milner formula* [14, 42] is a tuple $\mathcal{H} = (X, X^0, \Delta)$ consisting of finite sets $X \supseteq X^0$ of *variables* and *initial* variables, respectively, and a *declaration* $\Delta : X \rightarrow \mathsf{HML}(X)$. The set of such formulae is denoted HML^R. The semantics of a formula $\mathcal{H} \in \mathsf{HML}^\mathsf{R}$ is a set $[\![\mathcal{H}]\!] \in \mathsf{LTS}$ which is defined as a maximal fixed point, see [3, 42]; we do not go into these details here because we will give another, equivalent, semantics below.

The *characteristic formula* [42] of $(S, s^0, T) \in \mathsf{LTS}$ is now the HML^R formula $(S, \{s^0\}, \Delta)$ given by

$$\Delta(s) = \bigwedge_{(s,a,t) \in T} \langle a \rangle t \wedge \bigwedge_{a \in \Sigma} [a]\Big(\bigvee_{(s,a,t) \in T} t \Big).$$

Note how $\Delta(s)$ precisely specifies all labels which must be available from s (the first part of the conjunction) and, for each label, which properties must be satisfied after its occurrence (the second part of the conjunction).   □

4   Specification Theories

Definition 7 [31]. *A behavioral specification theory for* (Mod, $\sim$) *consists of a set* Spec *of specifications, a relation* $\models \subseteq \mathsf{Mod} \times \mathsf{Spec}$, *a mapping* $\chi : \mathsf{Mod} \rightarrow \mathsf{Spec}$, *and a preorder* $\leq$ *on* Spec, *called* refinement, *subject to the following conditions:*

(1) (Spec, $\models$) *is adequate for* (Mod, $\sim$);
(2) for every $\mathcal{M} \in \mathsf{Mod}$, $\chi(\mathcal{M})$ *is a characteristic formula for* $\mathcal{M}$;
(3) for all $\mathcal{M} \in \mathsf{Mod}$ *and all* $\mathcal{S} \in \mathsf{Spec}$, $\mathcal{M} \models \mathcal{S}$ *iff* $\chi(\mathcal{M}) \leq \mathcal{S}$.

We will generally omit "behavioral" from now and only speak about *specification theories*.

The equivalence relation $\equiv$ on Spec defined as $\leq \cap \geq$ is called *modal equivalence*. Some comments on the different ingredients above are in order.

1. By (2), (Spec, $\models$) is also *expressive* for (Mod, $\sim$).
2. χ is a *section* of $\models$: for all $\mathcal{M} \in$ Mod, $\mathcal{M} \models \chi(\mathcal{M})$.
3. (3) can be seen as *defining* $\models$, so we may omit $\models$ from the signature of specification theories.
4. For any $\mathcal{M} \in$ Mod, $\mathsf{Th}(\mathcal{M}) = \{\mathcal{S} \in \mathsf{Spec} \mid \chi(\mathcal{M}) \leq \mathcal{S}\} = \chi(\mathcal{M})\!\uparrow$ is the *upward closure* of $\chi(\mathcal{M})$ with respect to $\leq$.

Lemma 8 [31]. *Let* (Spec, χ, $\leq$) *be a specification theory for* (Mod, $\sim$).

(1) For all $\mathcal{S}_1, \mathcal{S}_2 \in$ Spec, $\mathcal{S}_1 \leq \mathcal{S}_2$ implies $[\![\mathcal{S}_1]\!] \subseteq [\![\mathcal{S}_2]\!]$.
(2) For all $\mathcal{M}_1, \mathcal{M}_2 \in$ Mod, $\mathcal{M}_1 \sim \mathcal{M}_2$ iff $\chi(\mathcal{M}_1) \leq \chi(\mathcal{M}_2)$.

Proof. For the first claim, $\mathcal{M} \in [\![\mathcal{S}_1]\!]$ implies $\chi(\mathcal{M}) \leq \mathcal{S}_1 \leq \mathcal{S}_2$, hence $\mathcal{M} \in [\![\mathcal{S}_2]\!]$.
    For the second claim, we have $\mathcal{M}_1 \sim \mathcal{M}_2$ iff $\mathcal{M}_1 \models \chi(\mathcal{M}_2)$ (as $\chi(\mathcal{M}_2)$ is characteristic for $\mathcal{M}_2$), iff $\chi(\mathcal{M}_1) \leq \chi(\mathcal{M}_2)$ by (3). □

Example 9. [14] introduces a *normal form* for HML^R formulae, showing that for any HML^R formula $\mathcal{H}_1 = (X_1, X_1^0, \Delta_1)$, there exists another formula $\mathcal{H}_2 = (X_2, X_2^0, \Delta_2)$ with $[\![\mathcal{H}_1]\!] = [\![\mathcal{H}_2]\!]$ and such that for any $x \in X_2$, $\Delta_2(x)$ is of the form

$$\Delta_2(x) = \bigwedge_{N \in \Diamond(x)} \left(\bigvee_{(a,y) \in N} \langle a \rangle y \right) \wedge \bigwedge_{a \in \Sigma} [a] \left(\bigvee_{y \in \Box^a(x)} y \right),$$

for finite sets $\Diamond(x) \subseteq 2^{\Sigma \times X_2}$ and, for each $a \in \Sigma$, $\Box^a(x) \subseteq X_2$. This may be seen as generalizing the characteristic formulae of HML^R: the first part of the conjunction in $\Delta_2(x)$ specifies all labels which must be available, and the second part, which properties must be satisfied after each label's occurrence.
    A *refinement* [14] of two HML^R formulae $\mathcal{H}_1 = (X_1, X_1^0, \Delta_1)$ and $\mathcal{H}_2 = (X_2, X_2^0, \Delta_2)$ in normal form is a relation $R \subseteq X_1 \times X_2$ such that for every $x_1^0 \in X_1^0$ there exists $x_2^0 \in X_2^0$ for which $(x_1^0, x_2^0) \in R$, and for any $(x_1, x_2) \in R$,

(1) for all $N_2 \in \Diamond_2(x_2)$ there is $N_1 \in \Diamond_1(x_1)$ such that for each $(a, y_1) \in N_1$, there exists $(a, y_2) \in N_2$ with $(y_1, y_2) \in R$;
(2) for all $a \in \Sigma$ and every $y_1 \in \Box_1^a(x_1)$, there is $y_2 \in \Box_2^a(x_2)$ for which $(y_1, y_2) \in R$.

Note how this corresponds to the intuition for the normal form above.
    Writing $\mathcal{H}_1 \leq \mathcal{H}_2$ whenever there exists a refinement as above, and denoting by $\chi(\mathcal{M})$ the characteristic formula of $\mathcal{M} \in$ LTS introduced in the previous example, it can be shown [14] that $(\mathsf{HML}^\mathsf{R}, \chi, \leq)$ is a specification theory for LTS under bisimulation. This also implies that the refinement semantics of HML^R agrees with the standard fixed-point semantics [3, 42]. □

Example 10. [14] exposes structural translations between HML^R and two other specification formalism: a generalization of the *disjunctive modal transition systems* (DMTS) introduced in [44] to multiple initial states, and a non-deterministic version of the *acceptance automata* (AA) of [19, 46]. This yields two other specification theories for LTS under bisimulation, one DMTS-based and one based on (non-deterministic) acceptance automata. □

Example 11. [31] introduces DMTS-based specification theories for $(\mathsf{LTS}, \cong)$, where $\cong$ is any equivalence in van Glabbeek's linear-time–branching-time spectrum [49]. Using the translations mentioned in the previous example, these also give rise to HML^R-based specification theories, and to specification theories based on acceptance automata, for all those equivalences.   □

5   Logical Operations on Specifications

Behavioral specifications typically come equipped with logical operations of conjunction and disjunction. Recall that $\equiv$ is defined as $\leq \cap \geq$.

Definition 12. *A specification theory* $(\mathsf{Spec}, \chi, \leq)$ *for* $(\mathsf{Mod}, \sim)$ *is* logical *if* $(\mathsf{Spec}, \leq)$ *forms a bounded distributive lattice up to* $\equiv$.

The above implies that Spec admits commutative and associative binary operations $\vee$ of least upper bound and $\wedge$ of greatest lower bound: disjunction and conjunction. It also entails that there is a bottom specification $\mathbf{ff} \in \mathsf{Spec}$, satisfying $[\![\mathbf{ff}]\!] = \emptyset$, and a top specification $\mathbf{tt} \in \mathsf{Spec}$, satisfying $[\![\mathbf{tt}]\!] = \mathsf{Mod}$. We sum up the properties of these operations:

$$\mathcal{S}_1 \vee \mathcal{S}_2 \leq \mathcal{S}_3 \quad \text{iff} \quad \mathcal{S}_1 \leq \mathcal{S}_3 \text{ and } \mathcal{S}_2 \leq \mathcal{S}_3 \tag{1}$$

$$\mathcal{S}_1 \leq \mathcal{S}_2 \wedge \mathcal{S}_3 \quad \text{iff} \quad \mathcal{S}_1 \leq \mathcal{S}_2 \text{ and } \mathcal{S}_1 \leq \mathcal{S}_3 \tag{2}$$

$$\mathcal{S}_1 \wedge (\mathcal{S}_2 \vee \mathcal{S}_3) \equiv (\mathcal{S}_1 \wedge \mathcal{S}_2) \vee (\mathcal{S}_1 \wedge \mathcal{S}_3)$$

$$\mathcal{S}_1 \vee (\mathcal{S}_2 \wedge \mathcal{S}_3) \equiv (\mathcal{S}_1 \vee \mathcal{S}_2) \wedge (\mathcal{S}_1 \vee \mathcal{S}_3)$$

$$\mathbf{ff} \wedge \mathcal{S} \equiv \mathbf{ff} \qquad \mathbf{tt} \wedge \mathcal{S} \equiv \mathcal{S}$$

$$\mathbf{ff} \vee \mathcal{S} \equiv \mathcal{S} \qquad \mathbf{tt} \vee \mathcal{S} \equiv \mathbf{tt}$$

Note that the properties of least upper bound and greatest lower bound in (1) and (2) above *define* $\vee$ and $\wedge$ uniquely: they are universal properties.

Example 13. Hennessy-Milner logic has disjunction and conjunction as part of the syntax, and [14] shows that on the specification theory $(\mathsf{HML}^R, \chi, \leq)$ from previous examples these are operations as above. The disjunction of two HML^R formulae in normal form is again in normal form; for conjunction it may be defined directly on normal forms as follows:

Let $\mathcal{H}_1 = (X_1, X_1^0, \Delta_1)$ and $\mathcal{H}_2 = (X_2, X_2^0, \Delta_2)$ be HML^R formulae in normal form and define $\mathcal{H} = (X_1 \times X_2, X_1^0 \times X_1^1, \Delta)$ by $\square^a((x_1, x_2)) = \square_1^a(x_1) \wedge \square_2^a(x_2)$ for every $a \in \Sigma$ and $(x_1, x_2) \in X$ and

$$\lozenge((x_1, x_2)) = \big\{\{(a, (y_1, y_2)) \mid (a, y_1) \in N_1, y_2 \in \square_2^a(x_2)\} \mid N_1 \in \lozenge_2(x_1)\big\}$$
$$\cup \big\{\{(a, (y_1, y_2)) \mid (a, y_2) \in N_2, y_1 \in \square_1^a(x_1)\} \mid N_2 \in \lozenge_2(x_2)\big\},$$

then $\mathcal{H} \equiv \mathcal{H}_1 \wedge \mathcal{H}_2$ [14].

Hence the three specification theories for $(\mathsf{Mod}, \sim)$ of [14]: HML^R, DMTS, and AA, are all logical.   □

As a variation, some specification theories only admit conjunction and no disjunction, thus forming a *bounded meet-semilattice*. We call such specification theories *semi-logical*.

6   Structural Operations on Specifications

Many behavioral specifications also admit structural operations of *composition*, denoted $\parallel$, and *quotient*, denoted $/$, in order to enable compositional design and verification.

Definition 14. *A* compositional specification theory *is a specification theory* (Spec, χ, $\leq$) *for* (Mod, $\sim$) *together with an operation* $\parallel$ *on* Spec *such that* (Spec, $\parallel$, $\leq$) *forms a commutative partially ordered semigroup up to* $\equiv$.

That is to say that the operation $\parallel$ is commutative and associative and additionally satisfies the following monotonicity law:

$$S_1 \leq S_2 \implies S_1 \parallel S_3 \leq S_2 \parallel S_3$$

Contrary to the logical operations $\vee$ and $\wedge$, $\parallel$ is *not* defined uniquely; indeed a specification theory may admit many different composition operations.

Corollary 15 (Independent implementability). *If* (Spec, $\parallel$, χ, $\leq$) *is compositional, then* $S_1 \leq S_3$ *and* $S_2 \leq S_4$ *imply* $S_1 \parallel S_2 \leq S_3 \parallel S_4$.

Proof. By monotonicity, $S_1 \parallel S_2 \leq S_3 \parallel S_2 \leq S_3 \parallel S_4$. $\square$

Note that independent implementability also *implies* the monotonicity law above.

If (Spec, $\parallel$, χ, $\leq$) is *compositional and logical*, then it is called a *lattice-ordered semigroup* (up to $\equiv$) as an algebraic structure; more precisely a bounded distributive lattice-ordered commutative semigroup. This entails that composition distributes over disjunction:

$$S_1 \parallel (S_2 \vee S_2) \equiv S_1 \parallel S_2 \vee S_1 \parallel S_3$$

Note that composition does *not* necessarily distributed over *conjunction*.

If composition $\parallel$ also admits a unit $\mathbb{1} \in$ Spec (up to $\equiv$), *i.e.* such that $S \parallel \mathbb{1} \equiv S$ for all $S \in$ Spec, then (Spec, $\parallel$, χ, $\leq$) is said to be *unital*, and "semigroup" is replaced by "monoid" above.

Definition 16. *A compositional specification theory* (Spec, $\parallel$, χ, $\leq$) *for* (Mod, $\sim$) *is* complete *if* (Spec, $\parallel$, $\leq$) *forms a* residuated *partially ordered commutative semigroup up to* $\equiv$.

That is, the operation $\parallel$ admits a *residual* $/$, in our context called *quotient*, satisfying the following property:

$$S_1 \parallel S_2 \leq S_3 \iff S_2 \leq S_3 / S_1 \tag{3}$$

This property is again universal, so that $/$ is uniquely defined by $\|$.

If $(\mathsf{Spec}, \|, \chi, \leq)$ is also unital, then it forms a *residuated poset* up to $\equiv$. In that case, the following holds for all $\mathcal{S}_1, \mathcal{S}_2 \in \mathsf{Spec}$:

$$\mathcal{S}_1 \| (\mathbb{1}/\mathcal{S}_2) \leq \mathcal{S}_1/\mathcal{S}_2$$

We refer to [37] for a survey on residuated posets and the residuated lattices we will encounter in a moment; we only highlight a few properties here.

Lemma 17 [37]. *The following hold in any complete compositional specification theory:*

$$\mathcal{S}_1 \| (\mathcal{S}_2/\mathcal{S}_3) \leq (\mathcal{S}_1 \| \mathcal{S}_2)/\mathcal{S}_3 \qquad \mathcal{S}_1/\mathcal{S}_2 \leq (\mathcal{S}_1 \| \mathcal{S}_3)/(\mathcal{S}_2 \| \mathcal{S}_3)$$
$$(\mathcal{S}_1/\mathcal{S}_2) \| (\mathcal{S}_2/\mathcal{S}_3) \leq \mathcal{S}_1/\mathcal{S}_3 \qquad (\mathcal{S}_1/\mathcal{S}_2)/\mathcal{S}_3 \equiv (\mathcal{S}_1/\mathcal{S}_3)/\mathcal{S}_2$$
$$\mathcal{S}_1/(\mathcal{S}_2 \| \mathcal{S}_3) \equiv (\mathcal{S}_1/\mathcal{S}_2)/\mathcal{S}_3 \qquad \mathcal{S} \| (\mathcal{S}/\mathcal{S}) \equiv \mathcal{S}$$
$$(\mathcal{S}/\mathcal{S}) \| (\mathcal{S}/\mathcal{S}) \equiv \mathcal{S}/\mathcal{S}$$

If $(\mathsf{Spec}, \|, \mathbb{1}, \chi, \leq)$ is *complete compositional and logical*, then it is called a *residuated lattice-ordered semigroup* (up to $\equiv$); more precisely a bounded distributive residuated lattice-ordered commutative semigroup. Distributivity of composition over disjunction now follows from residuation, and also the quotient is well-behaved with respect to the logical operations:

$$(\mathcal{S}_1 \wedge \mathcal{S}_2)/\mathcal{S}_3 \equiv \mathcal{S}_1/\mathcal{S}_3 \wedge \mathcal{S}_2/\mathcal{S}_3 \qquad \mathcal{S}_1/(\mathcal{S}_2 \vee \mathcal{S}_3) \equiv \mathcal{S}_1/\mathcal{S}_2 \wedge \mathcal{S}_1/\mathcal{S}_3$$

Additionally, composition and quotient interact with the bottom and top elements as follows:

$$\mathcal{S} \| \mathbf{ff} \equiv \mathbf{ff} \qquad \mathcal{S}/\mathbf{ff} \equiv \mathbf{tt} \qquad \mathbf{tt}/\mathcal{S} \equiv \mathbf{tt}$$

Finally, if $(\mathsf{Spec}, \|, \mathbb{1}, \chi, \leq)$ is complete compositional, unital, and logical, then it is called a *residuated lattice*. We sum up the different algebraic structures we have encountered in Fig. 1.

Example 18. In [14] it is shown that the specification theory $(\mathsf{HML}^\mathsf{R}, \chi, \leq)$, and thus also the specification theories based on DMTS and AA, are unital complete compositional when enriched with CSP-style composition $\|$. (In [27] this is generalized to other types of composition.)

The composition $\mathcal{H}_1 \| \mathcal{H}_2$ is defined by translation between HML^R and AA. Also quotient is defined through AA, and it is shown in [14] that due to these translations, composition may incur an exponential blow-up and quotient a double-exponential blow-up. □

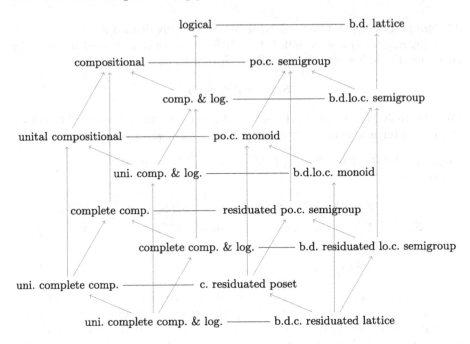

Fig. 1. Spectrum of specification theories and the corresponding algebraic structures. Abbreviations: b.—bounded; d.—distributive; c.—commutative; po.—partially ordered; lo.—lattice-ordered

7 Specification Theories for Real-Time and Probabilistic Systems

We quickly survey a few different specification theories for real-time and probabilistic systems.

7.1 Modal Event-Clock Specifications

Modal event-clock specifications (MECS) were introduced in [15]. They form a specification theory for event-clock automata (ECA) [5], a determinizable subclass of timed automata [4], under timed bisimilarity. Models and specifications are assume to be deterministic, thus $S_1 \leq S_2$ iff $[\![S_1]\!] \subseteq [\![S_2]\!]$ in this case.

In [15] it is shown that MECS admit a conjunction, thus forming a meet-semilattice up to $\equiv$. The authors also introduce composition and quotient; but computation of quotient incurs an exponential blow-up. Altogether, MECS form a complete compositional semi-logical specification theory: a bounded residuated semilattice-ordered commutative semigroup.

7.2 Timed Input/Output Automata

[20,21] introduce a specification theory based on a variant of the timed input/output automata (TIOA) of [38,39]. Both models and specifications are

Table 1. Algebraic taxonomy of some specification theories. Abbreviations: L—logical; C—compositional; Q—complete

Specifications	Models	L	C	Q	Notes
HML^R, DMTS, AA	LTS, bisim.	✓	✓	✓	[14]; bisimulation
HML^R, DMTS, AA	LTS, any	✗	✗	✗	[31]; any equivalence in LTBT spectrum [49]
DMTS	LTS, fail./div.	≈	✓	✗	[17]; failure/divergence equivalence; no disjunction
MECS	ECA, t.bisim.	≈	✓	✓	[15]; timed bisim.; no disjunction
TIOA	TIOA, t.bisim.	≈	✓	≈	[20]; no disjunction; weak quotient
IMC	PA, p.bisim.	✗	✗	✗	[25]; probabilistic bisim
APA	PA, p.bisim.	≈	✓	✗	[24]; no disjunction

TIOA which are action-deterministic and input-enabled; but models are further restricted using conditions of output urgency and independent progress. The equivalence on models being specified is timed bisimilarity.

In [20] it is shown that TIOA admit a conjunction, so they form a meet-semilattice up to ≡. The paper also introduces a composition operation and a quotient, but the quotient is only shown to satisfy the property that

$$\mathcal{S}_1 \| \mathcal{M} \leq \mathcal{S}_3 \iff \mathcal{M} \leq \mathcal{S}_3/\mathcal{S}_1$$

for all specifications $\mathcal{S}_1, \mathcal{S}_3$ and all *models* $\mathcal{M}$, which is strictly weaker than (3). With this caveat, TIOA form a complete compositional semi-logical specification theory: a bounded residuated semilattice-ordered commutative semigroup.

7.3 Abstract Probabilistic Automata

Abstract probabilistic automata (APA), introduced in [23,24], form a specification theory for probabilistic automata (PA) [48] under probabilistic bisimilarity. They build on earlier models of interval Markov chains (IMC) [25], see also [7,26] for a related line of work.

In [24] it is shown that APA admit a conjunction, but that IMC do not. Also a composition is introduced in [24], and it is shown that composing two APA with interval constraints (an IMC) may yield an APA with *polynomial* constraints (not an IMC); but APA with polynomial constraints are closed under composition. APA form a compositional semi-logical specification theory: a bounded semilattice-ordered commutative semigroup.

Table 1 sums up the algebraic properties of the different specification theories we have surveyed here, plus the specification theory for failure/divergence semantics based on DMTS from [17].

References

1. Aceto, L., Fábregas, I., de Frutos-Escrig, D., Ingólfsdóttir, A., Palomino, M.: On the specification of modal systems. Sci. Comput. Program. **78**(12), 2468–2487 (2013)
2. Aceto, L., Fokkink, W., van Glabbeek, R.J., Ingólfsdóttir, A.: Nested semantics over finite trees are equationally hard. Inf. Comput. **191**(2), 203–232 (2004)
3. Aceto, L., Ingólfsdóttir, A., Larsen, K.G., Srba, J.: Reactive Systems. Cambridge University Press, Cambridge (2007)
4. Alur, R., Dill, D.L.: A theory of timed automata. Theor. Comput. Sci. **126**(2), 183–235 (1994)
5. Alur, R., Fix, L., Henzinger, T.A.: Event-clock automata: a determinizable class of timed automata. Theor. Comput. Sci. **211**(1–2), 253–273 (1999)
6. Antonik, A., Huth, M., Larsen, K.G., Nyman, U., Wąsowski, A.: 20 years of modal and mixed specifications. Bull. EATCS **95**, 94–129 (2008)
7. Bart, A., Delahaye, B., Fournier, P., Lime, D., Monfroy, E., Truchet, C.: Reachability in parametric interval Markov chains using constraints. Theor. Comput. Sci. **747**, 48–74 (2018)
8. Bauer, S.S.: Moving from specifications to contracts in component-based design. In: de Lara, J., Zisman, A. (eds.) FASE 2012. LNCS, vol. 7212, pp. 43–58. Springer, Heidelberg (2012). https://doi.org/10.1007/978-3-642-28872-2_3
9. Bauer, S.S., Fahrenberg, U., Juhl, L., Larsen, K.G., Legay, A., Thrane, C.: Quantitative refinement for weighted modal transition systems. In: Murlak, F., Sankowski, P. (eds.) MFCS 2011. LNCS, vol. 6907, pp. 60–71. Springer, Heidelberg (2011). https://doi.org/10.1007/978-3-642-22993-0_9
10. Bauer, S.S., Fahrenberg, U., Juhl, L., Larsen, K.G., Legay, A., Thrane, C.: Weighted modal transition systems. Form. Meth. Syst. Des. **42**(2), 193–220 (2013)
11. Bauer, S.S., Juhl, L., Larsen, K.G., Legay, A., Srba, J.: Extending modal transition systems with structured labels. Math. Struct. Comput. Sci. **22**(4), 581–617 (2012)
12. Beneš, N., Černá, I., Křetínský, J.: Modal transition systems: composition and LTL model checking. In: Bultan, T., Hsiung, P.-A. (eds.) ATVA 2011. LNCS, vol. 6996, pp. 228–242. Springer, Heidelberg (2011). https://doi.org/10.1007/978-3-642-24372-1_17
13. Beneš, N., Delahaye, B., Fahrenberg, U., Křetínský, J., Legay, A.: Hennessy-Milner logic with greatest fixed points as a complete behavioural specification theory. In: D'Argenio, P.R., Melgratti, H. (eds.) CONCUR 2013. LNCS, vol. 8052, pp. 76–90. Springer, Heidelberg (2013). https://doi.org/10.1007/978-3-642-40184-8_7
14. Beneš, N., Fahrenberg, U., Křetínský, J., Legay, A., Traonouez, L.-M.: Logical vs. behavioural specifications. Inf. Comput. **271**, 104487 (2020)
15. Bertrand, N., Legay, A., Pinchinat, S., Raclet, J.-B.: Modal event-clock specifications for timed component-based design. Sci. Comput. Program. **77**(12), 1212–1234 (2012)
16. Brookes, S.D., Hoare, C.A.R., Roscoe, A.W.: A theory of communicating sequential processes. J. ACM **31**(3), 560–599 (1984)
17. Bujtor, F., Sorokin, L., Vogler, W.: Testing preorders for dMTS. ACM Trans. Embed. Comput. Syst. **16**(2), 41:1–41:28 (2017)
18. Bujtor, F., Vogler, W.: Failure semantics for modal transition systems. ACM Trans. Embed. Comput. Syst. **14**(4), 67 (2015)
19. Caillaud, B., Raclet, J.-B.: Ensuring reachability by design. In: Roychoudhury, A., D'Souza, M. (eds.) ICTAC 2012. LNCS, vol. 7521, pp. 213–227. Springer, Heidelberg (2012). https://doi.org/10.1007/978-3-642-32943-2_17

20. David, A., Larsen, K.G., Legay, A., Nyman, U., Traonouez, L.-M., Wąsowski, A.: Real-time specifications. Softw. Tools Technol. Transf. **17**(1), 17–45 (2015)
21. David, A., et al.: Compositional verification of real-time systems using Ecdar. Softw. Tools Technol. Transf. **14**(6), 703–720 (2012)
22. Delahaye, B., Fahrenberg, U., Guldstrand Larsen, K., Legay, A.: Refinement and difference for probabilistic automata. In: Joshi, K., Siegle, M., Stoelinga, M., D'Argenio, P.R. (eds.) QEST 2013. LNCS, vol. 8054, pp. 22–38. Springer, Heidelberg (2013). https://doi.org/10.1007/978-3-642-40196-1_3
23. Delahaye, B., Fahrenberg, U., Larsen, K.G., Legay, A.: Refinement and difference for probabilistic automata. Log. Meth. Comput. Sci. **10**(3), 1–32 (2014)
24. Delahaye, B.: Abstract probabilistic automata. Inf. Comput. **232**, 66–116 (2013)
25. Delahaye, B., Larsen, K.G., Legay, A., Pedersen, M.L., Wąsowski, A.: Consistency and refinement for interval Markov chains. Log. Algebr. Program. **81**(3), 209–226 (2012)
26. Delahaye, B., Lime, D., Petrucci, L.: Parameter synthesis for parametric interval Markov chains. In: Jobstmann, B., Leino, K.R.M. (eds.) VMCAI 2016. LNCS, vol. 9583, pp. 372–390. Springer, Heidelberg (2016). https://doi.org/10.1007/978-3-662-49122-5_18
27. Fahrenberg, U., Křetínský, J., Legay, A., Traonouez, L.-M.: Compositionality for quantitative specifications. Soft. Comput. **22**(4), 1139–1158 (2018)
28. Fahrenberg, U., Legay, A.: A robust specification theory for modal event-clock automata. In: Bauer, S.S., Raclet, J.-B. (eds.) FIT 2012. EPTCS, vol. 87, pp. 5–16 (2012)
29. Fahrenberg, U., Legay, A.: General quantitative specification theories with modal transition systems. Acta Inf. **51**(5), 261–295 (2014)
30. Fahrenberg, U., Legay, A.: A linear-time–branching-time spectrum of behavioral specification theories. In: Steffen, B., Baier, C., van den Brand, M., Eder, J., Hinchey, M., Margaria, T. (eds.) SOFSEM 2017. LNCS, vol. 10139, pp. 49–61. Springer, Cham (2017). https://doi.org/10.1007/978-3-319-51963-0_5
31. Fahrenberg, U., Legay, A.: A linear-time-branching-time spectrum for behavioral specification theories. J. Log. Algebraic Meth. Program. **110**, 100499 (2020)
32. Fahrenberg, U., Legay, A., Traonouez, L.-M.: Structural refinement for the modal nu-calculus. In: Ciobanu, G., Méry, D. (eds.) ICTAC 2014. LNCS, vol. 8687, pp. 169–187. Springer, Cham (2014). https://doi.org/10.1007/978-3-319-10882-7_11
33. Girard, J.-Y.: Linear logic. Theor. Comput. Sci. **50**, 1–102 (1987)
34. Groote, J.F., Vaandrager, F.W.: Structured operational semantics and bisimulation as a congruence. Inf. Comput. **100**(2), 202–260 (1992)
35. Hennessy, M., Milner, R.: Algebraic laws for nondeterminism and concurrency. J. ACM **32**(1), 137–161 (1985)
36. Hoare, C.A.R.: Communicating sequential processes. Commun. ACM **21**(8), 666–677 (1978)
37. Jipsen, P., Tsinakis, C.: A survey of residuated lattices. In: Martínez, J. (ed.) Ordered Algebraic Structures. Developments in Mathematics, vol. 7. Springer, Boston (2002). https://doi.org/10.1007/978-1-4757-3627-4_3
38. Kaynar, D.K., Lynch, N.A., Segala, R., Vaandrager, F.W.: Timed I/O automata: a mathematical framework for modeling and analyzing real-time systems. In: RTSS, pp. 166–177. IEEE Computer Society (2003)
39. Kaynar, D.K., Lynch, N.A., Segala, R., Vaandrager, F.W.: The Theory of Timed I/O Automata. Synthesis Lectures on Distributed Computing Theory, 2nd edn. Morgan & Claypool Publishers (2010)

40. Larsen, K.G.: Modal specifications. In: Sifakis, J. (ed.) CAV 1989. LNCS, vol. 407, pp. 232–246. Springer, Heidelberg (1990). https://doi.org/10.1007/3-540-52148-8_19

41. Guldstrand Larsen, K.: Ideal specification formalism = expressivity + compositionality + decidability + testability + ... In: Baeten, J.C.M., Klop, J.W. (eds.) CONCUR 1990. LNCS, vol. 458, pp. 33–56. Springer, Heidelberg (1990). https://doi.org/10.1007/BFb0039050

42. Larsen, K.G.: Proof systems for satisfiability in Hennessy-Milner logic with recursion. Theor. Comput. Sci. **72**(2&3), 265–288 (1990)

43. Larsen, K.G., Skou, A.: Bisimulation through probabilistic testing. In: POPL, pp. 344–352. ACM Press (1989)

44. Larsen, K.G., Xinxin, L.: Equation solving using modal transition systems. In: LICS, pp. 108–117. IEEE Computer Society (1990)

45. Pnueli, A.: Linear and branching structures in the semantics and logics of reactive systems. In: Brauer, W. (ed.) ICALP 1985. LNCS, vol. 194, pp. 15–32. Springer, Heidelberg (1985). https://doi.org/10.1007/BFb0015727

46. Raclet, J.-B.: Residual for component specifications. Electr. Notes Theor. Comput. Sci. **215**, 93–110 (2008)

47. Raclet, J.-B., Badouel, E., Benveniste, A., Caillaud, B., Legay, A., Passerone, R.: A modal interface theory for component-based design. Fundam. Inf. **108**(1–2), 119–149 (2011)

48. Segala, R., Lynch, N.A.: Probabilistic simulations for probabilistic processes. Nord. J. Comput. **2**(2), 250–273 (1995)

49. van Glabbeek, R.J.: The linear time–branching time spectrum I, chap. 1. In: Bergstra, J.A., Ponse, A., Smolka, S.A. (eds.) Handbook of Process Algebra, pp. 3–99. Elsevier (2001)

50. Vogler, W.: Failures semantics and deadlocking of modular Petri nets. Acta Inf. **26**(4), 333–348 (1989)

51. Vogler, W. (ed.): Modular Construction and Partial Order Semantics of Petri Nets. LNCS, vol. 625. Springer, Heidelberg (1992). https://doi.org/10.1007/3-540-55767-9

Approximating Euclidean by Imprecise Markov Decision Processes

Manfred Jaeger$^{(\boxtimes)}$, Giorgio Bacci$^{(\boxtimes)}$, Giovanni Bacci$^{(\boxtimes)}$,
Kim Guldstrand Larsen$^{(\boxtimes)}$, and Peter Gjøl Jensen$^{(\boxtimes)}$

Department of Computer Science, Aalborg University, Aalborg, Denmark
{jaeger,grbacci,giovbacci,kgl,pgj}@cs.aau.dk

Abstract. Euclidean Markov decision processes are a powerful tool for modeling control problems under uncertainty over continuous domains. Finite state imprecise, Markov decision processes can be used to approximate the behavior of these infinite models. In this paper we address two questions: first, we investigate what kind of approximation guarantees are obtained when the Euclidean process is approximated by finite state approximations induced by increasingly fine partitions of the continuous state space. We show that for cost functions over finite time horizons the approximations become arbitrarily precise. Second, we use imprecise Markov decision process approximations as a tool to analyse and validate cost functions and strategies obtained by reinforcement learning. We find that, on the one hand, our new theoretical results validate basic design choices of a previously proposed reinforcement learning approach. On the other hand, the imprecise Markov decision process approximations reveal some inaccuracies in the learned cost functions.

1 Introduction

The traditional goal of software development is correctness with respect to a given specification. However, in the presence of uncertainty, such as faced in the construction of software agents acting in stochastic environments, often no strict notions of correctness exist. One then has to aim instead for optimality with regard to a given performance measure, and in expectation with respect to the stochastic system behavior. The construction of optimal agents often leads to intractable optimization problems. However, it may be sufficient to construct near-optimal solutions with provable bounds on the deviation from optimality. When agents are learned from data, then instead of (near-)optimality by construction, one has to aim for convergence to optimality as the available data increases. In this paper we are primarily concerned with the first question of constructing near-optimal solutions for systems in complex environments described by a continuous state space, and performance measures given by a time-bounded objective. Some implications for the reinforcement learning approach introduced in [8] will also be discussed.

Our work is based on Markov Decision Processes (MDP) [11] as the model for an agent and its environment. MDPs provide a unifying framework for modeling

© Springer Nature Switzerland AG 2020
T. Margaria and B. Steffen (Eds.): ISoLA 2020, LNCS 12476, pp. 275–289, 2020.
https://doi.org/10.1007/978-3-030-61362-4_15

decision making in situations where outcomes are partly random and partly under the control of an agent. Optimal strategies for MDPs can be obtained via dynamic programming or reinforcement learning. They are used in many areas, including economics, control, robotics and autonomous systems. In its simplest form, an MDP comprises a finite set of states $\mathcal{S}$, and a finite set of control actions Act, which for each state s and action a specifies the transition probabilities $P_a(s, s')$ to successor states s'. In addition, transitioning from a state s an action a has an immediate cost $C(s, a)$[1]. The overall problem is to find a strategy σ that specifies the action $\sigma(s)$ to be made in state s in order to optimize some objective (e.g. the expected cost of reaching a goal state).

For many applications, however, such as queuing systems, epidemic processes (e.g. COVID19), and population processes the restriction to a finite state-space is inadequate. Rather, the underlying system has an infinite state-space and the decision making process must take into account the continuous dynamics of the system. In this paper, we consider a particular class of infinite-state MDPs, namely Euclidean Markov Decision Processes [8], where the state space $\mathcal{S}$ is given by a (measurable) subset of $\mathbb{R}^K$ for some fixed dimension K.

As an example, consider the semi-random walk illustrated on the left of Fig. 1 with state-space $\mathcal{S} = [0, x_{max}] \times [0, t_{max}]$ (one dimensional space, and time). Here the goal is to cross the $x = 1$ finishing line before $t = 1$. The agent has two actions at its disposal: to move fast and expensive (cost 3), or to move slow and cheap (cost 1). Both actions have uncertainty about distance traveled and time taken. This uncertainty is modeled by a uniform distribution over a successor state square: given current state (x, t) and action $a \in \{slow, fast\}$, the distribution over possible successor states is the uniform distribution over $[x + \delta(a) - \varepsilon, x + \delta(a) + \varepsilon] \times [t + \tau(a) - \varepsilon, t + \tau(a) + \varepsilon]$, where $(\delta(a), \tau(a))$ represents the direction of the movement in space and time which depends on the action a, while the parameter ε models the uncertainty. Now, the question is to find the strategy that will minimize the expected cost of reaching a goal state.

In [8], we proposed two reinforcement learning algorithms implemented in UPPAAL STRATEGO [4], using online partition refinement techniques. In that work we experimentally demonstrated its improved convergence tendencies on a range of models. For the semi-random walk example, the online learning algorithm returns the strategy illustrated on the right of Fig. 1.

However, despite its efficiency and experimentally demonstrated convergence properties, the learning approach of [8] provides no hard guarantees as to how far away the expected cost of the learned strategy is from the optimal one. In this paper we propose a step-wise partition refinement process, where each partitioning induces a finite-state imprecise MDP (IMDP). From the induced IMDP we can compute by value iteration strategies whose expected costs are upper and lower bounds on the expected cost of the original infinite-state Euclidean MDP. As a crucial result, we prove the correctness of these bounds, i.e., that they

---

[1] In several alternative but essentially equivalent definitions of MDPs transitions have associated rewards rather than cost, and the reward may be depend on the successor state as well.

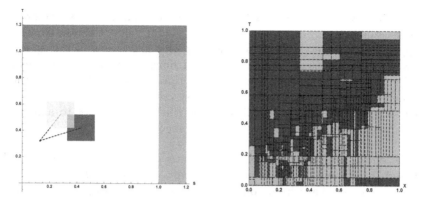

Fig. 1. Left: a Semi-Random Walk on $\mathcal{S} = [0, 1.2] \times [0, 1.2]$. Green: goal area, red: failure area, blue dot: current state, yellow/blue squares: successor state squares for *fast* (blue) and *slow* (yellow) actions. Right: partition of $[0, 1] \times [0, 1]$ and strategy learned by UPPAAL STRATEGO; partition regions colored according to actions prescribed by the strategy. (Color figure online)

are always guaranteed to contain the true expected cost. Furthermore, under a restriction to time-bounded objectives, we will also show that upper and lower bounds converge to the true expected cost, and therefore the associated strategies become near-optimal. Figure 2 shows upper and lower bounds on the expected cost over the regions shown in Fig. 1.

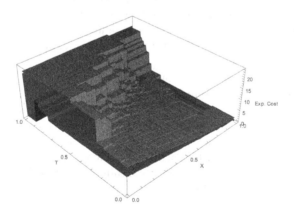

Fig. 2. Lower and upper cost bounds for the learned partition.

Applying the IMDP value iteration procedures to the partition learned by UPPAAL STRATEGO therefore allows us to compute guaranteed lower and upper bounds on the true expected cost, and thereby evaluate the results of reinforcement learning. The main contributions of this paper can by summarized as follows:

- We define IMDP abstractions of infinite state Euclidean MDPs, and establish as key theoretical properties: the correctness of value iteration to compute upper and lower expected cost functions, the correctness of the upper and lower cost functions as bounds on the cost function of the original Euclidean MDP, and, under a restriction to finite time horizons, the convergence of upper and lower bounds to the actual cost values.
- We demonstrate the applicability of the general framework to analyze the accuracy of strategies learned by reinforcement learning.

Related Work. Our work is closely related to various types of MDP models proposed in different areas. *Imprecise Markov Chains and Imprecise Markov Decision processes* have been considered in areas such as operations research and artificial intelligence [3,13,14]. The focus here typically is on approximating optimal policies for fixed, finite state spaces. In the same spirit, but from a verification point of view, [2] focuses on reachability probabilities.

Lumped Markov chains are obtained by aggregating sets of states of a Markov Chain into a single state. Much work is devoted to the question of when and how the resulting process again is a Markov chain (it rarely is) [5,12]. The interplay of lumping and imprecision is considered in [6]. Most work in this area is concerned with finite state spaces. Abstraction by state space partitioning (lumping) can be understood as a special form of *partial observability* (one only observes which partition element the current state belongs to). A combination or partial observability with imprecise probabilities is considered in [7].

[9] introduce *abstractions of finite state MDPs* by partitioning the state space. Upper and lower bounds for reachability probabilities are obtained from the abstract MDP, which is formalized as a two player stochastic game. [10] is concerned with obtaining accurate specifications of an abstraction obtained by state space partitioning. The underlying state space is finite, and a fixed partition is given.

Thus, while there is a large amount of closely related work on abstracting MDPs by state space partitioning, and imprecise MDPs that can result from such an abstraction, to the best of our knowledge, our work is distinguished from previous work by: the consideration of infinite continuous state spaces for the underlying models of primary interest, and the focus on the properties of refinement sequences induced by partitions of increasing granularity.

An extended version of this paper containing all proofs can be found at https://arxiv.org/abs/2006.14923.

2   Euclidean MDP and Expected Cost

Definition 1 (Euclidean Markov Decision Processes). *A Euclidean Markov decision process (EMDP) is a tuple $\mathcal{M} = (\mathcal{S}, \mathcal{G}, Act, T, \mathcal{C})$ where:*

- *$\mathcal{S} \subseteq \mathbb{R}^K$ is a measurable subset of the K-dimensional Euclidean space equipped with the Borel σ-algebra $\mathcal{B}^K$.*
- *$\mathcal{G} \subseteq \mathcal{S}$ is a measurable set of goal states,*

- *Act is a finite set of actions,*
- $T : \mathcal{S} \times Act \times \mathcal{B}^K \to [0, 1]$ *defines for every* $a \in Act$ *a transition kernel on* $(\mathcal{S}, \mathcal{B}^K)$, *i.e.,* $T(s, a, \cdot)$ *is a probability distribution on* $\mathcal{B}^K$ *for all* $s \in \mathcal{S}$, *and* $T(\cdot, a, B)$ *is measurable for all* $B \in \mathcal{B}^K$. *Furthermore, the set of goal states is absorbing, i.e. for all* $s \in \mathcal{G}$ *and all* $a \in Act$: $T(s, a, \mathcal{G}) = 1$.
- $\mathcal{C} : \mathcal{S} \times Act \to \mathbb{R}_{\geq 0}$ *is a cost-function for state-action pairs, such that for all* $a \in Act$: $\mathcal{C}(\cdot, a)$ *is measurable, and* $\mathcal{C}(s, a) = 0$ *for all* $s \in \mathcal{G}$.

A run π of an MDP is a sequence of alternating states and actions $s_1 a_1 s_2 a_2 \cdots$. We denote the set of all runs of an EMDP $\mathcal{M}$ as $\Pi_{\mathcal{M}}$. We use π_i to denote (s_i, a_i), $\pi_{\leq i}$ for the prefix $s_1 a_1 s_2 a_2 \cdots s_i a_i$, and $\pi_{>i}$ for the tail $s_{i+1} a_{i+1} s_{i+2} a_{i+2} \cdots$ of a run. The *cost* of a run is

$$\mathcal{C}^\infty(\pi) := \sup_N \sum_{i=1}^N \mathcal{C}(\pi_i) \in [0, \infty].$$

The set $\Pi_{\mathcal{M}}$ is equipped with the product σ-algebra $(\mathcal{B}^K \otimes 2^{Act})^\infty$ generated by the cylinder sets $B_1 \times \{a_1\} \times \cdots \times B_n \times \{a_n\} \times (\mathcal{S} \times Act)^\infty$ $(n \geq 1, B_i \in \mathcal{B}^K, a_i \in Act)$. We denote with $\mathcal{B}_+$ the Borel σ-algebra restricted to the non-negative reals, and with $\bar{\mathcal{B}}_+$ the standard extension to $\bar{\mathbb{R}}_{\geq 0} := \mathbb{R}_{\geq 0} \cup \{\infty\}$, i.e. the sets of the form B and $B \cup \{\infty\}$, where $B \in \mathcal{B}_+$.

Lemma 1. $\mathcal{C}^\infty$ *is* $(\mathcal{B}^K \otimes 2^{Act})^\infty - \bar{\mathcal{B}}_+$ *measurable.*

We next consider strategies for EMDPs. We limit ourselves to memoryless and stationary strategies, noting that on the rich Euclidean state space $\mathcal{S}$ this is less of a limitation than on finite state spaces, since a non-stationary, time dependent strategy can here be turned into a stationary strategy by adding one real-valued dimension representing time.

Definition 2 (Strategy). *A (memoryless, stationary) strategy for an MDP $\mathcal{M}$ is a function* $\sigma : \mathcal{S} \to (Act \to [0, 1])$, *mapping states to probability distributions over Act, such that for every* $a \in Act$ *the function* $s \in \mathcal{S} \mapsto \sigma(s)(a)$ *is measurable.*

The following lemma is mostly a technicality that needs to be established in order to ensure that an MDP in conjunction with a strategy and an initial state distribution defines a Markov process on $\mathcal{S} \times Act$, and hence a probability distribution on $\Pi_{\mathcal{M}}$.

Lemma 2. *If σ is a strategy, then*

$$
\begin{aligned}
T_\sigma : (\mathcal{S} \times Act) \times (\mathcal{B}^K \times 2^{Act}) &\to [0, 1] \\
((s, a), (B, A)) &\mapsto \int_B \sigma(s')(A) T(s, a, ds')
\end{aligned}
\tag{1}
$$

is a transition kernel on $(\mathcal{S} \times Act, \mathcal{B}^K \times 2^{Act})$.

Usually, an initial state distribution will be given by a fixed initial state $s = s_1$. We then denote the resulting distribution over $\Pi_{\mathcal{M}}$ by $P_{s,\sigma}$ (this also depends on the underlying $\mathcal{M}$; to avoid notational clutter, we do not always make this dependence explicit in the notation).

Definition 3 (Expected Cost). *Let $s \in S$. The expected cost at s under strategy σ is the expectation of C^∞ under the distribution $P_{s,\sigma}$, denoted $\mathbb{E}_\sigma(C, s)$. The expected cost at initial state s then is defined as*

$$\mathbb{E}(C, s) := \inf_\sigma \mathbb{E}_\sigma(C, s) \in [0, \infty].$$

Example 1. If $s \in \mathcal{G}$, then for any strategy σ: $P_{s,\sigma}(\bigcap_{i \geq 1}\{s_i \in \mathcal{G}\}) = 1$, and hence $\mathbb{E}(C, s) = 0$. However, $\mathbb{E}(C, s) = 0$ can also hold for $s \notin \mathcal{G}$, since $C(s, a) = 0$ also is allowed for non-goal states s.

Note that, for any strategy σ, the functions $\mathbb{E}_\sigma(C, \cdot)$ and $\mathbb{E}(C, \cdot)$ are $[0, \infty]$-valued measurable functions on S. This follows by measurability of $C(\cdot, a)$ and $\sigma(\cdot)(a)$, for all $a \in Act$, and [1, Theorem 13.4].

2.1   Value Iteration for EMDPs

We next show that expected costs in EMDPs can be computed by value iteration. Our results are closely related to Theorem 7.3.10 in [11]. However, our scenario differs from the one treated by Puterman [11] in that we deal with uncountable state spaces, and in that we want to permit infinite cost values. Adapting Puterman's notation [11], we introduce two operators, $\mathcal{L}$ and $\mathcal{L}^\sigma$, on $[0, \infty]$-valued measurable functions E on S, defined as follows:

$$\mathcal{L}E(s) := \min_{a \in Act} \left(C(s, a) + \int_{t \in S} E(t)\, T(s, a, \mathrm{d}t) \right),$$

$$\mathcal{L}^\sigma E(s) := \sum_{a \in Act} \sigma(s)(a) \cdot \left(C(s, a) + \int_{t \in S} E(t)\, T(s, a, \mathrm{d}t) \right),$$

The operators above are well-defined:

Lemma 3. *If E is measurable, so are $\mathcal{L}E$ and $\mathcal{L}^\sigma E$.*

The set of $[0, \infty]$-valued measurable functions on S forms a complete partial order under the point wise order $E \leq E'$ iff $E(s) \leq E'(s)$, for all $s \in S$. The top $\top$ and bottom $\bot$ are respectively given by the constant functions $\top(s) := \infty$, $\bot(s) := 0$, for $s \in S$. Meet and join are the point-wise infimum and point-wise supremum, respectively. By their definition, it is easy to see that both $\mathcal{L}$ and $\mathcal{L}^\sigma$ are monotone operators.

Since the set of actions Act is finite, for every E we can define a deterministic strategy d, such that $\mathcal{L}E = \mathcal{L}^d E$. We can establish an even stronger relation:

Lemma 4. $\inf_\sigma \mathcal{L}^\sigma = \mathcal{L}$.

As a first main step we can show that the expected cost under the strategy σ is a fixed point for the operator $\mathcal{L}^\sigma$:

Proposition 1. *For any strategy σ, $\mathbb{E}_\sigma(C, \cdot) = \mathcal{L}^\sigma \mathbb{E}_\sigma(C, \cdot)$.*

As a corollary of Lemma 4 and Proposition 1, $\mathbb{E}(\mathcal{C}, \cdot)$ is a pre-fixpoint of the $\mathcal{L}$ operator. Moreover, we can show that it is the least pre-fixpoint of $\mathcal{L}$.

Proposition 2. $\mathbb{E}(\mathcal{C}, \cdot) \geq \mathcal{L}\mathbb{E}(\mathcal{C}, \cdot)$. *Moreover, if* $E \geq \mathcal{L}E$, *then* $E \geq \mathbb{E}(\mathcal{C}, \cdot)$.

By Proposition 2 and Tarski fixed point theorem, $\mathbb{E}(\mathcal{C}, \cdot)$ is the least fixed point of $\mathcal{L}$. The following theorem, provides us with a stronger result. Let L be the supremum of the point-wise increasing chain $\perp \leq \mathcal{L}\perp \leq \mathcal{L}^2\perp \leq \mathcal{L}^3\perp \leq \ldots$ The following theorem then states that value iteration converges to $\mathbb{E}(\mathcal{C}, \cdot)$.

Theorem 1. $\mathbb{E}(\mathcal{C}, \cdot) = L$.

3   Imprecise MDP

The value iteration of Theorem 1 is a mathematical process, not an algorithmic one, as it is defined pointwise on the uncountable state space $\mathcal{S}$. Our goal, therefore, is to approximate the expected cost function $\mathbb{E}(\mathcal{C}, \cdot)$ of an EMDP by expected cost functions on finite state spaces consisting of partitions of $\mathcal{S}$. In order to retain sufficient information of the original EMDP to be able to derive provable upper and lower bounds for $\mathbb{E}(\mathcal{C}, \cdot)$, we approximate the EMDP by an *Imprecise Markov Decision Processes (IMDPs)* [14].

Definition 4 (Imprecise Markov Decision Processes). *A finite state, imprecise Markov decision process (IMDP) is a tuple* $\mathcal{M} = (\mathcal{S}, \mathcal{G}, Act, T^*, \mathcal{C}^*)$ *where:*

- $\mathcal{S}$ *is a finite set of states*
- $\mathcal{G} \subseteq \mathcal{S}$ *is the set of goal states,*
- *Act is a finite set of actions,*
- $T^* : \mathcal{S} \times Act \to 2^{(\mathcal{S} \to \mathbb{R}_{\geq 0})}$ *assigns to state-action pairs a closed set of probability distributions over* $\mathcal{S}$*; the set of goal states is absorbing, i.e., for all* $s \in \mathcal{G}$ *and all* $T(s, a) \in T^*(s, a)$*:* $\sum_{t \in \mathcal{G}} T(s, a)(t) = 1$,
- $\mathcal{C}^* : \mathcal{S} \times Act \to 2^{\mathbb{R}_{\geq 0}}$ *assigns to state-action pairs a closed set of costs, such that for all* $s \in \mathcal{G}, a \in Act$*:* $\mathcal{C}^*(s, a) = \{0\}$.

Memoryless, stationary strategies σ are defined as before. In order to turn an IMDP into a fully probabilistic model, one also needs to resolve the choice of a transition probability distribution and cost value.

Definition 5 (Adversary, Lower/Upper expected cost). *An adversary* α *for an IMDP consists of two functions*

$$\alpha_T : (s, a) \mapsto \alpha_T(s, a) \in T^*(s, a) \ ((s, a) \in \mathcal{S} \times Act),$$
$$\alpha_C : (s, a) \mapsto \alpha_C(s, a) \in \mathcal{C}^*(s, a) \ ((s, a) \in \mathcal{S} \times Act).$$

A strategy σ*, an adversary* α*, and an* initial state s *together define a probability distribution* $P_{s,\sigma,\alpha}$ *over runs* π *with* $s_1 = s$*, and hence the expected cost* $\mathbb{E}_{\sigma,\alpha}(\mathcal{C}^*(\pi), s)$*. We then define the lower and upper expected cost as*

$$\mathbb{E}^{\min}(\mathcal{C}^*(\pi), s) := \min_\sigma \min_\alpha \mathbb{E}_{\sigma,\alpha}(\mathcal{C}^*(\pi), s) \qquad (2)$$

$$\mathbb{E}^{\max}(\mathcal{C}^*(\pi), s) := \min_\sigma \max_\alpha \mathbb{E}_{\sigma,\alpha}(\mathcal{C}^*(\pi), s) \qquad (3)$$

Since $T^*(s,a)$ and $C^*(s,a)$ are required to be closed sets, we can here write $\min_\alpha$ and $\max_\alpha$ rather than $\inf_\alpha$, $\sup_\alpha$. Furthermore, the closure conditions are needed to justify a restriction to stationary adversaries, as the following example shows (cf. also Example 7.3.2 in [11]).

Example 2. Let $\mathcal{S} = \{s_1, s_2, s_3\}$, $Act = \{a\}$, We write (p_1, p_2, p_3) for a transition probability distribution T with $T(s_i) = p_i$. Then let $T^*(s_1, a) = \{(p_1, p_2, p_3) : p_1 \in]0, 1[, p_2 = 1-p_1\}$, $T^*(s_2, a) = T^*(s_3, a) = \{(0,0,1)\}$. $C^*(s_1, a) = C^*(s_3, a) = \{0\}$, $C^*(s_2, a) = \{1\}$. Since there is only one action, there is only one strategy σ. For $i \geq 1$ let $\epsilon_i \in]0, 1[$ such that $\prod_{i=1}^\infty \epsilon_i = \delta > 0$. Then, if the adversary at the i'th step selects transition probabilities $(\epsilon_i, 1 - \epsilon_i, 0)$ one obtains $\mathbb{E}^{\min}(C^*(\pi), s_1) = 1-\delta$. For every stationary adversary the transition from s_1 to s_2 will be taken eventually with probability 1, so that here $\mathbb{E}^{\min}(C^*(\pi), s_1) = 1$.

We note that only in the case of $\mathbb{E}^{\max}$ does α act as an "adversary" to the strategy σ. In the case of $\mathbb{E}^{\min}$, σ and α represent co-operative strategies. In other definitions of imprecise MDPs only the transition probabilities are set-valued [14]. Here we also allow an imprecise cost function. Note, however, that for the definition of $\mathbb{E}^{\min}(C^*, s)$ and $\mathbb{E}^{\max}(C^*, s)$ the adversary's strategy α_C will simply be to select the minimal (respectively maximal) possible costs, and that we can also obtain $\mathbb{E}^{\min}, \mathbb{E}^{\max}$ as the expected lower/upper costs on IMDPs with point-valued cost functions

$$C^{\min}(s,a) := \min C^*(s,a), \qquad C^{\max}(s,a) := \max C^*(s,a),$$

where then the adversary has no choice for the strategy α_C.

3.1 Value Iteration for IMDPs

We now characterize $\mathbb{E}^{\min}, \mathbb{E}^{\max}$ as limits of value iteration, again following the strategy of the proof of Theorem 7.3.10 of [11]. In this case, the proof has to be adapted to accommodate the additional optimization of the adversary, and, as in Subsect. 2.1, to allow for infinite costs. We again start by defining suitable operators $\mathcal{L}^{\min}, \mathcal{L}^{\max}$ on $[0, \infty]$-valued functions C defined on $\mathcal{S}$:

$$(\mathcal{L}^{\mathrm{opt}} C)(s) := \min_{a \in Act} \left(C^{\mathrm{opt}}(s,a) + \mathop{\mathrm{opt}}_{T \in T^*(s,a)} \sum_{s'} T(s') C(s') \right), \tag{4}$$

where opt $\in \{\min, \max\}$. The mapping

$$\alpha_T^{\mathrm{opt}}(C) : (s,a) \mapsto \mathop{\mathrm{arg\,opt}}_{T \in T^*(s,a)} \sum_{s'} T(s') C(s') \tag{5}$$

defines the α_T of an adversary. Similarly

$$\sigma^{\mathrm{opt}}(C) : s \mapsto \mathop{\mathrm{arg\,min}}_{a \in Act} \left(C^{\mathrm{opt}}(s,a) + \sum_{s'} \alpha_T^{\mathrm{opt}}(C)(s,a) C(s') \right) \tag{6}$$

defines a strategy.

Let $\perp$ be the function that is constant 0 on $\mathcal{S}$. Denote

$$L^{\mathrm{opt},n} := (\mathcal{L}^{\mathrm{opt}})^n \perp, \quad \text{and} \quad L^{\mathrm{opt}} := \sup_{n \geq 0} L^{\mathrm{opt},n} \tag{7}$$

We can now state the applicability of value iteration for IMDPs as follows:

Theorem 2. *Let* opt $\in \{\min, \max\}$. *Then* $\mathbb{E}^{\mathrm{opt}}(\mathcal{C}^*(\pi), \cdot) = L^{\mathrm{opt}}$

We note that even though $\mathcal{L}^{\mathrm{opt}}$, in contrast to the $\mathcal{L}$ operator for EMDPs, now only needs to be computed over a finite state space, we do not obtain from Theorem 2 a fully specified algorithmic procedure for the computation of $\mathbb{E}^{\mathrm{opt}}$, because the optimization over $T^*(s, a)$ contained in (4) will require customized solutions that depend on the structure of the $T^*(s, a)$.

4 Approximation by Partitioning

From now on we only consider EMDPs whose state space $\mathcal{S}$ is a compact subset of $\mathbb{R}^K$. We approximate such a Euclidean MDP by IMDPs constructed from finite partitions of $\mathcal{S}$. In the following, we denote with $\mathcal{A} = \{\nu_1, \ldots, \nu_{|\mathcal{A}|}\} \subset 2^{\mathcal{S}}$ a finite partition of $\mathcal{S}$. We call an element $\nu \in \mathcal{A}$ a *region* and shall assume that each such ν is Borel measurable. For $s \in \mathcal{S}$ we denote by $[s]_{\mathcal{A}}$ the unique region $\nu \in \mathcal{A}$ such that $s \in \nu$. The *diameter* of a region is $\delta(\nu) := \sup_{s,s' \in \nu} \| s - s' \|$, and the diameter of a partition $\mathcal{A}$ is defined as $\delta(\mathcal{A}) := \max_{\nu \in \mathcal{A}} \delta(\nu)$. We say that a partition $\mathcal{B}$ refines a partition $\mathcal{A}$ if for any $\nu \in \mathcal{B}$ there exist $\mu \in \mathcal{A}$ with $\nu \subseteq \mu$. We write $\mathcal{A} \sqsubseteq \mathcal{B}$ in this case.

A Euclidean MDP $\mathcal{M} = (\mathcal{S}, \mathcal{G}, Act, T, \mathcal{C})$ and a partition $\mathcal{A}$ of $\mathcal{S}$ induces an abstracting IMDP [9,10] according to the following definition.

Definition 6 (Induced IMDP). *Let* $\mathcal{M} = (\mathcal{S}, Act, s_{init}, T, \mathcal{C}, \mathcal{G})$ *be an MDP, and let* $\mathcal{A}$ *be a finite partition of* $\mathcal{S}$ *consistent with* $\mathcal{G}$ *in the sense that for any* $\nu \in \mathcal{A}$ *either* $\nu \subseteq \mathcal{G}$ *or* $\nu \cap \mathcal{G} = \emptyset$. *The IMDP defined by* $\mathcal{M}$ *and* $\mathcal{A}$ *then is* $\mathcal{M}_{\mathcal{A}} = (\mathcal{A}, \mathcal{G}_{\mathcal{A}}, Act, T^*_{\mathcal{A}}, \mathcal{C}^*_{\mathcal{A}})$, *where*

- $\mathcal{G}_{\mathcal{A}} = \{\nu \in \mathcal{A} | \nu \subseteq \mathcal{G}\}$

$$T^*_{\mathcal{A}}(\nu, a) = cl(\{T_{\mathcal{A}}(s, a) \mid s \in \nu\}),$$

where $T_{\mathcal{A}}(s, a)$ *is the marginal of* $T(s, a, \cdot)$ *on* $\mathcal{A}$, *i.e.* $T_{\mathcal{A}}(s, a)(\nu') = \int_{\nu'} T(s, a, dt)$, *and* cl *denotes topological closure.*

$$\mathcal{C}^*_{\mathcal{A}}(\nu, a) = cl(\{C(s, a) | s \in \nu\})$$

The following theorem states how an induced IMDP approximates the underlying Euclidean MDP. In the following, we use sub-scripts on expectation operators to identify the (I)MDPs that define the expectations.

Theorem 3. *Let $\mathcal{M}$ and $\mathcal{A}$ as in Definition 6. Then for all $s \in \mathcal{S}$:*

$$\mathbb{E}^{\min}_{\mathcal{M}_{\mathcal{A}}}(\mathcal{C}^*_{\mathcal{A}}, [s]_{\mathcal{A}}) \leq \mathbb{E}_{\mathcal{M}}(\mathcal{C}, s) \leq \mathbb{E}^{\max}_{\mathcal{M}_{\mathcal{A}}}(\mathcal{C}^*_{\mathcal{A}}, [s]_{\mathcal{A}}). \tag{8}$$

If $\mathcal{A} \sqsubseteq \mathcal{B}$, then $\mathcal{B}$ improves the bounds in the sense that

$$\mathbb{E}^{\min}_{\mathcal{M}_{\mathcal{A}}}(\mathcal{C}^*_{\mathcal{A}}, [s]_{\mathcal{A}}) \leq \mathbb{E}^{\min}_{\mathcal{M}_{\mathcal{B}}}(\mathcal{C}^*_{\mathcal{A}}, [s]_{\mathcal{B}}), \tag{9}$$

$$\mathbb{E}^{\max}_{\mathcal{M}_{\mathcal{A}}}(\mathcal{C}^*_{\mathcal{A}}, [s]_{\mathcal{A}}) \geq \mathbb{E}^{\max}_{\mathcal{M}_{\mathcal{B}}}(\mathcal{C}^*_{\mathcal{B}}, [s]_{\mathcal{B}}). \tag{10}$$

Our goal now is to establish conditions under which the approximation (8) becomes arbitrarily tight for partitions of sufficiently low diameter. This will require certain continuity conditions for $\mathcal{M}$ as spelled out in the following definition. In the following,

$$d_{tv}(P, P') := sup_{S \subseteq \mathcal{S}} |P(S) - P'(S)|$$

denotes the total variation distance between distributions P, P' on a state space $\mathcal{S}$. We will be using d_{tv} both when $\mathcal{S} = \mathcal{A}$ is finite, and for continuous spaces $\mathcal{S}$. In the latter case, the supremum over $S \subseteq \mathcal{S}$ is restricted to measurable subsets.

Definition 7 (Continuous Euclidean MDP). *A Euclidean MDP $\mathcal{M}$ is continuous if*

- *For each $\epsilon > 0$ there exists $\delta > 0$, such that: for all partitions $\mathcal{A}$, if $\delta(\mathcal{A}) \leq \delta$, then for all $\nu \in \mathcal{A}$, $s, s' \in \nu$, $a \in Act$: $d_{tv}(T(s, a), T(s', a)) \leq \epsilon$.*
- *$\mathcal{C}$ is continuous on $\mathcal{S}$ for all $a \in Act$.*

We observe that due to the assumed compactness of $\mathcal{S}$, the first condition of Definition 7 is satisfied if T is defined as a function $T(s, a, t)$ on $\mathcal{S} \times Act \times \mathcal{S}$ that for each a as a function of s, t is continuous on $\mathcal{S} \times \mathcal{S}$, and such that $T(s, a, \cdot)$ is for all s, a a density function relative to Lebesgue measure.

We next introduce some notation for N-step expectations and distributions. In the following, we use τ to denote strategies for induced IMDPs defined on partitions $\mathcal{A}$, whereas σ is reserved for strategies defined on Euclidean state spaces $\mathcal{S}$. For a given partition $\mathcal{A}$ and strategy τ for $\mathcal{M}_{\mathcal{A}}$ let α^+, α^- denote two strategies for the adversary (to be interpreted as strategies that are close to achieving $sup_\alpha \mathbb{E}_{\tau,\alpha}(\mathcal{C}^*(\pi), \cdot)$ and $inf_\alpha \mathbb{E}_{\tau,\alpha}(\mathcal{C}^*(\pi), \cdot)$, respectively, even though we will not explicitly require properties that derive from this interpretation). We then denote with $P^N_{\tau,\alpha^+}, P^N_{\tau,\alpha^-}$ the distributions defined by τ, α^+ and τ, α^- on run prefixes of length N, and with $\mathbb{E}^N_{\tau,\alpha^+}, \mathbb{E}^N_{\tau,\alpha^-}$ the corresponding expectations for the sum of the first N costs $\sum_{i=1}^{N} \alpha_C^{+[-]}(\nu_i, a_i)$. The P^N and $\mathbb{E}^N$ also depend on the initial state ν_1. To avoid notational clutter, we do not make this explicit in the notation. We then obtain the following approximation guarantee:

Theorem 4. *Let $\mathcal{M}$ be a continuous EMDP. For all N, $\epsilon > 0$ there exists $\delta > 0$, such that for all partitions $\mathcal{A}$ with $\delta(\mathcal{A}) \leq \delta$, and all strategies τ defined on $\mathcal{A}$:*

$$|\mathbb{E}^N_{\tau,\alpha^+} - \mathbb{E}^N_{\tau,\alpha^-}| \leq \epsilon \tag{11}$$

and

$$d_{tv}(P^N_{\tau,\alpha^+}, P^N_{\tau,\alpha^-}) \leq \epsilon. \tag{12}$$

Theorem 4 is a strengthening of Theorem 2 in [8]. The latter applied to processes that are guaranteed to terminate within N steps. Our new theorem applies to the expected cost of the first N steps in a process of unbounded length. When the process has a bounded time horizon of no more than N steps, and if we let τ, α^+, α^- be the strategy and the adversaries that achieve the optima in (2), respectively (3), then (11) becomes

$$|\mathbb{E}_{\mathcal{M}_\mathcal{A}}^{\max} - \mathbb{E}_{\mathcal{M}_\mathcal{A}}^{\min}| \leq \epsilon. \tag{13}$$

We conjecture that this actually also holds true for arbitrary continuous EMDPs:

Conjecture 1. Let $\mathcal{M}$ be a continuous Euclidean MDP. Let $\mathcal{A}_0 \sqsubseteq \mathcal{A}_1 \sqsubseteq \cdots \sqsubseteq \mathcal{A}_i \sqsubseteq \cdots$ be a sequence of partitions consistent with $\mathcal{G}$ such that $\lim_{i \to \infty} \delta(\mathcal{A}_i) = 0$. Then for all $s \in \mathcal{S}$:

$$\lim_{i \to \infty} \mathbb{E}_{\mathcal{M}_{\mathcal{A}_i}}^{\min} (\mathcal{C}_{\mathcal{A}_i}^*, [s]_{\mathcal{A}_i}) = \mathbb{E}_\mathcal{M}(\mathcal{C}, s) = \lim_{i \to \infty} \mathbb{E}_{\mathcal{M}_{\mathcal{A}_i}}^{\max} (\mathcal{C}_{\mathcal{A}_i}^*, [s]_{\mathcal{A}_i}).$$

5   Examples and Experiments

We now use our semi-random walker example to illustrate the theory presented in the preceding sections, and to demonstrate its applicability to the validation of machine learning models.

5.1   IMDP Value Iteration

We first illustrate experimentally the bounds and convergence properties expressed by Theorems 3 and 4. For this we consider a nested sequence of partitions of the continuous state space $\mathcal{S} = [0, x_{max}] \times [0, t_{max}]$ consisting of regular grid partitions $\mathcal{A} = \mathcal{A}(\Delta)$ defined by a width parameter Δ for the regions. We run value iteration to compute $\mathbb{E}_{\mathcal{M}_\mathcal{A}(\Delta)}^{\min}$ and $\mathbb{E}_{\mathcal{M}_\mathcal{A}(\Delta)}^{\max}$ for the values $\Delta \in \{0.1, 0.05, 0.025\}$. For illustration purposes, we plot expected cost functions along one-dimensional sections $\mathcal{S}_t' = [0, x_{max}] \times \{t\}$ for the two fixed time points $t = 0$ and $t = 0.7$.

Figure 3 shows the upper and lower expected costs that we obtain from the induced IMDPs. One can see how the intervals narrow with successive partition refinements. The bounds on the section $\mathcal{S}_0'$ are closer and converge more uniformly than on $\mathcal{S}_{0.7}'$. This shows that in the upper left region of the state space ($x < 0.5, t \geq 0.7$) the adversary has a greater influence on the process than at the lower part of the state space ($x \sim 0$), and the difference between a cooperative and a non-cooperative adversary is more pronounced.

Ultimately, induced strategies are of greater interest than the concrete cost functions. Once upper and lower expectations define the same strategy, further refinement may not be necessary. Figure 4 illustrates for the whole state space $\mathcal{S}$ the strategies σ obtained from the lower (Eq. (2)) and upper (Eq. (3)) approximations. On regions colored blue and yellow, both strategies agree to take the

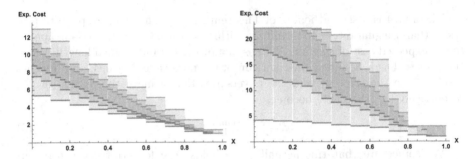

Fig. 3. Upper (yellow) and lower (blue) expected cost functions of IMDPs $\mathcal{M}_{\mathcal{A}}(\Delta)$ for $\Delta \in \{0.1, 0.05, 0.025\}$ on $\mathcal{S}'_0$ (left) and $\mathcal{S}'_{0.7}$ (right). (Color figure online)

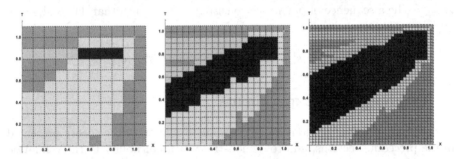

Fig. 4. Strategies obtained from lower and upper expected cost approximations for $\mathcal{M}_{\mathcal{A}}(\Delta)$ for $\Delta = 0.1, 0.05, 0.025$ (left to right). (Color figure online)

fast and *slow* actions, respectively. The regions colored light green are those where the lower bound strategy chooses the *fast* action, and the upper bound strategy the *slow* action. Conversely for the regions colored light red. One can observe how the blue and yellow areas increase in size with successive partition refinements. However, this growth is not entirely monotonic: for example, some regions in the upper left that for $\Delta = 0.1$ are yellow are sub-divided in successive refinements $\Delta = 0.05, 0.025$ into regions that are partly yellow, partly light green.

5.2   Analysis of Learned Strategies

We now turn to partitions computed by the reinforcement learning method developed in [8], and a comparison of the learned cost functions and strategies with those obtained from the induced IMDPs. We have implemented the semi-random walker in UPPAAL STRATEGO and used reinforcement learning to learn partitions, cost functions and strategies. Our learning framework produces a sequence of refinements, based on sampling 100 additional runs for each refinement. In the following we consider the models learned after $k = 27$ and $k = 205$ refinements.

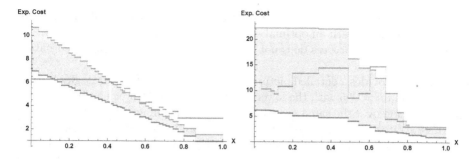

Fig. 5. Expected cost functions along S'_0 (left) and $S'_{0.7}$ (right). Green: learned cost function; yellow/blue: upper/lower expected cost function obtained from IMDP. (Color figure online)

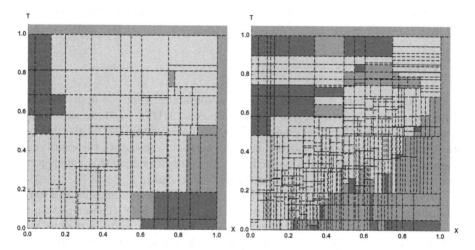

Fig. 6. Comparison of the strategies obtained for the IMDP induced by the partition $\mathcal{A}(27)$ (left) and $\mathcal{A}(205)$ (right). (Color figure online)

Figure 5 illustrates expected costs functions for the partition learned at $k = 205$. One can observe a strong correlation between the bounds and the learned costs. Nevertheless, the learned cost function sometimes lies outside the given bounds. This is to be expected, since the random sampling process may produce data that is not sufficiently representative to estimate costs for some regions.

Turning again to the strategies obtained on the whole state space, we first note that the learned strategy at $k = 205$, which is shown in Fig. 1 (right) exhibits an overall similarity with the strategies illustrated in Fig. 4, with the *fast* action preferred along a diagonal region in the middle of the state space. To understand the differences between the learning and IMDP results, it is important to note that in the learning setting $s_0 = (0, 0)$ is taken to be the initial state of interest, and all sampling starts there. As a result, regions that are unlikely to be reached (under any choice of actions) from this initial state will obtain very little relevant data, and therefore unreliable cost estimates. This is not necessarily a disadvantage, if we want to learn an optimal control strategy for processes starting at s_0. The value iteration process does not take into account the distinguished nature of s_0.

Figure 6 provides a detailed picture of the consistency of the strategies learned at $k = 27$ and $k = 205$ with the lower and upper bound strategies obtained from value iteration over the same partitions. Drawn in green are those regions where all three strategies pick the same action. Yellow and red are those regions, where the learned strategy agrees with one, respectively none, of the upper/lower bound strategies. As Fig. 6 shows, the areas of greatest discrepancies (red) are those in the top left and bottom right, which are unlikely to be reached from initial state $(0,0)$, and therefore have little data support in learning. The figure also indicates that unlike for the rightmost partition in Fig. 4, the upper and lower bound strategies here do not yet reach agreement on taking the *fast* action along the middle diagonal.

6   Conclusion

In this paper we have developed theoretical foundations for the approximation of Euclidean MDPs by finite state space imprecise MDPs. We have shown that bounds on the cost function computed on the basis of the IMDP abstractions are correct, and that for bounded time horizons they converge to the exact costs when the IMDP abstractions are refined. We conjecture that this convergence also holds for the total cost of (potentially) infinite runs.

The results we here obtained provide theoretical underpinnings for the learning approach developed in [8]. At the very fundamental level, Theorems 3 and 4 show that the hypothesis space of strategies defined over finite partitions that underlies our reinforcement learning approach is adequate in the sense that it contains strategy representations that approximate the optimal strategy for the underlying continuous domain arbitrarily well. To go from here to a proof of asymptotic optimality of learned strategies, one still needs to analyze the interplay of convergence of Q-learning on finite state spaces with the iterative refinement steps of our learning approach.

Upper and lower bounds computed from induced IMDPs can be used to check the accuracy of learned value functions. As we have seen, data sparsity and sampling variance can make the learned cost functions fall outside computed bounds. One can also use value iteration on IMDP approximations directly as a tool for computing cost functions and strategies, which then would come with stronger guarantees than what we obtain through learning. However, compared to the learning approach, this has important limitations: first, we will usually only obtain a partial strategy that is uniquely defined only where upper and lower bounds lead to the same actions. Second, we will require a full model of the underlying EMDP, from which IMDP abstractions then can be derived, and the optimization problem over adversaries that is part of the value iteration process must be tractable. Reinforcement learning, on the other hand, can also be applied to black box systems, and its computational complexity is essentially independent of the complexities of the underlying dynamic system.

References

1. Billingsley, P.: Probability and Measure, 2nd edn. Wiley, Hoboken (1986)
2. Chen, T., Han, T., Kwiatkowska, M.: On the complexity of model checking interval-valued discrete time Markov chains. Inf. Process. Lett. **113**(7), 210–216 (2013)
3. Crossman, R., Coolen-Schrijner, P., Škulj, D., Coolen, F.: Imprecise Markov chains with an absorbing state. In: Proceedings of the 6th International Symposium on Imprecise Probability: Theories and Applications (ISIPTA), pp. 119–128. Citeseer (2009)
4. David, A., Jensen, P.G., Larsen, K.G., Mikučionis, M., Taankvist, J.H.: Uppaal Stratego. In: Baier, C., Tinelli, C. (eds.) TACAS 2015. LNCS, vol. 9035, pp. 206–211. Springer, Heidelberg (2015). https://doi.org/10.1007/978-3-662-46681-0_16
5. Derisavi, S., Hermanns, H., Sanders, W.H.: Optimal state-space lumping in Markov chains. Inf. Process. Lett. **87**(6), 309–315 (2003)
6. Erreygers, A., De Bock, J.: Computing inferences for large-scale continuous-time markov chains by combining lumping with imprecision. In: Destercke, S., Denoeux, T., Gil, M.Á., Grzegorzewski, P., Hryniewicz, O. (eds.) SMPS 2018. AISC, vol. 832, pp. 78–86. Springer, Cham (2019). https://doi.org/10.1007/978-3-319-97547-4_11
7. Itoh, H., Nakamura, K.: Partially observable Markov decision processes with imprecise parameters. Artif. Intell. **171**(8–9), 453–490 (2007)
8. Jaeger, M., Jensen, P.G., Guldstrand Larsen, K., Legay, A., Sedwards, S., Taankvist, J.H.: Teaching Stratego to play ball: optimal synthesis for continuous space MDPs. In: Chen, Y.-F., Cheng, C.-H., Esparza, J. (eds.) ATVA 2019. LNCS, vol. 11781, pp. 81–97. Springer, Cham (2019). https://doi.org/10.1007/978-3-030-31784-3_5
9. Kwiatkowska, M.Z., Norman, G., Parker, D.: Game-based abstraction for Markov decision processes. In: QEST 2006, pp. 157–166. IEEE Computer Society (2006). ISBN 0-7695-2665-9. https://doi.org/10.1109/QEST.2006.19
10. Lun, Y.Z., Wheatley, J., D'Innocenzo, A., Abate, A.: Approximate abstractions of Markov chains with interval decision processes. In: Abate, A., Girard, A., Heemels, M. (eds.) ADHS 2018. IFAC-PapersOnLine, vol. 51, pp. 91–96. Elsevier (2018). https://doi.org/10.1016/j.ifacol.2018.08.016
11. Puterman, M.L.: Markov Decision Processes. Wiley, Hoboken (2005)
12. Rubino, G., Sericola, B.: A finite characterization of weak lumpable Markov processes. Part i: the discrete time case. Stoch. Process. Appl. **38**(2), 195–204 (1991)
13. Troffaes, M., Gledhill, J., Škulj, D., Blake, S.: Using imprecise continuous time Markov chains for assessing the reliability of power networks with common cause failure and non-immediate repair. In: SIPTA 2015 (2015)
14. White III, C.C., Eldeib, H.K.: Markov decision processes with imprecise transition probabilities. Oper. Res. **42**(4), 739–749 (1994)

Shield Synthesis for Reinforcement Learning

Bettina Könighofer[1,2(✉)], Florian Lorber[3], Nils Jansen[4], and Roderick Bloem[1]

[1] Institute IAIK, Graz University of Technology, Graz, Austria
bettina.koenighofer@iaik.tugraz.at
[2] Silicon Austria Labs, TU-Graz SAL DES Lab, Graz, Austria
[3] Department of Computer Science, Aalborg University, Aalborg, Denmark
[4] Radboud University Nijmegen, Nijmegen, The Netherlands

Abstract. Reinforcement learning algorithms discover policies that maximize reward. However, these policies generally do not adhere to safety, leaving safety in reinforcement learning (and in artificial intelligence in general) an open research problem. Shield synthesis is a formal approach to synthesize a correct-by-construction reactive system called a shield that enforces safety properties of a running system while interfering with its operation as little as possible. A shield attached to a learning agent guarantees safety during learning and execution phases. In this paper we summarize three types of shields that are synthesized from different specification languages, and discuss their applicability to reinforcement learning. First, we discuss deterministic shields that enforce specifications expressed as linear temporal logic specifications. Second, we discuss the synthesis of probabilistic shields from specifications in probabilistic temporal logic. Third, we discuss how to synthesize timed shields from timed automata specifications. This paper summarizes the application areas, advantages, disadvantages and synthesis approaches for the three types of shields and gives an overview of experimental results.

1 Introduction

Advances in machine learning enabled a new paradigm for developing controllers for autonomous systems that accomplish complicated tasks in uncertain and dynamic environments. The increasing use of learning-based controllers in physical systems in the proximity of humans strengthens the concern of whether these systems will operate safely. While convergence, optimality and data-efficiency of learning algorithms are well understood, ensuring the *safety* of decision-making for systems employing AI is still a major challenge [10].

Reinforcement learning (RL) [20] lets an agent *explore* its environment by sequential decision-making. During the exploration of the underlying Markov decision process (MDPs) [18] of the environment, the current policy may be unsafe in the sense that it harms the agent or the environment. This shortcoming

© Springer Nature Switzerland AG 2020
T. Margaria and B. Steffen (Eds.): ISoLA 2020, LNCS 12476, pp. 290–306, 2020.
https://doi.org/10.1007/978-3-030-61362-4_16

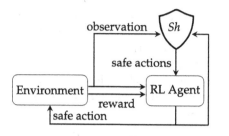

Fig. 1. Pre-shielding.

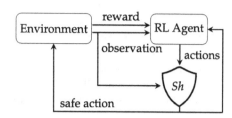

Fig. 2. Post-shielding.

restricts the application of RL mainly to application areas where safety is not a concern and has triggered the direction of *safe RL* [10].

In this paper, we approach the problem of ensuring safety in RL from a formal methods perspective. We discuss *shielded learning*, a framework that allows to apply RL while enforcing correctness w.r.t. a given safety specification. In the traditional RL setting, the learning agent chooses an action in every time step and sends it to the environment. The environment evolves accordingly and sends the agent an observation of its state and a reward for the underlying transition. The objective of the agent is optimizing the accumulated reward.

Our approach introduces a *shield* [1] into the traditional RL setting. The shield is computed upfront from the safety part of the given system specification and an abstraction of the agent's environment dynamics. We say that an action is *wrong*, if it may cause the violation of the safety specification; and *correct* otherwise. A shield prevents any wrong decisions from the agent. Shields fulfill the following requirements:

1. **Guaranteed correctness:** If the sequential decision-making of the learning agent is shielded, the safety specification is satisfied during the learning and execution phase (as long as the shield is used).
2. **Minimal interference:** The shield restricts potential decisions as little as possible.

We discuss two types of shields. In *pre-shielding*, see Fig. 1, the shield is implemented before the learning agent and each time the learning agent is to make a decision, it restricts the choices for the learner to a list of correct actions. In *post-shielding*, see Fig. 2, the shield monitors the actions selected by the agent and corrects them if and only if the chosen action is wrong.

Advantages. Shielded learning provides the following key advantages:

Separation of concerns. The synthesis algorithms for the computation of shields make relatively mild assumptions on the input/output structure of the learning algorithm (rather than its inner working). Thus, the correctness guarantees are agnostic to the learning algorithm of choice. The shielding setup introduces a clear boundary between the learning agent and the shield, helping to separate the concerns, e.g., correctness on one side and convergence and optimality on the other.

Scalability. A key advantage of using a separate safety objective is that we may analyze safety on just a fraction of the system. In our experiments, these MDP fragments are at least ten orders of magnitude smaller than a full model of the system, rendering model-based verification techniques applicable to realistic scenarios and enabling their usage to compute a shield. The learner itself has to consider the full model to increase performance, but may do so using either model-based or model-free approaches.

This paper summarizes the three papers on shielded RL [1,5,11] using the safety fragments of LTL [17], PLTL [4], and timed automata [2] as specification language, and gives a survey on how shields have been used in RL so far. Using a shield synthesized from an LTL specification, or a timed automata specification, a learning agent avoids safety violations altogether. Therefore, such shields guaranty correctness during the learning and execution phase and thereby justifying the deployment of learned controllers in safety critical applications. While both types of shields guarantee correctness, LTL is not expressible enough to capture real time behavior and thus the corresponding shields cannot protect against timing related faults. Therefore, if the learning agent has to learn complex timing behavior, timed shields are preferable. While guaranteed safety is necessary for some applications, in other cases this tight restriction limits the agent's exploration and understanding of the environment, and policies satisfying the restrictions may not even exist. Without randomness, all states are either absolutely safe or unsafe. However, in the presence of randomness, safety may be seen as a quantitative measure: in some states, all actions may induce a considerable risk, while in other states, one action may be considered relatively safe. Probabilistic shields from safety specifications given in PLTL incorporate more liberal constraints that enforce safety violations to occur only with small probability.

Related Work. Most approaches to safe RL [10] rely on reward engineering and changing the learning objective. As rewards are specialized for particular environments, reward engineering runs the risk of triggering negative side effects or hiding potential bugs. The area of *safe exploration* aims at restricting decision-making to adhere to safety requirements during the exploration of an environment [3]. Such restrictions may cause *insufficient progress* in following the original objective of the decision-maker or even *deadlocks.*

First approaches to safe RL that incorporate formal methods tackle this problem with pre-computations. First, a safe, permissive strategy is computed. Then, exploration is constrained to this strategy and thereby meets the imposed safety requirements. This requires strong assumptions on the available information about the environment [6,9,15].

An alternative to ensure safety is runtime enforcement (RE) [8,19] which enforces the expected behavior at runtime. Shields are correct-by-construction runtime enforcers, with the additional goal of interfering with the RL agent's choices as little as possible. The concept of a shield to ensure the correctness of reactive systems was proposed in [12].

Outline. In this work we summarize how to construct shields from different specification languages. We start with the shield synthesis from safety specifications in LTL in Sect. 2. Next, probabilistic shields are summarized in Sect. 3. Finally, we give an overview on timed shields in Sect. 4. We conclude in Sect. 5.

2   Safe RL via Shielding

In this section, we first discuss how we introduce a shield into the traditional RL setting, and discuss post- and pre-shielding. Next, we discuss the synthesis procedure to compute shields from safety specifications expressed in LTL, as proposed in [1], and conclude the section with the results of their case study.

2.1   Setting for Shielded RL

The loop between the learning agent and its environment can be modified in two alternative ways. Based on the location at which the shield is applied, the shielding setting is called *pre-shielding* and *post-shielding*, respectively.

Pre-shielding. The interaction between the agent, the environment and the shield is as follows: at every time step t, the shield computes a set of all correct actions $\{a_t^1, \ldots, a_t^k\}$. i.e., it takes the set of all actions available, and removes all wrong actions that would violate the safety specification. The agent receives the list and picks a correct action $a_t \in \{a_t^1, \ldots, a_t^k\}$. The environment executes action a_t, moves to a next state s_{t+1}, and computes the reward r_{t+1}. The task of the shield is basically to modify the set of available actions of the agent in every time step, such that only correct actions remain.

Post-shielding. The shield monitors the actions of the agent, and substitutes the selected actions by correct actions whenever this is necessary to prevent the violation of the specification. In each step t, the agent selects an action a_t^1. The shield forwards a_t^1 to the environment; i.e., $a_t = a_t^1$. Only if a_t^1 is wrong w.r.t. the specification, the shield selects a different correct action $a_t \neq a_t^1$. The environment executes a_t, moves to s_{t+1} and computes r_{t+1}. The agent receives a_t and r_{t+1}, and performs policy updates based on that information. For the executed action a_t, the agent updates its policy using r_{t+1}. This raises the question what the reward for a_t^1 should be, in case that $a_t \neq a_t^1$. Two different approaches are the following:

1. **Assign a punishment r_{t+1}' to a_t^1.** The agent assigns a punishment $r_{t+1}' < 0$ to the wrong action a_t^1 and learns that selecting a_t^1 at state s_t is wrong, without ever violating the specification. However, there is no guarantee that wrong actions are not part of the final policy. Therefore, the shield has to remain active even after the learning phase.
2. **Assign the reward r_{t+1} to a_t^1.** The agent updates the wrong action a_t^1 with the reward r_{t+1}. Therefore, picking wrong actions could be part of an optimal policy by the agent. Since a_t is always correct as it was selected by the shield,

this does not pose a problem and the agent never has to learn to avoid wrong actions. Consequently, the shield is needed during the learning and execution phase.

Properties of Pre-shielding and Post-shielding:

- Post-shielding has the advantage, that the learning algorithm is treated as a total back box. In order for pre-shielding to work, an agent needs to choose the actions w.r.t. the suggestions of the shield, in other words, the shield needs to be able to influence the set of actions per state from the agent.
- Another big advantage of post-shielding is that it works even if the learning algorithm is already in the execution phase and therefore follows a fixed policy. In every step, the shield just takes the provided action from the agent and corrects it if necessary to ensure safe operation of the system. The learning agent does not even need to know that it is shielded.
- In general, post-shielding is more restrictive than pre-shielding. Instead of overruling the agent, a pre-shield leaves the choice of all safe actions to the agent. Thus, pre-shielding in general has more potential to speed up the learning performance than post-shielding.
- In order to be less restrictive to the agent in the post-shielding setting, in every time step, the agent can provide a ranking $rank_t = \{a_t^1, \ldots, a_t^k\}$ on the actions to the shield, i.e., the agent wants a_t^1 to be executed the most, a_t^2 the second most, etc. The shield selects the first action $a_t \in rank_t$ that is correct. Only if all actions in $rank_t$ are wrong, the shield selects a correct action $a_t \notin rank_t$. Both approaches for updating the policy discussed before can naturally be extended for a ranking of several actions. A second advantage of having a ranking on actions is that the learning agent can perform several policy updates at once; e.g. if all actions in $rank_t$ are wrong, the agent can perform $|rank_t| + 1$ policy updates in one step.

2.2   Construction of Shields

Given is an RL problem in which an agent has to learn an optimal policy for an unknown environment that can be modelled by an MDP while satisfying a safety specification given in the safety fragment of LTL. The reactive synthesis algorithm to create a shield works as follows:

Step 1. Construct an abstraction of the environment dynamics. Reactive synthesis does not require the environment dynamics to be completely known in advance. However, to reason about when exactly a specification violation cannot be avoided, we have to give a (coarse finite-state) abstraction of them. Such an abstraction has to be conservative w.r.t. the behavior of the real MDP. This approximation may have finitely many states, even if the MDP has infinitely many states or is only approximately known. An abstraction of an MDP describes how its executions can possibly evolve, and provides the needed information about the environment to allow planning ahead w.r.t. the safety properties.

Step 2. Construct a safety automaton. Translate the given safety specifications in LTL to a deterministic safety word automaton [12] with a set of safe states F, i.e., an automaton in which only safe states in F may be visited.

Step 3. Construct and solve the safety game. The MDP abstraction that represents the environment and the safety automaton are transformed into a safety game. In the construction, the state space of the game is the product between the specification automaton state set and the abstraction state set. The game is played between two players. In the game, player 0 chooses the next observations from the MDP state, and player 1 chooses the next action. The safe states in the game are the ones at which the specification automaton is in a safe state and that are reachable within the abstraction. The play is won by player 1, if only safe states are visited during the play. In order to win, player 1 has to plan ahead: it can never allow the play to visit a state, from which the player 0 can force the play to visit an unsafe state in the future.

This planning ahead is the true power of synthesis. Think about an autonomous car that is heading towards a cliff. It is to late, if the shield notices that something bad is happening, if the car is already falling down. The shield has to avoid all states from which avoiding the cliff is no longer possible.

In the next step, the set W of winning states for player 1 is computed by standard safety game solving [12].

Step 4. Construct a shield. The safety game and its winning region W are translated into a reactive system that constitutes the shield in the following way: the shield *allows all actions that are guaranteed to lead to a state in W*, no matter what the next observation is. Since these winning states are exactly the ones from which player 1 can enforce not to ever visit a state not in F, the shield is minimally interfering. The shield disables all actions that may lead to an error state (according to the abstraction).

Step 5a. Pre-shielding. The shield is attached before the agent and at runtime applied in the following way: at every time step, the shield sends the set of correct actions to the agent. The agent picks one and sends it to the environment.

Step 5b. Post-shielding. The shield is attached after the agent and applied in the following way: at every time step it takes an action from the agent. If the action is correct it forwards it to the environment, else it picks a correct one.

2.3   Implementation and Experiments

We give one of the case studies of [1]. This example considers an agent that learns to drive around a block in a clockwise direction in an environment with the size of 480×480 pixels. The car has 8 sensors, distributed evenly around the car, that trigger whenever the agent is less than 60 pixels away from a wall. In each step, the car moves 3 pixels in the direction of its heading and can make a maximum turn of $7.5°$ in either direction. The safety specification in this example is to avoid crashing into a wall. A corresponding post-shield was synthesized in 2 s. In each step, a positive reward is given if the car moves a step in a clockwise direction along its track and a penalty is given if it moves in a counter-clockwise

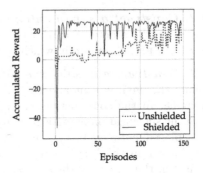

Fig. 3. Still image from the environment (left) and the accumulated reward per episode (right) for the self driving car example. (Color figure online)

direction. A crash into the wall results in a penalty and a restart. The agent uses a Deep Q-Network with a Boltzmann exploration policy. This network consists of 4 input nodes, 8 outputs nodes and 3 hidden layers. Figure 3(left) shows a snapshot of the environment, where the car is moving anti-clockwise. The plot in Fig. 3(right) shows that the accumulated rewards for unshielded RL (red, dashed) increase over time, but the car still crashes at the end of the simulation. The post-shielded version without punishment (blue, solid) learns more rapidly than the unshielded learner and never crashes.

3   Safe RL via Probabilistic Shields

We discussed deterministic shields as a suitable technique to guarantee correctness with certainty in RL in Sect. 2. Deterministic shields prevent an agent from taking any unsafe actions at runtime. To this end, the performance objective of the learning agent is extended with a constraint, the safety objective, specifying that unsafe states are *never* visited, i.e., there are no safety violations. However, in many cases, this tight restriction on the decision-making of the agent to adhere to the safety requirements limits the agent's exploration and understanding of the environment [3,16]. Such restrictions may cause *insufficient progress* in following the original objective of the decision-maker, or policies satisfying the restrictions may not exist. Thus, there is a *trade-off* between *safety* and *progress*. In this section, we discuss *probabilistic shields* [11] that incorporate more liberal constraints enforcing that safety violations occur *only with a small probability*. *If an action increases the probability of a safety violation by more than a factor δ w.r.t. the optimal safety probability, a probabilistic shield considers this action to be wrong.*

Advantages. Probabilistic shielding has the following key benefits:

Adaptivity. The shield is *adaptive* w.r.t. δ, as a high value for δ yields a stricter and a smaller value a more permissive shield. The value for δ can be changed on-the-fly and may depend on the individual minimal safety probabilities at each state. Without randomness, all states are either absolutely safe or unsafe. However, in the presence of randomness, safety may be seen as a quantitative measure: in some states, all actions may induce a large risk, while one action may be considered *relatively* safe. Therefore, it is essential to have an *adaptive* notion of shielding, in which the pre-selection of actions is not based on absolute thresholds, i.e., if necessary, the shield needs to dynamically adapt to allow more, potentially less safe, decisions.

Trade-off between safety and progress. Shielding may *restrict* exploration and lead to suboptimal policies. Therefore, it should not be considered in isolation. The trade-off between optimizing the performance objective and the achieved safety is intricate. Intuitively, taking a bit of additional risk short-term may allow for efficient exploration and limit the risk long-term. To this end, the value for δ can be adjusted based on such observations.

The formal notion of a probabilistic shield is based on MDPs. Safety is assessed using probabilistic temporal logic constraints [4] that limit, for example, the probability for reaching a set of critical states in the MDP.

In the remainder of this section, we describe the setting, outline the construction of probabilistic shields, state optimizations towards a computationally tractable implementation, and conclude with the results of a case study.

3.1   Probabilistic Shielding Setting

We first define the setting in which apply the probabilistic shield and discuss several potential applications. Next, we give a problem statement about what we would like to achieve by applying a shield in the discussed setting.

Setting. The setting is a partially-controlled multi-agent system, where one controllable agent (the *avatar*) and several uncontrollable agents (the *adversaries*) operate within a finite graph representation of an arena. The arena is a compact, high-level description of the underlying model. From this arena, the potential states and actions of all agents may be inferred. For safety considerations, the reward structure can be neglected, effectively reducing the state space for our model-based safety computations. Some combinations of agent positions are safety-critical (e.g., they may correspond to collisions). A safety property may describe reaching such positions, or any other property expressible in the safety fragment of temporal logic. To encode a *performance criterion*, edges of the arena are associated with a (partial) *token* function, indicating the status of some edge. Tokens have an associated *reward* that is, e.g., either earned as long as the token is present, or upon visiting an edge. In fact, tokens build a simple representation of a *state-space extension which is not relevant for the safety specification*. The performance objective is the maximization of the expected reward.

Problem Statement. Let us consider an environment described by an arena as above and a safety specification, and let us assume stochastic behaviors for the adversaries, e.g., obtained using RL in a training environment. In fact, this stochastic behavior determines all actions of the adversaries via probabilities.

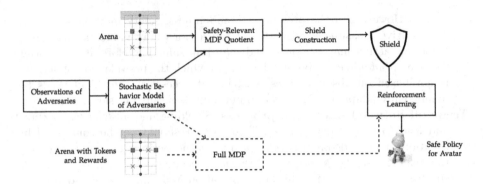

Fig. 4. Workflow of the Shield Construction

The underlying model is then an MDP: the avatar executes an action, and upon this execution, the next exact positions (the state of the system) are determined stochastically. *A probabilistic shield prevents avatar decisions that violate this specification by more than a threshold δ w.r.t. the optimal safety probability.*

Application. The formal setting is defined to be applicable to a series of scenarios. As an example, take a factory floor plan with several corridors. The nodes of the arena describe crossings, and the edges the corridors with machines. The adversaries are (possibly autonomous) transporters moving parts within the factory. The avatar models a service unit moving around and inspecting machines where an issue has been raised (as indicated by a token), while accounting for the behavior of the adversaries. Corridors might be too narrow for multiple robots, which poses a safety critical situation. Several notions of cost can be induced by the tokens, indicating the costs of a broken machine or for inspecting the machine.

3.2 Construction of Probabilistic Shields

Figure 4 outlines the synthesis procedure for probabilistic shields, which consists of the following steps (see [11] for more details):

Step 1. Construct behavior models for adversaries. An adversary model is learned by observing behavior in a set of similar (small) arenas, until sufficient confidence is gained that more training data would not change the behavior significantly. An upper bound on the necessary data may be obtained using Hoeffding's inequality [22]. Data augmentation techniques using domain knowledge of the arenas [21] can be used to reduce training set size.

Step 2. Compute the safety-relevant quotient MDP. Combining the models for the adversaries with a concrete arena yields an MDP. At this point, the token function is ignored, so the MDP may be seen as a quotient of the full MDP that models the real system within which only safe behavior is assessed.

Therefore, the MDP is called the *safety-relevant quotient*. The real scenario incorporates the *token function*. Rewards may be known or only be observed during learning. The underlying *full MDP* including tokens constitutes an *exponential blowup of the safety-relevant quotient*, rendering probabilistic model checking or planning practically infeasible, and is never needed to construct the shield.

Step 3. Construct the probabilistic shield. Using probabilistic model checking, the shield is computed from the safety-relevant MDP and the safety specification. For any state and any possible decision, the synthesis procedure computes precise probabilities for violating the safety specification. Based on these values and δ, the shield considers all actions inducing a too large risk to be *wrong*.

Step 4a. Pre-shielding: Attach the shield before the agent. The probabilistic shield then readily augments either model-free or model-based RL. In pre-shielding, the shield is placed *before* the learning agent. At each time step, the shield provides a list of correct actions, i.e., the actions that are too risky are deactivated. RL now aims to maximize the reward according to the original scenario, while wrong actions are blocked by the shield.

Step 4b. Post-shielding: Attach the shield after the agent. In post-shielding, the probabilistic shield is implemented *after* the agent and overwrites wrong actions with correct ones.

Faster construction of shields. Even with the restriction to the safety-relevant MDP, automatic analysis is challenging for realistic applications. Therefore the following optimizations can be applied:

- **Finite Horizon.** A policy for the avatar in the shielded MDP is then only guaranteed to be safe for the next n steps.
- **Piece-wise Construction.** The shield is computed for each state independently, enabling multi-threaded computations.
- **Independent Agents.** It may be possible to make the assumptions that the agents operate independently from each other. In such situations, the computations can be performed for each adversary separately and then composed to obtain the final shield.
- **Abstractions.** Several abstractions can be exploited, e.g., adversaries that are far away are not considered for the computation of the shield.

3.3   Implementation and Experiments

We summarize the results on probabilistic shielding of an agent for the arcade game Pac-Man. The task is to eat *food* in a *maze* and not get eaten by *ghosts*. Pac-Man achieves a high *score* if it eats all the food as quickly as possible while minimizing the number of times it gets eaten by the ghosts.

Each instance of the game is modeled as an arena, where Pac-Man is the avatar and the ghosts are adversaries. The safety specification is that the avatar

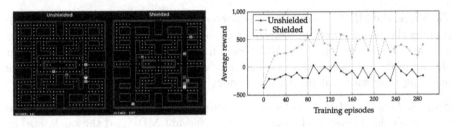

Fig. 5. Still image from video (left) and training scores (right) on Pac-Man.

does not get eaten with a high probability. Tokens represent the food at each position in the maze, such that food is either present or already eaten. Food earns reward (+10), while each step causes a small penalty (−1). A large reward (+500) is granted, if Pac-Man eats all the food in the maze. If Pac-Man gets eaten, a large penalty (−500) is imposed and the game is restarted.

The ghost behavior is learned from the original Pac-Man game for each ghost. Transferring the resulting stochastic behavior to any arena (without tokens) yields the safety-relevant MDP. For that MDP, a shield is computed via the model checker STORM [7] for a horizon of 10 steps.

The implementation uses an approximate Q-learning agent (using $\alpha = 0.2$, $\gamma = 0.8$ and $\epsilon = 0.05$) with the following feature vector: (1) how far away the next food is, (2) whether a ghost collision is imminent, and (3) whether a ghost is one step away. Figure 5(left) show a screenshot of a series of videos[1]. Each video compares how RL performs either shielded or unshielded on a Pac-Man instance. In the shielded version, the risk of potential decisions is indicated by the colors green (low), orange (medium), and red (high). Figure 5 (right) depicts the *scores* obtained during RL, composed by rewards and penalties mentioned above. Table 1 shows the results. The table lists the number of model checking calls, the time to construct the shield, the scores with and without shield, and the winning rate. For all instances, we see a large difference in scores due to the fact that Pac-Man is often saved by the shield. For the two largest instances with 3 and 4 ghosts, a shield that plans 10 steps ahead is not enough to always avoid Pac-Man from being encircled by the ghosts. Nevertheless, the shield still saves Pac-Man in many situations, leading to superior scores. Moreover, the shield helps to learn an optimal policy much faster because viewer restarts are needed.

4 Safe RL via Timed Shields

In this section, we focus on the enforcement of regular timed properties and automatically synthesize *timed shields* from *timed automata* specifications.

An especially challenging task for RL is to learn complex timing behavior. Shielding against timing properties is especially important for learned controllers, where a deadline violation comes with serious consequences. Since LTL

---

[1] https://seafile.iaik.tugraz.at/f/58f6043bad/.

Table 1. Average scores and win rates for Pac-Man.

Size, num Ghosts	Num MC	Time (s)	Score		Win rate	
			No shield	Shield	No shield	Shield
$9 \times 7,1$	5912	584	−359,6	535,3	0,04	0,84
$17 \times 6,2$	5841	1072	−195,6	253,9	0,04	0,4
$17 \times 10,3$	51732	3681	−220,79	−40,52	0,01	0,07
$27 \times 25,4$	269426	19941	−129,25	339,89	0,00	0,00

is not expressible enough to capture real time behavior, the corresponding shields cannot prevent timing related faults. Therefore, we summarize the synthesis procedure presented in [5] which computes timed shields from timed safety properties given as timed automata.

The timed pre-shield and timed post-shield settings are mostly similar as in the untimed case. A timed pre-shield provides *a set of correct actions* for the agent to choose from. If this set contains a *delay action*, the agent is permitted to wait without performing any discrete action. Otherwise, the agent has to produce an action immediately. A *timed post-shield* simply forwards any correct actions from the learning agent to the environment without altering them. If an action is wrong, or once an invariant is reached and any delay would violate the specification, the shield is allowed pick an action.

This section summarizes the construction of timed shields and concludes with a case study.

4.1 Construction of Timed Shields

In this section, we outline the construction of timed shields (for more details see [5]). The synthesis procedure consists of the following steps:

Step 1. Construct and solve a timed safety game. The safety specification is given in form of a network of timed input/output automata [2]. In the first step of the synthesis procedure, these automata are transformed into timed game automata [14] with a safety objective, i.e., the control objective is that bad states should never be visited. Solving the safety game leads to a winning strategy.

Step 2. Construct a timed shield. A timed shield is constructed by composing the timed game automata with the derived winning strategy; meaning that in the timed automaton that depicts the shield, all unsafe transitions are removed. The timed shield may still permit multiple correct actions in a given state.

Step 3. Construct the set of correct actions via zones. For a given state of the timed shield, the set of correct actions is computed via zones. From any given state, its zones can be calculated straightforwardly, see [2].

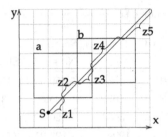

Fig. 6. The zones reachable by delay from a state s in a timed automaton with two clocks, x and y. The squares represent constraints for the actions a and b.

Example. *The concept of zones is illustrated in Fig. 6, where the X and Y axis depict different clocks, and the squares represent the constraints in which different actions a and b are correct. We have for $a : \{1 < x < 5, 2 < y < 5\}$ and for $b : \{4 < x < 8, 3 < y < 6\}$.*

Step 4a. Pre-shielding. The set of correct actions is kept up to date by monitoring the current state of the timed shield. Whenever a new input is received, the state is updated. From the new state, all zones that can be reached via delay are calculated and the correct actions in each zone determined.

Example. *In Fig. 6, the correct actions per zone are $z1 = \{\}$, $z2 = \{a\}$, $z3 = \{a,b\}$, $z4 = \{b\}$, $z5 = \{\}$. Thus, in the state S which is in $z1$, the set of correct actions is empty, after one time unit the set contains a, and so on.*

The set of correct actions for the current zone is sent to the agent. In case the end of the zone is not met yet, this includes a delay action. If enough time passes so that the end of the current zone is met, the shield needs to check whether future zones permit actions. If so, the set of actions of the next zone is passed to the agent. Otherwise, the current set of actions is transmitted again, this time without a delay action.

Step 4b. Post-shielding. The set of actions is kept up-to-date and is used to determine, whether the actions from the agent are correct, i.e., included in the current set. If this is the case, the action is forwarded to the environment. If not, the action is overwritten by an action that is contained in the current set.

4.2   Implementation and Experiments

We summarize the case-study of [5] in which an RL agent controls n *follower* vehicles in the platoon following an (environment controlled) *leader* vehicle[2]. All vehicles can drive a maximum of $20\,\mathrm{m/s}$ and have three different possible accelerations modes: $-2\,\mathrm{m/s^2}$, $0\,\mathrm{m/s^2}$ and $2\,\mathrm{m/s^2}$ which can be changed at every time unit. The goal of the RL agent is to control the followers in the platoon

---

[2] The source code, including some demonstrative videos and the running example used in the paper, is available at https://doi.org/10.5281/zenodo.3903227.

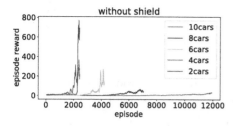 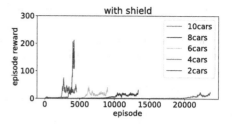

Fig. 7. Results training phase.

such that the total distance between all vehicles is minimized. Furthermore, the RL agent receives a negative reward if the distance between two cars is outside a safe region (≤ 5 m) or is too large (above 200 m).

The hyper-parameters for the DQN were chosen in the following way. The input features consist of the distances between the cars and the velocities of the cars. There are DNNs for actor and critic, containing 3 hidden layers with rectified linear units and a linear layer for the output. Networks are optimized with an Adamax optimizer. The hidden layers consist of 16 units. The learning rate is $\alpha = 0.002$, and the exponential decay rates are $\beta_1 = 0.9$ and $\beta_2 = 0.9999$. The reward function is designed such that the total spacing between the vehicle is minimized. If the distance between any two cars is either ≤ 5 m or ≥ 200 m, then the reward is set to -1. In all other cases, the distances between the cars are used within a logarithmic scale to determine the reward $0 \leq r \leq 1$ per step. The models from [13] were used to synthesize timed post-shields with the tool UPPAAL TIGA. The behaviour of RL agents was studied in the context of 1. no shielding, 2. post-shielding during execution, and 3. post-shielding during both training and execution. The learning curves during the training phase and the performances in the execution phase for $\{2, 4, 6, 8, 10\}$ cars are reported.

Training. Each training episode starts with random but safe initial distances and velocities of all cars. During the simulation, the environment picks the accelerations of the leading car via a uniform distribution. A training episode lasts for 2000 time units, or until the distance between two cars gets smaller than 5 m or larger than 200 m. Note, that with a shield, a training episode always lasts 2000 time units, since safety is always guaranteed.

Figure 7 compares the learning curves as a mean of 20 training phases, for the unshielded case (left) and the shielded case (right). The reward in the unshielded case is considerably higher than in the shielded setting. We observe that the agent exploits the relatively low risk of a crash and makes potentially unsafe choices. Since the accelerations of the leading car are picked via an uniform distribution, it is unlikely that e.g., the leading car accelerates to the maximum speed and then immediately hits the brake until it reaches zero. Such risk tolerance is not allowed when deploying the shield as even a potential but unlikely future crash should be shielded against.

Table 2. Results of the exploitation phase using 10000 simulations. Number of crashes is given in absolute values over all simulations, reward and time measures as averages. Time and crash values are omitted when shielding, as these are 2000 and 0, resp. Time denotes time-units of simulation before a crash.

#Cars	No shield			Shield E	Shield T+E
	#Crashes	Time	Reward	Reward	Reward
2	703	1133	747	915	603
4	13	1989	1070	685	393
6	0	2000	638	617	375
8	85	1908	477	495	386
10	983	544	170	608	342

Execution Phase. All controller combinations were tested for 1000 simulations, and each simulation lasts until a crash or for 2000 time units. Table 2 depicts the results. Note, that we learned a global controller for each number of cars (but use local shields) and that the controllers optimize a local minimum, therefore the controllers performances differ from each other. Interestingly, we observe that the combination of unshielded training (Shield E) provides better results in our setting than a RL agent utilizing the shield also during training (Shield T+E). More experiments are needed to discern this effect in detail.

5   Conclusion

We gave an overview of three types of shields that have already been applied to RL: deterministic, probabilistic, and timed shields and discussed their pros and cons in shielding RL agents. For future work, we will extend shields to richer models such as partially-observable MDPs. Furthermore, we want to exploit techniques from model repair and model refinement to deal with dynamic environments, and adapt the shields during runtime if needed. Additionally, we want to investigate techniques how shielding can be used for speeding up the learning performance in addition to providing safety. Another interesting direction is to explore (possibly model free) learning of shields, instead of employing model-based model checking. Moreover, we will extend our shielding approaches to industrial applications, employing deep recurrent neural networks as means of decision making, and justifying via our provided correctness guarantees the application of learned controllers in safety critical applications.

References

1. Alshiekh, M., Bloem, R., Ehlers, R., Könighofer, B., Niekum, S., Topcu, U.: Safe reinforcement learning via shielding. In: Proceedings of the Thirty-Second AAAI Conference on Artificial Intelligence (AAAI 2018), New Orleans, Louisiana, USA, 2–7 February 2018, pp. 2669–2678 (2018)

2. Alur, R., Dill, D.L.: A theory of timed automata. Theoret. Comput. Sci. **126**(2), 183–235 (1994)
3. Amodei, D., Olah, C., Steinhardt, J., Christiano, P., Schulman, J., Mané, D.: Concrete problems in AI safety. CoRR, abs/1606.06565 (2016)
4. Baier, C., Katoen, J.: Principles of Model Checking. MIT Press, Cambridge (2008)
5. Bloem, R., Jensen, P., Könighofer, B., Larsen, K.G., Lorber, F., Palmisano, A.: It's time to play safe: shield synthesis for timed systems. CoRR, abs/2006.16688 (2020)
6. David, A., Jensen, P.G., Larsen, K.G., Mikučionis, M., Taankvist, J.H.: UPPAAL STRATEGO. In: Baier, C., Tinelli, C. (eds.) TACAS 2015. LNCS, vol. 9035, pp. 206–211. Springer, Heidelberg (2015). https://doi.org/10.1007/978-3-662-46681-0_16
7. Dehnert, C., Junges, S., Katoen, J.-P., Volk, M.: A storm is coming: a modern probabilistic model checker. In: Majumdar, R., Kunčak, V. (eds.) CAV 2017. LNCS, vol. 10427, pp. 592–600. Springer, Cham (2017). https://doi.org/10.1007/978-3-319-63390-9_31
8. Falcone, Y., Pinisetty, S.: On the runtime enforcement of timed properties. In: Proceedings of the 19th International Conference on Runtime Verification, RV 2019, Porto, Portugal, 8–11 October 2019, pp. 48–69 (2019)
9. Fulton, N., Platzer, A.: Verifiably safe off-model reinforcement learning. In: Proceedings of the 25th International Conference on Tools and Algorithms for the Construction and Analysis of Systems, TACAS 2019, Prague, Czech Republic, 6–11 April 2019, pp. 413–430 (2019)
10. García, J., Fernández, F.: A comprehensive survey on safe reinforcement learning. J. Mach. Learn. Res. **16**, 1437–1480 (2015)
11. Jansen, N., Könighofer, B., Junges, S., Bloem, R.: Shielded decision-making in MDPs. CoRR, abs/1807.06096 (2018)
12. Könighofer, B., et al.: Shield synthesis. Formal Methods Syst. Des. **51**(2), 332–361 (2017)
13. Larsen, K.G., Mikucionis, M., Taankvist, J.H.: Safe and optimal adaptive cruise control. In: Proceedings of Correct System Design - Symposium in Honor of Ernst-Rüdiger Olderog on the Occasion of His 60th Birthday, Oldenburg, Germany, 8–9 September 2015, pp. 260–277 (2015)
14. Maler, O., Pnueli, A., Sifakis, J.: On the synthesis of discrete controllers for timed systems. In: Mayr, E.W., Puech, C. (eds.) STACS 1995. LNCS, vol. 900, pp. 229–242. Springer, Heidelberg (1995). https://doi.org/10.1007/3-540-59042-0_76
15. Mason, G., Calinescu, R., Kudenko, D., Banks, A.: Assured reinforcement learning with formally verified abstract policies. In: ICAART, vol. 2, pp. 105–117. SciTePress (2017)
16. Pecka, M., Svoboda, T.: Safe exploration techniques for reinforcement learning – an overview. In: Hodicky, J. (ed.) MESAS 2014. Lecture Notes in Computer Science, vol. 8906, pp. 357–375. Springer, Cham (2014). https://doi.org/10.1007/978-3-319-13823-7_31
17. Pnueli, A.: The temporal logic of programs. In: 18th Annual Symposium on Foundations of Computer Science, Providence, Rhode Island, USA, 31 October–1 November 1977, pp. 46–57 (1977)
18. Puterman, M.L.: Markov Decision Processes: Discrete Stochastic Dynamic Programming, 1st edn. Wiley, New York (1994)
19. Renard, M., Falcone, Y., Rollet, A., Jéron, T., Marchand, H.: Optimal enforcement of (timed) properties with uncontrollable events. Math. Struct. Comput. Sci. **29**(1), 169–214 (2019)

20. Sutton, R.S., Barto, A.G.: Reinforcement learning: an introduction. IEEE Trans. Neural Networks **9**(5), 1054 (1998)
21. Witten, I.H., Frank, E., Hall, M.A., Pal, C.J.: Data Mining: Practical Machine Learning Tools and Techniques. Morgan Kaufmann, Los Altos (2016)
22. Ziebart, B.D., Maas, A.L., Bagnell, J.A., Dey, A.K.: Maximum entropy inverse reinforcement learning. In: AAAI, pp. 1433–1438. AAAI Press (2008)

Inferring Performance
from Code: A Review

Emilio Incerto[(⊠)], Annalisa Napolitano[(⊠)], and Mirco Tribastone[(⊠)]

IMT School for Advanced Studies, 55100 Lucca, Italy
{emilio.incerto,annalisa.napolitano,mirco.tribastone}@imtlucca.it

Abstract. Performance is an important non-functional property of software that has a direct impact on the end-user's perception of quality of service since it is related to metrics such as response time, throughput, and utilization. *Performance-by-construction* can be defined as a development paradigm where executable code carries some kind of guarantee on its performance, as opposed to the current practice in software engineering where performance concerns are left to the later stages of the development process by means of profiling or testing. In this paper we argue that performance-by-construction techniques need to be probabilistic in nature, leveraging accurate models for the analysis. In support of this idea, here we carry out a literature review on methods that can be used as the basis of performance-by-construction development approaches. There has been significant research—reviewed elsewhere—on performance models derived from high-level software specifications such as UML diagrams or other domain-specific languages. This review, instead, focuses on methods where performance information is extracted directly from the code, a line of research that has arguably been less explored by the software performance engineering community.

1 Introduction

Non-functional (also called *extra-functional*) properties of software are related to issues concerning *how* a system works, as opposed to functional properties which establish what it does. Among many relevant such properties including security, dependability, and reliability is software performance. Briefly, it can be understood as a property analyzable through a number of quantitative metrics related to *how fast* the software system can yield the desired output. Typical performance metrics of interest are *response time*, i.e., how long it takes to obtain a reply since a request has been issued; *throughput*, i.e., how many requests can be

This work has been partially supported by the Italian Ministry for Education under grant SEDUCE no. 2017TWRCNB.

Electronic supplementary material The online version of this chapter (https://doi.org/10.1007/978-3-030-61362-4_17) contains supplementary material, which is available to authorized users.

T. Margaria and B. Steffen (Eds.): ISoLA 2020, LNCS 12476, pp. 307–322, 2020.
https://doi.org/10.1007/978-3-030-61362-4_17

served per unit time; and *utilization*, i.e., the percentage of time that a software resource is busy servicing some request.

Performance metrics can be defined mathematically (e.g., [11]), in which case it is possible to easily see how they can be formally related to each other. They can also be related to other metrics such as energy consumption (via appropriate models [41]) and availability (e.g., excessively long response times of a web application causing server crashes).

Performance is a key property that directly affects the end-user's perception of quality of a software system. It is such an important aspect that, as claimed by Harman and O'Hearn [29], "in many practical deployment scenarios, particularly mobile, **performance is the new correctness**." Despite its relevance, however, the practice of software engineering does not seem to make use of principled criteria to reason about performance. For example, the Android developers' guide suggests a rule of thumb for improving the performance of an app by means of multithreading [1]:

> "You can use trial-and-error to discover the minimum number of threads you can use without running into problems."

Such state of affairs is unsatisfactory for at least two reasons. First, conducting performance analysis only through testing or runtime profiling raises several issues about the cost and the degree of coverage of the experiments. Indeed, it implies a software development process where performance issues are left to the latest stages, which may make serious flaws too expensive to fix, such as in the notable case of halting a NASA space mission due to on-board software producing unacceptably large response times [2]. The second limitation is that testing approaches can detect the presence of performance issues, but they do not carry explanatory and generalization power on their own. Specifically, they do not provide a *model* of the software system under investigation that can be used for the analysis of further *what-if* scenarios or for formal verification.

A paradigm based on *performance-by-construction* principles aims instead at the development of software with guarantees of achieving given performance objectives [57]. In order to achieve this, it appears inescapable that this paradigm leverage appropriate models of software systems that can yield (accurate) performance predictions. Traditionally, performance models of computer and communication systems are probabilistic [11,56]. Essentially, this can be motivated by two orthogonal modeling choices to capture *external* and *internal* uncertainty, respectively [45]. With the former we refer to the typical use of stochastic processes to model the workload of software system (i.e., the pattern of arrivals of requests) as well as to abstract from the details of other environmental features such as the hardware on which the software system runs. With the latter we refer to the explicit use of programming primitives that generate samples from given probability distributions, as in the context of probabilistic programming [27].

A model capable of predicting performance properties is necessarily a distinct artifact than the software system under consideration. Of course, it could be built by hand by the software architect/engineer. However this would not fit with the need of providing automated support within a development process. Moreover, in general it is likely difficult to find engineers who have competences both in the problem domain and in the performance modeling techniques—recognized as a main obstacle to model-based performance analysis in software engineering [63].

More automated support to model building can be offered by model-driven development techniques where the performance model is algorithmically derived from software specifications such as behavioral UML diagrams (e.g., [58,59,64]) or domain-specific languages (e.g., [10]) annotated with quantitative information. Some of the vast literature on this topic has already been reviewed [7,35].

Model-driven approaches may not always be applicable, for instance when the code that is automatically generated from the higher-level specification is likely to undergo manual modifications. Indeed, after these, the related performance model may not be a faithful representation of the actual system under consideration any longer [23]. In order to avoid this problem, another approach might be to use the code as the model of the software system itself, thus inferring performance models directly from the code. Of course, this rules out the possibility of conducting performance analysis at the very early stages of the software development. However, it fits well with agile processes based on successive iterations, where changes in the codebase can be reflected onto changes in the associated performance model.

In this paper we present a literature review on the state of the art of techniques which produce performance predictions for code analysis in order to evaluate their feasibility as tools to be used within a performance-by-construction development framework. The literature analyzed, consisting of 24 research papers published with the period 1982–2019, is mostly located in the sub-fields of computer science regarding programming languages and software engineering. In addition to a brief description of each method, we provide a classification in terms of the assumptions on the input program, the type of technique employed (i.e., whether it uses static or dynamic analysis), and the output provided (i.e., if it yields a model or directly a performance prediction). We conclude the paper with a discussion of the main limitations of the state of the art for their use in realistic development processes based on performance-by-construction.

Search and Selection. The research was conducted by selecting from a search engine a set of representative and highly cited papers from the literature, which deal with the issue of extracting performance from the code, specifically [13,18, 21,24,25,38,51,65]. We then evaluated the ongoing and outgoing citation links of these papers and the most interesting, as well as the most cited, were selected for analysis in this semi-systematic review.

2 Analysis Dimensions

In this section, we analyze the several aspects that distinguish the analyzed methods of performance generation from code. They concern learning techniques, exploration techniques, the type of the output model or performance metrics, and the scalability level.

2.1 Learning Techniques

Although they differ greatly from each other, all performance learning techniques from software can be condensed into two categories:

- **Static analysis:** the source-code of the program is systematically inspected to infer performance. Often, an intermediate model is created, e.g. differential equations [61], Markov processes [47], or a step-counting function [50] which simplifies the software by focusing only on performance evaluation.
- **Dynamic analysis:** an instrumented version of the program is executed, and by analyzing traces, the necessary information to build the performance model is gathered (e.g., which parts of the code have been actually explored, the number of calls issued to a particular functions). While some approaches are based on one single run to inspect one specific profile [28], others perform several runs with different workloads to obtain metrics, models and trend functions of different profiles such as worst-, average-, best-case scenarios [65]. This could be costly if the program needs to be executed numerous times with different input sizes. There are several techniques to select the workloads (e.g., load-testing, probabilistic symbolic execution, random sampling), which we will analyze later in Subsect. 2.2.

Notice that often these techniques are combined together for the definition of hybrid approaches. For example, static analysis is used to create an instrumented version of the program that is then executed with dynamic analysis [21].

2.2 Exploration Techniques

In this subsection, we will describe the different techniques that can be used both for exploring the program's paths in the static analysis and to generate the workload input sequences that guide the dynamic analysis.

- **Runtime monitoring** implies analyzing the logs or execution traces of the real (instrumented) system. Approaches that exploit runtime monitoring care about instrumenting the program as efficiently as possible, so that to leave the system performance unchanged [6].
  This kind of exploration technique does not make any assumption on the input features and thus the resulting performance models show the typical system behavior and not a peculiar case.
- **Load testing** is an input generation technique that tries to stress the software by evaluating it with a workload of increasing size [25]. This may imply evaluating a particular scenario for a given size e.g., worst and best cases, trying to find out the right workload based on user-specified features, heuristics on the complexity of the data structures, or observations.
- **Random sampling** implies testing the program under an input randomly distributed according to some probability distribution [55]. Random sampling is efficient and easy to implement; in addition, sometimes it might be the

only viable option when the program is too complex or some source-code portions are unknown [19]. However, the main limitation is that without any heuristic it could be extremely unlikely to observe interesting but rare system behaviors [14].

- **Symbolic execution** exhaustively explores the execution tree of a program using symbolic values for the input instead of concrete ones [5,33]. Each execution edge could be described by a condition formula on the input variables. A path is described with the conjunction of all conditional formulas of its edges, called the *path condition*. The execution tree can be explored with any algorithms for traversing trees, such as breadth-first search. The search is done by trying to symbolically satisfy the (partial) path condition: if the set of solutions is not empty the search continues, by evaluating also child edges conditions; otherwise, the path condition is impossible to satisfy and thus that branch of the tree is marked as unreachable. Probabilistic symbolic execution [24] arises when symbolic execution is combined with model counting [26] in order to obtain not only reachability/unreachability information but also path probabilities, by comparing the number of path solutions, i.e., the cardinality of the path condition admissibility set, with the cardinality of the input set [18]. While in random testing the input distribution can be arbitrarily chosen, probabilistic symbolic execution works only for uniformly distributed input.

2.3   Output Model

The output models of the surveyed methods differ in many aspects, such as the amount of information they encode, the predictive power or the efficiency of the analysis techniques. They can be categorized as follows.

- **Enriched call graphs and control-flow graphs.** Mostly path or edges probabilities obtained through the code analysis are stored in a compact form in (enriched) control flow graphs or call graphs [6]. Since the total amount of program's paths is often exponential with respect to the number of visited branches, these techniques typically limit the exploration of the *hottest* ones, i.e., those that have the greatest impact on performance.
- **Performance metrics.** Often profiling approaches deal with discovering some static or dynamic performance metrics, e.g., number of procedure calls [20] and average runtimes [9]. The information level of this kind of model is low since it has no predictive power and it gives no indication as to the reason why the program execution shows those performance metrics.
- **Bottlenecks detection** provides insight on the worst case of the program execution, which can be given in terms of *hot paths* detection [16], or input values that trigger performance bottlenecks [3]. We consider this model to have a low information level since the worst-case scenario does not capture exhaustively the whole program's behavior.
- **Cost functions.** All the approaches that provide some kind of cost-function in terms of the size of input belong to this category. This function could

represent the average-case [65] as the asymptotic one [25]. Cost functions provide insight on how the program behaves as the input grows and thus they are considered medium-level informative. For instance, these techniques do not allow to select the best alternative of an algorithm among a set of functionally and asymptotically equivalent ones.

- **Markov processes** [47]. Markov processes are a fundamental model for software systems [11]. To build a Markov model that is compact and has an analytical solution in a closed form (i.e., a Markov chain) it is necessary that the analyzed program is memoryless. This implies that the probabilities of the edges are all mutually independent.
- **Target events probabilities** [38,51]. These approaches aim to evaluate the probability that certain target events happen. Even if these techniques are typical of bug finding and do not give directly a performance measure, they can provide insight on performance, since the target events could be previously selected as costly functions or inefficient blocks of code.

3   Model Construction Methods

In this section, we briefly describe all the methods that infer performance from code, presented in chronological order.

Gprof [28] periodically samples the program counter in a single program run with a certain workload, and counts the number of calls and execution times of each procedure. A post-processing step then propagates the sampled values to the program call-graph to estimate the total running time in each procedure.

Sarkar et al. [52] propose a framework for obtaining the mean and variance of the execution times for program's procedures. These values are obtained by a counter-based execution profile of the program and then inserted in the program's extended control flow graph. The proposed solution assumes that the average execution time of a procedure call is independent of the call site and thus the observed time value is multiplied by the frequency of that procedure call, without any concern about the program history and data flow.

Ramalingam et al. [47] study the problem of determining *how often*, i.e., with *what probability*, a fact holds true during program execution. The input is the program control flow graph whose edges are labeled with a probability. The program is simply modeled as a first-order Markov chain, by assuming the probability of the program execution following a particular branch is independent of the execution history, which does not hold in general for real programs.

Ball et al. [6] focus on path profiling, i.e., computing paths' frequencies and performance metrics. They claim that since edges probabilities are not independent, it is impossible to obtain paths frequencies by simply combining edges frequencies. In many cases the next visited program instructions are dependent on the execution history, thus making path profiling essential for finding accurate performance models of programs. Unfortunately while edge profiling is linear respect to the program size, path profiling is exponential. In order to tame such issue, the authors provide a solution for runtime estimation of intra-procedural path frequencies of an acyclic version of the program, by minimizing the overhead of the instrumentation. To further mitigate the scalability issues they only consider dynamic paths, i.e., those that have been actually executed during the program runtime monitoring.

Whole Program Paths (WPP) [36] is an approach to learn and represent the program's dynamic control flow, i.e., the set of executed paths. Differently from previous approaches, it considers loop iterations as well as interprocedural paths. The work shows also how to compute *hot subpaths*. The instrumentation and path discovery phase is done relying on the published work [6]; the novelty of WPP is the compression algorithm, which, by finding regularities (i.e., repeated code), transforms the traces more compactly into the directed acyclic graph.

JinsightEx [54] samples performance metrics (i.e., execution time, memory and other resource usage) of a Java program's *execution slices*, which are user-defined through dynamic or static criteria. The slices represent the primary view of the performance models and they can be grouped in workloads to facilitate larger analysis procedures. JinsightEx allows the user to browse this data to evaluate the number of called objects, allocations, method calls; and to find performance and memory problems in many industrial applications.

Magpie is an online performance modeling service that collects detailed end-to-end traces from users on the running system and constructs probabilistic models of its behavior [8,9]. It instruments the system using black-box approaches such as kernel-level tracing for Windows [53] or WinPcap packet capture library [48]. *Magpie* constructs a model of the observed behavior, by clustering requests features and performance. Using these behavioral clusters it is possible to detect anomalous requests and system malfunctions.

Ammons et al. [4] find bottlenecks, given some kind of profiles (e.g. call tree) of the system execution. There are two algorithms: one that finds expensive paths of a program and another that computes how the path cost differs from similar execution runs. They build a summarized model of the program that is based on heuristics, by collecting cost metrics of execution paths, and they provide an interface for querying this model and comparing paths cost metrics to find the worst-case. The approach is evaluated on a real-world case study.

Trend-prof [25] derives the asymptotic behavior of a program by computing its empirical computational complexity. This is done by executing the program on workloads of different sizes and user-specified numerical features, for example the number of bytes of the input file. Measured execution times of program blocks are fit against linear or power law models. *Trend-prof* is evaluated on several large programs; the authors report cases in which the program meets its expected bounds, performs better than its worst-case, or shows performance bugs.

Buse et al. [16] provide a descriptive statistical model of paths frequencies that is obtained by static analysis of the source code with *path enumeration*. The approach is validated on several benchmarks. The qualitative analysis provides insights on which source code features characterize hot paths. Since the number of program paths could be exponential, only interprocedural paths within one single class are considered; calls across class boundaries are ignored. The idea that underlines the approach is that the most likely hot paths are those that have little impacts on the program state, intended in terms of changes of global variables and stack. With this idea in mind, any machine learning algorithm could be trained to select the source-level features that identify hot paths; in the paper, Weka [31] is used. This approach suffers from overfitting, and in case the behavior of the program is not fully captured by a single class, it may reveal unuseful.

Zaparanuks et al. [65] exploit heuristics to determine a program's approximated cost functions from traces of representative program executions. This approach automatically determines the input size, measures the program's cost for each input, and fits a cost function. Several cost measures are supported such as algorithmic steps, number and size of reads/writes on data structures and the number of objects creations. The program input type (e.g., recursive data structures, arrays, and so on) and the input size are obtained by computing the number of elements of the structure or its memory occupation. A limitation of this approach is that it cannot infer the input size of programs that do not work with data structures but on primitive types, and that since it is based on heuristics, it returns an approximate cost-function rather than an exact one.

Geldenhuys et al. [24] propose an extension of Java Symbolic PathFinder [44] that estimates probabilities of each particular program locations using probabilistic symbolic execution. Although the cost of symbolic execution is mitigated by implementing some heuristics, the scalability of this technique is still a concerning issue. In the paper, the authors present case studies involving 4 and 5 operations on a data structure, i.e., insertions and deletions from Binomial-Heap, TreeMap, and BinaryTree. They claim the infeasibility of the analysis for programs having a sequence of 14 operations.

Coppa et al. [21] present a profiling methodology to discover hidden asymptotic inefficiencies from program traces. Grow rates of routines as a function of the input size is dynamically measured with a metric—the read memory size (RMS)—that counts the accessed numbers of memory cells. Thee supporting tool, named *aprof*, builds upon Valgrind [42] for the instrumentation. It determines the RMS and the minimum and maximum cost of executing routines and exploits curve fitting and curve bounding to obtain the functions that best describe their asymptotic behavior.

Sankaranarayanan et al. [51] statically analyze probabilistic programs, characterized by variables that assume uncertain values during execution, by assigning them probability distributions. They provide bounds on the probability that a certain event happens and claim that to determine those bounds only an adequate subset of program's execution paths is needed. The initial set of paths is obtained using random simulations and statistical tests, while probability bounds are obtained using symbolic execution, a heuristic they implement for the problem of computing the volume of an n-dimensional convex polyhedron, namely *probabilistic volume bound computation* and Monte Carlo sampling.

Like the previous work, Luckow et al. [38] consider the probability of a target event in case of nondeterministic programs, e.g., multithreaded or distributed programs. They firstly implement a symbolic tree scheduler to handle uncertainties using Markov decision processes [46] (exact algorithm) or Monte Carlo sampling (approximated algorithm) on the symbolic tree generated with a bounded symbolic execution of the program. Then they exploit reinforcement learning [32] to iteratively improve the tree of the approximate algorithm. Finally, model counting techniques and some heuristics are used to compute branch probabilities until reaching the target event.

Filieri et al. [22] propose a method for computing the probability of a target event for a program. The method is based on Monte Carlo sampling to improve Bayesian estimates of the sought probability. To speed up convergency they propose the *informed sampling* technique, with which paths with high statistical significance are explored first.

Borges et al. [12] describe a methodology for the automatic estimation of the probability of a target event given an input profile described via continuous probability distribution over the floating-point domain. The method supports three strategies, based on gradient descent optimization [43] and on heuristics, to improve the learning phase (hence, the scalability of the approach) that are based on ranking the edge condition constraints of the symbolic execution according to their impact on the convergence of the statistical analysis and counting.

Brünink et al. [13] present an approach to infer the performance specification of a running system by creating runtime models and subsequently producing performance assertions. These models are graphs that describe the expected behavior of the system in its hot functions, tracing probabilities in a context-sensitive or insensitive way, as needed. The context information is inserted when the performance metrics (i.e., the runtimes) of the procedures, evaluated for different contexts, belong to different clusters of values. Although they do not exploit analytical rigorous models they succeed to obtain accurate performance.

PerfPlotter [18] is a framework for performance analysis of a program that takes as input the source code and a usage profile and generates a probability density cost function. *PerfPlotter* extends Java Symbolic PathFinder [44] using probabilistic symbolic execution to detect paths with low and high probabilities under the given usage profile, and the resulting set of paths are executed to measure the effective runtime (precisely the subset chosen is that of the paths with high or low probability whose termination within a certain number of steps has been established). Finally, these results are combined and weighted with paths' probabilities to obtain the probability density function (PDF). This approach can infer the PDF, still having a scalability limitation due to the usage of probabilistic symbolic execution.

Luckow et al. [37] propose a technique based on *guided* symbolic execution to generate the worst-case complexity function of the input size. First, symbolic execution is run with a small value of input size, which is subsequently increased. The symbolic execution is guided by selecting only the paths that account for the worst cases. To be more accurate, during path selection the history of choices is taken into account when deciding which branch to execute next. Thus, the method produces a context-sensitive model of worst-case paths that are analyzed to fit the cost function using some resource consumption metrics (e.g., execution time or memory usage).

Wang et al. [60] present an approach to analyze the performance of applications deployed on Cloud. The approach first tests the Cloud infrastructure with typical micro-benchmarks and evaluates the performance distribution of each resource, e.g., memory and CPU. Then it tests the user-defined application with a given input that characterizes the program's typical workload, resulting in the *resource usage profile* of the target application. Finally, it conducts the same tests on the application deployed in the cloud producing the *baseline performance*. By combining these models the approach provides statistics that allow the developer to understand which kind of performance specification the application meets.

Speedoo [20] is an approach to identify groups of methods that are crucial to the program's performance and whose optimization would lead to the best speed-up possible. It suggests optimization opportunities for these methods based on performance (anti-)patterns detection, e.g., cyclic invocation, expensive recursion. *Speedoo* ranks the methods based on metrics of architectural importance (e.g. the size of the sub-calls tree) according to the Design Rule Hierarchy algorithm (DRH), defined by Cai et al. and Wong et al. [17,62], dynamic execution metrics (e.g., CPU time), and static complexity metrics (e.g., the number of loops).

PT4Cloud [30] is concerned about obtaining performance models of application developed on the cloud, addressing the issue of performance uncertainty due to IaaS resource managing. Their purpose is to find reliable stop conditions to test runs to cut down the cost of performance testing. They test the selected benchmarks with their pre-specified workloads and compute the performance distribution of the deployed application. By using a non-parametric statistical approach, they stop testing when they find that two subsequent distribution are statistically equivalent.

PerfXRL [3] presents an approach to find input values that trigger the performance bottlenecks of the system. Given an input space, possibly very large with multiple possible combinations, *PerfXRL* dynamically analyzes the system by executing it with a certain input and then guiding the analysis with the resulting cost reward value, using reinforcement learning.

4   Conclusion and Future Lines of Reseach

Performance is a crucial non-functional property that affects the user's perception of the software's quality. While it could be useful to know performance from early development stages, model-driven approaches may not always be applicable. When the code is continuously developed the real software source-code may differ considerably from model artifacts. In this scenario, performance models should be inferred directly from the deployed system. In this work we present a

Table 1. Summary of the analyzed methods

Method	Learning Techn.	Exploration Techn.	Output Model	Info. Level	Scalability
[28]	Dynamic analysis	Runtime monitoring	Enriched call-graph	Low	Medium
[52]	Static and dynamic analysis	Offline monitoring with given input	Performance metrics (sub-routines execution times and variance)	Low	Low
[47]	Static analysis	CFG sequential exploration	Markov Chain	Medium	Medium-low
[6]	Dynamic analysis	Runtime monitoring	Enriched CFG with acyclic intraprocedural path frequencies DAG (Directed Acyclic Graph)	Medium	Medium-high
[36]	Dynamic analysis	Uses [6]	Whole program paths and hot subpaths detection	Medium	Medium-high
[54]	Dynamic analysis	Realistic traces as input	Performance metrics organized in execution slices	Low	Medium
[9]	Dynamic analysis	Runtime monitoring	Performance metrics organized in clusters of request features	Low	High
[4]	Dynamic analysis	Profiles navigation searching the longest path	Bottlenecks detection	Medium-low	Medium-high
[25]	Dynamic analysis	Offline monitoring of chosen workloads described with numerical features	Computational complexity function of user-specified features	Medium	Medium
[16]	Static analysis	Loop bounded static path enumeration and counting with machine learning	Hot paths identification	Medium-low	Medium
[65]	Dynamic analysis	Realistic traces as input	Approximate descriptive cost function	Medium-low	Medium
[24]	Static analysis	Symbolic execution	Paths probabilities	Medium	Low
[21]	Dynamic analysis	Traces as input	Asymptotic cost function	Medium	Medium
[51]	Simulation + Static analysis	Random sampling with Monte Carlo + symbolic execution	Target events probabilities	Medium	Medium
[38]	Static analysis + simulation	Symbolic execution + Monte Carlo sampling and reinforcement learning	Target event probability	Low	Medium-high
[22]	Static analysis + simulation	Symbolic execution + Monte Carlo sampling and Hypothesis testing (i.e. *Importance Sampling*)	Target event probability	Low	Medium-high
[12]	Static analysis	Symbolic execution	Target event probability	Low	Medium
[13]	Dynamic analysis	Runtime monitoring	Performance metrics of hot functions (context sensitive profiling)	Medium-high	Medium
[18]	Static analysis	Symbolic execution	Probability density function of program runtime	High	Medium-low
[37]	Static analysis	Symbolic execution + policy guided exploration	Asymptotic cost-function	Medium	High
[60]	Dynamic analysis	Offline monitoring with typical benchmarks (Cloud) and typical input (stand-alone)	Cloud application performance statistics	Medium	High (Cloud)
[20]	Static and dynamic analysis	Design Rule Hierarchy algorithm + profiling tools	Optimization suggestions	Medium-low	High
[30]	Dynamic analysis	Testing with given inputs + non-parametric statistical approach for stop conditions	Cloud application performance distributions	High	High (Cloud)
[3]	Dynamic analysis	Reinforcement learning guided testing	Input values that trigger performance bottlenecks	Low	High

literature review of methods that produce performance information from code, trying to underline typical inefficiencies and future lines of research. Table 1 presents a summary of the evaluated methodologies and a comparison according to the proposed analysis dimensions.

Initially, the focus of the literature was on system profiling (mainly through dynamic analysis), using runtime monitoring [6,9,36] or offline monitoring starting from some realistic representative traces of program executions [25,34,54]. Recently, efforts have moved toward improving the applicability and scalability of symbolic execution (mainly with static analysis) [22,37,38]. Heuristics tried to speed up learning by approximating the paths probabilities [51] or by limiting the set of paths considered by the analysis to the most representative ones, i.e., worst-case, best-case, average-case [18].

In addition, most of the methodologies analyzed are able to learn low or medium *information content* models, such as performance metrics [13,54] or identification of hot paths [4,16]. The work presented by Ramalingam and Ganesan [47] is the only approach that extracts a model with a high predictive power like a Markov chain. Unfortunately, their model needs the memoryless assumption, i.e., the probability of the program execution following a particular branch is independent of the execution history, which obviously does not hold true in many cases. Also noteworthy are all the approaches that learn the probability density functions of the execution cost of the program [18,30], a compact but at the same time informative performance model, as it encapsulates the execution probabilities and the runtime.

Another interesting consideration, present in works of Brünink et al. and Luckow et al. [13,37], is to consider the impact of the context information on the probabilities of execution of the path, creating a context-aware model. It is evident, indeed, that the future behavior of the program is highly dependent on the state (i.e., the values of the variables) and therefore on past history. Explicitly considering this information in the performance model can provide a new and interesting view and allow the developer to better understand the reasons behind the performance behavior of a program. One could envisage the use of models with high predictive and implicitly context-sensitive content such as variable-length Markov chains [15,49], typically used for text analysis and pattern recognition. These techniques, never used for performance, have been used by Mazeroff et al. [39,40] to describe the behavior of the system in order to identify anomalies and malicious behaviors.

References

1. Android Developers' Guide: Threading performance. https://developer.android.com/topic/performance/threads.html. Accessed 23 July 2020
2. NASA delays satellite launch after finding bugs in software program. https://fcw.com/Articles/1998/04/19/NASA-delays-satellite-launch-after-finding-bugs-in-software-program.aspx. Accessed 4 Feb 2018
3. Ahmad, T., Ashraf, A., Truscan, D., Porres, I.: Exploratory performance testing using reinforcement learning. In: 2019 45th Euromicro Conference on Software Engineering and Advanced Applications (SEAA), pp. 156–163. IEEE (2019)

4. Ammons, G., Choi, J.-D., Gupta, M., Swamy, N.: Finding and removing performance bottlenecks in large systems. In: Odersky, M. (ed.) ECOOP 2004. LNCS, vol. 3086, pp. 172–196. Springer, Heidelberg (2004). https://doi.org/10.1007/978-3-540-24851-4_8

5. Baldoni, R., Coppa, E., D'elia, D.C., Demetrescu, C., Finocchi, I.: A survey of symbolic execution techniques. ACM Comput. Surv. (CSUR) **51**(3), 1–39 (2018)

6. Ball, T., Larus, J.R.: Efficient path profiling. In: Proceedings of the 29th Annual IEEE/ACM International Symposium on Microarchitecture, MICRO 29, pp. 46–57. IEEE (1996)

7. Balsamo, S., Di Marco, A., Inverardi, P., Simeoni, M.: Model-based performance prediction in software development: a survey. IEEE Trans. Softw. Eng. **30**(5), 295–310 (2004)

8. Barham, P., Donnelly, A., Isaacs, R., Mortier, R.: Using magpie for request extraction and workload modelling. In: OSDI, vol. 4, p. 18 (2004)

9. Barham, P., Isaacs, R., Mortier, R., Narayanan, D.: Magpie: online modelling and performance-aware systems. In: HotOS, pp. 85–90 (2003)

10. Becker, S., Koziolek, H., Reussner, R.: Model-based performance prediction with the palladio component model. In: Proceedings of the 6th International Workshop on Software and Performance (WOSP), pp. 54–65 (2007)

11. Bolch, G., Greiner, S., De Meer, H., Trivedi, K.S.: Queueing Networks and Markov Chains: Modeling and Performance Evaluation with Computer Science Applications. Wiley, Hoboken (2006)

12. Borges, M., Filieri, A., d'Amorim, M., Păsăreanu, C.S.: Iterative distribution-aware sampling for probabilistic symbolic execution. In: Proceedings of the 2015 10th Joint Meeting on Foundations of Software Engineering, pp. 866–877 (2015)

13. Brünink, M., Rosenblum, D.S.: Mining performance specifications. In: Proceedings of the 2016 24th ACM SIGSOFT International Symposium on Foundations of Software Engineering, pp. 39–49 (2016)

14. Bucklew, J.: Introduction to Rare Event Simulation. Springer, New York (2013). https://doi.org/10.1007/978-1-4757-4078-3

15. Bühlmann, P., Wyner, A.J., et al.: Variable length Markov chains. Ann. Stat. **27**(2), 480–513 (1999)

16. Buse, R.P., Weimer, W.: The road not taken: estimating path execution frequency statically. In: 2009 IEEE 31st International Conference on Software Engineering, pp. 144–154. IEEE (2009)

17. Cai, Y., Sullivan, K.J.: Modularity analysis of logical design models. In: 21st IEEE/ACM International Conference on Automated Software Engineering (ASE 2006), pp. 91–102. IEEE (2006)

18. Chen, B., Liu, Y., Le, W.: Generating performance distributions via probabilistic symbolic execution. In: Proceedings of the 38th International Conference on Software Engineering, pp. 49–60 (2016)

19. Chen, T.Y., Kuo, F.C., Merkel, R.G., Tse, T.: Adaptive random testing: the art of test case diversity. J. Syst. Softw. **83**(1), 60–66 (2010)

20. Chen, Z., et al.: Speedoo: prioritizing performance optimization opportunities. In: Proceedings of the 40th International Conference on Software Engineering, pp. 811–821 (2018)

21. Coppa, E., Demetrescu, C., Finocchi, I.: Input-sensitive profiling. ACM SIGPLAN Not. **47**(6), 89–98 (2012)

22. Filieri, A., Păsăreanu, C.S., Visser, W., Geldenhuys, J.: Statistical symbolic execution with informed sampling. In: Proceedings of the 22nd ACM SIGSOFT International Symposium on Foundations of Software Engineering, pp. 437–448 (2014)

23. Garcia, J., Krka, I., Mattmann, C., Medvidovic, N.: Obtaining ground-truth software architectures. In: Proceedings of the 35th International Conference on Software Engineering (ICSE), pp. 901–910 (2013)
24. Geldenhuys, J., Dwyer, M.B., Visser, W.: Probabilistic symbolic execution. In: Proceedings of the 2012 International Symposium on Software Testing and Analysis, pp. 166–176 (2012)
25. Goldsmith, S.F., Aiken, A.S., Wilkerson, D.S.: Measuring empirical computational complexity. In: Proceedings of the 6th Joint Meeting of the European Software Engineering Conference and the ACM SIGSOFT Symposium on the Foundations of Software Engineering, pp. 395–404 (2007)
26. Gomes, C.P., Sabharwal, A., Selman, B.: Model counting (2008)
27. Gordon, A.D., Henzinger, T.A., Nori, A.V., Rajamani, S.K.: Probabilistic programming. In: Proceedings of the Future of Software Engineering (FOSE), pp. 167–181 (2014)
28. Graham, S.L., Kessler, P.B., Mckusick, M.K.: Gprof: a call graph execution profiler. ACM Sigplan Not. **17**(6), 120–126 (1982)
29. Harman, M., O'Hearn, P.: From start-ups to scale-ups: opportunities and open problems for static and dynamic program analysis. In: SCAM (2018)
30. He, S., Manns, G., Saunders, J., Wang, W., Pollock, L., Soffa, M.L.: A statistics-based performance testing methodology for cloud applications. In: Proceedings of the 2019 27th ACM Joint Meeting on European Software Engineering Conference and Symposium on the Foundations of Software Engineering, pp. 188–199 (2019)
31. Holmes, G., Donkin, A., Witten, I.H.: WEKA: a machine learning workbench. In: Proceedings of ANZIIS 1994-Australian New Zealnd Intelligent Information Systems Conference, pp. 357–361. IEEE (1994)
32. Kaelbling, L.P., Littman, M.L., Moore, A.W.: Reinforcement learning: a survey. J. Artif. Intell. Res. **4**, 237–285 (1996)
33. King, J.C.: Symbolic execution and program testing. Commun. ACM **19**(7), 385–394 (1976)
34. Kluge, M., Knüpfer, A., Nagel, W.E.: Knowledge based automatic scalability analysis and extrapolation for MPI programs. In: Cunha, J.C., Medeiros, P.D. (eds.) Euro-Par 2005. LNCS, vol. 3648, pp. 176–184. Springer, Heidelberg (2005). https://doi.org/10.1007/11549468_22
35. Koziolek, H.: Performance evaluation of component-based software systems: a survey. Perform. Eval. **67**(8), 634–658 (2010)
36. Larus, J.R.: Whole program paths. ACM SIGPLAN Not. **34**(5), 259–269 (1999)
37. Luckow, K., Kersten, R., Pǎsǎreanu, C.: Symbolic complexity analysis using context-preserving histories. In: 2017 IEEE International Conference on Software Testing, Verification and Validation (ICST), pp. 58–68. IEEE (2017)
38. Luckow, K., Pǎsǎreanu, C.S., Dwyer, M.B., Filieri, A., Visser, W.: Exact and approximate probabilistic symbolic execution for nondeterministic programs. In: Proceedings of the 29th ACM/IEEE International Conference on Automated Software Engineering, pp. 575–586 (2014)
39. Mazeroff, G., De, V., Jens, C., Michael, G., Thomason, G.: Probabilistic trees and automata for application behavior modeling. In: 41st ACM Southeast Regional Conference Proceedings (2003)
40. Mazeroff, G., Gregor, J., Thomason, M., Ford, R.: Probabilistic suffix models for API sequence analysis of windows XP applications. Pattern Recogn. **41**(1), 90–101 (2008)

41. Möbius, C., Dargie, W., Schill, A.: Power consumption estimation models for processors, virtual machines, and servers. IEEE Trans. Parallel Distrib. Syst. **25**(6), 1600–1614 (2014)
42. Nethercote, N., Seward, J.: Valgrind: a framework for heavyweight dynamic binary instrumentation. ACM Sigplan Not. **42**(6), 89–100 (2007)
43. Nocedal, J., Wright, S.: Numerical Optimization. Springer, Heidelberg (2006). https://doi.org/10.1007/978-0-387-40065-5
44. Păsăreanu, C.S., Rungta, N.: Symbolic pathfinder: symbolic execution of Java bytecode. In: Proceedings of the IEEE/ACM International Conference on Automated Software Engineering, pp. 179–180 (2010)
45. Perez-Palacin, D., Mirandola, R.: Uncertainties in the modeling of self-adaptive systems: a taxonomy and an example of availability evaluation. In: Proceedings of the 5th ACM/SPEC International Conference on Performance Engineering, pp. 3–14 (2014)
46. Puterman, M.L.: Markov decision processes. Handb. Oper. Res. Manag. Sci. **2**, 331–434 (1990)
47. Ramalingam, G.: Data flow frequency analysis. ACM SIGPLAN Not. **31**(5), 267–277 (1996)
48. Risso, F., Degioanni, L.: An architecture for high performance network analysis. In: Proceedings of the Sixth IEEE Symposium on Computers and Communications, pp. 686–693. IEEE (2001)
49. Ron, D., Singer, Y., Tishby, N.: The power of amnesia: learning probabilistic automata with variable memory length. Mach. Learn. **25**(2–3), 117–149 (1996). https://doi.org/10.1023/A:1026490906255
50. Rosendahl, M.: Automatic complexity analysis. In: Proceedings of the Fourth International Conference on Functional Programming Languages and Computer Architecture, pp. 144–156 (1989)
51. Sankaranarayanan, S., Chakarov, A., Gulwani, S.: Static analysis for probabilistic programs: inferring whole program properties from finitely many paths. In: Proceedings of the 34th ACM SIGPLAN Conference on Programming Language Design and Implementation, pp. 447–458 (2013)
52. Sarkar, V.: Determining average program execution times and their variance. In: Proceedings of the ACM SIGPLAN 1989 Conference on Programming Language Design and Implementation, pp. 298–312 (1989)
53. Schlabach, T.: Insight into event tracing for windows (2019)
54. Sevitsky, G., De Pauw, W., Konuru, R.: An information exploration tool for performance analysis of Java programs. In: Proceedings Technology of Object-Oriented Languages and Systems, TOOLS 38, pp. 85–101. IEEE (2001)
55. Sharir, M., Pnueli, A., Hart, S.: Verification of probabilistic programs. SIAM J. Comput. **13**(2), 292–314 (1984)
56. Stewart, W.J.: Probability, Markov Chains, Queues, and Simulation. Princeton University Press, Princeton (2009)
57. Tribastone, M.: Towards software performance by construction. In: Margaria, T., Steffen, B. (eds.) ISoLA 2018. LNCS, vol. 11244, pp. 466–470. Springer, Cham (2018). https://doi.org/10.1007/978-3-030-03418-4_27
58. Tribastone, M., Gilmore, S.: Automatic extraction of PEPA performance models from UML activity diagrams annotated with the MARTE profile. In: Proceedings of the Seventh International Workshop on Software and Performance (WOSP) (2008)

59. Tribastone, M., Gilmore, S.: Automatic translation of UML sequence diagrams into PEPA models. In: Fifth International Conference on the Quantitative Evaluation of Systems (QEST), pp. 205–214 (2008)

60. Wang, W., et al.: Testing cloud applications under cloud-uncertainty performance effects. In: 2018 IEEE 11th International Conference on Software Testing, Verification and Validation (ICST), pp. 81–92. IEEE (2018)

61. Wegbreit, B.: Mechanical program analysis. Commun. ACM **18**(9), 528–539 (1975)

62. Wong, S., Cai, Y., Valetto, G., Simeonov, G., Sethi, K.: Design rule hierarchies and parallelism in software development tasks. In: 2009 IEEE/ACM International Conference on Automated Software Engineering, pp. 197–208. IEEE (2009)

63. Woodside, M., Franks, G., Petriu, D.C.: The future of software performance engineering. In: Proceedings of the Future of Software Engineering (FOSE), pp. 171–187 (2007)

64. Woodside, M., Petriu, D.C., Petriu, D.B., Shen, H., Israr, T., Merseguer, J.: Performance by unified model analysis (PUMA). In: Proceedings of the 5th International Workshop on Software and Performance, pp. 1–12. ACM, New York (2005)

65. Zaparanuks, D., Hauswirth, M.: Algorithmic profiling. In: Proceedings of the 33rd ACM SIGPLAN Conference on Programming Language Design and Implementation, pp. 67–76 (2012)

30 Years of Statistical Model Checking!

30 Years of Statistical Model Checking

Kim G. Larsen[1,2(✉)] and Axel Legay[1,2(✉)]

[1] Aalborg University, Aalborg, Denmark
kgl@cs.aau.dk, axel.legay@uclouvain.be
[2] INRIA Rennes – Bretagne Atlantique, Rennes, France

Abstract. This short note introduces statistical model checking and gives a brief overview of the *Statistical Model Checking, past present and future* session at ISOLA 2020.

1 Context

Quantitative properties of stochastic systems are usually specified in logics that allow one to compare the measure of executions satisfying certain temporal properties with thresholds. The model checking problem for stochastic systems with respect to such logics is typically solved by a numerical approach [BHHK03, CG04] that iteratively computes (or approximates) the exact measure of paths satisfying relevant subformulas; the algorithms themselves depend on the class of systems being analysed as well as the logic used for specifying the properties.

Another approach to solve the model checking problem is to *simulate* the system for finitely many runs, and use *hypothesis testing* to infer whether the samples provide *statistical* evidence for the satisfaction or violation of the specification. This approach was first applied in [LS91], where it was shown that hypothesis testing could be used to settle probabilistic modal logic properties with arbitrary precision, leading in the limit to probabilistic bisimulation. More recently [You05a] this approach has been known as statistical model checking (SMC) and is based on the notion that since sample runs of a stochastic system are drawn according to the distribution defined by the system, they can be used to obtain estimates of the probability measure on executions. Starting from time-bounded PCTL properties [You05a], the technique has been extended to handle properties with unbounded until operators [SVA05b], as well as to black-box systems [SVA04, You05a]. Tools, based on this idea have been built [HLMP04, SVA05a, You05a, You05b, BDD+11, DLL+11, BCLS13], and have been used to analyse many systems that are intractable numerical approaches.

The SMC approach enjoys many advantages. First, the algorithms require only that the system be simulatable (or rather, sample executions be drawn according to the measure space defined by the system). Thus, it can be applied to larger class of systems than numerical model checking algorithms, including black-box systems and infinite state systems. In particular, SMC avoids the 'state explosion problem' [CES09]. Second the approach can be generalized to a

© Springer Nature Switzerland AG 2020
T. Margaria and B. Steffen (Eds.): ISoLA 2020, LNCS 12476, pp. 325–330, 2020.
https://doi.org/10.1007/978-3-030-61362-4_18

larger class of properties, including Fourier transform based logics. Third, SMC requires many independent simulation runs, making it easy to parallelise and scale to industrial-sized systems.

While it offers solutions to some intractable numerical model checking problems, SMC also introduces some additional problems. First, SMC only provides probabilistic guarantees about the correctness of the results. Second, the required sample size grows quadratically with respect to the required confidence of the result. This makes rare properties difficult to verify. Third, only the simulation of purely probabilistic systems is well defined. Nondeterministic systems, which are common in the field of formal verification, are especially challenging for SMC.

2   On Statistical Model Checking

Consider a stochastic system S and a logical property φ that can be checked on finite executions of the system. Statistical Model Checking (SMC) refers to a series of simulation-based techniques that can be used to answer two questions: (1) *Qualitative*: Is the probability for S to satisfy φ greater or equal to a certain threshold? and (2) *Quantitative*: What is the probability for S to satisfy φ? In contrast to numerical approaches, the answer is given up to some correctness precision.

In the sequel, we overview two SMC techniques. Let B_i be a discrete random variable with a Bernoulli distribution of parameter p. Such a variable can only take 2 values 0 and 1 with $Pr[B_i = 1] = p$ and $Pr[B_i = 0] = 1 - p$. In our context, each variable B_i is associated with one simulation of the system. The outcome for B_i, denoted b_i, is 1 if the simulation satisfies φ and 0 otherwise.

Qualitative Answer. The main approaches [You05a,SVA04] proposed to answer the qualitative question are based on *sequential hypothesis testing* [Wal45]. Let $p = Pr(\varphi)$. To determine whether $p \geq \theta$, we can test $H : p \geq \theta$ against $K : p < \theta$. A test-based solution does not guarantee a correct result but it is possible to bound the probability of error. The *strength* of a test is determined by two parameters, α and β, such that the probability of accepting K (respectively, H) when H (respectively, K) holds, called a Type-I error (respectively, a Type-II error) is less or equal to α (respectively, β). A test has *ideal performance* if the probability of the Type-I error (respectively, Type-II error) is exactly α (respectively, β). However, these requirements make it impossible to ensure a low probability for both types of errors simultaneously (see [Wal45,You05a] for details). A solution is to use an *indifference region* $[p_1, p_0]$ (given some δ, $p_1 = \theta - \delta$ and $p_0 = \theta + \delta$) and to test $H_0 : p \geq p_0$ against $H_1 : p \leq p_1$. We now sketch the Sequential Probability Ratio Test (SPRT). In this algorithm, one has to choose two values A and B $(A > B)$ that ensure that the strength of the test is respected. Let m be the number of observations that have been made so far. The test is based on the following quotient:

$$\frac{p_{1m}}{p_{0m}} = \prod_{i=1}^{m} \frac{Pr(B_i = b_i \mid p = p_1)}{Pr(B_i = b_i \mid p = p_0)} = \frac{p_1^{d_m}(1 - p_1)^{m - d_m}}{p_0^{d_m}(1 - p_0)^{m - d_m}},$$

where $d_m = \sum_{i=1}^{m} b_i$. The idea is to accept H_0 if $\frac{p_{1m}}{p_{0m}} \geq A$, and H_1 if $\frac{p_{1m}}{p_{0m}} \leq B$. The algorithm computes $\frac{p_{1m}}{p_{0m}}$ for successive values of m until either H_0 or H_1 is satisfied. This has the advantage of minimizing the number of simulations required to make the decision.

Quantitative Answer. In [HLMP04] Peyronnet et al. propose an estimation procedure to compute the probability p for $\mathcal{S}$ to satisfy φ. Given a *precision* δ, the *Chernoff bound* of [Oka59] is used to compute a value for p' such that $|p' - p| \leq \delta$ with *confidence* $1 - \alpha$. Let $B_1 \ldots B_m$ be m Bernoulli random variables with parameter p, associated to m simulations of the system considering φ. Let $p' = \sum_{i=1}^{m} b_i/m$, then the Chernoff bound [Oka59] gives $Pr(|p' - p| \geq \delta) \leq 2e^{-2m\delta^2}$. As a consequence, if we take $m = \lceil \ln(2/\alpha)/(2\delta^2) \rceil$, then $Pr(|p' - p| \leq \delta) \geq 1 - \alpha$.

3   Content of the Session

SMC has been implemented in prototypes/tools, which includes UPPAAL-SMC [DLL+11], PLASMA [BCLS13], YMER [You05b], or COSMOS [BDD+11]. Those tools have been applied to several complex problems coming from a wide range of areas. This includes systems biology (see e.g., [Zul14]), automotive and avionics (see e.g., [BBB+12]), energy-centric systems (see e.g., [DDL+13]), or power grids (see e.g., [HH13]).

This year, the session is mostly focused on real-world applications of SMC on emerging industrial and societal topics such as automotive or COVID19. Some papers consider the integration of blackbox aspects, while others focus on combining the SMC approach with machine learning. It is worth observing that SMC reached a level of maturity that is sufficient for the approach to be integrated to real-life projects such as WABLIEFT or BEOCOVID presented hereafter. The program includes the following contributions.

– In [AKW20], the authors discuss the advantages gained when SMC is applied to white-box systems, utilizing the knowledge of their internals. The authors focus on the setting of unbounded-horizon properties such as reachability or LTL. The suggested approach is compared to other statistical and numerical techniques both conceptually as instantiations of the same framework, and experimentally. It not only clearly preserves scalability advantages of blackbox SMC compared to classical model checking (while providing high level of guarantees), but it also scales yet better than either of the two for a wide class of models.
– In [GESL20], the authors focus on Mission planning. This is one of the crucial problems in the design of Multi-Agent Systems (MAS) because it requires the agents to calculate collision-free paths and efficiently schedule their tasks. The complexity of this problem greatly increases when realistic assumptions are included, e.g. such as increase in number of agents, and timing requirements, as well as the stochastic behavior of the agents. In the paper, the authors

propose a novel method that integrates statistical model checking and reinforcement learning to overcome those difficulties. Additionally, the authors employ hybrid automata to model the continuous movement of agents and moving obstacles, and estimate the possible delay of the agents' traveling time when facing unpredictable obstacles, in order to synthesize mission plans that are statistically optimal. The authors show the result of synthesizing mission plans, analyzing bottlenecks, and the re-planning ability of the method in case of the sudden appearance of pedestrians by modeling and verifying a real industrial use case using UPPAAL SMC.

- In [BtBG+20], the authors provide a brief comparison of the modelling and analysis capabilities of two different formalisms and their associated simulation-based tools, acquired from experimenting with these methods and tools on one specific case study. The case study is a cyber-physical system from an industrial railway project, namely a railroad switch heater, and the quantitative properties concern energy consumption and reliability. The authors model and analyse the case study with stochastic activity networks and Möbius on the one hand and with stochastic hybrid automata and Uppaal SMC on the other hand. The authors give an overview of the performed experiments and highlight specific features of the two methodologies. This yields usefull pointers for future research and improvements.

- In [JLM+20], the authors present the BEOCOVID project. During the spring of 2020, the BEOCOVID project has been funded to investigate the use of stochastic hybrid models, statistical model checking and machine learning to analyse, predict and control the rapid spreading of COVID19. The overall aim of BEOCOVID is to support government in decision making. In the paper the authors focus on the SEIRH epidemiological model instance of COVID19 pandemics and show how the risk of viral exposure, the impact of superspreader events as well as other scenarios can be modelled, estimated and controlled in a variety of ways using the tool UPPAAL SMC.

- In [BLGW20], the authors present the WABLIEFT project. This project explores how to improve medical service delivery through a shared marketplace for service providers. This shared marketplace allows patients to choose services from providers and so support improved service delivery and patient satisfaction. Having a shared marketplace raises some service reliability and correctness challenges, as well as creates opportunities for improved information gathering. This work formalises the shared marketplace to prove correct behaviour and properties of the marketplace behaviour. The information available to the shared marketplace is also used to improve predictions of medical scenarios such as pandemics, and thus improve service delivery.

References

[AKW20] Ashok, P., Kretinsky, J., Weininger, M.: Statistical model checking: black or white? In: Margaria, T., Steffen, B. (eds.) ISoLA 2020. LNCS, vol. 12476, pp. 331–349 (2020)

[BBB+12] Basu, A., Bensalem, S., Bozga, M., Delahaye, B., Legay, A.: Statistical abstraction and model-checking of large heterogeneous systems. STTT **14**(1), 53–72 (2012). https://doi.org/10.1007/s10009-011-0201-2

[BCLS13] Boyer, B., Corre, K., Legay, A., Sedwards, S.: PLASMA-lab: a flexible, distributable statistical model checking library. In: Joshi, K., Siegle, M., Stoelinga, M., D'Argenio, P.R. (eds.) QEST 2013. LNCS, vol. 8054, pp. 160–164. Springer, Heidelberg (2013). https://doi.org/10.1007/978-3-642-40196-1_12

[BDD+11] Ballarini, P., Djafri, H., Duflot, M., Haddad, S., Pekergin, N.: COSMOS: a statistical model checker for the hybrid automata stochastic logic. In: QEST, pp. 143–144. IEEE Computer Society (2011)

[BHHK03] Baier, C., Haverkort, B.R., Hermanns, H., Katoen, J.-P.: Model-checking algorithms for continuous-time Markov chains. IEEE Trans. Softw. Eng. **29**(6), 524–541 (2003)

[BLGW20] Baranov, E., Legay, A., Given-Wilson, T.: Improving secure and robust patient service delivery. In: Margaria, T., Steffen, B. (eds.) ISoLA 2020. LNCS, vol. 12476, pp. 404–418 (2020)

[BtBG+20] Basile, D., ter Beek, M., Di Giandomenico, F., Gnesi, S., Fantechi, A., Spagnolo, G.: 30 years of simulation-based quantitative analysis tools: a comparison experiment between möbius and UPPAAL SMC. In: Margaria, T., Steffen, B. (eds.) ISoLA 2020. LNCS, vol. 12476, pp. 368–384 (2020)

[CES09] Clarke, E.M., Emerson, E.A., Sifakis, J.: Model checking: algorithmic verification and debugging. Commun. ACM **52**(11), 74–84 (2009)

[CG04] Ciesinski, F., Größer, M.: On probabilistic computation tree logic. In: Baier, C., Haverkort, B.R., Hermanns, H., Katoen, J.-P., Siegle, M. (eds.) Validation of Stochastic Systems. LNCS, vol. 2925, pp. 147–188. Springer, Heidelberg (2004). https://doi.org/10.1007/978-3-540-24611-4_5

[DDL+13] David, A., Du, D., Guldstrand Larsen, K., Legay, A., Mikučionis, M.: Optimizing control strategy using statistical model checking. In: Brat, G., Rungta, N., Venet, A. (eds.) NFM 2013. LNCS, vol. 7871, pp. 352–367. Springer, Heidelberg (2013). https://doi.org/10.1007/978-3-642-38088-4_24

[DLL+11] David, A., Larsen, K.G., Legay, A., Mikučionis, M., Wang, Z.: Time for statistical model checking of real-time systems. In: Gopalakrishnan, G., Qadeer, S. (eds.) CAV 2011. LNCS, vol. 6806, pp. 349–355. Springer, Heidelberg (2011). https://doi.org/10.1007/978-3-642-22110-1_27

[GESL20] Gu, R., Enoiu, E., Seceleanu, C., Lundqvist, K.: Probabilistic mission planning and analysis for multi-agent systems. In: Margaria, T., Steffen, B. (eds.) ISoLA 2020. LNCS, vol. 12476, pp. 350–367 (2020)

[HH13] Hermanns, H., Hartmanns, A.: An internet inspired approach to power grid stability. IT Inf. Technol. **55**(2), 45–51 (2013)

[HLMP04] Hérault, T., Lassaigne, R., Magniette, F., Peyronnet, S.: Approximate probabilistic model checking. In: Steffen, B., Levi, G. (eds.) VMCAI 2004. LNCS, vol. 2937, pp. 73–84. Springer, Heidelberg (2004). https://doi.org/10.1007/978-3-540-24622-0_8

[JLM+20] Jensen, P., Larsen, K.G., Mikuconis, M., Muniz, M., Poulsen, D., Jorgensen, K.: Fluid model-checking in UPPAAL for Covid-19. In: Margaria, T., Steffen, B. (eds.) ISoLA 2020. LNCS, vol. 12476, pp. 385–403 (2020)

[LS91] Kim Guldstrand Larsen and Arne Skou: Bisimulation through probabilistic testing. Inf. Comput. **94**(1), 1–28 (1991)

[Oka59] Okamoto, M.: Some inequalities relating to the partial sum of binomial probabilities. Ann. Inst. Stat. Math. **10**, 29–35 (1959). https://doi.org/10.1007/BF02883985

[SVA04] Sen, K., Viswanathan, M., Agha, G.: Statistical model checking of black-box probabilistic systems. In: Alur, R., Peled, D.A. (eds.) CAV 2004. LNCS, vol. 3114, pp. 202–215. Springer, Heidelberg (2004). https://doi.org/10.1007/978-3-540-27813-9_16

[SVA05a] Sen, K., Viswanathan, M., Agha, G.A.: VESTA: a statistical model-checker and analyzer for probabilistic systems. In: QEST, pp. 251–252. IEEE Computer Society (2005)

[SVA05b] Sen, K., Viswanathan, M., Agha, G.: On statistical model checking of stochastic systems. In: Etessami, K., Rajamani, S.K. (eds.) CAV 2005. LNCS, vol. 3576, pp. 266–280. Springer, Heidelberg (2005). https://doi.org/10.1007/11513988_26

[Wal45] Wald, A.: Sequential tests of statistical hypotheses. Ann. Math. Stat. **16**(2), 117–186 (1945)

[You05a] Younes, H.L.S.: Verification and planning for stochastic processes with asynchronous events. Ph.D. thesis, Carnegie Mellon (2005)

[You05b] Younes, H.L.S.: Ymer: a statistical model checker. In: Etessami, K., Rajamani, S.K. (eds.) CAV 2005. LNCS, vol. 3576, pp. 429–433. Springer, Heidelberg (2005). https://doi.org/10.1007/11513988_43

[Zul14] Zuliani, P.: Statistical model checking for biological applications. Int. J. Softw. Tools Technolo. Transfer **17**(4), 527–536 (2014), CoRR, abs/1405.2705, https://doi.org/10.1007/s10009-014-0343-0

Statistical Model Checking: Black or White?

Pranav Ashok[(✉)], Przemysław Daca, Jan Křetínský[(✉)],
and Maximilian Weininger[(✉)]

Technical University of Munich, Munich, Germany
ashok@in.tum.de, jan.kretinsky@tum.de, maxi.weininger@tum.de

Abstract. One of the advantages of statistical model checking (SMC) is its applicability to black-box systems. In this paper, we discuss the advantages gained when SMC is applied to white-box systems, utilizing the knowledge of their internals. We focus on the setting of unbounded-horizon properties such as reachability or LTL. We compare our approach to other statistical and numerical techniques both conceptually as instantiations of the same framework, and experimentally. It not only clearly preserves scalability advantages of black-box SMC compared to classical model checking (while providing high level of guarantees), but it also scales yet better than either of the two for a wide class of models.

1 Introduction

Classical *probabilistic verification* techniques rely on iterative approximation algorithms for linear equation systems and linear programs, such as *value iteration (VI)*, e.g. [Put14]. However, the scalability of such numeric analyses is severely limited, compared to standard non-quantitative (hardware or software) verification, since exact transformations, such as abstraction or partial-order reduction, are more difficult to use. Consequently, weaker guarantees such as *probably approximately correct (PAC)* results become acceptable even for completely known systems (*white box*) and not only in contexts where the system is executable but unknown (*black box*), and where thus absolute guarantees are principally impossible.

Example 1. Consider the task of model checking a reachability property of a probabilistic communication protocol, which starts by generating a few, say k, random bits. Thus the execution immediately branches into 2^k states. If there are only few or hard-to-find symmetries in the behaviour, standard analysis quickly becomes infeasible. In the following, we discuss drawbacks of previously studied alternative approaches; then we suggest a new one that overcomes the difficulties for a wide class of models.

This research was funded in part by TUM IGSSE Grant 10.06 (PARSEC) and the German Research Foundation (DFG) project 383882557 *Statistical Unbounded Verification* (KR 4890/2-1).

ⓒ Springer Nature Switzerland AG 2020
T. Margaria and B. Steffen (Eds.): ISoLA 2020, LNCS 12476, pp. 331–349, 2020.
https://doi.org/10.1007/978-3-030-61362-4_19

The exponential state-space explosion quickly renders explicit VI unable to propagate information by more than a single step. Besides, if the transition probabilities depend on the generated bits, even the symbolic variants of VI [BCH+97] cannot help much. There have been two major alternatives proposed, both relying on extensive use of simulations.

- (I) For large and possibly *unknown* systems, *statistical model checking (SMC)* [YS02] reincarnates the Monte Carlo method. It runs simulations of the system; the resulting statistics then yields confidence intervals, i.e. PAC results. However, for unbounded-horizon properties, such as reachability or linear temporal logic (LTL) [Pnu77], performing simulations of finite length requires some information about the model [Kře16]:

  1. Either the second eigenvalue of the transition matrix can be bounded [LP08,YCZ10], which requires essentially the complete knowledge of the system (white box) and is as hard as solving the model checking problem, or
  2. the topology of the underlying state-graph is known [YCZ10,HJB+10] (sometimes called *grey box*, e.g. [AKW19]) and the whole system is preprocessed, which beats the purpose of sublinear analysis, or
  3. a bound on the minimum transition probability $p_{\min}$ is known as is the case in [BCC+14,DHKP17]. This is the closest to black box, thus called *black SMC* here.

  In black SMC, long enough simulations can be run to ensure the system passes from the transient to the recurrent part and reliable information on the whole infinite run is obtained. While the a-priori length is practically infeasible [BCC+14], early detection of recurrent behaviour has been proposed [DHKP17] as follows. Based on the observed part of a simulation run, a hypothesis on the topology of the system is made, answering what bottom strongly connected component (BSCC) this run ends up in. With repetitive observations of transitions over the run, the confidence grows that what currently looks as a BSCC indeed is a BSCC. Since quite a few repetitions of *all* transitions in the BSCC are required, this approach turns out practical only for systems with small BSCCs and not too small $p_{\min}$.

  In this paper, assuming knowledge of the system (white-box setting), we twist the technique to a more efficient one as follows. After quickly gaining (unreliably low) confidence that the run entered a BSCC, we use the knowledge of the topology to confirm this information—again very quickly since not the whole model is built but only the *local* BSCC. Consequently, BSCCs are detected fast even in the case with larger BSCCs or small $p_{\min}$. As the information used turns out quite limited, corresponding to the grey-box setting, we call this approach *grey SMC*.

- (II) The other alternative to VI, now in the context or large but *known* systems, is the *asynchronous value iteration*, e.g. [BT89], a generalization of the Gauss-Seidel method and the core of reinforcement learning and approximate dynamic programming. There, the VI updates on states of the system are performed in varying orders, in particular possibly entirely skipping some states.

The class of algorithms providing guarantees is represented by *bounded real-time dynamic programming (BRTDP)* [MLG05,BCC+14,AKW19] where the states to be updated at each moment are those appearing on a current simulation run. Consequently, states with low probability of visiting and thus low impact on the overall value are ignored. While this allows for treating very "wide" systems with lots of unimportant branches, the scalability problem persists as soon as the branching is very uniform (see also Example 5 on Fig. 2b). From this perspective, grey SMC relaxes the rigorous approximation in the transient part and replaces it with a statistical estimate.

Overall, grey SMC fills the gap in the following spectrum:

VI	BRTDP	grey SMC	black SMC
analysis	analysis with simulation inside	simulation with analysis inside	simulation

On the one end, numeric analysis (VI) provides reliable results; in BRTDP, simulations are additionally used in the analysis to improve the performance while preserving the guarantees. On the other end, simulations (SMC) provide PAC guarantees; grey SMC then improves the performance by additional analysis in the simulation.

Our contribution can be summarized as follows:

– We modify the black SMC for unbounded properties of [DHKP17] to perform better in the white-box (and actually also in the so-called grey-box) setting.
– We compare our grey SMC to black SMC, BRTDP and VI both conceptually, illustrating advantages on examples, as well as experimentally, comparing the runtimes on standard benchmarks.
– We present all algorithms within a unified framework, which in our opinion eases understanding and comparison, provides a more systematic insight, and is pedagogically more valuable.

Outline of the Paper: After recalling necessary definitions in Sect. 2, we describe and exemplify the algorithms in Sect. 3 and the respective key sub-procedure in Sect. 4. Then we compare the algorithms and other related work in Sect. 5, discussing the expected implications, which we confirm experimentally in Sect. 6. For a broader account on related work on SMC in the context of unbounded-horizon properties, we refer the interested reader to the survey [Kře16].

2 Preliminaries

A *probability distribution* on a finite set X is a mapping $\delta : X \to [0, 1]$, such that $\sum_{x \in X} \delta(x) = 1$. The set of all probability distributions on X is denoted by $\mathcal{D}(X)$.

Definition 1 (MC). *A* Markov chain *(MC) is a tuple* (S, s_0, δ)*, where* S *is a finite set of* states *with a designated* initial state $s_0 \in S$*, and* $\delta : S \to \mathcal{D}(S)$

is a transition function *that given a state* s *yields a probability distribution* $\delta(s)$ *over successor states. For ease of notation, we write* $\delta(s, t)$ *instead of* $\delta(s)(t)$ *and* Post(s) := $\{t \mid \delta(s, t) > 0\}$ *to denote the set of successors of a state.*

The semantics of an MC is given in the usual way by the probability space on paths. An *infinite path* ρ is an infinite sequence $\rho = s_0 s_1 \cdots \in (S)^\omega$, such that for every $i \in \mathbb{N}$ we have $s_{i+1} \in$ Post(s_i). A finite path is a finite prefix of an infinite path. The Markov chain together with a state s induces a unique probability distribution $\mathbb{P}_s$ over measurable sets of infinite paths [BK08, Ch. 10].

Definition 2 (Reachability probability). *For a target set* T $\subseteq$ S, *we write* $\Diamond$T := $\{s_0 s_1 \cdots \mid \exists i \in \mathbb{N} : s_i \in$ T$\}$ *to denote the (measurable) set of all infinite paths which eventually reach* T. *For each* s $\in$ S, *we define the value in* s *as*

$$V(s) := \mathbb{P}_s(\Diamond T).$$

The reachability probability *is then the value of the initial state* V(s_0).

The value function V satisfies the following system of equations, which is referred to as the *Bellman equations*:

$$V(s) = \begin{cases} 1 & \text{if } s \in T \\ \sum_{s' \in S} \delta(s, s') \cdot V(s') & \text{otherwise} \end{cases} \tag{1}$$

Moreover, V is the *least* solution to the Bellman equations, see e.g. [CH08].

Certain parts of the state space are of special interest for the analysis of MC with respect to unbounded-horizon properties, such as reachability:

Definition 3 (SCC, BSCC). *A non-empty set* $T \subseteq$ S *of states is* strongly connected *if for every pair* s, s' $\in$ S *there is a path (of non-zero length) from* s *to* s'. *Such a set* T *is a* strongly connected component (SCC) *if it is maximal w.r.t. set inclusion, i.e. there exists no strongly connected* T' *with* $T \subsetneq T'$. *An SCC* T *is called* bottom (BSCC), *if for all states* s $\in T$ *we have* Post(s) $\subseteq T$, *i.e. no transition leaves the SCC.*

Note that the SCCs of an MC are disjoint and that, with probability 1, infinitely often reached states on a path form a BSCC.

We consider algorithms that have a limited information about the MC:

Definition 4 (Black box and grey box setting). *An algorithm inputs an MC as* black box *if it cannot access the whole tuple, but*

- *it knows the initial state,*
- *for a given state, it can sample a successor* t *according to* $\delta(s)$,[1]

---

[1] Up to this point, this definition conforms to black box systems in the sense of [SVA04] with sampling from the initial state, being stricter than [YS02] or [RP09], where simulations can be run from any desired state.

– *it knows* $p_{\min} \leq \min\limits_{s \in S, t \in \mathsf{Post}(s)} \delta(s, t)$, *an under-approximation of the minimum transition probability.*

When input as grey box, *it additionally knows the number* $|\mathsf{Post}(s)|$ *of successors for each state* s.[2]

3 Description of Algorithms

In this section, we describe all of the algorithms that we compare in this paper. They all use the framework of Algorithm 1. The differences are in the instantiations of the functions (written in capital letters). This allows for an easy and modular comparison.

Algorithm 1. Framework for all considered algorithms

Input: MC M, reachability objective T
Output: (An estimate of) $\mathbb{P}_{s_0}(\lozenge T)$
1: **procedure** COMPUTE REACHABILITY PROBABILITY
2:     INITIALIZE
3:     **repeat**
4:         $X \leftarrow$ GET_STATES
5:         UPDATE(X)
6:     **until** TERM_CRIT

3.1 Value Iteration

Value iteration (VI), e.g. [Put14], computes the value for all states in the MC. As memory, it saves a rational number (the current estimate of the value) for every state. In INITIALIZE, the estimate is set to 1 for target states in T and to 0 for all others. GET_STATES returns the whole state space, as the estimate of all values is updated simultaneously. The UPDATE works by performing a so called *Bellman backup*, i.e.g.iven the current estimate function L_i, the next estimate L_{i+1} is computed by applying the Bellman Equation (1) as follows:

$$L_{i+1}(s) = \sum_{s' \in S} \delta(s, s') \cdot L_i(s')$$

Example 2. Consider the MC from Fig. 1a, with $\delta(s_2, s_2) = \delta(s_2, t) = \delta(s_2, s_3) = \frac{1}{3}$ and the reachability objective $\{t\}$. The estimates that VI computes in the first 4 iterations are depicted in Fig. 1b. The target state t is initialized to 1, everything else to 0. The estimate for s_3 stays at 0, as it is a BSCC with no possibility to

---

[2] This requirement is slightly weaker than the knowledge of the whole topology, i.e. $\mathsf{Post}(s)$ for each s.

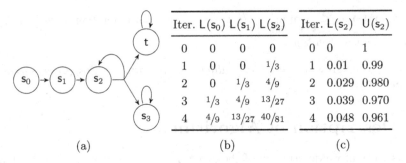

Iter.	L(s_0)	L(s_1)	L(s_2)	Iter.	L(s_2)	U(s_2)
0	0	0	0	0	0	1
1	0	0	$1/3$	1	0.01	0.99
2	0	$1/3$	$4/9$	2	0.029	0.980
3	$1/3$	$4/9$	$13/27$	3	0.039	0.970
4	$4/9$	$13/27$	$40/81$	4	0.048	0.961

(a)   (b)   (c)

Fig. 1. (a) Example Markov chain (b) Under approximations computed by value iteration, see Example 2 (c) Under- and over-approximations computed by bounded value iteration, see Example 3.

reach the target state. Since these two states do not change, they are omitted in the figure. In every iteration, the estimates are updated and become more precise, coming closer to the true value 0.5 for s_0, s_1 and s_2. However, they converge to 0.5 only in the limit, as for any finite number of iterations there is a positive probability to remain in s_2. Note that s_0 always is two steps behind s_2, as it takes two iterations to backpropagate the current estimate.

VI converges to the true value only in the limit, hence we need some termination criterion TERM_CRIT to stop when we are close enough. However, to be certain that the estimate is close, one has to perform an exponential number of iterations [CH08], which is infeasible. Hence, usually this version of VI does not give convergence guarantees, but instead just runs until the difference between two successive iterations is small. The result of this heuristic is guaranteed to be a lower bound, but can be arbitrarily imprecise [HM18], as we will also see in Example 3.

3.2 Bounded Value Iteration

To be able to give convergence guarantees, *Bounded value iteration* (BVI, also called interval iteration) was introduced more generally for Markov decision processes in [BCC+14, HM18]. In this paper, we only focus on Markov chains, i.e. Markov decision processes with a single action in every state. In addition to the under-approximation computed by VI, this approach also computes a convergent over-approximation. For this, it stores a second rational number for every state. Dually to the under-approximation, INITIALIZE sets the estimate to 0 in states that cannot reach the target and 1 everywhere else. Note that finding the states with value 0, i.e. BSCC that do not contain the target, BVI has to perform a graph analysis, e.g. a backwards search from the targets. BVI still works on the whole state space and the update is completely analogous to VI, only this time updating both approximations. As TERM_CRIT, BVI checks that difference between the over- and under-approximation in the initial state is smaller than a given precision ε. This guarantees that the returned value is ε-precise.

Example 3. Consider the MC from Fig. 1a with the same objective, but this time with $\delta(s_2, s_2) = 0.98$ and $\delta(s_2, t) = \delta(s_2, s_3) = 0.01$. Note that by pre-processing we set the over approximation $U(s_3)$ to 0, as it is a BSCC with no possibility of reaching the target. The estimates BVI computes for s_2 in the first 4 iterations are depicted in Fig. 1c.

If we were running VI only from below, we might stop after iteration 4, as the lower bound changes by less than 0.01 between these iterations and hence it seems to have converged close to the value. However, the difference between upper and lower bounds is still very high, so BVI knows that there still is a huge uncertainty in the values, as it could be anything between 0.048 and 0.961. Eventually, both estimates converge close enough to 0.5; for example, after around 400 iterations the lower bound is 0.49 and the upper bound 0.51. Then BVI can return the value 0.5 (the center of the interval) with a precision of 0.01, as this value is off by at most that.

3.3 Simulation-Based Asynchronous Value Iteration

The biggest drawback of the two variants we introduced so far is that they always work on the whole state space. Because of the state-space explosion, this is often infeasible. In contrast, asynchronous value iteration only updates parts of the state space in every iteration of the loop, i.e. GET_STATES does not return the whole state space, but instead heuristically selects the states to update next. This not only speeds up the main loop, but also allows the algorithm to reduce the memory requirements. Indeed, instead of storing estimates for all states, one stores estimates only for the partial model consisting of previously updated states. In [BBS95,MLG05,BCC+14], the heuristic for selecting the states is based on simulation: a path is sampled in the model, and only the states on that path are updated. The partial model contains all states that have been encountered during some of the simulations. If the part of the state space that is relevant for convergence of value iteration is small, this can lead to enormous speed-ups [BCC+14,KM19]. For more details on why this happens and a formal definition of 'state space relevant for convergence', we refer the interested reader to [KM19].

Algorithm 2. Simulation-based implementation of GET_STATES

Input: MC M, reachability objective T, s_0
Output: A set of states $X \subseteq S$
1: **procedure** SIMULATE
2:     $\rho \leftarrow s_0$
3:     **repeat**
4:         $s' \leftarrow$ sample from $\delta(\text{last}(\rho))$ according to NEXT_STATE
5:         $\rho \leftarrow \rho s'$
6:     **until** $\text{last}(\rho) \in T$ or STUCK
7:     **return** ρ

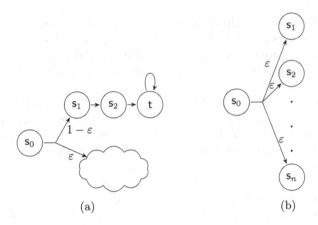

(a)   (b)

Fig. 2. (a) A Markov chain where exploring the whole state space can be avoided. ε denotes a transition probability. The cloud represents an arbitrarily large state space. (b) A Markov chain with high branching. From s_0, there is a uniform probabilistic choice with $n = \frac{1}{\varepsilon}$ successors.

Algorithm 2 shows how states can be sampled through simulations, as done in [BCC+14]: Starting from the initial state, in every step of the simulation a successor is chosen from the distribution of the last state on the path. Note that this choice depends on another heuristic NEXT_STATE. The successor can be chosen according to the transition probabilities δ, but it has proven to be advantageous to additionally consider the difference between the upper and lower bound in the successor states [MLG05, BCC+14]. In consequence, states where we already know a lot (under- and over-approximations are close to each other) are given less priority than states where we still need information.

The simulation is stopped in two cases: Either (i) it reaches a target state or (ii) it is stuck in a BSCC with no path to the target. Different heuristics for checking whether the simulation is stuck are discussed in depth in Sect. 4. Note that being able to differentiate between targets and non-target BSCCs during the simulations allows us not to do anything in INITIALIZE; we can set the value to 1 when reaching a target and 0 in the other case. The UPDATE function for simulation based asynchronous value iteration again uses the Bellman equation (1) to update the estimates of all states on the path; moreover, it can utilize additional information: Since GET_STATES returns a path, there is a notion of order of the states. Updating the states in reverse order backpropagates information faster.

Example 4. Consider the MC in Fig. 2a, again with reachability objective $\{t\}$. The cloud represents an arbitrarily large state space. However, since it is only reachable with a very small probability ε (and we are interested in an ε-precise solution), it need not be explored. Let the first sampled path be $s_0 s_1 s_2 t$. This happens with high probability, as the only other possibility would be to select a successor from the cloud in state s_0, but since the selection process depends on the transition probabilities δ, going to s_1 has a higher probability. After the simulation reaches t, this value is backpropagated in reverse order. First the lower estimate $L(s_2)$ is set to 1, then $L(s_1)$ is set to 1, then $L(s_0)$ is set to $1 - \varepsilon$. At this point the algorithm has converged, as difference between the lower and upper bound is ε.

So in this example, sampling the most probable path a single time gives a good approximation. The algorithm avoids exploring the large cloud and back-progagates values faster than synchronous VI.

Example 5. As an adversarial example, consider the MC in Fig. 2b. Here, the model exhibits high branching, so every single path has a low probability, and only by aggregating all paths we actually get a high value. Unlike the previous example, there is no part of the state space that is clearly irrelevant. In fact, to achieve precision of ε the algorithm has to see so many paths that their cumulative probability is $1 - \varepsilon$, which in this case means seeing all but one transition from the starting state. This needs at least $\frac{1}{\varepsilon}$ simulations, but since the successors are chosen probabilistically, most likely a lot more.

Note that similarly to synchronous VI, there are versions of asynchronous VI without (RTDP [BBS95]) and with (BRTDP [MLG05, BCC+14])[3] guaranteed error bounds.

3.4 Statistical Model Checking

Algorithms for statistical model checking (SMC), [YS02], are different from all previously described ones in two ways, namely what they store and what they return. The VI-based algorithms store estimates for every (seen) state and they update these values to be ever more precise. Thus, the returned bounds on the values are certainly correct, although possibly quite loose. In contrast, SMC stores only a single accumulator (for the value of the initial state) and the returned value is probably approximately correct (PAC [Val84]). Being PAC with probability α and approximation $\epsilon > 0$ guarantees the following: with high probability (α), the returned value is close to the true value (off by at most ε). However, the returned confidence interval is not guaranteed to be a valid under- and over-approximation; if we are unlucky (i.e. with the remaining probability $1 - \alpha$), there is no guarantee whatsoever on the returned value.

SMC does not need to do anything in INITIALIZE. It only stores a single accumulator to remember how often a target state was reached. GET_STATES works as in Algorithm 2 with NEXT_STATE typically sampling the successor according to the transition probabilities δ (in some settings, importance sampling may also be possible, e.g. [JLS12, BDH17]). UPDATE remembers whether we reached the target or not; in the end we can divide the number of reaches by the total number of samples to get the probability estimate. TERM_CRIT is a (typically low) number of samples that depends on the required probability of

---

[3] While all are more generally applicable to Markov decision processes, [MLG05] only ensures convergence if no end components [BK08] are present (for MC, no BSCCs without a target are present) and [BCC+14] lifts this restriction.

the guarantee and the width of the confidence interval; see [DHKP17, Section 2.2] for details or [JSD19] for more advanced techniques.

Example 6. Consider again the MC depicted in Fig. 1a. Let the first sampled path be $s_0s_1s_2s_2t$. At this point the simulation stops, as we have reached a target state, and we remember that we have seen a target once. Let the second path be $s_0s_1s_2s_2s_2s_3s_3\ldots$. On the one hand, the STUCK function has to let the simulation continue, even though s_2 is seen 3 times and it looks like a cycle. On the other hand, it has to detect that the simulation will loop forever in s_3 and has to stop it. Ways to detect this are discussed in Sect. 4. After detecting that we are stuck, we remember that the simulation did not reach the target.

Let the required probability of the guarantee be $\alpha = 0.9$ and the width of the confidence interval $\varepsilon = 0.1$. Using Hoeffding's inequality [Hoe63] we can show that the required number of samples for this is 461. So assume that after 461 simulations we have seen the target 223 times. Then we know that with probability at least 0.9, the value is in the interval $223/461 \pm 0.05$, i.e. $[0.434, 0.534]$. Increasing the number of simulations can both increase the confidence or decrease the width of the interval.

Note that this number of simulations is independent of the system. While 461 simulations are a lot for this small system, the number would be the same if we were considering a model with several billion states where value iteration is impossible.

4   STUCK

In this section, we discuss heuristics for detecting whether a simulation is stuck in a BSCC with no path to a target state. We also propose one new such heuristic with convenient theoretical properties.

For simulation-based asynchronous value iteration, previous work either excluded the existence of non-target BSCCs in their assumptions [BBS95, MLG05] or used a heuristic with no false negatives, but the possibility of false positives [BCC+14]. This means that if the simulation is stuck in a BSCC, the simulation definitely is stopped, which is required for termination. However, if the simulation is not stuck in a BSCC, it might still be stopped, guessing the value of the last state in the path is 0, although it might not be. The STUCK-heuristics used in previous work either depend on the path length ([BCC+14, Ujm15, Chapter 7.5]) or simply stops exploring when any state is seen twice [AKW19, Appendix A.3].

SMC has to be sure with high probability that the simulation is stuck, as otherwise it loses the probabilistic guarantee. In [YCZ10], two approaches are described. The first approach requires knowledge of the second eigenvalue of the MC in order to guarantee asymptotic convergence. However, getting the second eigenvalue is as hard as the verification problem itself. The second approach works in the grey-box setting and pre-processes the MC so that all potentially infinite paths are eliminated. A similar transformation, using white-box information, was suggested in [HJB+10]. However, both of these approaches transform the whole model and thus face problems in the case of very large models.

An alternative was suggested in [DHKP16]. It monitors the finite path sampled during the simulation, implicitly constructing a graph with all seen states as nodes and all seen transitions as edges. The *candidate* of the current path is the (possibly empty) set of states forming the maximal BSCC of this graph. Intuitively, it is what we believe to be a BSCC given the observation of the current simulation. This candidate has to be validated, because as we saw in Example 6, a state set can look like a BSCC for several steps before being exited. In the black-box setting, this validation works by continuing the simulation until the probability of overlooking some transition exiting the candidate becomes very small [DHKP16].

In this paper, we pinpoint that in the grey-box or white-box setting, this costly type of validation is not necessary. Instead of validating the candidate by running around in it for a huge number of steps, one can verify it using the additional information on the model. If no successor of any state in the candidate is outside of the candidate, then it indeed is a BSCC. Formally, for a candidate T, we check that $\{s \mid \exists t \in T : s \in \mathsf{Post}(t)\} \subseteq T$ (if the topology is known), or alternatively that $\forall t \in T : |\widehat{\mathsf{Post}}(t)| = |\mathsf{Post}(t)|$ (in what we defined as the grey-box setting) where $\widehat{\mathsf{Post}}$ yields the number of successors within the observed candidate.

Example 7. Consider again the MC depicted in Fig. 1a. When a simulation enters s_3, STUCK should return true in order to stop the simulation, as it has reached a BSCC with no path to a target. In the black box setting of [DHKP16], this is only possible after continuing the simulation for another huge amount of steps. For example, even in a BSCC with only a single state, hundreds of further steps can be necessary to reach the required confidence. Given the grey-box information, the algorithm can determine that all successors of the states in the candidate ($\{s_3\}$) have been seen and conclude that the candidate is indeed a BSCC.

However, this check stops the simulation and can incur an overhead if there are many SCCs in the transient part of the state space. Hence, we can delay it, not checking at the first occurrence of a cycle, but e.g. only when every state in the candidate has been seen twice. Alternatively, one can only allow the check every n (e.g. hundred) steps of the simulation. Depending on the model and the implementation of the algorithm, these heuristics can have some impact on the runtime.

Furthermore, one might modify this heuristic even further. If a state of the BSCC is only reached with low probability, it takes many steps for the simulation to reach it. When we check whether the current candidate is a BSCC, this state might not have occurred in the simulation yet. Instead of concluding that the information is insufficient and the simulation has to continue, one could deterministically explore the unknown successors and *compute* the BSCC. On the one hand, for small to medium sized BSCCs, this could result in a speed-up. On the other hand, it increases the overhead when transient SCCs are checked by STUCK. Consequently, in the available benchmarks, this heuristic did not prove advantageous. Hence we do not even report on it in the evaluation section.

5 Discussion

5.1 Dependency of Simulation Length on Topology

Although the number of samples in SMC is independent of the model size, the length of the simulations is highly dependent on the model size and even more on the structure. Indeed, any kind of cyclic behaviour in the transient part of the state space increases the simulation time for two reasons. Firstly, the simulation loops in transient SCCs and does not make progress towards a target or a BSCC. Secondly, the check whether the simulation is stuck in transient SCCs incurs an overhead. An adversarial handcrafted worst-case example where simulations struggle is given in [HM18, Figure 3]. Moreover, the structure of BSCCs affects the length of the simulation. For cyclic BSCCs, the simulation easily encounters all states of the BSCC and can quickly terminate. For more complex topologies, some states are typically only seen with very low frequency and thus the simulation takes longer.

If the model exhibits many transient SCCs, using any simulation-based technique is problematic.

5.2 Black, Grey and White SMC

The difference between the variants of SMC we report on are their knowledge of the transition system: p_{min} corresponds to black, the number of successors to grey and the exact successors and probabilities to the white-box setting. This information can be used in the STUCK-check; apart from that, the algorithms are the same.

Comparing grey and black box, it is apparent that simulations in grey box can be much shorter, as upon detection of a candidate that is a BSCCs the simulation is immediately stopped, whereas in the black box setting it has to continue for a number of steps. This number of steps depends on two things: (i) The size of the BSCC, as larger BSCC take longer to explore, especially since all states, no matter how improbable, need to be seen a certain amount of times, and (ii) the given under-approximation of the minimum transition probability p_{min}, as this determines how often every state in the candidate has to be seen until the probability of a false positive is small enough.

Thus, for large BSCCs or small p_{min}, grey SMC is clearly better, as we also experimentally validate in Table 3 (large BSCC) and Table 2 (various p_{min}) in the next section. For small BSCCs (e.g. only of size 1) and not so small p_{min}, black and grey SMC become more comparable, but grey SMC still has shorter simulations. However, practically, the overhead of verifying the candidates in grey SMC can be so large that black SMC can even be slightly faster than grey SMC (see e.g., leader6_11 in Table 1).

Heuristically reducing the number of checks in grey SMC (as described in Sect. 4) can make it faster again, but the effectiveness of the heuristics depends on the models. So, if it is known that the BSCC-detection is very easy for black SMC (e.g. they are of size 1 or cyclic and p_{min} is not too small), black SMC can be a viable choice. However, as black SMC is never far better, using grey SMC is the safer variant when facing models with uncertain topology.

5.3 Comparison of Algorithms

Finally, we compare the (dis-)advantages of the different algorithms, giving a practical decision guidance. If hard guarantees are required, then BVI or BRTDP are to be used. The latter is simulation based, and thus good if only a small part of the state space is relevant for convergence. Additionally, if the model is too large for BVI, BRTDP still has a chance, but quite possibly the partial model will also be too large. Conversely, if the model contains lots of transient SCCs, BVI is preferable, as simulation based approaches fail on this kind of model, see Sect. 5.1. Note that, if there are small probabilities present, it might take very long for BVI and BRTDP to converge, see Example 3.

For a quick estimate, or if PAC guarantees are sufficient, or if the system is too large, so that it is not possible to provide hard guarantees, SMC is to be used, if possible (white or grey box setting) in our grey variant. As both the memory and the termination criterion are independent of the size of the system, SMC always has a chance to yield an estimate, which additionally comes with a probabilistic guarantee.

There is no case in which un-guaranteed (synchronous or asynchronous) VI are preferable, as they suffer from the same drawbacks as BVI and BRTDP, but additionally do not provide guarantees. Whenever hard guarantees are not of interest and the system is not strongly connected, grey SMC should be used for a quick estimate.

5.4 Extensions to Other Unbounded-Horizon Properties

For more complex unbounded-horizon properties [BK08], such as Until (avoid-reach), LTL or long-run average reward, (B)VI pre-processes the state space to analyze the BSCCs [BK08] and BRTDP [BCC+14] can either do the same or analyze the encountered BSCCs only. Black SMC of [DHKP17] is applicable through additional analysis of the BSCC candidates after they have been found likely to be BSCCs. This is directly inherited by grey SMC and makes it available for these specifications with low overhead.

6 Experimental Evaluation

We implemented grey SMC in a branch of the PRISM Model Checker [KNP11] extending the implementation of black SMC [DHKP17]. We ran experiments on (both discrete- and continuous-time) Markov chains from the PRISM Benchmark

Table 1. Runtime (in seconds) comparison of black and grey SMC for various benchmarks. BVI runtimes are also presented as a baseline.

Model/property	Size	p_{min}	BSCC (no., max. size)	SMC		BVI
				Black	Grey	
bluetooth(10)time_qual	>569K	7.81×10^{-3}	>5.8K, 1	9	**7**	TO
brp_nodl(10K,10K)p1_qual	>40M	1×10^{-2}	>4.5K, 1	86	**84**	TO
crowds_nodl(8,20)positive_qual	68M	5×10^{-2}	>3K, 1	10	**8**	TO
egl(20,20)unfairA_qual	1719T	5×10^{-1}	1, 1	43	**25**	TO
gridworld(400,0.999)prop_qual	384M	1×10^{-3}	796, 160K	15	**8**	TO
herman-174tokens	10G	4.7×10^{-7}	1, 34	TO	**73**	98
leader6_11elected_qual	>280K	5.6×10^{-7}	1, 1	**106**	152	OOM
nand(50,3)reliable_qual	11M	2×10^{-2}	51, 1	11	**10**	455
tandem(2K)reach_qual	>1.7M	2.4×10^{-5}	1, >501K	**7**	**7**	62

Suite [KNP12a]. In addition to a comparison to black SMC, we also provide comparisons to VI and BVI of PRISM and BRTDP of [BCC+14]. An interested reader may also want to refer [DHKP17, Table II] for a comparison of black SMC against two unbounded SMC techniques of [YCZ10].

For every run configuration, we run 5 experiments and report the median. In black SMC, the check for candidates is performed every 1000 steps during path simulations, while in grey SMC the check is performed every 100 steps. Additionally, grey SMC checks if a candidate is indeed a BSCC once every state of the candidate is seen at least twice. In all our tables, 'TO' denotes a timeout of 15 min and 'OOM' indicates that the tool ran out of memory restricted to 1GB RAM.

6.1 Comparison of Black and Grey SMC

Table 1 compares black SMC and grey SMC on multiple benchmarks. One can see that, except in the case of leader6_11 and brp_nodl, grey SMC finishes atleast as soon as black SMC. In bluetooth, gridworld, leader and tandem, both the SMC methods are able to terminate without encountering any candidate (i.e. either the target is seen or the left side of the until formula is falsified). In brp_nodl, crowds_nodl and nand, the SMC methods encounter a candidate, however, since the candidate has only a single state (all BSCCs are trivial), black SMC is quickly able to confidently conclude that the candidate is indeed a BSCC. The only interesting behaviour is observed on the herman-17 benchmark. In this case, every path eventually encounters the only BSCC existing in the model. Grey SMC is able to quickly conclude that the candidate is indeed a BSCC, while black SMC has to sample for a long time in order to be sufficiently confident.

Table 2. Effect of p_{min} on black SMC runtimes (in seconds) on some of the benchmarks. Lower p_{min} demands stronger candidates, due to which black SMC has to sample longer paths.

Model	Black SMC/p_{min}				Grey SMC
	1×10^{-2}	1×10^{-3}	1×10^{-4}	1×10^{-5}	
brp_nodl(10K,10K)	86	93	183	TO	84
crowds_nodl(8,20)	11	41	334	TO	9
egl(20,20)	47	106	875	TO	44

The performance of black SMC is also a consequence of the p_{min} being quite small. Table 2 shows that black SMC is very sensitive towards p_{min}. Note that grey SMC is not affected by the changes in p_{min} as it always checks whether a candidate is a BSCC as soon as all the states in the candidate are seen twice.

6.2   Grey SMC vs. Black SMC/BRTDP/BVI/VI

We now look more closely at the self-stabilization protocol herman [KNP12b, Her90]. The protocol works as follows: herman-N contains N processes, each possessing a local boolean variable x_i. A token is assumed to be in place i if $x_i = x_{i-1}$. The protocol proceeds in rounds. In each round, if the current values of x_i and x_{i-1} are equal, the next value of x_i is set uniformly at random, and otherwise it is set equal to the current value of x_{i-1}. The number of states in herman-N is therefore 2^N. The goal of the protocol is to reach a stable state where there is exactly one token in place. For example, in case of herman-5, a stable state might be $(x_1 = 0, x_2 = 0, x_3 = 1, x_4 = 0, x_5 = 1)$, which indicates that there is a token in place 2. In every herman model, all stable states belong to the single BSCC. The number of states in the BSCC range from 10 states in herman-5 to 2,000,000 states in herman-21.

For all herman models in Table 3, we are interested in checking if the probability of reaching an unstable state where there is a token in places 2–5, i.e. $(x_1 = 1, x_2 = 1, x_3 = 1, x_4 = 1, x_5 = 1)$ is less than 0.05. This property, which we name 4tokens, identifies 2^{N-5} states as target in herman-N. The results in Table 3 show how well grey SMC scales when compared to black SMC, BRTDP, BVI[4] and VI. Black SMC times out for all models where $N \geq 11$. This is due to the fact that the larger models have a smaller p_{min}, thereby requiring black SMC to sample extremely long paths in order to confidently identify candidates as BSCCs. BVI and VI perform well on small models, but as the model sizes grow and transition probabilities become smaller, propagating values becomes extremely slow. Interestingly, we found that in both grey SMC and black SMC, approximately 95% of the time is spent in computing the next transitions, which

---

[4] We refrain from comparison to other guaranteed VI techniques such as sound VI [QK18] or optimistic VI [HK19] as the implementations are not PRISM-based and hence would not be too informative in the comparison.

Table 3. Runtime (in seconds) of the various algorithms on the Herman self-stabilization protocol [KNP12b] with the property **4tokens**. The median runtimes are reported for grey SMC, black SMC [DHKP17], BRTDP [BCC+14], Bounded value iteration (BVI) and Value iteration (VI). The SMC algorithms use SPRT method with parameters $\alpha = 0.01$ and $\beta = 0.01$. BRTDP, BVI and VI run until a relative error of 0.01 is obtained.

Model	States	Grey SMC	Black SMC	BRTDP	BVI	VI
herman-5	32	11	15	TO	1	1
herman-7	128	12	57	TO	1	1
herman-9	512	10	775	TO	1	1
herman-11	2048	19	TO	TO	1	1
herman-13	8192	18	TO	TO	1	1
herman-15	33K	17	TO	TO	9	3
herman-17	131K	49	TO	TO	98	21
herman-19	524K	252	OOM	TO	602	113
herman-21	2M	759	OOM	OOM	TO	TO

grow exponentially in number; an improvement in the simulator implementation can possibly slow down the blow up in run time, allowing for a fairer comparison with the extremely performant symbolic value iteration algorithms.

Finally, we comment on the exceptionally poor performance of BRTDP on **herman** models. In Table 4, we run BRTDP on three different properties: (i) tokens in places 2–3 (**2tokens**); (ii) tokens in places 2–4 (**3tokens**); and (iii) tokens in places 2–5 (**4tokens**). The number of states satisfying the property decrease when going from 2 tokens to 4 tokens. The table shows that BRTDP is generally better in situations where the target set is larger.

In summary, the experiments reveal the following:

- For most benchmarks, black SMC and grey SMC perform similar, as seen in Table 1. As expected, the advantages of grey SMC do not show up in these examples, which (almost all) contain only trivial BSCCs.
- The advantage of grey SMC is clearly visible on the **herman-N** benchmarks, in which there are non-trivial BSCCs. Here, black SMC quickly fails while grey SMC is extremely competitive.
- Classical techniques such as VI and BVI fail when either the model is too large or the transition probabilities are too small. However, they are still to be used for strongly connected systems, where the whole state space needs to be analysed for every run in both SMC approaches, but only once for (B)VI.

Table 4. Effect of restrictive properties (satisfied in fewer states) on the runtime (in seconds) of BRTDP in the herman benchmarks.

Model	Property		
	2tokens	3tokens	4tokens
herman-5	1	2	TO
herman-7	1	1	TO
herman-9	1	2	TO
herman-11	2	2	TO
herman-13	2	2	TO
herman-15	3	3	TO
herman-17	5	6	TO
herman-19	9	9	TO
herman-21	104	111	TO
herman-23	OOM	OOM	OOM

7   Conclusion

While SMC has found its use also in the white-box setting as a scalable alternative, we introduce the first approach that utilizes the knowledge in a local way, without globally processing the state space, and thus preserves the efficiency advantages of black-box SMC. We call this approach grey SMC since we utilize only the topological information and not the quantitative information (sometimes referred to as grey box). On the one hand, this is useful as the quantitative information is often unavailable or imprecise w.r.t. the modelled reality. On the other hand, while the full quantitative information is irrelevant in BSCCs, it plays a major role in the transient phase and could be used to further enhance the approach. For instance, it could be used for importance sampling in order to handle rare events efficiently [JLS12,BDH17] even in the context of unbounded-horizon properties.

References

[AKW19] Ashok, P., Křetínský, J., Weininger, M.: PAC statistical model checking for Markov decision processes and stochastic games. In: Dillig, I., Tasiran, S. (eds.) CAV 2019. LNCS, vol. 11561, pp. 497–519. Springer, Cham (2019). https://doi.org/10.1007/978-3-030-25540-4_29

[BBS95] Barto, A.G., Bradtke, S.J., Singh, S.P.: Learning to act using real-time dynamic programming. Artif. Intell. **72**(1–2), 81–138 (1995)

[BCC+14] Brázdil, T., et al.: Verification of Markov decision processes using learning algorithms. In: Cassez, F., Raskin, J.-F. (eds.) ATVA 2014. LNCS, vol. 8837, pp. 98–114. Springer, Cham (2014). https://doi.org/10.1007/978-3-319-11936-6_8

[BCH+97] Baier, C., Clarke, E.M., Hartonas-Garmhausen, V., Kwiatkowska, M., Ryan, M.: Symbolic model checking for probabilistic processes. In: Degano, P., Gorrieri, R., Marchetti-Spaccamela, A. (eds.) ICALP 1997. LNCS, vol. 1256, pp. 430–440. Springer, Heidelberg (1997). https://doi.org/10.1007/3-540-63165-8_199

[BDH17] Budde, C.E., D'Argenio, P.R., Hartmanns, A.: Better automated importance splitting for transient rare events. In: Larsen, K.G., Sokolsky, O., Wang, J. (eds.) SETTA 2017. LNCS, vol. 10606, pp. 42–58. Springer, Cham (2017). https://doi.org/10.1007/978-3-319-69483-2_3

[BK08] Baier, C., Katoen, J.-P.: Principles of Model Checking. MIT Press, Cambridge (2008)

[BT89] Bertsekas, D.P., Tsitsiklis, J.N.: Parallel and Distributed Computation: Numerical Methods. Prentice-Hall Inc., Upper Saddle River (1989)

[CH08] Chatterjee, K., Henzinger, T.A.: Value iteration. In: Grumberg, O., Veith, H. (eds.) 25 Years of Model Checking. LNCS, vol. 5000, pp. 107–138. Springer, Heidelberg (2008). https://doi.org/10.1007/978-3-540-69850-0_7

[DHKP16] Daca, P., Henzinger, T.A., Křetínský, J., Petrov, T.: Faster statistical model checking for unbounded temporal properties. In: Chechik, M., Raskin, J.-F. (eds.) TACAS 2016. LNCS, vol. 9636, pp. 112–129. Springer, Heidelberg (2016). https://doi.org/10.1007/978-3-662-49674-9_7

[DHKP17] Daca, P., Henzinger, T.A., Kretínský, J., Petrov, T.: Faster statistical model checking for unbounded temporal properties. ACM Trans. Comput. Log. 18(2), 12:1–12:25 (2017)

[Her90] Herman, T.: Probabilistic self-stabilization. Inf. Process. Lett. 35(2), 63–67 (1990)

[HJB+10] He, R., Jennings, P., Basu, S., Ghosh, A.P., Wu, H.: A bounded statistical approach for model checking of unbounded until properties. In: ASE, pp. 225–234 (2010)

[HK19] Hartmanns, A., Kaminski, B.L.: Optimistic value iteration. CoRR, abs/1910.01100 (2019)

[HM18] Haddad, S., Monmege, B.: Interval iteration algorithm for MDPs and IMDPs. Theor. Comput. Sci. 735, 111–131 (2018)

[Hoe63] Hoeffding, W.: Probability inequalities for sums of bounded random variables. J. Am. Stat. Assoc. 58(301), 13–30 (1963)

[JLS12] Jegourel, C., Legay, A., Sedwards, S.: Cross-entropy optimisation of importance sampling parameters for statistical model checking. In: Madhusudan, P., Seshia, S.A. (eds.) CAV 2012. LNCS, vol. 7358, pp. 327–342. Springer, Heidelberg (2012). https://doi.org/10.1007/978-3-642-31424-7_26

[JSD19] Jégourel, C., Sun, J., Dong, J.S.: Sequential schemes for frequentist estimation of properties in statistical model checking. ACM Trans. Model. Comput. Simul. 29(4), 25:1–25:22 (2019)

[KM19] Křetínský, J., Meggendorfer, T.: Of cores: a partial-exploration framework for Markov decision processes. (2019, Submitted)

[KNP11] Kwiatkowska, M., Norman, G., Parker, D.: PRISM 4.0: verification of probabilistic real-time systems. In: Gopalakrishnan, G., Qadeer, S. (eds.) CAV 2011. LNCS, vol. 6806, pp. 585–591. Springer, Heidelberg (2011). https://doi.org/10.1007/978-3-642-22110-1_47

[KNP12a] Kwiatkowska, M.Z., Norman, G., Parker, D.: The PRISM benchmark suite. In: QEST, pp. 203–204. IEEE Computer Society (2012)

[KNP12b] Kwiatkowska, M.Z., Norman, G., Parker, D.: Probabilistic verification of Herman's self-stabilisation algorithm. Formal Asp. Comput. **24**(4–6), 661–670 (2012). https://doi.org/10.1007/s00165-012-0227-6

[Kře16] Křetínský, J.: Survey of statistical verification of linear unbounded properties: model checking and distances. In: Margaria, T., Steffen, B. (eds.) ISoLA 2016. LNCS, vol. 9952, pp. 27–45. Springer, Cham (2016). https://doi.org/10.1007/978-3-319-47166-2_3

[LP08] Lassaigne, R., Peyronnet, S.: Probabilistic verification and approximation. Ann. Pure Appl. Logic **152**(1–3), 122–131 (2008)

[MLG05] Mcmahan, H.B., Likhachev, M., Gordon, G.J.: Bounded real-time dynamic programming: RTDP with monotone upper bounds and performance guarantees. In: ICML 2005, pp. 569–576 (2005)

[Pnu77] Pnueli, A.: The temporal logic of programs. In: FOCS, pp. 46–57 (1977)

[Put14] Puterman, M.L.: Markov Decision Processes: Discrete Stochastic Dynamic Programming. Wiley, Hoboken (2014)

[QK18] Quatmann, T., Katoen, J.-P.: Sound value iteration. In: Chockler, H., Weissenbacher, G. (eds.) CAV 2018. LNCS, vol. 10981, pp. 643–661. Springer, Cham (2018). https://doi.org/10.1007/978-3-319-96145-3_37

[RP09] El Rabih, D., Pekergin, N.: Statistical model checking using perfect simulation. In: Liu, Z., Ravn, A.P. (eds.) ATVA 2009. LNCS, vol. 5799, pp. 120–134. Springer, Heidelberg (2009). https://doi.org/10.1007/978-3-642-04761-9_11

[SVA04] Sen, K., Viswanathan, M., Agha, G.: Statistical model checking of black-box probabilistic systems. In: Alur, R., Peled, D.A. (eds.) CAV 2004. LNCS, vol. 3114, pp. 202–215. Springer, Heidelberg (2004). https://doi.org/10.1007/978-3-540-27813-9_16

[Ujm15] Ujma, M.: On verification and controller synthesis for probabilistic systems at runtime. Ph.D. thesis, University of Oxford, UK (2015)

[Val84] Valiant, L.G.: A theory of the learnable. Commun. ACM **27**(11), 1134–1142 (1984)

[YCZ10] Younes, H.L.S., Clarke, E.M., Zuliani, P.: Statistical verification of probabilistic properties with unbounded until. In: Davies, J., Silva, L., Simao, A. (eds.) SBMF 2010. LNCS, vol. 6527, pp. 144–160. Springer, Heidelberg (2011). https://doi.org/10.1007/978-3-642-19829-8_10

[YS02] Younes, H.L.S., Simmons, R.G.: Probabilistic verification of discrete event systems using acceptance sampling. In: Brinksma, E., Larsen, K.G. (eds.) CAV 2002. LNCS, vol. 2404, pp. 223–235. Springer, Heidelberg (2002). https://doi.org/10.1007/3-540-45657-0_17

Probabilistic Mission Planning and Analysis for Multi-agent Systems

Rong Gu$^{(\boxtimes)}$, Eduard Enoiu, Cristina Seceleanu$^{(\boxtimes)}$, and Kristina Lundqvist

Mälardalen University, Västerås, Sweden
{rong.gu,eduard.enoiu,cristina.seceleanu,kristina.lundqvist}@mdh.se

Abstract. Mission planning is one of the crucial problems in the design of autonomous Multi-Agent Systems (MAS), requiring the agents to calculate collision-free paths and efficiently schedule their tasks. The complexity of this problem greatly increases when the number of agents grows, as well as timing requirements and stochastic behavior of agents are considered. In this paper, we propose a novel method that integrates statistical model checking and reinforcement learning for mission planning within such context. Additionally, in order to synthesise mission plans that are statistically optimal, we employ hybrid automata to model the continuous movement of agents and moving obstacles, and estimate the possible delay of the agents' travelling time when facing unpredictable obstacles. We show the result of synthesising mission plans, analyze bottlenecks of the mission plans, and re-plan when pedestrians suddenly appear, by modelling and verifying a real industrial use case in UPPAAL SMC.

Keywords: MAS · Mission planning · Q-learning · Statistical model checking

1 Introduction

Multi-Agent Systems (MAS) draw a wide interest in academia and industry, mostly due to their autonomous functions that ease people's daily lives and improve industrial productivity. Mission planning for MAS involves path planning and task scheduling, and is one of the most critical problems when designing such systems [4]. There are path-planning algorithms that have already proved useful for autonomous systems, e.g., RRT [15] and Theta* [5]. These algorithms are able to calculate collision-free paths towards a destination, yet they do not consider complex requirements and uncertainties in the environment. For instance, if agents need to prioritize or repetitively execute some tasks, path planning is not enough. In addition, when the task execution time is uncertain, or some moving objects such as humans and other machines appear irregularly in the environment, autonomous agents need to consider these factors when synthesising mission plans so that the resulting plans are comprehensive. Task scheduling algorithms are designed to solve the above problems. However, since

© Springer Nature Switzerland AG 2020
T. Margaria and B. Steffen (Eds.): ISoLA 2020, LNCS 12476, pp. 350–367, 2020.
https://doi.org/10.1007/978-3-030-61362-4_20

task scheduling is an NP-hard problem, when the number of agents becomes large, traditional methods cannot manage to produce a result even for a simple instance with very restrictive constraints [1].

In our previous work, we have formally defined and modeled the movement and task execution of MAS [9], and proposed a combined model-checking and reinforcement learning method [10], to synthesise mission plans that are proved to satisfy complex requirements obtained from industry. However, when the agents perform some uncertain actions, e.g., unstable time of moving and operating, or the environment contains some stochastic phenomena, e.g., humans crossing the roads unpredictably, the proposed method does not provide quantitative verification and analysis, which is best suited in these cases.

In this paper, we propose an adjusted version of our method called MCRL (Model Checking + Reinforcement Learning) [10] to provide a means of synthesizing and analyzing mission plans for MAS with uncertainties of the type mentioned above. The method is based on Stochastic Timed Automata (STA) and statistical model checking (by employing UPPAAL SMC), and combines the latter with reinforcement learning. Instead of exhaustively exploring the state space of the model and looking for the execution traces that satisfy certain requirements, MCRL uses the simulation function of UPPAAL SMC to execute the model. Then, it adopts a reinforcement learning algorithm, namely Q-learning [21], to accumulate the rewards of the state-action pairs gathered in the simulation, and populate a Q-table that is used to guide the agents to move safely and finish tasks within a prescribed time limit. As the STA describe the stochastic behavior of the agents and uncertain events in the environment by probability distributions, based on which the simulation is executed, the collected state-action pairs reflect the possible scenarios that the agents would probably meet in the environment. Therefore, as long as the simulation generates enough data, the synthesised mission plans are comprehensive and optimal.

To estimate the possible delays of executing mission plans when the agents encounter unexpected situations, e.g., pedestrians, we adopt a hybrid-automata (HA) model of the agents that are equipped with a state-of-the-art collision-avoidance algorithm based on dipole flow fields [19]. By simulating and statistically verifying the HA model, we can get the estimated travelling time of the agents [11], respectively, which is then used to construct the STA model that is used for synthesising mission plans. Next, statistical verification and simulation of the STA are conducted in UPPAAL SMC in order to analyze the synthesised mission plans in an environment model containing uncertainties, which is not feasible by purely using reinforcement learning algorithms. To summarize, the contributions of this paper are:

- An innovative approach based on MCRL for synthesizing and analyzing mission plans for MAS that exhibit stochastic behavior.
- An effective combination of the STA and HA models of MAS, which enables the estimation of travelling time considering unexpected situations, and thus produces comprehensive mission plans.

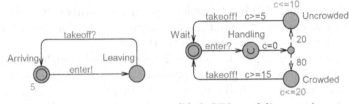

(a) A STA modeling passengers   (b) A STA modeling an airport

Fig. 1. STA modeling a scenario of passengers arriving at an airport and taking off

- An evaluation of the method showing the ability of analyzing the bottleneck of mission plans and re-planning when facing unpredictable moving obstacles.

The remainder of the paper is organized as follows. In Sect. 2, we introduce the preliminaries of this paper. Sect. 3 presents the problem and challenges. In Sect. 4, we introduce the adjusted version of MCRL and its combination with the HA model. Section 5 presents the bottleneck analysis as well as the ability of re-planning. In Sect. 6, we compare to related work, before concluding and outlining possible future work in Sect. 7.

2 Preliminaries

In this section, we introduce Stochastic Timed Automata and UPPAAL SMC, reinforcement learning, and a two-layer framework that we have proposed previously for formal modeling and verification of autonomous agents.

2.1 Stochastic Timed Automata and UPPAAL SMC

UPPAAL SMC [6] is an extension of the tool UPPAAL [14], which supports Statistical Model Checking (SMC) of Stochastic Timed Automata (STA). STA is a widely used paradigm for modeling the probabilistic behavior of real-time systems. The basic elements of STA are locations and edges connecting them. Time can elapse at locations, which is reflected by the increased values of clock variables in delayed transitions of STA, whereas transitions between locations are non-delayed. The delays at locations follow probabilistic distributions, which are either uniform distributions for time-bounded delays, or exponential distributions (with user-defined rates) for unbounded delays. The choices between multiple enabled non-delayed transitions are also probabilistic.

Figure 1 depicts a network of STA modeling the scenario of passengers arriving at an airport and taking off. Figure 1(a) shows the model of passengers, who randomly arrive at the airport. The arriving time follows the exponential distribution as it is modeled by an unbounded delay at location *Arriving*. The constant "*5*" is the exponential rate that can be replaced by any rational number. The channels (e.g., *enter* and *takeoff*) model the handshaking interaction between

STA. Note that UPPAAL SMC only supports broadcast channels for a clean semantics of purely non-blocking automata. When a passenger enters an airport, the corresponding STA moves to location *Leaving* simultaneously with the airport STA (Fig. 1(b)) moving from location *Wait* to *Handling*, synchronized via the channel *enter*. Next, the airport STA goes to a branch point leading to two locations, namely *Crowded* and *Uncrowded*, respectively. The constants, *"20"* and *"80"*, are the probability weights of the edges marked by the dashed lines in Fig. 1(b), meaning that the probability of entering a crowded airport is *80%*, and *20%* for an uncrowded one. Delays at locations such as location *Crowded* are time-bounded, as the locations are constrained by invariants (e.g., $c \leq 10$), so the delay time at these locations should not surpass the upper boundary specified by the invariants, respectively. If the outgoing edges of such locations are guarded by conditions, e.g., $c \geq 5$ in our case, the STA cannot leave the locations until the lower boundaries of the guards are exceeded. A uniform distribution is set for the time-bounded delays by default in UPPAAL SMC, which is also adopted in this paper. Variables can be updated by assignments (e.g., $c = 0$) or C-code functions on the edges.

2.2   Reinforcement Learning

Reinforcement learning is a branch of machine learning that enables agents to learn how to take actions by themselves, in an environment. In this paper, we employ *Q-learning* [21] as the reinforcement learning algorithm to generate policies of movement and task execution for agents. A policy is associated with a state action value function called *Q function*, where "Q" stands for "quality". The optimal Q function satisfies the Bellman optimality equation:

$$q^*(s, a) = \mathbb{E}[R(s, a) + \gamma \max_{a'} q^*(s', a')], \tag{1}$$

where $q^*(s, a)$ represents the expected reward of executing action a at state s, $\mathbb{E}$ denotes the expected value function, $R(s, a)$ is the reward obtained by taking the action a at state s, γ is a constant of discounting, s' is the new state coming from state s by taking action a, $\max_{a'} q^*(s', a')$ represents the maximum reward that can be achieved by any possible next state-action pair (s', a'). The equation means that the expected reward of the state-action pair (s, a) is the sum of the current reward and the discounted maximum future reward. The Bellman equation accumulates the Q-values of state-action pairs and guarantees the values to converge to the maximum Q-value during the learning process [13]. In this paper, we use the simulation function in UPPAAL SMC to gather the information of state-action pairs in files, and invoke a Java program to parse the data and run the Q-learning algorithm, so that a Q-table is populated.

2.3   A Two-Layer Framework for Formal Modelling and Verification of Autonomous Agents

To provide a separation of concerns for the formal modeling and verification of autonomous agents, we have proposed a two-layer framework [11]. In this framework, a static layer is responsible for mission planning and only concerns static obstacles and milestones where the tasks are carried out. The dynamic layer uses hybrid automata (HA) [12] to model the continuous movement and operations of the agents in UPPAAL SMC. In addition, UPPAAL SMC provides a "spawning" function to dynamically generate instances of HA models during the verification, which enables one to mimic the sudden appearance of obstacles (e.g., pedestrians), which are considered unpredictable before the agents get close to them.

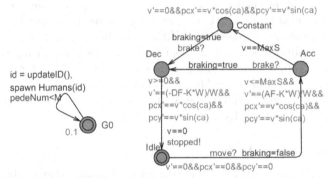

(a) An example of HA gen-   (b) An example of HA modeling the
erating pedestrians   linear movement of agents

Fig. 2. Examples of HA model in the dynamic layer of the framework

Figure 2(a) shows the HA that generates pedestrians. As long as the number of pedestrians does not exceed a maximum number (i.e., "pedeNum<M"), the self-loop edge of location *G0* is enabled, which invokes the spawning function to generate an instance of the pedestrian model. The constant *"0.1"* denotes the rate of the exponential probability distribution of the pedestrians' appearance. Figure 2(b) depicts the HA that models the continuous linear movement of agents. The model contains four locations, representing the four moving statuses of agents: idle, acceleration, constantly moving, and deceleration. At the each of the locations, the derivatives of speed and positions are regulated by Newtonian laws of motion in the form of ordinary differential equations (ODE). In a nutshell, the HA model describes the continuous movement of agents, and thus the simulation of the model reflects the agents' moving trajectories when circumventing obstacles. For brevity, we refer readers to the literature [11] for details. In this paper, we use this HA model to generate the moving trajectories of pedestrians and agents, and UPPAAL SMC to estimate the prolonged traveling time of the agents caused by collision avoidance, which is used for re-planning.

3 Problem Description

In this section, we introduce the research problem that originates from an industrial use case of an autonomous quarry, containing various autonomous vehicles, e.g., trucks, wheel loaders, etc. For example, as shown in Fig. 3, in an autonomous quarry, a wheel loader digs stones at stone piles and loads them into trucks, which carry the stones to a primary crusher, where stones are crushed into fractions, and proceed to carry the crushed stones to the secondary crushers, which is the destination. To accomplish their tasks and guarantee a certain level of productivity, these autonomous vehicles need to calculate collision-free paths and schedule their tasks (e.g., digging stones) to finish their jobs within a time frame. In this paper, henceforth, we name path planning and task scheduling as mission planning in general. As our solution is generic and suits all kinds of autonomous systems that need to synthesise mission plans, the autonomous vehicles in this paper are referred to as autonomous agents [8].

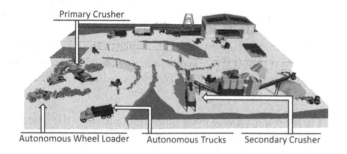

Fig. 3. An example of an autonomous quarry

In this paper, path planning is accomplished by the Theta* algorithm [5] as the environment in the problem is a 2D map and the algorithm is especially good at generating smooth paths with any-angle turning points in 2D maps. Task scheduling acquires satisfaction of various requirements, e.g., task assignment, execution order, and timing requirements. We extract the requirements of the autonomous quarry from our industrial partner, and generically categorize them as follows:

- *Task Assignment.* The task must be assigned to the right milestone containing the corresponding device.
- *Execution Order.* The task execution order must be correct, e.g., unloading into the primary crusher can start only after digging stones finishes.
- *Milestone Exclusion.* Some milestones containing a device that only allows one agent to operate at a time are exclusive when they are occupied.
- *Timing.* Tasks must be completed within a prescribed time frame.

The complexity of path planning of multiple agents increases linearly as the number of agents grows, because the path-planning algorithm runs on each individual agent and it does not consider the paths of other agents, as the collision

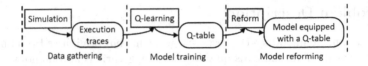

Fig. 4. The process of the MCRL method

avoidance is dealt with when the agents are actually moving. In other words, the time to calculate paths for multiple agents is the sum of the computation time of each agent. However, the task-scheduling problem is NP-hard and involves uncertainties that traditional methods do not consider [1].

- *Uncertain execution time of tasks.* The execution time of tasks is not a fixed value, but it is a time interval between the best-case execution time (BCET) and worst-case execution time (WCET), which are usually different.
- *Uncertain movement time.* Since some milestones are exclusive, when an agent approaches an occupied milestone, it most probably should wait until it is released. The waiting time is uncertain.
- *Uncertain environment.* Human workers sometimes appear in the sites but do not always stay there. This requires the agents to avoid those workers at all cost, and adjust their mission plans accordingly, in order to maintain productivity.

These features make our problem even more difficult than the classic scheduling problem. For example, if human workers appear irregularly, it is hard to estimate their influence on the traveling time of agents. We formulate the target problems of this paper as follows.

Overall Challenge. Given a confined environment containing multiple autonomous agents, several predefined milestones and static obstacles, some unpredictable moving objects or humans, a set of tasks for the agents to finish in order to satisfy some requirements, the goal is to synthesize mission plans for these agents, such that:

- The mission plans satisfy the requirements that are categorized previously;
- The mission plans consider the uncertainties in the environment and handle them effectively so that the agents could finish tasks under various conditions;
- The solution provides a means of statistical analysis of the synthesised mission plans to investigate the bottleneck of the plans, and an ability of re-planning when facing disturbance, e.g., pedestrians.

4   Mission Planning Based on Reinforcement Learning and Stochastic Timed Automata

In this section, we introduce the modelling of MAS using STA, which is based on a method called MCRL [10]. MCRL combines model checking and reinforcement learning, which enables the method to cope with large numbers of agents and verify the synthesised mission plans. The use of stochastic timed automata in this paper extends MCRL with the ability of modelling stochastic behaviors. We also present some queries that are used in this method for statistical analysis of the mission plans.

4.1 MCRL: Combining Model Checking and Reinforcement Learning for Mission Planning

Previously, we have presented the formal definitions of agent movement and task execution and the model-generation algorithms to generate Timed Automata (TA) for mission-plan synthesis [9]. This initial work provides a theoretical foundation and a tool called TAMAA, based on which a novel approach is designed to synthesise mission plans, namely MCRL.

Overall Description of MCRL. As Fig. 4 depicts, MCRL consists of three phases. First, it simulates the TA that models the movement and task execution of autonomous agents by running the Monte Carlo simulation query in UPPAAL SMC. The introduction of the TA model is in the literature [10]. The multi-round simulation produces the execution traces of the model. Some of them satisfy our requirements, e.g., finishing tasks in time, correct execution order of tasks; some traces fail, e.g., exceeding the time limit. The successful traces are assigned with positive values, which are calculated by $(ST - FT)^2$, where ST is the simulation time, FT is time of reaching the desired state, e.g., finishing all tasks; whereas a fixed negative value is assigned to all the failed traces.

Next, the traces and their values are input into the model-training phase, where a reinforcement learning algorithm, namely Q-learning, is performed to generate a Q-table. The Q-table contains the state-action pairs and their values that are accumulated by running Eq. (1) using the data of the input traces. This equation guarantees that the values of state-action pairs converge, as long as the simulation has produced enough data of execution traces. Eventually, the Q-table is injected back to the TA model of agents, where a new TA named conductor is created so that the behavior of the agent model is controlled by it. The conductor TA looks up the Q-table and chooses the action that owns the highest value among the available actions at the current state for the agents to perform. Each agent model has its own conductor TA so that the agents can make decisions distributedly. However, as the Q-table contains the state-action pairs of all agents, when their actions conflict, e.g., moving to the same exclusive milestone simultaneously, the agents can compare their rewards of actions with others, and let the one having the highest reward to perform. In this way, the Q-table serves as the mission plan we intend to synthesise. In addition, since the method utilizes random simulation and reinforcement learning instead of pure exhaustive model checking, the solution is scalable for systems with large numbers of agents. For a detailed introduction of the method, we refer readers to the literature [10].

Although Q-learning strengthens MCRL's ability of handling large numbers of agents, the method provides no means of handling unpredictable events, which is important as the environment is uncertain. This limitation stems from the use of timed automata. This modelling language cannot depict the stochastic events in the environment. For example, when human workers sporadically appear in the environment, MCRL cannot estimate the possible delay that is caused by the detour taken by the agents to avoid humans. In addition, industries always focus on productivity. The waiting time of agents at exclusive milestones is an unnecessary consumption of time, but it is hard to capture as the waiting time depends on multiple factors. Original MCRL is not able to provide this kind of analysis, as it does not use any statistical analysing techniques.

4.2   Stochastic Timed Automata for MCRL

To overcome these shortcomings, we improve MCRL by adopting stochastic timed automata (STA) as the modelling language and statistical model checking for verification and analysis. In this section, we present the STA model in detail such that readers understand how the movement and task execution is modelled as STA, and how the stochastic behavior is handled by this model.

STA of Task Execution. Tasks in this paper are operations of the agents that need to be carried out in a right order and at the specific milestones. For instance, in the scenario of an autonomous quarry in Fig. 3, tasks for autonomous trucks can be unloading stones into the primary crushers, charging, etc. Collaborative tasks are the ones that need more than one agent to perform, e.g., loading stones at stones piles needs a wheel loader and a truck to accomplish. For mission planning, a task can be abstracted as time duration between the BCET and WCET, which is only permitted to start when a set of conditions is satisfied, e.g., precedent tasks are finished, and staying at the right milestone. The formal definition of tasks is presented in literature [9].

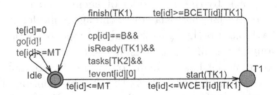

Fig. 5. The STA modeling an agent executing task *T1*

Figure 5 depicts an example of the STA modelling an agent executing one of its tasks, namely *T1*. For brevity, the execution of other tasks for the same agent, which should be modelled in the same STA, is not shown in this figure. Note that the variable *id* in this figure is the index of the agent. The STA starts from the location named *Idle* that represents the status of running no tasks. Agents are only allowed to move at this status, hence, this location has a self-loop edge labelled by a synchronization channel *go[id]* that is used to inform the movement STA to start moving. Since the milestone that the agent is approaching to might be occupied and exclusive, the agent probably has to wait. The invariant on the location *Idle* (e.g., *te[id]* ≤ *MT*) and the guard on its self-loop edge (e.g., *te[id]* ≥ *MT*) is for triggering the "moving" command every *MT* time units, so that the agent would not wait forever and periodically detects whether the target milestone is available. The detection is done by the STA of agent movement, which is introduced in the next section.

If the agent decides to execute task *T1*, its task execution STA transfers to location *T1*. This edge is guarded by a Boolean expression that is composed of four parts (see Fig. 5). The first Boolean expression *cp[id]==B* checks if the agent is at milestone *B* currently, where the task is permitted. The following function *isReady(TK1)* returns a Boolean value indicating whether task *T1* is not finished yet. If *T1* is a collaborative task, this function also decides if the collaborating agents are ready for this task by checking if they are staying at the same right position, which is milestone *B* in this case. The Boolean array named *tasks* stores the execution status of tasks, namely finished or not, so *tasks[TK2]* here checks if the precedent task of *T1* is finished. The Boolean expression *!event[id][0]* indicates that the event monitored by this agent is not active, where the number "*0*" is the index of the event that can be replaced. An event can be a battery-level-low warning, or a critical-damage alert, etc., which needs to be prioritized than regular tasks, and responded within a time frame. The task execution time is between the BCET and WCET. Therefore, the invariant on location *T1* regulates that the clock variable should not exceed the WCET of *T1*, whereas the guard on the outgoing edge of this location decides the earliest time to leave this location to be later than the BCET. In UPPAAL SMC, the default probability distribution of time-bounded delays is uniform distribution. Hence, the execution time of task *T1* here is between the BCET and WCET with equal possibilities.

When the guards hold, agents can take the transition with the execution of function *start(TK1)* to start *T1*. This function changes the variable of the current task of the agent, and stores the current state of the agent, as well as the corresponding action taken at this moment into an array. The array, which represents the execution trace, will be printed by UPPAAL SMC in the end of the data gathering phase (see Fig. 4). The function *finish(TK1)* simply changes the variable of the current task to *Idle*, and checks if all the tasks have been finished when the agent should leave the environment and stop.

STA of Agent Movement. Figure 6(a) depicts a scenario containing an intersection where pedestrians keep crossing the road every once a while. An autonomous vehicle starting from position *A1* intends to go to *A2*. Though going straightly to *A2* is the shortest path, potential collision avoidance might increase the travelling time, as shown by the blue trajectory. Therefore, the vehicle can alternatively choose to detour via position *B1*, as shown by the violet trajectory. As the HA described in Sect. 2.3 model the probable appearance of human workers and the continuous movement of agents equipped with a collision-avoidance algorithm based on dipole flow fields [19], we can verify the HA model against queries in the following forms in order to obtain the prolonged travelling time and its probabilities.

$$Pr[<=T](<> \text{ arrived})$$ (2)

$$Pr[<=T]([] \text{ arrived imply t} <= TL),$$ (3)

where T is the simulation time, `arrived` is a Boolean variable indicating if the agent arrives at the destination or not, t is a clock variable, and TL is an integer indicating the time limit. Query (2) calculates the probability of the agent reaching the destination, and Query (3) further calculates the probability of always arriving at the destination within TL time units. The results are probability intervals and we use the average value to estimate the probability of travelling time, which is used in the STA of movement.

Figure 6(b) shows a part of the movement STA modelling the movement from *A1* to *A2*. As there are two alternative paths, the STA starts with a non-deterministic choice between two transitions to location *A1B1A2* or a branch point. The function *isOver()* returns a Boolean value of whether the agent has finished all tasks and should stop. The update function *move(0, A1, A2)* changes the current position of the agent, and stores the current state-action pair into the array, which is similar to the function *start()* in Fig. 5. When the agent chooses to go via position *B1*, which does not have any pedestrians, the STA transfers to the location *A1B1A2* representing the duration of travelling. When the least travelling time has passed, e.g., *15* time units travelling via *B1*, the STA can transfer to location `PA2`, as long as the milestone *A2* is not occupied. If the travelling time is uncertain by the influence of pedestrians, the STA transfers to a branch point that leads to different locations representing different probable travelling duration, e.g., location `A1A2_1`. After verifying the HA of agents (see Fig. 2 for an example) against queries similar to Queries (2) and (3), and replacing *TL* with different numbers, we can obtain that going to position *A2* straightly can cost *10* or *18* time units, and their probabilities are 40% and 60%, respectively, which are depicted in Fig. 6(b). In the STA of movement, a synchronization channel named *go[id]* is used to get commands from the task execution STA (Fig. 5). So the verification of agents is for an integrated model composing the STA of agent movement and task execution.

In UPPAAL SMC, a simulation query composed as following randomly executes the model for R rounds and T time units in each round,

$$\text{simulate}[<=T;R] \{ds[0].cs,ds[0].act,ds[0].value,...\}:tasks[TK1],$$ (4)

where `ds` is the array variable whose type is a structure, `cs` and `act` are the elements of the structure representing the current state and action, respectively, `value` is the reward or penalty assigned to the pair. The definitions of the states and actions are in the literature [10]. The predicate in the end of the query regulates that the data in the curly brackets are printed only when the predicate

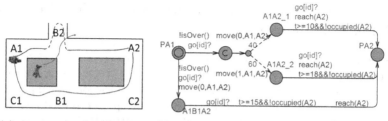

(a) A scenario of an intersection containing pedestrians

(b) The STA modeling the possible movement of agents

Fig. 6. A scenario of intersection and the STA modeling the movement of agents

is true. In this query, when the agent finishes task *T1*, the elements in `ds` are printed. The simulation needs to run multiple runs for obtaining enough state-action pairs that simulate various situations that the agents would encounter. Hence, the Q-learning algorithm, which uses the state-action pairs as input, would cover various cases comprehensively so that the final mission plans can satisfy various properties in an environment model containing uncertainties.

MCRL Revisited. Now that the TA of task execution and movement are adjusted to STA, the simulation query in UPPAAL SMC would explore the state space of the model based on the probability distributions defined in the STA. The model-training phase that uses the state-action pairs representing the stochastic behavior of agents would generate mission plans that are statistically optimal.

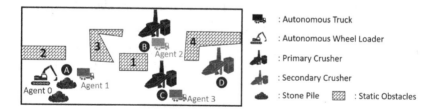

Fig. 7. An experimental scenario containing 4 autonomous agents

Table 1. Tasks for the autonomous agents in the experiment

	Task	BCET	WCET	Precedent task	Milestone
Wheel loader	Dig	2	2	none	Stone pile (A)
	Unload	1	4	Dig	Stone pile (A)
Truck	Load I	1	4	Dig	Stone pile (A)
	Unload I	4	4	Load I	Primary crusher (B or C)
	Load II	2	3	Unload I	Primary crusher (B or C)
	Unload II	3	5	Load II	Secondary crusher (D)

5   Statistical Verification and Analysis of the Use Case: An Autonomous Quarry

In this section, we evaluate our method by demonstrating a statistical verification and analysis on our use case: an autonomous quarry (as shown in Fig. 3). The experiments are conducted in UPPAAL 4.1.24. Most of the statistical parameters are set to the default values in UPPAAL SMC, except the probability of false negatives (α), which is 0.001, and probability uncertainty (ε), which is 0.001. The experimental scenario is depicted in Fig. 7. Tasks for those agents are shown in Table 1. Milestones A to D are exclusive, thus only one truck is allowed at one time. As there are two primary crushers, the trucks need to choose one of them to perform tasks, which take uncertain execution time. The agents must carry all the stones to the secondary crusher, and the job need to be accomplished within a time frame.

5.1   Mission Plan Synthesis

After building the STA and running MCRL by using UPPAAL SMC and our Java program of the Q-learning algorithm, we successfully synthesize mission plans for agents. By verifying queries as following, we demonstrate the synthesized mission plans satisfy different kinds of requirements that are described in Sect. 3.

- *Task Assignment.* Query (5) checks the probability of agent n performing task T_i at milestone P_i. The results for all tasks in Table 1 are above 99.8%.

$$\texttt{Pr[<=T]([] te}_n\texttt{.T}_i \texttt{ imply m}_n\texttt{.P}_i\texttt{)} \tag{5}$$

- *Execution Order.* Query (6) checks the probability that when agent n is performing task T_i, its precedent task T_j has finished. UPPAAL SMC returns that the results for tasks that have precedent tasks are above 99.8%.

$$\texttt{Pr[<=T]([] te}_n\texttt{.T}_i \texttt{ imply te}_n\texttt{.tasks[j])} \tag{6}$$

- *Milestone Exclusion.* Query (7) checks the probability that when agent n is at an exclusive milestone named P_i, other agents are not there. The results for milestones A to D are above 99.8%.

$$\texttt{Pr[<=T]([] m}_n\texttt{.P}_i \texttt{ imply !(m}_0\texttt{.P}_i \texttt{ \&\& } \ldots \texttt{ \&\& m}_{n-1}\texttt{.P}_i \texttt{ \&\& m}_{n+1}\texttt{.P}_i \ldots\texttt{))} \tag{7}$$

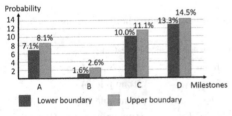
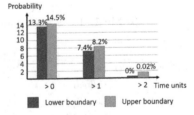

(a) Probabilities of waiting at milestones   (b) Waiting time at milestone D

Fig. 8. Bottleneck analysis of the scenario in Fig. 7

– *Timing.* Query (8) checks the probability of agent n travelling through all milestones and finishing all tasks within *TL* time units. If we set *TL* to be *10* and *25* for wheel loaders and trucks, the results are above 99.8%.

$$\text{Pr[<=T]([] (te}_n\text{.tasks[0] \&\& ... \&\& te}_n\text{.tasks[M-1]) imply x < TL)} \quad (8)$$

In these queries, te_n and m_n are the task execution STA and movement STA of agent n, respectively, te_n.tasts is a Boolean array for storing the task execution status of agent n, namely *true* for finished tasks, and *false* for unfinished ones, M is the number of tasks, and x is a global clock variable that is only reset when all tasks finish.

5.2   Bottleneck Analysis

To perform this analysis, we verify the reformed model equipped with Q-tables against queries in the following form of Query (9) to get the waiting time at different milestones during the process of transferring stones.

$$\text{Pr[<=T](<> m0.wt[i] + m1.wt[i] + ... + mn.wt[i] > TL)}, \quad (9)$$

where T is the simulation time, m0 to mn are the movement STA of agents *0* to n, wt[i] refers to the waiting time at milestone i, and TL is an integer estimating the waiting time. By setting TL to zero and replacing the index i with the indices of milestones A to D, one can investigate the probability of waiting at each milestone (see Fig. 8(a)). By replacing the integer TL with different values and fixing the index i to some certain milestone, one can estimate the waiting time at the milestone and the corresponding probability (see Fig. 8(b)). In UPPAAL SMC, the result of a probability estimation property (e.g., Query (9)) is given as a probability interval with a confidence level. Hence, the probabilities in Fig. 8 are presented as ranges from the lower boundaries to the upper boundaries. As shown in Fig. 8(a), the probabilities of waiting at milestones A to D are always larger than zero, and the average probability of waiting at milestone D is the highest. We specifically estimate the waiting time at milestone D. As shown in Fig. 8(b), the waiting time is most likely less than 2 time units.

5.3   Travelling Timed Estimation and Re-planning

When the autonomous agents encounter pedestrians, they must run collision-avoidance algorithms to compute a new path to bypass the pedestrians, and that would possibly affect the travelling time significantly such that it is even quicker to take another path. We call the ability of agents choosing another path when encountering moving obstacles re-planning. In the scenario depicted in Fig. 7, if the number of autonomous trucks is decreased to one, the truck is free to choose between primary crushers at milestones B and C, as no other trucks are competing with it. Since the primary crusher at milestone C is closer to the secondary crusher, the Q-learning algorithm enables the autonomous truck to choose milestone C rather than milestone B as the precedent position of milestone D. We can verify this phenomenon by checking Query (10):

$$\texttt{Pr[<=T] ([] m0.D imply (viaC \&\& !viaB)),} \tag{10}$$

where `viaC` and `viaB` are Boolean variables, which are turned to *true* when the agent sets off from the starting point, i.e., milestone A, and reaches milestones C and B, respectively, and are turned back to *false* when the agent leaves milestone D. Hence, Query (10) checks the probability of an agent going to location D via location C but not location B.

However, if pedestrians keep walking near milestone C and thus block the path (see Fig. 7), it could take longer time if the agent sticks to the original path plan (i.e., travelling via milestone C). By using the HA model depicted in Fig. 2(a), we can generate instances of the pedestrian model dynamically during verification. Then we verify the HA model that describes the continuous movement of agents (see Fig. 2(b) for an example of linear movement) together with the pedestrian model against queries in the form of Queries (2) and (3), in order to estimate the prolonged travelling time between milestones A and C, and the corresponding probabilities. Next, we encode the new travelling time and its probabilities into the movement STA and synthesize mission plans.

Figure 9 shows two situations of the scenario, where pedestrians are few and crossing the road quickly (Fig. 9(a)), as well as pedestrians are many and walking slowly (Fig. 9(c)), which causes congestion on the road. The situation with fewer pedestrians results in the movement STA that is partly shown in Fig. 9(b), where the probability of going to milestone C quickly is 83% (i.e., $t \geq 3$), whereas 33% is the probability of moving slowly (i.e., $t \geq 10$). Similarly, the situation containing many pedestrians results in the movement STA partly depicted in Fig. 9(d), where the chance of agents moving slowly is much larger than the chance of moving quickly.

Verifying Query (10) against the model that is partly shown in Fig. 9(d) produces a result of a range of low probabilities, where as if query is changed to check the probability of agents going via milestone B, the result is much higher. This shows that MCRL enables the agents to re-plan a better path when the irregular appearance of pedestrians influences the path plans.

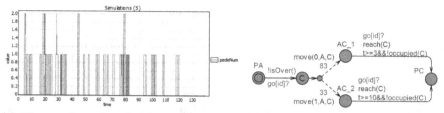

(a) The number of pedestrians. Exponential rate of the generator: 0.1. Existing time: 1

(b) The resulting movement STA in the situation with a few pedestrians

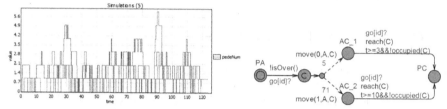

(c) The number of pedestrians. Exponential rate of the generator: 0.2. Existing time: 5

(d) The resulting movement STA in the situation with many pedestrians

Fig. 9. The Number and frequency of pedestrians and the movement STA

6   Related Work

Motion-plan synthesis has arisen a wide interest of research in recent years. Nikou et al. [16] present a method of automatic controller synthesis for multi-agent systems under the presence of uncertainties. Sadraddini et al. [17] propose an approach of synthesising control strategies for positive and monotone systems, which satisfy requirements formalized by Signal Temporal Logic, and demonstrate their method on a traffic management case study. Wang et al. [20] propose a novel formulation based on Partially Observable Markov Decision Processes to synthesis policies over a vast space of probability distributions. Although having promising results, these methods are not applied in industrial systems, which requires solutions to be practically usable and scalable.

To model the uncertain behavior of the autonomous agents and environment, Markov Decision Process and Probabilistic Computation Tree Logic (PCTL) have been adopted by many studies. A solution of behavior verification of autonomous vehicles (AV) proposed by Sekizawa et al. [18] considers the disturbance that causes the AV to swerve from the planned path. Their solution uses the probabilistic model checker PRISM to conduct the verification against PCTL properties. Al-Nuaimi et al. [2] also employs PRISM in their design of a stochastically verifiable decision making framework for AV. The authors demonstrate the applicability of their framework in a scenario of parking bay containing one AV, a pedestrian, and another vehicle. Ayala et al. [3] present a solution to find control strategies for mobile robotic systems moving in environments containing entities that are not completely observable. Compared with these studies, our approach systematically estimates the disturbance caused by unpredictable moving obstacles, and enables re-planning for the autonomous agents. UPPAAL STRATEGO is designed to synthesize strategies for stochastic priced timed games [7], and it also implements the Q-learning algorithm as one of its algorithms for synthesis. The main difference between MCRL and UPPAAL STRATEGO is that the former supports a larger numbers of agents, and we refer the interested readers to previous work [10] for a detailed comparison between the methods.

7   Conclusion and Future Work

We present a method for automatic synthesis of mission plans for multi-agent systems. The method is based on MCRL, which combines model checking with reinforcement learning, and extends MCRL with the ability of handling uncertainties in the environment by employing Stochastic Timed Automata and Statistical Model Checking. We demonstrate the applicability of the method in an industrial use case: an autonomous quarry, provided by VOLVO CE. The demonstration shows that the method is capable of synthesising mission plans for MAS that satisfy various requirements, and further analyse the bottleneck of the mission plans. When encountering disturbance of unpredictable moving obstacles, e.g., pedestrians, the method is able to estimate the delays of traveling time of the agents, and conduct a re-planning when it is necessary. Future work includes integrating the new MCRL with our tool called TAMAA [9], so that a complete solution of mission-plan synthesis for MAS together with a user-friendly GUI is accomplished. Automating the transformation of requirements into temporal logic queries is another possible direction.

Acknowledgement. The research leading to the presented results has been undertaken within the research profile DPAC - Dependable Platform for Autonomous Systems and Control project, funded by the Swedish Knowledge Foundation, grant number: 20150022.

References

1. Abdeddaı, Y., Asarin, E., Maler, O., et al.: Scheduling with timed automata. Theor. Comput. Sci. **354**(2), 272–300 (2006)
2. Al-Nuaimi, M., Qu, H., Veres, S.M.: A stochastically verifiable decision making framework for autonomous ground vehicles. In: 2018 IEEE International Conference on Intelligence and Safety for Robotics (ISR), pp. 26–33. IEEE (2018)
3. Ayala, A.M., Andersson, S.B., Belta, C.: Temporal logic control in dynamic environments with probabilistic satisfaction guarantees. In: 2011 IEEE/RSJ International Conference on Intelligent Robots and Systems, pp. 3108–3113. IEEE (2011)
4. Chandler, P., Pachter, M.: Research issues in autonomous control of tactical UAVs. In: Proceedings of the 1998 American Control Conference. ACC (IEEE Cat. No. 98CH36207). IEEE (1998)

5. Daniel, K., Nash, A., Koenig, S., Felner, A.: Theta*: any-angle path planning on grids. J. Artif. Intell. Res. **39**, 533–579 (2010)
6. David, A., et al.: Statistical model checking for stochastic hybrid systems. arXiv preprint arXiv:1208.3856 (2012)
7. David, A., Jensen, P.G., Larsen, K.G., Mikučionis, M., Taankvist, J.H.: UPPAAL STRATEGO. In: Baier, C., Tinelli, C. (eds.) TACAS 2015. LNCS, vol. 9035, pp. 206–211. Springer, Heidelberg (2015). https://doi.org/10.1007/978-3-662-46681-0_16
8. Franklin, S., Graesser, A.: Is it an agent, or just a program?: A taxonomy for autonomous agents. In: Müller, J.P., Wooldridge, M.J., Jennings, N.R. (eds.) ATAL 1996. LNCS, vol. 1193, pp. 21–35. Springer, Heidelberg (1997). https://doi.org/10.1007/BFb0013570
9. Gu, R., Enoiu, E.P., Seceleanu, C.: TAMAA: UPPAAL-based mission planning for autonomous agents. In: 35th ACM/SIGAPP Symposium on Applied Computing SAC2020. ACM (2019)
10. Gu, R., Enoiu, E., Seceleanu, C., Lundqvist, K.: Verifiable and scalable mission-plan synthesis for autonomous agents. In: ter Beek, M.H., Ničković, D. (eds.) FMICS 2020. LNCS, vol. 12327, pp. 73–92. Springer, Cham (2020). https://doi.org/10.1007/978-3-030-58298-2_2
11. Gu, R., Marinescu, R., Seceleanu, C., Lundqvist, K.: Towards a two-layer framework for verifying autonomous vehicles. In: Badger, J.M., Rozier, K.Y. (eds.) NFM 2019. LNCS, vol. 11460, pp. 186–203. Springer, Cham (2019). https://doi.org/10.1007/978-3-030-20652-9_12
12. Henzinger, T.A.: The theory of hybrid automata. In: Inan, M.K., Kurshan, R.P. (eds.) Verification of Digital and Hybrid Systems NATO ASI Series (Series F: Computer and Systems Sciences), vol. 170, pp. 265–292. Springer, Heidelberg (2000). https://doi.org/10.1007/978-3-642-59615-5_13
13. Kochenderfer, M.J.: Decision Making Under Uncertainty: Theory and Application. MIT press, Cambridge (2015)
14. Larsen, K.G., Pettersson, P., Yi, W.: UPPAAL in a nutshell. Int. J. Softw. Tools Technol. Transf. **1**(1–2), 134–152 (1997)
15. LaValle, S.M.: Rapidly-exploring random trees: a new tool for path planning. Technical report, Computer Science Department, Iowa State University, October 1998
16. Nikou, A., Tumova, J., Dimarogonas, D.V.: Probabilistic plan synthesis for coupled multi-agent systems. IFAC-PapersOnLine **50**(1), 10766–10771 (2017)
17. Sadraddini, S., Belta, C.: Formal synthesis of control strategies for positive monotone systems. IEEE Trans. Autom. Control **64**(2), 480–495 (2018)
18. Sekizawa, T., Otsuki, F., Ito, K., Okano, K.: Behavior verification of autonomous robot vehicle in consideration of errors and disturbances. In: 2015 IEEE 39th Annual Computer Software and Applications Conference, vol. 3, pp. 550–555. IEEE (2015)
19. Trinh, L.A., Ekström, M., Cürüklü, B.: Toward shared working space of human and robotic agents through dipole flow field for dependable path planning. Front. Neurorobot. **12**, 28 (2018)
20. Wang, Y., Chaudhuri, S., Kavraki, L.E.: Bounded policy synthesis for POMDPs with safe-reachability objectives. In: International Conference on Autonomous Agents and Multi Agent Systems. IFAAMS, ACM (2018)
21. Watkins, C.J.C.H.: Learning from delayed rewards, King's College, Cambridge (1989)

30 Years of Simulation-Based Quantitative Analysis Tools: A Comparison Experiment Between Möbius and Uppaal SMC

Davide Basile[1]([✉]) [iD], Maurice H. ter Beek[1]([✉]) [iD], Felicita Di Giandomenico[1] [iD], Alessandro Fantechi[1,2] [iD], Stefania Gnesi[1] [iD], and Giorgio O. Spagnolo[1] [iD]

[1] ISTI–CNR, Pisa, Italy
{basile,terbeek,digiandomenico,fantechi,gnesi,spagnolo}@isti.cnr.it
[2] University of Florence, Florence, Italy

Abstract. We provide a brief comparison of the modelling and analysis capabilities of two different formalisms and their associated simulation-based tools, acquired from experimenting with these methods and tools on one specific case study. The case study is a cyber-physical system from an industrial railway project, namely a railroad switch heater, and the quantitative properties concern energy consumption and reliability. We modelled and analysed the case study with stochastic activity networks and Möbius on the one hand and with stochastic hybrid automata and Uppaal SMC on the other hand. We give an overview of the performed experiments and highlight specific features of the two methodologies. This yields some pointers for future research and improvements.

1 Introduction

Industrial critical, cyber-physical systems typically need to satisfy a number of quantitative properties. The formal modelling and efficient analysis of such systems is challenging and has been extensively studied recently. Indeed, simulation-based analysis techniques and tools have been used for decades to perform quantitative analysis, well before the NSF workshop on cyber-physical systems in October 2006 made them fashionable. In particular, stochastic model-based analysis has a longstanding and rich history in Mathematics, well preceding Computer Science as a discipline [4,29]. Statistical Model Checking (SMC) may be traced back to hypothesis testing in the context of probabilistic bisimulation [1,21], but the notion has become popular during the last two decades as a result of Younes's Ph.D. thesis [22,34,35]. Tools that support SMC are more recent [1]. For instance, the first version of Uppaal SMC [17] was released in 2014. The stochastic analysis tool Möbius [15] can be traced back much further, to its predecessors UltraSAN [16,32] and MetaSAN [33]. The latter offer analysis techniques for performability models based on stochastic activity networks (SAN), which are a generalization of stochastic Petri nets [2], which are considered to

© Springer Nature Switzerland AG 2020
T. Margaria and B. Steffen (Eds.): ISoLA 2020, LNCS 12476, pp. 368–384, 2020.
https://doi.org/10.1007/978-3-030-61362-4_21

mark the starting point of cross-fertilization between the fields of performance evaluation and formal verification [4].

In this paper, we continue this cross-fertilization by providing a brief comparison of some of the modelling and analysis capabilities of Möbius and Uppaal SMC, their two different modelling formalisms and their simulation-based quantitative analysis techniques, acquired by experimenting with these methods and tools on one and the same case study. The case study is a cyber-physical system from the railway domain, namely a railroad switch heater, and the quantitative properties concern energy consumption and reliability. This case study comes from our industrial partners in STINGRAY (SmarT station INtelliGent RAilwaY), a project funded by the Tuscany region, which advocates the study of energy-saving algorithms in the railway domain. The models and analyses with stochastic activity networks (SAN) and Möbius have originally been presented in [5], while those with stochastic hybrid automata (SHA) and Uppaal SMC have originally been presented in [9].

The agenda of compared features ranges from modelling features (e.g. communication primitives and delay distributions) to properties specification (e.g. measures of interest) and experiments and presentation of results (e.g. experiment parameter setup), cf. the leftmost column of Table 1 in Sect. 5. While most of the findings of our comparison are likely well known by the communities around Möbius and Uppaal SMC, this might be less so for someone who is facing her first attempt at modelling a real-time system with the aim of performing quantitative analyses. Our comparison can help such user evaluate which method and tool better fits her specific needs, or at least make her aware of possible limitations and specificities of the chosen methodology. Furthermore, we conclude our comparison by providing some possible pointers to future research and improvements, from the point of view of usability, for both methodologies.

Finally, our approach to model and analyse one and the same case study with two different formalisms and their associated tools also responds to the call for formal methods diversity in the railway sector as put forward in [27,28]. This call, inspired by code/design diversity [24], is based on the assumption that the application of different, non-certified analysis tools on a replication of the same design may increase confidence in the correctness of the analysis results. We believe this to be a useful concept.

Outline. After this Introduction, we provide a short description of the case study and its context in Sect. 2. In Sect. 3, we briefly describe the two tools, followed by a description of the models and experiments that our comparison is based on in Sect. 4. The main contribution of our paper is presented in Sect. 5, where we present a detailed comparison of a number of specific features of the two methodologies, concluded by some pointers to possible improvements for the future. Section 6, finally, wraps up the paper.

2   Context of the Case Study

In this section, we provide a brief description of the case study and project where it originates from. Traditionally, railway stations have a private energy distribution and communication system. The main reasons for this are to ensure uninterrupted power supply and security, but this isolation has two main drawbacks. First, it prohibits integration with 'smart cities', in which, ideally, information between different transport systems (i.e. bike sharing, car sharing, urban transport, etc.) is synergically exploited. Second, the station system fails to benefit from modern energy-saving techniques.

The project STINGRAY (SmarT station INtelliGent RAilwaY), funded by the Tuscany region, aims to enhance the integration of railway stations into smart cities of the future as well as to study advanced energy-saving techniques. To this aim, the design and development of a station communication infrastructure is studied, integrating powerline and wireless technologies. Powerlines are utilised to enable a more efficient management of machinery and energetic resources. The goals of the project are:

- to realise a LAN over the station plants using power line and wireless technologies;
- to allow the control and monitoring of station equipment via Supervisory Control And Data Acquisition (SCADA), and in particular railroad switch heaters as studied in this paper;
- to create value-added services for both customers and railway staff, such as connectivity, monitoring fault prediction service (FPS), video surveillance, environmental surveying and integration and access to so-called smart city infomobility services; in particular the energy management service (EMS) is addressed;
- to optimise existing strategies for managing energy consumption within the station, to avoid wasting energy.

The case studies of STINGRAY provided by the industrial partners from the railway domain are station lighting and the heating of the railroad switches in ice conditions (cf. Fig. 1). In this paper, we address the latter case study.

Railroad switch heaters assure correct working of switches in case of ice and snow through a central control unit in charge of managing policies of energy consumption while satisfying reliability constraints. Although apparently a rather focused system, with restricted functionalities, it represents very well the peculiarities of a cyber-physical system: physical components (the heater), cyber components (the heating policies and the related coordinator), stochastic aspects (failure events and weather forecasts), and logical/physical dependencies.

3   Description of the Tools

Before providing the models, we briefly describe Möbius and Uppaal SMC.

Fig. 1. Gas heating keeping a railroad switch free from snow and ice (Di Fabian Grunder (FabiBerg) – Opera propria, CC BY-SA 3.0, https://commons.wikimedia.org/w/index.php?curid=641923)

3.1 Möbius

Möbius [15] offers a distributed discrete-event simulator, and, for Markovian models, explicit state-space generators and numerical solution algorithms. It is possible to analyse both transient and steady-state reward models. Möbius supports different formalisms, among which the aforementioned SAN, and models specified in different formalisms can be composed in different ways. Reward models are used to define the measures under analysis. A SAN is composed of the following primitives: *places*, *activities*, *input gates*, and *output gates*. Places and activities have the same interpretation as places and transitions in Petri nets [30]. Input gates control the enabling conditions of an activity and define the change of marking when an activity completes. Output gates define the change of marking upon completion of the activity. Activities can be of two types: *instantaneous* or *timed*. Instantaneous activities complete once the enabling conditions are satisfied. Timed activities take an amount of time to complete, following a temporal stochastic distribution function which can be, e.g., exponential or deterministic. Cases are associated to activities, and are used to represent probabilistic uncertainty about the action taken upon completion of the activity. Primitives of the SAN models are defined using C++ code.

3.2 Uppaal SMC

Statistical Model Checking (SMC) concerns running a sufficient number of (probabilistically distributed) simulations of a system model to obtain statistical evidence (with a predefined level of statistical confidence) of the quantitative properties to be checked [1,22]. UPPAAL SMC [17] is an extension of UPPAAL [11], a well-known toolbox for the verification of real-time systems modelled by (extended) timed automata. Timed automata are finite-state automata enhanced with real-time modelling through *clock* variables; their stochastic extension replaces non-determinism with probabilistic choice and time delays with probability distributions (uniform for bounded time and exponential for unbounded time). These automata may communicate via (broadcast) channels and shared variables. The resulting stochastic hybrid automata (SHA) form the input models of UPPAAL SMC. UPPAAL SMC allows to check (quantitative) properties over simulation runs of an UPPAAL SMC model (i.e. a network of SHA). These properties must be expressed in a dialect [12] of the Metric Interval Temporal Logic (MITL) [3].

4   Models and Experiments

To contextualize the comparison between the two methodologies, in this section we briefly describe the models and experiments performed in [5,9].

Although the modeling studies on the railroad switch heating system have since been further extended to focus on other aspects (mainly, to account for more sophisticated weather dynamics and representation, e.g. in [14]), these only exploited the SAN formalism and Möbius. Hence for our comparison experiment the two works mentioned in the beginning of this section are the most suitable.

4.1   Modelling Approaches

The aforementioned energy-saving policies for railroad switch heaters are based on dynamic power management, according to which energy is turned on and off based on predefined temperature thresholds. Moreover, the system can be constrained to not exceed a given maximum amount of power. This is especially useful in case of degraded operational modes which forbid to exceed a certain amount of power. In particular, once the system temperature falls below a temperature warning threshold (T_{wa}), the heating needs to be activated, otherwise the associated switch fails. Once the temperature rises and reaches the working threshold (T_{wo}), the heating system can be safely turned off.

The models (in both tools) are parameterized based on these two temperature thresholds T_{wa} and T_{wo}, and on NH_{max}, which is the maximum power that the system can provide at every instant of time, expressed as the percentage of heaters that can be turned on at the same time.

The continuous physical behaviour concerning the increment and decrement of the temperature of the railroad track when the heater is turned on or off, respectively, is modelled by an ordinary differential equation (ODE) representing the balance of energy.

When the temperature of the railroad track is below the freezing threshold (i.e. $0\,°C$ in the performed experiments), a switch may experience a failure. In

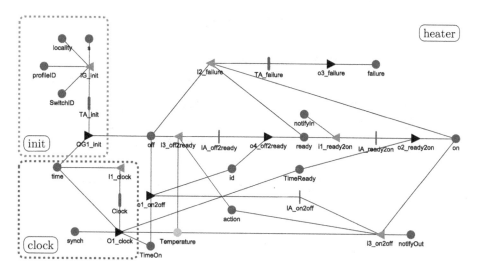

Fig. 2. The SAN model *RailRoadSwitchHeater* from [5]

this case, the time-to-failure is modelled with an exponential distribution with fixed rate, which is based on the temperature of the railroad track. This rate is an input parameter.

To model the external weather conditions, the model takes as input data structures containing profiles of average temperatures in those days for which the analysis is relevant (e.g. winter days). Different daily weather profiles retrieved from the Internet are used in the performed experiments. The time window under analysis is divided into intervals to which an average reference temperature is assigned.

The two main logical components describing the discrete cyber part of the analysed system are the *heater* and the *central coordinator*. The overall model is then composed of n heaters and the coordinator. The heater model implements the policy for activating and deactivating the heating phase. The central coordinator manages the activation and deactivation of each heater, by interacting with the network of heaters, to notify the activation or deactivation, respectively, of a heater, according to a specific communication protocol designed by the authors.

SAN Model. We first describe the SAN model of the railroad switch heating system, built with the functionalities provided by Möbius.

The main SAN model concerning the railroad switch heater is depicted in Fig. 2, reproduced from [5]. It is partitioned into three logical components: the *init* subnet, the *clock* subnet, and the *heater* subnet.

The *init* subnet initialises the data structures used by the SAN model. The *clock* subnet models the evolution of time (during one day in our analysis) and it is used to update the environment temperature and the temperature of the railroad track. In [5], we considered as unit of time one hour. The activity Clock

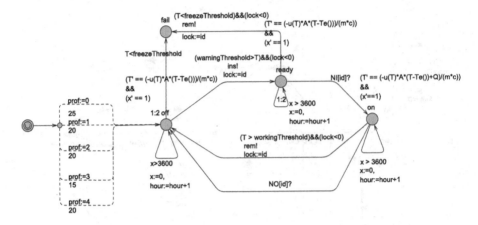

Fig. 3. SHA H from [9], modelling an instance of a railroad switch heater

has a deterministic distribution of time (non-Markovian) and completes each hour. When Clock completes, the place Temperature is updated: if the heater is turned on then the temperature increases, otherwise the temperature will be updated according to the temperature of the environment. Indeed, the time-step has been discretized to account for the temperature profile windows.

The *heater* subnet represents the status of the railroad switch heater. The *heater* subnet interacts with a SAN model *Coordinator* (not depicted here) through places that are shared among all the replicas of the heater model and the coordinator model.

The function representing the heating exchange is defined in C++, and it is called by the output gate O1_clock shown in Fig. 2 to update the temperature of the railroad each interval of time t. The activity TA_failure models the failure of a heater. It has an exponential distribution of time based on the temperature of the railroad track: the more the temperature is below the freezing threshold the more likely the activity will fire, according to the rate of the distribution which is an input parameter of the model.

The SAN model *Coordinator* represents the central management unit and it interacts with all heaters in the network by activating, deactivating, or moving them into a waiting state.

SHA Model. Next we describe the SHA model of the railroad switch heating system, built with the functionalities provided by Uppaal SMC. SHA allow to capture discrete, continuous, and stochastic aspects in a single framework. We briefly outline the formalisation of the system of (remotely controlled) railroad switch heaters as a product of SHA.

The ODE is expressed in the SHA model H in Fig. 3, where the temperature T is a *continuous clock* and the flow function F (i.e. the ODE) is similar in different states. Indeed, when H is in state on, F adds the term Q (i.e. power), which does not occur in states off and ready.

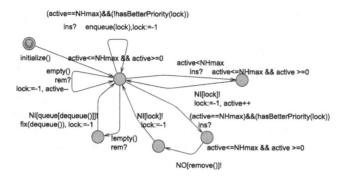

Fig. 4. SHA K from [9], modelling the coordinator

The two main logical components describing the discrete cyber part of the analysed system are the *heater* H and the *central coordinator* K, depicted in Figs. 3 and 4, respectively, both reproduced from [9]. The network composed of n heaters and the coordinator is realised by the product of K and the replicas of the SHA H_{id}, $id \in 1, \ldots, n$, where each heater is uniquely identified by its id, i.e. $(\bigotimes_{id \in 1, \ldots, n} H_{id}) \otimes K$.

The SHA heater model depicted in Fig. 3 implements the policy for activating and deactivating the heating phase, similarly to the SAN heater model depicted in Fig. 2. In particular, the dotted transitions are urgent (i.e. instantaneous) probabilistic transitions used for selecting one of the available weather profiles. The main states are on, off, ready, and fail, which correspond to the places of the SAN model *RailRoadSwitchHeater*. Note that each state has an inner cycle modelling the decrease and increase of the internal temperature according to the flow function, and that both incoming transitions to state fail have an exponential distribution of time, whose rates are input parameters to fine tune the model. During a simulation, the current time is stored in the clock x and a variable hour stores the current hour. The function Te(), used in the flow function of T, selects the actual external temperature based on the current hour, and it is implemented in Uppaal.

The SHA model depicted in Fig. 4 implements the coordinator model. Its behaviour is similar to that of the SAN model *Coordinator* mentioned above. The queue of pending heaters is modelled with the array queue[ ] of length equal to NH_{max}, and the functions enqueue(int id) and dequeue() are used for inserting and removing elements, while empty() returns true if the queue of pending heaters is empty.

The coordinator sends messages to the network of heaters through two arrays of channels, NI[id] and NO[id], both indexed by the identifiers of the heaters, to notify the activation and deactivation, respectively, of a heater. Note that Uppaal SMC only allows broadcast channels, hence an array of channels has been adopted in order to implement one-to-one communications. Following the de facto standard notation in component-based systems, sending a message through a channel a is denoted as a!, while reading is denoted as a?. Upon reception of the notification NI[id]?, the heater with identifier id switches from state ready to state on.

The heaters communicate to the coordinator their transition from off to ready through the channel ins, asking to be activated, and their transition from on to off through the channel rem; both channels are many-to-one. All channels are *urgent*: no delay will occur in case a synchronisation is available.

While the coordinator is in a busy state, a shared variable lock is used as a semaphore to prevent a heater from sending messages that cannot be elaborated, and it is used by the heaters for communicating their identifiers to the coordinator.

4.2   Quantitative Analyses

The conducted analyses focussed on reliability as well as energy consumption indicators. More precisely, the two measures of interest concerning energy consumption and reliability of the system under analysis were defined as follows.

1. The time (in hours) a generic heater is activated in a specific time interval. By multiplying such measurement for the power consumed (kilowatt per hour), it is possible to derive the energy consumed by the system.
2. The probability that a generic switch fails (becomes frozen). Reliability is computed as the probability that no failure occurs in the interval of time under analysis.

In Möbius, reward structures were used for evaluating the measures of interest, while in Uppaal SMC they were defined as formulae in the aforementioned MITL [3], which are enriched with quantification operators on the replicated models and expected values.

First consider the SAN model. The first measure of interest was computed as the sum of the time that each heater model spends in markings encoding its operative state, that is the time that each heater is activated. The second measure of interest, the probability of failure, instead was computed as the probability that there is one token in the place encoding a failure state in the heater model at the end of the experiment.

Next consider the SHA model. In Uppaal SMC, a discrete clock energy was used to count the hours each heater is activated. For the first measure of interest, the energy consumption, the number of hours in which the heaters are active was estimated as the formula:

$$E[<= 24; 10000] \; (\texttt{max} : \sum_{i:id_t} H_i.\texttt{energy})$$

In this formula, E stands for the expected value, 24 is the considered interval of time (24 h) and 10000 is the number of simulations executed by the tool. The overall energy consumption is the sum for all H_i of all clocks energy.

The second measure of interest, the probability of failure, was instead estimated by Uppaal SMC through the formula:

$$\mathbb{P}(\Diamond_{h \leq 24} \exists (i : id_t)(H_i.\texttt{fail}))$$

This formula evaluates the probability that in the interval $[t, t + l]$ (24h) there exists at least a switch H_i in the network which has failed, i.e. H_i is in state `fail`.

Experiments conducted on a system of 10 switches, grouped according to their priority, confirmed that both modelling and analysis methodologies, i.e. SAN and Möbius on the one hand and SHA and Uppaal SMC on the other hand, are suitable to address the analyses. Results were aligned in spite of some differences in the models, thus also serving as mutual cross-validation, as advocated by formal methods diversity (cf. Introduction).

As expected, the analyses confirmed how energy consumption and reliability are contrasting requirements: by reducing the energy consumption the overall system reliability decreases. However, experiments made it possible to find a parameter setup that represents the best compromise between these two measures. Of course, the nature of the adopted approaches did generate differences in the evaluation experience, as discussed in the next section.

5 Comparison

In this section, we present the main contribution of our paper, in the form of a number of considerations subjective to our experiences with applying the two methodologies to the above mentioned case study. Our aim is merely to highlight some specific features that the two methodologies offer, to be used by potential modellers in deciding which one better suits their need for the particular case study at hand. In addition, we underline that the comparison carried out touches only those functionalities of the two modeling and evaluation environments that were involved given the needs of the case study under analysis. Therefore, we cannot claim that we exhaustively considered all features, and consequently our goal is by no means to pronounce a definitive verdict concerning the methodologies' suitability, let alone quality. Generally speaking, we note that Möbius is a mature tool that has been widely adopted in the evaluation of performance and dependability aspects of real-world systems, while Uppaal is a mature tool oriented to the quantitative verification of properties of real-time systems of which Uppaal SMC is a recent, as yet less mature extension.

Our comparison should be seen in the light of a recent study, reported in [10], of the outcomes of three questionnaires on the adoption of formal methods and tools in the railway domain, which were performed within three different projects of the EU Shift2Rail innovation programme (cf. https://shift2rail.org/). As part of an analysis of the respondents' expectations on tools, the paper reports that the most relevant functionalities are formal verification and support for formal modelling, followed by traceability, simulation, test and code generation. Instead, the most relevant quality features are related to the maturity, usability, and learnability of the tools.

Our comparison addresses the following three groups of features (summarised in the leftmost column of Table 1 below) in the next three sections.

Modelling Features: these concern the composition of, and interactions between, different models (i.e. *heterogeneous formalisms, replicated models,* *dynamic process instantiation, communication primitives*) and the ability towards modelling hybrid and stochastic systems (i.e. *delay distributions, hybrid variables*);

Properties Specification: these concern the definition of measures of interest (i.e. *measures of interest*) and the ability to verify properties of the defined models (i.e. *property verification*);

Experiments and Presentation of Results: these concern the setup and execution of experiments, as well as data collection and plotting the results (i.e. *experiment parameter setup*).

We note that, for this comparison experiment that is focused on usability and expressiveness, we specifically consider whether features are primitively supported by the tool. Of course, for features that are not built-in, both tools may rely on external software packages or libraries for accessing extended functionalities at the cost of an extra modelling effort. In the end, we provide some pointers to future research and improvements for both methodologies.

5.1   Modelling Features

Systems under analysis are often composed of different types of components, and in general more components of the same type may be involved, as is the case for the railroad switch heater system of our case study. Möbius allows to develop a composite overall model where individual models can be replicated, joined, and defined in different formalisms (e.g. Petri nets [30,31], PEPA [19], Fault trees [23], etc.). However, replication operators treat models as anonymous, so in case non-anonymous instantiations are required, as in our case study, a specific mechanism to assign a unique identifier to each replica model needs to be added to the model under development. Anticipating the discussion, we mention that the replication operator in Möbius has recently been enhanced in efficiency [26], thus alleviating to some extent the additional computational overhead required by the mechanism to implement non-anonymity. Moreover, efficient solutions to non-anonymous model replication have been also proposed (cf., e.g., [13,25]), which resort to a script on top of primitive facilities provided by Möbius.

Similarly, Uppaal offers template models that can be replicated, but each replica has its own built-in identifier. Identifiers can be used for quantifying formulae, as we did for the measures of interest in our case study. It is also possible to dynamically create new processes during a simulation, through a *fork* primitive. Several instances of models can be joined through the composition operator. Accordingly, when different formalisms are necessary for designing the system under analysis and the replicas are anonymous, Möbius is more adequate. If the replicas are instead non-anonymous, Möbius requires to distinguish them through ad-hoc networks that result in a larger state space. Moreover, if the system to be modelled comprehends the dynamic generation of new processes, then this feature is primitively available in Uppaal, making it very suitable.

Concerning the interaction between different instances of models, in the SAN models defined in Möbius communication is implemented through shared places (i.e. places where different networks can read/write). Indeed, through tokens in different places it is possible to codify the identifiers of the interacting parties and the messages sent. The SHA models defined in Uppaal SMC are endowed with primitives for I/O communication, allowing to describe interactions among entities in a high-level language. When modelling communication-based systems, SHA models thus offer both I/O primitives at message level and shared variables, while SAN models interact through shared places (acting as shared variables). We note in passing that shared places/variables are part of the state space, while synchronous messages may reduce the state space by avoiding interleavings (e.g. places `notifyIn` and `notifyOut` in Fig. 2 are rendered as communication channels `NI` and `NO` in Fig. 3).

Concerning modeling stochastic and hybrid Systems, both SAN and SHA models are capable of describing probabilistic transitions and stochastic delays. Through SAN models it is possible to describe Markovian and non-Markovian models with several probability distributions for delays in firing a transition, whereas only uniform and exponential distributions for delays are available for SHA models. Therefore, in general, SAN models allow for a more accurate representation of physical phenomena. Both formalisms can model instantaneous transitions, which are called instantaneous activities in SAN models and urgent transitions in SHA models.

SHA models allow to describe discrete and hybrid clocks for updating values according to given ODE, whereas SAN models do not provide a built-in solver of ODE. Instead, the equations have to be solved and implemented in, for example, C++ functions or via calls to external solvers. The hybrid clocks are stored in Uppaal SMC through double precision types, while Möbius provides extended places for storing high precision values.

Hence, Uppaal SMC deals with hybrid systems by primitively supporting ODE. Möbius, on the other hand, primitively allows to model several stochastic distributions in SAN models.

5.2 Properties Specification

Concerning definition of measures of interest, in Möbius, measures of interest (performance variables) on the composed model are defined through reward models. A reward model defines the data that needs to be collected from the model (using C++ code), through analytic solvers or simulations. Rate rewards on the measures of interest specify whether the reward is collected based on the marking of the SAN models or the firing of activities, and if it is collected at a specific instant of time, over an interval of time, over a time-averaged interval of time, or after the system reaches a steady state.

In Uppaal SMC, measures of interest are introduced by means of formulae in a weighted extension of MITL [12]. The available evaluation methods are probability estimation, hypothesis testing, and probability comparison. It is also possible to perform simulations to monitor the values of interest. The possibility of expressing measures of interest as formulae in a temporal logic has the advantage that a precise formal semantics endows those measures. Moreover, it is possible to define fine-grained properties directly through the available temporal operators. For example, the formula $\mathbb{P}(\Diamond_{[0,24]}\exists(\mathtt{i}:\mathtt{id_t})(\Box_{[0,2]}\mathtt{H_i.on}))$ evaluates the probability that there exists, in the interval of 24 hours, a component $\mathtt{H_i}$ (where i is its index) in state on, for at least 3 consecutive time units.

Uppaal offers high-level expressions for the formal definition of varieties of indicators to be analysed, while Möbius typically requires to enrich the model to properly account for sophisticated properties, such as the one described by the temporal logic formula above (e.g., by adding ad-hoc places and transitions to code the property to be analysed, thus resulting in a more complex model). Continuing the example, an extra place should be added to Fig. 2 with a token being added once the heater is on for more than 3 time units, and the reward model should be based upon this extra place.

Concerning the verification of the models and performances, Uppaal provides the possibility of verifying properties such as for example the absence of deadlocks. It is also possible to perform trace analysis and simulation of the models for debugging purposes, and in case a property is violated the tool reports the trace which violates it as counterexample.

Möbius does not provide any built-in verification of properties expressed in some kind of logic. The property must be encoded in a Markov Reward Model, thus requiring more effort from the point of view of the user. However, it is possible to perform LTL model checking on traces obtained from the logs of the simulations in Möbius by means of external prototypical tools, such as for example Traviando [20].

Summing up, Uppaal supports model checking of temporal logic formulae, while Möbius offers a more prototypical trace-based analysis.

Finally, in relation to the specific experiments carried out in [5,9], Möbius showed better performances than Uppaal SMC. This might be due to the fact that Uppaal SMC solves the defined ODE during simulation and the number of simulations is fixed. No general conclusions can be drawn from two experiments.

5.3   Experiments and Presentation of Results

The experiments in Möbius can be organised in batches, called studies. Each study contains the parameter setup of the experiment (such as temperature thresholds and energy available in our case), which can then be executed in series or in parallel. This feature enhances efficiency, by allowing to perform all required experiments in background. In Uppaal SMC, instead, the parameters must be instantiated manually for each experiment to be evaluated.

The results of the experiments performed by Möbius are stored into tabular data, ready to be analysed and plotted through a database (PostgreSQL) or external tools. Uppaal provides built-in graphic visualisers of, for example, the density and cumulative distribution of the evaluated property.

In the specific case study presented in this paper, Möbius proved effective in dealing with several parameter setups and a large amount of resulting data concerning the experiments. From the viewpoint of presentation of the results, Uppaal automatically generates the visualisation of results while Möbius requires a pre-processing phase.

5.4 Discussion

The comparison performed in this section so far is summarised in Table 1, which reflects one of the main contributions of this paper. In the remainder of this section, we highlight some directions for future developments for both Möbius and Uppaal SMC to address some of the points discussed so far.

Table 1. Comparison between SAN + Möbius and SHA + Uppaal SMC

Features	SAN + Möbius	SHA + Uppaal SMC
Measures of interest	Reward Models	MITL formulae
Experiments parameter setup	Batches	Single
Replicated models	Anonymous	Distinguished
Dynamic process instantiation	Not available	Available
Heterogeneous formalisms	Available (SAN, PEPA, etc.)	Not available (SHA)
Communication primitives	Shared places	Channels
Delay distributions	Various distributions	Exponential, Uniform
Hybrid variables	No primitive support	ODE solver available
Property verification	Not available	Temporal logics

Concerning SAN and Möbius, improvement of the anonymous replication aspect appears to be a major advancement to pursue. Actually, this is already ongoing activity (involving a subset of the authors), aiming at implementing the principles at the basis of the replication mechanism defined in [13] as a native Möbius operator.

A further interesting extension of Möbius, from the point of view of usability, would be the automatic generation of plot graphs from predefined measures of interest. Indeed, although Möbius is conceived as a meta-tool to be coupled with a variety of other tools (including visual tools and other functionalities), offering an internal visualization facility would be certainly appreciated by those users that prefer to have all they need within the same working environment. Motivated by the same reasoning, also a primitive support for ODE solving would be a step towards making easier the modeling effort of cyber-physical systems, without requiring the knowledge of software libraries tailored to specific needs.

Moving to SHA and Uppaal SMC, we note that the tool lacks the possibility of organising experiments in batches, where each batch has a specific parameter setup. In the current version, this has to be done manually or by means of external scripts. An interesting facility from the point of view of usability would be to equip the tool with the possibility to automatically execute batches of experiments (and collect the results). The possibility to primitively express other distribution delays (different from exponential distributions) would increase the expressiveness of the SHA formalism. For example, the SAN model presented previously discretises the time-steps by simply having a deterministic distribution delay that fires each specific time unit. We note in passing that such behaviour (deterministic time) is typical of many real-time specifications, i.e. interacting periodically with a fixed period. This behaviour can be obtained in Uppaal by an encoding of an invariant on a state of the form $x \leq t$ and an outgoing transition from that state of the form $x \geq t$. This ensures that the transition is fired exactly at time t. Note that in Uppaal invariants are defined for each state individually. Making such behaviour primitively expressible in the tool would improve its usability, as well as the readability of the models. Furthermore, it would typically reduce the state space (in the above example, we would need to instantiate a clock x and a parameter t).

Finally, we envisage that a formal mapping from SHA to SAN models would pave the way for automatic replicas of analyses, thus increasing the confidence in results and the soundness of the tools' implementations. In [7], a subset of the authors already provided a formal translation from contract automata [6] to SAN. Contract automata are similar to the SHA formalism used in Uppaal, and a timed extension also exists [8]. This former translation could be extended to deal with stochastic delays (to be encoded in SAN activities) and real-time clocks.

6   Conclusion

We have compared the modelling and analysis capabilities offered by SAN and Möbius with those offered by SHA and Uppaal SMC. This comparison experiment is based on modelling and analysing a single, small cyber-physical system from an industrial railway project (cf. [18] for a judgement study involving Uppaal SMC and 8 other tools). We have provided an overview of the performed experiments and based on those we have highlighted some specific features of the two methodologies. This has resulted in a few pointers for future research and improvements for both, to be considered during the next 30 years.

Acknowledgements. Supported by POR FESR 2014–2020 project STINGRAY (SmarT station INtelliGent RAilwaY) and MIUR PRIN 2017FTXR7S project IT MaTTerS (Methods and Tools for Trustworthy Smart Systems).

References

1. Agha, G., Palmskog, K.: A survey of statistical model checking. ACM Trans. Model. Comput. Simul. **28**(1), 6:1–6:39 (2018). https://doi.org/10.1145/3158668
2. Ajmone Marsan, M., Bobbio, A., Donatelli, S.: Petri nets in performance analysis: an introduction. In: Reisig, Rozenberg, [30], pp. 211–256. https://doi.org/10.1007/3-540-65306-6_17
3. Alur, R., Feder, T., Henzinger, T.A.: The benefits of relaxing punctuality. J. ACM **43**(1), 116–146 (1996). https://doi.org/10.1145/227595.227602
4. Baier, C., Haverkort, B.R., Hermanns, H., Katoen, J.P.: Performance evaluation and model checking join forces. Commun. ACM **53**(9), 76–85 (2010). https://doi.org/10.1145/1810891.1810912

5. Basile, D., Chiaradonna, S., Di Giandomenico, F., Gnesi, S.: A stochastic model-based approach to analyse reliable energy-saving rail road switch heating systems. J. Rail Transp. Plan. Manag. **6**(2), 163–181 (2016). https://doi.org/10.1016/j.jrtpm.2016.03.003
6. Basile, D., Degano, P., Ferrari, G.L.: Automata for specifying and orchestrating service contracts. Log. Methods Comp. Sci. **12**(4) (2016). https://doi.org/10.2168/LMCS-12(4:6)2016
7. Basile, D., Di Giandomenico, F., Gnesi, S.: A refinement approach to analyse critical cyber-physical systems. In: Cerone, A., Roveri, M. (eds.) SEFM 2017. LNCS, vol. 10729, pp. 267–283. Springer, Cham (2018). https://doi.org/10.1007/978-3-319-74781-1_19
8. Basile, D., ter Beek, M.H., Legay, A.: Timed service contract automata. Innov. Syst. Softw. Eng. **16**(2), 199–214 (2019). https://doi.org/10.1007/s11334-019-00353-3
9. Basile, D., Di Giandomenico, F., Gnesi, S.: Statistical model checking of an energy-saving cyber-physical system in the railway domain. In: Proceedings of the 32nd Symposium on Applied Computing (SAC), pp. 1356–1363. ACM (2017). https://doi.org/10.1145/3019612.3019824
10. ter Beek, M.H., et al.: Adopting formal methods in an industrial setting: the railways case. In: ter Beek, M.H., McIver, A., Oliveira, J.N. (eds.) FM 2019. LNCS, vol. 11800, pp. 762–772. Springer, Cham (2019). https://doi.org/10.1007/978-3-030-30942-8_46
11. Behrmann, G., et al.: UPPAAL 4.0. In: QEST. pp. 125–126. IEEE (2006). https://doi.org/10.1109/QEST.2006.59
12. Bulychev, P., David, A., Larsen, K.G., Legay, A., Li, G., Poulsen, D.B.: Rewrite-based statistical model checking of WMTL. In: Qadeer, S., Tasiran, S. (eds.) RV 2012. LNCS, vol. 7687, pp. 260–275. Springer, Heidelberg (2013). https://doi.org/10.1007/978-3-642-35632-2_25
13. Chiaradonna, S., Di Giandomenico, F., Masetti, G.: A stochastic modeling approach for an efficient dependability evaluation of large systems with non-anonymous interconnected components. In: Proceedings of the 28th International Symposium on Software Reliability Engineering (ISSRE), pp. 46–55. IEEE (2017). https://doi.org/10.1109/ISSRE.2017.17
14. Chiaradonna, S., Di Giandomenico, F., Masetti, G., Basile, D.: A refined framework for model-based assessment of energy consumption in the railway sector. In: ter Beek, M.H., Fantechi, A., Semini, L. (eds.) From Software Engineering to Formal Methods and Tools, and Back. LNCS, vol. 11865, pp. 481–501. Springer, Cham (2019). https://doi.org/10.1007/978-3-030-30985-5_28
15. Clark, G., et al.: The Möbius modeling tool. In: Proceedings of the 9th International Workshop on Petri Nets and Performance Models (PNPM), pp. 241–250. IEEE (2001). https://doi.org/10.1109/PNPM.2001.953373
16. Couvillion, J.A., et al.: Performability Modeling with UltraSAN. IEEE Softw. **8**(5), 69–80 (1991). https://doi.org/10.1109/52.84218
17. David, A., Larsen, K.G., Legay, A., Mikučionis, M., Poulsen, D.B.: UPPAAL SMC tutorial. Int. J. Softw. Tools Technol. Transf. **17**(4), 397–415 (2015). https://doi.org/10.1007/s10009-014-0361-y
18. Ferrari, A., Mazzanti, F., Basile, D., ter Beek, M.H., Fantechi, A.: Comparing formal tools for system design: a judgment study. In: Proceedings of the 42nd International Conference on Software Engineering (ICSE), pp. 62–74. ACM (2020). https://doi.org/10.1145/3377811.3380373

19. Hillston, J.: A Compositional Approach to Performance Modelling. Cambridge University Press (1996). https://doi.org/10.1017/CBO9780511569951
20. Kemper, P., Tepper, C.: Traviando - debugging simulation traces with message sequence charts. In: QEST, pp. 135–136. IEEE (2006). https://doi.org/10.1109/QEST.2006.58
21. Larsen, K.G., Skou, A.: Bisimulation through probabilistic testing. Inf. Comput. **94**(1), 1–28 (1991). https://doi.org/10.1016/0890-5401(91)90030-6
22. Legay, A., Lukina, A., Traonouez, L.M., Yang, J., Smolka, S.A., Grosu, R.: Statistical model checking. In: Steffen, B., Woeginger, G. (eds.) Computing and Software Science. LNCS, vol. 10000, pp. 478–504. Springer, Cham (2019). https://doi.org/10.1007/978-3-319-91908-9_23
23. Limnios, N.: Fault Trees. ISTE (2007). https://doi.org/10.1002/9780470612484
24. Littlewood, B., Popov, P., Strigini, L.: Modeling software design diversity: a review. ACM Comput. Surv. **33**(2), 177–208 (2001). https://doi.org/10.1145/384192.384195
25. Masetti, G., Chiaradonna, S., Di Giandomenico, F.: Model-based simulation in Möbius: an efficient approach targeting loosely interconnected components. In: Reinecke, P., Di Marco, A. (eds.) EPEW 2017. LNCS, vol. 10497, pp. 184–198. Springer, Cham (2017). https://doi.org/10.1007/978-3-319-66583-2_12
26. Masetti, G., Chiaradonna, S., Di Giandomenico, F., Feddersen, B., Sanders, W.H.: An efficient strategy for model composition in the Möbius modeling environment. In: Proceedings of the 14th European Dependable Computing Conference (EDCC), pp. 116–119 (2018). https://doi.org/10.1109/EDCC.2018.00029
27. Mazzanti, F., Ferrari, A.: Ten diverse formal models for a CBTC automatic train supervision system. In: Gallagher, J.P., van Glabbeek, R., Serwe, W. (eds.) MARS/VPT. EPTCS, vol. 268, pp. 104–149 (2018). https://doi.org/10.4204/EPTCS.268.4
28. Mazzanti, F., Ferrari, A., Spagnolo, G.O.: Towards formal methods diversity in railways: an experience report with seven frameworks. Int. J. Softw. Tools Technol. Transfer **20**(3), 263–288 (2018). https://doi.org/10.1007/s10009-018-0488-3
29. Pinsky, M.A., Karlin, S.: An Introduction to Stochastic Modeling, 4th edn. Academic Press, Cambridge (2011). https://doi.org/10.1016/C2009-1-61171-0
30. Reisig, W., Grzegorz, R. (eds.): ACPN 1996. LNCS, vol. 1491. Springer, Heidelberg (1998). https://doi.org/10.1007/3-540-65306-6
31. Reisig, W., Grzegorz, R. (eds.): ACPN 1996. LNCS, vol. 1492. Springer, Heidelberg (1998). https://doi.org/10.1007/3-540-65307-4
32. Sanders, W., Obal II, W., Qureshi, M., Widjanarko, F.: The UltraSAN modeling environment. Perform. Eval. **24**(1), 89–115 (1995). https://doi.org/10.1016/0166-5316(95)00012-M
33. Sanders, W.H., Meyer, J.F.: METASAN: a performability evaluation tool based on stochastic acitivity networks. In: Proceedings of the 1986 Fall Joint Computer Conference, pp. 807–816. IEEE (1986)
34. Sen, K., Viswanathan, M., Agha, G.: Statistical model checking of black-box probabilistic systems. In: Alur, R., Peled, D.A. (eds.) CAV 2004. LNCS, vol. 3114, pp. 202–215. Springer, Heidelberg (2004). https://doi.org/10.1007/978-3-540-27813-9_16
35. Younes, H.L.S.: Verification and Planning for Stochastic Processes with Asynchronous Events. Ph.D. thesis, Carnegie Mellon University, January 2005. http://reports-archive.adm.cs.cmu.edu/anon/2005/CMU-CS-05-105.pdf

Fluid Model-Checking in UPPAAL
for Covid-19

Peter G. Jensen, Kenneth Y. Jørgensen, Kim G. Larsen[✉],
Marius Mikučionis, Marco Muñiz, and Danny B. Poulsen[✉]

Department of Computer Science, Aalborg University, Aalborg, Denmark
{pgj,kyrke,kgl,marius,muniz,dannybpoulsen}@cs.aau.dk

Abstract. During the spring of 2020, the BEOCOVID project has been funded to investigate the use of stochastic hybrid models, statistical model checking and machine learning to analyse, predict and control the rapid spreading of Covid-19. In this paper we focus on the SEIHR epidemiological model instance of Covid-19 pandemics and show how the risk of viral exposure, the impact of super-spreader events as well as other scenarios can be modelled, estimated and controlled using the tool UPPAAL SMC.

1 Introduction

Epidemic modelling has gained tremendous interest in both news and research communities in 2020 due to the rapid spread of Covid-19. In the news most of the interest has been to use modelling as a way to explain the spread of Covid-19 while much research is about using models to predict and control the spread.

In Denmark three (collaborating) initiatives on combating Covid-19 using mathematical models has been made:

- In March an expert group headed by Statens Serum Institut (SSI[1]) was established with the task of developing mathematical models to predict the impact of Covid-19 spread in the Danish society and to evaluate the effect of preventive measures.
- In early April researchers at Danmarks Tekniske Universitet (DTU) and Aalborg Universitet (AAU) started a research project funded by Novo Nordisk Fonden (NNF) to develop and improve modelling tools of Covid-19 to assist decision makers to evaluate the effectiveness and impact of preventive measures. The project has been carried out in collaboration with SSI.
- On April 20th researchers from the Distributed, Embedded and Intelligent systems group at Department of Computer Science, Aalborg University (AAU) received a grant by Poul Due Jensens Foundation (PDJ) to further aid development of Covid-19 models. The PDJ project has been working in close collaboration with the NNF project.

---

[1] https://www.ssi.dk.

The project was funded by Poul Due Jensens Foundation grant.

T. Margaria and B. Steffen (Eds.): ISoLA 2020, LNCS 12476, pp. 385–403, 2020.
https://doi.org/10.1007/978-3-030-61362-4_22

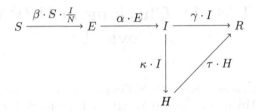

Fig. 1. Rate diagram of the basic compartmental SEIHR model.

The key research question addressed in the NNF and PDJ projects has been to identify the best strategy for social restrictions dependent on age and region in Denmark for protecting the population and society from Covid-19 mortalities caused by exceeding the intensive care capacity in the Danish hospital system.

An ambition of the two projects has been to provide a strategic decision tool for the Danish authorities. The projects involved dissemination to Statens Serum Institute (SSI), through a number of scheduled meetings. These have not only included the concepts behind the models, but also effects of changing the underlying assumptions and the uncertainties inherent in the different input data and estimations, as well as the predictive power of the analysis methods.

Classically epidemics are modelled using so-called *compartmental* models [5–7] where a population is divided into a number of different compartments, e.g. the following five compartments of the so-called SEIHR model:

- *susceptible* (S) being those that can affected by the disease,
- *exposed* (E) being those that have the disease but not yet infectious,
- *infectious* (I) being those that have the disease and can infect others,
- *recovered/removed* (R) being those that have had the disease and either recovered (with an assumed immunity), in quarantine or died, and
- *hospitalised* (H) being those that are hospitalised.

The dynamic change of the distribution of a population over compartments may be described using a rate diagram such as Fig. 1. In the rate diagram the expression above an arrow describes the rate of the flow between different compartments, e.g. the arrow $E \xrightarrow{\alpha \cdot E} I$ means a conversion from E to I with a rate α multiplied by the number of E elements. Similarly $S \xrightarrow{\beta \cdot S \cdot \frac{I}{N}} E$ is a conversion from S to E with a rate β multiplied by the number of S, except this conversion is facilitated by the number of infectious I elements where the probability of meeting one is I/N, therefore the overall conversion rate is scaled with this probability. As we shall see later, the rate diagram may be analysed using a number of different mathematical models.

Remark 1. Importantly it should be mentioned, that at the time of writing details concerning immunity in respect to Covid-19 (especially duration) are not yet established. If immunity is later discovered to be only temporary and lasts shortly, then our models need to be refined.

A crucial aspect of epidemic modelling is estimation of the $\beta, \alpha, \gamma, \kappa$ and τ parameters. After the outbreak of Covid-19 Chinese researchers [8] have estimated the parameters based on data observed in Wuhan. These parameters are however not directly transferable from one country to another as they depend on the health and the behavior of each society. The NNF-project has fitted Danish data to a SEIHR model and estimated the parameters for Danish conditions. These parameter values are used in our modelling and analysis effort.

In this paper we focus on the PDJ project, with the purpose of illustrating how statistical model checking in the tool UPPAAL SMC [3] has been used to model, analyse and synthesise a variety of scenarios relevant for Covid-19 [4], ranging from abstract (continuous) population models to detailed (stochastic) agent-based models as well as (fluid) mixtures of these, allowing to reason about health risks of selected individuals in the setting of particular populations.

2   SEIHR Models in UPPAAL SMC

The rate diagram in Fig. 1 describing how individuals move between the different compartments of the SEIHR model can be captured by a number of different mathematical models. Traditionally, rate diagrams are most often interpreted as ordinary differential equations (ODE) which are deterministic. However, the diagrams can also be viewed as stochastic models, where the rates of the reactions are used as parameters of exponential distributions. The stochastic models may either be aggregated or be agent-based. In the latter, the health-status (i.e. compartment) for each individual is faithfully reflected, whereas in the former only the number of individuals in each compartment is maintained. The stochastic models are more realistic than the ODE models, but also come with a significantly increased complexity in their analysis: the analysis of agent-based models are exponentially[2] more complex than the analysis of aggregate models. A well-known fact about the aggregate stochastic model is that it can be easily translated into a set of ODEs capturing the expected behaviour of the model in the limit. Furthermore, the aggregated stochastic model can be proven to be a correct abstraction of the agent-based stochastic model using the notion of probabilistic bisimulation. To mediate between the accuracy of modelling and the complexity of analysis, it is possible to have mixed models – so-called fluid models – where selected individuals are modelled as agents, whereas the remaining population are modelled using either ODE or aggregated models.

In the remainder of this section we will show how the tool UPPAAL SMC [3] can easily model and analyse all the three (four) above types of models for reaction networks.

2.1   Ordinary Differential Equation Models

Figure 2 shows the ODE model of the SEIHR reaction network in UPPAAL. The main ingredients of the model are the five continuous state-variables S,

---

[2] Assuming a fixed number of compartments.

```
typedef int[0,1<<31-1] int32_t;
const int32_t N = 10000;
const double eps = 0.01;
const double BRN = 2.4;
const double alpha = 1.0/5.1;
const double gamma = 1.0/3.4;
const double beta0 = BRN * gamma;
const double pH = 0.9e-3;
const double kappa =
    gamma*pH/(1.0-pH);
const double tau = 1.0/10.12;
clock S = (1.0-eps)*N;
clock E = eps * N;
clock I = 0.0;
clock H = 0.0;
clock R = 0.0;
```

(a) Declarations.

◎ Quantities

```
S' == -beta0*I*S/N              &&
E' == beta0*I*S/N - alpha*E     &&
I' == alpha*E - (gamma+kappa)*I &&
H' == kappa*I - tau*H           &&
R' == gamma*I + tau*H
```

(b) SEIHR hybrid automaton.

(c) Simulation.

Fig. 2. ODE model of SEIHR rate diagram.

E, I, H and R declared as (initialised) clocks in the declaration part Fig. 2a. The declaration part also sets a number of constants for the various rates of the reaction network to fit the evolution of Covid-19 in Denmark. Here we are looking at small sub-population of Denmark with 10,000 people and with 1% being exposed initially. The behavioural part of the model is given in Fig. 2b, being a one-location automata, with an invariant describing the behaviour of the state-variables as a system of ODEs. The ODEs are derived from the SEIHR reaction network in a very simple manner: for any state-variable X there is an ODE expressing that the derivative of X equals the difference between the total rate of the incoming edges and the total rate of outgoing edges, i.e.:

$$X' = \sum_{Y \xrightarrow{E} X} E - \sum_{X \xrightarrow{E} Z} E$$

Finally, we see the evolution of the state-variables over a period of 100 days in Fig. 2c. In particular, we note that out the total population of 10,000 some 1,403 will get exposed, 900 infected and 1,98 hospitalised. The time for the simulation was 0.077 s.

2.2 Aggregated Stochastic Models

In Fig. 3(a)–(e), we show the aggregated stochastic model of the SEIHR rate diagram. In this model the different compartments are represented as integer variables (counters S, E, I, H and R) representing at any given point in time the number of individuals being in that state. A key assumption is that $S + E + I +$

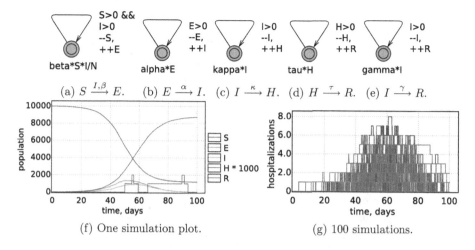

Fig. 3. Aggregated CTMC model of SEIHR rate diagram.

H + R = N, where N is the number of individuals. As for the rate-expressions of the SEIHR rate diagram, these are used as rates of exponentially distributed transitions incrementing/decrementing the relevant counters. E.g. the (looping) transition of Fig. 3(b) indicates that one individual is transferred from E to I with rate kappa*I – of course provided that E is larger than 0 as expressed by the guard E>0. The resulting aggregated model is a continuous time Markov chain (CTMC) with states being vectors (S, E, I, H, R) and where the five transitions of Fig. 3(a)–(e) are racing against each other.

In Fig. 3(f) we see the evolution of the state counters resulting from a single simulation over a period of 100 days. Despite the randomness of the simulation, the evolution of S, E, I and R seems indistinguishable from that of the ODE model Fig. 2. However, considering the variable H, we see a variation between 0, 1 and 2 over the 100 day period. Figure 3(g) visualises 100 random simulations with H ranging between 0 and 8. In fact, based on the 100 random simulations the expected value of H in the aggregated CTMC model is found to be 3.82 ± 0.24. Moreover, using 291 random simulations the probability that H will exceed 4 is found to be in the confidence interval $[0.183, 0.282]$ with 5% confidence. These stochastic analyses significantly refines the expected behaviour analysis provided by the deterministic ODE model, where H was below 2. For this aggregated CTMC model the time to perform a single simulation is approximately 0.702 s (a factor of 10 more than the ODE model).

2.3 Agent-Based Stochastic Models

Both the ODE model and the aggregated CTMC model provide sufficient information to address[3] the key question as to whether the capacity at hospitals will

---

[3] Assuming, of course, that the given model is valid with respect to reality.

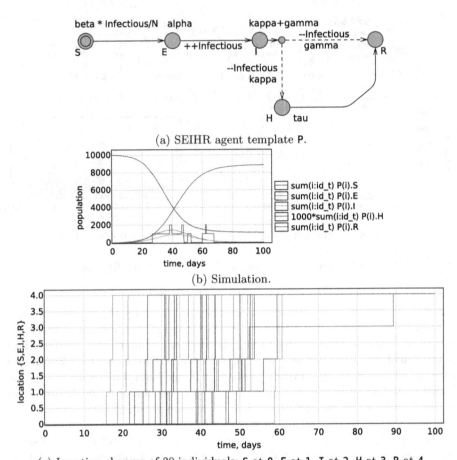

(a) SEIHR agent template P.

(b) Simulation.

(c) Location changes of 30 individuals: S at 0, E at 1, I at 2, H at 3, R at 4.

Fig. 4. Agent-based CTMC model of SEIHR rate diagram.

be exceeded within a given period. However, questions such as "how many different individuals will be hospitalised" and "what is the expected time before a given individual becomes exposed" cannot be readily answered by these two models. To answer such questions, we need an agent-based model, where the healthiness status of each individual is accounted for. Figure 4(a) provides a SEIHR agent automaton (template) to be instantiated for each individual of the population. In the automaton, the five locations S, E, I, H and R are used to represent healthiness status. The time of transitions between the last four states are exponentially distributed with rates alpha, kappa and gamma respectively The rate of the transition between S and E has rate beta*infectious/N, where infectious keeps count on the total number of infected individuals, i.e. infectious/N is the probability that a random individual is infected.

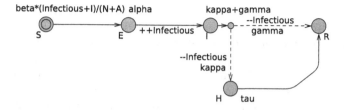

Fig. 5. Fluid SEIHR agent template P.

Instantiating the template 10,000 times we see in Fig. 4(b) the evolution of the number of individuals in the different states resulting from a single simulation over a period of 100 days. During the simulation we are tracking expressions such as `sum(i:id_t) P(i).S`. Here `P(i)` refer to the i'th instance of the template P, and `P(i).S` is a Boolean indicating whether `P(i)` is in state S. Summing over all instances i the overall expression `sum(i:id_t) P(i).S` provides the total number of individuals in state S. We see that the evolution matches that of the aggregated CTMC.

Now we select 30 individuals out of the total population of 10,000. In Fig. 4(c) we track the state of these selected 30 individuals during one simulation. In particular, we note a wide variation in the time of becoming exposed as well as in the length of time being in the various states. Out of the 30 randomly selected individuals one a single person becomes hospitalised. The time for the simulation for 10,000 individuals was 407.49 s (several orders of magnitude larger than the aggregated CTMC model).

2.4   Fluid Models

For agent-based models – as described in the previous section – simulations involve *all* individuals of the total population resulting in significant increase in simulation time. However, if the properties of interests only refer to a limited number of selected individuals it may be advantageous to apply the method of *fluid model checking*.

In [2] a potential use of fluid approximation techniques in the context of stochastic model checking has been investigated. Here the focus is on properties describing the behaviour of a single agent in a (large) population of agents, exploiting a limit result known also as fast simulation. In particular, the behaviour of the single agent is approximated with a time-inhomogeneous CTMC, which depends on the environment and on the other agents only through the solution of the ODE. This approach has been proven asymptotically correct in terms of satisfiability of logical properties including reachability probabilities. In our context the advantage of fluid model checking is that it allows us reduce simulation efforts while preserving the reachability probabilities (e.g. probability of getting exposed) of the few agents we are concerned with.

In Fig. 5 we revise the agent-based CTMC model from the previous section with the purpose of exploiting fluid model checking. For each of the 30 selected individuals, the template P will be instantiated. To model the behaviour of the remaining 9,970 individuals we will use the ODE model of Fig. 2 (with $N = 9,970$). Importantly, the template P of Fig. 5 describes a time-inhomogeneous CTMC as the rate of the transition of leaving S given by the expression beta *

(infectious+I)/(N+A) is time dependent. Here infectious is the number of individuals infected out of the 30 selected ones, and the I one of the five state-variables of the ODE describing the number of infected individuals out of the 9,970 large population. Finally, A respectively N is the number of selected individuals (30) respectively the amount of individuals of the ODE model (9,970). The time for a single simulation of the resulting fluid model is 0.164 s being several orders of magnitude faster than simulation of the corresponding agent-based model (407.49 s).

3   Covid-19 in Denmark

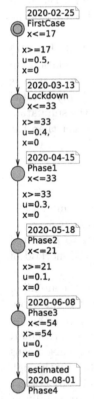

Fig. 6. Phases.

Covid-19 was first identified at December 2019 in Wuhan, China and from there quickly spread throughout the world. On February 27th the first case of Covid-19 was confirmed in Denmark.

On March 11th 2020 the Danish prime minister Mette Frederiksen announced a countrywide quarantine (lockdown) taking effect from March 13th. The order closed down all non-essential public services, including daycare, primary- and secondary schools, upper secondary schools and universities. All non-essential public sector staff were required to stay and work from home, the order urged the private sector to follow the same procedure. On March 16th a new order closely followed restricting public gatherings of more than 10 people, as well as closing down shopping centers and stores where people are in close proximity, including bars, restaurants, fitness centers, hairdressers, dentists and shopping centers.

The lockdown was kept into effect until April 15th when a gradual reopening of the country started. The reopening was planned and approved by politicians in collaboration with the government, assisted by modelling and expert input by SSI. The plan consisted of 4 phases gradually lifting the quarantine:

Phase 1: daycare and primary schools (1.-5 grade) as well as hairdressers, dentists.

Phase 2: starting May 18th, included the opening of shopping centers, bars and restaurants (with reduced opening hours), secondary schools, upper secondary schools, outdoor sports clubs, churches and professional sports and athletics.

Phase 3: staring from June 8th, included universities, public swimming pool, gyms, sports, tourist attractions, parties and larger gatherings of up to 500.

Phase 4: everything else including lifting the ban on public gatherings of more than 500 people. The phase is planned to start in August.

Figure 6 shows an extended timed automaton modelling the four phase of the gradual lifting of the quarantine. Here u is a floating point variable between 0 and 1 giving the degree of quarantine, i.e. 0 corresponds to the complete lifting of quarantine. Figure 7 is a slightly modified version of the ODE SEIHR model, taking into account the degree of quarantine at any given point in time.

In Figs. 8, 9 and 10 we compare the planned lifting of quarantine with a hypothetical plan, where quarantine is completely lifted after phase 1. The three Figures focus on different subsets of S, E, I, H and R. In the first two figures the values of H as well as u are so small that a scaling has been used. From Fig. 8 we see that the planned lifting of quarantine slowly brings R close to the level needed for herd immunity in Denmark at approximately 3,267,000 (at the time of writing this paper we are in the middle of Phase 3). In contrast the alternative plan of early reopening herd immunity would have been achieved already now.

○ Quantities

S' == -(1.0-u)*beta0*I*S/N   &&
E' == (1.0-u)*beta0*I*S/N - alpha*E &&
I' == alpha*E - (gamma+kappa)*I   &&
H' == kappa*I - tau*H   &&
R' == gamma*I + tau*H

Fig. 7. SEIHR model for Denmark with quarantine.

Figure 10 focuses on the number of hospitalised individuals. Here the predictions of the two models are compared to the actual Covid-19 hospitalised numbers as published by SST (Sundhedsstyrelsen)[4]. We see that the trajectory in Fig. 10(a) obtained from the ODE model under the planned quarantine phases is extremely close to the actual observed data. Most importantly we see that the maximum number of hospitalised individuals at any given point in time is less

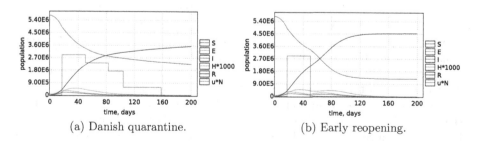

(a) Danish quarantine.   (b) Early reopening.

Fig. 8. SEIHR trajectories.

[4] https://www.sst.dk/da/corona/tal-og-overvaagning.

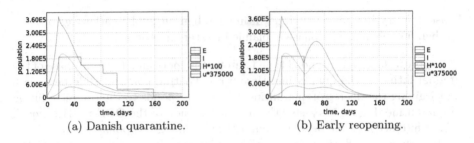

Fig. 9. EIH trajectories.

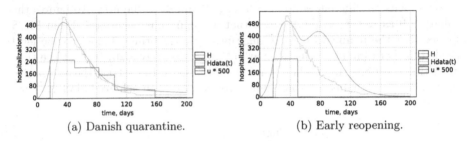

Fig. 10. Hospitalizations.

than 520, well below the capacity of Danish hospitals. In Fig. 10(b) we see that the early complete lifting of quarantine results in a small temporary increase in the number of hospitalisations.

4   Family Routines in Cities

In this section, we consider a scenario focusing on the healthiness of a family with three members, a mother, a father and a son, living in Copenhagen. Besides living in Copenhagen (613,288 inhabitants) the members of the family spend considerable time at work and at school and occasionally enjoy some leisure activity. More precisely, the mother works at Maersk (estimated 2,000 employees at Esplanaden), the father works at ITU (estimated 2,300 employees) and the son goes at Vesterbro Ny school (752 pupils). As for leisure, the father is fanatic about FCK (FC Copenhagen) and has season tickets for home matches at Parken (capacity of 38,000 spectators) twice a week. During weekend the mother and father enjoy a dinner at one of restaurants in Nyhavn (some 5,000 people may gather there). In this scenario the son enjoys no leisure activities.

Now the city of Copenhagen as well as the 5 locations relevant for this particular family, i.e. Parken, ITU, Maersk, Vesterbro Ny School and Nyhavn, will have their own SEIHR ODE-based model. Each location has a population-size as well as a specific transition-rate for flow between susceptible (S) and exposed (E) reflecting the differences in being exposed at various locations. Figure 11(a) is an instantiation of the ODE SEIHR model for Copenhagen, where KBH_N is

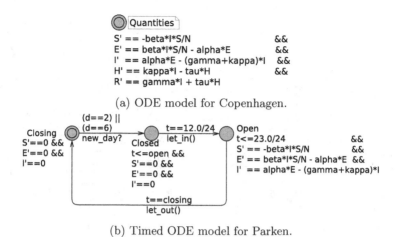

(a) ODE model for Copenhagen.

(b) Timed ODE model for Parken.

Fig. 11. SEIHR models for locations.

the number of inhabitants in Copenhagen and beta is an array with a distinct values for each location e.g. beta[kbh] is the exposure rate for Copenhagen.

The SEIHR model for Parken is essentially the product of an ODE SEIHR model with a timed automaton [1] indicating the opening hours of Parken. In Fig. 11(b) we see that on Tuesdays (d==2) and Saturdays (d==60) the opening hours are between 12:00–23:00. Only in the Open location, the ODE for Parken is activated. The function (not shown here) let_in() (let_out()) will "transfer" a number of spectators from (to) Copenhagen into (from) Parken upon opening (closing). The SEIHR models of the remaining four locations are similar to that of Parken taking the opening hours into account.

As for the three members of the family we will use two components: an agent-based model for recording the health status and a timed automaton describing the weekly itinerary reflecting work-hours and leisure activities. For example Fig. 12(a) is a timed automaton describing the whereabouts of the Father over a week. Here x is a clock used to determine the precise timing of the various location-visits. As such we see that he leaves Home at 7 o'clock in the morning and reaches ITU at 8 o'clock. At 16 o'clock he leaves either for Home in order to go to Nyhavn or to Parken. Figure 12(b, c) describes the itineraries for the mother and son. Figure 12(d) is the agent-based SEIHR model used to describe the health status of each family member. Here we note that the rate for leaving S is a composite expression essentially picking the index of the array beta corresponding to current location of the family member (given by the expression l[id], where l is an array holding the location of all three family members). Note here the final case, where the family member is at home (potentially the location with highest exposure), where the integer variable Home_I counts the number of family members being infected.

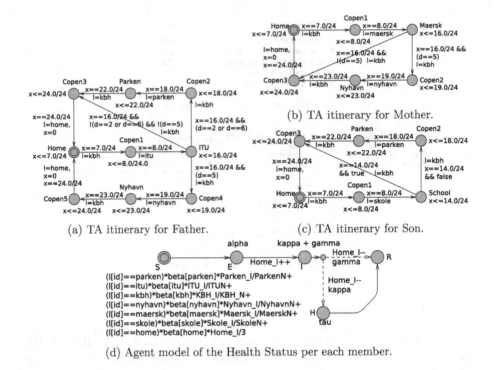

(a) TA itinerary for Father.   (b) TA itinerary for Mother.

(c) TA itinerary for Son.

(d) Agent model of the Health Status per each member.

Fig. 12. Models for family members.

In Fig. 13 we see the result of a single simulation of the SEIHR model Copenhagen. In Fig. 13(a) we notice that twice a week a significant part of the Copenhagen population goes to Parken. Also, in Fig. 13(b) we note that the number of hospitalized peaks on day 42 at approximately 125 people.

In Fig. 14 we estimate the probability for each family member that one becomes exposed during a duration of 300 days. For the father (similar for the mother) the returned 95% confidence intervals are 0.738 ± 0.025, whereas the confidence interval for the son is only slightly below being 0.731 ± 0.025. Note that in all cases the exposure happens within the first 100 days – after this the number of infections in the relevant locations becomes too low.

The very marginal difference between the exposure of the son and the parents may seem strange as the son in this scenario does not enjoy any leisure activities (where the beta has been set substantially higher than at work-places). However, the son meets his father and mother regularly and for a substantial amount of time at their home. Thus, we investigated an alternative scenario, where the son lives alone (still not enjoying leisure activities). The result becomes significantly different as shown in Fig. 14(c), where the estimated 95% confidence interval becomes 0.661 ± 0.025. Thus the lesson is: it is not enough that you yourself stay away from highly exposed places, you should avoid spending long time-periods with others having this behaviour.

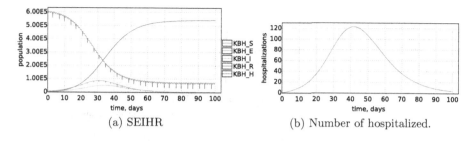

(a) SEIHR   (b) Number of hospitalized.

Fig. 13. Copenhagen.

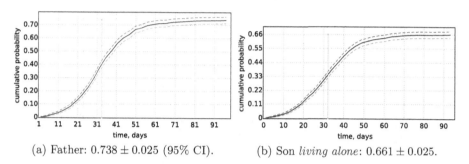

(a) Father: 0.738 ± 0.025 (95% CI).   (b) Son *living alone*: 0.661 ± 0.025.

Fig. 14. Probabilities of becoming exposed within 300 days.

5 Super-Spreading and Bars

In this section we consider a scenario of a super-spreader, being a single individual who is infected and has a personal extremely high rate for spreading the virus to other people at the same location. For locations, we consider five bars (say at Nyhavn in Copenhagen) each with a capacity of 300 persons (out of which 3 are assumed to be exposed already). For each bar we instantiate the aggregate CTMC model of Fig. 3(a). Thus a complete state will be captured by five arrays of counters S, E, I, H and R, e.g. E[2] will be the number of exposed people in bar number 2, Bar[2].

In this scenario the super-spreader walks between bars in a periodic manner. In fact, to demonstrate the damage of the super-spreader only Bar[1] and Bar [2] are visited. The periodic behaviour of the super-spreader is given as a timed automaton in Fig. 15(a), where we note that the period is 2 days. spread is a Boolean array where spread[i] is **true** when the super-spreader is in Bar[i]. In Fig. 15(b) we see the extra reaction rule added to Bar[i]. We see that the rule causes a susceptible person to be exposed with extremely high rate (beta=10) but only if the super-spreader is in Bar[i]. In Fig. 15(c) we see 10 simulations tracking the number exposed people in each of the five bars over a period of 100 days. Clearly, there are many more people being exposed in the bars visited by the super-spreader in comparison to the other bars. Also the exposure happens much faster in these bars with a peak around day 13 compared to day 40. In

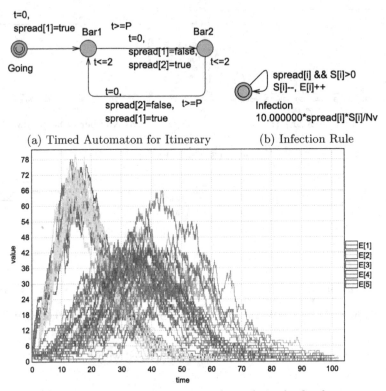

(a) Timed Automaton for Itinerary   (b) Infection Rule

(c) Evolution of number of exposed people in the five bars.

Fig. 15. Super-spreader

fact, the expected number of people becoming exposed in `Bar[1]` is 72.58 ± 1.38 compared to that of `Bar[5]` being 48.04 ± 2.43.

6   Tracing Covid-19

One strategy for limiting the spread of epidemic diseases is containment: isolate infected people and rapidly determine who they infected and also isolate them. This strategy works very well if:

1. we can discover initially infected people through testing, and
2. we can trace their interactions.

The smitte|stop smartphone application[5], mandated by the Danish government[6], has recently made such a trace-and-isolate strategy possible. The

---

[5] https://smittestop.dk/.

[6] https://sum.dk/Aktuelt/Nyheder/Coronavirus/2020/Maj/~/media/Filer%20-%20dokumenter/01-corona/App/Politisk-aftale-om-smittessporingsappen.pdf.

application is build atop frameworks of Apple and Google for their respective smartphone platforms.

After being installed smitte|stop periodically emits unique IDs to nearby phones running smitte|stop. It also stores IDs of phones it has received (been in close contact with) during a 15 min interval. These ID exchanges are sufficient for infected individuals running the smitte|stop app to notify people whom they have plausible infected.

Part of the strategy of the Danish government to stop a second wave relies on the smitte|stop app having a significant reduction in the number of new infections. However, the impact of such an app relies heavily on the adoption of the population. We thus demonstrate the use of UPPAAL to asses the impact of smitte|stop with varying adoption rates.

To model the effect of the smitte|stop application, we extend the agent based model presented in Sect. 2.3. However, to reduce the complexity, we make the following assumptions:

1. infected one who has been tested positive immediately warns other users using the app,
2. people who receive a warning are tested immediately,
3. test results are received after a fixed number of testDelay days, and
4. the interaction with disease transmission is accurately and specifically captured by smitte|stop.

We believe that assumptions 1–3 are quite realistic. However, we can see that assumption 4 is a crude simplification as it may fail to register when *a)* two users do not interact long enough, or *b)* two users each were infected by separate third parties but caught by the smitte|stop accidentally.

Nonetheless, we expect these effects to be minor. Furthermore, we restrict ourselves to a 1,000-agent simulation due to the required computational effort, as noted in Sect. 2.3

Each individual in our world is modelled by two different automata: one automaton (Health) models the health condition of each person while a second automaton (Test) models a persons behaviour in regards to testing policies.

Notice that the Health automaton (Fig. 16) is a modified version of Fig. 4: an extra location Q for quarantine has been added while the hospitalisation has been merged into the R location. We merged the hospitalisation into R as the number of hospitalisations is not interesting for this particular scenario. The extra Q location captures the (assumed) non-interaction of persons in quarantine – a health state reached via a synchronisation on the person-specific quarantine channel. During location changes Health also updates a shared variable s to reflect its new health status such that the behaviour of the Test template is modified accordingly.

Figure 17 shows the Test automaton. Initially a choice is made as to whether this person uses smitte|stop. Afterwards (in S) we wait for the Health automaton to signal it has been exposed. Upon exposure an existing infected individual is selected (at random) as the source of the exposure; if no-one is infected, the edge

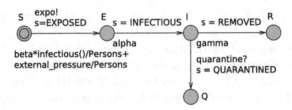

Fig. 16. Health of the smitte|stop model. The `external_pressure/Persons` models people might be exposed from outside (e.g. travels)

guarded by `no_infectious()` can be taken, in which case the source of infection is assumed to be external. Notice the increment of `frandom` and `fapp`: these are counters of how many infected are found using random testing and how many are found using the app.

In the location **E** a person can either be selected for random testing through synchronisation on `test`, or via a warning from smitte|stop, modelled via synchronisation on (`positive_c[who]?`). The automaton follows a similar pattern in both cases: we go to a location where it waits for a test result for `testDelay` days. If the test is positive (with probability weight `testInf()`) then the individual moves to isolation – if the individual is using smitte|stop, the person emits a warning via smitte|stop (`pos`, received on `positive_c[who]` when who matches the ID of the transmitting individual). If the test is negative (with probability weight `testNInf()`) then for the random testing path (red rectangle) the individual returns to **E** while the current protocol (blue rectangle) for a smitte|stop case mandates a second test after a two day waiting/incubation period[7].

Remark 2. We mentioned above that people could be selected for random testing by synchronisation on `test`, but did not mention who controls this channel. It is controlled by an additional automaton that continuously chooses a delay from an exponential distribution. After that delay it selects a person to be tested a uniformly. The exponential distribution has rate T which corresponds to the number of people tested each day.

To assess the potential effect of using smitte|stop, we estimated the number of people found using the app within 200 days, and the number of people found using random testing within 200 days for different adoption rates of smitte|stop, and for different levels of testing accuracy. As our model is fully stochastic each simulation used for estimation does not have the same number of infected.

Table 1 summarises the results of these simulations. Worth noting is:

1. The number of infected using smitte|stop (smitte|stop column) does increase with higher adoption rate of the app,
2. the `Random+smitte|stop` column indicates that we do find more infected in total with higher adoption rates,

---

7 https://smittestop.dk/spoergsmaal-og-svar.

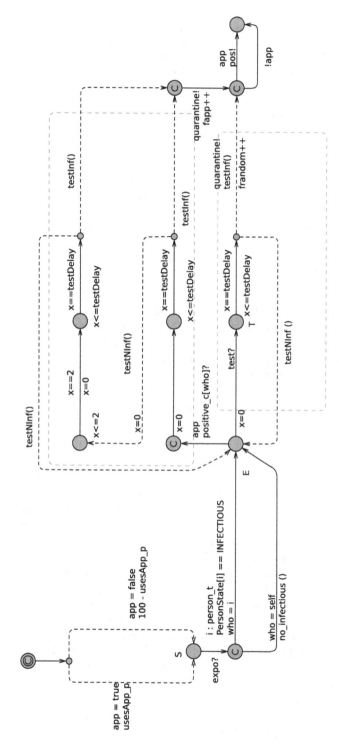

Fig. 17. Excerpt of Test of the smitte|stop model. The area in the blue rectangle is the smitte|stop testing procedure and the area red rectangle is the random test procedure. (Color figure online)

Table 1. Estimation Data for the smitte|stop model: `Persons` is total size of the population, `TestAcc` is the accuracy of the tests, `Tests/day` is the amount of people tested using random testing per day, %smitte|stop is the percentage of people using smitte|stop, `Random` is the number of infected found using random testing while smitte|stop is the amount found using the smitte|stop app. The `Random` and smitte|stop columns are estimated over 10000 runs.

Persons	TestAcc	Tests/day	%smitte|stop	Random	smitte|stop	Random+smitte|stop
1000	.25	2	.25	1.75	0.02	1.79
1000	.25	2	.50	1.75	0.07	1.82
1000	.25	2	.75	1.70	0.17	1.87
1000	.50	2	.25	3.35	0.05	3.40
1000	.50	2	.50	3.25	0.23	3.48
1000	.50	2	.75	3.22	0.59	3.81
1000	.75	2	.25	4.72	0.11	4.83
1000	.75	2	.50	4.69	0.49	5.18
1000	.75	2	.75	4.59	1.14	5.73

3. A superficial scan over Table 1 could easily lead to the conclusion that smitte|stop is not useful: with the highest adoption rate (highlighted in Table 1) it only finds 1.14 infected. However, one should consider that random testing finds only 4.59 infected, and random testing needs to find an infected individual before smitte|stop can alert people. Increasing test capacity should have a positive effect on both the number of infected found by random testing and the number of infected found using smitte|stop.

7   Conclusion

In this paper we have demonstrated how UPPAAL SMC may be used to model the ongoing Covid-19 epidemic in several ways. The span of models allows for a range of analyses to be made. This includes analysis at population level for crucial estimation of the sufficiency of hospital capacity. Also analyses at the level of individuals is possible using fluid models, where consequences of various social behavioural patterns may be predicted.

We are convinced that the graphical and rich modelling formalism of UPPAAL SMC has been crucial for the rapid speed by which these models have been constructed and analysed. As for the analyses the current efficiency of UPPAAL SMC has proven adequate with respect to the scenarios considered. However, we have a number of ideas for optimisations (e.g. precomputing the solutions to the ODE component of fluid models, sweeping of parameters, exploiting cluster computing facilities) that will be needed for scaling to more complex scenarios.

In the NNF project domain specific modelling-notations and ways of visualising results more suited for end-users (doctors, politicians, etc.) are being developed. We plan to support these notations.

One overall important aspect that we have not considered is the estimation of parameters and initial condition based on real observed measurements. In the sister NNF project a number of approaches for this has been examined.

References

1. Alur, R., Dill, D.L.: A theory of timed automata. Theor. Comput. Sci. **126**(2), 183–235 (1994)
2. Bortolussi, L., Hillston, J.: Fluid model checking. In: Koutny, M., Ulidowski, I. (eds.) CONCUR 2012. LNCS, vol. 7454, pp. 333–347. Springer, Heidelberg (2012). https://doi.org/10.1007/978-3-642-32940-1_24
3. David, A., Larsen, K.G., Legay, A., Mikučionis, M., Poulsen, D.B.: Uppaal SMC tutorial. Int. J. Softw. Tools Technol. Transf. **17**(4), 397–415 (2015)
4. Jensen, P.G., Jørgensen, K.Y., Larsen, K.G., Mikucionis, M., Muñiz, M., Poulsen, D.B.: Fluid models in uppaal for covid-19 - full models. https://github.com/DEIS-Tools/uppaal-models/tree/master/CaseStudies/Covid-19
5. Kermack, W.O., McKendrick, A.G.: Contributions to the mathematical theory of epidemics–I. Bull. Math. Biol. **53**(1), 33–55 (1991)
6. Kermack, W.O., McKendrick, A.G.: Contributions to the mathematical theory of epidemics-II. The problem endemicity. Bull. Math. Biol. **53**(1), 57–87 (1991)
7. Kermack, W.O., McKendrick, A.G.: Contributions to the mathematical theory of epidemics-III. Further studies of the problem of endemicity. Bull. Math. Biol. **53**(1), 89–118 (1991)
8. Peng, L., Yang, W., Zhang, D., Zhuge, C., Hong, L.: Epidemic analysis of covid-19 in China by dynamical modeling (2020)

Improving Secure and Robust Patient Service Delivery

Eduard Baranov[✉], Thomas Given-Wilson[✉], and Axel Legay[✉]

Université Catholique de Louvain, Ottignies-Louvain-la-Neuve, Belgium
{eduard.baranov,thomas.given-wilson,axel.legay}@uclouvain.be

Abstract. The Wablieft project explores how to improve medical service delivery through a shared marketplace for service providers. This shared marketplace allows patients to choose services from providers and so support improved service delivery and patient satisfaction. Having a shared marketplace raises some service reliability and correctness challenges, as well as creates opportunities for improved information gathering. This work formalises the shared marketplace to prove correct behaviour and properties of the marketplace behaviour. The information available to the shared marketplace is also used to improve predictions of medical scenarios such as pandemics, and thus improve service delivery.

1 Introduction

The Wablieft project considers how to improve the delivery of services to patients by using a shared marketplace [5]. Current service providers may be over- or under-utilised due to patients being assigned to a specific service provider by their hospital. By pooling the information on services and allowing patients to choose the service provider (and hence timing, locations, etc.) of the service that is best for them, the goal is to improve the utilisation and overall delivery of services. This pooling of information is done through a shared marketplace where service providers offer their services, and patients are able to choose the service and service provider that best matches them.

This shared marketplace is designed to benefit all parties involved, hospitals, patients, service providers (and others such as payment options, legislation, etc.). For hospitals they do not need to manage a single or multiple service providers directly and can instead use the marketplace to offer many services (and service providers). For patients this provides options to choose service providers according to patient preferences, e.g., more convenient location, better appointment times, etc. For service providers this allows many more potential patients to find services, and to more efficiently schedule services (ensuring more consistent utilisation). There are also advantages for other actors in the Wablieft project related to patient compliance, auditing, financial services, and legal protections, although these are not detailed in this work.

Having a shared marketplace raises some service reliability and correctness challenges, as well as creates opportunities for improved information gathering.

© Springer Nature Switzerland AG 2020
T. Margaria and B. Steffen (Eds.): ISoLA 2020, LNCS 12476, pp. 404–418, 2020.
https://doi.org/10.1007/978-3-030-61362-4_23

By using this new approach to service provisioning there are potential concerns with implementation.

One of the main challenges is to ensure that the shared marketplace behaves correctly and fairly toward all users. This requires some delicacy in how the different users can interact with the shared marketplace, and how to ensure this cannot be exploited. Also by having a shared marketplace system, the common behaviours to all users of the same class should be handled in a consistent manner, e.g., all service providers should have the same experience. There are also questions of accountability in a shared marketplace, where all the users may wish to have consistent, immutable, and reliable records of the usage of the system.

The information available to the shared marketplace is also potentially able to provide benefits to users of the system. The shared marketplace has a global view of how the market is behaving and can use this to improve outcomes for all parties. For example, consider when service provisioning may be interrupted by emergency service requirements (e.g., an operating theatre that was scheduled for one patient is required for an emergency). Then in the case of some larger occurrence like a pandemic, predicting the spread to other regions can improve service delivery by preventing too many services being offered and cancelled.

This work formalises the shared marketplace in Uppaal SMC [1] and uses statistical model checking [4,6,8] to analyse key behavioural properties. The models were made easily reconfigurable, thus allowing many experiments with differing input parameters (number of patients, services, kind of blockchain, kind of pandemic model etc.). To model the occurrence of a pandemic and predictive power of the shared marketplace, we used a simplified version of the model, optimised to improve performance while considering a large number of patients. The main contributions of this work are as follows.

- A formal model for a shared marketplace of the Wablieft project.
- Prove the correctness of the model of the Wablieft project.
- Demonstrate the predictive advantage of global knowledge from a shared marketplace as in the Wablieft project.

The structure of the paper is as follows. Section 2 recalls important background for understanding this paper. Section 3 overviews the Wablieft project and its goals. Section 4 presents the models of the Wablieft project. Section 5 experiments with how to improve service delivery in the face of a pandemic. Section 6 concludes and considers future work.

2   Background

This paper makes use of formal verification techniques. The key concepts are briefly introduced here for those unfamiliar with the field. In formal verification both the system and the requirements are represented via mathematical models and formulas on which (mathematical) operations are applied. The usage of a model allows for validation at design time, in particular early in the project life cycle. One common approach to verification is *Model Checking* (MC) (see [3] for a detailed survey) where the system is represented by a *Transition System* (TS) or graph where nodes represent states of the system and ordered edges between nodes represent transitions between those states. The execution of the system is represented by a sequence $n_0\ e_0\ n_1\ e_1\ n_2...$, where n_is are nodes and e_is are edges from n_i to n_{i+1}. Requirements are represented by temporal logic formulas [3]. For example, both linear and branching temporal logics (resp. LTL/CTL) are sufficient to represent requirements that make (temporal) hypothesis on a given set of executions. Such logics extend classical Boolean logics with temporal operators over sequences of states. As an example, the LTL formula "[]*a*" says that proposition "*a*" must be true in each state of each execution, while "<> *a*" says that for each execution there must be a state in the execution where "*a*" is true.

The advantages of MC are that 1. it can be deployed at all steps of conception time, and 2. it is exhaustive as it explores the entire behaviors of the system.

A wide range of works have focused on quantitative systems. Such systems are TS where transitions are equipped with quantitative values such as cost or probabilities. This allows us to express quantitative measures, e.g., duration of an execution or probability/cost of an action. In such cases, logics are themselves extended with quantitative operators, which allows us to pose quantitative questions like "what is the probability of termination", or "what is the probability that we avoid a deadlock", or "what is the timing cost of a specific execution".

Unfortunately, MC requires exploration of all executions and this is infeasible for large models. This problem is also known as the state-space explosion problem. To address this problem, an alternative approach was proposed based on algorithms from statistics. The core idea of *Statistical Model Checking* (SMC) [6–8] is to make many simulations of the model during which properties are monitored. Then, the statistical algorithm (e.g., Monte-Carlo) is used to decide the probability of the property to be satisfied with some degree of confidence. The level of confidence can be tuned with the number of simulations. Being based on simulation techniques, SMC is known to be less time and memory consuming than exhaustive methods. SMC is usually used to monitor bounded executions, therefore Bounded LTL/CTL logics are used - versions that can be decided on finite executions.

Uppaal SMC [1,4] is a statistical model checker using stochastic timed automata models [2]. The stochastic extension adds probabilistic choice between transitions and probability distributions for time delays. Uppaal SMC provides several queries for statistical model checking: "probability estimation" - probability of the property to be satisfied within the given timebound; "hypothesis testing" - comparing the probability of the property to be satisfied with a threshold; "probability comparison" of two properties. In addition Uppaal SMC supports evaluation of expected values of an expression.

3   The Wablieft Project

The motivation for the Wablieft project is to improve the delivery of healthcare services through a shared marketplace.

3.1   The Wablieft Marketplace

The Wablieft shared marketplace is designed to bring together various actors in the healthcare sector, including: hospitals, patients, and service providers amongst others. (Note this work will focus on the interactions between these three and the shared marketplace.)

A typical interaction of these actors without the shared marketplace in as follows. The patient visits a hospital and is prescribed to receive a treatment. The hospital then assigns a service provider to provide the treatment to the patient. The patient arranges an appointment for the treatment with the service provider. The patient receives the treatment at the appointed time from the (hospital) chosen service provider.

One main inefficiency in this approach is that the hospital chooses the service provider. In practice other service providers may also be able to provide the same service, often at a more convenient time or location for the patient. This is where the shared marketplace is designed to improve the service.

A typical interaction of the above actors with the shared marketplace is as follows. The patient visits a hospital and prescribed to receive a treatment. The hospital provides the patient with a voucher to use in the shared marketplace. The patient uses this voucher to arrange an appointment with the service provider they prefer (and receive a coupon for this appointment). The patient receives the treatment at the appointed time from their chosen service provider.

The flow of interactions with the shared marketplace is not significantly changed, except that now the patient can choose a service provider taking into account their preferences. The hospital can also benefit by no longer needing to have a priori knowledge of all service providers, or working with many service providers (or being limited by the service providers they have a prior relationship with). Similarly the service providers benefit by having a larger pool of patients they can offer services to, and also not requiring direct relationships with many hospitals.

3.2   Safe and Secure Behaviour

There are several aspects of service delivery where safety and security are highly desirable. Here these do not necessarily depend upon the use of a shared marketplace. However, since the goal of the Wablieft project is to gain the advantages of a shared marketplace, this is an opportunity to ensure desired behaviours are guaranteed by this new approach to service delivery.

One central requirement from all of the actors is a fair use of the shared marketplace. This manifests in several ways. One is that all actors are treated equally in their role (all patients are equal to each other, all service providers are

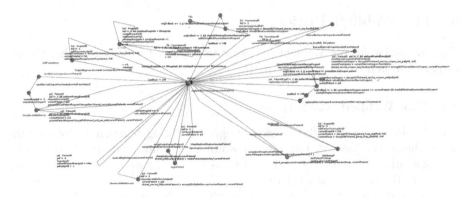

Fig. 1. Marketplace template for wablieft model.

equal to each other, all hospitals are equal to each other, etc.). In particular this means that no patient, service provider, or hospital is prioritised over another. Another is the capability to inspect and audit all sales done by the marketplace. This allows for all actors to examine the actions taken and ensure their actions are correctly recorded. This motivated the desire for an immutable record of the use of the shared marketplace.

There are also several properties related to how the marketplace supports coupons for patients to use services. The following are related to correct usage, and the inability for malicious usage of the marketplace.

- A coupon can be used only once. That is, a coupon can only be used to gain a service and never re-used.
- A revoked coupon cannot be used. Since a coupon may be lost or replaced, this coupon can be revoked. Once a coupon is revoked it cannot be used to gain a service.
- A forged coupon (i.e. not issued by the marketplace) cannot be used. This ensures that only coupons created by the shared marketplace can be used on the shared marketplace.

There are also privacy related properties, for example a patient cannot receive coupons issued to other patients. Similarly, service providers cannot see patients that are not using their service without a coupon, and hospitals only have knowledge about their own patients.

4 Modelling Wablieft

This section presents the models of the Wablieft project and the properties to ensure safe and secure operation of the market.

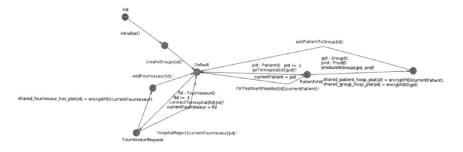

Fig. 2. Hospital template for wablieft model.

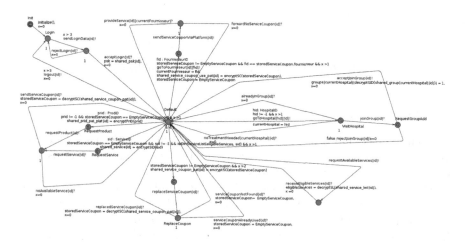

Fig. 3. Patient template for wablieft model.

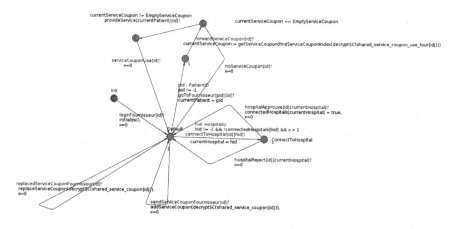

Fig. 4. Service Provider template for wablieft model.

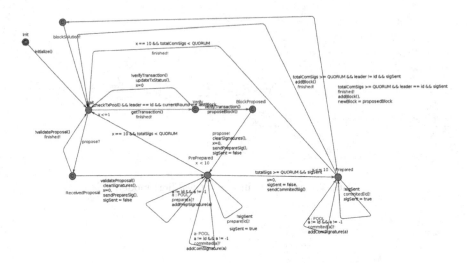

Fig. 5. Blockchain validator template for wablieft model.

4.1   The Wablieft Model

The marketplace and other actors have been modelled in Uppaal SMC. There are four templates for each of the actors: marketplace Fig. 1, hospitals Fig. 2, patients Fig. 3, and service providers Fig. 4.

The general workflow is as follows. The first step is when a patient goes to a hospital and if the patient needs treatment then the hospital adds information to the marketplace that the patient requires a particular medical service. Note that at this stage the patient must opt-in to using the shared marketplace and thus the addition of their information. The next step is when the patient goes to the shared marketplace and requests the prescribed medical service from any service provider of the patient's choice. The marketplace generates a coupon that is securely transferred to the patient which can be used at a service provider. As a additional option, a patient can request a coupon be reissued, e.g., in case of losing the coupon.

There are several mechanism included in the model that help ensure required safety and security properties. Patients and service providers are required to "login" to the marketplace and obtain a session key. This key allows encryption of all communication between the actors and the marketplace preventing other actors from reading this communication. In the model this is abstracted to simply adding the key to the message and assuming the possibility of decryption only in case of knowing the key.

In order to keep track of all coupon issuing and usage, we have a blockchain that stores all this information. The presence of a blockchain keeps the data immutable and has two uses. The first is allowing actors to check the origin of each coupon, in particular whether it was really issued by the shared marketplace and whether the coupon has already been used or revoked. The second is allowing a later audit of the shared marketplace ensuring the proper behaviour.

There are several architectural decisions that have to be made during the project. The modular nature of Uppaal SMC models allows us to check different options without the considerable effort for complete remodelling the entire system. As an example of such required decision is the type of blockchain used in the project. The default option considered by industrial partners is to use a private blockchain, i.e. only the shared marketplace can create blocks in the blockchain. Another approach is to use a "consortium" blockchain that requires an agreement from several trusted partners (e.g., hospitals and service providers) to add a block to the blockchain. By simply adding two templates with validators Fig. 5 and leader controller necessary for Istanbul Byzantine Fault Tolerance consensus algorithm, it is possible to evaluate both options and prove their correct function.

4.2   The Wablieft Properties

Due to the size of the model, full verification of the properties is not feasible. Therefore, we use statistical model checking that is available at Uppaal SMC SMC.

For the privacy properties we checked the probability that service coupon received by a patient (and decrypted) does indeed belong to this patient, in particular we check that it always holds that the patient can either have his ID or is empty.

$$Pr[<= 1000]([] \bigwedge_{p:Patient} (p.storedServiceCoupon.patient == p.id$$

$$|| p.storedServiceCoupon.patient == -1)) \quad (1)$$

For the properties related to coupon misuse, we added a malicious patient template that intentionally attempts to reuse of forge a coupon. In case of a success, the malicious patient goes into a successful state, and we can evaluate the probability of reaching such state.

For the evaluation of properties we use an instantiation with two hospitals, ten patients, and two service providers. The blockchain size is bounded by two hundred blocks and the simulation lasts until the blockchain is full. Each property requires approximately $21\,s$ to evaluate and the satisfaction probability is above 98% with 99% confidence.

5   Marketplace Prediction Capabilities

In this section we consider two evolutions of the shared marketplace and a pandemic scenario.

The first evolution of the Wablieft model is that services may have multiple contributing components. Each service may require one or more doctors, one or more nurses, specialised room, and some medical devices. For one example, an operation service may require an operating theater, an anesthesiologist, and two nurses. Another example is a dialysis service that requires only a nurse and a dialysis machine. Clearly if a service provider has only a limited number of nurses, this may prevent offering too many services. If they had only six nurses, then they could offer 3 operation services, or 6 dialysis services, but not both. Ideally the service provider would like to be able to offer the maximum of both, and then reduce as these services are purchased through the marketplace.

The second evolution of the Wablieft model is that emergency patients may appear, i.e. a patient who was not predicted to appear scheduled but requires immediate medical service. In practice service providers may be required to provide services for emergency patients who cannot wait to go through the marketplace (or any other waiting list) to be treated. This creates a potential conflict for the service provider who would like to offer the maximum number of services possible, but also have facilities available for emergency patients. Here this is considered as a trade-off where normal services may be cancelled if too many emergency patients appear, but only if the service provider does not have enough components (i.e. doctors, nurses, etc.). Of course service providers can somewhat predict emergencies and so do not sell all possible services assuming no emergency patients, as service cancellations are extremely poor outcomes for patients.

Normally, number of emergency cases are expected to have some stable pattern, e.g., n emergencies per day with slightly more on Friday and Saturday night.

Observe that the two evolutions above together add some interesting complexity to service delivery. In particular the ability to predict how many services can be offered to normal patients without causing too many cancellations. This is made more complex (and realistic) here by the reality that some medical services may require more equipment than others, and that with limited resources (e.g., doctors, nurses, etc.) there is motivation to maximise service delivery.

This section considers how to improve service delivery, but also the advantages that can be gained by having a shared marketplace. Here we consider how the shared marketplace can improve outcomes for patients by using better information to predict emergency patient patterns. In particular we consider the scenario of a pandemic, where emergencies can grow exponentially requiring more and more resources each day. Here a single service provider may notice the fast growth and adapt their scheduling, however during the first days of pandemic multiple services could be cancelled due to unexpected number of emergency cases.

In such a scenario the marketplace's global knowledge of the population's health can better evaluate current needs. A pandemic does not start everywhere simultaneously, some locations are affected later than others. The marketplace has a capability to detect the start of the pandemic in the first location and notify service providers in other locations to be prepared.

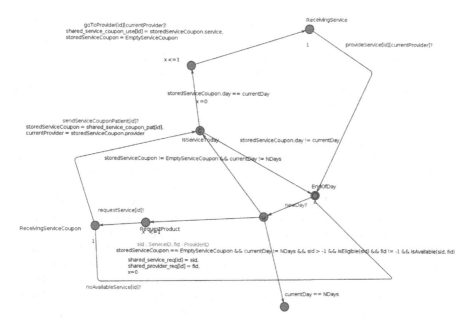

Fig. 6. Patient template for pandemic model.

To explore this scenario we developed a Uppaal SMC model focusing on three actors: a (shared) marketplace, several service providers, and many patients. Each day service providers select how much resources shall be kept for emergency cases and offer the remaining resources to be sold via the marketplace. Patients (as shown in Fig. 6) in turn can book services from the marketplace.

To focus on the predictive power of the service providers and the marketplace, the model is restricted to only selling services for the current or next day. This restriction is introduced in order to prevent the case when lots of services are already sold for several days in advance and so not allowing service providers to reserve more resources for emergency cases.

Each service provider encounters a number of emergencies during each day. This was originally modelled by a large pool of patients (who may require a normal service, or may have an emergency). However, this approach was too computationally expensive since to reasonably model both the normal services and emergency cases, a large pool of patients (with potential for these services) was required. To address this computational cost the model was simplified: each service provider model selects the number of emergencies (according to some function) and processes the emergencies at the beginning of each day. (This processing of emergencies first in effect preempts normal service delivery.) Note that while patients can book services from any service provider, emergency cases are considered to be cared for by the "nearest" service provider.

Number of patients, service providers, services and their requirements are parameters of the model. We have created a python script that is capable to modify these parameters of the model based on the desired configuration. There are two controlled sources of randomness in the model: the rates of service purchase and the rate of emergencies are parameters of the model. Both are selected with normal distribution where parameters define the mean value.

We consider several options for the service providers to predict the number of emergencies in the future.

1. Baseline - There is a fixed number of resources reserved for emergency cases. That is, each day the prediction is a fixed value.
2. Providers Separately - Each service provider makes predictions based on their local knowledge. Here the service providers can look at their history of emergency cases and attempt to predict future emergencies.
3. Total Emergencies - The shared marketplace makes prediction based on the total number of emergencies. Here the marketplace considers all the emergency cases across all service providers and uses this for prediction.
4. Worst Scenario Among Providers - The shared marketplace makes separate predictions based on data from each service provider then selects the worst scenario and this is propagated to all service providers. Here the marketplace finds the worst emergency numbers from any service provider uses this to predict a worst case scenario for all service providers.

The prediction function is identical in all cases except Baseline. The prediction function compares the growth of emergencies over the last 3 days and chooses among the constant, linear and exponential scenarios. The only difference between the options is the input data (source) given to the prediction function.

To evaluate the predictions we consider several outcomes.

1. Cancelled - This is the number of services that had to be cancelled due to emergency patients. The idea here is to measure how often patients must be turned away due to service providers over-selling their capabilities. This number also include undelivered emergency services in case of provider facilities overflow by emergency patients (although no special penalty is imposed here since emergency services are prioritised and this would overflow regardless of prediction).
2. Sold - This is the number of services sold through the marketplace. This is to balance against a naive approach that could only provide emergency services and so have almost no cancelled services, but also deliver very few services (i.e. only emergency services).
3. Delivered - This is the number of services that were successfully delivered. This measures *normal* services delivered, in practice this adjusts for the number of cancelled services except for cases when a service provider is overflown by emergency patients. Note that emergency services are not counted here since we are considering the shared marketplace delivery improvements.

The outcomes are evaluated with SMC engine of Uppaal SMC. Each service provider has counters of cancelled and delivered services, while the marketplace computes the sales. By running the simulation multiple times (100 in our experiments) Uppaal SMC can then report the expected values of outcomes.

5.1   Experiments

Our first experiment is a model of service providers that provide a simple set of services: a physician visit, several types of surgeries, a blood analysis and an x-ray scan. In total we have 5 medical professional types: physician, surgeon, anesthesiologist, radiographer, and nurse, also 4 types of equipment: x-ray, laser, pacemaker, and analysis laboratory. We consider an exponential emergency growth. We consider three service providers that are hit by the exponential growth not simultaneously but in consequent days. At the peak almost 80% of service provider resources would be required by emergency patients. Only one service is unaffected since it does not require professionals and tools involved into the emergency services. In order to reduce the computation complexity we simplified the model by replacing a single standard patient with 6, i.e. each patient would book and consume 6 units of resource instead of 1. This allows to gradually reduce the number of processes while, as we believe, having only minor effect on model applicability. In the experiment we considered 900 standard patients transformed into 150 processes after simplification.

Prediction	Cancelled	Delivered	Sold
Baseline	3677.4	7328.64	11006
Providers separately	22.92	7230.18	7253.1
Total emergencies	66.18	7077.78	7143.96
Worst scenario among providers	14.4	6096.36	6110.76

Fig. 7. Results for exponential scenario

We run 100 simulations of 20 days of marketplace work. The mean values for considered outcomes are shown in Fig. 7. The baseline is selling 80% of service provider resources resulting in 11006 bookings by patients. As expected, since emergency services require more than 20% of providers resources starting from day 8, the baseline has lots of overbookings resulted in high number of cancelled services. Using means for prediction, more resources are reserved for emergencies when the growth is detected and, even if the sales are lower, the number of cancelled services decreases immensely. Notice that despite the decrease in sales the number of delivered services is close to the baseline for 2 out of 3 prediction options. The best result in cancelled services is achieved when considering worst case scenario among providers. This is compensated by considerably lower level of sales due to high reservation of resources. The prediction based on counting total emergencies does not perform well in this experiment: large growth of emergencies for one provider is compensated by the stable situation of others. Simulation for each prediction option takes 15 min.

In order to see if the model can work in a more realistic scenario we take the number of COVID-19 cases per Belgian province for the period 01.03.2020-13.04.2020 reported by Belgian Institute of Public Health[1]. We assume that all

---

[1] https://epistat.wiv-isp.be/covid/.

patients used service providers of their municipality and we also assume that all patients added some load to the service providers. At each municipality we fixed the number of resources proportional to the population of the region such that the COVID-19 patients would add a significant resource consumption. In addition we added other patients that are trying to receive standard services. In this experiment we have 11 service providers, 2 standard services plus an emergency service, and 200 standard patients (as before each books and consumes 6 units of resource). Simulation for each prediction option takes about 2 h.

Prediction	Cancelled	Delivered	Sold
Baseline	645.53	49410.7	50027.44
Providers separately	307.35	47057.9	47336.12
Total emergencies	303.61	48465.9	48740.64
Worst scenario among providers	135.58	44429.1	44535.78

Fig. 8. Results for COVID-19 scenario

The results are shown in Fig. 8 and in Figs. 9 & 10.

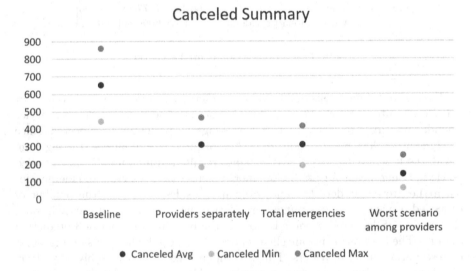

Fig. 9. Number of cancelled services or missed emergencies for COVID-19 scenario.

An overview of the cancelled results can be seen in Fig. 9. Clearly the number of cancelled medical services decreases with each choice of prediction. This is as expected, with the baseline having high cancelled numbers, localised and global knowledge marketplace prediction performing similarly (although the global

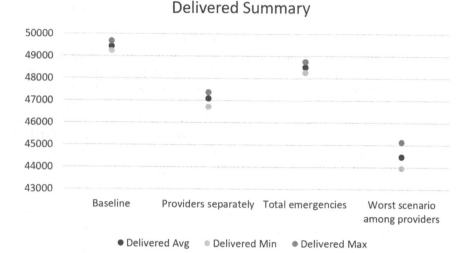

Fig. 10. Number of delivered services for COVID-19 scenario.

knowledge prediction has tighter bounds), and worst case scenario having the lowest number of cancelled services.

A graph of the delivered results can be seen in Fig. 10. As expected the baseline here performs the best. This is due to over-selling of services and then having a very high cancellation rate (as seen above). The prediction per service provider performs significantly worse than the global knowledge marketplace. This is most significant since they achieve approximately the same cancelled rate, and so the global prediction increases service delivery while also achieving a (very small) improvement in cancelled medical services. Finally, as expected the worse case scenario delivers the least medical services.

Overall these results show that using predictions can significantly reduce the number of cancelled services (more than 335 or 52% reduction for all prediction models). Also the global knowledge of the shared marketplace has a significant improvement on relative service delivery; reducing from the baseline by approximately 950 or <2%, compared with approximately 2350 or <5% less services delivered for local predictions. (That is, the global knowledge of the shared marketplace has an approximately 60% improvement in the reduction of delivered services.) The worst case scenario of course performs the worst in delivery, but was used here to indicate a (somewhat) reasonable bound for worst performance.

6 Conclusions

The Wablieft project proposes to use a shared marketplace to improve medical service delivery. The shared marketplace provides benefits for all actors; hospitals, patients, and service providers. By formalising this model in Uppaal SMC it is possible to prove that desirable properties about the shared marketplace can be proven. This in turn ensures that an implementation can meet these properties.

The shared marketplace also has access to greater information than individual service providers. We explore how this can be used to improve responses to events that span multiple service providers and impact their normal ability to offer and deliver services. Here we demonstrate the advantages of shared information from a shared marketplace by using this knowledge to improve prediction in a pandemic scenario. This is considered with two different models for the pandemic; simple exponential growth, and using real data from COVID-19 incidences in Belgium. Four different approaches to prediction are compared, demonstrating that the shared marketplace can improve both emergency and non-emergency service delivery.

Future Work. Future work on the Wablieft project will be to extend the Wablieft model with more actors to consider other entities such as financial and government services, and also blockchain-based records keeping. This will also require the development of more complex properties that address concerns related to GDPR regulations.

There are also opportunities to consider other ways that knowledge from the shared marketplace can be exploited to improve medical service delivery. Other kinds of larger scale responses or scenarios can be considered. Also the possibility to learn from patterns in one service provider or medical service, and apply the knowledge to other providers or medical services ina more fine-grained manner.

References

1. Uppaal. http://www.uppaal.org/
2. Alur, R., Dill, D.L.: A theory of timed automata. Theor. Comput. Sci. **126**(2), 183–235 (1994)
3. Baier, C., Katoen, J.P.: Principles of Model Checking (Representation and Mind Series). The MIT Press (2008)
4. David, A., Larsen, K.G., Legay, A., Mikučionis, M., Poulsen, D.B.: UPPAAL SMC tutorial. Int. J. Softw. Tools Technol. Transfer **17**(4), 397–415 (2015). https://doi.org/10.1007/s10009-014-0361-y
5. Given-Wilson, T., Baranov, E., Legay, A.: Building user trust of critical digital technologies. In: 2020 IEEE International Conference on Industrial Technology, ICIT 2020, Buenos Aires, Argentina, 26–28 February 2020, pp. 1199–1204. IEEE (2020). https://doi.org/10.1109/ICIT45562.2020.9067154
6. Hérault, T., Lassaigne, R., Magniette, F., Peyronnet, S.: Approximate probabilistic model checking. In: Steffen, B., Levi, G. (eds.) VMCAI 2004. LNCS, vol. 2937, pp. 73–84. Springer, Heidelberg (2004). https://doi.org/10.1007/978-3-540-24622-0_8
7. Legay, A., Delahaye, B., Bensalem, S.: Statistical model checking: an overview. In: Barringer, H., et al. (eds.) RV 2010. LNCS, vol. 6418, pp. 122–135. Springer, Heidelberg (2010). https://doi.org/10.1007/978-3-642-16612-9_11
8. Sen, K., Viswanathan, M., Agha, G.: On statistical model checking of stochastic systems. In: Etessami, K., Rajamani, S.K. (eds.) CAV 2005. LNCS, vol. 3576, pp. 266–280. Springer, Heidelberg (2005). https://doi.org/10.1007/11513988_26

Verification and Validation
of Concurrent and Distributed Systems

Verification and Validation of Concurrent and Distributed Systems (Track Summary)

Marieke Huisman[1]([✉]) and Cristina Seceleanu[2]

[1] University of Twente, Enschede, The Netherlands
m.huisman@utwente.nl
[2] Mälardalen University, Västerås, Sweden

Abstract. Usually, greater concurrency is the goal of any distributed system, yet distribution also introduces issues of consistency and separate failure domains. With the increase of device connectivity and virtualization techniques, developing correct and reliable concurrent and distributed systems characterized by high performance is notoriously difficult. This requires novel verification techniques, or extensions, adaptations and improvements of existing ones, to address emergent problems. The track on Verification and Validation of Concurrent and Distributed Systems aims to discuss key challenges that need to be tackled in order to enable the efficient and scalable assurance of modern concurrent and distributed systems, as well as present methods and tools that bear the promise to achieve the latter.

1 Motivation and Goals

Concurrent and distributed systems are becoming omnipresent for two reasons. First of all, concurrency and distribution are necessary to fulfill performance requirements of modern software. Second, such systems' paradigms are a natural fit with most underlying application domains. However, concurrent and distributed systems add a lot of extra complexity to systems, and allow many different kinds of errors to occur, which cannot happen in sequential software. As Leslie Lamport, known for his seminal work in distributed systems, famously said: "A distributed system is one in which the failure of a computer you did not even know existed can render your own computer unusable" [13]. Similarly, for concurrent systems, an error might occur in one execution, and then disappear in the next execution of the system.

Nevertheless, over the last years, we see a plethora of different tools and techniques to reason about distributed systems [7,12,17] and concurrent software [3,5,8,10,14,16] being developed and applied under different specific scenarios.

The next step is then to think about how to develop verification techniques for systems that combine distributed and concurrent aspects. One can refine

© Springer Nature Switzerland AG 2020
T. Margaria and B. Steffen (Eds.): ISoLA 2020, LNCS 12476, pp. 421–425, 2020.
https://doi.org/10.1007/978-3-030-61362-4_24

this ambition by asking: How can verification techniques for concurrent systems benefit from verification techniques for distributed systems, and vice versa?

The **Verification and Validation of Concurrent and Distributed Systems** (VVCDS) track focuses on providing answers to these questions, by presenting invited papers that propose models, techniques, and tools for the rigorous analysis of various concurrent and distributed systems. The included contributions give a good overview of the current state-of-the-art in the verification of concurrent and distributed systems, and propose solutions to difficult problems related to modern topics such as cloud-native microservice architectures, blockchain synchronization, or validation and dynamic monitoring of multi-threaded programs, but also to long-standing issues such as ensuring quality and correctness of distributed protocols used in industry, taming the complexity of distributed systems design via incremental development, or applying academic tools for verifying distributed systems in an industrial context. The track closes with a discussion to look further ahead: given the current-state-of-the-art, how can we combine verification and validation techniques for concurrency and distribution such that not only the systems' specific issues are tackled, but also the scalability and applicability in industry of the proposed approaches are achieved. For this, we would like to understand similarities and differences between concurrent yet not distributed, and truly distributed systems, and their respective techniques of verification and validation, in an attempt to leverage the key strengths of such approaches and reduce their potential weaknesses.

Finally, we would like to express our deep gratitude to the ISoLA organisers, in particular Prof. Tiziana Margaria and Prof. Bernhard Steffen, for working so hard to provide such a wonderful platform for our and other tracks, enabling lively and creative interaction between individuals and communities, helping us all to not forget the bigger picture of working for the development of systems that people can rely on.

2   Overview of Contributions

In *Step-wise Development of Provably Correct Actor Systems* [1], the authors Bernhard K. Aichernig and Benedikt Maderbacher present an approach for the incremental formal development of actor systems via refinement, in the Event-B tool. The assumption is that distributed software modeled using the actor-based paradigm benefits from the latter's simple asynchronous message passing for interprocess communication, and does not suffer from the common pitfall of shared mutable state. The technique is shown on Agha's classical factorial algorithm, which has been proven correct via a series of refinement steps, starting from an abstract description. The authors have also proven deadlock-freeness and convergence from which the termination of a single computation follows. The paper shows that the key to handling complexity is to keep the actor model simple enough yet as faithful to reality as possible, such that all proofs can be resolved automatically.

In *Violation Witnesses and Result Validation for Multi-Threaded Programs* [2], the authors Dirk Beyer and Karlheinz Friedberger present how the standard format for violation witnesses for program analysis tools is extended to multi-threaded programs. It discusses what information about threading needs to be captured in the witness. It turns out that the main information that is needed is the thread identifier that executes an instruction, whereas other information about monitors etc. does not have to be kept. The paper also presents a validation tool that can be used to confirm detected violations. An extensive experimental evaluation is done, which confirms that for larger problems validation time is faster than the original verification time.

In *Tendermint Blockchain Synchronization: Formal Specification and Model Checking* [4], the authors Sean Braithwaite, Ethan Buchman, Igor Konnov, Zarko Milosevic, Ilina Stoilkovska, Josef Widder, and Anca Zamfir present a formal specification of the blockchain synchronization protocol of Tendermint, called Fastsync. The protocol is firstly specified in English language, after which it is decomposed and abstracted in TLA+. Various safety and liveness properties are encoded in the property language of checkers TLC and Apalache, and the resulting specifications are model checked. The generated counter-examples have led to better understanding of different issues of both the specification and implementation of Fastsync. The authors discuss also the lessons learned, including the scalability issues that has forced them to resort to bounded model checking with Apalache, in order to account for faulty peers too.

In *Safe Sessions of Channel Actions in Clojure: A Tour of the Discourje Project* [6], the authors Ruben Hamers and Sung-Shik Jongmans give an overview of the Discourje project. Discourje supports dynamic monitoring of concurrent Clojure programs. The monitored properties describe the expected system behavior at an abstract level, and the monitor implementation then checks whether the implementation behaves as specified. The system is illustrated by three different examples, each illustrating different aspects of the specifications and implementations. It also discusses how the monitor is added into the implementation. The paper completes with a short summary of the Discourje formalization.

In *Modular Verification of Liveness Properties of the I/O Behavior of Imperative Programs* [9], the author Bart Jacobs describes a modular verification technique to reason about I/O behaviour of programs. The verification technique allows to verify properties such as eventually something will happen, response and reactive properties, and persistence properties (something will eventually become true forever). The paper first illustrates typical specifications for all these patterns. It then formalizes the verification technique, and discusses how verification proceeds for some of the examples discussed earlier.

In *Formal Verification of an Industrial Distributed Algorithm: an Experience Report* [11], the authors Nikolai Kosmatov, Delphine Longuet and Romain Soulat report on experiences with modeling and verification of some consensus algorithms. Their paper explains that even though the literature contains many verified consensus algorithms, in industrial practice slight variations are often needed, so we need techniques to reason about those easily. The paper sketches a consensus algorithm that is used at Thales on a distributed internet-of-things system. The algorithm is modeled in two different ways: fully explicitly and in the form of an abstract model, where a single node is modeled, interacting with a model that represents the rest of the network. The authors experiment with 3 different tools (SafeProver, CBMC and KLEE) to analyze the model, and they discuss the lessons learned from these experiments. In particular, the experiments show that it is indeed possible to use formal analysis tools in an industrial setting, but more work is needed to turn this into daily industrial practice.

In *Deploying TESTAR to enable remote testing in an industrial CI pipeline: a case-based evaluation* [15], the authors Fernando Pastor Ricós, Pekka Aho, Tanja Vos, Ismael Torres Boigues, Ernesto Calás Blasco, and Héctor Martínez Martínez describe the application of an academic tool for testing, called TESTAR, on a commercially-available distributed system. The technical challenges of a distributed software system, which the tool has not been initially designed for, are described, as well as how these gaps have been bridged. The paper also highlights the differences between industry and academia, in approaching problems and their corresponding classification, respectively.

In *A Formal Model of the Kubernetes Container Framework* [18], the authors Gianluca Turin, Andrea Borgarelli, Simone Donetti, Einar Broch Johnsen, S. Lizeth Tapia Tarifa, and Ferruccio Damiani develop a formal model of resource consumption and scaling for Kubernetes containerized micro-services. The framework, encoded in Real-time ABS, is intended to provide a platform in which various configurations can be assessed before the actual deployment. The authors validate the model by comparing an instance of the framework, under several scenarios, to observations of a real system running on a high-performance application cluster called HPC4AI. The work paves the way towards the model-based development of native-cloud solutions based on Kubernetes.

References

1. Aichernig, B.K., Maderbacher, B.: Step-wise development of provably correct actor systems. In: Margaria, T., Steffen, B. (eds.) ISoLA 2020. LNCS, vol. 12476, pp. 426–448. Springer, Cham (2020)
2. Beyer, D., Friedberger, K.: Violation witness and result validation for multi-threaded programs. Implementation and evaluation with CPAchecker. In: Margaria, T., Steffen, B. (eds.) ISoLA 2020. LNCS, vol. 12476, pp. 449–470. Springer, Cham (2020)
3. Blom, S., Darabi, S., Huisman, M., Oortwijn, W.: The VerCors tool set: verification of parallel and concurrent software. In: Polikarpova, N., Schneider, S. (eds.) IFM 2017. LNCS, vol. 10510, pp. 102–110. Springer, Cham (2017). https://doi.org/10.1007/978-3-319-66845-1_7
4. Braithwaite, S., et al.: Tendermint blockchain synchronization: formal specification and model checking. In: Margaria, T., Steffen, B. (eds.) ISoLA 2020. LNCS, vol. 12476, pp. 471–488. Springer, Cham (2020)
5. da Rocha Pinto, P., Dinsdale-Young, T., Gardner, P.: TaDA: a logic for time and data abstraction. In: Jones, R. (ed.) ECOOP 2014. LNCS, vol. 8586, pp. 207–231. Springer, Heidelberg (2014). https://doi.org/10.1007/978-3-662-44202-9_9

6. Hamers, R., Jongmans, S.-S.: Safe sessions of channel actions in clojure: a tour of the discourje project. In: Margaria, T., Steffen, B. (eds.) ISoLA 2020. LNCS, vol. 12476, pp. 489–508. Springer, Cham (2020)

7. Hawblitzel, C., et al.: IronFleet: proving practical distributed systems correct. In: Proceedings of the 25th Symposium on Operating Systems Principles, SOSP 2015, pp. 1–17. ACM (2015)

8. Jacobs, B., Smans, J., Philippaerts, P., Vogels, F., Penninckx, W., Piessens, F.: VeriFast: a powerful, sound, predictable, fast verifier for C and Java. In: Bobaru, M., Havelund, K., Holzmann, G.J., Joshi, R. (eds.) NFM 2011. LNCS, vol. 6617, pp. 41–55. Springer, Heidelberg (2011). https://doi.org/10.1007/978-3-642-20398-5_4

9. Jacobs, B.: Modular verification of liveness properties of the I/O behavior of imperative programs. In: Margaria, T., Steffen, B. (eds.) ISoLA 2020. LNCS, vol. 12476, pp. 509–524. Springer, Cham (2020)

10. Jung, R., et al.: Iris: monoids and invariants as an orthogonal basis for concurrent reasoning. In: POPL, pp. 637–650. ACM (2015)

11. Kosmatov, N., Longuet, D., Soulat, R.: Formal verification of an industrial distributed algorithm: an experience report. In: Margaria, T., Steffen, B. (eds.) ISoLA 2020. LNCS, vol. 12476, pp. 525–542. Springer, Cham (2020)

12. Krogh-Jespersen, M., Timany, A., Ohlenbusch, M.E., Gregersen, S.O., Birkedal, L.: Aneris: a mechanised logic for modular reasoning about distributed systems. In: Muller, P., et al. (eds.) ESOP 2020. LNCS, vol. 12075, pp. 336–365. Springer, Cham (2020). https://doi.org/10.1007/978-3-030-44914-8_13

13. Lamport, L.: Distribution, May 1987. Email message sent to a DEC SRC bulletin board at 12:23:29 PDT on 28 May 87

14. Müller, P., Schwerhoff, M., Summers, A.J.: Viper: a verification infrastructure for permission-based reasoning. In: Jobstmann, B., Leino, K.R.M. (eds.) VMCAI 2016. LNCS, vol. 9583, pp. 41–62. Springer, Heidelberg (2016). https://doi.org/10.1007/978-3-662-49122-5_2

15. Ricós, F.P., Aho, P., Vos, T., Boigues, I.T., Blasco, E.C., Martínez, H.M.: Deploying TESTAR to enable remote testing in an industrial CI pipeline: a case-based evaluation. In: Margaria, T., Steffen, B. (eds.) ISoLA 2020. LNCS, vol. 12476, pp. 543–557. Springer, Cham (2020)

16. Sergey, I., Nanevski, A., Banerjee, A.: Specifying and verifying concurrent algorithms with histories and subjectivity. In: Vitek, J. (ed.) ESOP 2015. LNCS, vol. 9032, pp. 333–358. Springer, Heidelberg (2015). https://doi.org/10.1007/978-3-662-46669-8_14

17. Sergey, I., Wilcox, J.R., Tatlock, Z.: Programming and proving with distributed protocols. In: Proceedings of PACMPL2(POPL), vol. 2, pp. 28:1–28:30. ACM (2018)

18. Turin, G., Borgarelli, A., Donetti, S., Johnsen, E.B., Tarifa, S.L.T., Damiani, F.: A formal model of the kubernetes container framework. In: Margaria, T., Steffen, B. (eds.) ISoLA 2020. LNCS, vol. 12476, pp. 558–577. Springer, Cham (2020)

Step-Wise Development of Provably Correct Actor Systems

Bernhard K. Aichernig$^{(\boxtimes)}$ and Benedikt Maderbacher$^{(\boxtimes)}$

Graz University of Technology, Graz, Austria
aichernig@ist.tugraz.at, benedikt.maderbacher@iaik.tugraz.at

Abstract. Concurrent and distributed software is widespread, but is inherently complex. The Actor model avoids the common pitfall of shared mutable state and interprocess communication is done via asynchronous message passing. Actors are used in Erlang, the Akka framework, and many others. In this paper we discuss the formal development of actor systems via refinement. We start with an abstract specification and introduce details until the final model can be translated into an actor program. In each refinement, we show that the abstract properties are still preserved. Agha's classical factorial algorithm serves as a demonstrating example. To the best of our knowledge we are the first who formally prove that his actor system computes factorials. We use Event-B as a modelling language together with interactive theorem proving and SMT solving for verification.

Keywords: Actors · Refinement · Proof-based development · Formal method · Event-B · Verification

1 Introduction

Modern computer systems rely heavily on concurrent and distributed software. Classic techniques using shared mutable state and explicit synchronization mechanisms are not ideal for these tasks. Instead, many systems are written using techniques that are designed to handle the challenges inherent to concurrent programs. A model that is widely used in this area are actor systems [19]. They are based on asynchronous communication via message passing. Each actor has its own memory and state that is isolated from the rest of the world. All interaction is done by sending messages between actors. This concept has been implemented in various programming languages such as Erlang [5,6] as well as in frameworks for other languages such as Akka [21] for Scala [27] and Java [7]. Many well-known distributed systems use various actor implementations in their backend. This includes network infrastructure by Cisco [9] and Ericsson's telecommunication systems [18]. The messenger WhatsApp uses Erlang on its servers [24,31]. Other usages of actors include various online games, for example LeagueOfLegends [11]. Actor systems can also be used to describe other distributed systems such as IoT devices.

© Springer Nature Switzerland AG 2020
T. Margaria and B. Steffen (Eds.): ISoLA 2020, LNCS 12476, pp. 426–448, 2020.
https://doi.org/10.1007/978-3-030-61362-4_25

Actor systems by design help to prevent many common bugs in concurrent programming, such as data races and many forms of deadlocks, but they do not guarantee that the software is correct. There are still many possibilities to introduce errors in software written with actors. The usage of such systems in critical areas such as communication systems makes them an attractive target for formal methods. Formal methods use mathematics and logic to model and analyse hardware and software. They aim to find errors or certify the conformance to a specification. This techniques help to create software with fewer errors. Large companies, such as Amazon [26] and Microsoft [8], use formal methods to improve the quality of their software. In this paper we will explore how the formal method Event-B [1] can be used to verify actor systems. Here, we will focus on one classical example, further examples can be found in Maderbacher's master thesis [23].

Actor Systems. The main component of the actor systems concurrency model are so called actors. These are similar to processes or threads but they cannot access any shared memory. Each actor can have its own local memory. Actors communicate by sending messages. An actor who receives a message can do three kinds of actions: (1) it can send messages to other actors, (2) create new actors, or (3) change its own state or behaviour. A behaviour defines how an actor reacts to messages. While an actor performs computations triggered by one message, no other message can interrupt it. This allows actors to avoid the classic data race problem [10, 28].

Event-B. Event-B is a modelling language and formal method based on set theory. One writes a model that captures the important behaviours of a system, instead of directly verifying a computer program. An Event-B model contains machines and contexts. A machine has a set of variables that define the state and guarded events that can change this state. An initial event defines the initial values of the variables. Contexts contain the static definitions of a model, including carrier sets, constants, and axioms. The models represent a discrete transition system: the initial state is defined via the initial event. The transitions are formed by enabled events with their guard expression evaluating to true in the current state. If more than one guard is enabled, the choice is non-deterministic. If no guard is enabled the system terminates or deadlocks depending on the interpretation. A model is developed by using step-wise refinement. At each step a new machine is created that is a refinement of the previous one. It is a more concrete version that contains more details and is closer to the modelled system. For each step a formal proof is required to demonstrate that this refinement relation holds. The Rodin Platform [2], an Event-B IDE based on Eclipse, supports the development and refinement of models with automatic generation and partial discharging of mathematical proof obligations.

Next, we introduce our demonstrating example in Sect. 2. Then, in Sect. 3 we discuss the modelling of actors in Event-B. Section 4 presents our formal development starting from the mathematical definition of the problem and ending in a correct actor system. Next, in Sect. 5 we briefly discuss a truly concurrent

Listing 1. Factorial with Scala's actor library Akka Typed.

```
1  final case class Request(value: Int, replyTo: ActorRef[Result])
2  final case class Result(value: Int)
3
4  val fact: Behavior[Request] = Behaviors.receive { (c, m) =>
5    m.value match {
6      case 0 => m.replyTo ! Result(1)
7      case n =>
8        val cont = c.spawnAnonymous(cont(m.value, m.replyTo))
9        c.self ! Request(m.value - 1, cont)
10   }
11   Behaviors.same }
12
13 def cont(i:Int, cust:ActorRef[Result]): Behavior[Result] =
14   Behaviors.receive { (c, m) =>
15     cust ! Result(i * m.value)
16     Behaviors.same }
```

extension of the previous actor system. Section 6 surveys related work. Finally, in Sect. 7 we discuss the results and draw our conclusions.

2 Demonstrating Example

As a demonstrating example we will develop Agha's classical factorial algorithm with actors [3]. The algorithm works recursively, but the computation is not solely done by one function. Instead, it works by creating continuations for each step. Each of these continuations is represented as its own actor. Additionally, there is one actor called *fact* that receives requests by customers, to calculate the factorial for a certain number. In response to these requests, it starts the continuation actors to do the actual work.

An implementation of this algorithm, using Scala [27] and Akka Typed [22], can be seen in Listing 1. The program contains two types of behaviours, *fact* and *cont*. There exists exactly one actor with the behaviour *fact*, therefore we will also refer to it as *fact*. It receives as a request the value that shall be processed and the address of the recipient of the result. If the number is 0, it will immediately send the result 1 to the recipient, otherwise it creates a new actor with the *cont* behaviour. This new actor keeps as state the value and the recipient of the request. After the new actor is created, *fact* sends itself an updated request, containing the decremented value and the newly created continuation as recipient. The *cont* actors await the result of the factorial of the number below the one stored by them. Once this is received, it is multiplied by the stored number and the result is sent to the stored recipient.

Figure 1 shows a sequence diagram computing the factorial of 3. At first, only the actor *Factorial* exists. It receives a request with the number 3 and the recipient address c. As a result the continuation actor m is created with the state 3 and c. The actor *Factorial* also sends itself the new request message containing 2 and the address of m. This is repeated two more times and the actors m' and m'' are created. When *Factorial* receives the request with the value 0, it responds to the newest actor m'' with the result 1. This triggers a chain of result messages. The actor m'' computes the value 1 and sends it to m'. This continues till m sends the final result 6 to the customer who sent the original request.

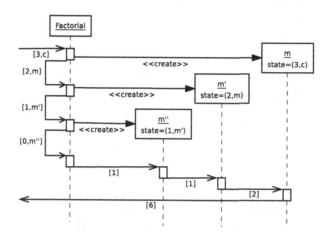

Fig. 1. Sequence diagram computing the factorial of 3 with actors.

Computing the factorial function in this way is not more efficient than using a sequential program. It might even consume more memory because the number of actors is linear in the size of the problem. One possible advantage of this program is that it can distribute the computation of multiple calls to factorial over multiple processors, instead of doing them one after another. In this case the factorial actor receives not only a single request, but multiple requests over time. The created continuation actors are distributed and can do all computations independently. The general pattern of using actors to represent continuation can also be used for more complicated computations. Thus, the techniques used to verify this case study, might be applied to other more complex distributed applications.

3   Modelling Actor Systems

To model actor systems in Event-B [1], it is necessary to define when a model represents an actor system. This requires us to assign Event-B constructs to all components of an actor system, we want to study. The two most important of these components are actors and messages.

Actors have unique identifiers. Hence, we define an Event-B context with a carrier set $ACTOR\_ID$. It contains identifiers for dynamically created actors, represented as natural numbers, and two special identifiers. The first one is *final_id* for the customer (main) actor who is outside the modelled system and who, in our example, should receive the final result. To simplify computations, it is represented by the number -1. In addition, we use *invalid_id* if a variable of type $ACTOR\_ID$ is not used at some point in time. These identifiers are formally defined as Event-B constants with the following axioms:

axm_0: $ACTOR\_ID = \mathbb{N} \cup \{-1, invalid\_id\}$
axm_1: $final\_id = -1$
axm_2: $invalid\_id \notin \mathbb{N}$
axm_3: $final\_id \neq invalid\_id$

To represent the actors, multiple new variables are introduced into an Event-B machine: *num_actors* stores the number of existing actors and *actor_id* is a set that stores all actor identifiers which are currently in use. These variables are defined by these invariants:

inv_1: $num\_actors \in \mathbb{N}$
inv_2: $actor\_id = 0 \mathinner{\ldotp\ldotp} (num\_actors - 1)$

Meaning that exactly the actor identifiers from 0 to $num\_actors - 1$ are valid and a newly created actor will get the next larger number as its identifier.

Actors may have a state. For example, the continuation actors in our example store their value and the target actor who will receive their response. Both of these state variables are represented as functions from *actor_id* to their respective types:

inv_3: $cont\_actors\_target \in actor\_id \rightarrow (actor\_id \cup \{final\_id\})$
inv_4: $cont\_actors\_value \in actor\_id \rightarrow \mathbb{N}_1$

Actors communicate asynchronously via message queues. Hence, the most general model would map actor ids to sequences (arrays) of messages. However, we may postulate assumptions in order to simplify the model and consequently verification. For example, for proving that the actor model computes the recursive definition of a factorial function, we may (initially) assume a slow environment, where a new request is only issued after a response has been received. With such a synchronized behaviour, at most one message at a time can exists in our factorial actor system. Hence, it is sufficient to use a single set of variables for all components of messages. The Boolean variable *msg_exists* stores if an unprocessed message exists. The variables *msg_content* and *msg_recipient* store the values of a message. If no message exists, the value of *msg_recipient* will be *invalid_id*. The variable *active_actor* stores the actor which receives the current message if a message exists. Otherwise, it is the identifier of the last actor that was created. We give the formal definition of these variables:

inv_5: $msg\_exists \in BOOL$
inv_6: $msg\_recipient \in actor\_id \cup \{final\_id, invalid\_id\}$
inv_7: $msg\_content \in \mathbb{N}_1$
inv_8: $msg\_exists = FALSE \Leftrightarrow msg\_recipient = invalid\_id$
inv_9: $active\_actor = num\_actors - 1$

Note, that we prefer to decompose a message into separate variables over defining a composite message type. Naturally, one would describe a message as a tuple of its fields, e.g., the pair $msg \in (actor\_id \cup \{final\_id, invalid\_id\}) \times \mathbb{N}_1$. The reason for our flat encoding is that the provers tend to have less difficulties with basic data types.

In contrast, in a fully concurrent model, we need to keep track of individual computation requests via a $REQUEST\_ID$. Hence, we model the message queues of the continuation actors as follows[1]:

invC_1: $cont\_mail\_msg\_content \in (ACTOR\_ID \times REQUEST\_ID) \nrightarrow \mathbb{N}_1$

This is the most general model, where each actor has a set of messages to be processed. In this model, too, it is beneficial to split the message queue of an actor into separate queues per message type.

Having discussed the representation of actors in Event-B, we are going to develop the actor model of the factorial.

4 Step-Wise Development

In this section we detail the development of the sequential actor model where the environment issues the next computation requests after receiving the result of the previous one. Our formal development of the provably correct factorial actor system follows a refinement strategy. We start with the standard recursive definition of factorial. Then, in five refinements, the details necessary for an actor system are added.

The initial model consists of an event that computes the factorial in one step. The first refinement changes the one step computation into an iterative algorithm. In the second refinement the used memory is made explicit in the form of a stack. We also separate the creation of the memory cells from performing the computation. Refinement 3 is the first one that resembles an actor system. At that point the stack elements are replaced by actors and the computations are triggered by messages. However, the process of creating the actors is still controlled by an iterative program. Refinement 4 turns this last part into an actor, controlled by sending updated messages to itself. Refinement 5 changes the shared mailbox to one mailbox per actor.

4.1 Specification

The specification is captured in an initial model comprising a context that defines the function *fact* and a machine (Fig. 2) that uses this function. The context defines two constants, the recursive factorial function *fact* and the *input*:

---

[1] An arrow with a vertical bar is Event-B's notation for a partial function.

axm0_0: $fact \in \mathbb{N} \rightarrow \mathbb{N}_1$
axm0_1: $fact(0) = 1$
axm0_2: $\forall n \cdot n \in \mathbb{N} \Rightarrow fact(n+1) = (n+1) * fact(n)$
axm0_3: $input \in \mathbb{N}$

The initial machine has only a single variable *result* of type $\mathbb{N}$. This variable is used to store the final result of the computation. For brevity, we do not display the variable definitions in the model listings, but show events only. There are two events:

The *Initialisation* event sets the value of *result* to 0.
The *Finish* event contains one action
   act0_0: $result := fact(input)$
that assigns *result* to the result computed by the *fact* function. This event contains no guard and may be repeated.

This model is sequential as it assumes that one factorial is computed after each other. A simulation consists of the execution of the *Initialisation* event followed by an unrestricted number of computation steps without any effect. Execution of the *Finish* event computes the factorial in one step. For simplicity, the input is a constant as we are only interested to prove that the refined actor system computes a factorial of an arbitrary input.

4.2   Refinement 1

The first refinement (Fig. 3) splits the computation into multiple steps. The new variables *tmp_result* and *val* are introduced to hold the intermediate state. The *result* variable stays part of the machine. The algorithm will do the calculation beginning with the smallest number 1. In each consecutive step the next factorial number is calculated based on the previous one which is stored in *tmp_result*. The number of remaining steps is stored in *val*. The types of this new variables are $\mathbb{N}$ for *val* and $\mathbb{N}_1$ for *tmp_result*.

```
MACHINE m0
EVENTS
Initialisation
begin
   act0_0: result := 0
end
Finish ⟨ordinary⟩ ≅
begin
   act0_0: result := fact(input)
end
END
```

Fig. 2. Events of the Specification.

```
MACHINE m1
EVENTS
Initialisation
begin
  act1_0: result := 0
  act1_1: val := input
  act1_2: tmp_result := 1
end
ComputeStep ⟨convergent⟩ ≙
when
  grd1_0:  val > 0
then
  act1_0: val := val − 1
  act1_1: tmp_result := tmp_result ∗ (input − val + 1)
end
Finish ⟨ordinary⟩ ≙
refines Finish
when
  grd1_0:  val = 0
then
  act1_0: result := tmp_result
end
END
```

Fig. 3. Events of Refinement 1.

The *Initialisation* assigns the variable *val* to *input*. We need to do as many steps as the value of the input. To start the computation properly, *tmp_result* is initialised to 1 the multiplicative identity. As in the previous machine, *result* is set to 0.

The event *ComputeStep* is new and we have to show that it is *convergent*. This means that the event must not be enabled infinitely often possibly preventing the other events. The guard states that this event can only be executed if val is not 0, meaning that there is still work to do. The two actions decrement *val* and update *tmp_result* to the next factorial number.

The event *Finish* refines the event of the same name. It now contains a guard. Also, instead of assigning the final result directly, the variable *tmp_result* is assigned to *result*. This event can now only be executed if there are no more computations to do and instead of doing the computation itself, the result is just copied.

In order to demonstrate that this machine is indeed a refinement of the previous machine, we need to confirm that all events refine their corresponding abstract event. It is also required to show that all convergent events are really convergent. That is, there exists a variant, an expression bounded from below which is decreased by every execution of the convergent event.

The event *ComputeStep* is new and the refinement relation is thus trivially satisfied, if we can shown convergence. The variant for this machine is the variable *val*. It is a natural number and thus cannot get infinitely small and it is decremented in *ComputeStep*. Thus, it turns out that *ComputeStep* is indeed convergent.

To justify that *Finish* refines its predecessor event, we need to demonstrate that whenever *val* is 0, the value in *tmp_result* is the correct final result. We can prove this with the following invariants added to the model:

inv1_2: $val \leq input$

inv1_3: $tmp\_result = fact(input - val)$

We need to prove that these invariants are preserved by all events. The initialisation satisfies both invariants. More interesting is the event *ComputeStep*. Before the event is executed $tmp\_result = fact(input - val)$ and afterwards $tmp\_result' = fact(input - val) * (input - val + 1) = fact(input - val')$ which proves that the invariant inv1_3 is preserved. Here, we use standard notation: primed variables refer to values after event execution while unprimed variables denote values before execution. Constants are always unprimed. The proof of inv1_2 follows from the observation that *val* is only decremented and *input* is a constant.

Finally, we prove deadlock freedom. The corresponding theorem states that at least one event must always be enabled, or expressed differently, the disjunction of all guards must be a valid expression:

thm_DLF: ⟨theorem⟩ $(val > 0) \lor (val = 0)$

This theorem follows directly from the type definition invariant of *val*, stating that $val \in \mathbb{N}$. All proof obligations for this refinement can be discharged by the included automatic solvers [14,17]. No manual proofs are required.

4.3   Refinement 2

In the second refinement (Fig. 4) the computation is split into two phases. First, all numbers are pushed on a stack, afterwards they are multiplied. This brings us one step closer to the actor system, where first actors are created, then they process messages to perform the actual computation.

For this stack-based model, we need to introduce several new variables: *counter* tracks how many more elements need to be pushed, *stack* is a function that models the stack and *stack_pointer* is the current size of the stack. They are defined by the following invariants:

inv2_1: $stack \in \mathbb{N} \nrightarrow \mathbb{N}_1$

inv2_2: $stack\_pointer \in \mathbb{N}$

inv2_3: $0 \mathbin{..} (stack\_pointer - 1) \subseteq dom(stack)$

inv2_4: $counter \in \mathbb{N}$

MACHINE m2
EVENTS
Initialisation
begin
   act2_0: $result := 0$
   act2_1: $counter := input$
   act2_2: $stack := \varnothing$
   act2_3: $stack\_pointer := 0$
   act2_4: $tmp\_result := 1$
end
Call ⟨convergent⟩ $\widehat{=}$
when
   grd2_0: $counter > 0$
   grd2_1: $tmp\_result = 1$
then
   act2_0: $counter := counter - 1$
   act2_1: $stack\_pointer := stack\_pointer + 1$
   act2_2: $stack(stack\_pointer) := counter$
end
Return ⟨convergent⟩ $\widehat{=}$
refines ComputeStep
when
   grd2_0: $counter = 0$
   grd2_1: $stack\_pointer > 0$
then
   act2_0: $tmp\_result := tmp\_result * stack(stack\_pointer - 1)$
   act2_1: $stack\_pointer := stack\_pointer - 1$
end
Finish ⟨ordinary⟩ $\widehat{=}$
refines Finish
when
   grd2_0: $counter = 0$
   grd2_1: $stack\_pointer = 0$
then
   act2_0: $result := tmp\_result$
end
END

Fig. 4. Events of Refinement 2.

In `inv2_3` the *dom* function is used to get the domain of a function. It means that *stack* is defined for all $\mathbb{N}$ up to, but not including *stack_pointer* which points to the next free space in the stack. The variables *result* and *tmp_result* are the same as in the previous machine. The variable *val* is no longer visible.

The event *Initialisation* sets *counter* to *input*, *stack* to an empty set, *stack_pointer* to 0. The old variables *result* and *tmp_result* are initialised as before to 0 and 1.

The event *Call* is a new convergent event. It is responsible for pushing the numbers on the stack. The guard states that there are numbers left and that the computation has not started. This is needed to satisfy some invariants. The actions push the value of counter and decrement it. To establish that this event is convergent, the variant *counter* is used.

The event *Return* is a refinement of *ComputeStep*. Its guard requires that all elements are pushed and that the stack is non-empty. When executed, it pops one element and multiplies it with *tmp_result*. The value of *tmp_result* is the same as in the previous refinement. The difference is that now it is computed based on a stack element and not based on a simple variable.

The event *Finish* is almost the same as in the previous refinement. Only the guard is slightly different.

To establish the refinement relationship, we need to relate the new variables to the old ones of the more abstract model. This relation is defined in so called gluing invariants as follows:

inv2_5: $\forall n \cdot n \in dom(stack) \Rightarrow stack(n) = input - n$
inv2_6: $stack\_pointer + counter = val$
inv2_7: $counter = 0 \Rightarrow val = stack\_pointer$
inv2_8: $counter \neq 0 \Rightarrow val = input$

The invariant `inv2_5` allows us to know the value on the stack, which is important for the proof obligations related to the *return* event. The other three invariants state how *counter*, *stack_pointer*, and *val* are related. While the event *Call* is executed, the value of *val* stays at *input*. At the same time *counter* and *stack_pointer* are decremented and incremented, but always both. Once *counter* is 0 and the execution of *return* starts, the *stack_pointer* takes the role of *val*. The invariant `inv2_7` follows directly from `inv2_6`, it could be marked as a theorem. Using these invariants, all proof obligations can be discharged by the automatic solvers [14,17]. The deadlock freedom theorem

thm_DLF: $\langle theorem \rangle$ $(counter > 0 \land tmp\_result = 1) \lor$
$(counter = 0 \land stack\_pointer > 0) \lor (counter = 0 \land stack\_pointer = 0)$

is also proven automatically.

4.4   Refinement 3

With the third refinement (Fig. 5), we start to introduce actors. The stack, used in the previous refinement, is now represented as actors and the computation phase is controlled by messages sent between these actors. Actor identifiers and the number of existing actors are defined as described in Sect. 3.

In this refinement step only the memory for the computation is represented as actors. This corresponds to the behaviour *cont* in Listing 1. The state of these actors consists of *value* and *target* as defined in Sect. 3. Also the simplified model for messages for these actors has been presented in Sect. 3. Furthermore, the two variables *result* and *counter* are taken from the previous refinement. The machine consists of five events, one more than in the previous refinement.

MACHINE m3
EVENTS
Create ⟨convergent⟩ ≙
refines Call
when

   grd3_0: $counter > 0$
then

   act3_0: $counter := counter - 1$

   act3_1: $actor\_id := 0 .. num\_actors$

   act3_2: $cont\_actors\_target(active\_actor + 1) := active\_actor$

   act3_3: $cont\_actors\_value(active\_actor + 1) := counter$

   act3_4: $active\_actor := active\_actor + 1$

   act3_5: $num\_actors := num\_actors + 1$
end
Created ⟨convergent⟩ ≙
when

   grd3_0: $counter = 0$

   grd3_1: $msg\_exists = FALSE$

   grd3_2: $active\_actor = input - 1$
then

   act3_0: $msg\_exists := TRUE$

   act3_1: $msg\_recipient := active\_actor$

   act3_2: $msg\_content := 1$
end
Compute ⟨convergent⟩ ≙
refines Return
when

   grd3_1: $msg\_exists = TRUE$

   grd3_2: $msg\_recipient \neq final\_id$

   grd3_3: $msg\_recipient = active\_actor$
then

   act3_0: $msg\_recipient := cont\_actors\_target(msg\_recipient)$

   act3_1: $msg\_content := msg\_content * cont\_actors\_value(msg\_recipient)$

   act3_2: $num\_actors := num\_actors - 1$

   act3_3: $actor\_id := 0 .. num\_actors - 2$

   act3_4: $cont\_actors\_target := \{msg\_recipient\} \lhd cont\_actors\_target$

   act3_5: $cont\_actors\_value := \{msg\_recipient\} \lhd cont\_actors\_value$

   act3_6: $active\_actor := cont\_actors\_target(msg\_recipient)$
end
Finish ⟨ordinary⟩ ≙
refines Finish
when

   grd3_1: $msg\_exists = TRUE$

   grd3_2: $msg\_recipient = final\_id$

   grd3_3: $msg\_recipient = active\_actor$
then

   act3_0: $result := msg\_content$
end
END

Fig. 5. Events of Refinement 3.

In the *Initialisation* event most variables are set to empty or default values. The variable *active_actor* is set to -1, meaning that no dynamic actor exists at that point. For brevity the initialisation event is not shown in Fig. 5.

The event *Create* refines the event *Call*. It creates continuation actors. The guard is a subset of the guard of *Call*. When executed, the counter is decremented and a new continuation actor is created. To create this new actor the *num_actors* variable is incremented, the *actor_id* variable is extended, and the state is added to *cont_actors_target* and *cont_actors_value*. Additionally, the *active_actor* variable is set to the id of the newly created actor.

The newly introduced event *Created* is enabled when the counter reaches zero, but no message was sent to a continuation actor. It is responsible for starting the computation by sending the first message to the continuation actor that was created last. To do so, the *msg_exists* flag is set to *true* and the other *msg* variables are filled. This event is introduced in this refinement and marked as convergent. So we need to provide a suitable variant. We know that this event is only executed once and it is the only event that changes *msg_exists*. To build a variant out of this Boolean variable, we need an auxiliary function that turns the Boolean value into an integer and decreases when the input changes from *false* to *true*. The following definition is part of the context:

axm3_4: $boolToNat \in BOOL \to \mathbb{N}$
axm3_5: $boolToNat(TRUE) = 0$
axm3_6: $boolToNat(FALSE) = 1$

By using it, the variant can be defined as *boolToNat(msg_exists)*.

The event *Compute* is the receive function of the continuation actors. It is enabled whenever there exists a message for one of these actors. It also contains two additional guards to keep the system synchronized. When the event is executed, a message is sent to the stored target. The message contains the product of the stored value and the value received via the latest message. This corresponds to the *cont* behaviour in the actor algorithm in Listing 1. Additionally, the actor who processed the message is deleted, as there will be no more messages for it to process. This is done by removing it from the *cont_actors* functions and from the *actor_id* set.

The *Finish* event corresponds to the customer who receives the final result. It is enabled if a message arrives at this customer. When executed, the variable *result* is set to the received result in the message.

In order to demonstrate that this third machine is a refinement of the second machine, we need to provide some gluing invariants. These relate the now invisible variables of the stack system, to the new variables of the actor system. The roles of *tmp_result* and *stack_pointer* are now taken by *msg_content* and *num_actor*. In fact, these variables are equivalent to its predecessors, they are just renamed to be a better fit for describing an actor system. The content of the continuation actors is equivalent to stack frames in the second refinement. The gluing invariants are formally stated as:

inv3_8: $msg\_exists = TRUE \Rightarrow counter = 0$
inv3_11: $msg\_content = tmp\_result$
inv3_12: $num\_actors = stack\_pointer$
inv3_14: $\forall x \cdot x \in dom(cont\_actors\_value) \Rightarrow stack(x) = cont\_actors\_value(x)$
inv3_15: $\forall x \cdot x \in dom(cont\_actors\_target) \Rightarrow cont\_actors\_target(x) = x - 1$

As for all the previous machines, we need to provide a deadlock freedom theorem. In this case we need to provide additional invariants to prove it because our existing invariants are not strong enough. The value of *msg_recipient* needs to be derived correctly from the other information known in a guard. There is no way to guarantee its values independently.

inv3_16: $msg\_exists = TRUE \Rightarrow msg\_recipient = active\_actor$
inv3_17: $(counter = 0 \wedge msg\_exists = FALSE) \Rightarrow active\_actor = input - 1$

With this additional invariants the deadlock freedom theorem, i.e. the disjunction of all guards equals true, can be proven. The proof obligations from the invariants and the deadlock freedom theorem are all automatically discharged by the solvers [14,17]. The only manual intervention was the creation of the two additional invariants for deadlock freedom.

4.5 Refinement 4

In the fourth refinement (Fig. 6), we replace the counter variable by a message. This message is sent by the factorial actor to itself. It corresponds to the *Request* message and the *fact* actor in Listing 1. To model this message, we introduce a new channel consisting of the variables *msgC_exists* and *msgC_content*. The *msgC* prefix expresses that these variables belong to the message that sends the counter. The variable *counter* from the previous refinement is removed, all other variables stay the same. The variables are defined, including the gluing invariant, as follows:

inv4_0: $msgC\_exists \in BOOL$
inv4_1: $msgC\_content \in \mathbb{N}$
inv4_2: $msgC\_content = counter$

The number and names of the events are unchanged, compared to the previous refinement.

The *Initialisation* is the same as before, except for the new variables.

The event *Create* is modified to handle the new message. Instead of checking the value of the *counter*, the existence of the message and its value are checked. The decremented *counter* is not updated directly, but instead sent as a message. The *msgC_exists* flag is already *true*, thus unchanged, and the message content is written to *msgC_content*.

The event *Created* is also modified to work with the counter message. The guard now checks the existence of the message and whether its content is 0. An additional action supplements the actions of the event. After the last counter message was handled, the channel will be empty, as this event does not create a new one. Thus, the value of the *msgC_exists* flag needs to be changed.

MACHINE m4
EVENTS
Create ⟨convergent⟩ ≙
refines Create
when
   grd3_0: $msgC\_exists = TRUE$
   grd3_1: $msgC\_content > 0$
then
   act3_0: $msgC\_content := msgC\_content - 1$
   act3_1: $actor\_id := 0 .. num\_actors$
   act3_2: $cont\_actors\_target(active\_actor + 1) := active\_actor$
   act3_3: $cont\_actors\_value(active\_actor + 1) := msgC\_content$
   act3_4: $active\_actor := active\_actor + 1$
   act3_5: $num\_actors := num\_actors + 1$
end
Created ⟨convergent⟩ ≙
refines Created
when
   grd3_0: $msgC\_exists = TRUE$
   grd3_1: $msgC\_content = 0$
   grd3_2: $msg\_exists = FALSE$
   grd3_3: $active\_actor = input - 1$
then
   act3_0: $msg\_exists := TRUE$
   act3_1: $msg\_recipient := active\_actor$
   act3_2: $msg\_content := 1$
   act3_3: $msgC\_exists := FALSE$
end
END

Fig. 6. Events of Refinement 4. The events *Compute* and *Finish* are the same as in Fig. 5.

The events *Compute* and *Finish* are the same as in the previous refinement.

The proofs for refinement and deadlock freedom are done automatically [14,17]. To establish the deadlock freedom theorem, we need this additional invariant:

inv4_3: $msgC\_exists = FALSE \Rightarrow msg\_exists = TRUE$

4.6   Refinement 5

The fifth and last refinement (see Appendix) changes the mailboxes to arrays and uses separate ones for each actor. This follows the technique for truly concurrent systems described in Sect. 3 and gives a model that better resembles an actor system.

We introduce the new variables for the mailboxes of the *fact* and *cont* actors. They replace the variables *msg_exists*, *msg_content*, *active_actor*, *msgC_exists* and *msgC_content*. Their types are defined by the following invariants:

inv5_0: $fact\_mail\_msgC\_content \in \mathbb{N} \nrightarrow \mathbb{N}$
inv5_3: $fact\_index\_msgC \in \mathbb{N}$
inv5_4: $cont\_mail\_msg\_content \in (ACTOR\_ID \times \mathbb{N}) \nrightarrow \mathbb{N}$
inv5_6: $cont\_index\_msg \in \mathbb{N}$

The state variables as well as the *result* and *actor_id* variables are unchanged compared to the previous refinement. The events are adapted to the new message encoding in a relatively straightforward way. There is no change in the processing logic.

To satisfy the refinement condition, we need gluing invariants to link the old mailbox variables to the new ones. Note that the model still adheres to the restriction that there can be only one message in all the continuation actor mailboxes. This message must be in the mailbox of the actor identified by the now hidden *active_actor* variable. The Boolean *exists* flags are replaced by using an empty set instead. This gives us these gluing invariants:

inv5_1: $msgC\_exists = TRUE \Leftrightarrow$
$ran(fact\_mail\_msgC\_content) = \{msgC\_content\}$
inv5_2: $msgC\_exists = FALSE \Leftrightarrow fact\_mail\_msgC\_content = \varnothing$
inv5_7: $msg\_exists = TRUE \Leftrightarrow ran(cont\_mail\_msg\_content) = \{msg\_content\}$
inv5_8: $msg\_exists = FALSE \Leftrightarrow cont\_mail\_msg\_content = \varnothing$
inv5_9: $\exists n \cdot msg\_exists = TRUE \Rightarrow$
$dom(cont\_mail\_msg\_content) = \{active\_actor \mapsto n\}$

Again, with these invariants all proofs are found fully automatically.

5   Concurrent Version

The previous model has one major limitation: it can only perform the computation once and, hence, behaves like a sequential program. Even though the actor program in Listing 1 can compute the solution for multiple requests, these requests can also occur while the previous computation is still running. In that case the two computations are performed concurrently and can be interleaved. In this section we adapt our previous factorial model to handle concurrent requests like the Scala version.

It is not possible to realize this as a refinement of the previous machine. Instead we create a new specification machine and refine it to an actor system as in the previous section. The concurrent machines follow the same structure as before, but we introduce a task identifier to associate each continuation actor and message with a task.

The concurrent specification (Fig. 7) contains variables for *tasks* and for *results*. The *start* event expects as parameters an input and a unique task

```
MACHINE m0c
EVENTS
Initialisation
begin
   act0_0: tasks := ∅
   act0_1: results := ∅
end
Start ⟨ordinary⟩ ≙
any
   input
   task
where
   grd0_0: input ∈ ℕ
   grd0_1: task ∉ dom(tasks)
then
   act0_0: tasks(task) := input
end
Finish ⟨ordinary⟩ ≙
any
   task
where
   grd0_0: task ∈ dom(tasks)
   grd0_1: task ∉ dom(results)
then
   act0_0: results(task) := fact(tasks(task))
end
END
```

Fig. 7. Events of the concurrent specification.

identifier, it adds these to the set of tasks. Analogue to the *Finish* event in the previous section the *Finish* event here calculates the factorial number in one step. Instead of accessing the constant *input* it processes one of the tasks that do not yet have an associated result. The newly computed number is inserted into the results. That way the model is able to handle arbitrary many requests instead of only one.

All refinements closely follow the ones from the previous section. The events are similar, but they all expect a task parameter to know which task is processed. Variables and invariants need to be lifted to the set of tasks. An invariant that previously had the form $\varphi(input, result)$ becomes in this model $\forall task : \varphi(tasks(task), results(task))$. Except for the newly added *Start* event all machines contain the same events as in the sequential case.

Changing all of the variables to functions leads to some proofs requiring manual intervention. Table 1 shows how many proof obligations where generated for each refinement and how many of them where done automatically. We can see that 29 out of 305 proof obligations required interactive proof. This is contrast to the sequential actor model where all proofs were done automatically. This demonstrates the effect of more complex data structures (here functions) to proof automation.

Table 1. Proof statistics for the concurrent model.

Element	Total	Auto	Manual
ctx0c	2	1	1
ctx3c	0	0	0
m0c	8	8	0
m1c	26	24	2
m2c	50	47	3
m3c	129	110	19
m4c	33	33	0
m5c	57	53	4
Σ	305	276	29

6 Related Work

Type systems have been used in conjunction with actors. Charalambides et al. [12] apply session types to actor systems. This has been extended to also prove liveness properties of actor systems [13]. Our method on the other hand uses refinement to develop a model in multiple steps. The specification is built gradually and the model is separate from a possible program.

Rebeca is a modelling language and model checker for actor systems [29,30]. However, Rebeca cannot deal with the dynamic creation of actors necessary for the factorial case study. Another actor modelling language is ABS [20]. It is an executable and formally specified language based on the active object variant of actor systems. ABS has been used in large industrial case studies [4]. KeY-ABS [15,16] allows tool-based reasoning about ABS specifications. However, ABS does not support refinement.

Musser and Varela [25] developed an actor theory in the Athena proof assistant. Using Athena, they proved properties about actor systems like uniqueness of addresses or fairness. Their theory supports the creation of actors and the exchange of actor identifiers. Another implementation of actor systems was done in the Coq proof assistant by [32]. They also modelled Agha's factorial example [3] but without a complete correctness prove. Their system can export Erlang code and they proved uniqueness for their address generation and fairness. Both of these works use correctness properties as theorems. However, they do not use stepwise refinement or any other iterative process to develop the final program from the specification.

7   Conclusion

In this paper we studied the formal development of actor systems in Event-B using refinement. Starting from a mathematical recursive specification, we have proven with five refinement steps that Agha's classical factorial actor system is correct. We have also proven deadlock-freeness and convergence from which the termination of a single computation follows. With the assumption that requests are issued synchronously, we could keep the actor model flat and all proofs could be resolved automatically—once the necessary invariants have been added. Our actor models use a naming scheme and actor code could be generated from it, in principle, although this has not been implemented.

To the best of our knowledge, we are the first who formally verified that Agha's factorial actor system implements its recursive definition. Furthermore, we think that we are the first who developed actor systems in Event-B. The example might be simple, but it shows how recursive definitions can be turned into actor systems. Furthermore, the case study demonstrates the proof power of the available provers. The key to this high automation is to keep the actor model as simple as possible: we exploited the synchronous nature of the recursive definition and kept the actor model flat, avoiding composite data structures.

The full development of the truly concurrent factorial model discussed in Sect. 5 can be found in [23]. It uses the insights from the synchronous development and shows that with the more involved data structures we loose proof automation: 9.5% of the 305 proof obligations needed manual intervention, which is still acceptable. Maderbacher also develops a messaging client-server system which demonstrates the applicability of the method beyond the factorial example.

We strongly believe that abstract models and refinement are essential to the development of dependable distributed systems. An abstract model provides the necessary global view and complexity needs to be added incrementally. Starting at the actor or code level is too late and one has difficulties in stating the correctness properties. This is demonstrated by the observation that we seem to be the first who formally proved the correctness of the classical factorial actor system—which was quite surprising to us.

Acknowledgement. This work is supported by the TU Graz LEAD project "Dependable Internet of Things in Adverse Environments". The authors wish to thank the three anonymous reviewers for their constructive feedback in order to improve the paper.

Appendix

The complete model of the final actor model computing a factorial number (Refinement 5).

MACHINE m5
REFINES m4
SEES ctx5
VARIABLES
  result
  num_actors
  actor_id
  cont_actors_target
  cont_actors_value
  fact_mail_msgC_content
  fact_index_msgC
  cont_mail_msg_content
  cont_index_msg
INVARIANTS
  inv5_0: $fact\_mail\_msgC\_content \in \mathbb{N} \nrightarrow \mathbb{N}$
  inv5_1: $msgC\_exists = TRUE \Leftrightarrow ran(fact\_mail\_msgC\_content) = \{msgC\_content\}$
  inv5_2: $msgC\_exists = FALSE \Leftrightarrow fact\_mail\_msgC\_content = \varnothing$
  inv5_3: $fact\_index\_msgC \in \mathbb{N}$
  inv5_4: $cont\_mail\_msg\_content \in (ACTOR\_ID \times \mathbb{N}) \nrightarrow \mathbb{N}$
  inv5_6: $cont\_index\_msg \in \mathbb{N}$
  inv5_7: $msg\_exists = TRUE \Leftrightarrow ran(cont\_mail\_msg\_content) = \{msg\_content\}$
  inv5_8: $msg\_exists = FALSE \Leftrightarrow cont\_mail\_msg\_content = \varnothing$
  inv5_9: $\exists n \cdot msg\_exists = TRUE \Rightarrow dom(cont\_mail\_msg\_content) = \{active\_actor \mapsto n\}$
EVENTS
Initialisation
begin
  act5_0: $result := 0$
  act5_5: $num\_actors := 0$
  act5_6: $actor\_id := \varnothing$
  act5_7: $cont\_actors\_target := \varnothing$
  act5_8: $cont\_actors\_value := \varnothing$
  act5_9: $fact\_mail\_msgC\_content := \{0 \mapsto input\}$
  act5_10: $fact\_index\_msgC := 1$
  act5_11: $cont\_mail\_msg\_content := \varnothing$
  act5_13: $cont\_index\_msg := 0$
end
Create ⟨convergent⟩ $\widehat{=}$
refines Create
any
  content
  index
where
  grd5_0: $index \in dom(fact\_mail\_msgC\_content)$
  grd5_1: $fact\_mail\_msgC\_content(index) = content$
  grd5_2: $content > 0$
then
  act5_0: $fact\_mail\_msgC\_content := \{fact\_index\_msgC \mapsto content - 1\}$

act5_1: $fact\_index\_msgC := fact\_index\_msgC + 1$
act5_2: $actor\_id := 0 \mathinner{..} num\_actors$
act5_3: $cont\_actors\_target(num\_actors) := num\_actors - 1$
act5_4: $cont\_actors\_value(num\_actors) := content$
act5_6: $num\_actors := num\_actors + 1$
end
Created $\langle$convergent$\rangle$ $\hat{=}$
refines Created
any
  index
where
  grd5_0: $\{index\} = dom(fact\_mail\_msgC\_content)$
    we need to guarante that there is only one msg, because of the previous machines
  grd5_1: $fact\_mail\_msgC\_content(index) = 0$
  grd5_2: $cont\_mail\_msg\_content = \varnothing$
  grd5_3: $num\_actors = input$
then
  act5_0: $cont\_mail\_msg\_content := \{(num\_actors - 1 \mapsto cont\_index\_msg) \mapsto 1\}$
  act5_3: $fact\_mail\_msgC\_content := \{index\} \vartriangleleft fact\_mail\_msgC\_content$
end
ContCompute $\langle$ordinary$\rangle$ $\hat{=}$
refines Compute
any
  actor
  index
where
  grd5_0: $\{actor \mapsto index\} = dom(cont\_mail\_msg\_content)$
  grd5_1: $actor \neq final\_id$
then
  act5_1: $cont\_mail\_msg\_content := \{(cont\_actors\_target(actor) \mapsto cont\_index\_msg) \mapsto (cont\_mail\_msg\_content(actor \mapsto index) * cont\_actors\_value(actor))\}$
  act5_2: $num\_actors := num\_actors - 1$
  act5_3: $actor\_id := 0 \mathinner{..} num\_actors - 2$
  act5_4: $cont\_actors\_target := \{actor\} \vartriangleleft cont\_actors\_target$
  act5_5: $cont\_actors\_value := \{actor\} \vartriangleleft cont\_actors\_value$
end
Finish $\langle$ordinary$\rangle$ $\hat{=}$
refines Finish
any
  actor
  index
where
  grd5_0: $\{actor \mapsto index\} = dom(cont\_mail\_msg\_content)$
  grd3_1: $actor = final\_id$
then
  act3_0: $result := cont\_mail\_msg\_content(actor \mapsto index)$
end
END

References

1. Abrial, J.R.: Modeling in Event-B: System and Software Engineering. Cambridge University Press, Cambridge (2010)
2. Abrial, J.R., Butler, M.J., Hallerstede, S., Hoang, T.S., Mehta, F., Voisin, L.: Rodin: an open toolset for modelling and reasoning in Event-B. Int. J. Softw. Tools Technol. Transfer **12**(6), 447–466 (2010)
3. Agha, G.: Actors: A Model of Concurrent Computation in Distributed Systems. MIT Press, Cambridge (1986)
4. Albert, E., et al.: Formal modeling and analysis of resource management for cloud architectures: an industrial case study using Real-Time ABS. Serv. Oriented Comput. Appl. **8**(4), 323–339 (2014)
5. Armstrong, J.: Programming Erlang: Software for a Concurrent World. Pragmatic Programmers, The Pragmatic Bookshelf, 2nd edn (2013)
6. Armstrong, J., Virding, R., Williams, M.: Concurrent Programming in ERLANG. Prentice Hall, Upper Saddle River (1993)
7. Arnold, K., Gosling, J., Holmes, D.: The Java Programming Language. Addison-Wesley, Boston (2000)
8. Ball, T., Cook, B., Levin, V., Rajamani, S.K.: SLAM and static driver verifier: technology transfer of formal methods inside Microsoft. In: Boiten, E.A., Derrick, J., Smith, G. (eds.) IFM 2004. LNCS, vol. 2999, pp. 1–20. Springer, Heidelberg (2004). https://doi.org/10.1007/978-3-540-24756-2_1
9. Bevemyr, J.: How Cisco is using Erlang for intent-based networking (2018). https://youtu.be/077-XJv6PLQ, Code Beam Stockholm
10. Boehm, H.J., Adve, S.V.: Foundations of the C++ concurrency memory model. In: Gupta, R., Amarasinghe, S.P. (eds.) Proceedings of the ACM SIGPLAN 2008 Conference on Programming Language Design and Implementation, Tucson, AZ, USA, 7–13 June 2008, pp. 68–78. ACM (2008)
11. Cesarini, F.: Which companies are using Erlang, and why?, 11 September 2019. https://www.erlang-solutions.com/blog/which-companies-are-using-erlang-and-why-mytopdogstatus.html
12. Charalambides, M., Dinges, P., Agha, G.: Parameterized concurrent multi-party session types. In: Kokash, N., Ravara, A. (eds.) Proceedings 11th International Workshop on Foundations of Coordination Languages and Self Adaptation, FOCLASA 2012, Newcastle, U.K., 8 September 2012. EPTCS, vol. 91, pp. 16–30 (2012)
13. Charalambides, M., Palmskog, K., Agha, G.: Types for progress in actor programs. In: Boreale, M., Corradini, F., Loreti, M., Pugliese, R. (eds.) Models, Languages, and Tools for Concurrent and Distributed Programming. LNCS, vol. 11665, pp. 315–339. Springer, Cham (2019). https://doi.org/10.1007/978-3-030-21485-2_18
14. Clearsy: Atelier B (2016). https://www.atelierb.eu/en/atelier-b-tools/
15. Din, C.C., Bubel, R., Hähnle, R.: KeY-ABS: a deductive verification tool for the concurrent modelling language ABS. In: Felty, A.P., Middeldorp, A. (eds.) CADE 2015. LNCS (LNAI), vol. 9195, pp. 517–526. Springer, Cham (2015). https://doi.org/10.1007/978-3-319-21401-6_35
16. Din, C.C., Tapia Tarifa, S.L., Hähnle, R., Johnsen, E.B.: History-based specification and verification of scalable concurrent and distributed systems. In: Butler, M., Conchon, S., Zaïdi, F. (eds.) ICFEM 2015. LNCS, vol. 9407, pp. 217–233. Springer, Cham (2015). https://doi.org/10.1007/978-3-319-25423-4_14

17. Déharbe, D., Fontaine, P., Guyot, Y., Voisin, L.: SMT solvers for Rodin. In: Derrick, J., et al. (eds.) ABZ 2012. LNCS, vol. 7316, pp. 194–207. Springer, Heidelberg (2012). https://doi.org/10.1007/978-3-642-30885-7_14

18. Ericsson: Erlang celebrates 20 years as open source, 31 May 2018. https://www.ericsson.com/en/news/2018/5/erlang-celebrates-20-years-as-open-source

19. Hewitt, C.: Actor model of computation: scalable robust information systems. arXiv (2010). http://arxiv.org/abs/1008.1459

20. Johnsen, E.B., Hähnle, R., Schäfer, J., Schlatte, R., Steffen, M.: ABS: a core language for abstract behavioral specification. In: Aichernig, B.K., de Boer, F.S., Bonsangue, M.M. (eds.) FMCO 2010. LNCS, vol. 6957, pp. 142–164. Springer, Heidelberg (2011). https://doi.org/10.1007/978-3-642-25271-6_8

21. Lightbend: Akka Documentation (2019). https://doc.akka.io/docs/akka/2.5/index.html

22. Lightbend: Akka Typed Documentation (2019). https://doc.akka.io/docs/akka/2.5/typed/actors.html

23. Maderbacher, B.: Proof-based development of actor systems. Master's thesis, Graz University of Technology, Institute of Software Technology, December 2019. Supervisor: Bernhard K. Aichernig

24. Metz, C.: Why WhatsApp Only Needs 50 Engineers for Its 900M Users. WIRED (2015). https://www.wired.com/2015/09/whatsapp-serves-900-million-users-50-engineers/

25. Musser, D.R., Varela, C.A.: Structured reasoning about actor systems. In: Jamali, N., Ricci, A., Weiss, G., Yonezawa, A. (eds.) Proceedings of the 2013 Workshop on Programming Based on Actors, Agents, and Decentralized Control, AGERE!@SPLASH 2013, Indianapolis, IN, USA, 27–28 October 2013, pp. 37–48. ACM (2013)

26. Newcombe, C., Rath, T., Zhang, F., Munteanu, B., Brooker, M., Deardeuff, M.: How Amazon web services uses formal methods. Commun. ACM 58(4), 66–73 (2015)

27. Odersky, M., Spoon, L., Venners, B.: Programming in Scala. Artima Inc. (2008)

28. Savage, S., Burrows, M., Nelson, G., Sobalvarro, P., Anderson, T.E.: Eraser: a dynamic data race detector for multithreaded programs. ACM Trans. Comput. Syst. 15(4), 391–411 (1997)

29. Sirjani, M.: Power is overrated, go for friendliness! expressiveness, faithfulness, and usability in modeling: the actor experience. In: Lohstroh, M., Derler, P., Sirjani, M. (eds.) Principles of Modeling. LNCS, vol. 10760, pp. 423–448. Springer, Cham (2018). https://doi.org/10.1007/978-3-319-95246-8_25

30. Sirjani, M., Movaghar, A., Shali, A., de Boer, F.S.: Modeling and verification of reactive systems using Rebeca. Fundamenta Informaticae 63(4), 385–410 (2004). http://content.iospress.com/articles/fundamenta-informaticae/fi63-4-05

31. WhatsApp: 1 million is so 2011, 06 January 2012. https://blog.whatsapp.com/196/1-million-is-so-2011

32. Yasutake, S., Watanabe, T.: Actario: a framework for reasoning about actor systems. Technical report, Tokyo Institute of Technology (2015)

Violation Witnesses and Result Validation for Multi-Threaded Programs
Implementation and Evaluation with CPAchecker

Dirk Beyer⑩ and Karlheinz Friedberger⑩

LMU Munich, Munich, Germany

Abstract. Invariants and error traces are important results of a program analysis, and therefore, a standardized exchange format for verification witnesses is used by many program analyzers to store and share those results. This way, information about program traces and variable assignments can be shared across tools, e.g., to validate verification results, or provided to users, e.g., to visualize and explore the results in order to fix bugs or understand the reason for a program's correctness. The standard format for correctness and violation witnesses that was used by SV-COMP for several years was only applicable to sequential (single-threaded) programs. To enable the validation of results for multi-threaded programs, we extend the existing standard exchange format by adding information about thread management and thread interleaving. We contribute a reference implementation of a validator for violation witnesses in the new format, which we implemented as component of the software-verification framework CPACHECKER. We experimentally evaluate the format and validator on a large set of violation witnesses. The outcome is promising: several verification tools already produce violation witnesses that help validating the verification results, and our witness validator can re-verify most of the produced witnesses.

Keywords: Verification witness · Result validation · Software verification · Proof format · Program analysis · Violation witness · Counterexample · CPAchecker

1 Introduction

Reliable and correct software is a basic dependency of today's society and industry. For proving programs correct as well as for finding errors in programs, formal verification is a powerful technique. Given a program and a specification, a software verifier either finds an error path through the program that exposes the specification violation or proves that the specification is satisfied by the program. In most cases, the analysis produces some kind of data that is valuable for the user and can

Replication package available on Zenodo [14].

Funded in part by Deutsche Forschungsgemeinschaft (DFG) – 378803395 (ConVeY).

T. Margaria and B. Steffen (Eds.): ISoLA 2020, LNCS 12476, pp. 449–470, 2020.
https://doi.org/10.1007/978-3-030-61362-4_26

be used in further applications. Several tool chains support the direct reuse of verification results [5,6,25]. In general, information about the program analysis can be provided in form of a verification witness, either as correctness witness [10] (e.g., describing invariants from the correctness proof) or as violation witness [11,12] (e.g., representing an abstract counterexample towards a property violation).

The standard witness exchange format was specified and continuously improved by the verification community (especially SV-COMP) over the last years.[1] The specification was first supporting only sequential programs (since SV-COMP 2015 [4,11]), and we later extended it to multi-threaded programs as well (SV-COMP 2018–2020). In this paper, we describe the necessary extensions to the witness format and provide evidence that violation witnesses for concurrent tasks are not only *produced* by many verification tools (in SV-COMP 2020: CBMC [29], CPACHECKER [18], CPALOCKATOR [1], DARTAGNAN [33], DIVINE [3], ESBMC [32], LAZY-CSEQ [39], PESCO [31], ULTIMATE AUTOMIZER [37], ULTIMATE TAIPAN [35], YOGAR-CBMC [40]), but that most of the violation witnesses for concurrent programs can also be *validated* by our implementation of a validation tool.

Contributions. The paper makes the following contributions:

- Extension of the existing violation witness format by additional hints on thread management: (i) thread interleavings are represented using thread-ids at all edges and (ii) thread creation is added to the witness.
- Implementation of an approach for validation of violation witnesses for multi-threaded programs in the verification framework CPACHECKER and make the source code available as reference implementation for others.[2]
- Experimental evaluation of the new format and validator on a large number of verification tasks with violation witnesses from several verifiers to show that the approach is effective and helps validating the existence of error traces in multi-threaded programs.
- Availability of all experimental results, including raw data, tables, experiment setup, etc. (see Sect. 6).

Related Work. As we extend an existing standardized witness format and validation technology, this work is based on a number of existing ideas, which we outline in the following.

Verification Artifacts. Many program-analysis techniques are efficient at discovering proofs or failures. However, it is often difficult to evaluate results, such as program paths towards property violations. Artifacts [24] from verifier executions are valuable for users [2,28,36]. The standard exchange format for verification witnesses [11] is the basis of our work; we describe and extend it in this paper and apply it in our evaluation.

---

[1] https://github.com/sosy-lab/sv-witnesses
[2] https://cpachecker.sosy-lab.org

Test Execution and Harnesses. While it is comparatively simple to create an executable harness for a sequential program [12,27,30,34], the situation for multi-threaded programs is more complex. Simple test cases can not capture the difficulty of nondeterministically interleaved threads and can only be used to heuristically execute a sample of all possible program traces. The scheduling of threads needs to be encoded into the harness in such a way that all statements are interleaved in the correct ordering.

Sequentialization. Tools like LAZY-CSEQ [38,39] apply sequentialization techniques before verification and can thus provide data about multi-threaded counterexample traces via a sequentialized program. However, the mapping from a sequentialized program (and the found counterexample path in it) back to its multi-threaded origin needs to be supported.

2   Background

We provide only a short overview of some basic concepts and definitions that we use to describe our approach, including the program representation, the format for violation witnesses, and the multi-threaded program analysis in CPACHECKER.

2.1   Program Representation

For presentation, we restrict our programs to a simple imperative programming language that contains only assignments, assumptions, declarations, function calls, and function returns. The language supports simple thread management via the calls of *pthread_create* and *pthread_join*, and assumes that each statement in the code is atomic on its own, i.e., uses a strong memory model providing sequential consistency, such that an update of a shared variable is immediately visible to all threads and the verification approach does not need to care about asynchronous memory accesses like simultaneously updating the same memory cell from multiple threads or unit-local caching of values that might happen on hardware level. This is not a theoretical restriction, as each statement could be decomposed into a sequence of reading and writing statements, where each statement involves at most one shared variable. For simplicity and generality, the witnesses ignore further thread-management methods like *mutex locks*, *wait*, and *cancel* operations, as well as interrupts. In violation witnesses such operations do not need to be specified for the validation tool.

The violation witnesses for multi-threaded programs that are produced by the verifiers all support the C programming language as input language and may support a wider range of thread-management operations. We will analyze the quality of those witnesses in the evaluation (Sect. 5).

A program is represented by a *control-flow automaton* (CFA) (L, l_{init}, G), which consists of a set L of program locations (modeling the program counter), a set $G \subseteq L \times Ops \times L$ of control-flow edges (modeling the control flow with assignment and assumption operations as well as declarations and function calls

```
1   int NUM = 4,  FIB = 55;
2   int  i = 1,  j = 1;
3
4   void *t1 () {
5     for (int  k = 0;  k < NUM;  k++) {
6       i += j;
7     }
8     pthread_exit (0);
9   }
10
11  void *t2 () {
12    for (int  k = 0;  k < NUM;  k++) {
13      j += i;
14    }
15    pthread_exit (0);
16  }
17
18  int main () {
19    pthread_t  id1,  id2;
20    pthread_create(&id1,  0,  t1,  0);
21    pthread_create(&id2,  0,  t2,  0);
22    if (i >= FIB || j >= FIB) {
23      __VERIFIER_error ();
24    }
25    return 0;
26  }
```

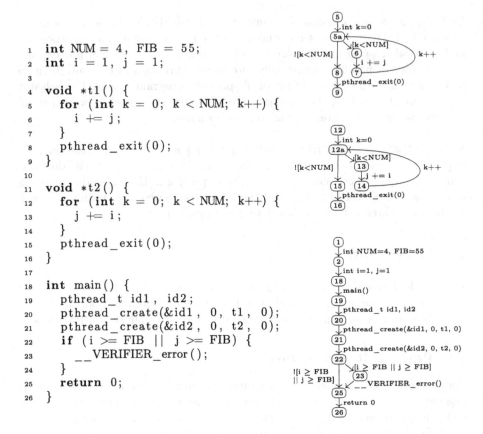

Fig. 1. Source code and CFAs for multi-threaded example program, adopted from program https://github.com/sosy-lab/sv-benchmarks/blob/svcomp20/c/pthread/fib_bench-2.c

and returns from Ops), and a program-entry location $l_{init} \in L$. A sequence $<g_1, g_2, ..., g_n>$ of CFA edges from G is called *program path* if it starts from the program-entry location (i.e., $g_1 = (l_{init}, \cdot, \cdot)$). As we analyze multi-threaded programs, this sequence consists of potentially interleaved edges from different threads, e.g., there is no need that the end location l of a CFA edge $g_i = (\cdot, \cdot, l)$ is identical with the start location l' of its directly succeeding CFA edge $g_{i+1} = (l', \cdot, \cdot)$, but the next CFA edge along the sequence from the same thread must start with program location l. At the program entry and at each thread entry, there is no matching previous program location in a valid program path.

The example in Fig. 1 shows a short multi-threaded program and the corresponding CFAs. The program is build around the Fibonacci sequence, even if the source itself does not directly reveal this. We will later examine this example and find a sequence of operations such that $fib(10) = 55$ was computed (this is modeled as a violation of the specification G ! call(__VERIFIER_error()) i.e., a call to function __VERIFIER_error is not reachable).

2.2 Violation Witnesses

Witnesses in software verification are based on the concept of protocol automata [11] that are matched against a CFA for validation. A protocol automaton consists of control states with invariants and edges between control states that represent program transitions. An edge contains a source guard, which restricts the transition to a specific set $S \subseteq G$ of edges from the CFA, and a state-space guard, which restricts the state space by giving additional constraints on variables.

For exporting a violation witness to a file, the protocol automaton is converted into *GraphML* [26], enriched with additional meta-data (like a hash of the analyzed program). When importing a violation witness from a file, the *GraphML* data structure is transformed into a protocol automaton, such that it can be used internally in parallel to any of CPACHECKER's program analyses.

2.3 Analysis of Multi-Threaded Programs in CPACHECKER

CPACHECKER is based on the concept of configurable program analysis (CPA) [15,16]. Different concerns of a program are analyzed by different components (denoted as CPAs). To track variables and their assigned values, we can choose from a predicate-abstraction analysis [19], an explicit-value analysis [21], a BDD-based analysis [23], a symbolic execution [20], and several more. For the analysis of program locations in multi-threaded programs, the multi-threading analysis [13] explores the state space, computes possible thread interleavings on-the-fly, and maintains abstract states, where each abstract state consists of several program locations (one per thread) together with their call stacks (also one per thread). Additional optimizations like partial-order reduction are available in the implementation, but not considered here.

To avoid collisions of identifiers during a program analysis, e.g., as it might happen if the same function is called in two different threads at the same time, CPACHECKER uses different function names for parallel running threads. If necessary, we use several copies of the CFA for a function of the program, using indexed names. For exporting a violation witness, the indexes are removed, because changed function names are not compatible across different tools. When using an existing violation witness for validating a multi-threaded program, we reintroduce a matching of available thread identifiers in the witness and indexed function copies of the CFAs.

3 Detailed Example

In the following, we explain an example step by step. First we start a verifier to verify an example program and produce a witness, and second we start a validator to validate the verification result using the produced witness.

3.1 Producing a Violation Witness

The program from Fig. 1 creates two threads id1 and id2, which run in parallel and increase the value of the variables i and j. If any of the variables i

Program Path	Operation Scheduling			Variable Values				Line
	main	id1	id2	i	j	k_{t1}	k_{t2}	
$(1,.,2),(2,.,18),(18,.,19),(19,.,20)$	i=1, j=1			1	1			2
$(20,.,21),(5,.,5a)$		$k_{t1}=0$				0		5
$(5a,.,6),(6,.,7)$		i+=j		2				6
$(7,.,5a)$		k_{t1}++				1		5
$(21,.,22),(12,.,12a)$			$k_{t2}=0$				0	12
$(12a,.,13),(13,.,14)$			j+=i		3			13
$(14,.,12a)$			k_{t2}++				1	12
$(5a,.,6),(6,.,7)$		i+=j		5				6
$(12a,.,13),(13,.,14)$			j+=i		8			13
$(14,.,12a)$			k_{t2}++				2	12
$(7,.,5a)$		k_{t1}++				2		5
$(5a,.,6),(6,.,7)$		i+=j		13				6
$(12a,.,13),(13,.,14)$			j+=i		21			13
$(14,.,12a)$			k_{t2}++				3	12
$(7,.,5a)$		k_{t1}++				3		5
$(5a,.,6),(6,.,7)$		i+=j		34				6
$(12a,.,13),(13,.,14)$			j+=i		55			13
$(22,.,23)$	j >= FIB							22

Fig. 2. Counterexample trace represented by program path, scheduling of operations, data state as variable assignment, and line number as reference

or j reaches their limit (which is $fib(10)$), then function __VERIFIER_error is reached and a standard verifier can check this by using the specification G ! call(__VERIFIER_error()) and let it produce a counterexample path. This case can happen if the assignments i+=j and j+=i in the two threads id1 and id2 are executed in alternating order for all iterations of the loops. The rest of the loop statements in both threads, i.e., checking the loop bound, can be executed in arbitrary ordering here and allows a wide range of possible thread interleaving.

The following command line runs CPACHECKER as a verifier, configured to use an explicit-value-based analysis for verifying multi-threaded programs:

```
scripts/cpa.sh \
    -outputpath verification \
    -setprop counterexample.export.graphml=witness.graphml \
    -setprop counterexample.export.compressWitness=false \
    -spec config/properties/unreach-call.prp \
    -valueAnalysis-concurrency \
    fib.c
```

This command specifies the directory for all output (including the witness file), the name of the witness file (without compressing it), the specification (which searches for the function call __VERIFIER_error), the domain-specific analysis for the verification process, and the subject program.

Fig. 3. Graphical representation of a violation witness and the available data

The verification process starts the analysis at the program entry and explores the reachable state space. In this example, it finds and reports an error trace as a program path (first column of Fig. 2) and provides the violation witness in Fig. 3, which is written into the file verification/witness.graphml.gz. Both, the counterexample trace and the violation witness specify the interleaved thread execution and variable assignments, such that a user or a witness validator can directly follow the path until reaching the property violation in the program. We highlight the information that is relevant for the thread interleaving. The violation witness uses sink nodes for branches or thread interleavings that do not follow the counterexample path. For simplicity, we avoid them in the graphical representation.

Using the explicit-value domain allows us to export detailed data about the counterexample trace, such as assignments for all variables at many program locations. The verification witness is enriched with these assignments, such that the validator can use them as additional constraints.

The information about which thread is executed, and how the interleaving looks like, is important for the user (and also for the validator). In a program with threads created from the same function (that is, with identical line numbers), the thread identifier is the only way to distinguish between different contexts. Therefore, a witness must contain a thread identifier for every transition (edge) in the witness. In this example, the executed threads have different function scopes (t1 and t2) which makes it easier for the reader to find the correct trace towards the property violation.

3.2 Validating Results Based on a Violation Witness

In order to validate the information from the witness, the violation witness is matched against the program source code. As the violation witness describes a limited set of paths (best case: exactly one path), the validation process is expected to be efficient and to only analyze a small portion of the reachable state space of the whole program.

The following command line runs CPACHECKER as a validator based on the provided violation witness for the multi-threaded program:

```
scripts/cpa.sh \
    -outputpath validation \
    -spec config/properties/unreach-call.prp \
    -witnessValidation \
    -witness verification/witness.graphml \
    fib.c
```

This command specifies the directory for all output (including the newly generated witness file), the specification (which searches for the function call __VERIFIER_error), the validation analysis that will select the strategy to analyze multi-threaded programs, the witness that will be used for the validation (as second, parallel specification), and the subject program. Figure 4

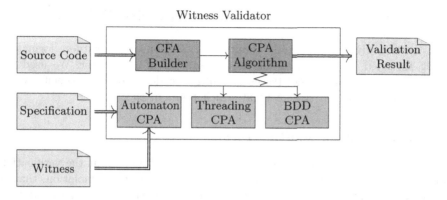

Fig. 4. Overview of CPACHECKER's control flow for violation witness validation for multi-threaded programs

shows the architecture of CPACHECKER for the witness validation for multi-threaded programs. The program is parsed into a CFA and then given to an analysis based on the CPA concept [17]. The property specification and the violation witness are used as protocol automata.

The validation proceeds with the following steps: The witness validator CPACHECKER converts the GraphML file (from Fig. 3) into its internal protocol automaton [11], which includes the constraints of the witness. The analysis then runs this automaton in parallel to the default analysis (reduced product) and strengthens the transition relation of the analysis with the additional constraints from the witness. The analysis starts with an initial abstract state built from the program-entry location in the CFA and the entry node in the witness automaton. Then it computes successors for each state and follows a strategy that aims at getting as deep as possible into the witness automaton. This corresponds with strict guidance from the protocol automaton.

By the definition of the witness and the CFA, it is guaranteed that each step through the violation witness matches one or more edges in the program's CFA. The witness structure guides the search towards the property violation in the program. The validator only confirms a property violation from a violation witness, if both the witness automaton and the program location refer to a property violation according to the specification.

For the example, the validation process reports a property violation and confirms the violation witness. The framework reports the validated counterexample trace in form of a new violation witness, which looks quite similar to the existing one. As our validation process uses the BDD-based domain, intermediate steps can be different and more precise than with the previously used explicit-value analysis. However, exporting data from BDDs is more difficult and CPACHECKER does not (yet) support it for the witness export.

4   Violation Witnesses for Multi-threaded Programs

This section gives some details about the extension of the witness format to multi-threaded programs and the implementation of a validator. We used the most obvious way to model traces in multi-threaded programs: specify which thread executes which statement at which point in the trace.

4.1   Extending the Existing Format

A violation witness should contain sufficient information about the verification task, such that a validator can efficiently replay the property violation, that is, without re-analyzing the whole state space of the program. This means that for guiding the validator towards a certain property violation, the witness needs to contain sufficient information about all branching choices. While branching points are obvious in sequential programs —just mark all if-then-else statements—, the situation in a multi-threaded program is more complex. The difficulty is to determine the correct ordering of thread interleavings along the counterexample trace. A detailed look provides us insights about the encoding of thread interleavings in CPAchecker: Each program state represents multiple program counters (i.e., one program location per thread) and thus allows the execution of the follower statement from any available thread. We identified only one single information that is critical for the validator to successfully validate a violation witness for a multi-threaded program: a unique *thread identifier* to identify the actual thread that executes a statement given in the witness. Along a violation witness, the thread identifier is required for two different steps:

- Whenever a new thread is started via a control-flow edge calling `pthread_create`, we insert the information `createThread=<ID>`, where ID is a new thread identifier for the new thread. Using these hints on *thread creation*, the validator can register a new thread and follow its control flow.
- The thread interleaving is encoded with the *thread identifier* that is given for each statement in the witness. The information `threadId=<ID>` is added to all control-flow edges in the witness, where the thread `<ID>` executes the statement along the control-flow edge.

To keep the witness format as simple as possible, our extension of the witness format consists of only the two above pieces of information (and even those two are optional, i.e., just act as hints for the validator to find the property violation faster). Overall, this allows verification tools that already have support for exporting violation witness and can analyze concurrent programs to directly export violation witnesses for concurrent programs without larger changes to their code base. We considered to include an explicit notion of thread exit or thread join into the set of critical information, but it turned out that none of these actually helped or improved the performance of the validator. In other words, terminating a single thread is unimportant and the validator can automatically infer such information, whenever a single thread reaches the end of its control flow.

Limitations of the Format. The current witness format does not support assumptions using thread-local scopes of identifiers, such as *x from thread 1 is larger than x from thread 2*. The validator could in principle overcome this limitation by heuristically choosing which thread is responsible for which identifier. This could make validation slow due to a potentially large overhead. Alternatively, we could extend the assumption format, which are currently plain C statements, with fully qualified names. However, that requires several changes to the syntax (parser and exporter) of the assumptions in both producer and consumer of the witness format. Thus, our validator currently ignores assumptions for which it can not deterministically assign the corresponding thread.

The current witness format does not support quantifiers. For a possibly unbounded number of threads in the program, a correctness witness has to provide information (invariants) over all threads, i.e., uses quantifiers such as *forall threads: property violation can not happen*.

4.2   Implementation of the Validator in CPACHECKER

CPACHECKER transforms a given GraphML-based witness into its internal automaton format, which is then applied along the program analysis to restrict the reachable state space. Additional assumptions over program variables that are given in the witness can be used to strengthen domain-specific transfer relations or cut off the state-space exploration, e. g., if an assumption about a program variable does not satisfy its current assignment.

The validator uses the information from the violation witness for two different features: (1) The state-space exploration is configured to prioritize the search in the direction of the violation witness, i.e., as soon as any control-flow edge from the witness is matching, CPACHECKER directly follows that direction. This does not exclude other traces of the program, as they will just be scheduled later in the exploration algorithm. (2) If an assumption is available in the witness, the validator applies *strengthening* and allows to exchange of information between CPAs.

Matching Thread Identifiers. The validator needs to combine the information provided in the witness automaton with its own thread model. The important information for multi-threading is provided as an (optional) thread identifier for each single control-flow edge. The validator assumes that the identifier is unique for any particular state in the witness, and we allow to reuse a thread identifier if its previous usage is out of scope, i.e., the corresponding thread has already exited and was joined.

Our internal thread model uses indices to refer to threads in an abstract state. When validating the violation witness, we create a mapping of the thread identifier from the witness to a possible thread index of our own thread model. This allows the validator to be independent from any concrete representation of a thread identifier in the witness.

Analyses in CPACHECKER with Support for Multi-threaded Programs. The validation for violation witnesses uses the default CPA algorithm [17], which provides an efficient state-space exploration and can be combined with CEGAR.

With the CPA concept, we combine independent analyses (CPAs) that work for different aspects of the program analysis. The automaton analysis handles the matching against the specification automaton and the witness automaton, The threading analysis [13] manages the thread scheduling and interleaving. Additional CPAs like an explicit-value analysis [21], a BDD-based [23], or interval-based analysis allow to reason about assignments of variables.

For validation of violation witnesses, we additionally *strengthen* the abstract threading state with information provided in the witness automaton, in order to track the mapping of thread identifiers and thread indices, and to cut off irrelevant branches in the state space eagerly.

Limitations of the Validator. There are some conceptional or implementation-defined limitations of the current implementation of the validator. We discuss these limitations to encourage developers of future validators for multi-threaded programs to improve the approach in our tool, to extend other validators for sequential programs by support for multi-threaded tasks, or to provide new validators.

Based on the requirement to prepare a CFA for each thread of a multi-threaded program, there is a fixed upper bound in the number of threads (default value is 5). The validator ignores traces that use more than the given number of threads, which is an unsound approximation. Note that this is no general limitation of the witness format or the validator. Each concrete error trace for a violation witness has a bounded length and thus can only use a bounded number of thread interleavings. (For example, the number of threads could be added to the metadata of the violation witness and the limit value could be set appropriately.) For the evaluated verification tasks, the default limit was sufficient. If the violation witness is to imprecise and the program allows to create more threads than given in the violation witness, the validator can of course also apply the analysis for more threads. Due to our simple threading analysis, we can only track threads with simple thread-identifier assignments, i.e., where the thread itself is not assigned to an array element or complex pointer structure.

CPAchecker currently supports two domains concretely for analyzing multi-threaded programs, which are explicit-value analysis and BDD-based analysis. The default is to use the BDD-based approach, as it can also handle symbolic values. The validator inherits the limitations of those domains, e.g., it has only limited support for heap-related data structures, such that we need to ignore most array- or pointer-related operations, which can make the validation process imprecise and in some cases even unsound (in case of pointer assignments). This leads to two general cases in which a validator can be wrong: (a) there could be a perfectly valid violation witness but the validator cannot replay it and rejects it due to missing feature support and (b) there could be an invalid violation witness (does not describe a feasible error path) but the validator still finds a different feasible counterexample itself and accepts it due to imprecise information in the witness. There were a few such cases in SV-COMP 2020. The following examples are extracted from the results of SV-COMP 2020 by manual investigation, to give an impression for unsupported features and how they show up in the results[3]:

---

[3] SV-COMP published all referenced witnesses [9] and verification tasks [8].

- CBMC provides a valid (rather short) violation witness[4] for the task `tls_destructor_worker.yml`[5]. The validator with BDD-based analysis can not confirm this witness due to missing support for `pthread_create_key` and pointer operations.
- ESBMC provides a valid violation witness[6] for the task `race-2_3-container_of.yml`[7], which the validator with BDD-based analysis can not confirm due to missing support for structs.
- YOGAR-CBMC provides a valid violation witness[8] for the task `bigshot_p.yml`[9], for which the validator aborts due to an unexpected assignment of a thread identifier into an array element.

So far, the presented validator is the only validator for multi-threaded programs, and it participated already three years in the competition of software verification (since SV-COMP 2018).

5 Experimental Evaluation

We perform an experimental evaluation on violation witnesses for multi-threaded programs to provide qualitative and quantitative insights on how well the result validation based on violation witnesses for multi-threaded programs works.

5.1 Evaluation Questions

We split our experimental evaluation into the following evaluation questions:

Q1: Which verifiers already support the export of violation witnesses for multi-threaded programs after a successful verification run and what kind of information about the counterexample trace is provided within the witness.

Q2: Is the format sufficient and concrete enough for the validator to re-verify the counterexample trace?

Q3: Is the validation process faster than the verification process?

---

[4] https://sv-comp.sosy-lab.org/2020/results/fileByHash/
c4a519d36a719304f05e0af3675a0bcf40a7ce4d5000fba784365eed63105ee0.
graphml

[5] https://github.com/sosy-lab/sv-benchmarks/blob/svcomp20/c/
pthread-divine/tls_destructor_worker.yml

[6] https://sv-comp.sosy-lab.org/2020/results/fileByHash/
784befbee140f91b180268f489a6cdce2471ffc6f8578fb0e361c3d2953313d1.
graphml

[7] https://github.com/sosy-lab/sv-benchmarks/blob/svcomp20/c/ldv-races/
race-2_3-container_of.yml

[8] https://sv-comp.sosy-lab.org/2020/results/fileByHash/
f197f473759cc28e4845bcfc6f92af00c0d3ad27e020ee9db1029bfd7c854dba.
graphml

[9] https://github.com/sosy-lab/sv-benchmarks/blob/svcomp20/c/pthread/
bigshot_p.yml

5.2 Benchmark Set

We evaluate the witness format and the validator on a large set of verification tasks, which is taken from the SV-Benchmarks collection [8][10], in the same version as used for SV-COMP 2020. We limit the benchmark set to the subset of verification tasks that exactly matches the category *ConcurrencySafety* in SV-COMP 2020, i.e., multi-threaded programs with a reachability property as specification.

5.3 Setup

Our experiments were executed on computers with Intel Xeon E3-1230 v5 CPUs, 3.40 GHz CPU frequency, and 33 GB of RAM. We limited the CPU time to 15 min and the memory to 15 GB.

We evaluated our validator on violation witnesses from SV-COMP [9] that were produced by several different software verifiers. We selected those verifiers that participated in SV-COMP 2020 [7], support violation witnesses (produced more than 100 such witnesses that were confirmed), and have publicly available archives on GitLab[11]. Those verifiers are the following seven: CBMC, CPA-SEQ, DIVINE, ESBMC, LAZY-CSEQ, PESCO, and YOGAR-CBMC. In addition to the witnesses that we took from SV-COMP [9], we also used an updated version of CPACHECKER (revision r33531) to produce witnesses, where a small extension for the export of violation witnesses was applied (add all beneficial information about thread identifiers to the violation witness and consider more thread interleavings). We include this additional verifier to show that a small and inexpensive extension can lead to a significant improvement of the validation results. The CPU time and memory consumption for each verification run was measured by SV-COMP using BENCHEXEC [22], and the number of nodes and transitions was counted using the GraphML witness files.

Currently, there is only one validator available for violation witnesses of multi-threaded programs, which is the validator explained in Sect. 4.2 and implemented in the CPACHECKER framework[2]. We use revision r33531 for the experiments.

5.4 Results and Discussion

Q1: Verifier Support and Available Information. All verifiers that we considered in our experiments support (1) the verification of multi-threaded programs and (2) the export of violation witnesses. Some tools include the beneficial information about thread interleaving in the violation witness. That specific feature was already requested in SV-COMP 2018, when the organizers extended the validation of violation witnesses to the category of concurrent tasks. This shows that our extension was already adopted to other verification tools. However, the availability and the quality of the integration differs between the tools.

---

[10] https://github.com/sosy-lab/sv-benchmarks/tree/svcomp20
[11] https://gitlab.com/sosy-lab/sv-comp/archives-2020/-/tree/svcomp20/2020

Table 1. Statistical description of the generated witnesses for the verifiers

Verifier	Number of states				Number of transitions			
	Median	Mean	Max	Sum	Median	Mean	Max	Sum
CBMC	6.00	6.05	10	4 790	4.00	4.05	8	3 210
CPA-SEQ	48.0	48.7	662	38 700	82.0	84.4	744	67 000
CPACHECKER (r33531)	141	140	1 480	112 000	207	202	1 620	161 000
DIVINE	3.00	3.05	5	1 820	2.00	2.05	4	1 220
ESBMC	3.00	5.19	30	4 140	2.00	4.19	29	3 340
LAZY-CSEQ	66.0	64.1	156	52 100	64.0	62.1	154	50 500
PESCO	51.0	49.5	662	38 600	83.0	85.9	744	67 000
YOGAR-CBMC	86.0	84.7	188	68 300	84.0	82.7	186	66 700

Table 2. Properties of the exported violation witnesses

Verifier	Thread id	Thread creation	All thread interleavings
CBMC		✓	
CPA-SEQ	✓	✓	
CPACHECKER (r33531)	✓	✓	✓
DIVINE			
ESBMC			
LAZY-CSEQ	✓	✓	✓
PESCO	✓	✓	
YOGAR-CBMC	✓	✓	✓

Table 1 gives a statistical overview of the provided violation witnesses and shows how many states and transitions are available in the violation witnesses. Figure 5a shows the distribution of sizes of the violation witnesses for different verifiers. As most tasks have roughly equal difficulty and length of the counterexample trace, the sizes of the violation witnesses are in a certain range. The noticeable difference comes with the tools themselves, i.e., some tools export more details than others.

We also inspected the witnesses for the kind of information they contain. Table 2 shows the different kinds of information available in the witnesses produced by the verifiers. We analyzed whether the violation witnesses contain the *thread id* for every transition, information about *thread creation* for newly started threads during the counterexample trace, and information about thread interleaving. CBMC, DIVINE, and ESBMC only export the main thread of the multi-threaded program, which is not suitable for a counterexample trace with interleaving thread statements, because all information about other threads is missing.

Q2: Validation Results. The validation results for the produced violation witnesses show whether the information from the violation witness was sufficient to guide the validator towards confirming the given counterexample trace. Overall, the performance of the validation run is determined by two factors: first, how well the violation witness itself guides the state-space exploration and defines the thread

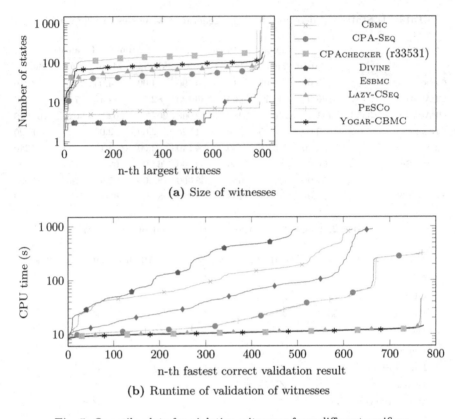

(a) Size of witnesses

(b) Runtime of validation of witnesses

Fig. 5. Quantile plots for violation witnesses from different verifiers

scheduling, and second, how precise the data in the violation witness are. The less information is provided in the violation witness, the more work is left to the validator with its heuristics to recover the error trace. In other words, more precise violation witnesses are often validated faster than less precise witnesses. Figure 5b shows the CPU time of the validator for violation witnesses from different verification tools. Comparing the results with the annotations exported by the tools (Table 2) leads us to a first conclusion: exporting thread interleavings is critical for finding a concrete counterexample path through the program during validation.

As CBMC, DIVINE, and ESBMC produce violation witnesses that contain only a minimal set of nodes and transitions, especially only consisting of the main function of the program and ignoring any additional threads, the validation can not follow the given trace sufficiently and performs worse than for other violation witnesses. CPA-SEQ and PESCO use the same underlying analysis, i.e., both tools apply CPACHECKER's BDD-based concurrency analyzer with nearly identical options. Thus, they produce nearly identical violation witnesses which also results in similar validation performance.

For the three tools that export thread interleavings in the violation witness, the validation is fast and precise for most of the available verification tasks. Apart from the startup time of the validator (due to starting the Java VM), the

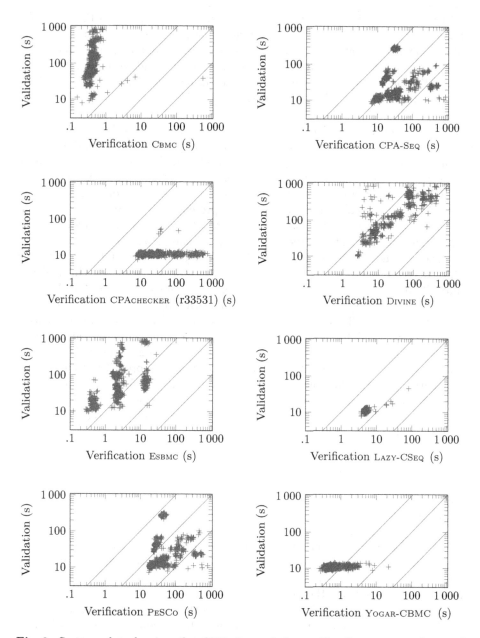

Fig. 6. Scatter plot showing the CPU time of the verification process of several tools against the CPU time of the validation process

runtime of the validation itself is negligible. The violation witness guides the validator in the right direction, i.e., all scheduling information is available and nearly no overhead from unimportant program traces appears in the validation process. Only some validation tasks suffer from a high runtime, but these cases also suffer from a rather long and complex to find counterexample trace, such that the violation witness itself contains several thousands of nodes. Note that depending on the verifier, a different path might have been determined, resulting in violation witnesses of different length for each verification task.

Q3: Performance of Validation Compared to Verification. Based on the CPU time consumed by the verifiers and the CPU time consumed by the validator, we can compare the performance of the validation with the performance of the verification per verifier. Figure 6 shows several scatter plots, each comparing for a given verifier the CPU times for successful validation runs against the corresponding verification runs. Each data point in the scatter plots represents a verification task that was verified and the resulting violation witness was then successfully validated. The three diagonal lines indicate the factors of 0.1, 1, and 10 between the coordinates.

The overall picture for all scatter plots is as follows: The validator (as part of CPACHECKER) is written in Java and has a large startup overhead. This makes it difficult to see a clear performance difference for the small and fast verification tasks. For CBMC and ESBMC, which are tools with only very imprecise witnesses, the validation usually needs much more CPU time than the actual verification took, i.e., the validator needed much more time to find a counterexample trace matching the rudimentary information in the violation witness. DIVINE not only has quite imprecise witnesses, but also requires more CPU time for the verification process; thus the difference to the time required for the validation is smaller. For more precise witnesses, as produced by LAZY-CSEQ, YOGAR-CBMC, and CPACHECKER (r33531), the validation process is often faster, or at least requires mostly a nearly constant time (about 10 s).

5.5   Threats to Validity

The validity of our experiments is limited by certain choices that we made in the ex- periment setup.

External Validity. The verifiers are all state-of-the-art and seven of them are taken from SV-COMP 2020. We applied the same options and a similar en- vironment that was used in the competition execution, and collected the vi- olation witnesses from the selected verifiers.

There exists only a single validator for multi-threaded violation witnesses, and it might be possible that our results (sufficient information in the witness format) does not apply to other, future validators for multi-threaded programs. We based our validator on the verification framework CPACHECKER, because mechanisms for witness export and validation was already integrated. The configuration using a BDD-based analysis is currently the most performant approach for multi-threaded programs in the framework. The heuristics for exploring the abstract state space are tuned to match witnesses from a broad range of verifiers.

The community-based SV-Benchmarks repository is a largest and most divers collection of verification tasks for the language C. We used all verification tasks that were also used by the most recent competition: category *ConcurrencySafety*.

Internal Validity. The validator might contain programming bugs, but we based our validator on the infrastructure that is used by the verifier CPA-Seq, which performed extremely well in the recent competitions. Thus, we believe that the implementation has a high quality. Also, previous versions of our validator participated in the competition since SV-COMP 2018. Limitations of the validator were discussed in depth in Sect. 4.2.

The execution of the verification and validation runs was done with BENCHEXEC [22], the (only available) state-of-the-art benchmarking tool, which is also used by the StarExec competition infrastructure and competitions like SV-COMP and Test-Comp. BENCHEXEC is used to enforce the limits and collect measurements for the consumed resources (CPU time and memory).

6 Conclusion

While validation of verification results for sequential programs has been thoroughly described in 2015, validation support for multi-threaded programs was not yet described in the literature. This paper closes this gap by describing the (only available) validator for multi-threaded programs, which was already used three times as validator in the competition on software verification (SV-COMP 2018-2020).

In our evaluation, we report the available features that the witnesses produced by several verifiers expose to the validator, and we report the performance. The results are promising, but it would be better for the verification community to have more such validators available: There are six validators for violation witnesses for sequential programs, but only one for multi-threaded programs.

Data Availability Statement. We make the violation witnesses, a ready-to-run archive of CPACHECKER, and all experimental results (including raw data, tables, and plots) available on a supplementary web site[12] and in a Zenodo archive [14]. The verifiers that participated in SV-COMP 2020 have publicly available archives in a GitLab repository.[11] More witnesses and results from SV-COMP can be found in the archives mentioned in the report [7] (Table 4).

References

1. Andrianov, P., Mutilin, V., Khoroshilov, A.: Predicate abstraction based configurable method for data race detection in Linux kernel. In: Proc. TMPA, CCIS, vol. 779. Springer (2018). https://doi.org/10.1007/978-3-319-71734-0_2

---

[12] https://www.sosy-lab.org/research/witnesses-concurrency

2. Artho, C., Havelund, K., Honiden, S.: Visualization of concurrent program executions. In: Proc. COMPSAC, pp. 541–546. IEEE (2007). https://doi.org/10.1109/COMPSAC.2007.236
3. Baranová, Z., Barnat, J., Kejstová, K., Kučera, T., Lauko, H., Mrázek, J., Ročkai, P., Štill, V.: Model checking of C and C++ with DIVINE 4. In: Proc. ATVA, LNCS, vol. 10482, pp. 201–207. Springer (2017). https://doi.org/10.1007/978-3-319-68167-2_14
4. Beyer, D.: Software verification and verifiable witnesses (Report on SV-COMP 2015). In: Proc. TACAS, LNCS, vol. 9035, pp. 401–416. Springer (2015). https://doi.org/10.1007/978-3-662-46681-0_31
5. Beyer, D.: Reliable and reproducible competition results with BENCHEXEC and witnesses (Report on SV-COMP 2016). In: Proc. TACAS, LNCS, vol. 9636, pp. 887–904. Springer (2016). https://doi.org/10.1007/978-3-662-49674-9_55
6. Beyer, D.: Software verification with validation of results (Report on SV-COMP 2017). In: Proc. TACAS, LNCS, vol. 10206, pp. 331–349. Springer (2017). https://doi.org/10.1007/978-3-662-54580-5_20
7. Beyer, D.: Advances in automatic software verification: SV-COMP 2020. In: Proc. TACAS (2), LNCS, vol. 12079, pp. 347–367. Springer (2020). https://doi.org/10.1007/978-3-030-45237-7_21
8. Beyer, D.: SV-Benchmarks: Benchmark set of 9th Intl. Competition on Software Verification (SV-COMP 2020). Zenodo (2020). https://doi.org/10.5281/zenodo.3633334
9. Beyer, D.: Verification witnesses from SV-COMP 2020 verification tools. Zenodo (2020). https://doi.org/10.5281/zenodo.3630188
10. Beyer, D., Dangl, M., Dietsch, D., Heizmann, M.: Correctness witnesses: Exchanging verification results between verifiers. In: Proc. FSE, pp. 326–337. ACM (2016). https://doi.org/10.1145/2950290.2950351
11. Beyer, D., Dangl, M., Dietsch, D., Heizmann, M., Stahlbauer, A.: Witness validation and stepwise testification across software verifiers. In: Proc. FSE, pp. 721–733. ACM (2015). https://doi.org/10.1145/2786805.2786867
12. Beyer, D., Dangl, M., Lemberger, T., Tautschnig, M.: Tests from witnesses: Execution-based validation of verification results. In: Proc. TAP, LNCS, vol. 10889, pp. 3–23. Springer (2018). https://doi.org/10.1007/978-3-319-92994-1_1
13. Beyer, D., Friedberger, K.: A light-weight approach for verifying multi-threaded programs with CPACHECKER. In: Proc. MEMICS, EPTCS, vol. 233, pp. 61–71 (2016). https://doi.org/10.4204/EPTCS.233.6
14. Beyer, D., Friedberger, K.: Replication package for article 'Violation witnesses and result validation for multi-threaded programs'. Zenodo (2020). https://doi.org/10.5281/zenodo.3885694
15. Beyer, D., Gulwani, S., Schmidt, D.: Combining model checking and data-flow analysis. In: Handbook of Model Checking, pp. 493–540. Springer (2018). https://doi.org/10.1007/978-3-319-10575-8_16
16. Beyer, D., Henzinger, T.A., Théoduloz, G.: Configurable software verification: Concretizing the convergence of model checking and program analysis. In: Proc. CAV, LNCS, vol. 4590, pp. 504–518. Springer (2007). https://doi.org/10.1007/978-3-540-73368-3_51
17. Beyer, D., Henzinger, T.A., Théoduloz, G.: Program analysis with dynamic precision adjustment. In: Proc. ASE, pp. 29–38. IEEE (2008). https://doi.org/10.1109/ASE.2008.13

18. Beyer, D., Keremoglu, M.E.: CPACHECKER: A tool for configurable software verification. In: Proc. CAV, LNCS, vol. 6806, pp. 184–190. Springer (2011). https://doi.org/10.1007/978-3-642-22110-1_16

19. Beyer, D., Keremoglu, M.E., Wendler, P.: Predicate abstraction with adjustable-block encoding. In: Proc. FMCAD, pp. 189–197. FMCAD (2010)

20. Beyer, D., Lemberger, T.: CPA-SymExec: Efficient symbolic execution in CPAchecker. In: Proc. ASE, pp. 900–903. ACM (2018). https://doi.org/10.1145/3238147.3240478

21. Beyer, D., Löwe, S.: Explicit-state software model checking based on CEGAR and interpolation. In: Proc. FASE, LNCS, vol. 7793, pp. 146–162. Springer (2013). https://doi.org/10.1007/978-3-642-37057-1_11

22. Beyer, D., Löwe, S., Wendler, P.: Reliable benchmarking: Requirements and solutions. Int. J. Softw. Tools Technol. Transfer 21(1), 1–29 (2017). https://doi.org/10.1007/s10009-017-0469-y

23. Beyer, D., Stahlbauer, A.: BDD-based software verification: Applications to event-condition-action systems. Int. J. Softw. Tools Technol. Transfer 16(5), 507–518 (2014). https://doi.org/10.1007/s10009-014-0334-1

24. Beyer, D., Wehrheim, H.: Verification artifacts in cooperative verification: Survey and unifying component framework. arXiv/CoRR 1905(08505) (May 2019). https://arxiv.org/abs/1905.08505

25. Beyer, D., Wendler, P.: Reuse of verification results: Conditional model checking, precision reuse, and verification witnesses. In: Proc. SPIN, LNCS, vol. 7976, pp. 1–17. Springer (2013). https://doi.org/10.1007/978-3-642-39176-7_1

26. Brandes, U., Eiglsperger, M., Herman, I., Himsolt, M., Marshall, M.S.: GraphML progress report. In: Graph Drawing, LNCS, vol. 2265, pp. 501–512. Springer (2001). https://doi.org/10.1007/3-540-45848-4_59

27. Cadar, C., Ganesh, V., Pawlowski, P.M., Dill, D.L., Engler, D.R.: EXE: Automatically generating inputs of death. In: Proc. CCS, pp. 322–335. ACM (2006). https://doi.org/10.1145/1180405.1180445

28. Castaño, R., Braberman, V.A., Garbervetsky, D., Uchitel, S.: Model checker execution reports. In: Proc. ASE, pp. 200–205. IEEE (2017). https://doi.org/10.1109/ASE.2017.8115633

29. Clarke, E.M., Kröning, D., Lerda, F.: A tool for checking ANSI-C programs. In: Proc. TACAS, LNCS, vol. 2988, pp. 168–176. Springer (2004). https://doi.org/10.1007/978-3-540-24730-2_15

30. Csallner, C., Smaragdakis, Y.: Check 'n' crash: Combining static checking and testing. In: Proc. ICSE, pp. 422–431. ACM (2005). https://doi.org/10.1145/1062455.1062533

31. Czech, M., Hüllermeier, E., Jakobs, M.C., Wehrheim, H.: Predicting rankings of software verification tools. In: Proc. SWAN, pp. 23–26. ACM (2017). https://doi.org/10.1145/3121257.3121262

32. Gadelha, M.Y.R., Ismail, H.I., Cordeiro, L.C.: Handling loops in bounded model checking of C programs via k-induction. Int. J. Softw. Tools Technol. Transfer 19(1), 97–114 (2017). https://doi.org/10.1007/s10009-015-0407-9

33. Gavrilenko, N., Ponce de León, H., Furbach, F., Heljanko, K., Meyer, R.: BMC for weak memory models: Relation analysis for compact SMT encodings. In: Proc. CAV, LNCS, vol. 11561, pp. 355–365. Springer (2019). https://doi.org/10.1007/978-3-030-25540-4_19

34. Gennari, J., Gurfinkel, A., Kahsai, T., Navas, J.A., Schwartz, E.J.: Executable counterexamples in software model checking. In: Proc. VSTTE, LNCS, vol. 11294, pp. 17–37. Springer (2018). https://doi.org/10.1007/978-3-030-03592-1_2

35. Greitschus, M., Dietsch, D., Podelski, A.: Loop invariants from counterexamples. In: Proc. SAS, LNCS, vol. 10422, pp. 128–147. Springer (2017). https://doi.org/10.1007/978-3-319-66706-5_7

36. Gunter, E.L., Peled, D.A.: Path exploration tool. In: Proc. TACAS, LNCS, vol. 1579, pp. 405–419. Springer (1999). https://doi.org/10.1007/3-540-49059-0_28

37. Heizmann, M., Hoenicke, J., Podelski, A.: Software model checking for people who love automata. In: Proc. CAV, LNCS, vol. 8044, pp. 36–52. Springer (2013). https://doi.org/10.1007/978-3-642-39799-8_2

38. Inverso, O., Tomasco, E., Fischer, B., La Torre, S., Parlato, G.: Lazy-CSeq: A lazy sequentialization tool for C (competition contribution). In: Proc. TACAS, LNCS, vol. 8413, pp. 398–401. Springer (2014). https://doi.org/10.1007/978-3-642-54862-8_29

39. Inverso, O., Trubiani, C.: Parallel and distributed bounded model checking of multi-threaded programs. In: Proc. PPoPP. ACM (2020)

40. Yin, L., Dong, W., Liu, W., Wang, J.: On scheduling constraint abstraction for multi-threaded program verification. IEEE Trans. Softw. Eng. (2018). https://doi.org/10.1109/TSE.2018.2864122

Tendermint Blockchain Synchronization: Formal Specification and Model Checking

Sean Braithwaite[2], Ethan Buchman[1], Igor Konnov[3(✉)], Zarko Milosevic[2], Ilina Stoilkovska[3], Josef Widder[3], and Anca Zamfir[2]

[1] Informal Systems, Toronto, Canada
ethan@informal.systems
[2] Informal Systems, Lausanne, Switzerland
{sean,zarko,anca}@informal.systems
[3] Informal Systems, Vienna, Austria
{igor,ilina,josef}@informal.systems

Abstract. Blockchain synchronization is one of the core protocols of Tendermint blockchains. We describe our recent efforts on formal specification of the protocol and its implementation, and present model checking results for small parameters. We demonstrate that the protocol quality and understanding can be improved by writing specifications and applying model checking to verify their properties.

1 Introduction

Tendermint is a state-of-the art Byzantine-fault-tolerant state machine replication (BFT SMR) engine equipped with a flexible interface supporting arbitrary state machines written in any programming language [6]. Tendermint is particularly popular for proof-of-stake blockchains, and constitutes a core component of the Cosmos Project [7]. At the heart of the Cosmos Project is the InterBlockchain Communication protocol (IBC) for reliable communication between independent BFT SMs; what TCP is for computers, IBC aims to be for blockchains.

Multiple Tendermint-based blockchains run in production on the public Internet for over a year, with new ones launching regularly. They carry billions of dollars of cumulative value in the market capitalizations of their respective cryptocurrencies. One of the primary deployments is the Cosmos Hub blockchain [24]. It is operated by a diverse set of 125 consensus forming nodes; they are connected over an open-membership gossip network consisting of hundreds of other nodes.

Tendermint was the first proof-of-stake blockchain system to apply traditional BFT consensus protocols at its core [18]. The Tendermint BFT consensus protocol constitutes a modern implementation of the consensus algorithm for Byzantine faults with Authentication from [11], built on top of an efficient gossiping layer. The latest description of the consensus protocol can be found in the technical report [8]. Tendermint has been a source of inspiration for a wide variety of blockchain systems that have followed [9,26], though few, if any, have achieved its level of maturity in production.

Supported by Interchain Foundation (Switzerland).

T. Margaria and B. Steffen (Eds.): ISoLA 2020, LNCS 12476, pp. 471–488, 2020.
https://doi.org/10.1007/978-3-030-61362-4_27

The reference implementation of the Tendermint software is written in Go [25]. Under the hood, it consists of several fault-tolerant distributed protocols that interact to ensure efficient operation:

Consensus. Core BFT consensus protocol including the gossiping of proposals, blocks, and votes.

Evidence. To incentivize consensus participants to follow the consensus protocol (and not behave faulty), in the proof-of-stake systems, misbehavior is punished by destroying stake. This protocol gossips evidence of malicious behavior in the form of conflicting signatures.

Mempool. A protocol to gossip transactions, ensuring transactions that should eventually end up in a block are distributed to all participants.

Peer Exchange. Gossiping is based on communication only with a subset of the peers. Managing the list of available peers and selecting peers based on performance metrics is done by this protocol.

Blockchain synchronization (Fastsync). If a peer gets disconnected by the network for some time, it might miss the most recent blocks in the blockchain. A node that recovers from such a disconnection uses the blockchain synchronization protocol to learn blocks without going through consensus.

We are conducting a project to formally specify and model check these protocols. The first protocol we considered was the blockchain synchronization protocol called *Fastsync*. Specifications can be found in English [13] and TLA$^+$ [14].

Fastsync. A full node that connects to a Tendermint blockchain needs to synchronize its state to the latest global state of the network. This network state is defined by the sequence of blocks that the system has decided upon. These blocks are numbered continuously, and a block's number is called its height, and the height of the most recently added block is called the current height of the blockchain. Thus, another way to put the blockchain synchronization problem is the need to catch-up to a recent height of the blockchain. One way to achieve this is using Fastsync: Initially, the node has a local copy of a blockchain prefix and the corresponding application state that may be out of date. The node queries its peers for the blocks that were decided on by the Tendermint blockchain since the time the full node was disconnected from the system. (Fastsync can be also used by a fresh node that connects to a blockchain; the node starts with the genesis file, i.e., the initial block.) After receiving these blocks, the protocol executes the transactions that are stored in the blocks, in order to synchronize to the current height of the blockchain and the corresponding application state.

Figure 1 shows a typical execution of the Blockchain Synchronization protocol. In this execution, a new node connects to two full nodes: a correct peer and a faulty peer. The node requests the blockchain heights of the peers by issuing `statusReq`. Once a peer replies with its height, e.g., with `statusRes(10)`, the node can request for a block i by sending the message `blockReq(i)`. In our example, the correct peer receives the request `blockReq(1)` for block 1 and replies with the message `blockRes(b1)` that contains the block. In a Tendermint blockchain, the commit (signed votes messages) for block `h` is contained

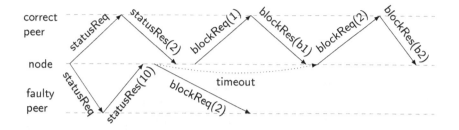

Fig. 1. A Fastsync execution for a fully unsynchronized node of height 1

in block **h+1**, and thus a node performing Fastsync must receive two sequential blocks before it can verify fully the first of them. If verification succeeds, the first block is accepted; if it fails, both blocks are rejected, as it is unknown which block was faulty. When the node rejects a block, it suspects the sending peer of being faulty and evicts this peer from the set of peers. The same happens when a peer does not reply within a predefined time interval. In our example, the faulty peer is evicted, and the node finishes synchronization with the correct peer.

The above example may produce an impression that it is easy to specify and verify correctness of Fastsync. (The authors of this paper thought so.) By writing several protocol specifications in English and TLA$^+$ and by running model checkers, we have found that the specifications are intricate, in particular due to the presence of faulty peers. Moreover, the intuitive safety and liveness properties often fail to hold, and one has to refine the temporal formulas used to encode these properties. This effort significantly improves understanding of the protocol boundaries and of its guarantees.

2   Architecture

The most recent implementation of the Fastsync protocol, called V2, is the result of significant refactoring to improve testability and determinism, as described in the Architectural Decision Record [1]. In the original design, a go-routine (thread of execution) was spawned for each block requested, and was responsible for both protocol logic and network IO. In the V2 design, the protocol logic is decoupled from IO by using three concurrent threads of execution: a `scheduler`, a `processor`, and a `demuxer`, as per Fig. 2.

Both the scheduler and processor are structured as finite state machines with input and output events. Inputs are received on an unbounded priority queue, with higher priority for error events. Output events are emitted on a blocking, bounded channel. Network IO is handled by the Tendermint p2p subsystem, where messages are sent in a non-blocking manner. The demuxer routine is responsible for all IO, including translating between internal events and network IO messages, and routing events between components.

The task of the scheduler is to ensure that a number of blocks are always available for verification by the processor. To achieve this, the scheduler tracks

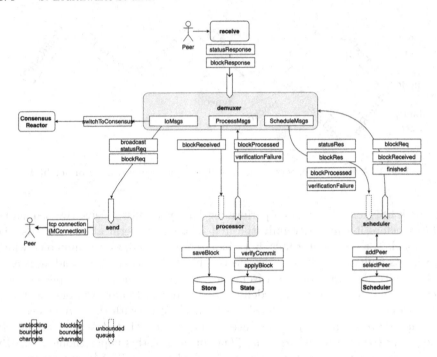

Fig. 2. Communication between components in the Fastsync implementation [1].

peers and their heights (via `statusReq` and `statusRes` messages and events) and makes block requests (`blockReq`) to peers. In order not to overload any one peer, the block requests are equally spread across the peers. The block responses (`blockRes`) are forwarded to the processor (`blockReceived`) for verification. The scheduler maintains lists of pending block requests and block responses for each peer. Peers that (i) are unresponsive, (ii) sent blocks which cause verification failure, or (iii) sent unsolicited blocks, are removed, together with any unprocessed blocks from these peers. In case there are pending block requests associated with the removed peers, these blocks are requested from other peers.

The processor performs block processing, including verification of consensus signatures and execution of all transactions, which is performed in increasing order of the block height. The blocks that are successfully verified are stored in `Store`, and the chain `State` is updated with the result of transaction execution (cf. Fig. 2). The result of the block processing (`blockProcessed` or `verificationFailure`) is sent to the scheduler via the **demuxer** routine. The scheduler keeps track of the block execution height and triggers termination—at the maximum peer height (`finished`). Once a node terminates executing Fastsync, it continues by executing the Tendermint consensus protocol to stay up to date with the latest blockchain changes.

3   Specifications in English and TLA$^+$

In addition to protocol verification, we are elaborating a verification-driven development process. Our goal is to have a design process that has researchers, verification engineers, and software engineers in the loop during the design and development of protocols. Fastsync was the first protocol where we adopted that process in part. By the time we started our verification efforts, the blockchain synchronization protocol had already been designed using a classic engineering process, whose artifacts include architecture decision records and English specifications that focus on data structures and APIs. There had already been two implementations of the protocol (V0 and V1), and our software engineering team was in the process of wrapping-up a third implementation (called V2) whose primary goal was increased testability.

In this project we started with joint sessions of software engineers, researchers and verification engineers, in which we wrote first TLA$^+$ specifications together. In order to better understand how TLA$^+$ can be of most help to us, we then wrote different specifications that focus, e.g., on the business logic, the local concurrency architecture of the implementation of V2, and the protocol level; we published the latter at [14]. While TLA$^+$ specifications provide precise semantics, we found that English specifications are a valuable tool for communication, both within the project, but also to others who are interested in the protocols. We thus developed a structure for English specifications [13]. While in the Fastsync project, this structured English specification was written after-the-fact, in the verification-driven development process and our current projects, it is the origin and deals as reference both for implementations written by the software engineers as well as for the TLA$^+$specification written by the verification engineers.

We chose TLA$^+$ for two reasons: (1) We have acquired a good understanding of the language by developing the APALACHE model checker [16], and (2) TLA$^+$ has been successfully used by systems designers, e.g., at Amazon [5, 23].

Structured Specification in English. We start our formalization by a structured English specification [13], that consists of four parts:

1. *Blockchain.* Formalization of relevant properties of the chain and its blocks.
2. *Sequential problem statement.* Here we consider the blockchain as a growing list of blocks, and define what we expect from the blockchain synchronization protocol with respect to this list. This specification is sequential. It ignores that the blockchain is implemented in a distributed system, in which validators may be faulty. Even if they are correct, they locally have prefixes of different lengths, which introduces uncertainty that has to be reflected in the distributed protocol as well as in the distributed problem statement.
3. *Distributed aspects.* Here we introduce the computational model and the refinement of the sequential problem statement. The computational model specifies assumptions about the system, such as assumptions on the message delays, process faults, etc. As a result, the problem statement is restricted to some fairness constraints, e.g., it is preconditioned by the process being connected to at least one correct peer.

4. *Distributed protocol.* Specification of the protocol, where we describe inputs, outputs, variables, and functions used by the protocol. We specify functions mainly in terms of preconditions, postconditions, and error conditions. Further, we provide invariants over the protocol variables. These inform both the implementation and the verification efforts.

Specifications in TLA$^+$. The structure of the English specification highlights interesting properties of the protocols and points to some issues. As it is written in natural language, the English specification is ambiguous. We have written three TLA$^+$ specifications that provide precise semantics, which focus on different aspects of the protocol and its architecture:

- *High-level specification (HLS).* This specification contains the minimal set of interactions in the synchronization protocol. Its primary purpose is to highlight safety and termination properties. HLS was mainly written by the distributed system researchers.
- *Low-level specification (LLS).* While HLS captures the distributed protocol, there was a significant gap between HLS and the implementation. For instance, the implementation uses additional messages and contains detailed error codes, which are missing in HLS. The low-level specification is closer to the implementation. It is mainly written by distributed system engineers.
- *Concurrency specification (CRS).* As discussed above, the V2 implementation uses several threads that communicate via queues. To formally capture this, we wrote a specification that models threads and message queues.

In the following, we focus on the high-level specification in English and TLA$^+$ [14]. In Sects. 4–7, we give the main abstractions and insights about the specifications. The TLA$^+$ specification has about 800 lines, hence we omit presenting it in full detail. In addition, it is parameterized by the blockchain length, and the set of peers. By fixing these parameters, we check its safety and liveness with TLC [17] and APALACHE [16], detailed in Sect. 8.

4   The Blockchain Specification in English and TLA$^+$

A block is a data structure that contains application information (e.g., transactions) as well as metadata needed for the protocols. As we are interested in the blockchain synchronization, some of this metadata is relevant for our formal model. Figure 3 illustrates three blocks of a Tendermint blockchain. The blocks are consecutively numbered, and each block is assigned a number, called its *height*. As the blocks are a result of consensus by *validators*, the validity of a block is confirmed if a quorum of the validators signed (a hash of) a block. The validator membership in Tendermint changes over time, and is indeed a result of consensus itself. Moreover, the validators have an associated voting power, which is not necessarily uniform. For a block, a *validator set* is a set of pairs of IDs of validators and their associated voting power. The quorum we referred to

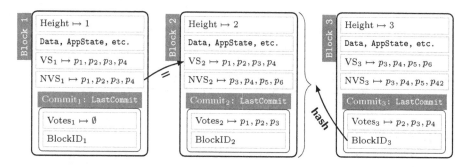

Fig. 3. The block structure in Tendermint blockchain. The fields VS and NVS denote the current and next *validator sets* of a block. Note that $Votes_3$ contains more than $2/3$ of voting power in NVS_1.

above thus corresponds to the set of validators that have more than $2/3$ of the total voting power in a given validator set.

To capture this, in a block of height i, the validator set of the current block is stored in the field VS_i, the validator set for the next block is stored in NVS_i, and the signed messages that confirm block i are stored in the field $Commit_{i+1}$ of the block at height $i + 1$. The nodes whose signatures are in $Commit_{i+1}$ must be a subset of the set VS_i of validators at height i. A node running the blockchain synchronization protocol checks the quorums and signatures in order to locally confirm whether a downloaded block originates from the blockchain. Therefore, it is crucial to capture validator sets and commits in our formal specification.

TLA^+ *Specification.* The blockchain data structures in the implementation are quite rich. To render model checking possible, we abstract blocks so that the safety and liveness properties of the protocol are preserved, while the potential search space becomes finite and relatively small. We call this model Tinychain, and present it below. A compact version of TLA^+ code is shown in Listing 1.

First, note that in general, the number of blocks on a blockchain may grow unboundedly. As a result, the field height is also an unbounded integer. Hence, we parameterize the blockchain with the maximal height MAX_HEIGHT in line 3.

Second, the structure of the validator sets is not essential for the protocol. The few required properties of the blocks, hashes, and validator sets are axiomatized at an abstract level. Hence, we add two more parameters to the specification in lines 4–5: VALIDATOR_SETS and NIL_VS. The parameter VALIDATOR_SETS can be a set of any values, not necessarily sets. We usually define it as a set of uninterpreted constants, e.g., as $\{$ "S1", "S2", "S3" $\}$. The parameter NIL_VS encodes an abstract set outside of VALIDATOR_SETS, e.g., "Nil".

Third, the field blockID in a commit and a block hash are needed only to test block equality, when trying to find out whether a block has been sent by a faulty or a correct peer. Hence, for every block, instead of its hash and the hash of the previous block in the commit, we introduce two predicates: hashEqRef and blockIdEqRef. These predicates restrict the behavior of faulty peers by comparing

Listing 1. Abstract blockchain for Fastsync in TLA$^+$

```
1  -------------- module Tinychain -------------------
2  EXTENDS Integers
3  CONSTANTS MAX_HEIGHT, \* the maximal number of blocks
4           VALIDATOR_SETS, \* a set of abstract sets
5           NIL_VS \* a special abstract set outside of the above set
6
7  IsCorrectBlock(chain, h) ≜
8    ∧ chain[h].height = h \* the height is right
9    ∧ h > 1 ⇒
10     ∧ chain[h].VS = chain[h − 1].NVS \* the validators are from the prev. block
11     ∧ chain[h].lastCommit.voters = chain[h − 1].VS \* and they are the voters
12
13 IsCorrectChain(chain) ≜
14   LET OkCommits ≜ [blockIdEqRef: {TRUE}, voters: VALIDATOR_SETS]
15       OkBlocks ≜ [height: 1..MAX_HEIGHT, hashEqRef: {TRUE},
16                   wellFormed: {TRUE}, VS: VALIDATOR_SETS,
17                   NVS: VALIDATOR_SETS, lastCommit: OkCommits]
18   IN
19     ∧ chain ∈ [1..MAX_HEIGHT → OkBlocks]
20     ∧ ∀ h ∈ 1..MAX_HEIGHT: IsCorrectBlock(chain, h)
21 ============================================================
```

a block against the reference chain. We explain this in Sect. 6. Finally, we abstract all simple structure tests with the predicate wellFormed, whose negation models that a block by a faulty peer does not pass simple consistency tests.

Having the abstract block structure, we define the predicate IsCorrectChain in lines 13–20 that constrains the block sequence chain. Line 19 restricts chain to be a function of a block height to a block from OkBlocks, that is, a set of records that is defined in lines 15–17. (The notation 'a: B' constrains the record field a to range over the set B). Using the predicate IsCorrectChain, we define the *reference chain*, to which the correct peers are synchronized.

5   The Blockchain Synchronization Problem in English

Sequential Problem Statement. The synchronization protocol must satisfy:

Sync. Let k be the height of the blockchain at the time Fastsync starts. When the protocol terminates, it outputs a list of all blocks from its initial height to some height *terminationHeight* $\geq k - 1$. (Fastsync cannot synchronize to the maximum height k as in Tendermint, verification of block at height h requires the commit from the block at height $h + 1$.)

Liveness. Fastsync eventually terminates.

Safety. Upon termination, the application state is the one that corresponds to the blockchain at height *terminationHeight*.

Observe that **Sync** requires $terminationHeight \geq k - 1$. As in Tendermint the verification of a block at height h requires the commit from the block at height $h + 1$, Fastsync cannot synchronize to the height k. Also note that the blockchain may grow during the execution of Fastsync, that is, its height may increase before Fastsync terminates. In **Sync** we require to reach at least the height of the blockchain when the protocol starts (it is a minimal requirement), while we allow the protocol to go larger heights in case the blockchain grows.

Distributed Aspects and Faulty Peers. We consider a node FS that performs Fastsync by communicating with peers from a set *PeerIDs*, some of which may be faulty. We assume the authenticated Byzantine fault model [11] in which no peer (faulty or correct) may break digital signatures, but otherwise, no additional assumption is made about the internal behavior of faulty peers. That is, faulty peers are only limited in that they cannot forge messages. We do not make any assumptions about the number or ratio of correct/faulty peers.

Communication between the node FS and all correct peers is reliable and bounded in time: there is a message end-to-end delay Δ such that if a message is sent at time t by a correct process to a correct process, then it will be received and processed by time $t + \Delta$.

Without the assumption that *PeerIDs* contains a correct full node, no protocol can solve the sequential problem. To relax the problem in the unreliable distributed setting, we consider two kinds of termination (successful and failure). We specify below under what conditions Fastsync ensures successful termination and still solves the sequential problem.

Distributed Problem Statement. In the distributed setting, the synchronization protocol must satisfy:

Sync. Let $maxh$ be the maximum height of a correct peer to which the node is connected at the time Fastsync starts. If the protocol terminates successfully, it is at some height $terminationHeight \geq maxh - 1$.

Liveness. Fastsync eventually terminates: either successfully or with failure.

Non-abort. If there is one correct process in *PeerIDs*, Fastsync never terminates with failure.

Safety. The same as Safety in the sequential problem statement.

In the distributed setting, non-abort in conjunction with liveness ensures that if there is a correct process in *PeerIDs*, then Fastsync never terminates with failure, that is, it will terminate successfully.

6   Correct and Faulty Peers in TLA$^+$

Section 5 introduces a number of assumptions about correct and faulty peers. In this section, we give an idea about formalization of these assumptions in TLA$^+$. The node starts with a finite set of peers, which can shrink when the node suspects peers of being faulty. The initial set of peers is partitioned into two

Listing 2. Alternating composition of the node and peers in TLA$^+$

```
1   CONSTANTS CORRECT, FAULTY, ... \* the sets of correct and faulty peers
2   VARIABLES state, blockPool \* the node's state variables
3   VARIABLES peersState \* the peer's state variables
4   VARIABLES turn, inMsg, outMsg \* the composition variables
5   /* specification of the node and the peers */
6   ...
7   Init ≜
8      ∧ IsCorrectChain(chain) \* initialize the chain up to MAX_HEIGHT
9      ∧ InitNode ∧ InitPeers \* initialize the node and the peers
10     ∧ turn = "Peers" \* the first turn is by the peers
11     ∧ inMsg = NoMsg \* no incoming message from the peers to the node
12     ∧ outMsg = [type ↦ "statusRequest"] \* a request from the node to a peer
13
14  Next ≜
15     IF turn = "Peers"
16     THEN NextPeers ∧ turn' = "Node" ∧ UNCHANGED ⟨state, blockPool, chain⟩
17     ELSE NextNode ∧ turn' = "Peers" ∧ UNCHANGED ⟨peersState⟩
```

subsets: CORRECT and FAULTY. As expected, the node specification must not refer to either of these subsets, as the node is not able to distinguish the faulty nodes from the correct ones in the distributed setting.

Composition. Listing 2 shows the specification structure. The predicate Init constrains the initial states, whereas the predicate Next constrains the transition relation of the system. We model the distributed system as two components: the node and its peers. They communicate via two variables: outMsg, that keeps an output message from the node to a peer, and inMsg, that keeps an input message from a peer to the node; both variables may be set to None, indicating that there is no message. The components alternate their steps by flipping the variable turn: The odd turns belong to the node, and the even turns to the peers.

This approach is simple yet powerful. On one hand, it dramatically decreases the state space, as there are no queues, and alternation produces significantly fewer states than the disjunction, which would correspond to interleaving: NextNode ∨ NextPeers. On the other hand, it does not decrease precision, as the peers consume and produce messages independently of one another. Moreover, this approach allows us to easily formulate fairness in the system as weak fairness over the variable turn.

Correct Peers. The correct peers non-deterministically send their status (the chain height) to the node and respond to its requests. For example, if the node requests a block of height 5 from a peer "c3", the peer "c3" sends its block. The peers may also join and leave the network. We omit the technical details.

Faulty Peers. The faulty peers are authenticated Byzantine: In addition to the behavior of the correct peers, they may send unsolicited or corrupt messages, or ignore the requests. As discussed in Sect. 4, the blockchain uses hashes, which limits the power of the faulty peers in sending blocks. This is where the hashing predicates come into play. The essential piece of TLA$^+$ code is given below:

```
1   SendBlockResponseMessage(...) ≜
2     ∨ ... \* a response by a correct peer to a node's request
3     ∨ ∃ peerId ∈ FAULTY: \* a faulty peer can always send a block
4       ∃ block ∈ Blocks:
5         ∧ block.height = height \* height mismatch is easy to detect
6         ∧ block.hashEqRef ⇒ block = chain[height] \* no hash forging
7         ∧ (height > 1 ∧ block.lastCommit.voters = chain[height − 1].VS)
8           ⇒ block.lastCommit.blockIdEqRef \* no equivocation by the validators
9         ∧ inMsg' = [type ↦ "blockResponse", peerId ↦ peerId, block ↦ block]
10        ∧ ...
```

Line 6 forces a faulty peer to produce the block as on the chain, when the predicate block.hashEqRef holds true, that is, the block hash matches the hash of the reference block on the chain. This is exactly the semantics of a perfect hash. Line 8 is perhaps less obvious. Intuitively, it says that if the block contains a commit for the previous block, and the voters in the commit coincide with the validators of the previous block on the chain, then the hash in the commit must be equal to the hash of the previous block on the chain. (The implementation tests whether voters constitute over 2/3 of the VS voting power. However, we find our approximation sufficient for model checking.) Importantly, with Boolean hashEqRef and blockIdEqRef, we model the scenarios: (1) the hashes are equal to the reference hash; (2) the hashes are equal to a number different from the reference hash; and (3) the hashes are not equal.

7 The Node Protocol in English and TLA$^+$

Recall Fig. 1, that shows a typical execution of Fastsync. Using statusReq, the node FS asks a peer about its current height, that is, the length of the prefix of the blockchain the peer has stored. Each peer responds with statusRes(h), where h is its current height. By collecting these responses, FS gets information about which peer has which blocks, and uses this information (1) to compute its target height (the maximum height its peers know of) and (2) to decide which blocks to request from which peer. It requests a block of height h from a peer by sending blockReq(h), and a peer responds by sending blockRes(bh), that contains a block of height h. FS stores all the received blocks locally, and checks all the signatures and hashes to make sure that there are no invalid blocks that could have been provided by faulty peers.

As the implementation uses external events (message reception) and timeouts to make progress, we have chosen to describe the model in terms of the following functions, that are triggered by events:

QueryStatus(): regularly (at least 2Δ, now 10 s) queries all peers from *PeerIDs* for their current heights by sending statusReq to all peers.

CreateRequest(): regularly checks whether certain blocks have no open request. If a block does not have an open request and its height is h, FS requests one from a peer. It does so by sending `blockReq(h)` to one peer.

In our specification, we leave the strategy of peer selection unspecified. Various implementations of Fastsync differ in this aspect. Version V2 (see Sect. 2) selects a peer p with the minimum number of pending requests that can serve the required height h, that is, whose height is greater than or equal to h.

When the messages `statusRes(h)` or `blockRes(b)` are returned from the peer at address `addr`, the following functions are called, respectively:

OnStatusResponse(addr Address, h int): The full node with address *addr* returns its current height. The function updates the height information about *addr*, and may also increase the target height.

OnBlockResponse(addr Address, b Block): The full node with address *addr* returns a block. It is added to blockstore. Then the auxiliary function `Execute` is called.

Execute(): Iterates over the received blocks. It checks soundness of the blocks (hashes, signatures, etc.), and executes the transactions of a sound block and updates the application state.

FS keeps track of several performance metrics: the last time a peer responded, the throughput to a peer, etc. If a peer p has not provided a block recently or it has not provided a sufficient amount of data, then p is removed from *PeerIDs*. Fastsync V2 schedules a timeout whenever a block is executed, that is, when the height is incremented. If the timeout expires before the next block is executed, Fastsync terminates. If this happens, then Fastsync terminates with failure. Otherwise it terminates successfully when it reaches the target height.

We omit the details about the other functions. Figure 4 shows an example of how we specify functions in the English specification. Rather than using pseudo code, we specify functions mainly using preconditions and postconditions. They have a clear meaning to verification engineers, but also give the software engineers a precise understanding of what the function should do without restricting them in how to satisfy these requirements in the source code.

TLA$^+$ *Specification*. We omit technical details of encoding the node communication. The implementation V2 relies on several timeouts to guarantee termination. Although precise modeling of time and timeouts is possible in TLA$^+$ [20], it obviously leads to state explosion. Hence, we simply model timeouts with non-determinism and weak fairness.

Listing 3 shows the block verification logic. Interestingly, VerifyCommit checks the predicates commit.blockIdEqRef and block.hashEqRef. There are two valid options with respect to the hash *hash* of the reference block: Either both the hashes are equal to *hash*, or they are both different from *hash*.

```
func OnBlockResponse(addr Address, b Block)
```
– Comment
  • if after adding block b, blocks of heights $height$ and $height+1$ are in $blockstore$, then Execute is called
– Expected precondition
  • $pendingblocks(b.Height) = addr$
  • b satisfies basic soundness
– Expected postcondition
  • if function Execute has been executed without error or was not executed:
    * $receivedBlocks(b.Height) = addr$
    * $blockstore(b.Height) = b$
    * $peerTimeStamp[addr]$ is set to a time between invocation and return of the function.
    * $peerRate[addr]$ is updated according to size of received block and time passed between current time and last block received from this peer (addr)
– Error condition: if precondition is violated: $addr$ not in $PeerIDs$; reset $pendingblocks(b.Height)$ to nil;

Fig. 4. Example of a function definition in the English specification

Listing 3. Block execution logic in TLA$^+$

```
1  VerifyCommit(block, commit) ≜
2    commit.voters = block.VS ∧ commit.blockIdEqRef = block.hashEqRef
3
4  ExecuteBlocks(pool) ≜
5    ... \* get stored blocks b0, b1, b2 for heights h−1, h, h+1
6    IF b1 = Nil ∨ b2 = Nil \* no two next consecutive blocks
7    THEN pool
8    ELSE IF b0.NVS ≠ b1.VS ∨ ¬VerifyCommit(b0, b1.lastCommit)
9        THEN RemovePeers({Sender(b1.height)}, pool)
10       ELSE IF ¬VerifyCommit(b1, b2.lastCommit)
11           THEN RemovePeers({Sender(b1.height), Sender(b2.height)}, pool)
12           ELSE [pool EXCEPT !.height = pool.height + 1]
```

8 Model Checking with TLC and Apalache

While developing TLA$^+$ specifications, we were using TLA$^+$ Toolbox and the model checker TLC [17]. We also checked the safety properties with the new symbolic model checker APALACHE [2,16]. So far, we have checked the specifications for tiny parameters, such as 1 to 3 peers and Blockchain height from 3 to 5. Table 1 summarizes the results and running times of TLC and APALACHE. A central temporal property is the protocol's Termination:

$$\text{WF}_{turn}(FlipTurn) \Rightarrow \diamond(state = \text{``finished''})$$

where $\text{WF}_x(A)$ in TLA$^+$ forces weak fairness of action A, if it changes x.

In 7 min, TLC finds a bug: Faulty peers may keep the node busy by sending blocks or joining and leaving the network. The more precise property TerminationByTO states that the protocol terminates, if there is a global timeout:

$$\mathrm{WF}_{turn}(Flip\,Turn) \wedge \Diamond(\mathsf{inMsg.type} = \text{``}syncTimeout\text{''}$$
$$\wedge\ blockPool.height \leq blockPool.syncHeight) \Rightarrow \Diamond(state = \text{``}finished\text{''})$$

In this case, TLC finds no bug, though it does not finish state exploration. (We did not run APALACHE, as it only supports safety.) We found that it is extremely hard to formulate the "normal" termination property in the presence of faults, i.e., without involving a timeout. We also formulated the property TerminationCorrect: The protocol terminates without a timeout, provided that all peers are correct. TLC exhaustively proves this property for one correct peer.

The more interesting property is "synchronization", whose intuitive meaning is that by the time Fastsync terminates, it reaches the height of the blockchain. Let us formalize this as Sync1: To see that our modeling is precise, we start with a property that is slightly wrong, namely, when the protocol finishes, it reaches the maximum height among the heights of the correct peers, i.e.,

$$\Box\big(state = \text{``}finished\text{''} \Rightarrow blockPool.height \geq MaxCorrectPeerHeight(blockPool)\big)$$

Both model checkers report counterexamples. One reason is that to verify a block h, one needs the commit signatures from block $h + 1$. We also observe, that the node running Fastsync is not always connected to correct peers. Hence, we fix it in Sync2, by stating that height $MaxCorrectPeerHeight(blockPool) - 1$ should be reached when the node is connected to correct peers. This property also fails. This time we observe that a global timeout — that guarantees TerminationByTO — may terminate Fastsync before it has reached the maximal height. We add a precondition for "no timeout", and call the property Sync3. Neither TLC, nor APALACHE produce a counterexample (for executions up to 20 steps).

We formulated the invariant CorrectBlocks: The synchronized blocks have enough votes and contain correct signatures and hashes (the correct peers produce only the blocks that satisfy this property). By running APALACHE, we found that this property was violated by the specification. After code inspection, we realized that the implementation executes an extra consistency test that was not captured in the specification (as it was not clear that it is part of the protocol). After fixing the specification, we have found no further counterexamples.

Both model checkers quickly find counterexamples for the following two properties that might appear to be correct. SyncFromCorrect states that the accepted blocks originate only from the correct processes. This property fails, as it does not account for the cases where faulty peers behave correct in an execution prefix (before showing faulty behavior). NoSuspectedCorrect states that the correct peers are never removed from the peer set. This would be a desirable property, but the current implementation V2 does not guarantee it.

Finally, TLC is quite fast when checking properties in the configuration with one correct peer. However, adding just one faulty peer blows up the state space,

Table 1. Model checking results for TLC and APALACHE against the high-level specification for 1 correct peer, 0/1 faulty peers, and 4 blocks. The experiments were run in an AWS instance equipped with 32GB RAM and a 4-core Intel® Xeon® CPU E5-2686 v4 @ 2.30GHz CPU. The notation: ✗ for "found a bug at depth k", $[✓]_{<k}$ for "found no bug up to depth k", ✓ for "correct" (exhaustive search), TO for "timeout" (24 h).

Property	TLC (4 CPUs, 28 GB)							APALACHE (1 CPU)	
	1 correct/0 faulty/4 blocks				1 correct/1 faulty/4 blocks			1 correct/1 faulty/4 blocks	
	result	time	#states	diameter	result	time	#states	result	time
Sync1	$[✗]_{=5}$	13s	9K	5	$[✗]_{=5}$	28s	1.1M	$[✗]_{=5}$	16s
Sync2	$[✗]_{=5}$	7s	9K	5	$[✗]_{=5}$	28s	1.1M	$[✗]_{=5}$	16s
Sync3	✓	37s	68K	15	$[✓]_{<15}$	TO	875M	$[✓]_{<21}$	1h25m
Termination	$[✗]_{=8}$	11s	25K	8	$[✗]_{=7}$	7m25s	2.9M	not supported	
TerminationByTO	✓	33s	68K	15	$[✓]_{<14}$	TO	461M	not supported	
TerminationCorrect	✓	42s	68K	15	not applicable			not supported	
CorrectBlocks	✓	31s	68K	15	$[✓]_{<15}$	TO	873M	$[✓]_{<16}$	1h53m
SyncFromCorrect	$[✗]_{=9}$	9s	33K	9	$[✗]_{=9}$	8m34s	4.5M	$[✗]_{=9}$	1m23s
NoSuspectedCorrect	$[✗]_{=3}$	6s	1K	9	$[✗]_{=3}$	4s	126K	$[✗]_{=3}$	9s

which prevents TLC from finishing state exploration. In this case APALACHE performs better. However, it runs bounded model checking, which gives us only bounded safety, that is, up to the predefined execution length.

9 Conclusions and Future Work

We approach this work with a process-oriented goal in mind: By *Verification-Driven Development* [15] we understand a design process for distributed systems that makes it easier to test and verify the software. The re-design of the Fastsync protocol that resulted in a decomposition into state machines should be understood under this aspect. The English and the TLA$^+$ specifications are artifacts of this design process, and are means of communication between researchers, software engineers, and verification engineers. The structured English specification strikes a balance between mathematical rigor and readability. It serves as a base for (i) formal verification efforts in TLA$^+$, that provide precise semantics, and (ii) implementations. The annotations with invariants, pre- and postconditions are very helpful for the software engineers to guide the implementation.

The gap between informal English specifications, and formal TLA$^+$ specifications and the implementations is still a research challenge. As future work we will consider semi-formal methods that address this formalization gap. For instance, we have found that the distributed system engineers have a hard time specifying precise liveness properties, which truly requires one to think about temporal operators. Specifying fairness is the most challenging specification task in case of fault-tolerant distributed systems. Instead of asking the engineers to write the temporal properties directly, we could instantiate specification patterns [4] that collect the most-often occurring shapes of temporal formulas. This can be done with the help of graphical tools such as PROPAS [12]. In a more general setting, we could use the boilerplates approach offered by CESAR [3]. This is a specification method that uses restricted English grammar, where a designer selects the boilerplates that fit the specific requirement, and fills the details to arrive at a complete specification.

The formalization also led to a better understanding of the liveness properties that we expect and want from blockchain synchronization protocols, and to an improved awareness regarding the differences between the current implementations (Fastsync V0, V1, and V2). We have found several liveness issues that come from unexpected behavior of faulty peers. For instance, rather than reporting bad blocks, faulty peers may be very slow in reporting good blocks. If they report them slower than the blockchain grows, but fast enough to not lead to a timeout at the node, V2 may never terminate. This highlights that a vital requirement had not been captured before, namely, a relationship between timeout duration, block generation rate, and message end-to-end delays. As this issue is closely related to real-time, we are not able to directly capture it and reproduce it with TLA$^+$. However, TLA$^+$ counterexamples and the English specifications helped us in isolating this scenario.

For safety verification, we can replace a timeout by a non-deterministic event that may occur at any time. For liveness, we have to treat the relation of timeouts to message delays and processing times precisely. The extensive use of timeouts in the current implementation poses future research challenges to liveness verification. Some of our current research questions are: How to limit timeouts in the implementation? What is the most effective way to use timeouts in the implementation in order to stay precise in the verification? How can we capture the relation of the (local) timeouts to (global) message delays in model checking?

The counterexamples produced by the model checkers were quite helpful in understanding and refining the protocol properties. After refining the protocol with small hashes, which resulted in a larger state space, TLC could not reach error states within the reasonable time frame of one hour. In contrast, APALACHE was finding errors within 10 min, which was still interactive enough for us. Once we felt confident in the protocol after debugging it with APALACHE, we shrinked the state space by introducing Boolean abstraction of hashes, allowing TLC to also report errors. As future work, we plan to find an inductive invariant and prove its correctness with APALACHE (for fixed but larger parameters).

The language of TLA$^+$ built around refinement [19,21]. In the classical approach, one starts with an abstract specification A of a protocol and produces a more detailed specification C. To show refinement, the user substitutes the variables of A with expressions over the variables of C, which results in a specification $\gamma(A)$, and then proves that the behaviors of C can be replayed by $\gamma(A)$. It suffices to prove two statements: (1) the initial states of C are a subset of the initial states of $\gamma(A)$, formally, $C!Init \Rightarrow \gamma(A)!Init$; and (2) the transitions of C are a subset of the transitions of $\gamma(A)$, formally, $C!Next \Rightarrow \gamma(A)!Next$. To prove the steps (1) and (2) for all values of the parameters, the user has to use TLA$^+$ Proof System [10]. To debug the statements (1) and (2) for small parameters, one can use the model checkers TLC and APALACHE.

In our case, the design flow was in the opposite direction. We started with the existing implementation and wrote several specifications of the protocol in TLA$^+$. Technically, we could construct a refinement mapping between the low-level specification and the high-level specification and check it with the model checkers for the small parameters. However, the potential feedback from this step seemed to be negligible, in comparison to checking safety and liveness of the protocol. A more pressing issue for us is how to establish conformance of the protocol implementation (in Google Go) to the TLA$^+$ specification. To this end, we are currently developing a model-based testing tool, which produces system tests out of TLA$^+$ traces, as generated by TLC and APALACHE as output.

An alternative approach would be to use Ivy [22] instead of TLA$^+$ tools. The authors of Ivy demonstrated how one can do refinement and parameterized verification of consensus protocols with their tool. Their approach requires creative massaging of the specification with the goal of simplifying the SMT theory and transforming the constraints in the EPR form. We found that is much easier to explain TLA$^+$ to the engineers than uninterpreted first-order logic. It would be great to unite the clarity of TLA$^+$ and effectiveness of Ivy.

References

1. ADR 043: Blockhchain reactor riri-org (2020). https://github.com/tendermint/tendermint/blob/master/docs/architecture/adr-043-blockchain-riri-org.md
2. APALACHE: a symbolic model checker for TLA$^+$ (2020). https://github.com/informalsystems/apalache/. Accessed 10 Aug 2020
3. Arora, C., Sabetzadeh, M., Briand, L.C., Zimmer, F., Gnaga, R.: Automatic checking of conformance to requirement boilerplates via text chunking: an industrial case study. In: ESEM (2013)
4. Dwyer, M.B., Avrunin, G.S., Corbett, J.C.: Property specification patterns for finite-state verification. In: FMSP, pp. 7–15 (1998)
5. Brooker, M., Chen, T., Ping, F.: Millions of tiny databases. In: USENIX, pp. 463–478 (2020)
6. Buchman, E.: Tendermint: Byzantine fault tolerance in the age of blockchains. Master's thesis, University of Guelph (2016). http://hdl.handle.net/10214/9769
7. Buchman, E., Kwon, J.: Cosmos whitepaper: a network of distributed ledgers (2016). https://cosmos.network/resources/whitepaper
8. Buchman, E., Kwon, J., Milosevic, Z.: The latest gossip on BFT consensus. arXiv preprint arXiv:1807.04938 (2018). https://arxiv.org/abs/1807.04938
9. Buterin, V., Griffith, V.: Casper the friendly finality gadget. arXiv preprint arXiv:1710.09437 (2017)
10. Cousineau, D., Doligez, D., Lamport, L., Merz, S., Ricketts, D., Vanzetto, H.: TLA$^+$ proofs. In: Giannakopoulou, D., Méry, D. (eds.) FM 2012. LNCS, vol. 7436, pp. 147–154. Springer, Heidelberg (2012). https://doi.org/10.1007/978-3-642-32759-9_14
11. Dwork, C., Lynch, N., Stockmeyer, L.: Consensus in the presence of partial synchrony. J. ACM **35**(2), 288–323 (1988)
12. Filipovikj, P., Seceleanu, C.: Specifying industrial system requirements using specification patterns: a case study of evaluation with practitioners. In: ENASE, pp. 92–103 (2019)

13. Informal Systems: Fastsync - English specification (2020). https://github.com/informalsystems/tendermint-rs/blob/master/docs/spec/fastsync/fastsync.md
14. Informal Systems: Fastsync - TLA$^+$ specification (2020).https://github.com/informalsystems/tendermint-rs/blob/master/docs/spec/fastsync/fastsync.tla
15. Informal Systems: Verification-Driven Development: An Informal Guide (2020). https://github.com/informalsystems/VDD/blob/master/guide/guide.md
16. Konnov, I., Kukovec, J., Tran, T.: TLA+ model checking made symbolic. PACMPL **3**(OOPSLA), 123:1–123:30 (2019)
17. Kuppe, M.A., Lamport, L., Ricketts, D.: The TLA+ toolbox. In: F-IDE@FM 2019, pp. 50–62 (2019)
18. Kwon, J.: Tendermint: consensus without mining. Draft v. 0.6, fall **1**(11) (2014)
19. Lamport, L.: Specifying Systems: The TLA+ Language and Tools for Hardware and Software Engineers. Addison-Wesley (2002)
20. Lamport, L.: Real-time model checking is really simple. In: Borrione, D., Paul, W. (eds.) CHARME 2005. LNCS, vol. 3725, pp. 162–175. Springer, Heidelberg (2005). https://doi.org/10.1007/11560548_14
21. Lamport, L.: Byzantizing Paxos by refinement. In: Peleg, D. (ed.) DISC 2011. LNCS, vol. 6950, pp. 211–224. Springer, Heidelberg (2011). https://doi.org/10.1007/978-3-642-24100-0_22
22. McMillan, K.L., Padon, O.: Ivy: a multi-modal verification tool for distributed algorithms. In: Lahiri, S.K., Wang, C. (eds.) CAV 2020. LNCS, vol. 12225, pp. 190–202. Springer, Cham (2020). https://doi.org/10.1007/978-3-030-53291-8_12
23. Newcombe, C., Rath, T., Zhang, F., Munteanu, B., Brooker, M., Deardeuff, M.: How Amazon web services uses formal methods. Comm. ACM **58**(4), 66–73 (2015)
24. Tendermint Inc.: Cosmos hub (2020). https://hub.cosmos.network
25. Tendermint core, reference implementation in Go (2020). https://github.com/tendermint/tendermint
26. Yin, M., Malkhi, D., Reiter, M.K., Gueta, G.G., Abraham, I.: Hotstuff: BFT consensus with linearity and responsiveness. In: PODC, pp. 347–356 (2019)

Safe Sessions of Channel Actions in Clojure: A Tour of the Discourje Project

Ruben Hamers[1] and Sung-Shik Jongmans[1,2(✉)]

[1] Open University, Heerlen, The Netherlands
ssj@ou.nl
[2] CWI, Amsterdam, The Netherlands

Abstract. To simplify shared-memory concurrent programming, in addition to low-level synchronisation primitives, several modern programming languages have started to offer core support for higher-level communication primitives as well, in the guise of message passing through channels. Yet, a growing body of evidence suggests that channel-based programming abstractions for shared memory also have their issues.

The Discourje project aims to help programmers cope with message-passing concurrency bugs in Clojure programs, based on run-time verification and dynamic monitoring. The idea is that programmers write not only implementations, but also specifications (of sessions of channel actions). Discourje then offers a library to ensure that implementations run safely relative to specifications (= "bad" channel actions never happen).

This paper gives a tour of the current state of Discourje, by example; it is intended to serve both as a general overview for readers who are unfamiliar with previous work on Discourje, and as an introduction to new features for readers who are familiar.

1 Introduction

Background. To take advantage of today's and tomorrow's multi-core processors, shared-memory concurrent programming—a notoriously complex enterprise—is becoming increasingly important. To alleviate some of the complexities, in addition to low-level *synchronisation primitives*, several modern programming languages have started to offer core support for higher-level *communication primitives* as well, in the guise of message passing through *channels* (e.g., Go [21], Rust [40], Clojure [11]). The idea is that, beyond their usage in distributed computing, channels can also serve as a *programming abstraction* for shared memory, supposedly less prone to concurrency bugs than locks, semaphores, and the like. Notably, the official Go documentation recommends programmers to "not communicate by sharing memory; instead, share memory by communicating" [20].

Yet, a growing body of evidence suggests that channel-based programming abstractions for shared memory also have their issues. For instance, in the 2016–2018 editions of the annual Go survey [16–18], "[respondents] *least agreed* that

© Springer Nature Switzerland AG 2020
T. Margaria and B. Steffen (Eds.): ISoLA 2020, LNCS 12476, pp. 489–508, 2020.
https://doi.org/10.1007/978-3-030-61362-4_28

they are able to effectively debug uses of Go's concurrency features", while in the 2019 edition [19], "debugging concurrency" has the *lowest satisfaction rate* of all eleven "very or critically important" topics (as indicated by the majority of respondents). Moreover, after studying 171 concurrency bugs in popular open source Go programs [45], Tu et al. find that "message passing does not necessarily make multi-threaded programs less error-prone than shared memory."

Recently, several research projects emerged that aim to help programmers cope with concurrency bugs in Go programs [7,30,31,36,43], based on compile-time verification and static analysis; the resulting tools complement Go's static type-checker in a natural fashion, and their compile-time usage integrates well—at least potentially—with established Go programming practices. However, while similar *compile-time techniques* may suit other *statically typed languages* (e.g., Rust) at least as well, their appropriateness seems less obvious for *dynamically typed languages* (e.g., Clojure): for such languages, technical and cultural differences mean that *run-time techniques* may be preferable. The Discourje project is a research vehicle to develop and study such techniques: ultimately, the aim is to help programmers cope with concurrency bugs in Clojure programs,[1] based on run-time verification and dynamic monitoring.

The Discourje Project. Discourje,[2] pronounced "discourse", addresses the following problem: given a specification S of the *roles* (threads), the *infrastructure* (channels between threads), and the *sessions* (communications through channels) that an implementation I in Clojure should fulfill, how to check—at run-time—that an execution of I is indeed *safe* relative to S? Safety means that "bad" channel actions never happen: <u>if</u> a channel action happens in I, <u>then</u> it can happen in S. For instance, typical specifications rule out common channel-based concurrency bugs [45], such as sends without receives, receives without sends, and type mismatches (actual type sent $\neq$ expected type received).

Roughly, the idea is to execute specification S—as if it were a state machine—alongside implementation I, in "perfect synchrony"; this means that, to provide safety, a channel action in I happens if and only if a corresponding transition happens in S. To achieve this, following standard run-time verification practices [3], two extra components are needed: a *monitor* (of S) and *instrumentation* (of I). Specifically, every time that a channel action is about to happen in I, the instrumentation quickly intervenes and first asks the monitor if S can make a corresponding transition. If the monitor answers "yes", both the channel action in I and the corresponding transition in S happen; if "no", an exception is thrown, while the channel action is aborted (= safe). Facilitating this approach, Discourje offers the programmer easy-to-learn libraries to write specifications, add monitors, and add instrumentation to Clojure programs.

---

[1] Clojure [11,23] is a dynamically typed, functional language (impure) that compiles to Java bytecode. As a dialect of Lisp, Clojure follows the code-as-data philosophy, offers a powerful macro system, and is written in parenthesised prefix notation.

[2] https://github.com/discourje.

In recent editions of the annual Clojure survey [9,10], respondents indicated that "ease of development" is one of Clojure's most important strengths (more important than "runtime performance"). For this reason, and to make Discourje non-invasive to deploy and start using, we emphasise *ergonomics* (including expressiveness) in the design and implementation of the libraries. Notably:

1. We leverage Clojure's macro system to offer the specification language as a library of macros. As a result, the programmer can write specifications and implementations in the same syntactic style, using the same editor (no external tools needed), towards a seamless specification–implementation experience. Monitors can subsequently be added with simple function calls.
2. Control-flow operators in the specification language have the same names as those in Clojure, for a gentle learning curve.
3. Normally, in Clojure, channel-based programming abstractions can be used by loading standard library `clojure.core.async`. To add instrumentation, the only thing the programmer needs to change, is load `discourje.core.async` instead, for the primitives Discourje currently supports: **thread** (new thread), **chan** (new channel; unbuffered or buffered),[3] **close!** (close), **>!!** (send), **<!!** (receive), and **alts!!|** (select). This means, in particular, that the programmer does not need to write the implementation with Discourje in mind: instrumentation can straightforwardly be added afterwards.

When `clojure.core.async` was introduced in 2013 [8], already, it was suggested that "certain kinds of automated correctness analysis" are possible, but at the time, "no work ha[d] been done on that front". To our knowledge, Discourje is the first project that addresses this open problem.

This Paper. This paper gives a tour of the current state of Discourje, by example. It is geared towards demonstrating two core concepts of `clojure.core.async` that we did not support before [22], and which significantly improve applicability: *unbuffered channels* (to perform handshake communications) and *selects* (to await enabledness of one of several channel actions). This paper has two aims and intends to address two audiences: **(i)** for readers who *are not* familiar with previous work on Discourje [22], this paper serves as a gentle overview of the general idea and expressiveness; **(ii)** for readers who *are* familiar with previous work, this paper introduces our new support for unbuffered channels and selects.

The tour consists of three Clojure programs, each of which simulates a game: it starts in Sect. 2 with Tic–Tac–Toe; it continues in Sect. 3 with Rock–Paper–Scissors; it ends in Sect. 4 with Go Fish. In each of these examples, essentially,

---

[3] With *unbuffered channels*, in the absence of a buffer, both sends and receives are blocking until a reciprocal channel action is performed on the other end of the channel. With *buffered channels*, in the presence of a bounded, n-capacity, order-preserving buffer, sends are blocking until the buffer is not full (then, a message is added to the back of the buffer), while receives are blocking until the buffer is not empty (then, a message is removed from the front of the buffer).

```
1 (defrole :alice) (defrole :bob)        6 (defsession :ttt-turn [r1 r2]
2                                         7   (cat (--> Long r1 r2)
3 (defsession :ttt []                     8     (alt (:ttt-turn r2 r1)
4   (alt (:ttt-turn :alice :bob)          9       (par (close r1 r2)
5        (:ttt-turn :bob :alice)))       10             (close r2 r1)))))
```

Fig. 1. Specification of Tic–Tac–Toe

the safety property that we aim to ensure is that players never violate the "inter-action rules" of the game (e.g. proper turn-taking), as prescribed by the specifications; however, we do not check full functional correctness (e.g., we check if players properly take turns to make moves, but we do not check if every move is actually valid in the current state of the game). In Sect. 5, we give a brief overview of the underlying formal foundation. For reference, a summary of Clojure's core functions and macros is given in Appendix A. Full code (specifications and implementations) can be downloaded via the project's website (footnote 2).

2   The Tour: Tic–Tac–Toe

Overview. We start the tour with a program that simulates a game of Tic–Tac–Toe.[4] The program consists of two threads and two oppositely directed channels through which these threads communicate. The threads take turns to make plays on thread-local copies of the grid; at the end of its turn, the active thread sends its play to the other thread and becomes passive, while the other thread receives the play, becomes active, updates its copy of the grid accordingly, and makes the next play. This example demonstrates the following features:

- SPECIFICATION: roles; unbuffered communication (binary);[5] close; concatenation; choice; parallel; session parameters (roles).
- IMPLEMENTATION: channels; send; receive; close; monitor; instrumentation.

Specification. A Discourje specification of Tic–Tac–Toe is shown in Fig. 1. Core Discourje functions and macros are typeset in `font`.

Line 1 defines two roles (`defrole`), identified by `:alice` and `:bob`. Lines 3–10 define two sessions (`defsession`), identified by `:ttt` (zero formal parameters) and `:ttt-turn` (two formal parameters for roles, identified by `r1` and `r2`).

Session `:ttt-turn` represents one turn of `r1` (active) against `r2` (passive). It prescribes a concatenation (`cat`):

1. First, a message of type `Long` is communicated from `r1` to `r2`, unbuffered (`-->`). The idea is that `r1` sends its play this turn to `r2`.

---

[4] Tic–Tac–Toe is a two-player game played on a 3 × 3 grid. Players take turns to fill the initially blank spaces of the grid with crosses ("X") and noughts ("O"). The first player to fill three consecutive spaces, in any direction, with the same symbol wins.

[5] A version of this example with buffered communication appears elsewhere [22].

2. Then, there is a choice (`alt`):
   (a) Either, there is another instance of session `:ttt-turn`, but now with `r2` active and `r1` passive. The idea is that `r1` did not win or draw this turn, so the game continues.
   (b) Or, channels are closed (`close`), in parallel (`par`). The idea is that `r1` did win or draw this turn, so the game ends.
       We note that the closes may happen in any order; this is crucial, as neither one of the closes is causally related to the other. In the implementation, additional "covert interaction" (= synchronisation/ communication outside the specification) would be needed to order them.

Session `:ttt` represents the whole game. It prescribes a choice between either an initial instance of session `:ttt-turn` with actual parameters `:alice` and `:bob`, or `:bob` and `:alice`, depending on who takes the first turn. Thus, at the specification level, it is undecided who goes first; this is an implementation detail.

As concatenation, choice, and recursion are supported, any regular expression (over unbuffered communications and closes) can be written. However, for convenience, shorthands are available for the following patterns: 0-or-more repetitions (`*`), 1-or-more (`+`), and 0-or-1 (`?`). Thus, the programmer never needs to use recursion to write regular expressions. The syntax and semantics of the remaining five macros are the same as those in standard library `clojure.spec.alpha`, to make Discourje easy to learn. For the same reason, the notation to define and "call" sessions is similar to the notation to define and call functions.

Implementation. A Clojure implementation of Tic–Tac–Toe is shown in Fig. 2. Core Clojure functions and macros are typeset in `font`.

Line 1 loads five functions and macros from `clojure.core.async`. Lines 3–11 define constants (`blank`, `cross`, `nought`, `initial-grid`) and functions (`get-blank`, `put`, `not-final?`) to represent Tic–Tac–Toe concepts. Lines 11–12 define unbuffered channels (`a->b` and `b->a`) that implement the infrastructure through which the threads communicate. As these channels are unbuffered, sends and receives block until reciprocal channel actions are performed.

Lines 16–26 and 27–37 define threads that implement roles `:alice` and `:bob`. Both threads execute a loop, starting with a blank initial grid. In each iteration, `:alice` first gets the index of a blank space on the grid, then plays a cross in that space, then sends a message to `:bob` to communicate the index (a message of type `Long`), then awaits a message from `:bob`, and then updates the grid accordingly; `:bob` acts symmetrically. After every grid update, `:alice` or `:bob` checks if it has reached a final grid; if so, the loop is exited and channels are closed.[6]

---

[6] Many data structures in Clojure—including the vector that implements the grid—are *persistent* and, thus, effectively *immutable*: every operation on an old data structure leaves it unmodified and, instead, returns a new data structure. In concurrent programs, including Tic–Tac–Toe, persistent data structures can be used as thread-local copies of data, but modifications need to be explicitly communicated. Persistence also means that classical data races cannot happen: if threads communicate only persistent data structures through channels, freedom of data races is guaranteed.

```
1  (require '[clojure.core.async :refer [thread chan close! >!! <!!]])
2
3  (def blank " ") (def cross "x") (def nought "o")
4
5  (def initial-grid [blank blank blank    ;; an initial 3x3 grid of blank spaces,
6                     blank blank blank    ;;   implemented as a vector of length 9
7                     blank blank blank])  ;;   (persistent data structure)
8
9  (def get-blank  (fn [g]          ...)) ;; returns a blank space in g
10 (def put        (fn [g i x-or-o] ...)) ;; returns g, but with i set to x-or-o
11 (def not-final? (fn [g]          ...)) ;; returns true iff g is not final
12
13 (def a->b (chan)) (def b<-a a->b) ;; b<-a is an alias of a->b
14 (def b->a (chan)) (def a<-b b->a) ;; a<-b is an alias of b->a
15
16 (thread ;; for :alice              27 (thread ;; for :bob
17   (loop [g initial-grid]           28   (loop [g initial-grid]
18     (let [i (get-blank g)          29     (let [i (<!! b<-a)
19           g (put g i cross)]       30           g (put g i cross)]
20       (>!! a->b i)                 31       (if (not-final? g)
21       (if (not-final? g)           32         (let [i (get-blank g)
22         (let [i (<!! a<-b)         33               g (put g i nought)]
23               g (put g i nought)]  34           (>!! b->a i)
24           (if (not-final? g)       35           (if (not-final? g)
25             (recur g))))))         36             (recur g))))))
26   (close! a->b))                   37   (close! b->a))
```

Fig. 2. Implementation of Tic–Tac–Toe (dashed arrows: matching send/receive)

Safety. The implementation in Fig. 2 runs fine—*supposedly*—but to really ensure that it satisfies the specification in Fig. 1 (written independently), the programmer can add a monitor and instrumentation. The few changes needed, are shown in Fig. 3: to add instrumentation, on line 1 (which replaces line 1 in Fig. 2), discourje.core.async is loaded instead of clojure.core.async; to add a monitor, on lines 12–14 (which replace line 12–14), a monitor is created for session :ttt, and then, channels a->b and b->a are associated with a sender, receiver, and monitor. No other changes are needed: notably, the code that implement roles :alice and :bob in Fig. 2 stays exactly the same. This shows that Discourje is non-invasive to deploy and start using.

With these changes in place, safety is guaranteed: if a non-compliant channel action were to be attempted, the monitor prevents it from happening and throws an exception. Because the implementation in Fig. 2 actually satisfies the specification in Fig. 1, an exception is *never* thrown. In contrast, if the programmer were to change Long to String on line 7 in Fig. 1, an exception is *always* thrown; if they were to change par to cat on line 9, an exception is *sometimes* thrown, depending on the execution and scheduling of threads.

```
1  (require '[discourje.core.async :refer [thread chan close! >!! <!!]])

12 (def m (monitor (session :ttt [])))
13 (link a->b (role :alice) (role :bob) m)
14 (link b->a (role :bob) (role :alice) m)
```

Fig. 3. Ensuring safety of Tic–Tac–Toe

```
1  (defrole :player)
2
3  (defsession :rps [ids]
4    (:rps-round ids empty-set))
5
6  (defsession :rps-round [ids co-ids]
7    (if (> (count ids) 1)
8      (cat (par-every [i ids
9                       j (disj player-ids i)]
10          (--> String (:player i) (:player j)))
11       (alt-every [winner-ids (power-set ids)]
12         (let [loser-ids (difference ids winner-ids)]
13           (par (:rps-round winner-ids (union co-ids loser-ids))
14             (par-every [i loser-ids
15                         j (disj (union ids co-ids) i)]
16               (close (:player i) (:player j)))))))))))
```

Fig. 4. Discourje specification of Rock–Paper–Scissors

3 The Tour: Rock–Paper–Scissors

Overview. We continue the tour with a program that simulates a game of Rock–Paper–Scissors.[7] The program consists of k threads and $k^2 - k$ directed channels from every thread to every other thread. In every round, every thread chooses an item—rock, paper, or scissors—and sends it to every other thread; then, when all items have been received, every thread determines if it goes to the next round. This example demonstrates the following features:

- SPECIFICATION: indexed roles; unbuffered communication (multiparty); conditional; local bindings; quantification (existential; unordered universal); session parameters (role indices); set operations; non-determinism (implicit).
- IMPLEMENTATION: select; external synchronisation.

---

[7] Rock–Paper–Scissors is a multiplayer game played in rounds. In every round, every remaining player chooses an item—rock, paper, or scissors—and reveals it. A player goes to the next round, unless some other player defeats them, while they defeat no other player, based on the chosen items in the current round ("scissors cuts paper, paper covers rock, rock crushes scissors"). The last player to remain wins.

Specification. A Discourje specification of Rock–Paper–Scissors is shown in Fig. 4. Auxiliary Discourje functions for operations on sets are typeset in `font`.

Line 1 defines one role, identified by `:player`. Lines 3–16 define two sessions, identified by `:rps` (one formal parameter for role indices) and `:rps-round` (two formal parameters). There are two key differences with Fig. 1 in Sect. 2:

- Whereas roles `:alice` and `:bob` in Tic–Tac–Toe are enacted each by a *single* thread, role `:player` in Rock–Paper–Scissors is enacted by *multiple* threads. To distinguish between different threads that enact the same role, roles can be *indexed* in specifications. For instance, with 0-based indexing, (`:player 5`) represents the thread that implements the sixth player.
- Whereas formal parameters of session `:ttt-turn` in Tic–Tac–Toe range over roles, those of sessions `:rps` and `:rps-round` range over (sets of) role indices. This exemplifies that session parameters can range over arbitrary values.

Session `:rps-round` represents one round of the game; threads indexed by elements in set `ids` are still in, while threads indexed by elements in set `co-ids` are already out. If fewer than two threads are still in (`if`), the session is effectively empty. Otherwise, session `:rps-round` prescribes a concatenation:

1. First, there is an unordered universal quantification (`par-every`) of local variable `i` over domain `ids`, and simultaneously, local variable `j` over domain "`ids` without `i`" (`disj`). In general, an unordered universal quantification gives rise to a "big parallel" of branches, each of which is formed by binding values in domains to local variables (cf. parallel for-loops). In this particular example, every such branch prescribes a communication of a message of type `String` from (`:player i`) to (`:player j`), unbuffered. The idea is that every (`:player i`) sends its chosen item to every other in-game (`:player j`), in no particular order; the order is an implementation detail.
2. Then, there is an existential quantification (`alt-every`) of local variable `winner-ids` over domain "set of subsets of `ids`" (`power-set`). Similar to unordered universal quantification, in general, existential quantification gives rise to a "big choice" of branches. In this particular example, every such branch prescribes a binding (`let`) of local variable `loser-ids` to "`ids` without `winner-ids`" (`difference`), after which there is a parallel:
   (a) Concurrently, there is another instance of session `:rps-round`, but now with only `winner-ids` retained from `ids`, and with `loser-ids` added to `co-ids` (`union`). The idea is that only every (`:player i`) that is a winner this round goes to the next round.
   (b) Concurrently, there is an unordered universal quantification of `i` over `loser-ids`, and simultaneously, `j` over "all indices except `i`". Every branch of this "big parallel" prescribes a close of the channel from (`:player i`) to (`player j`). The idea is that every (`:player i`) that is a loser this round closes its channel to every other in-game or out-game (`:player j`).

   Thus, the idea of the existential quantification is, for every possible subset of winners, that the winners stay in the game, while the losers go out.

   We note that the usage of existential quantification in this way makes the

```
1  (def k ...) ;; number of threads (e.g., read from stdin)
2
3  (def rock "rock") (def paper "paper") (def scissors "scissors") ;; items
4
5  (def rock-or-paper-or-scissors (fn []      ...)) ;; returns an item
6  (def winner-ids                (fn [r]     ...)) ;; returns winners in round r
7  (def winner-or-loser?          (fn [r i] ...)) ;; returns true iff thread i is
8                                                  ;;  winner or loser in round r
9  (def chans    (mesh chan (range k)))
10 (def barrier (java.util.concurrent.Phaser. k))
11
12 (doseq [i (range k)]
13   (thread ;; for role (:player i)
14     (loop [ids (range k)]
15       (let [item (rock-or-paper-or-scissors)
16             opponent-ids (remove #{i} ids)
17             round (loop [acts (into (puts chans [i item] opponent-ids)
18                                     (takes chans opponent-ids i))
19                          round {}] ;; map from ids to items (initially empty)
20                     (if (empty? acts)
21                       (assoc round i item)
22                       (let [[v c] (alts!! acts)]
23                         (recur (remove #{[c item] c} acts)
24                                (assoc round (putter-id chans c) v)))))]
25         (.arriveAndAwaitAdvance barrier)
26         (if (winner-or-loser? round i)
27           (do (.arriveAndDeregister barrier)
28               (doseq [j (remove #i (range k))]
29                 (close! (chans i j))))
30           (recur (winner-ids round)))))))
```

Fig. 5. Implementation of Rock–Paper–Scissors, excerpt

specification implicitly *non-deterministic*: different branches may start with the exact same (sequence of) channel action(s), until a "distinguishing" channel action happens. This requires non-trivial bookkeeping to support.

Session :rps represents the whole game. It prescribes an initial instance of session :rps-round, where all threads are in, and no threads are out (empty-set).

In addition to existential quantification and unordered universal quantification, there is support for ordered universal quantification (cat-every): similar to the former two, the latter one gives rise to a "big concatenation" of branches (cf. sequential for-loops). We note that quantification domains need to be finite to ensure that checking whether a channel action is safe can happen in finite time.

The syntax and semantics of the functions for operations on sets are the same as those in standard library clojure.set, to make Discourje easy to learn.

Implementation. A Clojure implementation of Rock–Paper–Scissors is shown in Fig. 5 (excerpt; some details are left out to save space). Auxiliary Discourje functions are typeset in `font`; shading indicates external Java calls.

Line 1 defines a constant for the number of threads k. Lines 3–7 define constants and functions to represent Rock–Paper–Scissors concepts. Line 9 defines a collection of $k^2 - k$ unbuffered channels that implement the infrastructure, intended to be used as a fully connected mesh network; the threads are represented by indices in the range from 0 to k (exclusive). We note that `mesh` is "merely" an auxiliary Discourje function to simplify defining collections of channels; just as the other auxiliary Discourje functions used in Fig. 5, it works also without adding a monitor or instrumentation. Line 10 defines a reusable synchronisation barrier, imported from Java standard library `java.util.concurrent`, leveraging Clojure's interoperability with Java; shortly, we clarify the need for this.

Lines 12–30 define k copies of a thread that implements role `:player`. Every such thread executes two parametrised loops: an outer one, each of whose iterations comprises a round, and an inner one, each of whose iterations comprises a channel action (send or receive, indirectly using select). Salient aspects:

- According to the specification (Fig. 4), in the first half of every round (lines 8–10), the items that are chosen by in-game threads are communicated among them. This can be problematic: as channels are unbuffered, sends and receives are blocking until reciprocal channel actions are performed, so unless threads agree on a global order to perform such individual channel actions, deadlocks are looming. But, global orders are hard to get right and brittle to maintain. An alternative solution is to use *selects*: in general, a select consumes a collection of channel actions as input, then blocks until one of those actions becomes enabled, then performs that action, then unblocks, and then produces that action's output as output. Thus, a select performs *one* channel action from a collection, depending on its enabledness at run-time. In this particular example, instead of performing globally ordered individual sends and receives, every thread performs a series of selects (`alts!!`) in the inner loop. Initially, the collection of channel actions consists of all sends (`puts`) and receives (`takes`) that a thread needs to perform in a round. When a select finishes, the channel action that was performed is removed from the collection, and the inner loop continues. Because every thread behaves in this way, reciprocal channel actions are always enabled, so every thread makes progress. Thus, by using selects, the order in which communications happen, is not implemented (nor is it specified), but deadlocks are still avoided.
- According to the specification (Fig. 4), there is a strict order between the first half of every round (lines 8–10) and the second half (lines 11–16): *all* channel actions that belong to the first half need to have happened before proceeding to the second half. This can be problematic: additional synchronisation or timing measures are needed to ensure that "fast threads"—those that perform their channel actions early—wait for "slow threads" to catch up.

One solution is to extend the session with additional communications. An alternative solution is to mix communication primitives with synchronisation primitives. In this particular example, we adopt the latter solution: we mix channels with a barrier from `java.util.concurrent` (shaded code in Fig. 5). This demonstrates that channel-based programming abstractions (checked using Discourje) can be mixed seamlessly with other concurrency libraries (not checked), which is common practice [44,45].

Safety. A monitor and instrumentation can be added as in Fig. 3.

4   The Tour: Go Fish

Overview. We end the tour with a program that simulates a game of Go Fish.[8] Like the Rock–Paper–Scissors program in Sect. 3, the Go Fish program consists of $k + 1$ threads (players, plus dealer), and $k^2 + k$ channels from every thread to every other thread; unlike the Rock–Paper–Scissors program, however, all interactions among threads happen through channels (no need for external barriers, locks, etc.). This example demonstrates the following features:

– SPECIFICATION: user-defined message types; repetition (0-or-more); quantification (ordered universal); non-determinism (explicit).
– IMPLEMENTATION: message type-based control flow.

Specification. A Discourje specification of Go Fish is shown in Fig. 6.

Line 1 defines two roles, identified by :`dealer` (enacted by a single thread) and :`player` (multiple threads). Lines 3–29 define two sessions, identified by :`gf` and :`gf-turn`. Lines -7–0 define six user-defined message types.

Session :`gf-turn` represents one turn of (:`player i`). It prescribes a "big choice". In every branch, the idea is as follows. First, (:`player i`) asks (:`player j`) for some card. Then, there is a choice:

1. Either, (:`player j`) replies with the card that it was asked for, which happens to be the last card that (:`player i`) needs (to complete its last group), so it informs (:`dealer`), and the game ends.
2. Or, (:`player j`) replies with the card that it was asked for, which does not happen to be the last card that (:`player i`) needs, so (:`player i`) takes another turn, and the game continues.

We note that the specification is explicitly non-deterministic: the first branch and the second branch both start with the same channel action.

---

[8] Go Fish is a multiplayer game played with a standard 52-card deck. A dealer shuffles the deck and deals an initial hand to every player. Then, players take turns to collect groups of cards of the same rank. Every turn, the active player asks a passive player for a card. If the asked player has it, the asking player gets it and takes another turn; if not, the asked player tells the asking player ("go"), the asking player gets a card from the dealer ("fish"), and the turn is passed to the asked player. The first player to hold only complete groups wins. (This version of Go Fish is due to Parlett [38].).

```
 1 (defrole :dealer) (defrole :player)          -7 (defrecord Turn [])
 2                                               -6 (defrecord Ask [s r])
 3 (defsession :gf [ids]                         -5 (defrecord Card [s r])
 4   (cat (par-every [i ids]                      -4 (defrecord OutOfCards [])
 5         (cat-every [_ (range 5)]               -3 (defrecord Go [])
 6           (--> Card :dealer (:player i))))     -2 (defrecord Fish [])
 7        (alt-every [i ids]                      -1 ;; above, parameters s and r
 8         (cat (--> Turn :dealer (:player i))     0 ;;  abbreviate suit and rank
 9          (:gf-turn i ids)))
10        (par-every [i ids]
11         (cat (close :dealer (:player i))
12          (par (cat (* (--> Card (:player i) :dealer))
13                (close (:player i) :dealer))
14           (par-every [j (disj ids i)]
15            (close (:player i) (:player j)))))))))
16
17 (defsession :gf-turn [i ids]
18   (alt-every [j (disj ids i)]
19     (cat (--> Ask (:player i) (:player j))
20       (alt (cat (--> Card (:player j) (:player i))
21             (--> OutOfCards (:player i) :dealer))
22         (cat (--> Card (:player j) (:player i))
23          (:gf-turn i ids))
24         (cat (--> Go (:player j) (:player i))
25          (--> Fish (:player i) :dealer)
26          (alt (--> Card :dealer (:player i))
27               (--> OutOfCards :dealer (:player i)))
28          (--> Turn (:player i) (:player j))
29          (:gf-turn j ids)))))))
```

Fig. 6. Discourje specification of Go Fish, including message types

3. Or, (:player j) does not reply with the card that it was asked for, so (:player i) tries to "fish" a card from :dealer, after which (:player i) passes the turn to (:player j), and the game continues.

Session :gf represents the whole game. It prescribes a concatenation:

1. First, there is a "big parallel". The idea is that :dealer deals every player an initial hand of five cards, in no particular order (implementation detail).
2. Then, there is a "big choice". The idea is that :dealer passes the first turn to one of the players (implementation detail). During the game, the players pass the turn among themselves unbeknownst to :dealer.
3. Then, there is a "big parallel". The idea is that the game has ended at this point, so :dealer closes its channel to every (:player i), in no particular order (implementation detail), after which every (:player i) sends its hand back to :dealer through the oppositely directed channel, closes that channel, and closes its channel to every other (:player j), in no particular order.

```
1 (doseq [i (range k)]                    11 (thread ...) ;; for :dealer
2   (thread ;; for (:player i)
3     (... (let [[v c] (alts!! ...)]
4         (condp = (type v)
5           Turn (... (let [v (<!! ...)]
6                  (condp = (type v)
7                    Card ...
8                    Go   ...)))  ;; another <!! and condp in this case
9           Ask  ...
10          nil  ...))))))
```

Fig. 7. Implementation of Rock–Paper–Scissors, excerpt

Implementation. A Clojure implementation of Go Fish is shown in Fig. 7 (excerpt; many details are left out to save space).

To demonstrate that Discourje supports message type-based control flow, Fig. 7 shows fragments of code where messages are received—directly with <!! and indirectly with alts!!—by threads that implement role :player. Specifically:

- On line 3, alts!! is used to receive a message v from another :player or from :dealer. This message is either of type Turn (received from another :player), or of type Ask (idem), or nil ("received" from :dealer).
  We note that a "receive" of nil happens only, and automatically, when the channel from :dealer to (:player i) is closed. Such a degenerate "receive" is used by (:player i) to detect that the game has ended.
- On line 5, <!! is used to receive a message of type Card or Go from (:player j), to which a message of type Ask was sent previously (not shown).

Safety. A monitor and instrumentation can be added as in Fig. 3.

5   Foundation

Overview. Discourje is built on a formal foundation, inspired by process algebra (e.g., [15]) and multiparty session types (e.g., [46]). In a nutshell, let $\mathbb{S}$ and $\mathbb{I}$ be sets of specifications and implementations. Then, given a specification $S \in \mathbb{S}$ and an implementation $I \in \mathbb{I}$, the "game" is to check if a trace of I is also a trace of S. We briefly summarise the theory (for unbuffered channels), based on [22].

Specification. Let $\mathbb{R}$ be a set of roles, ranged over by p, q, r. Let $\mathbb{F}$, $\mathbb{V}$, $\mathbb{X}$, and $\mathbb{E}$ be sets of functions, values, variables, and expressions, ranged over by f, v, x, and e, such that $\mathbb{F} \subseteq \mathbb{V} \subseteq \mathbb{E}$ and $\mathbb{X} \subseteq \mathbb{E}$; for simplicity, we leave the elements of $\mathbb{F}$, $\mathbb{V}$, $\mathbb{E}$, and $\mathbb{X}$ unspecified (although, we stipulate that $\mathbb{E}$ contains at least boolean, numerical, and lambda expressions). Let $\tilde{\mathbb{X}}$ and $\tilde{\mathbb{E}}$ be sets of lists of variables and lists of expressions, ranged over by $\tilde{e}$ and $\tilde{x}$. The syntax of specifications is defined as follows (with corresponding Discourje macros):

$$S \in \mathbb{S} ::= \underset{\longrightarrow}{\mathbf{1}} \mid \underset{\text{par}}{r_1[e_1] \twoheadrightarrow r_2[e_2] : f} \mid \underset{\text{close}}{r_1[e_1] \nrightarrow r_2[e_2]} \mid \underset{\text{cat}}{S_1 \cdot S_2} \mid \underset{\text{alt}}{S_1 + S_2} \mid$$

$$\underset{\text{par}}{S_1 \parallel S_2} \mid \underset{\text{if}}{e \triangleright S_1 \diamond S_2} \mid \underset{\text{“call”}}{X(\tilde{e})} \mid \underset{\text{defsession}}{\langle S \mid X_1(\tilde{x}_1) = S_1, \ldots, X_n(\tilde{x}_n) = S_n \rangle}$$

Term $\mathbf{1}$, which represents a *skip*, is the only term for which no corresponding Discourje macro exists; its shading indicates that it is used primarily/ only to define the operational semantics (it should not be used directly). Conversely, Discourje macro calls for which no corresponding term exist, are encodable. For instance, (cat-every [x (range 5)] ...), with x free in the ellipses, corresponds with $\langle X(5) \mid X(x) = (x > 1 \triangleright (\ldots \cdot X(x-1)) \diamond (x > 0 \triangleright \ldots \diamond \mathbf{1}) \rangle$.

$$\frac{}{\mathbf{1} \downarrow} \text{ [S}\downarrow\text{-One]} \qquad \frac{S_1 \downarrow \text{ and } S_2 \downarrow}{S_1 \cdot S_2 \downarrow} \text{ [S}\downarrow\text{-Cat]} \qquad \frac{S_{i \in \{1,2\}} \downarrow}{S_1 + S_2 \downarrow} \text{ [S}\downarrow\text{-Alt]}$$

Fig. 8. Operational semantics of specifications (termination), excerpt

$$\frac{e_i \Downarrow i \text{ and } e_j \Downarrow j \text{ and } (f\ v) \Downarrow \text{true}}{p[e_i] \twoheadrightarrow q[e_j] : f \xrightarrow{p[i]q[j]!?v} \mathbf{1}} \text{ [S-Unbuf]} \qquad \frac{e_i \Downarrow i \text{ and } e_j \Downarrow j}{p[e_i] \nrightarrow q[e_j] \xrightarrow{p[i]q[j]\bullet} \mathbf{1}} \text{ [S-Close]}$$

$$\frac{S_1 \xrightarrow{\alpha} S_1'}{S_1 \cdot S_2 \xrightarrow{\alpha} S_1' \cdot S_2} \text{ [S-Cat1]} \qquad \frac{S_1 \downarrow \text{ and } S_2 \xrightarrow{\alpha} S_2'}{S_1 \cdot S_2 \xrightarrow{\alpha} S_2'} \text{ [S-Cat2]} \qquad \frac{S_{i \in \{1,2\}} \xrightarrow{\alpha} S'}{S_1 + S_2 \xrightarrow{\alpha} S'} \text{ [S-Alt]}$$

Fig. 9. Operational semantics of specifications (reduction), excerpt

The operational semantics of specifications is defined in terms of evaluation relation $\Downarrow$, termination predicate $\downarrow$, and labelled reduction relation $\rightarrow$. Labels, ranged over by α, are of the form $p[i]q[j]!?v$ (unbuffered send and receive; handshake) and $p[i]q[j]\bullet$ (close). A subset of rules are shown in Figs. 8–9; they are standard (cf. Basic Process Algebra [15], plus merge, conditional and recursion).

Implementation. The syntax of implementations is defined as follows (it does not cover all features of Clojure used in Sects. 2–4, but a smaller core set):

$$I \in \mathbb{I} ::= \text{skip} \mid \text{if } I_1\ I_2\ I_3 \mid \text{loop } \tilde{x}\ \tilde{e}\ I \mid \text{recur } \tilde{e} \mid I_1 \cdot I_2 \mid$$

$$I_1 \parallel I_2 \mid \text{chan} \mid \text{close } e \mid \text{send } e_1\ e_2 \mid \text{recv } e\ x \mid \text{select } \tilde{I}$$

The operational semantics of the calculus is defined in terms of labelled reductions of pairs $(I, \mathcal{H})$, where $\mathcal{H}$ is a heap (map from locations to channel

$$\frac{e \Downarrow v \quad (I_v, \mathcal{H}) \xrightarrow{\alpha} (I', \mathcal{H}')}{(\text{if } e \; I_{\text{true}} \; I_{\text{false}}, \mathcal{H}) \xrightarrow{\alpha} (I', \mathcal{H}')} \; [\text{I-If}] \qquad \frac{\tilde{e} \Downarrow \tilde{v} \text{ and } I[\text{loop } \tilde{x} \; \tilde{e} \; I/\text{recur}][\tilde{v}/\tilde{x}] \xrightarrow{\alpha} I'}{(\text{loop } \tilde{x} \; \tilde{e} \; I, \mathcal{H}) \xrightarrow{\alpha} (I', \mathcal{H})} \; [\text{I-Loop}]$$

$$\frac{\begin{array}{c}\ell \notin \mathcal{H} \text{ and} \\ (I[\ell/x], \mathcal{H}[\ell \mapsto \top]) \xrightarrow{\alpha} (I', \mathcal{H}')\end{array}}{(\text{chan } x \cdot I, \mathcal{H}) \xrightarrow{\alpha} (I', \mathcal{H}')} \; [\text{I-Chan}] \qquad \frac{e \Downarrow \ell \text{ and } \ell \in \mathcal{H}}{(\text{close } e \cdot I, \mathcal{H}) \xrightarrow{\ell\bullet} (I, \mathcal{H}[\ell \mapsto \bot])} \; [\text{I-Close}]$$

$$\frac{\begin{array}{c}\text{send } e_1 \; e_v \in \mathcal{I}_1 \text{ and recv } e_2 \; x \in \mathcal{I}_2 \text{ and} \\ e_1 \Downarrow \ell \text{ and } e_v \Downarrow v \text{ and } e_2 \Downarrow \ell \text{ and } \mathcal{H}(\ell) = \top\end{array}}{((\text{select } \mathcal{I}_1 \cdot I_1) \; \| \; (\text{select } \mathcal{I}_2 \cdot I_2), \mathcal{H}) \xrightarrow{\ell!?v} (I_1 \; \| \; I_2[v/x], \mathcal{H})} \; [\text{I-Unbuf}]$$

$$\frac{(I_1, \mathcal{H}) \xrightarrow{\alpha} (I_1', \mathcal{H}')}{(I_1 \; \| \; I_2, \mathcal{H}) \xrightarrow{\alpha} (I_1' \; \| \; I_2, \mathcal{H}')} \; [\text{I-Par1}] \qquad \frac{(I_2, \mathcal{H}) \xrightarrow{\alpha} (I_2', \mathcal{H}')}{(I_1 \; \| \; I_2, \mathcal{H}) \xrightarrow{\alpha} (I_1 \; \| \; I_2', \mathcal{H}')} \; [\text{I-Par2}]$$

Fig. 10. Operational semantics of implementations, excerpt

states). As we cover only unbuffered channels in this paper (buffered channels are covered elsewhere [22]), a channel state is represented by $\top$ (if the channel is open) of $\bot$ (closed). Labels are of the form $\ell!?v$ and $\ell\bullet$. A subset of rules are shown in Fig. 10 (notably, a structural congruence rule has been omitted).

Safety. Let $\dagger$ be a function from heap locations to sender–receiver pairs; it corresponds with the linkage of channels to a monitor (Fig. 3). Abusing notation, we write $\dagger(\ell!?v)$ and $\dagger(\ell\bullet)$ instead of $\dagger(\ell)!?v$ and $\dagger(\ell)\bullet$.

We formalise safety ("bad channel actions never happen") in terms of *simulation*. Specifically, implementation I is $\dagger$-simulated by specification S if there exists a $\preceq \subseteq \mathbb{I} \times \mathbb{S}$ such that: (1) $I \preceq S$, and (2) for all $\hat{I}, \hat{I}' \in \mathbb{I}$ and $\hat{S} \in \mathbb{S}$, if $\hat{I} \preceq \hat{S}$ and $\hat{I} \xrightarrow{\alpha} \hat{I}'$, then there exists an $\hat{S}' \in \mathbb{S}$ such that $\hat{I}' \preceq \hat{S}'$ and $\hat{S} \xrightarrow{\dagger(\alpha)} \hat{S}'$.

To ensure safety at run-time, a monitor dynamically constructs a simulation relation to check if the implementation is simulated by the specification, incrementally, as channel actions are performed. A subtle—but important—detail is that the relation is constructed not for the whole reduction relation of the implementation, but only for a "linear" subrelation (a trace; the actual execution).

6   Conclusion

Related Work. The Discourje project is strongly influenced by work on *multiparty session types* (MPST) [24]. The idea of MPST is to specify protocols as behavioural types [1,28] against which threads are subsequently type-checked; the theory guarantees that static well-typedness of threads at compile-time implies dynamic safety of their channel actions at run-time. In recent years, several practical implementations were developed, mostly for statically typed languages (e.g., C [37], Java [26,27], Scala [42], F# [34], Go [7]), and to lesser extent for dynamically typed languages (e.g., Python [25], Erlang [35]).

Discourje takes advantage of two key properties of the application domain to offer higher expressiveness than existing MPST tools: we apply run-time verification instead of compile-time analysis, and we target shared-memory programs instead of distributed systems. The former means that no implementations are conservatively rejected (so, Discourje supports more implementations); the latter means that no decomposition of "global" specifications into "local" specifications—one for every role—is required, which is needed in existing MPST tools, but often not possible [7] (so, Discourje supports more specifications). Notably, we support non-deterministic choice and value-dependent control flow in specifications. To our knowledge, in the context of MPST, we are the first to leverage run-time verification and shared memory together, although they have been considered in isolation:

- There are MPST approaches that combine static type-checking with a form of distributed run-time monitoring and/or assertion checking [4,5,13,33,34]. In contrast to Discourje, however, these dynamic techniques still rely on decomposition; none of the specifications in this paper are supported.
- Decomposition-free MPST has also been explored by López et al. [32,41]. Their idea is to specify MPI communication protocols in an MPI-tailored DSL, inspired by MPST, and verify the implementation against the specification using deductive verification tools (VCC [12] and Why3 [14]). However, this approach does not support push-button verification: considerable manual effort is required. In contrast, Discourje is fully automated.

Verification of shared-memory concurrency with channels has received attention in the context of Go [30,31,36,43]. However, in addition to relying on static techniques (unlike Discourje), emphasis in these works is on checking deadlock-freedom, liveness, and generic safety properties, while we focus on program-specific protocol compliance. Castro et al. [7] also consider protocol compliance for Go, but their specification language is substantially less expressive than ours; none of the specifications in this paper are supported.

We are aware of only two other works that use formal techniques to reason about Clojure programs: Bonnaire-Sergeant et al. [6] formalized the optional type system for Clojure and proved soundness, while Pinzaru et al. [39] developed a translation from Clojure to Boogie [2] to verify Clojure programs annotated with pre/post-conditions. Discourje seems the first to target concurrency in Clojure.

Future Work. We are currently working towards several new features: (1) automated *recovery* when a violation is detected, instead of throwing an exception; (2) *meta-verification* of specifications, to detect "insensible" specifications; (3) first-class support for histories, to improve expressiveness with history-based conditionals. Also, we are interested to explore "weaving", as in aspect-oriented programming [29], to further reduce the effort of adding instrumentation [3].

Finally, research is needed to better understand the *effectiveness* of Discourje (e.g., in terms of reduced development costs). In particular, we would like to gain insight into difficulties that programmers face when writing specifications. We try to make Discourje easy to learn and use by supporting standard Clojure idioms wherever possible (e.g., for regular expressions; Sect. 2), but scientific evidence on usability is still to be gathered.

Acknowledgements. We thank Luc Edixhoven and anonymous reviewers for comments on an earlier version of this paper. Funded by the Netherlands Organisation of Scientific Research (NWO): 016.Veni.192.103.

A Clojure

Standard library `clojure.core`:

- **(def** x e): first evaluates e to v; then binds x to v in the global environment.
- **(if** e_1 e_2 e_3): first evaluates e_1; if **true**, evaluates e_2; else, evaluates e_3.
- **(let** [x_1 e_1 ... x_n e_n] e): first evaluates e_1 to v_1; then evaluates e_2 to v_2 with x_1 bound to v_1; ...; then evaluates e_n to v_n with x_1, ..., x_{n-1} bound to v_1, ..., v_{n-1}; then evaluates e with x_1, ..., x_n bound to v_1, ..., v_n.
- **(fn** [x_1 ... x_n] e_1 ... e_m): evaluates to a function with parameters x_1, ..., x_n and creates a recursion point; then, when applied to arguments v_1, ..., v_n, sequentially evaluates e_1, ..., e_m with x_1, ..., x_n bound to v_1, ..., v_n.
- **(loop** [x_1 e_1 ... x_n e_n] e): same as **let**, but also creates a recursion point.
- **(recur** e_1 ... e_n): first evaluates e_1, ..., e_n to v_1, ..., v_n; then evaluates the nearest recursion point with x_1, ..., x_n bound to v_1, ..., v_n.

Standard library `clojure.core.async`:

- **(thread** e): starts a new thread that evaluates e.
- **(chan)**: evaluates to a new unbuffered channel.
- **(close!** e): first evaluates e to channel c; then closes c.
- **(>!!** e_1 e_2): first evaluates e_1 to channel c; then evaluates e_2 to v; then sends v through c.
- **(<!!** e): first evaluates e to channel c; then receives a value through c.
- **(alts!!** [a_1 ... a_n]): for every a_i of the form [$e_{i,1}$ $e_{i,2}$] (send) or e_i (receive), evaluates $e_{i,1}$ and e_i to channel c_i, and then, evaluates $e_{i,2}$ to v; then, waits until one of these channel actions can be performed; then, performs a channel action that can be performed (non-deterministically selected).

References

1. Ancona, D., et al.: Behavioral types in programming languages. Found. Trends Program. Lang. **3**(2–3), 95–230 (2016)
2. Barnett, M., Chang, B.-Y.E., DeLine, R., Jacobs, B., Leino, K.R.M.: Boogie: a modular reusable verifier for object-oriented programs. In: de Boer, F.S., Bonsangue, M.M., Graf, S., de Roever, W.-P. (eds.) FMCO 2005. LNCS, vol. 4111, pp. 364–387. Springer, Heidelberg (2006). https://doi.org/10.1007/11804192_17

3. Bartocci, E., Falcone, Y., Francalanza, A., Reger, G.: Introduction to runtime verification. In: Bartocci, E., Falcone, Y. (eds.) Lectures on Runtime Verification. LNCS, vol. 10457, pp. 1–33. Springer, Cham (2018). https://doi.org/10.1007/978-3-319-75632-5_1

4. Bocchi, L., Chen, T., Demangeon, R., Honda, K., Yoshida, N.: Monitoring networks through multiparty session types. Theor. Comput. Sci. **669**, 33–58 (2017)

5. Bocchi, L., Honda, K., Tuosto, E., Yoshida, N.: A theory of design-by-contract for distributed multiparty interactions. In: Gastin, P., Laroussinie, F. (eds.) CONCUR 2010. LNCS, vol. 6269, pp. 162–176. Springer, Heidelberg (2010). https://doi.org/10.1007/978-3-642-15375-4_12

6. Bonnaire-Sergeant, A., Davies, R., Tobin-Hochstadt, S.: Practical optional types for Clojure. In: Thiemann, P. (ed.) ESOP 2016. LNCS, vol. 9632, pp. 68–94. Springer, Heidelberg (2016). https://doi.org/10.1007/978-3-662-49498-1_4

7. Castro, D., Hu, R., Jongmans, S., Ng, N., Yoshida, N.: Distributed programming using role-parametric session types in go: statically-typed endpoint APIs for dynamically-instantiated communication structures. PACMPL **3**(POPL), 29:1–29:30 (2019)

8. Clojure Team: Clojure - Clojure core.async Channels, 28 June 2013. https://clojure.org/news/2013/06/28/clojure-clore-async-channels. Accessed 1 Sept 2019

9. Clojure Team: Clojure - State of Clojure 2019 Results, 04 February 2019. https://clojure.org/news/2019/02/04/state-of-clojure-2019. Accessed 1 Sept 2019

10. Clojure Team: Clojure - State of Clojure 2020 Results, 20 February 2019. https://clojure.org/news/2020/02/20/state-of-clojure-2020. Accessed 28 May 2020

11. Clojure Team: Clojure (nd). https://clojure.org. Accessed 1 Sept 2019

12. Cohen, E., et al.: VCC: a practical system for verifying concurrent C. In: Berghofer, S., Nipkow, T., Urban, C., Wenzel, M. (eds.) TPHOLs 2009. LNCS, vol. 5674, pp. 23–42. Springer, Heidelberg (2009). https://doi.org/10.1007/978-3-642-03359-9_2

13. Demangeon, R., Honda, K., Hu, R., Neykova, R., Yoshida, N.: Practical interruptible conversations: distributed dynamic verification with multiparty session types and python. Formal Methods Syst. Des. **46**(3), 197–225 (2015)

14. Filliâtre, J.-C., Paskevich, A.: Why3—where programs meet provers. In: Felleisen, M., Gardner, P. (eds.) ESOP 2013. LNCS, vol. 7792, pp. 125–128. Springer, Heidelberg (2013). https://doi.org/10.1007/978-3-642-37036-6_8

15. Fokkink, W.: Introduction to Process Algebra. Texts in Theoretical Computer Science. An EATCS Series. Springer, Heidelberg (2000). https://doi.org/10.1007/978-3-662-04293-9

16. Go Team: Go 2016 Survey Results - The Go Blog, 03 June 2017. https://blog.golang.org/survey2016-results. Accessed 1 Sept 2019

17. Go Team: Go 2017 Survey Results - The Go Blog, 26 February 2018. https://blog.golang.org/survey2017-results. Accessed 1 Sept 2019

18. Go Team: Go 2018 Survey Results - The Go Blog, 28 March 2019. https://blog.golang.org/survey2018-results. Accessed 1 Sept 2019

19. Go Team: Go Developer Survey 2019 Results - The Go Blog, 20 April 2020. https://blog.golang.org/survey2019-results. Accessed 8 May 2020

20. Go Team: Effective Go - The Go Programming Language (nd). https://golang.org/doc/effective_go.html. Accessed 8 May 2020

21. Go Team: The Go Programming Language (nd). https://golang.org. Accessed 1 Sept 2019

22. Hamers, R., Jongmans, S.-S.: Discourje: runtime verification of communication protocols in Clojure. In: Biere, A., Parker, D. (eds.) TACAS 2020. LNCS, vol. 12078, pp. 266–284. Springer, Cham (2020). https://doi.org/10.1007/978-3-030-45190-5_15

23. Hickey, R.: The Clojure programming language. In: DLS, p. 1. ACM (2008)

24. Honda, K., Yoshida, N., Carbone, M.: Multiparty asynchronous session types. In: POPL, pp. 273–284. ACM (2008)

25. Hu, R., Neykova, R., Yoshida, N., Demangeon, R., Honda, K.: Practical interruptible conversations. In: Legay, A., Bensalem, S. (eds.) RV 2013. LNCS, vol. 8174, pp. 130–148. Springer, Heidelberg (2013). https://doi.org/10.1007/978-3-642-40787-1_8

26. Hu, R., Yoshida, N.: Hybrid session verification through endpoint API generation. In: Stevens, P., Wąsowski, A. (eds.) FASE 2016. LNCS, vol. 9633, pp. 401–418. Springer, Heidelberg (2016). https://doi.org/10.1007/978-3-662-49665-7_24

27. Hu, R., Yoshida, N.: Explicit connection actions in multiparty session types. In: Huisman, M., Rubin, J. (eds.) FASE 2017. LNCS, vol. 10202, pp. 116–133. Springer, Heidelberg (2017). https://doi.org/10.1007/978-3-662-54494-5_7

28. Hüttel, H., et al.: Foundations of session types and behavioural contracts. ACM Comput. Surv. **49**(1), 3:1–3:36 (2016)

29. Kiczales, G., et al.: Aspect-oriented programming. In: Akşit, M., Matsuoka, S. (eds.) ECOOP 1997. LNCS, vol. 1241, pp. 220–242. Springer, Heidelberg (1997). https://doi.org/10.1007/BFb0053381

30. Lange, J., Ng, N., Toninho, B., Yoshida, N.: Fencing off go: liveness and safety for channel-based programming. In: POPL, pp. 748–761. ACM (2017)

31. Lange, J., Ng, N., Toninho, B., Yoshida, N.: A static verification framework for message passing in go using behavioural types. In: ICSE, pp. 1137–1148. ACM (2018)

32. López, H.A., et al.: Protocol-based verification of message-passing parallel programs. In: OOPSLA, pp. 280–298. ACM (2015)

33. Neykova, R., Bocchi, L., Yoshida, N.: Timed runtime monitoring for multiparty conversations. Formal Aspects Comput. **29**(5), 877–910 (2017). https://doi.org/10.1007/s00165-017-0420-8

34. Neykova, R., Hu, R., Yoshida, N., Abdeljallal, F.: A session type provider: compile-time API generation of distributed protocols with refinements in f#. In: CC, pp. 128–138. ACM (2018)

35. Neykova, R., Yoshida, N.: Let it recover: multiparty protocol-induced recovery. In: CC, pp. 98–108. ACM (2017)

36. Ng, N., Yoshida, N.: Static deadlock detection for concurrent go by global session graph synthesis. In: CC, pp. 174–184. ACM (2016)

37. Ng, N., Yoshida, N., Honda, K.: Multiparty session C: safe parallel programming with message optimisation. In: Furia, C.A., Nanz, S. (eds.) TOOLS 2012. LNCS, vol. 7304, pp. 202–218. Springer, Heidelberg (2012). https://doi.org/10.1007/978-3-642-30561-0_15

38. Parlett, D.: The Penguin Book of Card Games. Penguin (2008)

39. Pinzaru, G., Rivera, V.: Towards static verification of Clojure contract-based programs. In: Mazzara, M., Bruel, J.-M., Meyer, B., Petrenko, A. (eds.) TOOLS 2019. LNCS, vol. 11771, pp. 73–80. Springer, Cham (2019). https://doi.org/10.1007/978-3-030-29852-4_5

40. Rust Team: Rust Programming Language (nd). https://rust-lang.org. Accessed 1 Sept 2019

41. Santos, C., Martins, F., Vasconcelos, V.T.: Deductive verification of parallel programs using why3. In: ICE. EPTCS, vol. 189, pp. 128–142 (2015)
42. Scalas, A., Dardha, O., Hu, R., Yoshida, N.: A linear decomposition of multiparty sessions for safe distributed programming. In: ECOOP. LIPIcs, vol. 74, pp. 24:1–24:31. Schloss Dagstuhl - Leibniz-Zentrum fuer Informatik (2017)
43. Stadtmüller, K., Sulzmann, M., Thiemann, P.: Static trace-based deadlock analysis for synchronous mini-go. In: Igarashi, A. (ed.) APLAS 2016. LNCS, vol. 10017, pp. 116–136. Springer, Cham (2016). https://doi.org/10.1007/978-3-319-47958-3_7
44. Tasharofi, S., Dinges, P., Johnson, R.E.: Why do Scala developers mix the actor model with other concurrency models? In: Castagna, G. (ed.) ECOOP 2013. LNCS, vol. 7920, pp. 302–326. Springer, Heidelberg (2013). https://doi.org/10.1007/978-3-642-39038-8_13
45. Tu, T., Liu, X., Song, L., Zhang, Y.: Understanding real-world concurrency bugs in go. In: ASPLOS, pp. 865–878. ACM (2019)
46. Yoshida, N., Gheri, L.: A very gentle introduction to multiparty session types. In: Hung, D.V., D'Souza, M. (eds.) ICDCIT 2020. LNCS, vol. 11969, pp. 73–93. Springer, Cham (2020). https://doi.org/10.1007/978-3-030-36987-3_5

Modular Verification of Liveness Properties of the I/O Behavior of Imperative Programs

Bart Jacobs[✉][iD]

Department of Computer Science, imec-DistriNet Research Group, KU Leuven,
Leuven, Belgium
bart.jacobs@cs.kuleuven.be

Abstract. One way of verifying systems whose components interact by exchanging messages, such as distributed systems or certain types of concurrent systems, is by defining a protocol that governs the communication between the components and then verifying that each component's input and output (I/O) actions comply with its role in the protocol.

In this paper, we propose a separation logic-based approach for specifying and verifying liveness properties of the I/O behavior of such components implemented as imperative programs, such as the property that a server eventually responds to each request. Our approach builds on earlier work for specifying safety properties of the I/O behavior of programs in separation logic by means of abstract nested Hoare triples, and encodes a liveness property verification problem into a termination verification problem by specifying that some appropriately chosen I/O operation (for example, the response to the N'th request, for some unknown but fixed N) will cause the program to terminate.

1   Introduction

Consider the following program:

$$\textbf{loop } (\textbf{let } \mathsf{msg} = \mathsf{recv}() \textbf{ in } \mathsf{send}(\mathsf{msg}))$$

This program implements a simple echo server. It sits in an infinite loop. In each iteration, it receives a message and echoes it back out. The problem we address in this paper is: how to specify and verify the safety and liveness properties of the I/O behavior of programs such as this one in Hoare logic [4]? We target Hoare logic so that we obtain a modular verification approach. For the example program specifically, we want to be able to specify the safety property that it only sends messages that it has received, and that it sends a message at most once[1]; furthermore, we want to be able to specify the liveness property that it sends each message it has received at least once.

---

[1] For simplicity, in this paper we assume a program never receives the same message more than once.

© Springer Nature Switzerland AG 2020
T. Margaria and B. Steffen (Eds.): ISoLA 2020, LNCS 12476, pp. 509–524, 2020.
https://doi.org/10.1007/978-3-030-61362-4_29

For specifying the safety properties of the I/O behavior, we apply our earlier work [7–9] on *abstract nested Hoare triples* in *separation logic* [11]. For specifying liveness properties, we build on earlier work [5] on verification of *basic liveness*. We combine and extend this work to obtain an approach that supports specifying a wide range of liveness properties. Adopting the terminology of Chang *et al.* [2], we show how our approach supports not just *guarantee properties* (of the form $\Diamond p$, *eventually p* in temporal logic) (example: the program eventually terminates) and *simple response properties* (of the form $\Box\Diamond p$, *always eventually p*) (example: the program always eventually responds to each request), but also *general response properties* (of the form $\bigwedge_i \Box\Diamond p_i$) (example: the program always eventually responds to each request and always eventually emits a heartbeat signal), *simple reactivity properties* (of the form $\Box\Diamond p \Rightarrow \Box\Diamond q$) (example: if the program always eventually receives a request, it always eventually responds to each request), *general reactivity properties* (of the form $\bigwedge_i(\Box\Diamond p_i \Rightarrow \Box\Diamond q_i)$) (example: the program always eventually emits a heartbeat signal, and if it always eventually receives a request, it always eventually responds to each request) and *persistence properties* (of the form $\Diamond\Box p$) (example: the program eventually always sends messages using the new message format).

The structure of this paper is as follows. In Sect. 2, we present our approach informally. In Sect. 3, we formalize the syntax and semantics of a simple programming language with I/O. In Sect. 4, we formalize our logic for liveness. We discuss related work in Sect. 5 and offer a conclusion in Sect. 6.

2   Our Approach, Informally

In this section, we present our approach informally. In subsequent sections, we formalize the programming language and the logic.

2.1   Safety

For specifying the safety properties of the I/O behavior, we apply our earlier work [7–9]: we use *abstract nested Hoare triples* in *separation logic* [11]. For example, a specification for the program send("Hello"); send("world!") could look as follows:

$$\{P_1 \wedge \mathsf{send\_}(P_1, \texttt{"Hello"}, P_2) \wedge \mathsf{send\_}(P_2, \texttt{"world!"}, P_3)\}$$
$$\texttt{send("Hello"); send("world!")}$$
$$\{P_3\}$$

where the specification for send is

$$\{P \wedge \mathsf{send\_}(P, m, Q)\} \ \mathsf{send}(m) \ \{Q\}$$

and $\mathsf{send\_}(P, m, Q)$ is a *higher-order predicate* that states that any resource that satisfies separation logic predicate P is sufficient to send message m; doing so consumes such a resource and produces a resource that satisfies separation logic predicate Q. We refer to higher-order predicates such as send_ as *abstract nested Hoare triples* because their meaning is similar to that of the Hoare triple $\{P\}$ send(m) $\{Q\}$. The difference between abstract nested Hoare triples and actual nested Hoare triples is that the abstract ones are in fact just user-defined predicates, so their meaning is entirely defined by the user, rather than having a fixed meaning assigned by the logic. The meaning of predicate send_, for example, is defined by the author of the module that implements function send.

We can read the specification for the "Hello, world!" example as follows: for any P_1, P_2, and P_3, if a resource (satisfying) P_1 allows me to send "Hello" and obtain a resource P_2, and P_2 allows me to send "world!" and obtain P_3, and I have P_1, then I can run safely and if I terminate, I will end up with P_3.

In a similar fashion we can specify programs that perform both input and output. For example, the body of the echo loop can be specified as follows:

$$\{P_1 \land \mathsf{recv\_}(P_1, m, P_2) \land \mathsf{send\_}(P_2, m, P_3)\}$$
$$\mathsf{let}\ \mathsf{msg} = \mathsf{recv}()\ \mathsf{in}\ \mathsf{send}(\mathsf{msg})$$
$$\{P_3\}$$

where the specification for recv is

$$\{P \land \mathsf{recv\_}(P, m, Q)\}\ \mathsf{recv}()\ \{Q \land \mathsf{res} = m\}$$

In postconditions, we use res to denote the result of a command. The predicate recv_(P, m, Q) means that if you have P, you are allowed to receive. This will consume P and produce Q. Furthermore, the message you will receive is m. It follows that the specification for the single echo iteration states that it is allowed to receive a message, and then send the message it received, and that if it terminates, it shall indeed have performed these actions.

Using these ingredients, we can specify the full echo server, by first coinductively defining two predicates for expressing permission to receive and send an infinite sequence of messages, respectively:

$$\mathsf{recv\_stream}(P, m \cdot \mu) = \exists Q.\ \mathsf{recv\_}(P, m, Q) \land \mathsf{recv\_stream}(Q, \mu)$$
$$\mathsf{send\_stream}(P, m \cdot \mu) = \exists Q.\ \mathsf{send\_}(P, m, Q) \land \mathsf{send\_stream}(P, \mu)$$

We use μ to range over infinite sequences of messages[2], and $m \cdot \mu$ to denote the sequence with head m and tail μ. One possible specification for the safety of the echo server is then:

$$\{P_r * P_s \land \mathsf{recv\_stream}(P_r, \mu) \land \mathsf{send\_stream}(P_s, \mu)\}$$
$$\mathsf{loop}\ (\mathsf{let}\ \mathsf{msg} = \mathsf{recv}()\ \mathsf{in}\ \mathsf{send}(\mathsf{msg}))$$
$$\{\mathsf{False}\}$$

This is where separation logic's separating conjunction $-*-$ comes in; it allows us to express that I have permission P_r to receive, and *separately* I have permission P_s to send. We can apply separation logic's *frame rule*

---

[2] For simplicity, we assume the same message does not appear twice in such a sequence. As a result, "echoing out the message at position i in μ" is equivalent to "responding to the i'th request".

$$\frac{\{P\} \, c \, \{Q\}}{\{P * R\} \, c \, \{Q * R\}}$$

to the triple

$$\{P_r \wedge \mathsf{recv\_stream}(P_r, m \cdot \mu)\} \; \mathsf{recv}() \; \{\exists P_r'. \, P_r' \wedge \mathsf{recv\_stream}(P_r', \mu) \wedge \mathsf{res} = m\}$$

taking *frame* $R = (P_s \wedge \mathsf{send\_stream}(P_s, m \cdot \mu))$ to obtain

$$\{P_r * P_s \wedge \mathsf{recv\_stream}(P_r, m \cdot \mu) \wedge \mathsf{send\_stream}(P_s, m \cdot \mu)\}$$
$$\mathsf{recv}()$$
$$\{\exists P_r'. \, P_r' * P_s \wedge \mathsf{recv\_stream}(P_r', \mu) \wedge \mathsf{send\_stream}(P_s, \mathsf{res} \cdot \mu)\}$$

If we only had $P_r \wedge P_s$ instead of $P_r * P_s$, we would not be able to conclude that recv() preserves P_s.

Note, however, that this specification requires that the server reply to requests in the order in which it receives them. This is overly strict, and forbids concurrent implementations. To allow the server to reply to requests in any order, we replace predicate send_stream by send_all, defined as follows:

$$\mathsf{send\_all}(P, m \cdot \mu) = \exists P_1, P_2. \, (P \Rrightarrow P_1 * P_2) \wedge \mathsf{send\_}(P_1, m, \mathsf{True}) \wedge \mathsf{send\_all}(P_2, \mu)$$

where $P \Rrightarrow Q$, called a *view shift* [6], essentially simply means that P implies Q.[3]

2.2 Basic Liveness

By itself, the logic we proposed in earlier work for verification of safety properties of the I/O behavior of programs guarantees that the program does not perform any I/O that is not permitted by the specification, and that *if* the program terminates, it will have performed the I/O prescribed by the specification, but it does not guarantee that the program will indeed perform the prescribed I/O. It might instead go into a silent infinite loop, and not perform any I/O from some point on. Or it might respond to some requests, but allow others to starve.

Of course, we could combine the I/O logic with any logic for verifying termination, such as the one we proposed in earlier work [5]. Interpreted in such a combined logic, the specifications shown above for the "Hello, world!" example and for the single echo loop iteration express full total correctness. However, this approach is not appropriate for the complete echo server: it is not supposed to terminate. (Indeed, the specification for the echo server shown above, interpreted in a total logic, is unimplementable.)

---

[3] More precisely, $P \Rrightarrow Q$ means that a state satisfying P can be transformed into a state satisfying Q by optionally performing an update of the *ghost state*. However, the reader can ignore the concept of ghost state for now.

In earlier work [5], we proposed an approach for verifying *basic liveness* of non-terminating programs. Basic liveness means that the program always eventually performs I/O, i.e. that it never completely stops responding. Our approach was to reduce the basic liveness verification problem to a termination verification problem by imagining that the N'th I/O operation performed by the program, for some fixed but unknown N, causes abrupt termination of the program. For example, in this approach, we can prove basic liveness of **loop** (beep()) by assuming the following specification for beep():

$$\{\mathsf{IO}(n)\}\ \mathsf{beep}()\ \{0 < n \wedge \mathsf{IO}(n-1)\}$$

where $\mathsf{IO}(n)$ means the $(n+1)$'th next I/O operation will terminate the program (so, in particular, $\mathsf{IO}(0)$ means that the very next I/O operation will terminate the program), and then proving

$$\{\mathsf{IO}(n)\}\ \mathbf{loop}\ (\mathsf{beep}())\ \{\mathsf{False}\}$$

in a total logic. In words, this specification states that, assuming that the $(n+1)$'th I/O operation performed by the program terminates the program, the program terminates, and furthermore, the program does not terminate normally (because the postcondition is False, so **skip** and beep(); beep() do not satisfy this specification[4]). Here, the number of I/O operations left before the program is terminated can be used as a loop variant.

2.3 Simple Responsiveness

Notice that for the echo server, basic liveness is insufficient as a specification: an implementation could satisfy it simply by receiving requests, but not responding to any of them.

In this paper, we improve upon our earlier work by proposing an approach for specifying and verifying not just basic liveness, but richer, application-specific liveness properties of a program's I/O behavior as well, such as the property that our echo server eventually responds to each request. We again reduce the liveness property verification problem to a termination verification problem by imagining that a particular well-chosen I/O operation causes abrupt termination of the program. For example, to prove that the echo server eventually responds to each request, it is sufficient to prove that it terminates, under the assumption that the response to the k'th request, for some fixed but unknown k, terminates the program. Since the choice of which I/O operation terminates the program is application-dependent, we do not encode it directly into the I/O primitives' specification, as we did for basic liveness verification. Instead, we integrate it with the program's I/O safety specification, by stating in the program's precondition that the postcondition of the I/O operation that terminates the program is False.

---

[4] Actually, beep(); beep() does satisfy the specification for $n < 2$, but the point is that it does not satisfy the specification $\forall n.\ \{\mathsf{IO}(n)\}\ -\ \{\mathsf{False}\}$.

For example, if we apply this approach to the echo server, we obtain the following specification:

$$\{P_r * P_s \wedge \text{recv\_stream}(P_r, \mu) \wedge \text{send\_all}'(P_s, k, \mu) \wedge 0 \le k\}$$
$$\textbf{loop } (\textbf{let } msg = \text{recv}() \textbf{ in } \text{send}(msg))$$
$$\{\text{False}\}$$

where $\text{send\_all}'(P, k, \mu)$ is defined in exactly the same way that $\text{send\_all}(P, \mu)$ was defined above (so it means that resource P gives permission to send all of the messages in μ, in any order), except that the postcondition of sending the message at index k in μ is False (so sending the message at index k in μ terminates the program) (if $0 \le k$)[5]:

$$\text{send\_all}'(P, k, m \cdot \mu) =$$
$$\exists P_1, P_2. (P \Rightarrow P_1 * P_2) \wedge \text{send\_}(P_1, m, k \ne 0) \wedge \text{send\_all}'(P_2, k - 1, \mu))$$

where $k \in \mathbb{Z}$. Again, k can be used as a loop variant to prove termination of the loop.

This approach also allows us to verify other echo server implementations, such as one that performs buffering and reordering of requests, against the same specification:

$$\{P_r * P_s \wedge \text{recv\_stream}(P_r, \mu) \wedge \text{send\_all}'(P_s, k, \mu)\}$$
$$\textbf{loop } ($$
$$\quad \textbf{let } msg1 = \text{recv}() \textbf{ in}$$
$$\quad \textbf{let } msg2 = \text{recv}() \textbf{ in}$$
$$\quad \textbf{let } msg3 = \text{recv}() \textbf{ in}$$
$$\quad \text{send}(msg3);$$
$$\quad \text{send}(msg1);$$
$$\quad \text{send}(msg2)$$
$$)$$
$$\{\text{False}\}$$

Other simple responsiveness properties (i.e. properties of the form $\Box\Diamond p$) can be encoded similarly.

2.4   General Responsiveness

Suppose the echo server should eventually respond to each request, and also eventually log each request. We can reduce this property to termination by imagining that *either* the response to the k'th request, for some k, *or* logging the j'th request, for some j, terminates the program:

$$\left\{ \begin{array}{l} P_r * P_s * P_l \wedge \text{recv\_stream}(P_r, \mu) \wedge \\ \text{send\_all}'(P_s, k, \mu) \wedge \text{log\_all}'(P_l, j, \mu) \wedge (0 \le k \vee 0 \le j) \end{array} \right\}$$
$$\textbf{loop } (\textbf{let } msg = \text{recv}() \textbf{ in } \text{send}(msg); \text{log}(msg))$$
$$\{\text{False}\}$$

---

[5] Notice that if $k < 0$, $\text{send\_all}'(P, k, \mu)$ is equivalent to $\text{send\_all}(P, \mu)$.

Since the program only knows that *either* $0 \leq k$ *or* $0 \leq j$, it must *both* log all requests *and* respond to all of them to be sure of termination.

Other general responsiveness properties (i.e. properties of the form $\bigwedge_i \Box\Diamond p_i$) can be encoded similarly.

2.5 Reactivity

Suppose receiving can suffer transient failures. To prove that the echo server always eventually sends, we need to assume that receiving always eventually succeeds. This can be expressed as follows:

$$\{P_r * P_s \wedge \text{recv\_stream}'(P_r, \nu, \mu) \wedge \text{send\_all}'(P_s, k, \mu)\}$$
$$\textbf{loop } (\textbf{let msg} = \text{recv}() \textbf{ in if msg} \neq \bot \textbf{ then send(msg)})$$
$$\{\text{False}\}$$

where $\text{recv\_stream}'(P, \nu, \mu)$ means that receiving message μ_i will fail ν_i times before succeeding, for all $i \in \mathbb{N}$:

$$\text{recv\_stream}'(P, 0 \cdot \nu, m \cdot \mu) = \exists Q.\ \text{recv\_}(P, m, Q) \wedge \text{recv\_stream}'(Q, \nu, \mu)$$
$$\text{recv\_stream}'(P, (n+1) \cdot \nu, \mu) = \exists Q.\ \text{recv\_}(P, \bot, Q) \wedge \text{recv\_stream}'(Q, n \cdot \nu, \mu)$$

and $\nu \in \mathbb{N}^\omega$ ranges over infinite sequences of natural numbers.

Other reactivity properties (i.e. properties of the form $\Box\Diamond p \Rightarrow \Box\Diamond q$) can be encoded similarly.

2.6 General Reactivity

Suppose the echo server should always eventually emit a heartbeat signal, even if receiving fails persistently:

$$\left\{ \begin{array}{l} P_r * P_s * P_h \wedge \text{recv\_stream}'(P_r, \tilde{\nu}, \mu) \wedge \\ \text{send\_all}'(P_s, k, \mu) \wedge \text{heartbeats}'(P_h, j) \wedge (\tilde{\nu} \in \mathbb{N}^\omega \wedge 0 \leq k \vee 0 \leq j) \end{array} \right\}$$
$$\textbf{loop } (\textbf{let msg} = \text{recv}() \textbf{ in heartbeat}(); \textbf{if msg} \neq \bot \textbf{ then send(msg)})$$
$$\{\text{False}\}$$

where $\tilde{\nu} \in (\mathbb{N} \cup \{\infty\})^\omega$ and $\text{heartbeats}'$ is defined as follows:

$$\text{heartbeats}'(P, j) =$$
$$\exists P_1, P_2.\ (P \Rrightarrow P_1 * P_2) \wedge \text{heartbeat\_}(P_1, j \neq 0) \wedge \text{heartbeats}'(P_2, j-1)$$

Other general reactivity properties (i.e. properties of the form $\bigwedge_i(\Box\Diamond p_i \Rightarrow \Box\Diamond q_i)$) can be encoded similarly.

2.7 Persistence

Suppose the echo server is allowed to drop a finite number of requests:

$$\{\, P_r * P_s \wedge \mathsf{recv\_stream}(P_r, \mu) \wedge \mathsf{send\_all}''(P_s, \mu)\,\}$$

$\mathsf{commit}(\mathsf{false}); \mathsf{commit}(\mathsf{false}); \mathsf{commit}(\mathsf{false});$

$\mathsf{recv}(); \mathbf{let}\ \mathsf{msg} = \mathsf{recv}()\ \mathbf{in}\ \mathsf{send}(\mathsf{msg}); \mathsf{recv}();$

$\mathsf{commit}(\mathsf{true});$

$\mathbf{loop}\ (\mathbf{let}\ \mathsf{msg} = \mathsf{recv}()\ \mathbf{in}\ \mathsf{send}(\mathsf{msg}))$

$\{\mathsf{False}\}$

which uses the following auxiliary definition:

$\mathsf{send\_all}''(P, m \cdot \mu) =$
$\quad (\exists Q_1, Q_2.\ \mathsf{commit\_}(P, \mathsf{false}, Q_1 * Q_2) \wedge \mathsf{send\_}(Q_1, m, \mathsf{True}) \wedge \mathsf{send\_all}''(Q_2, \mu)) \wedge$
$\quad (\exists Q, k \geq 0.\ \mathsf{commit\_}(P, \mathsf{true}, Q) \wedge \mathsf{send\_all}'(Q, k, m \cdot \mu)$

To terminate, the program has to finish the phase where it is allowed to drop requests (represented by predicate $\mathsf{send\_all}''$) and enter the phase where it responds to each request (represented by predicate $\mathsf{send\_all}'$); it needs to signal this by performing the *ghost I/O action* $\mathsf{commit}(\mathsf{true})$.[6]

Other persistence properties (i.e. properties of the form $\Diamond\Box p$) can be encoded similarly.

3   A Programming Language with I/O

We present our approach in the context of a simplified ML-like programming language with support for I/O. Its grammar is as follows:

$$v \in \mathit{Vals}, x \in \mathit{Vars}, t \in \mathit{IOPrims}$$

$e \in \mathit{Exprs} ::= v \mid x$
$c \in \mathit{Cmds} ::= e \mid t(e) \mid \mathbf{if}\ e = e\ \mathbf{then}\ c\ \mathbf{else}\ c \mid \mathbf{let}\ x = c\ \mathbf{in}\ c \mid \mathbf{loop}\ c$

We assume a set Vals of values, Vars of program variables, and $\mathit{IOPrims}$ of I/O primitives.[7] We assume Vals contains at least the unit value ().

We define $c; c' = \mathbf{let}\ x = c\ \mathbf{in}\ c'$ where x does not appear in c'.

We define the I/O actions $\alpha \in \mathit{IOActions} ::= t(v, v)$; in $t(v, v')$, we call v the *argument* and v' the *result*. We coinductively define the set of traces $\tau \in \mathit{Traces} ::= \mathsf{Div} \mid \mathsf{Ret}(v) \mid t(v, v') \cdot \tau$. A trace ending in Div is called a *diverging trace*; it represents the behavior where the program eventually neither terminates nor performs I/O. A trace ending in $\mathsf{Ret}(v)$ is a finite trace; it represents the behavior where the program eventually terminates with result value v.

---

[6] The commit *ghost commands* are inserted into the program text for verification purposes only. Since they do not have any observable effect, any properties proven about the ghost-instrumented program hold also for the original program (also known as the *erased* program).

[7] In the examples, we assume $\mathsf{send}, \mathsf{recv}, \mathsf{beep}, \mathsf{log}, \mathsf{heartbeat}, \mathsf{commit} \in \mathit{IOPrims}$.

We define concatenation of traces coinductively as follows:

$$\mathsf{Ret}(v);_v \tau = \tau \qquad \mathsf{Div};_v \tau = \mathsf{Div} \qquad \frac{\tau;_v \tau' = \tau''}{t(v',v'') \cdot \tau;_v \tau' = t(v',v'') \cdot \tau''}$$

We define the language's semantics by means of a big-step relation $c \Downarrow \tau$, which relates a command c to a trace τ. We define the relation coinductively by means of the following rules:

$$v \Downarrow \mathsf{Ret}(v) \qquad \frac{c \Downarrow \tau}{\textbf{if } v = v \textbf{ then } c \textbf{ else } c' \Downarrow \tau} \qquad \frac{v \neq v' \quad c' \Downarrow \tau}{\textbf{if } v = v' \textbf{ then } c \textbf{ else } c' \Downarrow \tau}$$

$$\frac{c \Downarrow \tau \quad c'[v/x] \Downarrow \tau' \quad \tau;_v \tau' = \tau''}{\textbf{let } x = c \textbf{ in } c' \Downarrow \tau''} \qquad \frac{c; \textbf{loop } c \Downarrow \tau}{\textbf{loop } c \Downarrow \tau} \qquad t(v) \Downarrow t(v,v') \cdot \mathsf{Ret}(v')$$

Notice that we have **loop** () $\Downarrow$ Div. We also have **loop** () $\Downarrow \tau$ for any other trace τ as well; this imprecision is harmless, since we will be proving liveness.

3.1 Liveness Properties

If we define $c_{\mathsf{echo}} = \textbf{loop } (\textbf{let } \mathsf{msg} = \mathsf{recv}(())$ **in** $\mathsf{send}(\mathsf{msg}))$, we can state the responsiveness property of the echo server as follows:

$$\forall \tau, \mu. \; c_{\mathsf{echo}} \Downarrow \tau \wedge \tau|_{\mathsf{recv}} \preceq \mu \Rightarrow \forall m \in \mu. \; \mathsf{send}(m,()) \in \tau$$

where we define $\tau|_{\mathsf{recv}} \preceq \mu$ coinductively as follows:

$$\mathsf{Div}|_{\mathsf{recv}} \preceq \mu \qquad \mathsf{Ret}(v)|_{\mathsf{recv}} \preceq \mu \qquad \frac{\tau|_{\mathsf{recv}} \preceq \mu}{(\mathsf{recv}(\_, m) \cdot \tau)|_{\mathsf{recv}} \preceq m \cdot \mu}$$

$$\frac{\tau|_{\mathsf{recv}} \preceq \mu}{(\mathsf{send}(\_, ()) \cdot \tau)|_{\mathsf{recv}} \preceq \mu}$$

To make the link with temporal logic: this is more or less equivalent to

$$\forall \tau. \; c_{\mathsf{echo}} \Downarrow \tau \Rightarrow \tau \vDash \Box\Diamond(\exists m. \; \mathsf{recv}(\_, m)) \wedge \Box(\forall m. \; \mathsf{recv}(\_, m) \Rightarrow \Diamond\mathsf{send}(m, \_))$$

(It is equivalent if we ignore the possibility of messages being sent before they are received.)

In the next section, we define a separation logic for modularly verifying properties such as this one, and argue formally that it is indeed adequate for this purpose.

4   A Program Logic for I/O Liveness

4.1   Exit Actions and Exit Traces

We use the notation $\dot{v} \in \mathit{Vals} \cup \{\top\}$ to denote either a program value or the special *exit value* $\top$. An *exit action* $\dot{\alpha} = t(v, \dot{v})$ is like an action except that its result may be the exit value. An *exit trace* $\dot{\tau}$ is a finite sequence of exit actions. We say an exit action is *exiting* if its result is the exit value.

The I/O safety logic from our earlier work [8] proves that a program's partial traces are prefixes of a given set of traces. A total logic (such as [5]) proves that a program's traces end with Ret(_), or, equivalently, that they start with a partial trace that ends with Ret(_). By combining and slightly generalizing these, we can obtain a logic whose correctness judgments imply that each of a program's traces starts with one of the partial traces from a given set of *exit traces*, i.e. partial traces that, as soon as an exiting I/O action is performed, cause the program to be considered "terminated". Examples of such *exit sets* are: the set of partial traces T_1 where the program has responded to the first request, the set of partial traces T_2 where the program has responded to the second request, etc. By proving a universally quantified correctness judgment, we can obtain that a program's traces start with a partial trace from T_1 *and* with a partial trace from T_2, etc., that is, that the program responds to the first request *and* to the second request, etc., allowing us to conclude that the program satisfies the responsiveness property.

In the remainder of this section, we elaborate this approach.

4.2   Petri Nets

The I/O safety logic is based on the idea that the program must own particular resources in order to be allowed to perform a given I/O action. When using the logic, there is no need to specify the particular nature of those resources. However, for the sake of proving adequacy of the logic, we do need to introduce a particular ontology of resources. For this purpose, we here use a particular type of *Petri nets*. Indeed, these resources serve very much like *tokens* in a Petri net. If, in a Petri net, there is a token in each *pre-place* of a *transition*, the transition can *fire*, which removes one token from each pre-place and adds one to each *post-place*. This, in turn, can enable a new transition, and so on. If we label the transitions by I/O actions, we obtain that a *marking* $V \in \mathcal{P} \to \mathbb{N}$ of a Petri net (which maps each place to the number of tokens present at that place) defines a set of traces.

Specifically, we will be labeling transitions by exit actions, so that a marking defines a set of exit traces.

Let $\mathcal{P}$ be a set of places. We use p and q to range over places. We consider Petri nets where the set of transitions N is a subset of the set $\mathcal{N}$ defined as

$$\chi \in \mathcal{N} ::= t(V_{\mathsf{pre}}, v, \dot{v}, V_{\mathsf{post}}) \mid \mathbf{noop}(V_{\mathsf{pre}}, V_{\mathsf{post}})$$

where V_{pre} and V_{post} are multisets of places, called the *pre-places* and *post-places* of the transition, respectively.

A Petri net defines a labeled step relation $\rightarrow$ and a corresponding labeled reachability relation $\twoheadrightarrow$ on markings:

$$\frac{t(V_{\mathsf{pre}}, v, \dot{v}, V_{\mathsf{post}}) \in N}{V \uplus V_{\mathsf{pre}} \xrightarrow{t(v,\dot{v})} V \uplus V_{\mathsf{post}}} \qquad \frac{\mathbf{noop}(V_{\mathsf{pre}}, V_{\mathsf{post}}) \in N}{V \uplus V_{\mathsf{pre}} \xrightarrow{\epsilon} V \uplus V_{\mathsf{post}}} \qquad V \xrightarrow{\epsilon} V$$

$$\frac{V \xrightarrow{\dot{\tau}} V' \qquad V' \xrightarrow{\dot{\tau}'} V''}{V \xrightarrow{\dot{\tau}\cdot\dot{\tau}'} V''}$$

where $V \uplus V' = \lambda p.\ V(p) + V'(p)$. We define $\mathsf{Traces}_N(V) = \{\dot{\tau} \mid \exists V'.\ V \xrightarrow{\dot{\tau}} V'\}$.

4.3   Assertions, Correctness Judgments, View Shifts

We define the set of *assertions* semantically as the set of sets of markings. That is, an assertion describes a marking. An assertion $\mathbf{tokens}(V)$ describes a marking that includes V: $\mathbf{tokens}(V) = \{V' \mid \forall p.\ V'(p) \geq V(p)\}$. The separating conjunction $P * P'$ describes a marking that can be split into one that satisfies P and one that satisfies P': $P * P' = \{V \uplus V' \mid V \in P \wedge V' \in P'\}$.

We define the meaning of a correctness judgment $\{P\}\ c\ \{Q\}$, where precondition P is an assertion, c is a command, and postcondition Q maps a value to an assertion, as follows:

$$\{P\}\ c\ \{Q\} \Leftrightarrow \forall V, \tau.\ V \in P \wedge c \Downarrow \tau \Rightarrow \mathsf{safe}(\tau, \mathsf{Traces}_N(V), Q)$$

where $\mathsf{safe}(\tau, T, Q)$ is defined inductively by the following rules:

$$\frac{\exists V \in Q(v).\ \mathsf{Traces}_N(V) \subseteq T}{\mathsf{safe}(\mathsf{Ret}(v), T, Q)} \qquad \frac{t(v, \top) \in T}{\mathsf{safe}(t(v, v') \cdot \tau, T, Q)}$$

$$\frac{t(v, v'') \in T \qquad v' \neq v''}{\mathsf{safe}(t(v, v') \cdot \tau, T, Q)} \qquad \frac{t(v, v') \in T \qquad \mathsf{safe}(\tau, \{\dot{\tau}' \mid t(v, v') \cdot \dot{\tau}' \in T\}, Q)}{\mathsf{safe}(t(v, v') \cdot \tau, T, Q)}$$

The set T can be seen as a *specification* that expresses safety and liveness properties of the program, as well as assumptions about the environment. Notice that infinite or diverging traces are safe only if they contain an input that conflicts with the specification (i.e. the environment assumptions are violated) or perform an action that corresponds to an exiting action of the specification.

Informally, $\{P\}\ c\ \{Q\}$ states that for every marking V that satisfies P, assuming that the environment provides only inputs allowed by the traces of V, command c performs only outputs allowed by the traces of V and terminates, either by performing an exiting action, or by returning with a result v and a marking V' such that $V' \in Q(v)$.

We say that P view-shifts to Q, written as $P \Rrightarrow Q$, if $\forall V \in P. \ \exists V' \in Q. \ \mathsf{Traces}_N(V') \subseteq \mathsf{Traces}_N(V)$. That is, we can replace the current marking by another one that is equivalent or more restrictive in terms of the program outputs it allows.[8]

4.4 Proof Rules

Given these definitions, the following proof rules are admissible:

$$\{Q(v)\} \ v \ \{Q\} \qquad \frac{\{P \wedge v = v'\} \ c \ \{Q\} \qquad \{P \wedge v \neq v'\} \ c' \ \{Q\}}{\{P\} \ \text{if } v = v' \ \text{then } c \ \text{else } c' \ \{Q\}}$$

$$\frac{\{P\} \ c \ \{Q\} \qquad \forall v. \ \{Q(v)\} \ c'[v/x] \ \{R\}}{\{P\} \ \text{let } x = c \ \text{in } c' \ \{R\}} \qquad \frac{\forall n. \ \{P_n\} \ c \ \{\exists n' < n. \ P_{n'}\}}{\{P_m\} \ \text{loop } c \ \{\mathsf{False}\}}$$

$$\{\mathbf{tokens}(V_{\mathsf{pre}}) \wedge t(V_{\mathsf{pre}}, v, \dot{v}, V_{\mathsf{post}}) \in N\} \ t(v) \ \{\mathbf{tokens}(V_{\mathsf{post}}) \wedge \dot{v} \neq \top \wedge \mathsf{res} = \dot{v}\}$$

$$\frac{P \Rrightarrow P' \qquad \{P'\} \ c \ \{Q\} \qquad Q \Rrightarrow Q'}{\{P\} \ c \ \{Q'\}} \qquad \frac{\{P\} \ c \ \{Q\}}{\{P * R\} \ c \ \{Q * R\}}$$

$$\frac{\forall i \in I. \ \{P_i\} \ c \ \{Q\}}{\{\exists i \in I. \ P_i\} \ c \ \{Q\}} \qquad \frac{P \Rightarrow Q}{P \Rrightarrow Q} \qquad \frac{P \Rrightarrow Q}{P * R \Rrightarrow Q * R}$$

$$\frac{\mathbf{noop}(V_{\mathsf{pre}}, V_{\mathsf{post}}) \in N}{\mathbf{tokens}(V_{\mathsf{pre}}) \Rrightarrow \mathbf{tokens}(V_{\mathsf{post}})} \qquad \frac{P \Rrightarrow P' \qquad P' \Rrightarrow P''}{P \Rrightarrow P''}$$

We sometimes write postconditions as assertions with a free variable res.

4.5 Abstract Nested Hoare Triples Notation

We define the abstract nested Hoare triple notation $t_-(P, v, v', Q)$ as follows:

$$t_-(P, v, v', Q) =$$
$$P \Rrightarrow \exists V_{\mathsf{pre}}, V_{\mathsf{post}}. \ \mathbf{tokens}(V_{\mathsf{pre}}) \wedge$$
$$(t(V_{\mathsf{pre}}, v, v', V_{\mathsf{post}}) \in N \wedge \mathbf{tokens}(V_{\mathsf{post}}) \Rrightarrow Q \vee t(V_{\mathsf{pre}}, v, \top, V_{\mathsf{post}}) \in N)$$

It follows that we have $\{P \wedge t_-(P, v, v', Q)\} \ t(v) \ \{Q \wedge \mathsf{res} = v'\}$.

4.6 Example: Simple Responsiveness

We show now how we can use our logic to verify the responsiveness property of the echo server, repeated here:

$$\forall \tau, \mu. \ c_{\mathsf{echo}} \Downarrow \tau \wedge \tau|_{\mathsf{recv}} \preceq \mu \Rightarrow \forall m \in \mu. \ \mathsf{send}(m, ()) \in \tau$$

---

[8] Note: reducing the set of traces does not strengthen the assumptions on the environment, because if two traces of a specification make conflicting assumptions about environment behavior, the resulting assumption is the *conjunction* of these, i.e. False.

First of all, we fix μ. Again, we assume no message appears more than once in μ.

It is sufficient to prove

$$\forall k \geq 0, \tau. \; c_{\mathsf{echo}} \Downarrow \tau \wedge \tau|_{\mathsf{recv}} \preceq \mu \Rightarrow \mathsf{send}(\mu_k, ()) \in \tau$$

where μ_k denotes the message at index k in μ.

We fix k. We define exit set T as follows:

$$T = \{\dot{\tau} \mid \dot{\tau}|_{\mathsf{recv}} \preceq \mu \wedge (\forall \mathsf{send}(v, \dot{v}) \in \dot{\tau}. \; v = \mu_k \vee \dot{v} = ())\}$$

where we define $\dot{\tau}|_{\mathsf{recv}} \preceq \mu$ as follows:

$$\epsilon|_{\mathsf{recv}} \preceq \mu \qquad \frac{\dot{\tau}|_{\mathsf{recv}} \preceq \mu}{(\mathsf{recv}(\_, m) \cdot \dot{\tau})|_{\mathsf{recv}} \preceq m \cdot \mu} \qquad \frac{\dot{v} \in \{(), \top\} \qquad \dot{\tau}|_{\mathsf{recv}} \preceq \mu}{(\mathsf{send}(\_, \dot{v}) \cdot \tau)|_{\mathsf{recv}} \preceq \mu}$$

It is sufficient to prove

$$\forall \tau. \; c_{\mathsf{echo}} \Downarrow \tau \Rightarrow \mathsf{safe}(\tau, T, \mathsf{False})$$

where μ_k denotes the message at index k in μ.

Indeed, we can prove, by induction on the derivation of $\mathsf{safe}(\tau, T, \mathsf{False})$, that for any τ, if $\mathsf{safe}(\tau, T, \mathsf{False})$ and $\tau|_{\mathsf{recv}} \preceq \mu$, then $\mathsf{send}(\mu_k, ()) \in \tau$.

We construct a Petri net $(\mathcal{P}, N)$ and a marking V such that $\mathsf{Traces}_N(V) \subseteq T$. We define

$$\mathcal{P} = \{\mathsf{recv}_i \mid 0 \leq i\} \cup \{\mathsf{send}_i \mid 0 \leq i\}$$

and

$$\begin{aligned} N = &\{\mathsf{recv}(\{\!\{\mathsf{recv}_i\}\!\}, (), \mu_i, \{\!\{\mathsf{recv}_{i+1}\}\!\}) \mid i \geq 0\} \cup \\ &\{\mathsf{send}(\{\!\{\mathsf{send}_i\}\!\}, \mu_i, (), \mathbf{0}) \mid i \geq 0 \wedge i \neq k\} \cup \{\mathsf{send}(\{\!\{\mathsf{send}_k\}\!\}, \mu_k, \top, \mathbf{0})\} \end{aligned}$$

and

$$V = \lambda p. \begin{cases} 1 \text{ if } p = \mathsf{recv}_0 \\ 1 \text{ if } \exists i. \; p = \mathsf{send}_i \\ 0 \text{ otherwise} \end{cases}$$

where $\{\!\{p\}\!\}$ denotes the singleton multiset with a single token at p, and $\mathbf{0}$ denotes the empty multiset.

It is easy to check that indeed $\mathsf{Traces}_N(V) \subseteq T$, and that $V \in P$ where $P = \exists P_r, P_s. \; P_r * P_s \wedge \mathsf{recv\_stream}(P_r, \mu) \wedge \mathsf{send\_all}'(P_s, k, \mu)$.

Then, by the meaning of correctness judgments, we have that $\{P\} \; c_{\mathsf{echo}} \; \{\mathsf{False}\}$ implies the goal.

4.7   General Responsiveness

The adequacy of the verification approach for general responsiveness properties presented in Sect. 2 follows directly from the adequacy for simple responsiveness properties, combined with the observation that $\{P_1 \vee P_2\} \; c \; \{Q\}$ implies both $\{P_1\} \; c \; \{Q\}$ and $\{P_2\} \; c \; \{Q\}$. Therefore, given a successful verification of the program, each constituent simple responsiveness property can then be established separately as above.

4.8   Example: Persistence

We wish to prove that c'_{echo}, defined as

$$
\begin{aligned}
c'_{echo} = \\
&\text{recv}(); \text{let msg} = \text{recv}() \text{ in send(msg); recv}(); \\
&\textbf{loop } (\text{let msg} = \text{recv}() \text{ in send(msg)})
\end{aligned}
$$

drops only finitely many messages, i.e. that it eventually always responds. Formally:

$$
\forall \mu, \tau.\ c'_{echo} \Downarrow \tau \wedge \tau|_{recv} \preceq \mu \Rightarrow \exists k_0 \geq 0.\ \forall k \geq k_0.\ \text{send}(\mu_k, ()) \in \tau
$$

We consider a *ghost-instrumented* version $\tilde{c}'_{echo}$ of c'_{echo}, defined as follows:

$$
\begin{aligned}
\tilde{c}'_{echo} = \\
&\text{commit(false); commit(false); commit(false);} \\
&\text{recv}(); \text{let msg} = \text{recv}() \text{ in send(msg); recv}(); \\
&\text{commit(true);} \\
&\textbf{loop } (\text{let msg} = \text{recv}() \text{ in send(msg)})
\end{aligned}
$$

Obviously, it is sufficient to prove

$$
\forall \mu, \tau.\ \tilde{c}'_{echo} \Downarrow \tau \wedge \text{erasure}(\tau)|_{recv} \preceq \mu \Rightarrow \exists k_0 \geq 0.\ \forall k \geq k_0.\ \text{send}(\mu_k, ()) \in \tau
$$

where $\text{erasure}(\tau)$ removes the commit actions (replacing an infinite sequence of commit actions with Div). We define $\#\tau$ as the index of the first commit(true, _) action in τ, or 0 if it does not contain such an action. It is sufficient to prove

$$
\forall \mu, \tau.\ \tilde{c}'_{echo} \Downarrow \tau \wedge \text{erasure}(\tau)|_{recv} \preceq \mu \Rightarrow \forall k \geq 0.\ \text{send}(\mu_{\#\tau+k}, ()) \in \tau
$$

We fix μ and k and define exit set T as follows:

$$
T = \left\{ \dot{\tau} \left| \begin{array}{l} \text{erasure}(\dot{\tau})|_{recv} \preceq \mu \wedge \\ (\forall \text{send}(v, \dot{v}) \in \dot{\tau}.\ \text{commit(true, _)} \in \dot{\tau} \wedge v = \mu_{\#\dot{\tau}+k} \vee \dot{v} = ()) \end{array} \right. \right\}
$$

It is sufficient to prove

$$
\forall \tau.\ \tilde{c}'_{echo} \Downarrow \tau \Rightarrow \text{safe}(\tau, T, \text{False})
$$

Indeed, one can again show, by induction on the derivation of $\text{safe}(\tau, T, \text{False})$ that for all τ, if $\text{safe}(\tau, T, \text{False})$ and $\text{erasure}(\tau)|_{recv} \preceq \mu$, then $\text{send}(\mu_{\#\tau+k}, ()) \in \tau$.

The remainder of this example proceeds as above: we construct a Petri net and a marking that satisfies the precondition we used for verifying the persistence example in Sect. 2 and whose traces are included in T. Successful verification then implies the goal.

5   Related Work

We are not aware of existing work on Hoare logics for verifying liveness properties of the I/O behavior of programs. To the best of our knowledge, most approaches for verifying liveness properties of the I/O behavior of systems have so far been based on a representation of the system as some kind of a state machine, or a set of interacting processes or state machines, rather than a program. In these approaches, the liveness properties of interest are very often specified using temporal logic [2].

Even when it comes to Hoare logics for liveness properties of other aspects of program execution, there is very little existing work. We are aware of only two lines of work. Boström and Müller [1] verify that blocked threads in a multi-threaded program are always eventually unblocked. In ongoing work, D'Osualdo *et al.* [3] verify termination under a fair scheduler of multithreaded programs that involve synchronization based on busy-waiting.

For a discussion of related work on verifying safety of I/O behavior and on verifying program termination, we refer to our earlier work [5,9].

6   Conclusion

We presented a Hoare logic-based approach for the specification and verification of liveness properties of the I/O behavior of program modules. Our approach is based on the idea of reducing the problem to a termination verification problem and then applying existing approaches for I/O safety verification and termination verification. Our approach can be applied straightforwardly in existing verification tools that support separation logic, higher-order predicates, and termination verification, such as our VeriFast tool [12].

In this paper, we considered a very simple programming language with no dynamically allocated memory, higher-order functions or dynamic method binding, or concurrency. However, we believe the ideas of this paper can be integrated straightforwardly into the separation logic for total correctness of multithreaded object-oriented programs from our earlier work [5] to verify liveness properties of the I/O behavior of a large class of realistic programs.

A limitation of this earlier work, however, is that it does not support *busy waiting*, a common practice in programs for multiprocessor machines. In recent work [10], we propose a logic for verifying termination under fair scheduling of programs where threads busy-wait for other threads to abruptly terminate the program. By combining that logic with the ideas from this paper, one can obtain a logic for verifying responsiveness of a multithreaded server where one thread receives requests and another responds to them: the first thread can be seen as busy-waiting for the second thread to terminate the program by responding to the k'th request.

We have not addressed the question of completeness: does our approach support all possible liveness properties? Chang *et al.* [2] claim that any temporal logic formula is equivalent to a general reactivity formula. However, their setting is not quite the same as ours, as evidenced by the fact that we need to use ghost I/O operations to support persistence properties, whereas in their framework persistence properties are subsumed by reactivity properties. A thorough investigation of this question is future work.

References

1. Boström, P., Müller, P.: Modular verification of finite blocking in non-terminating programs. In: Boyland, J.T. (ed.) 29th European Conference on Object-Oriented Programming, ECOOP 2015, 5–10 July 2015, Prague, Czech Republic. LIPIcs, vol. 37, pp. 639–663. Schloss Dagstuhl - Leibniz-Zentrum für Informatik (2015)
2. Chang, E., Manna, Z., Pnueli, A.: The safety-progress classification. In: Bauer, F.L., Brauer, W., Schwichtenberg, H. (eds.) Logic and Algebra of Specification. NATO ASI Series (Series F: Computer & Systems Sciences), vol. 94, pp. 143–202. Springer, Berlin, Heidelberg (1993). https://doi.org/10.1007/978-3-642-58041-3_5
3. D'Osualdo, E., Farzan, A., Gardner, P., Sutherland, J.: TaDA live: compositional reasoning for termination of fine-grained concurrent programs. CoRR abs/1901.05750 (2019)
4. Hoare, C.A.R.: An axiomatic basis for computer programming. Commun. ACM 12(10), 576–580 (1969)
5. Jacobs, B., Bosnacki, D., Kuiper, R.: Modular termination verification of single-threaded and multithreaded programs. ACM Trans. Program. Lang. Syst. 40(3), 12:1–12:59 (2018)
6. Jung, R., Krebbers, R., Jourdan, J., Bizjak, A., Birkedal, L., Dreyer, D.: Iris from the ground up: a modular foundation for higher-order concurrent separation logic. J. Funct. Program. 28, e20 (2018)
7. Penninckx, W., Jacobs, B., Piessens, F.: Sound, modular and compositional verification of the input/output behavior of programs. In: Vitek, J. (ed.) ESOP 2015. LNCS, vol. 9032, pp. 158–182. Springer, Heidelberg (2015). https://doi.org/10.1007/978-3-662-46669-8_7
8. Penninckx, W., Timany, A., Jacobs, B.: Abstract I/O specification. CoRR abs/1901.10541 (2019)
9. Penninckx, W., Timany, A., Jacobs, B.: Specifying I/O using abstract nested Hoare triples in separation logic. In: Proceedings of the 21st Workshop on Formal Techniques for Java-like Programs. FTfJP 2019, Association for Computing Machinery, New York (2019)
10. Reinhard, T., Timany, A., Jacobs, B.: A separation logic to verify termination of busy-waiting for abrupt program exit. In: FTfJP (2020, to appear)
11. Reynolds, J.C.: Separation logic: a logic for shared mutable data structures. In: Proceedings of the 17th IEEE Symposium on Logic in Computer Science (LICS 2002), 22–25 July 2002, Copenhagen, Denmark, pp. 55–74. IEEE Computer Society (2002)
12. Vogels, F., Jacobs, B., Piessens, F.: Featherweight VeriFast. Log. Methods Comput. Sci. 11(3), 1–57 (2015)

Formal Verification of an Industrial Distributed Algorithm: An Experience Report

Nikolai Kosmatov$^{(\boxtimes)}$ ⓘ, Delphine Longuet$^{(\boxtimes)}$ ⓘ, and Romain Soulat$^{(\boxtimes)}$ ⓘ

Thales Research and Technology, Palaiseau, France
nikolaikosmatov@gmail.com,
{delphine.longuet,romain.soulat}@thalesgroup.com

Abstract. Verification of distributed software is a challenging task. This paper reports on modeling and verification of a consensus algorithm developed by Thales. The algorithm has an arbitrary number of processes (nodes), which can possibly fail and restart at any time. Communications between nodes are periodic, but completely asynchronous. The goal of this algorithm is that, after a given amount of time since the last status change, the network of nodes agrees on a list of working nodes. Our verification approach is based on modeling both the source code of the algorithm and the possible interleavings of executions. We present how we were able to scale up to 100 processes using the rely-guarantee based technique. Some of the initially expected properties did not hold, and generated counter-examples helped to fix and prove them. We also successfully verified other consensus algorithms at Thales with the same approach. We describe our experiments on applying several model-checking tools and a symbolic execution tool, and present some lessons learned.

Keywords: Distributed algorithm verification · Consensus algorithms · Symbolic model checking · Rely-guarantee · Symbolic execution

1 Introduction

Distributed software is largely used nowadays. The advance of Internet of Things (IoT) devices and autonomous systems promises their ever-growing use in the next generations of industrial systems. Design and verification of distributed algorithms for distributed software remain a very active research topic since several decades. Many efficient algorithms were proposed [17,18], and important impossibility results were established [11].

Distributed algorithms include in particular *consensus protocols*, where the processes (nodes) of a network, executing the same code, have to come to the agreement on some data. One example is *leader election protocols*, where several processes have to choose a unique leader. In the synchronous context, the nodes

© Springer Nature Switzerland AG 2020
T. Margaria and B. Steffen (Eds.): ISoLA 2020, LNCS 12476, pp. 525–542, 2020.
https://doi.org/10.1007/978-3-030-61362-4_30

exchange information on the common clock signal, while in the asynchronous one, they can communicate at different moments. A well-known synchronous leader election protocol is the so-called *Bully algorithm* [12] in which the node with the highest ID is elected as a leader after several rounds. In the asynchronous context, a leader election protocol was described by Leslie Lamport [15]. It was formally proved correct using several tools, in particular, in TLA$^+$ [16], or, more recently, in the timed model checking tool UPPAAL [6]. However, the existing automated proofs were performed only for a small number of processes, typically ≤ 10.

The verification of a given protocol is tightly linked to the considered setting: synchronous or asynchronous, specific fault models, expected properties, values of periods of message exchanges, the degree of possible period variations and communication delays in a given system, etc. While many protocols were proposed in the literature, the industrial practice shows that their assumptions and properties do not always correspond to those of the target real-life system, and some specific (variants of) algorithms can be needed. Of course, as soon as the initial assumptions are modified, each new algorithm should be verified again.

Thales designed several distributed consensus algorithms where an arbitrary number of processes are run and can possibly fail and restart at any moment. Thus, each node can be on or off, but these statuses can change. Communications between nodes are periodic, but completely asynchronous. The goal of these algorithms is that, after a given amount of time since the last status modification, the network of nodes agrees on a list of working nodes. Thus, the final property of interest states that after a given number of activations, each node identifies the same set of nodes as working, that is, the consensus is reached. They also ensure some partial consistency properties after a smaller amount of time, which express step-by-step progress of the algorithm towards the desired final property.

This paper presents an experience report on formal verification of a distributed consensus algorithm developed at Thales. This experience was mainly realized by the formal methods group of Thales Research and Technology, with participation of other Thales engineers. The algorithm itself is not detailed in the paper: first, it is broadly inspired by the existing algorithms, and second, the precise algorithm cannot be revealed due to confidentiality reasons. We describe the methodology used to model and formally prove the initial algorithm as well as some similar algorithms.

Our verification approach combines several ideas from previous work, in particular, on modeling the interleavings using a simulation loop to represent the whole system (e.g. [7]), and the technique of rely-guarantee [13] that allows us to focus on the behavior of a given node rather than the whole system. We first modeled the source code of the algorithm and simulated the possible interleavings of executions, and used synchronous model checkers to verify the model. Possible variations of communication periods and communication delays in the target system are simulated using *jitters*, slightly modifying the activation times of the nodes. However, this technique does not allow us to prove the algorithm for a large number of nodes. Then we created a second, abstracted model focusing on the execution of a unique node and modeling the behavior of other nodes by assumptions, and attempting to prove that each of them is indeed guaranteed by the current node. This allowed the proof to scale up to 100 processes, and to validate the C code against those assumptions. We also verified other consensus algorithms at Thales with the same approach. Some of the initially expected properties did not hold, and generated counter-examples helped to fix and prove them. We describe our experiments on applying several model-checking tools and a symbolic execution tool, and present some lessons learned.

This paper builds on a previously published case study [5] on verification of an industrial algorithm at Thales using the SAFEPROVER tool [10]. This work extends it with a clearer presentation of the methodology, additional experiments with two other verification tools, CBMC [9] and KLEE [8], and some lessons learned. Recent case studies for similar algorithms confirmed the applicability of this work.

Outline. The paper is organized as follows. Section 2 gives an overview of the target system and algorithm. The verification methodology is presented in Sect. 3. Our experiments using different verification tools are reported in Sect. 4. Finally, Section 5 concludes the paper with some lessons learned and future work.

2   Presentation of the System and the Algorithm

2.1   Overview of the System

For confidentiality reasons, we cannot disclose the exact real-life system and algorithm, but we believe it does not prevent from understanding our approach and results. In particular, system parameters were modified in the paper but the consistency of the presented algorithm and results was of course preserved.

The system is composed of several identical computing nodes. They can perform various tasks and receive a part of the workload. The nodes are fully interconnected, which means that any node can send messages to any other node in the network, for example, to communicate computation results. On top of those messages, periodically, each node sends to all other nodes a special kind of message indicating that the sender is still alive and providing some additional data. Our distributed algorithm uses these messages in order for each node to be able to compute a correct list of all working nodes in the network. This has several uses: workload balancing, clock synchronization, leader election, etc.

More formally, the system is a fixed set of p nodes $\mathcal{N} = \{node_1, \ldots, node_p\}$, $p \in \mathbb{N}$, given with integer timing constants $period_{min}$, $period_{max}$, $jitter_{min}$, $jitter_{max}$, $msgDelay_{min}$, $msgDelay_{max}$. Each node $node_i$ is a record containing the following fields:

1. a unique integer-valued *ID*: $id \in \mathbb{N}$,
2. an integer-valued *activation period*: $per \in [period_{min}, period_{max}]$,
3. an integer-valued *first activation time*: $start \in [0, per[$ (which can be seen as an *offset*, with the usual assumption that the offset is less than the period),

Constant	Value
period$_{min}$	49
period$_{max}$	51
jitter$_{min}$	−0.5
jitter$_{max}$	0.5
msgDelay$_{min}$	0
msgDelay$_{max}$	0

(a)

Node	per	start	jitter$_i^1$	jitter$_i^2$	jitter$_i^3$
$node_1$	49	0	0.5	−0.5	0.2
$node_2$	51	30	0	0.1	0
$node_3$	49	0.1	0.1	−0.5	0.5

(b)

Fig. 1. (a) Static constants (in ms), and (b) values chosen for the nodes in Example 1.

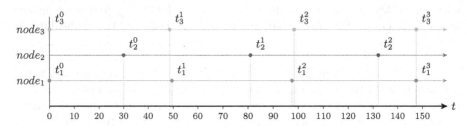

Fig. 2. Activation times (in ms) of the three nodes of Example 1.

4. a flag *failure*, *failure* ∈ {⊥, ⊤}, which corresponds to the state of the node, ⊤ means that the node has failed, ⊥ means that the node is running,
5. a *receive failure* flag, *rcvFailure* ∈ {⊥, ⊤}, indicating a failure in the capacity to receive messages (⊤ means that the node cannot receive messages, ⊥ means that the node can receive messages), and
6. a *send failure* flag, *sndFailure* ∈ {⊥, ⊤}, indicating a failure in the capacity of the node to send messages.
7. a field *state* represents the set of internal variables of the node,
8. a field *networkView* indicates the definitive belief of the node on the list of fully working nodes in the network.

In addition, we use the following constants to model uncertainties (time variations) in the system execution:

1. an integer $jitter_i^j \in [\text{jitter}_{min}, \text{jitter}_{max}]$, indicating a delay in the execution of $node_i$ for the j-th activation,
2. an integer $msgDelay_{ki}^j \in [\text{msgDelay}_{min}, \text{msgDelay}_{max}]$ giving a delay in message transmission between $node_k$ and $node_i$ for the j-th activation of $node_i$.

The j-th activation of node $node_i$ occurs at time $t_i^j = t_i^{j-1} + node_i.per + jitter_i^j$ for $j > 0$. We set besides: $t_i^0 = node_i.start$.

In all our models we use values in microseconds for periods, activation times, jitters, message delays, etc., in order to be as close as possible to a real-life execution and to be able to model all possible interleavings, while still using integer values, easier to read and often better supported by tools. (In the examples in this paper, we use milliseconds just to make the constants more readable.)

Algorithm 1: Pseudo-code of function *UpdateNode(i)*

---

1 **if** $node_i.EvenActivation$ **then**
2      $allMessages \leftarrow ReadMessages(i)$
3      $nodeState \leftarrow ComputeState(allMessages, nodeState)$
4      $message \leftarrow ComputeMessage(nodeState)$
5 **if** $\neg node_i.sndFailure$ **then**
6      $SendToAllNetwork(message, currentTime)$
7 $node_i.EvenActivation \leftarrow \neg node_i.EvenActivation$

Note that the periods of different nodes can be different, which makes the problem particularly challenging. While the period remains constant over the node's entire execution, its effective activation time can still be modified by a jitter, varying at each activation (this is the common definition of a jitter).

The static timing parameters are defined by the target system constraints. In this paper, we use the (anonymized) values given in Fig. 1a.

Example 1. Assume the system is made of three nodes. The periods, start times, and jitters for the first three activations of the nodes are given in Fig. 1b. We therefore have $t_1^0 = 0, t_1^1 = 49.5, t_1^2 = 98, t_1^3 = 147.2, t_2^0 = 30, t_2^1 = 81, t_2^2 = 132.1, t_2^3 = 183.1, t_3^0 = 0.1, t_3^1 = 49.2, t_3^2 = 97.7, t_3^3 = 147.2$. The first activations of the nodes are depicted in Fig. 2. Due to both uncertain periods and jitters, it can happen that, between two consecutive activations of a node, another node is activated twice: for example, between t_3^1 and t_3^2, node 1 is activated twice (i.e. t_1^1 and t_1^2), and therefore, between two consecutive activations, node 3 may receive two messages from node 1, while node 1 receives no new message from node 3.

Finally note that the number of activations of different nodes can increase at a different speed. The number of activations since the system start for nodes 1 and 3 having the same periods remains roughly the same at any timestamp: initially equal to at most 1, the difference can change very slowly (with the values of Fig. 1a, due to jitters, it can increase by 1 after at least j activations such that $(49-0.5)(j+1) < (49+0.5)j$, i.e. $j > 48.5$). The numbers of activations for node 2 and nodes 1 and 3 can evolve with a more rapidly increasing difference.

Nodes can fail and restart. We consider in our models 5 failure modes:

- F1: A node can stop and flush its internal memory. When restarting, the node will believe it is alone in the network until it receives messages from the other nodes. This corresponds to a node shutting down.
- F2: A node can stop and keep its internal memory. When restarting, the node will have the same state as before stopping, it will still assume the network in the same state as when it stopped, until it receives messages that will contradict this belief. This corresponds to a node freezing.
- F3: A node can stop sending and receiving messages. This corresponds to a disconnection from the network.

– F4/F5: A node can stop receiving (resp., sending) messages but still be able to emit (resp. receive) messages. This corresponds to a partial disconnection.

2.2 Overview of the Algorithm

We briefly describe how we modeled the node operation in this part. We assume that *currentTime*, the timestamp of the node execution, is a global variable that can be accessed by any node. (In practice, the view of the time by the node can be slightly imprecise. This imprecision is covered in the model by jitters and message delays.)

At each activation, each $node_i$ executes a code similar to the one given in Algorithm 1. Due to asynchronicity, the main part of the code treating received messages is executed only once every two activations (when the boolean flag $node_i.EvenActivation$ is true, cf. lines 1–4), while a working node sends a message at each activation. This ensures that if a node is present in the network, then any other node has received at least one message from it (cf. Fig. 2 for an example of when it is necessary).

When $node_i.EvenActivation$ is true, the node first reads the content of its mailbox (line 2). Then it computes its new state from the messages it received (line 3), and a message to be sent to the rest of the network (line 4). The code of these two parts is confidential. Finally, at every iteration, if the sending capacity has not failed, it sends a message to the rest of the network (using the $SendToAllNetwork$ function, cf. lines 5–6). The message is either the one that has just been computed, or the repetition of the old message but with the current timestamp. It then swaps the flag *EvenActivation*.

3   Methodology

One of our objectives was to develop a methodology and models that could be read by software developers not specialized in formal verification, and hence, must be as straightforward as possible. The first model, M_{sim}, simulating the whole network, is presented in Sect. 3.1. However, its verification was not able to scale up to the real number of nodes so we developed an abstract model, M_{abs}, presented in Sect. 3.2, that uses the rely-guarantee and abstraction techniques. The models were specified in a simple subset of an imperative C-like language (and were adapted to the input language of the tools used in our experiments). We present their simplified pseudo-code versions in this paper.

3.1   Modeling the Whole System by Simulation

The model M_{sim} simulates a network of a fixed, constant number of p processes. It explicitly represents all nodes, with their associated periods, first activation times, local memories, and mailboxes of received messages. A pseudo-code of M_{sim} is given in Algorithm 2. The mailbox of each node is represented as a

---

Algorithm 2: Pseudo-code of model M_{sim} simulating p nodes

```
// Network initialization for nodes i=1,2,...,p
```
1 **State** : $node_i.state$
2 **Integer** : $node_i.id, node_i.per, node_i.start, Activation_i, nextActivationTime_i$
3 **Boolean** :
   $node_i.EvenActivation, node_i.failure, node_i.rcvFailure, node_i.sndFailure$
4 **Assume** : AllDifferent($node_i.id \mid i \in 1, \ldots, p$) `// Identifiers are unique`
5 **foreach** $i \in \{1, \ldots, p\}$ **do**
6      $Activation_i \leftarrow 0$
7   **Assume** : $\mathsf{period}_{\mathsf{min}} \leq node_i.per \leq \mathsf{period}_{\mathsf{max}}$
8   **Assume** : $0 \leq node_i.start < node_i.per$
9      $nextActivationTime_i \leftarrow node_i.start$

```
// Mailbox initialization
```
10 ...
```
// Main algorithm simulating the network execution
```
11 **while** *true* **do**
12      $i \leftarrow indexMin(nextActivationTime)$ `// Node with the smallest time`
13   **if** $\neg node_i.failure$ **then**
14          $UpdateNode(i)$ `// Execute the node`
15          $Activation_i \leftarrow Activation_i + 1$
16      $jitter \leftarrow nondet()$ `// Choose an arbitrary value for a new jitter`
17   **Assume** : $\mathsf{jitter}_{\mathsf{min}} \leq jitter \leq \mathsf{jitter}_{\mathsf{max}}$ `// in the considered bounds`
18      $nextActivationTime_i \leftarrow nextActivationTime_i + node_i.per + jitter$
19   **Assert** : $P_1 \wedge \cdots \wedge P_\alpha$ `// Partial and final properties`

---

list containing the messages received from every other node (or nothing, if such messages were not received).

In the initialization phase, we assume (cf. lines 1–3 in Algorithm 2) that all variables are initialized by arbitrary values. It is equivalent to be initialized by a call to an uninterpreted function $nondet()$ (for which, by abuse of notation, the same function name will be used to return data of the relevant type). Necessary constraints (e.g. on the periods, cf. line 7) are introduced by the assume clause. The assumption on line 4 states that all node IDs are different. In this way, a symbolic initial state is created. (This notion of a symbolic initial state was earlier used to solve a challenge by Thales [19], also featuring uncertain periods.) The variable $Activation_i$ is used to store how many times $node_i$ has been executed.

The code of function $UpdateNode(i)$ is given by Algorithm 1. To take into account possible receiving failures and delays, the $ReadMessages(i)$ function selects the messages received by $node_i$ to consider (unless it lost the ability to receive messages, i.e. $node_i.rcvFailure$ is true). For each other node $node_k$, it checks when the latest message from $node_k$ has been sent. If the message has been sent since less than $\mathsf{msgDelay}_{\mathsf{min}}$, we consider that it has not yet reached $node_i$, and we use the previous message from $node_k$. If the latest message has been sent a long time ago (since more than $\mathsf{msgDelay_{max}}$), we consider it has reached $node_i$ and we use this message. If the message has been sent between $\mathsf{msgDelay_{min}}$ and $\mathsf{msgDelay_{max}}$, the message may or may not have reached the node, in that case we consider one of the two last messages to model both possible cases.

The main simulating loop of Algorithm 2 chooses $node_i$ to execute next as the node having the smallest $nextActivationTime$ (line 12). If $node_i$ did not fail, it is executed and its activation counter incremented (lines 13–15). Then a jitter is chosen and the next activation time computed (lines 16–18).

The final consensus achievement property P_α we want to prove for working nodes since the last node status change is of the form:

$$\forall k \in \{1,\ldots,p\}, (\ node_k \in networkState \ \wedge \ Activation_k \geq \alpha \ ) \qquad (P_\alpha)$$
$$\Rightarrow node_k.networkView = networkState$$

where $networkState$ is the list of all currently working nodes (i.e. without any failure), and $\alpha \in \mathbb{N}$ is a parameter depending on the system (in our system, $\alpha = 7$). Thus, to prove the consensus is reached, the loop on line 11 should execute each node at least α times. The consensus preservation (for any $j \geq \alpha$) can be proved using k-induction (or by checking in some way that the system returns to the same symbolic state as in the beginning). Our algorithm goes through several partial consistency properties before reaching the consensus. Such a partial property P_j, $1 \leq j < \alpha$, is of the form:

$$\forall k \in \{1,\ldots,p\}, (\ node_k \in networkState \ \wedge \ Activation_k \geq j \ ) \Rightarrow \ldots \qquad (P_j)$$

The right-hand side is a property of $node_k$'s state. It is not necessarily different for all j. For the M_{sim} model of our algorithm, only P_2, P_5 and of course P_7 are stronger than a previous one, so we will focus on them in our experiments and call them *key properties*. In our algorithm, properties P_j can also be expressed in terms of the message sent by $node_k$ at its j-th activation.

As suggested in Fig. 2, the number of different executions can grow very fast with the number of nodes and the execution length. A rough lower bound for the number of different execution orderings of M_{sim} can be computed as $(p!)^n$, where n is the number of activations of a node in the considered executions (so $n \geq \alpha$). The target Thales system is comprised of roughly 20 nodes, and the consensus is supposed to be reached after 7 activations of each node. Hence the number of execution paths of M_{sim} is greater than $(20!)^7 \approx 5 \cdot 10^{128}$.

As we will see in Sect. 4, model M_{sim} allows us to prove our algorithm for a small number of nodes. It is very useful to debug the implementation and iteratively check properties P_j or find counter-examples that are easily readable and understandable by the algorithm developers. To prove the same algorithm for a larger number of nodes, we need to abstract some behaviors.

3.2   Modeling One Node with an Abstraction of the System

We now explain how we construct an abstract model M_{abs} (cf. Algorithm 3). It is (manually) deduced from the original model M_{sim}. The idea is to model

---

Algorithm 3: Pseudo code for abstract model M_{abs} (for a proof of P_l)

```
// Initialization for nodes k=1,2,...,p
```
1   **Integer** : $node_k.id, Activation_k$
2   **Boolean** : $node_k.failure, node_k.rcvFailure, node_k.sndFailure$
3   **Assume** : AllDifferent$(node_k.id \mid k \in 1,\ldots,p)$ `// Identifiers are unique`
```
   // Initialization for node i
```
4   **Assume** : $i \in \{1,\ldots,p\}$
5    $Activation_i \leftarrow 0$
6   **Boolean** : $node_i.EvenActivation$
```
   // Main loop iteratively activating node i
```
7   **while** *true* **do**
8      $Mailbox \leftarrow \emptyset$ `// Model possible messages from other nodes`
9   **for** $k \in \{1,\ldots,p\} \setminus \{i\}$ **do**
10        $message_k \leftarrow nondet()$
11   **if** $\neg node_i.rcvFailure \wedge \neg node_k.sndFailure$ **then**
12          $Mailbox \leftarrow Mailbox \cup message_k$
13        $Activation_k \leftarrow Activation_k + |nondet()|$ `// An increasing value`
14   **Assume** : $P_{timed} \wedge P_1 \wedge \cdots \wedge P_{l-1}$ `// Assume up to` P_{l-1} `for all nodes`
15   **if** $\neg node_i.failure$ **then**
16        $UpdateNode(i)$
17      $Activation_i \leftarrow Activation_i + 1$
18   **Assert** : $(P_1 \wedge \cdots \wedge P_l)|_{node_i}$ `// Prove properties up to` P_l `for` $node_i$

---

the system as one node $node_i$ (the node of interest) interacting with the rest of the network. The model activates only $node_i$, which receives messages from the other nodes. The behavior of the other nodes is defined only by assumptions.

M_{abs} also abstracts away the timing information contained in M_{sim} and also ensures it by suitable assumptions, called P_{timed}. To infer and verify these assumptions, we consider a simple auxiliary model M_T of M_{sim} which merely contains relevant timing information. We then use a parametric timed model checker to infer properties on possible execution interleavings of nodes.

In our methodology, we use M_{abs}, with the integration of P_{timed} as assumptions, to iteratively prove properties P_j, $1 \leq j \leq \alpha$, on the (state and) messages of $node_i$. To prove P_l, we assume in addition P_j, $1 \leq j < l$, for all other nodes. Each time a new property P_l is proven, we add it as an assumption on the messages sent to $node_i$ by other nodes. After several steps, when $l = \alpha$, the proven property P_l is the consensus property P_α (cf. lines 14, 18 in Algorithm 3).

We now describe models M_{abs} and M_T in more detail.

Abstract Model M_{abs} and Proof of Properties P_j. This model considers only the activations of the node under study, $node_i$. The rest of the network is abstracted by the messages contained in the mailbox of $node_i$. Every other node $node_k$ ($k \neq i$) can have any state and send any message at any activation, provided it respects the assumptions (cf. line 14). Its behavior does not directly rely on its parity ($node_k.EvenActivation$), what the nodes sent previously, or what $node_i$ is sending. Thus, only some of the node fields are used in this model.

Algorithm 3 first initializes (non-deterministically) the useful fields of all nodes (lines 1–3), then those of the node under study $node_i$ (lines 4–6). The loop on lines 7–18 iteratively activates $node_i$ (lines 15–17) if it did not fail. Prior to that, it constructs a mailbox with any possible messages from the other nodes (lines 8–12) that can communicate with $node_i$ (cf. line 11). These messages have to respect the assumptions on line 14.

Notice that the number of activations $Activation_k$ of any other node $node_k$ is not tightly linked to that of $node_i$. The constraint for $Activation_k$ to be increasing follows from line 13, while having an acceptable difference with $Activation_i$ will follow from the assumption P_{timed}, as explained below. Thus, property P_{timed} will force some of the assumed properties P_j to constrain the messages received by $node_i$ from a working node $node_k$ in the case when $Activation_k \geq j$ follows from P_{timed}.

We iteratively prove the properties P_l for the messages sent by $node_i$, starting by $l = 1$. Once a new property is proved, we add it as an assumption on the messages sent by the other nodes. To prove property P_l ($1 \leq l \leq \alpha$) for $node_i$, we assume that all other nodes respect the properties for smaller numbers of activations P_j, $1 \leq j < l$, along with P_{timed} (cf. line 14). The assertion on line 18 requires to prove P_l for $node_i$ in addition to the previously proven $P_j, 1 \leq j < l$ (that are already true at this step if the proof is done iteratively). The notation $P_j|_{node_i}$ means that the property is reduced to $node_i$ (by removing the quantification and taking $k = i$ in the definition (P_j)).

In this way, if the assertion on line 18 is proved for $node_i$, we can deduce that P_l holds for any node and any execution, thanks to a non-deterministic choice of the node under study and symbolic states of all other nodes.

Interestingly, we observed that due to abstraction, the consensus property in the abstract model M_{abs} for our algorithm was not reached after $\alpha = 7$ activations as in the simulating model M_{sim}, but after $\alpha = 8$ activations. This extra delay was not an issue for system developers, a rigorous proof being more important. Therefore, we use $\alpha = 8$ in the specification and verification of M_{abs}. The other key properties P_2 and P_5 were still true for the same j.

Abstract Model M_T and Proof of Property P_{timed}. We give in this section only a very brief overview of the model M_T. More detail about it can be found in [5].

Our goal is to establish a property P_{timed} relating the numbers of executions of two nodes for the given system parameters. It has the following form:

$$\forall i, k \in \{1, \ldots, p\}, \ Activation_i \leq \beta$$
$$\Rightarrow \ | \ Activation_i - Activation_k \ | \ \leq \gamma \tag{P_{timed}}$$

for some $\beta, \gamma \in \mathbb{N}$. The value γ depends on the activation periods, the maximal jitter values, and of course the value of β. The value β must be sufficient in order to cover executions long enough to prove all properties P_j, $1 \leq j \leq \alpha$ needed to reach the consensus property. Example 1 illustrated some situations where the difference between such numbers of activations can (slightly) increase. In model M_{abs} of our target system, since we need at least $\alpha = 8$ activations of each node to reach a consensus, we can take $\beta = 8$ and have the bound $\gamma = 2$.

Given the current number of activations of $node_i$, this property allows us to deduce information on a possible number of activations of $node_k$. To prove it, we use a timed abstract model M_T of M_{sim}. It relies on an extension of the formalism of timed automata [1], a powerful extension of finite-state automata with clocks, i.e. real-valued variables that evolve at the same time. Timed automata were proven successful in verifying many systems with interactions between time and concurrency, especially with the state-of-the-art model-checker UPPAAL [6]. However, timed automata cannot model and verify arbitrary periods: while it is possible to model a different period at each round, it is not possible to first fix a period once for all (in an interval), and then use this period for the rest of the execution. We therefore use the extension *parametric timed automata* [2,3] allowing to consider *parameters*, i.e. unknown constants (possibly in an interval). IMITATOR [4] is a state-of-the-art model checker supporting this formalism. The timed abstract model M_T of M_{sim} is a product of two similar parametric timed automata representing the node under study $node_i$ and a generic node $node_k$.

Thanks to a more abstract view of the system in the model M_{abs}, where other nodes and timing constraints were abstracted away and replaced by assumptions relating the numbers of activations of nodes, and thanks to an iterative proof of partial properties P_j, the proof for M_{abs} scaled up to larger numbers of nodes.

4   Experiments with Various Tools

To perform our experiments, we selected three tools: SAFEPROVER [10], CBMC [9], and KLEE [8]. Our experiments were not specifically aimed at comparing the tools or judging their potential. Their goal was rather to report the results that industrial engineers without an advanced knowledge of these tools can obtain when using them on a real-life distributed algorithm.

4.1   Experiments with SafeProver

We describe here the results obtained by a commercial SMT solver called SAFE-PROVER [10] designed by the SafeRiver company. SAFEPROVER is designed to perform model-checking on Mathworks Simulink designs. It is a symbolic synchronous model checker, which fits with our modelings. However, it can be used with other input languages. In our case, we elected to use the Imperative Common Language (ICL) also designed by SafeRiver. ICL has some constraints that fitted with the use-case: all loops have to be statically bounded, all types and array sizes must be known statically. It forced us to use arrays for incoming messages, but this was coherent with the original implementation of the algorithm. SAFEPROVER uses several steps of proven model simplification, as outlined in [10], before sending the resulting model to a bit-blasting algorithm. The proof can then be performed by a choice of several SAT solvers.

(a)	#nodes variant	$p = 3$ Correct	$p = 4$ Correct	$p = 5$ Correct
	time	59.5 s	95m48 s	TO
	result	✓	✓	—

(b)	#nodes variant	$p = 3$ Correct	$p = 18$ Correct	$p = 42$ Correct	$p = 100$ Correct
	time	0.29 s	9.74 s	5min12 s	15min30
	result	✓	✓	✓	✓

Fig. 3. Experiments with SAFEPROVER for correct properties with all failure modes for models (a) M_{sim}, and (b) M_{abs}. TO means a timeout (set to 2 h).

We chose this language and tool as it is very close to a regular programming language for the algorithmic parts and offers the possibility to specify assumptions and assertions.

Models. We performed the proof of both models, M_{sim} and M_{abs}, with all failure modes. For these models, we ran SAFEPROVER on the proof of correction of P_7 (resp. P_8). We obtained that:

- The algorithm was correct when nodes could fail completely, or fail to send messages (F1, F2, F3, and F5);
- The algorithm was not correct if nodes could fail to receive messages, while still emitting new messages to the network (F4).

Results. For these models we ran SAFEPROVER on a full proof using k-induction. Contrary to the other tools tested for these experiments, it means that if a property is proven, it is true for all possible infinite executions. In order to establish this property, SAFEPROVER first performs a Bounded Model Checking (BMC) step with k steps and then tries to prove the k-induction step. In all our experiments, the hardest and most time-consuming part of the proof was the k-induction step. The tool did not report the time for the BMC part of the proof, so we are unable to provide it for a clearer comparison between the tools. We believe that these proof times are still interesting because it shows that this approach is also viable for industrial proof. Times in Fig. 3 are given for the models with all possible failure modes. It includes the proof when the algorithm is correct (failure modes F1, F2, F3, and F5) and the generation of counter-examples when it was not (F4). SAFEPROVER gave good results in terms of proof times and scaled up to $p = 100$ nodes for M_{abs}.

Next Steps. SAFEPROVER offers the possibility to work on Mathworks Simulink sheets. Simulink[1] allows to model multidomain dynamical systems and automatically generate the code. It is widely used in Thales entities for algorithm design. We plan on working on a framework that would allow engineers to develop their algorithm in Simulink, and have an automatic generation of a provable model. Counter-examples would be given as a test case in Simulink so that the engineer can correct their design.

---

[1] See https://fr.mathworks.com/products/simulink.html.

#nodes	$p = 3$				$p = 4$				$p = 5$			
variant	P_1^{err}	P_4^{err}	P_6^{err}	Correct	P_1^{err}	P_4^{err}	P_6^{err}	Correct	P_1^{err}	P_4^{err}	P_6^{err}	Correct
time	0.25 s	0.95 s	6.27 s	37.75 s	0.33 s	1.52 s	53.98 s	14 m52 s	0.57 s	8.4 s	2 m27 s	TO
result	CE	CE	CE	✓	CE	CE	CE	✓	CE	CE	CE	—
RDP	0.13 s	0.74 s	5.76 s	37.49 s	0.20 s	1.25 s	53.18 s	14 m51 s	0.35 s	7.95 s	2 m26 s	TO
#vars	30,898	70,488	96,542	87,797	47,765	111,735	153,802	143,204	68,448	162,716	224,677	212,182
#clauses	110,966	256,340	351,902	319,867	172,625	408,119	562,800	523,886	261,475	627,154	867,407	819,048

Fig. 4. Experiments on erroneous and correct versions of model M_{sim} simulating all nodes without failures with CBMC. TO means a timeout (set to 2 h). RDP stands for runtime decision procedure.

#nodes	$p = 3$				$p = 18$				$p = 42$			
variant	P_1^{err}	P_4^{err}	P_7^{err}	Correct	P_1^{err}	P_4^{err}	P_7^{err}	Correct	P_1^{err}	P_4^{err}	P_7^{err}	Correct
time	0.32 s	0.33 s	0.41 s	0.34 s	2.19 s	2.35 s	2.42 s	2.85 s	8.07 s	8.65 s	9.81 s	11.05 s
result	CE	CE	CE	✓	CE	CE	CE	✓	CE	CE	CE	✓
RDP	0.13 s	0.14 s	0.17 s	0.14 s	0.88 s	0.97 s	1.08 s	1.18 s	2.20 s	2.79 s	3.81 s	4.28 s
#vars	38,615	38,606	38,597	38,594	197,795	197,786	197,777	197,774	452,483	452,474	452,465	452,462
#clauses	116,705	116,411	116,009	115,851	578,390	577,736	576,434	575,856	1,317,086	1,315,856	1,313,114	1,311,864

Fig. 5. Experiments on erroneous and correct versions of the abstract model M_{abs} without failures with CBMC. TO means a timeout (set to 2 h).

4.2 Experiments with CBMC

CBMC is a bounded model-checker for C programs [9]. We chose to work on C code because the modelling language used for the initial model is very close to C so the translation was quite straightforward, which allowed to compare tools on similar models. We chose CBMC since it is a well-known state-of-the-art model-checker for C programs. We thought it was well fitted for this experiment since the core of the problem is naturally bounded: the consensus is reached after a given number of executions, so the proof only requires a fixed number of iterations. For a complete proof, one also needs to prove that once a consensus is reached, it is preserved by the following executions. Bounded model-checking is not able to prove such a property stated on infinite executions, but it helped us gain confidence in it by proving it for very long executions.

Models. In a first set of experiments, we worked on simpler variants of the two models M_{sim} et M_{abs}, where we do not consider message delays nor possible failures. For these models, we ran CBMC on the following properties:

- P_j^{err}, with $j = 1, 4, 6$ for M_{sim} and $j = 1, 4, 7$ for M_{abs}: an erroneous version of the key property P_{j+1} where the same property is stated after j executions instead of $j + 1$. This leads to the production of a counter-example.
- P_7 (resp. P_8): each node executed at least 7 (resp. 8) times knows the actual list of working nodes in M_{sim} (resp. M_{abs}). The proof should be successful.

In a second step we extended the two models to all possible failures (except those preventing a consensus to be reached). On these last models, we only ran CBMC on P_7 for M_{sim} (resp. P_8 for M_{abs}), to be able to compare the proof times to those of SAFEPROVER.

(a)

#nodes variant	$p = 3$ Correct	$p = 4$ Correct
time	4 min20 s	TO
result	✓	—
RDP	4 min19 s	TO
#vars	305,431	527,197
#clauses	986,574	1,713,053

(b)

#nodes variant	$p = 3$ Correct	$p = 18$ Correct	$p = 22$ Correct	$p = 23$ Correct
time	2.36 s	9 min2 s	55 min47 s	TO
result	✓	✓	✓	—
RDP	1.63 s	8 min46 s	55 min19 s	TO
#vars	371,265	2,007,225	2,436,945	2,543,945
#clauses	1,143,416	6,080,111	7,350,811	7,665,476

Fig. 6. Experiments with CBMC on correct versions of models (a) M_{sim} with failures, and (b) M_{abs} with failures. TO means a timeout (set to 2 h).

#nodes variant	$p = 2$ P_1^{err}	P_4^{err}	P_6^{err}	$p = 3$ P_1^{err}	P_4^{err}	P_6^{err}	$p = 4$ P_1^{err}	P_4^{err}	P_6^{err}	$p = 5$ P_1^{err}	P_4^{err}	P_6^{err}
time	0.6s	7s	48s	0.8s	12m33s	TO	1.15s	TO	TO	2.1s	TO	TO
result	CE	CE	CE	CE	CE	—	CE	—	—	CE	—	—
#instr.	2,299	595,279	4,231,836	4,820	51,662,006	?	12,288	?	?	44,118	?	?

Fig. 7. Experiments on erroneous versions of model M_{sim} simulating all nodes with KLEE. For correct versions, the tool timed out. TO means a timeout (set to 2 h).

Results. On model M_{abs} without failures, all properties are falsified or proved in less than 25s for a size of network ranging from 3 to 64 nodes (see Fig. 5). On model M_{sim} without failures, the exponentially growing complexity of the model prevents the termination of proofs for the more complex properties, except for a very small number of nodes (see Fig. 4).

On models with failures, proofs are much more difficult. For model M_{sim}, only the model with 3 nodes is proven in less than 2 h (with 4 nodes the proof takes almost 6 h). And even for model M_{abs}, the property is proven in less than 2 h only on models with less than 22 nodes. Results are shown in Fig. 6. This seems to make SAFEPROVER much more efficient on these models.

One may notice that for all the experiments, the total proof time is mainly the time of the runtime decision procedure (RDP), except for model M_{abs} without failures, where the time needed to build the formula takes two thirds of the total proof time. The complexity of the BMC problem is expressed in terms of the number of clauses and variables of the formula sent to the SAT solver.

The main advantage of CBMC in an industrial setting is to work directly on C code. Moreover, the tool is quite easy to handle and the default parameters seem to be sufficient for the proof of user-defined properties. It requires very few adaptations of the initial code to be run so the time needed to make ones first proof is quite short. One may regret that, with the command line interface, default counter-examples are not very easy to read, and that it is not possible to directly replay them.

#nodes variant	$p = 2$ P_1^{err}	P_4^{err}	P_7^{err}	$p = 3$ P_1^{err}	P_4^{err}	P_7^{err}	$p = 4$ P_1^{err}	P_4^{err}	P_7^{err}	$p = 5$ P_1^{err}	P_4^{err}	P_7^{err}
time	0.3s	27s	17m53s	0.5s	26m21s	TO	1s	60m53s	TO	1.7s	1h25m	TO
result	CE	CE	CE	CE	CE	—	CE	CE	—	CE	CE	—
#instr.	2,213	2,039,992	57,289,534	6,739	63,235,648	?	21,582	88,588,978	?	62,962	109,841,990	?

Fig. 8. Experiments on erroneous and correct versions of the abstract model M_{abs} with KLEE. For correct versions, the tool timed out. TO means a timeout (set to 2 h).

Next steps. A BMC proof of the original (real-life) code could be tried, thanks to the knowledge we gained on the tool.

4.3 Experiments with KLEE

In the last set of experiments, we used KLEE [8], a popular dynamic symbolic execution tool. It explores program paths using a combination of concrete and symbolic execution, offers several strategies, and generates test cases for a given C program, possibly enriched with assume and assert statements.

Models. We used KLEE on the same models and properties as in the first set of experiments with CBMC (see Sect. 4.2).

Results. The results for M_{sim} and M_{abs} are shown, resp., in Fig. 7 and 8. They show that KLEE was able to generate counter-examples for both models, but for the most complex properties it was possible only for 2 nodes. The execution was stopped at a first assertion failure so we do not have data on a complete session, but we report the number of instructions KLEE explored before a counter-example was found. They show the combinatorial complexity of the models. On the correct versions and for some properties for more nodes, KLEE timed out (and also reported that the memory cap was exceeded, so many paths were dropped).

5 Lessons Learned and Perspectives

Our experience shows that despite the existence of several verified consensus algorithms, *industrial users often need to verify a specific algorithm (variant) that precisely fits their needs.* The reasons can be grouped into two categories. System developers can be reluctant to changes and prefer to obtain a proof of the existing legacy algorithm, or adapted only with minor changes. Second, especially in embedded systems where performance is a key factor, the existing algorithms do not always meet the constraints of the target system, e.g., memory size, network usage, computational time, non-interference with other computations, relevant fault models and robustness constraints, the level of possible variations of the activation or communication times.

Generic verification methodologies applicable to large families of similar algorithms can be very helpful in this context. The existence of advanced verification tools and a large record of verification efforts in the area makes it possible today to suggest such methodologies for industrial engineers. After verifying one algorithm, the engineer may need to adapt it to a new system and to verify again. The present paper describes such a methodology for a family of consensus algorithms and reports on its application to some of them. The criteria for acceptance of the methodology include the capacity to perform the proof, the possibility to analyze the real-life code or a model as close as possible to the code, and to produce and easily read counter-examples.

As is often the case in distributed algorithms, the models of consensus algorithms we considered have *a high combinatorial complexity,* due to several free variables in the initial state and lots of possible interleavings. It is rapidly increasing with the number of nodes and executions. Therefore, we focused on symbolic tools: symbolic model checking and symbolic execution. Timed model checking did not seem to be a suitable candidate for two reasons. The timed model checkers we experimented with were enumerative. When experimenting with IMITATOR [4], we filled the 160GB RAM memory of the server before ending the proof. The second reason is the modeling language expected to be close to the code, and the need to easily generate and read counter-examples without having to invest too much time. Thus, Timed Petri nets or automata were not considered as suitable candidates to perform the whole study, but their application should be further investigated in the future. We restricted the usage of timed model checkers to one property, P_T, in order to perform the proof on the abstract model M_{abs}. The underlying model was simple enough to be reviewed.

Symbolic model checking tools we used (SAFEPROVER and CBMC) appeared to be very powerful both for finding counter-examples and proving the correct version of the algorithm. In particular, the support of bit operations was particularly useful to achieve better results thanks to a compact bit-level encoding of data in our models: the results became much better than for an earlier, naive array-based version.

We have also verified algorithms where message transmission can be delayed, using the SAFEPROVER tool and applying the same methodology. While this change did increase the time for the proof to be completed, it did not significantly change the number of nodes for which the proof worked.

Symbolic execution using KLEE also proved to be useful to detect counter-examples for small numbers of nodes and executions. Due to the combinatorial explosion of the number of paths, in this case study we were not able to use it to explore all paths in order to show the absence of errors on the correct models. KLEE was convenient for producing readable counter-examples since it directly handles the C code.

Abstracting the system model using the rely-guarantee based technique was essential for the proof to scale for a large number of nodes. While the proof of the properties on the complete model M_{sim} was successful for smaller numbers of nodes ($p < 10$), it ran out of time and memory for bigger numbers of nodes which were required in the target systems. The rely-guarantee based approach, dating back to the work of Jones [13] and well-established today, solved this issue for the family of algorithms we faced in this work.

Future Work. Future work directions include the application of the methodology to other industrial algorithms, proof of the assumptions for the real-life C code using deductive verification (using e.g. FRAMA-C [14]) and experiences using other verification tools (model checking and symbolic execution). More generally, collecting the engineers' needs and experience related to verification of distributed algorithms at Thales and supporting them in their verification work remains a priority for the formal methods group of Thales Research and Technology.

Acknowledgment. The authors are grateful to Etienne André, Laurent Fribourg and Jean-Marc Mota for their contribution to the previous case study [5], as well as to the anonymous reviewers for their useful comments.

References

1. Alur, R., Dill, D.L.: A theory of timed automata. Theor. Comput. Sci. **126**, 183–235 (1994)
2. Alur, R., Henzinger, T.A., Vardi, M.Y.: Parametric real-time reasoning. In: STOC. ACM (1993)
3. André, É.: What's decidable about parametric timed automata? Int. J. Softw. Tools Technol. Transf. **21**(2), 203–219 (2019)
4. André, É., Fribourg, L., Kühne, U., Soulat, R.: IMITATOR 2.5: a tool for analyzing robustness in scheduling problems. In: Giannakopoulou, D., Méry, D. (eds.) FM 2012. LNCS, vol. 7436, pp. 33–36. Springer, Heidelberg (2012). https://doi.org/10.1007/978-3-642-32759-9_6
5. André, É., Fribourg, L., Mota, J., Soulat, R.: Verification of an industrial asynchronous leader election algorithm using abstractions and parametric model checking. In: Enea, C., Piskac, R. (eds.) Verification, Model Checking, and Abstract Interpretation. VMCAI 2019 LNCS, vol. 11388, pp. 409–424. Springer, Cham (2019). https://doi.org/10.1007/978-3-030-11245-5_19
6. Behrmann, G., David, A., Larsen, K.G.: A tutorial on UPPAAL. In: Bernardo, M., Corradini, F. (eds.) SFM-RT 2004. LNCS, vol. 3185, pp. 200–236. Springer, Heidelberg (2004). https://doi.org/10.1007/978-3-540-30080-9_7
7. Blanchard, A., Kosmatov, N., Lemerre, M., Loulergue, F.: Conc2Seq: a frama-C plugin for verification of parallel compositions of C programs. In: SCAM. IEEE (2016)
8. Cadar, C., Dunbar, D., Engler, D.R.: KLEE: unassisted and automatic generation of high-coverage tests for complex systems programs. In: OSDI (2008)
9. Clarke, E., Kroening, D., Lerda, F.: A tool for checking ANSI-C programs. In: Jensen, K., Podelski, A. (eds.) TACAS 2004. LNCS, vol. 2988, pp. 168–176. Springer, Heidelberg (2004). https://doi.org/10.1007/978-3-540-24730-2_15
10. Étienne, J.F., Juppeaux, É.: SafeProver: a high-performance verification tool. ACM SIGAda Ada Lett. **36**(2), 47–48 (2017)
11. Fischer, M.J., Lynch, N.A., Paterson, M.: Impossibility of distributed consensus with one faulty process. J. ACM **32**(2), 374–382 (1985)
12. García-Molina, H.: Elections in a distributed computing system. IEEE Trans. Comput. **31**(1), 48–59 (1982)
13. Jones, C.B.: Tentative steps toward a development method for interfering programs. ACM Trans. Program. Lang. Syst. **5**(4), 596–619 (1983)
14. Kirchner, F., Kosmatov, N., Prevosto, V., Signoles, J., Yakobowski, B.: Frama-C: a software analysis perspective. Formal Asp. Comput. **27**(3), 573–609 (2015)
15. Lamport, L.: The part-time parliament. ACM Trans. Comput. Syst. **16**(2), 133–169 (1998)
16. Lamport, L.: Specifying Systems: The TLA+ Language and Tools for Hardware and Software Engineers. Addison-Wesley Longman Publishing Co., Inc. (2002)

17. Lynch, N.A.: Distributed Algorithms. Morgan Kaufmann Publishers Inc., Burlington (1996)
18. Raynal, M.: Fault-Tolerant Message-Passing Distributed Systems - An Algorithmic Approach. Springer, Heidelberg (2018). https://doi.org/10.1007/978-3-319-94141-7
19. Sun, Y., André, É., Lipari, G.: Verification of two real-time systems using parametric timed automata. In: WATERS (2015)

Deploying TESTAR to Enable Remote Testing in an Industrial CI Pipeline: A Case-Based Evaluation

Fernando Pastor Ricós[1]([✉]), Pekka Aho[2]([✉]), Tanja Vos[1,2]([✉]),
Ismael Torres Boigues[1,2,3]([✉]), Ernesto Calás Blasco[1,2,3],
and Héctor Martínez Martínez[3]

[1] Universitat Politècnica de València, 46002 Valencia, Spain
ferpasri@inf.upv.es
[2] Open Universiteit, Heerlen, The Netherlands
{pekka.aho,tanja.vos}@ou.nl
[3] Prodevelop, Valencia, Spain
{itorres,info}@prodevelop.es

Abstract. Companies are facing constant pressure towards shorter release cycles while still maintaining a high level of quality. Agile development, continuous integration and testing are commonly used quality assurance techniques applied in industry. Increasing the level of test automation is a key ingredient to address the short release cycles. Testing at the graphical user interface (GUI) level is challenging to automate, and therefore many companies still do this manually. To help find solutions for better GUI test automation, academics are researching scriptless GUI testing to complement the script-based approach. In order to better match industrial problems with academic results, more academia-industry collaborations for case-based evaluations are needed. This paper describes such an initiative to improve, transfer and integrate an academic scriptless GUI testing tool TESTAR into the CI pipeline of a Spanish company Prodevelop. The paper describes the steps taken, the outcome, the challenges, and some lessons learned for successful industry-academia collaboration.

Keywords: Automated testing · GUI level · TESTAR · CI · Technology transfer

1 Introduction

The development of cost-effective and high-quality software systems is getting more and more challenging for SMEs. Modern systems are distributed and become larger and more complex, as they connect multitude of components that interact in many different ways and have constantly changing and different types of requirements. Adequately testing these systems cannot be faced alone with traditional testing approaches.

© Springer Nature Switzerland AG 2020
T. Margaria and B. Steffen (Eds.): ISoLA 2020, LNCS 12476, pp. 543–557, 2020.
https://doi.org/10.1007/978-3-030-61362-4_31

New techniques for systematization and automation of testing are being researched in academia. To help the industry to keep up with the increasing quality requirements, it is important to guarantee the successful transfer of new techniques into use.

Unit tests are widely automated, especially if test-driven development process is followed. However, testing through graphical user interface (GUI) is more challenging to automate [1]. The most common way to automate GUI testing is based on scripts that are defined before the test execution. Manually recording or writing test scripts for all the possible paths of the GUI takes simply too much effort to be practical, and even if the test cases are built with keywords and a proper architecture, so many test scripts would result in serious maintenance issues [6]. To address this challenge, the academics are researching scriptless GUI testing to complement the script-based approach. In scriptless GUI testing, the test cases are generated during the test execution, based on observing the run-time state of the system under test (SUT).

The rest of this paper is structured as follows. First, in Sect. 2, we describe the context of this study. In Sect. 2.1, we describe TESTAR, an open source scriptless test automation tool developed in academia. In Sect. 2.2, we describe a Spanish company Prodevelop, their software product Posidonia that is used as the system under test (SUT) in this collaboration, and their continuous integration (CI) process. In Sect. 3, we describe the goals and the objectives to consider that the transfer of knowledge has been achieved. In Sect. 4, we describe the development improvements made into TESTAR in terms of functionality belonging to the tool. We discuss the results in Sect. 5 and summarize the lessons learnt about academia-industry collaboration in Sect. 6. Finally, we conclude in Sect. 7.

2   Context

The work described in this paper has been carried out within the context of the European ITEA3 TESTOMAT project[1]. Both the private company Prodevelop and the academic partners are funded through this project.

2.1   The TESTAR Tool

TESTAR[2] [14] is an academic open source tool for automated testing through the GUI currently being developed by the Polytechnic University of Valencia and the Open University of the Netherlands, funded by various national and European initiatives.

TESTAR is a tool for *scriptless* testing, meaning that it does not require the creation, use and maintenance of scripts to test and explore the SUT from the user's perspective. It is open source under BSD3 license and available on Github[3].

---

[1]   https://www.testomatproject.eu/.

[2]   https://testar.org/.

[3]   https://github.com/TESTARtool/TESTAR_dev.

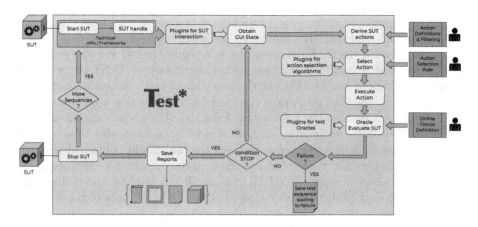

Fig. 1. TESTAR functional flow

The underlying principle of this testing approach is as follows (see Fig. 1): generate test sequences of (state, action)-pairs by starting up the SUT in its initial state and continuously select an action to bring the SUT in another state. The action selection characterizes the most basic problem of intelligent systems: *what to do next*. The difficult part is optimizing the action selection [ázar2018] to find faults, and recognizing a faulty state when it is found.

The default action selection of TESTAR focuses on random exploration of the SUT through processing of the state information extracted before and after each executed action. This way TESTAR can analyze the robustness of the SUT in a generic way and automate the testing of what we call *Non-User Stories*, detecting failures by implicit test oracles that check the violation of general-purpose system requirements, such as:

- the SUT should not *crash*,
- the SUT should not find itself in an *unresponsive* state (freeze), and
- the UI state should not contain any widget with *suspicious titles* like *error*, *problem*, *exception*, etc.

Implementing support for various technical APIs enables TESTAR to interact with different kinds of SUTs (desktop as well as Web). The modular architecture of TESTAR allows customizing and enriching the system specific protocol, for example, changing the action selection algorithms to take different exploratory paths, or defining system specific inputs or test oracles.

In addition to the SUT-specific protocol defining the behavior of TESTAR tool in terms of widgets interaction, actions exploration and test oracles, another set of configuration parameters is required to indicate how to connect to the desired SUT, define suspicious title patterns for SUT-specific test oracles or change between different protocols if these are customized to explore different parts of the SUT.

The configuration options for TESTAR are by default read from a local file, which allows to read and write the desired protocol implementation to adapt the functionality with the SUT requirements. For beginners and learning purposes, or facilitate the first SUT inspection and configuration of TESTAR, a GUI is offered to highlight the visibility of the most important configuration options. When changed, the GUI overwrites the local file with the new configuration.

As TESTAR obtains the information from the SUT about existing widgets, states, and available actions to execute, it selects and executes these actions generating the TESTAR test sequences. All the information obtained is stored in different formats and types of files creating output results for every sequence. After each executed action, TESTAR applies all the implicit and defined test oracles to obtain a verdict to determine whether the latest state of the sequence contains failures.

Every sequence creates the following types of files:

- Logs including step-by-step textual information about the executed actions, target widgets, and the verdicts from test oracles.
- Screenshots of each state and target widget on which an action is going to be executed, taken along the test sequence.
- HTML reports of each generated test sequence, including step-by-step screenshots and textual information about existing widgets and available actions of every state, and the executed action over the target widget.
- Binary files, used for saving the information about the executed actions in a form that allows a sequence to be replayed later.

2.2 Prodevelop

Prodevelop[4] is a Spanish company located in Valencia with an extensive network of clients in Europe, Africa, America and Oceania. From the beginning, Prodevelop has specialized on Geographic Information Systems and its application to the maritime transportation, especially in port domain.

The SUT used in this study is Posidonia Management, a web-based port management application developed and maintained by Prodevelop. Posidonia Management is conceived and designed to fulfil the management needs of different Port Authorities. The increasing port traffic and high competitiveness of the international market lead to increasingly complex systems. It is in this context that Posidonia Management, as a complete management system, can improve the efficiency, productivity, and competitiveness of a Port Authority.

Until a few years ago, Prodevelop followed the waterfall development cycle, but in the last few years, encouraged by the TESTOMAT Project, Prodevelop has oriented its development practices towards a more agile development cycle, with more frequent product deliveries, weekly in some products.

Continuous integration [8,10] (CI) is a process that focuses on increasing the client value through developing, updating, building and testing the software product as often as possible, for example after each code commit or once a day.

---

[4] https://www.prodevelop.es.

The continuous integration process of Prodevelop is made up of a series of linked and interrelated steps, illustrated in Fig. 2. The process begins when the Quality Assurance (QA) team configure the automatization orchestrator server Jenkins[5], a free and open source automation server that can be used to build, test and deploy software, facilitating continuous integration.

In parallel, the Business Analyst will gather the project requirements and analyse them to obtain the specification of the system. Based on this specification, on one hand, the testers will use TestLink[6] to define the Acceptance/Functional test, and on the other hand, the Developers will develop the system and create the Unit Tests. These tests will be evaluated by the task of Jenkins that performs the build of the deliverables.

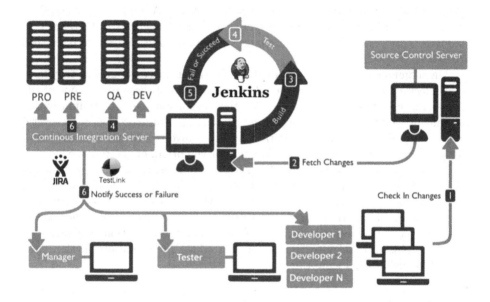

Fig. 2. Prodevelop CI/CD Pipeline

This automated process starts each time the Developers make a commit of source code to the repository. When a project that is assigned to a continuous integration environment receives an update of the source code, the Jenkins application will execute software code testing tasks: Static analysis, build and unit testing, to validate and compile the new source code.

If the build tasks in Jenkins end with the result "OK", the new version of the application will be deployed in the Quality Assurance (QA) environment, and the acceptance/functional tests are executed manually. If the tests are passed, the application will be deployed in the User Acceptance Test (PRE) and/or

---

[5] https://www.jenkins.io.
[6] http://testlink.org/.

Production (PRO) environment, which are located in the Client's own environments. The number of environments and deployment procedures are subject to the specific requirements of the Client.

In the case that any of the tasks that should be executed in Jenkins ends with "NOK" results, Jenkins informs the Developers detailing which test or tests have failed. In addition, Jenkins will generate an Incident-Ticket in Jira[7], an issue tracking and project management software, with all the necessary information, including also the phase of the process and specifically the test that fail, so that the Project Manager follows-up until the incident is resolved.

To ensure the quality of the software, Prodevelop relies mainly on functional testing. The QA staff assigned to a project defines functional test cases for each requirement and scenario using TestLink tool. These test cases are manually executed by the QA team when a new release is ready. A report with the results is generated and sent to the project manager to decide actions to be taken. On the other hand, developers are in charge of defining unit and static tests that are executed automatically.

The manual execution of functional tests is very time consuming as they have to be executed on each new delivery. The automation of these tests is one of the short-term objectives of Prodevelop. Another important issue to be improved is the time needed to solve an error. Since Posidonia is a large product with several million lines of code, and with several developers involved throughout the life of this product, a lot of time is spent looking for the origin of the problem.

To facilitate error detection and root cause analysis, the Posidonia Management application is instrumented with the intention to detect and debug all behaviour that is identified as an exception. All these exceptions are written to a log file with the information about the method where it occurred (the specific class and package it belongs to) and details about the exception that has been detected. This internal error information is added incrementally in the background log using local timestamps.

3   Objectives of the Study

From the academic point of view, the main goal of this collaboration was to evaluate the academic TESTAR tool on another real case in an industrial testing environment. TESTAR has already been evaluated in other industrial environments [2–4,7,9], and in order to be able to generalize these results based on individual cases [15] we need to study as many cases as we can and focus on their similarities. All the case studies so far shared one common aspect: before the introduction of TESTAR, GUI testing was done manually. For these studies we could see that TESTAR was considered a useful complement to the existing testing practices and interesting failures were found.

From the industrial point of view, Prodevelop is trying to achieve a high level of software quality by innovating its development processes. As indicated, the functional tests that are executed manually involve a high cost of running the

---

[7] https://www.atlassian.com/es/software/jira.

tests. For this reason, only a subset of them is executed in each release. So the objective of the study is clear: *integrate TESTAR into the current CI pipeline to automatically test Posidonia when the life cycle requires it and evaluate the performance.*

With TESTAR integrated into the CI pipeline, every time a new version is released and a nightly build is made, the following steps are taken:

- First, it will be checked whether there are failure sequences from previous versions, and in that case *replay* TESTAR test sequences to verify that errors were solved in the new release.
- Second, new test sequences will be *generated* with TESTAR to explore and verify the robustness of the application using the desired oracles and protocols. Depending on the configuration used, TESTAR can be steered to explore specific parts of Posidonia.
- Third, if a failure is detected, Prodevelop must verify that it is not a false positive, inspecting the sequence that found the failure. If it is not, all the logs generated during the test run should be filtered by the timestamps of the failure finding sequence, saved in a database and documented in TestLink. Then, a Jira ticket will be created with linked information about these results to be reviewed in the future.

To start the integration, Posidonia was tested with the default set-up of TESTAR to generate: test sequences, TESTAR logs, HTML test reports and GUI screenshots. All these artefacts generated by TESTAR were analyzed by Prodevelop. It was found that before the integration into CI could be realized, the following TESTAR extensions and improvements had to be implemented first:

1. Enable invocation of TESTAR through the CLI (Command Line Interface). This means that the configuration dialog should be disabled, and, instead of passing the test settings in a local file, they should be passed as parameters of the CLI command.
2. Enable TESTAR to correctly detect SUTs that have multiple processes handling the GUI, or that the GUI process change at run-time. Posidonia runs in a browser that starts with two main processes to which we should connect to properly verify the defined oracles.
3. Enable distributed execution of TESTAR by providing a remote API. This feature is fundamental if we want to integrate TESTAR into the CI methodology, or any other distributed process for that matter.
4. Improve the functionality of TESTAR Replay mode to observe changes between a previously executed and saved sequence and a newly executed test sequence.
5. Enable the synchronization of the logs produced by Posidonia with those of TESTAR. In order to find the root cause of the errors, it is important to be able to analyse the logs generated by Posidonia together with TESTAR logs. This information is needed by Prodevelop developers to understand and replicate the error.

These TESTAR adaptations will be described in the next section.

4   Extending TESTAR for the Case Study

This section describes the changes that had to be implemented into TESTAR to meet the requirements of Prodevelop and to be able to test Posidonia with TESTAR in the CI pipeline of Prodevelop.

4.1   Executing and Configuring TESTAR Through CLI

To allow TESTAR tool to be integrated into a CI pipeline, a new configuration option was added in addition to local settings files. When starting TESTAR through a CLI, the configuration can be passed on as parameters. This way any configuration setting can be overwritten through CLI, also disabling the GUI. This feature makes it easier to put TESTAR configuration into the settings of the CI job that starts TESTAR execution and change it from the CI tool.

4.2   Supporting SUTs with Multiple GUI Processes

By default, the execution of a SUT is started up by TESTAR using the path that contains the executable file, or in the case of web applications, by indicating the browser executable with the desired web URL. In case of running the SUT on Windows, first, we use this path to invoke a Windows function that will return the *process* handle of the SUT process that allow us to obtain the identifier of the SUT process, *pid*. However, to obtain the GUI state information (i.e., the widget tree and all the widget properties) through the Windows Accessibility API plugin, we need the *window handle*. To find the corresponding window handle, we probe all the existing window handles that are children of the Windows Desktop, to find the one that has the same *pid* as our SUT process.

The SUT in this case study, Posidonia, does not run in a single process. Instead, it starts execution with two GUI related processes. Some elements of one of these processes use warning pop-ups or lists of items. This prevented TESTAR from recognizing all the widgets. Therefore, TESTAR had to be changed to deal with SUTs that start with multiple GUI processes or launch new GUI handling processes at run-time. When a SUT starts up multiple processes, we do not have one main *pid*, but we have a list of *pids* (i.e., including the child *pids* of this main *pid*). In such cases we need to iterate over all the elements in the list to be able to get the GUI properties and information for each pid and merge them into one widget tree.

Supporting multiple GUI processes improved TESTAR's interaction with the SUT of the case study, making it possible to obtain the GUI information of both GUI handling processes. In addition to this, we also added a possibility to check whether there are new running processes in the environment after launching the SUT. If we find them, we save the *pids*. This way we are able to use different Windows API functions to check whether the process *pid* of the window handle that is in the foreground exists in our internal processes list. This makes it possible to iterate and create a widget tree also for this new visible window handle.

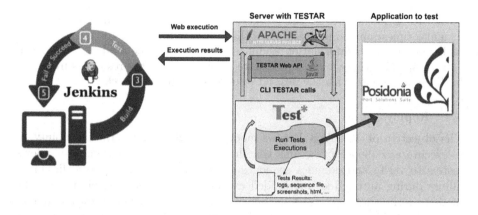

Fig. 3. Integration of TESTAR through an API in a distributed environment

4.3 Distributed TESTAR Execution with a Remote API

In order to integrate TESTAR into the Posidonia CI test cycle, the next step was to design a CI architecture [8,11] in which TESTAR can be invoked remotely in a distributed manner. First, suitable technologies were required for the communication between the: (1) CI server that launches the test execution, (2) the server that contains TESTAR, and (3) the server that executes the SUT.

Thinking about future deployments and enabling TESTAR execution in a test server environment, a Spring boot application was developed with an Apache Tomcat servlet that provides an API for TESTAR settings. Prodevelop offered the initial version of the API that was updated by the TESTAR developers with other necessary requirements, such as new settings parameters for remote login (instead of coding the user login inside the TESTAR Java protocol), and additional configuration options for the initialization of the GUI state model that is built during testing.

With the default implementation, the web API instance should be running in the same directory as the TESTAR tool. Subsequently, when receiving a POST request that is compatible with the TESTAR settings from the CI orchestrator, the contents of the web parameters will be parsed into CLI instructions using the configuration functionality described in 4.1. The flow of the invocation from the CI pipeline is depicted in Fig. 3. The main steps of the functionality are:

1. Upon receiving a web POST request, Posidonia CI orchestrator will send the desired configuration settings to run TESTAR. Only a couple of parameters were needed in the request payload.
2. The remote API is running in the same directory with TESTAR binaries to receive the requests and transform the parameters into a TESTAR configuration that is executed through the CLI.
3. If all the parameters were correct, TESTAR execution will start and a response will be sent back with the output information printed by TESTAR

on the CLI, which includes the test results, the path of the generated sequence and a timestamp to indicate when the sequence began.

4. If more detailed information about any sequence is required, a request will be sent indicating which sequence we want to obtain the resources from.
5. Then a response with the desired resources will be sent back.

4.4   Replay Mode

The objective of TESTAR Replay mode is to offer testers the possibility to re-execute a sequence of actions that has already been executed. This allows testers to verify and debug a sequence for which TESTAR reported finding a failure during automated unattended execution. It is also possible to use this mode to verify that a correct sequence of actions also does not throw any failure in the new SUT versions. Alternatively, we can use it to show that, after a bug fix, the sequence does no longer produce the failure.

A new sequence is started when TESTAR starts the SUT, and executed actions are saved in a Java object stream of the ongoing sequence every time TESTAR executes an action. Information about which action was executed is ready to be replayed, and the state of the SUT does not have to be used for deriving and selecting an available action. The discovered issue of the Replay mode was that TESTAR was not verifying if the SUT is changing between the desired states that we want to follow again by replaying a sequence.

To improve the Replay mode, the information related to the widget in which the action was executed and about the SUT states found, should be stored in the object stream associated with the action executed.

4.5   Output Results and the Structure of TESTAR Logs

The various logs and resources created by TESTAR could offer a large amount of information about the different GUI elements detected by TESTAR in the different states that conform the SUT. However, these files were not stored in a suitable structure for the case study. All the resources were stored in their corresponding directory (logs, sequences, HTML reports, screenshots), but they were stored incrementally according to the sequence number without taking into account the execution of TESTAR. With this structure the objective of synchronizing Prodevelop and TESTAR logs could not be achieved, and therefore, it had to be changed.

The solution was the creating an *index log* and restructuring the output directories according to the timestamp in which TESTAR was launched, in addition to the sequence number. This index can then be used by Posidonia every time it needs to obtain GUI information from TESTAR logs. Using its own logs and its own timestamps, Posidonia will filter the desired sequence in the TESTAR index and will be able to obtain the resource path with all the required information.

In Fig. 4 we can see that Posidonia creates its own logs based on its internal state. If an error occurs, a timestamp will be used to find the matching event from the TESTAR index log to obtain all existing resources and verify which front-end GUI action produced the back-end error.

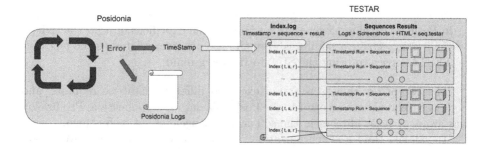

Fig. 4. Posidonia and TESTAR Logs Structure

5   Results

When doing academia-industry collaborations, there are several types of results. On the one hand, the academic tools have improved, they have successfully been adopted in an industrial context, and new ideas are generated for future research. On the other hand, the academic results are validated in an industrial context, and data shows that this improves the quality of the testing practices in the company. Naturally, our goal was to achieve all of these, but unfortunately the second part was not entirely achievable.

Due to various circumstances, the SUT Posidonia evolved into "maintenance only" phase, and Prodevelop decided not to make any changes to their existing testing processes because there are hardly any changes to the SUT anymore. This meant that, unfortunately, we could not really evaluate the performance of TESTAR in a real CI environment.

To try and get some data, we simulated a test with Posidonia by running TESTAR during 4 nightly builds for 12 h with random action selection protocol and a configuration of 30 sequences of 200 actions each night. Unfortunately, the SUT did not change in between, so the outcome of the runs could only differ due to the randomness of TESTAR. The runs showed that the CLI adaptions, the detection of multiple processes and the distributed execution did not fail during long unattended runs.

This outcomes of the test runs were:

– a total of 24000 actions in 120 test sequences
– 15 sequences resulting in *suspicious titles* (all found during the first run)
– 6 sequences resulting in *unexpected close* (all found during the first run)
– 0 sequences resulting in *unresponsiveness*

Analyzing these faulty sequences using the HTML report revealed that:

– 12 of the found *suspicious titles*-failures all lead back to a database connection error in Posidonia when TESTAR executed actions related to querying a port registry.

- the other 3 *suspicious titles*-failures lead to another database connection error in Posidonia trying to generate and obtain the expedient of a port activity.
- the 6 *unexpected close*-failures were all false positives related to the fact that TESTAR tries to bring the SUT to the foreground.

The two errors that were found executed different database requests, and both were related with an error in the Posidonia database connection. Prodevelop was aware of these glitches in the software, but decided not to fix them.

To validate the log synchronization, TESTAR and Posidonia logs were compared to check that the failure sequences found by TESTAR could be mapped to the internal error-logs from Posidonia. The mapping was found correctly and the names of the methods and classes that provoked the exception in Posidonia were meaningful in respect to the properties of the web elements on which the actions were executed. However, there was a delay of 5–10 s between timestamps. This is attributed to the time needed for the internal process to represent and detect the data at GUI level.

The mapping did not only help to verify the synchronization of errors after the execution of a sequence, but also motivated us to investigate the possibility of synchronizing TESTAR with other possible internal logs in order to find a way to improve the action selection based on the available internal methods.

6   Academia-Industry Collaboration

The fact that we could not validate the work completely in a real environment made us reflect again about the academia-industry collaboration. What went wrong here? Why did we find out that the company had stopped active development of the system we planned to test when we were ready with the adjustments to our tool to support their environment?

A myriad of articles [5,12,13] have been written with lessons learned from technology transfer. A simple Internet search with keywords such as university companies, academia industry, collaboration, cooperation, etc, will result in a massive number of hits discussing the issue. Looking at the factors mentioned in the literature, we had them covered (at least that is what we thought):

- we had *funding* through an European research project,
- that gave us the possibility to have *regular meetings*,
- as well as the *approval and commitment of the management* to do the study
- some practitioners at the company had been previously employed at a university, so we had their support and a *collaboration champion on site*
- the objectives of this collaboration were defined to address both the *needs* from academia as well as that of the company
- we worked in *agile sprints* due to the nature of the funded research project
- we *allowed solutions to emerge from the needs of the company* (e.g., the log synchronization, the multiple processes, the distributed execution) that were added to TESTAR to fulfill the requirements of the company)

Academics about industry:	Industry about academics:
- think all problems are solved by increased ROI - keep no track of data - talk lots of waffle - are short term focused - desperately need our solutions but do not (want to) understand this	- are single focused - have no eye for application - are stuck in theory - cannot write a catchy story - have no sense of urgency - only want to write papers - work with you for the funding but will not really give you a solution

Fig. 5. Preconceptions industry and academia have about each other

- a team of academics was *enthusiastic and committed* to contribute to the industry needs and had *previous experience* with working together with similar companies

We started a discussion round with the involved people to figure out what went wrong during the process that lead us to this situation and distill lessons learned for the next time.

We found out that it was mainly the preconceptions industry and academia have about each other, sometimes without even knowing it. These hindered the communication. Everybody thought we were on the same track, but we were not. Many of the preconceptions we detected are in Fig. 5. While the academics thought the company really needed their tool and because of that were working on the case study, the practitioners actually thought the academics only wanted to try this out for the sake of the project on some industrial system and so they provided us one. They were not really looking ahead to the future where the solution would be really used (before the system would go into maintenance).

Successful innovation transfer is about effective communication and emotional intelligence. Both soft skills should receive more attention in computer science curricula.

7   Summary, Conclusions and Future Work

We have presented a case-based evaluation of the academic TESTAR tool on the industrial SUT Posidonia. In order to do this, we integrated TESTAR into the existing CI pipeline of Prodevelop to automatically test Posidonia when the release cycle required it.

The results of this study are threefold. First, TESTAR has been extended with five new valuable features that will be useful also for other test environments (i.e., CLI invocation, multiple processes, distributed testing, replay mode and log synchronization). Second, it was shown to be a useful complement to the existing testing practices and find failures. Third, we learned some lessons on what went wrong during our seemingly perfect collaboration.

Although the collaboration was not without problems, both parties have shown mutual effort in understanding the cause of the problems with the intent to improve. Both parties are currently researching new ways to collaborate and improve their tools. Prodevelop has started the development of a new web application where modern web frameworks and technologies will be used. We intend to continue collaborating in this project. Having already integrated the TESTAR tool into a similar CI environment, the future work will additionally focus on:

1. Improving the visualization of HTML reports. Prodevelop already gave some initial proposals to improve the structure and aesthetic design of the information that TESTAR tool is currently generating.
2. Improving test oracles. In addition to searching for generic suspicious titles, such as error, exception, warning, and HTML error codes like 404, 40X, etc. at GUI level, we aim to define and analyze the usefulness of preparing TESTAR oracles more focused at the web level.
3. Evaluating the recently developed TESTAR functionality for automatically learning GUI state models capturing all the information found in the SUT.
4. Use these state models to optimize the action selection strategies, to automatically measure the GUI coverage, to find the shortest path to reproduce found failures, or to compare two state models from different versions of the same SUT to automatically detect changes at the GUI level.

Acknowledgment. This work has been funded through the ITEA3 TESTOMAT project (www.testomatproject.eu), the EU H2020 DECODER project (www.decoder-project.eu), the EU H2020 iv4XR project (iv4xr-project.eu) and the ITEA3 IVVES project (ivves.weebly.com).

References

1. Aho, P., Vos, T.: Challenges in automated testing through graphical user interface. In: 2018 IEEE International Conference on Software Testing. Verification and Validation Workshops (ICSTW), pp. 118–121. IEEE Computer Society, Los Alamitos, April 2018
2. Aho, P., Vos, T.E.J., Ahonen, S., Piirainen, T., Moilanen, P., Ricos, F.P.: Continuous piloting of an open source test automation tool in an industrial environment. Jornadas de Ingeniería del Software y Bases de Datos (JISBD) 1–4 (2019)
3. Bauersfeld, S., de Rojas, A., Vos, T.E.J.: Evaluating rogue user testing in industry: an experience report. In: 2014 IEEE Eighth International Conference on Research Challenges in Information Science (RCIS), pp. 1–10, May 2014
4. Bauersfeld, S., Vos, T.E.J., Condori-Fernández, N., Bagnato, A., Brosse, E.: Evaluating the TESTAR tool in an industrial case study. In: 2014 ACM-IEEE International Symposium on Empirical Software Engineering and Measurement, ESEM 2014, Torino, Italy, 18–19 September 2014, p. 4 (2014)
5. Beckman, K., Coulter, N., Khajenoori, S., Mead, N.R.: Collaborations: closing the industry-academia gap. IEEE Softw. 14(6), 49–57 (1997)
6. Coppola, R., Ardito, L., Torchiano, M.: Fragility of layout-based and visual GUI test scripts: an assessment study on a hybrid mobile application. In: Proceedings

of the 10th ACM SIGSOFT International Workshop on Automating TEST Case Design, Selection, and Evaluation, A-TEST 2019, pp. 28–34. ACM, New York (2019)

7. Chahim, H., Duran, M., Vos, T.E.J., Aho, P., Condori Fernandez, N.: Scriptless testing at the GUI level in an industrial setting. In: Dalpiaz, F., Zdravkovic, J., Loucopoulos, P. (eds.) RCIS 2020. LNBIP, vol. 385, pp. 267–284. Springer, Cham (2020). https://doi.org/10.1007/978-3-030-50316-1_16

8. Fowler, M.: Continuous integration (2006). https://www.martinfowler.com/articles/continuousIntegration.html. Accessed 12 Dec 2019

9. Martinez, M., Esparcia, A.I., Rueda, U., Vos, T.E.J., Ortega, C.: Automated localisation testing in industry with test*. In: Wotawa, F., Nica, M., Kushik, N. (eds.) ICTSS 2016. LNCS, vol. 9976, pp. 241–248. Springer, Cham (2016). https://doi.org/10.1007/978-3-319-47443-4_17

10. Meyer, M.: Continuous integration and its tools. Softw. IEEE **31**, 14–16 (2014)

11. O'Connor, R.V., Elger, P., Clarke, P.M.: Continuous software engineering: a microservices architecture perspective. J. Softw.: Evol. Process. **29**(11), e1866 (2017)

12. Rovegard, P., et al.: The success factors powering industry-academia collaboration. IEEE Softw. **29**(02), 67–73 (2012)

13. Sandberg, A., Pareto, L., Arts, T.: Agile collaborative research: action principles for industry-academia collaboration. IEEE Softw. **28**(4), 74–83 (2011)

14. Vos, T.E.J., Kruse, P.M., Condori-Fernández, N., Bauersfeld, S., Wegener, J.: TESTAR: tool support for test automation at the user interface level. Int. J. Inf. Syst. Model. Des. **6**(3), 46–83 (2015)

15. Wieringa, R., Daneva, M.: Six strategies for generalizing software engineering theories. Sci. Comput. Program. 101, 136–152 (2015). Towards general theories of software engineering

A Formal Model of the Kubernetes Container Framework

Gianluca Turin[1,2]($\boxtimes$), Andrea Borgarelli[2]($\boxtimes$), Simone Donetti[2]($\boxtimes$),
Einar Broch Johnsen[1]($\boxtimes$), Silvia Lizeth Tapia Tarifa[1]($\boxtimes$),
and Ferruccio Damiani[2]($\boxtimes$)

[1] Department of Informatics, University of Oslo, Oslo, Norway
{gianlutu,einarj,sltarifa}@ifi.uio.no
[2] Department of Computer Science, University of Turin, Turin, Italy
andrea.borgarelli@edu.unito.it,
{simone.donetti,ferruccio.damiani}@unito.it

Abstract. Loosely-coupled distributed systems organized as collections of so-called cloud-native microservices are able to adapt to traffic in very fine-grained and flexible ways. For this purpose, the cloud-native microservices exploit containerization and container management systems such as Kubernetes. This paper presents a formal model of resource consumption and scaling for containerized microservices deployed and managed by Kubernetes. Our aim is that the model, developed in Real-Time ABS, can be used as a framework to explore the behavior of deployed systems under various configurations at design time—before the systems are actually deployed. We further present initial results comparing the observed behavior of instances of our modeling framework to corresponding observations of real systems. These preliminary results suggest that the modeling framework can provide a satisfactory accuracy with respect to the behavior of distributed microservices managed by Kubernetes.

1 Introduction

Software that was considered scalable yesterday, may now be perceived as inflexible and overly entangled compared to the suites of so-called microservices that are today widely used [4]. Microservices are loosely coupled, independently deployed, cloud-native small services [26]. Kubernetes [16] is a framework to resiliently run distributed systems built from such microservices; it takes care of scaling and failover for the application, provides deployment patterns, service discovery, load balancing and other development-related functionalities.

The underlying technology for orchestrating microservices with Kubernetes, is containerization [11]. Containers encapsulate a microservice environment, abstracting details of machines and operating systems from the application

Supported by the Research Council of Norway through the project *ADAPt: Exploiting Abstract Data-Access Patterns for Better Data Locality in Parallel Processing* (www.mn.uio.no/ifi/english/research/projects/adapt/).

T. Margaria and B. Steffen (Eds.): ISoLA 2020, LNCS 12476, pp. 558–577, 2020.
https://doi.org/10.1007/978-3-030-61362-4_32

developer and the deployment infrastructure. Well-designed containers and container images are scoped to a single microservice, such that managing microservices means managing containers rather than machines. Thus, containerization enables a shift from machine-oriented to application-oriented orchestration of a system's deployment by managing containers to minimize the downtime for any deployed microservice, even when the system is flooded with requests.

In this paper, we develop a formal model of resource consumption and scaling for containerized microservices deployed and managed by Kubernetes. Although this model abstracts from many aspects of Kubernetes (e.g., self-healing, rollouts, rollbacks, and storage orchestration), it already allows system deployment under several configurations to be explored at the modeling level, *before the system is actually deployed.* Our objective with this work is to develop a modeling framework which can help the developer in finding a deployment strategy for a microservice-based system which meets the system's performance requirements. We aim to facilitate the comparison of different deployment strategies on a highly configurable and executable model. Although not addressed in this paper, the formal model can also be used to verify liveness and safety properties for workflows deployed as microservices with Kubernetes.

The Kubernetes model has been developed using Real-Time ABS [6,22], a formal executable modeling language targeting distributed and cloud-based systems. We present a preliminary validation of our work by comparing results obtained with the Kubernetes model to observations of a real system running on HPC4AI [3], a cluster for deploying high-performance applications. The results of this comparison suggest that the model-based analysis of an application's deployment complies with the observed performance of its actual deployment.

The main contributions of this paper can be summarized as follows:

- **Formalization:** We develop a succinct formal executable model of Kubernetes, a state-of-the-art management framework for monitoring resources consumption and scalability of microservices;
- **Configurable modeling framework:** The developed Kubernetes model can be configured to different client workloads and to different microservices running in parallel and affecting each others performance. By means of simulations, system administrators can easily compare how different parameter configurations affect the performance of their deployed microservices at the modeling level;
- **Evaluation:** The proposed modeling framework is validated by comparing an instance of the framework, modeling a real system deployed using Kubernetes, to the modeled system. We consider several scenarios in which different workloads will trigger the need for automatic autoscaling. The results suggest that our modeling framework can provide a satisfactory accuracy with respect to the behavior of real systems.

Paper Overview. Section 2 introduces microservices, Kubernetes and Real-Time ABS. Section 3 presents the developed Kubernetes model. Section 4 discusses how the model was validated. Section 5 surveys related work and Sect. 6 concludes the paper.

2   Background

2.1   Microservices, Containers and Their Management via Kubernetes

Microservices [26] are small basic services which are easy to adapt to distributed hardware. They stem from service-oriented architectures (SOA) [14] and service-oriented computing (SOC) [17]. Microservices are so-called *cloud native*; i.e., they are built to run scalable applications on cloud infrastructure. An application consists of a collection of loosely coupled microservices. This decoupling makes them easier to develop, deploy, scale, monitor and maintain in isolation. Microservice architectures facilitate scalability since new instances of the same microservice can be launched to split the workload locally, without scaling the overall service.

Containers encapsulate execution environments for microservices, abstracting from details of physical and virtual machines and operating systems from the application developer and the deployment infrastructure. Containers have been proposed instead of heavy VMs, and raise the level of abstraction from running a service on virtual hardware to running it using *logical resources*. Containers keep the advantages of virtualization such as modularity, but the unit of deployment is the container and not a full VM, which opens for better utilization of resources. Containers offer better scalability and maintainability because they can be added or updated easily, such that resources can be shared in clusters to which containers can be added or removed on-demand.

By encapsulating microservices in containers, the services can be monitored with respect to service performance and resource utilization. In contrast to VMs, which run all components, including an operating system on top of virtualized hardware, containers are *lightweight* but still keep their own filesystem, CPU, memory, and process space similar to a VM. However, they are decoupled from the underlying infrastructure, and additional containers can be created at execution time rather than only at deployment time. They are also *portable* across clouds and OS distributions [15], therefore they require much less space and have faster booting time.

Kubernetes is an open-source system[1] for managing containerized applications across multiple hosts. It provides basic mechanisms for deployment, maintenance, and scaling of applications. Figure 1 depicts a logical representation of a Kubernetes instance in a public or private cloud. Among all the components implementing its functionalities, in the rest of this section, we briefly introduce the main Kubernetes components related to resource management, load balancing and autoscaling[2] (for further details, see [16]).

Pods are the basic scheduling unit in Kubernetes. They are high-level abstractions for groups of containerized components. A pod consists of one or more containers that are guaranteed to be co-located on the host machine and

---

[1] https://github.com/kubernetes/kubernetes/.
[2] https://kubernetes.io/docs/concepts/.

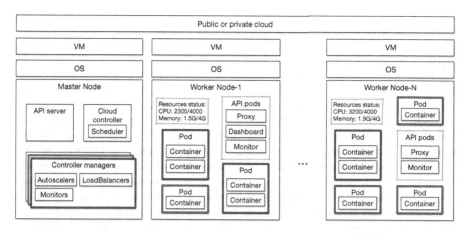

Fig. 1. A logical representation of Kubernetes components in a generic cloud infrastructure. The colors mark services deployed on the cluster, their controller managers reside on the master and their pods are distributed among the workers. (Color figure online)

can share resources. A pod is deployed according to its resource requirements and has its own specified resource limits. For two or more pods to be deployed in the same node, the sum of the minimum amounts of resources required for the pods needs to be available in the node. All pods have unique IP address, which allows applications to use ports without the risk of conflict. Within the pod, containers can reference each other directly, but a container in one pod cannot address a container in another pod without passing through a reference to a service; the service then holds a reference to the target pod at the specific pod IP address. The IP addresses of pods are ephemeral; i.e., they are reassigned on pod creation and system boot.

Services represent components that act as basic internal load balancers and ambassadors for pods. A service groups together a logical collection of pods that perform the same function and presents them as a single entity. This allows the Kubernetes framework to deploy a service that can keep track of and route to all the back-end containers of a particular type. Internal consumers only need to know about the stable endpoint provided by the service. Meanwhile, the service abstraction enables the scaling or replacing of back-end work units as necessary. The IP address of a service remains stable regardless of changes to the pods to which it routes requests. By deploying a service, the associated pods gain discoverability, which simplifies container designs. Whenever access to one or more pods needs to be provided to another application or to external consumers, a service can be configured. Although services, by default, are only available using an internally routable IP address, they can be made available outside of the cluster.

Autoscalers are responsible for ensuring that the number of pods deployed in the cluster matches the number of pods in its configuration. There is one autoscaler for each service, managing a group of identical, replicated pods which are created from pod templates and can be horizontally scaled. Autoscalers are processes that refer to a pod template and control parameters to scale identical replicas of a pod horizontally, i.e. by increasing or decreasing the number of running copies. Thus, autoscalers facilitate load distribution and increase availability natively within Kubernetes.

Nodes in a cluster are each given a role (master or worker) within the Kubernetes ecosystem. One node functions as the master node, it implements a server that acts as a gateway and controller for the cluster by exposing an API for developers and external traffic. It carries out scheduling, and orchestrates communication between other components. The master node acts as the primary point of contact with the cluster and is responsible for most of the centralized logic that Kubernetes provides. The workers host pods and form the larger part of a Kubernetes cluster. The worker nodes have explicit resource capabilities, which are known by the system. These are given as a set of labels attached to a worker node to specify its version, status and particular features.

Scheduler is in charge of assigning pods to specific nodes in the cluster. The scheduler matches the operating requirements of a pod's workload to the resources that are available in the current infrastructure environment, and places pods on appropriate nodes. The scheduler is responsible for monitoring the available capacity on each node to make sure that workloads are not scheduled in excess of the available resources. The scheduler needs to know the total capacity of each node as well as the resources already allocated to existing workloads on the nodes.

2.2 Real-Time ABS

The *abstract behavioral specification* language (ABS)[3] is an actor-based, object-oriented modeling language targeting concurrent and distributed systems and supports the design, verification, and execution of such systems [18]. ABS has a Java-like syntax and a concurrency model, based on active objects, which decouples communication and synchronization using asynchronous method calls, futures and cooperative scheduling [7]. ABS is an open-source research project.[4]

The functional layer of ABS is used to model computations on the internal data of objects. It allows designers to abstract from the implementation details of imperative data structures at an early stage in the software design. The functional layer combines parametric algebraic data types (ADTs) and a simple functional language with case distinction and pattern matching. ABS includes a library with predefined datatypes such as Bool, Int, String, Rat, Float, Unit, etc. It also has parametric datatypes such as lists, sets and maps. All other types and functions are user-defined.

The imperative layer of ABS allows designers to express communication and synchronization between active objects. In the imperative layer, threads are

---

encapsulated within COGs [18, 28] (concurrent objects groups). Threads are created automatically at reception of a method call and terminated after the execution of the method call is finished. ABS combines active (with a run method which is automatically activated) and reactive behavior of objects by means of cooperative scheduling: Inside COGs threads may suspend at explicitly defined scheduling points, after which control may be transferred to another thread. Suspension allows other pending threads to be activated. The suspending thread does not signal any other particular thread, instead the selection of the next thread to be executed is left to the scheduler. Between these scheduling points, only one thread is active inside a COG, which means that race conditions are avoided.

Real-Time ABS [6] extends ABS with support for the modeling and manipulation of dense time. This extension allows the logical execution time to be represented inside methods. The local passage of time is expressed in terms of **duration** statements (which constrain time advance, similar to guards in, e.g., UPPAAL [23] and Real-Time Maude [27]). To express dense time, we consider the two types Time and Duration Real-Time ABS provides. Time values capture points in time as reflected on a global clock during execution. In contrast, finite durations reflect the passage of time as local timers over time intervals.

ABS is supported by a range of analysis tools (see, e.g., [1]); for the analyses in this paper, we are using the simulation tool which generates Erlang code.

3   A Kubernetes Model in Real Time ABS

In this section, we present the Real-Time ABS model of Kubernetes, with a focus on resource management and autoscaling, by modeling the Kubernetes components involved in the deployment of a service. We aim for the model to be *executable* and to faithfully *reproduce* the behavior of Kubernetes. The precision of this model determines the predictive capabilities of the simulations of real world scenarios.

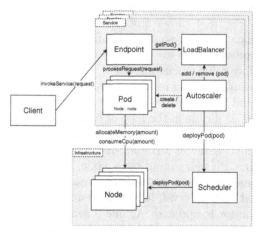

Figure 2 shows the structure of a modelled cluster. A service is composed from its pods, an endpoint, a load balancer and an autoscaler. Clients invoke the service by sending a request to the endpoint which gets a

Fig. 2. The architecture of the modeled Kubernetes cluster

selected pod using the load balancer. A pod is deployed on a node and consumes its resources while processing a request. The scheduler manages the number of pods for the service and calls the autoscaler to deploy new pods. In the remainder of this section, we discuss some selected aspects of this model.[5]

3.1 Modeling of Pods

A service is carried out by its pods, for simplicity in the proposed model pods are assumed to consist of a single container (a pod with many containers would correspond to a pod running one container which consumes the sum of their consumed resources). They are deployed onto nodes whose resources are consumed while processing requests.

Figure 3 shows the model of a pod using the PodObject class: a PodObject is instantiated by passing the configuration parameters which are serviceName, id, compUnitSize, cpuRequest, cpuLimit, monitor (used by the method processRequest in Fig. 4) and insufficientMemCooldown. After the underlying node is set by the setNode method, the refreshAvailableCpu cycle starts. The PodObject class has a custom scheduler which executes refreshAvailableCpu as the first method of every time interval. Note that the auxiliary function reset_availCpu_scheduler, which is set as custom scheduler of the COG by the expression inside square brackets (Fig. 3 Line 1), ensures that the scheduler gives priority to the execution of method refreshAvailableCpu and guarantees that every consumed CPU unit is counted in the right time interval. If availableCpu falls to zero the pod has reached its cpuLimit meaning no more CPU will be consumed within that time interval. The allocateMemory and releaseMemory methods manage memory allocation and deallocation on the Node, they are both called in the processRequest method. If the Node's free memory is not sufficient, the allocateMemory method waits for insufficientMemCooldown time before retrying.

Figure 4 shows processRequest method (called by clients) in a PodObject, which models resource consumption while processing a request. In our model, a Request is modeled as a pair of CPU and memory costs. The method first stores information about the CPU and memory cost, a time stamp started, for the calling time of a request, and a deadline for the request to be processed. At lines 2 and 3 the required memory is allocated, the request cost is then consumed one step at a time in the loop of lines 6–17. The size of the step is compUnitSize and is set in the pod configuration, which determines the amount of CPU the pod can consume in a round, having the same compUnitSize for every pod achieves fair CPU scheduling on a node. If the Node runs out of CPU resources, the consumption is suspended (consumeCpu sets the variable blocked to True) for that time interval, it is then resumed in the next time interval after the pod's monitor is updated. At line 9 availableCpu is checked, if it is equal to zero the pod limit is reached and no more cost is consumed within that time interval. Once the request cost is entirely consumed, at line 19 the previously allocated memory is released and at line 21 the total time spent in the process is computed subtracting started to the actual time. Line 22 shows how the spentTime is then compared to the deadline This approximates the quality of service related to the

---

[5] The full model is available at https://doi.org/10.5281/zenodo.3975006.

```
1   [Scheduler: reset_availCpu_scheduler(queue)] class PodObject(String serviceName, Int id,
2   Rat compUnitSize, Rat cpuRequest, Rat cpuLimit, ResourcesMonitor monitor,
3   Rat insufficientMemCooldown) implements Pod {
4      Bool blocked = False; Node node = null; Rat availableCpu = 0;
5
6      Unit setNode(Node n){ this.node = n; this!refreshAvailableCpu(); }
7
8      Unit refreshAvailableCpu(){
9        this.availableCpu = cpuLimit; // sets max available CPU for this time interval
10       this.blocked = False;
11       await duration(1,1);
12       this!refreshAvailableCpu();}
13
14     Bool processRequest(Request request, Time started, Duration deadline){ ... }
15
16     Rat allocateMemory(Rat requiredMemory){
17       Bool memoryAllocated = False;
18       Rat givenMemory = 0;
19
20       while (!memoryAllocated){
21         givenMemory = await node!allocateMemory(requiredMemory);
22         if (givenMemory > 0){ memoryAllocated = True; }
23         else {await duration(insufficientMemCooldown,insufficientMemCooldown);}}
24       return givenMemory;}
25
26     Rat releaseMemory(Rat amount){ Rat v = await node!releaseMemory(amount); return v;}
27   ...}
```

Fig. 3. PodObject class

```
1   Bool processRequest(Request request, Time started, Duration deadline) {
2     Rat cost = requestCost(request); Rat requiredMemory = memory(request);
3     this.allocateMemory(requiredMemory); // memory allocation
4     monitor!consumedMemoryUpdate(requiredMemory);
5
6     while (cost > 0){
7       ...
8       if (cost >= compUnitSize){
9         await this.availableCpu > 0; // check on the pod limit
10        await node!consumeCpu(compUnitSize,this); // consume node CPU
11        await !this.blocked; // refresh sync
12        availableCpu = availableCpu − compUnitSize;
13        monitor!consumeCpu(compUnitSize);
14        cost = cost − compUnitSize; // cost decreases
15      } else if (cost > 0){ ... } // consume remaining cost
16      ... suspend;}
17
18    this.releaseMemory(requiredMemory); // memory release
19    monitor!consumedMemoryUpdate(−requiredMemory);
20    Rat spentTime = timeDifference(now(),started); // deadline check
21    Bool success = (spentTime <= durationValue(deadline));
22    return success; }
```

Fig. 4. Pod processRequest method

```
1   interface ServiceLoadBalancer{
2     Pod getPod();
3     Unit addPod(Pod p, ResourcesMonitor rm);
4     Unit removePod(Pod p);
5     List⟨Pair⟨Pod,ResourcesMonitor⟩⟩ getPods();
6     ServiceState getConsumptions(); // Total service consumption
7     List⟨PodState⟩ getPodsConsumptions();}
```

Fig. 5. ServiceLoadBalancer interface

response time, separating served requests between successes and failures. The passing of time is a consequence of the limited amount of available CPU on a node in every time interval. As explained in Sect. 2.2, the value of time during the model execution is managed by the functions provided by Real-Time ABS.

3.2 Modeling of Services

A service is invoked through its endpoint which provides the service reference for the clients. As explained in Sec. 2.1, every service has its own load balancer that chooses the pod to which the endpoint forwards the request. The load balancer's policy for work distribution between all the pods of the service is round robin. Figure 5 shows the ServiceLoadBalancer interface of our model: getPod returns the pod for forwarding a request, addPod and removePods add and remove pods from the pods of the service, getPods returns the service's available pods and getConsumptions and getPodConsumptions return the total consumption and per pod consumption values in the current time interval.

Like in a real Kubernetes installation, a service in our model is configurable. Several parameters are passed on service instantiation as PodConfig and ServiceConfig. PodConfig specifies the CPU request and limit for the pods, the cool-down time for insufficient memory and the computation unit size. The memory cool-down is the time awaited before retrying in case there's not enough free memory on the node. The computation unit size is the amount of cost computed every time the pod is given the CPU. For example, if CompUnitSize for Service A is 1 and for Service B is 2, the pods of Service B will execute twice the cost of the pods of Service A every time they are scheduled. This allows control over the CPU time scheduling, setting all unit sizes to the same amount will provide a fair scheduling, while setting different values allows to set different priorities for the pods. ServiceConfig specifies the initial number of pods, the minimum and maximum number of pods for the service and the configuration of the autoscaler.

3.3 Modeling of Autoscalers

Every service in our model has also its own Autoscaler which creates and deletes pods. On service initialization it creates the specified starting number of pods and then periodically checks the average load on the pods. In case the given thresholds for scaling are reached, it creates or deletes pods accordingly. After creating a pod the Autoscaler calls the Scheduler to deploy it on a node. Figure 6 shows the resize method of the Autoscaler, it fetches the average pod CPU consumption ratio in the current time interval, waits for the next time interval to apply the scaling, then starts over. The Autoscaler has its own configuration: cycle period gives the frequency of resize execution, the thresholds for scaling (percentages of requested CPU) up and down are modeled by downscaleThreshold and upscaleThreshold and finally, downscalePeriod specifies how long a pod set has to stay idle before shrinking. While scaling up is immediate as soon as the threshold is hit, for scaling down the load is required to stay below the threshold for a configurable period of time before any pod is deleted.

```
1    Unit resize(){
2      ServiceState ss = await lb!getConsumptions(); // get service consumption
3      Rat serviceRatio = cpuRatio(ss);
4
5      if (serviceRatio < downscaleThreshold){ // updates the cumulative counter
6        underDsThresholdCounter = underDsThresholdCounter + 1;
7      } else { // reset it
8        underDsThresholdCounter = 0;}
9      await duration(cycle, cycle); // scale in the successive time interval
10     if (serviceRatio >= upscaleThreshold && nPods < maxPods){
11       ... // scale up}
12     if (underDsThresholdCounter >= downscalePeriod && nPods > minPods){
13       ... // scale down}
14     this!resize();}
```

Fig. 6. ServiceAutoscaler resize method

3.4 Modeling of Nodes

The Kubernetes master node is not explicitly modeled, its functionalities are implemented in the model logic, while Node models the Kubernetes worker node, which has a given amount of resources (CPU and memory) to be consumed by its running pods. CPU and memory capacities for a node are specified upon node creation:

- CPU is refreshed every time interval, the total amount of computed costs on a node in the time interval cannot exceed the node's CPU capacity.
- Memory is time independent, it can be decreased and restored, it is decreased when a pod starts the processing of a request and allocates memory cost on the node memory. If there is enough free memory then it is decreased for the whole computation time and the allocated amount is restored on request completion. In case the free memory is insufficient, the request remains pending until enough memory is available.

The available resources of the node are statically reserved when a pod is scheduled. The amount of CPU required by the pod serves as discriminant for the scheduler to find a suitable node. (This easily extends to matching over multiple resource capabilities using the aforementioned label mechanism, which we have left for future work.) Hence a node can be fully occupied while actually idle, since there can be many pods deployed on it, but none is receiving requests.

3.5 Modeling of Scheduler

The Scheduler deploys pods on nodes. Figure 7 shows the deployPod method of the Scheduler: it checks the pod CPU request and compares it to the available CPU in the least busy node. If there is enough available CPU, the pod is scheduled on that node, otherwise it remains pending, to be scheduled in another time interval.

```
1   Node deployPod(Pod p, ResourcesMonitor rm){
2       Bool deployed = False;
3       Rat requestedCpu = await rm!getCpuRequest();
4       Node result = null;
5
6       while (!deployed){
7           result = head(activeNodes);
8           Rat maxCpu = await result!getAvailableCpu(); // total cpu − total requested CPU
9           List⟨Node⟩ nodesToCheck = tail(activeNodes);
10          foreach ( n in nodesToCheck){ ... // get the node with maximum available CPU}
11          if (maxCpu >= requestedCpu){await result!addPod(p,rm); deployed = True;}
12          else{await duration(1,1);} }
13      return result;}
```

Fig. 7. Scheduler deployPod method

4   Validating the Model

We report on initial experiments to assess the precision of our model with respect to real microservices managed by Kubernetes.

4.1   Experimental Setup

We set up experiments in which we compare two simple scenarios of microservices running on a cluster to simulations in our model.

HPC4AI. The experiments have been performed on the HPC4AI infrastructure. HPC4AI [3] is a centre on High-Performance Computing for Artificial Intelligence at the University of Turin and the Polytechnic University of Turin, which offers on-demand provisioning of AI and BDA cloud services to a heterogeneous industrial community of Small-Medium Enterprises (SMEs) active in many different sectors and leaning towards Industry 4.0. The centre aims at an increasingly connected ecosystem of devices that produce digital data of increasing variety, volume, speed and volatility. To fully exploit its potential, the next generation of AI applications must embrace distributed High-Performance Computing (HPC) techniques and platforms, where computing and data management capabilities of distributed HPC are readily and easily accessible on-demand to data scientists, who are more used to perform their work locally on interactive platforms. The centre is currently looking at using containerized microservices for this purpose. The preliminary results of this paper contribute towards a modeling framework to equip HPC4AI with deployment decisions for this complex setup.

Simulations. We replicated two simple scenarios in the model, each simulating the execution of a stress test on a microservice system deployed on the HPC4AI cluster. The stress tests have been created with Apache Jmeter, a tool generating traffic to test web services. To reproduce the same circumstances, we modeled the cluster infrastructure and measured the load generated during the stress test for any type of service request. To this end, we represented stress tests as waves of requests (see Figs. 8a and 10c). To reproduce the load of a wave, the model instantiates a certain number of clients; by duplicating the number it will simulate twice the load of the original wave.

We consider single workload and mixed workload scenarios. In the *single workload scenario* the flow of requests is generated by three succeeding groups of threads targeting the same service and running at different speed, such that the central wave, with the highest load (see Fig. 8a) delivers twice the number of requests than the first and the third. Simulating complicated stress tests requires more measurements to be taken. In the *mixed workload scenario* we therefore considered two services sharing the available resources and affecting each others performance. In this setting, each service is targeted by a thread group generating a certain load for the service.

To provide a baseline for the resource consumption of the model, we tuned the model by stressing each service in isolation. After that, it is possible to simulate mixed workloads. To generate a group of clients that reproduces a certain load in the model, we needed to find the balance between the number and the cost of the requests sent at any step. Here we decide also on the granularity of the model: a large set of requests in the real system will be simulated in the model with few costly ones, as done with batch processing. This will keep the granularity of the simulations coarse, instead of fine-grained with many cheap requests, and will allow us to run big workloads in the model in a short amount of time.

The duration of a time interval in the model is decided during the model calibration, where the size of the waves in the requests determines the length of the stress test on the cluster, and the granularity of the model the number of time intervals of the simulation.

Experiments. We set up two experiments with a time interval corresponding to 2 s.

Experiment 1. The purpose of Experiment 1 is to check the precision of the modeling framework. We do this by running a single service stress test 10 min long, in order to measure the model's ability to reproduce Kubernetes autoscaling while the service is processing requests and then compare the load experienced on the cluster with the one seen in the simulation. In more detail, the cluster setting was one service deployed and three nodes available with 4000 millicores of CPU capacity each.

We start with one pod requiring 1000 millicores of CPU and limited to 2500. The autoscaling threshold was set to 80% of the required CPU busy and the downscale time was 300 s of inactivity. The load on the cluster has been generated with Jmeter:[6] a group of 50 threads send requests with a given timing for a three minutes, flooding the system with a wave. Then for the next three minutes they generate requests at twice the speed (the second wave) before sending the final requests again at their initial speed (see Fig. 8a). This stress test

---

[6] https://jmeter.apache.org/.

has been replicated in the model by bulking clients up to reach the first wave load, then twice that number of clients has been used to flood during the second wave, and finally return to the initial amount of request in the third wave (see Fig. 8c), to obtain the same total load in the simulation and real Kubernetes deployment. The ABS code emulating the clients can be found in the repository of the simulator along with the Jmeter stress test descriptor.[7]

Experiment 2. The purpose of Experiment 2 is to test the prediction ability of the modeling framework. Namely, given the same load of requests of two services to the model and the real system, can we predict the scaling behavior of the real system? We run a second stress test 13 min long in a scenario with the two services, where each service goes through variable load, so that we can simulate scheduling and autoscaling in a resource-intensive scenario under different configurations. The first service is the same as in Experiment 1 and configured similarly; the second service has a different profile of resource consumption, its pods require 1000 millicores of CPU and limited to 2500, but have an upscale threshold of 95% and a downscale time of 300 s. The stress test load can be divided into four phases and is different for both services: one uses the same thread group as the first simulation, but inverting the load of the three waves: it starts with a high load of requests, then reduces the load to half and finally increases it again to the double. The load on the second service has been calibrated separately, it starts low, turns high, then drops down again before finishing with a demand that is much higher than the previous high traffic wave.

4.2 Results of the Experiments

Experiment 1. Figure 8 reports on the results of the first experiment. The load in the real system, shown in Fig. 8a, triggers the scaling of pods, shown in Fig. 8b. The approximated load in the model, shown in Fig. 8c, triggers the scaling of pods, shown in Fig. 8d. The graphs suggest that the model is properly calibrated and can reproduce the scalability scenario with reasonable accuracy.

Experiment 2. The results of the second experiment are shown in Figs. 10, 11 and 12. In this case we first reproduced the load in the Kubernetes model, based on the measurements of the separate loads of the two services, then we executed the model with the two services, potentially affecting each others performance, and therefore affecting also the scalability of the services. Figure 10 shows the result of this calibration.

We then tested *different* configurations of the model before doing the corresponding runs on the real cluster. This carried two main benefits: it lowered the resources needed to test several configurations, and it emulated a real time interval with few seconds of computation time.

---

[7] https://github.com/giaku/abs-k8s-model.

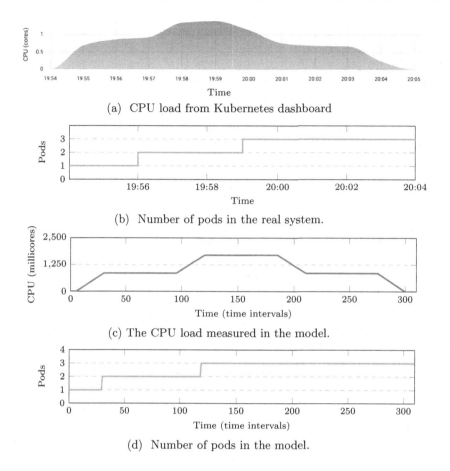

(a) CPU load from Kubernetes dashboard

(b) Number of pods in the real system.

(c) The CPU load measured in the model.

(d) Number of pods in the model.

Fig. 8. The results of the first experiment.

We considered two differ-ent configurations, changing the upscale threshold for the services. In the first configuration, shown in Fig. 11, we obtained similar graphs for the model and for the real system. The yellow line represents the number of pods for the

	Service 1	Service 2
Calibration	80%	95%
Configuration 1	95%	80%
Configuration 2	95%	95%

Fig. 9. Upscale thresholds for Experiment 2.

first service, which stayed beneath 2 as a result of having a 95% scaling threshold, the blue line represents the second service, which raised up to six with an upscale threshold of 80%. In the second configuration, shown in Fig. 12, we tested 95% as the threshold for the second service as well, its number of pod grew at most at 5 (blue line) both in the simulator and on the real cluster. Figure 9 summarizes the different configurations.

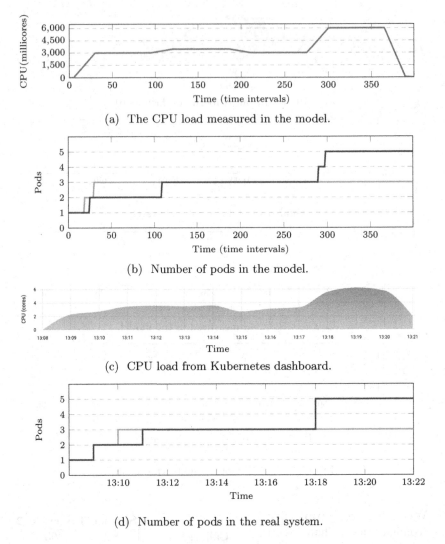

(a) The CPU load measured in the model.

(b) Number of pods in the model.

(c) CPU load from Kubernetes dashboard.

(d) Number of pods in the real system.

Fig. 10. Calibration for the mixed workload scenario of the second experiment. (Color figure online)

5   Related Work

Cloud-Based Models in ABS. Whereas there are many cloud modeling languages (see, e.g., [5]), this paper is part of a line of work on formal modeling of virtualized systems in ABS. The perspective on virtualized systems we have taken, is to focus on resource provisioning and quality-of-service, which typically affects the timing behavior of systems on the cloud. The underlying technical idea is to introduce a separation of concerns between resource-needs for different computational tasks, and resource-provisioning in the infrastructure [20–22]. This approach has been

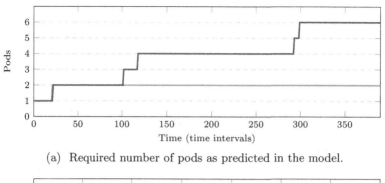

(a) Required number of pods as predicted in the model.

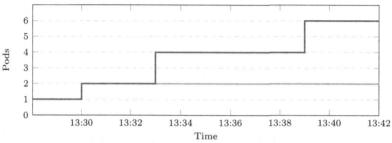

(b) Used number of pods as observed on the real system.

Fig. 11. Results for the first configuration, comparing the predicted need for pods in the model the observed use of pods on the real cluster. (Color figure online)

successfully applied to different kinds of virtualization infrastructure, including Amazon AWS [19], Hadoop YARN [25] and Hadoop Spark Streaming [24]. The concurrency model of ABS, based on actors, has also been used for verification to industrial case studies in a DevOps setting [1] and for parallel cost analysis [2], a novel static analysis method related to parallelism and maximal span. The formal model of Kubernetes presented in this paper differs from previous work in its *nested* virtualization; i.e., the containerization of microservices lead to two levels of book-keeping in the resource-sensitive architecture, corresponding to the pods ond nodes of the Kubernetes framework. Furthermore, the notion of indirection due to the service-concept and the auto-scaling groups add complexity compared to previous work.

Optimization of Microservice Management. It has been shown that deployment management can be formalized as finite state machines, such as the Aeolus [13] and TOSCA-compliant deployment models [10], which can be adapted to formally reason about the static deployment of microservices; i.e., to express component resilience and static links between components. For example, the static deployment of microservices can be encoded as a constraint problem [9]. This work, which is based on Aeolus, takes an ABS model as its starting point. In contrast to our work, the authors are not restricted to modelling and simulation but are able to decide on optimal deployment. However, the optimization can

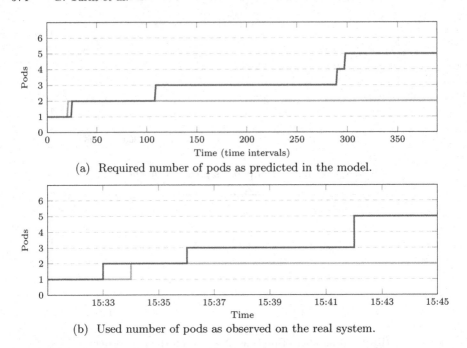

(a) Required number of pods as predicted in the model.

(b) Used number of pods as observed on the real system.

Fig. 12. Results for the second configuration, comparing the predicted need for pods in the model the observed use of pods on the real cluster.

only handle very limited forms of reconfiguration, and does not address dynamic scaling as modelled in our work.

Testing Environments for Cloud-Based Services. In order to perform tests on the real Kubernetes platform, we looked for a tool that allowed to simulate multiple requests in parallel to the service and to simulate behavior that varies over time. After a brief investigation about which tools are available on the market (eg: Apache JMeter[8], Locust[9], Tsung[10], etc.) we decided to use Apache JMeter since it is an open-source tool, it is multiplatform, multiprotocol, it comes with a simple GUI for configuration and to run the simulation from a shell, it presents the simulation results in textual or graphical format. Apache JMeter is used both by companies and in the scientific field to emulate traffic to network services [8,12].

The most significant KPIs that we are looking for in order to evaluate the service performance are the response time over time (which gives us an indication about the quality of the offered service) and the number of requests per second (to have an evaluation about the load our service undergoes).

---

[8] https://jmeter.apache.org/.
[9] https://locust.io/.
[10] http://tsung.erlang-projects.org/.

6   Conclusion and Future Work

In this paper, we present a formal model of resource consumption and scaling for containerized microservices deployed and managed by Kubernetes. The model focuses on how the deployment of such systems can behave under various configurations to be explored at design time and abstract from other aspects of Kubernetes such self-healing, rollouts, rollbacks, and storage orchestration. This preliminary model and results contribute towards the development of a modeling framework which can help developers in finding a deployment strategy for a microservice-based system which meets the system's performance requirements. The model is implemented in Real-Time ABS, it can be configured with different client workloads and different microservices running in parallel and affecting each others performance. The presented model can be used to explore different configurations for loosely coupled microservices at design time.

In future work, we plan to extend the model with aspects related to resiliency and reconfiguration of distributed and decoupled system, adding possible failures, volumes and stateful Kubernetes components. In particular, we plan to use the resulting model to assess quality-of-service aspects of different configuration choices by, e.g., predicting their response time and resource consumption. We also plan to trace data movement within the cluster and predict how this may affect the performance. We plan to validate such models using workloads collected from hours, weeks or months of running real systems. We further plan to investigate how such resiliency and reconfiguration can affect data access times and patterns.

References

1. Albert, E., et al.: Formal modeling and analysis of resource management for cloud architectures: an industrial case study using real-time ABS. Serv. Orient. Comput. Appl. **8**(4), 323–339 (2013). https://doi.org/10.1007/s11761-013-0148-0
2. Albert, E., Correas, J., Johnsen, E.B., Pun, K.I., Román-Díez, G.: Parallel cost analysis. ACM Trans. Comput. Logic **19**(4), 31:1–31:37 (2018). https://doi.org/10.1145/3274278
3. Aldinucci, M., et al.: HPC4AI: an AI-on-demand federated platform endeavour. In: Proceedings of 15th International Conference on Computing Frontiers (CF 2018), pp. 279–286. ACM (2018). https://doi.org/10.1145/3203217.3205340
4. Balalaie, A., Heydarnoori, A., Jamshidi, P.: Microservices architecture enables DevOps: migration to a cloud-native architecture. IEEE Softw. **33**(3), 42–52 (2016). https://doi.org/10.1109/MS.2016.64
5. Bergmayr, A., et al.: A systematic review of cloud modeling languages. ACM Comput. Surv. **51**(1), 22:1–22:38 (2018). https://doi.org/10.1145/3150227
6. Bjørk, J., de Boer, F.S., Johnsen, E.B., Schlatte, R., Tapia Tarifa, S.L.: User-defined schedulers for real-time concurrent objects. Innov. Syst. Softw. Eng. **9**(1), 29–43 (2013). https://doi.org/10.1007/s11334-012-0184-5
7. de Boer, F.S., et al.: A survey of active object languages. ACM Comput. Surv. **50**(5), 76:1–76:39 (2017). https://doi.org/10.1145/3122848

8. Brady, J.F., Gunther, N.J.: How to emulate web traffic using standard load testing tools. CoRR abs/1607.05356 (2016). http://arxiv.org/abs/1607.05356

9. Bravetti, M., Giallorenzo, S., Mauro, J., Talevi, I., Zavattaro, G.: Optimal and automated deployment for microservices. In: Hähnle, R., van der Aalst, W. (eds.) FASE 2019. LNCS, vol. 11424, pp. 351–368. Springer, Cham (2019). https://doi.org/10.1007/978-3-030-16722-6_21

10. Brogi, A., Canciani, A., Soldani, J.: Modelling and analysing cloud application management. In: Dustdar, S., Leymann, F., Villari, M. (eds.) ESOCC 2015. LNCS, vol. 9306, pp. 19–33. Springer, Cham (2015). https://doi.org/10.1007/978-3-319-24072-5_2

11. Burns, B., Grant, B., Oppenheimer, D., Brewer, E., Wilkes, J.: Borg, Omega, and Kubernetes. Queue 14(1), 70–93 (2016). https://doi.org/10.1145/2898442.2898444

12. Curiel, M., Pont, A.: Workload generators for web-based systems: characteristics, current status, and challenges. IEEE Commun. Surv. Tutorials 20(2), 1526–1546 (2018). https://doi.org/10.1109/COMST.2018.2798641

13. Di Cosmo, R., Mauro, J., Zacchiroli, S., Zavattaro, G.: Aeolus: a component model for the cloud. Inf. Comput. 239, 100–121 (2014). https://doi.org/10.1016/j.ic.2014.11.002

14. Erl, T.: Service-Oriented Architecture: Concepts, Technology, and Design. Prentice Hall, Upper Saddle River (2005)

15. Fazio, M., Celesti, A., Ranjan, R., Liu, C., Chen, L., Villari, M.: Open issues in scheduling microservices in the cloud. IEEE Cloud Comput. 3(5), 81–88 (2016). https://doi.org/10.1109/MCC.2016.112

16. Hightower, K., Burns, B., Beda, J.: Kubernetes: Up and Running Dive into the Future of Infrastructure. O'Reilly, Newton (2017)

17. Huhns, M.N., Singh, M.P.: Service-oriented computing: key concepts and principles. IEEE Internet Comput. 9(1), 75–81 (2005). https://doi.org/10.1109/MIC.2005.21

18. Johnsen, E.B., Hähnle, R., Schäfer, J., Schlatte, R., Steffen, M.: ABS: a core language for abstract behavioral specification. In: Aichernig, B.K., de Boer, F.S., Bonsangue, M.M. (eds.) FMCO 2010. LNCS, vol. 6957, pp. 142–164. Springer, Heidelberg (2011). https://doi.org/10.1007/978-3-642-25271-6_8

19. Johnsen, E.B., Lin, J.-C., Yu, I.C.: Comparing AWS deployments using model-based predictions. In: Margaria, T., Steffen, B. (eds.) ISoLA 2016. LNCS, vol. 9953, pp. 482–496. Springer, Cham (2016). https://doi.org/10.1007/978-3-319-47169-3_39

20. Johnsen, E.B., Pun, K.I., Tapia Tarifa, S.L.: Modeling deployment decisions for elastic services with ABS. In: Behjati, R., Elmokashfi, A. (eds.) Proceedings of First International Workshop on Formal Methods for and on the Cloud. Electronic Proceedings in Theoretical Computer Science, vol. 228, pp. 16–26. Open Publishing Association (2016). https://doi.org/10.4204/EPTCS.228.3

21. Johnsen, E.B., Pun, K.I., Tapia Tarifa, S.L.: A formal model of cloud-deployed software and its application to workflow processing. In: Begusic, D., Rozic, N., Radic, J., Saric, M. (eds.) Proceedings of 25th International Conference on Software, Telecommunications and Computer Networks (SoftCOM 2017), pp. 1–6. IEEE (2017). https://doi.org/10.23919/SOFTCOM.2017.8115501

22. Johnsen, E.B., Schlatte, R., Tapia Tarifa, S.L.: Integrating deployment architectures and resource consumption in timed object-oriented models. J. Logical Algebraic Methods Program. 84(1), 67–91 (2015). https://doi.org/10.1016/j.jlamp.2014.07.001

23. Larsen, K.G., Pettersson, P., Yi, W.: UPPAAL in a nutshell. Int. J. Softw. Tools Technol. Transf. **1**(1–2),134–152 (1997). https://doi.org/10.1007/s100090050010

24. Lin, J.-C., Lee, M.-C., Yu, I.C., Johnsen, E.B.: A configurable and executable model of spark streaming on apache YARN. IJGUC **11**(2), 185–195 (2020). https://doi.org/10.1504/IJGUC.2020.10026548

25. Lin, J.-C., Yu, I.C., Johnsen, E.B., Lee, M.-C.: ABS-YARN: a formal framework for modeling Hadoop YARN clusters. In: Stevens, P., Wąsowski, A. (eds.) FASE 2016. LNCS, vol. 9633, pp. 49–65. Springer, Heidelberg (2016). https://doi.org/10.1007/978-3-662-49665-7_4

26. Newman, S.: Building Microservices - Designing Fine-Grained Systems, 1st edn. O'Reilly (2015). http://www.worldcat.org/oclc/904463848

27. Ölveczky, P.C., Meseguer, J.: Semantics and pragmatics of real-time maude. High. Order Symb. Comput. **20**(1–2), 161–196 (2007). https://doi.org/10.1007/s10990-007-9001-5

28. Schäfer, J., Poetzsch-Heffter, A.: JCoBox: generalizing active objects to concurrent components. In: D'Hondt, T. (ed.) ECOOP 2010. LNCS, vol. 6183, pp. 275–299. Springer, Heidelberg (2010). https://doi.org/10.1007/978-3-642-14107-2_13

Author Index

582   Author Index

Printed in the United States
By Bookmasters